THE
BURGUNDIANS

THE BURGUNDIANS

A VANISHED EMPIRE
A HISTORY OF 1111 YEARS AND ONE DAY

BART VAN LOO

Translated by Nancy Forest-Flier

HEAD
ZEUS

An Apollo Book

First published in the Netherlands as *De Bourgondiërs* by De Bezige Bij in 2019
First published in English in the UK in 2021 by Head of Zeus Ltd
This paperback edition published in 2022 by Head of Zeus Ltd,
part of Bloomsbury Publishing Plc

9 7 5 3 4 6 8

A catalogue record for this book is available from
the British Library.

ISBN (PB): 9781789543445
ISBN (E): 9781789543452

Typeset by Palimpsest Book Production Limited, Falkirk, Stirlingshire
Cover images: Portrait of a Lady (1460) by Rogier van der Weyden (National
Gallery of Arts, Washington); Jean Wauquelin presenting his *Chroniques de
Hainaut* to Philip the Good (1447) by Rogier van der Weyden (Royal Library of
Belgium, Brussels); Portrait of Philip the Good (1445), copy of the lost original by
Rogier van der Weyden (Musée des Beaux-Arts, Dijon).

Printed and bound in Great Britain by
CPI Group (UK) Ltd, Croydon CRO 4YY

Head of Zeus Ltd
5–8 Hardwick Street
London EC1R 4RG

WWW.HEADOFZEUS.COM

This book was published with the support of
Flanders Literature (flandersliterature.be).

Dedicated to my Burgundian spouse, who made her home in Flanders.

The author received a grant from Flanders Literature to support the writing of this book.

'No vestige of fright
In the face of each knight,
But courtly and calm,
With steady aplomb,
They stare each other down.'

Paul van Ostaijen: 'Ridderstijd'
['The Age of Chivalry'] from *Music-Hall*, 1916

'...a sky full of bloody red, heavy and desolate with
threatening lead-grey, full of a false copper lustre.'

Johan Huizinga: *Autumntide of the Middle Ages*, 2020

'...and homesick with a pain that won't be quenched
to see the King for Whom I'd longed to fight,
I stride towards Death –
and he who hoped to be a man-at-arms
in that most passionate of bygone times,
must now report in long neglected words
on eras that have darkened into tales
– bleak and fearsome – of Crusades
and cathedrals.'

Hendrik Marsman: 'Heimwee'
['Homesickness'] from *Paradise Regained*, 1927

'En route to a scandalous joust,
in his iron accoutrements housed
he sings with a hushed virtuosity
of the world and its punctiliosity
thus describing himself to a fault
screwed into his ambulant vault.'

Hugo Claus: 'Ridder' ['The Knight']
from *Almanak*, 1982

TABLE OF CONTENTS

GENEALOGIES AND ROYAL HOUSES

THE ROYAL LINEAGE OF THE BURGUNDIANS

Gebicca
[mythical tribal king who, with his son Gundahar, united the various Burgundian kings under him, †407]

Gundahar
[king from 407 to 436, died in a battle with the Huns]

Gundioc
[437–74, contemporary of Attila, who ruled from 434 to 454]

Chilperic
[474–80]

Gundobad
[480–516, ruled for a time with his brother Godegisel, whom he murdered, and later with his son Sigismund, contemporary of Clovis]

Sigismund
[516–23]

Gundomar
[523–34]

According to Burgundian tradition, power was passed on to the next generation only when the last representative of the previous generation died. Sometimes brothers would reign together for a few years, which often led to fatal conflicts (as with Gundobad and Godegisel). Strictly speaking there were two kingdoms, with a discernible break between the slaughter by Aetius and the Huns in 436 on the one hand and the subsequent flight from Worms to the south on the other. I chose to regard them as one kingdom because in the end it was the same royal family that held sway, albeit over two different regions. It was from the southern region that the medieval and present-day Burgundy would develop.

ENGLISH KINGS

PLANTAGENET
Edward III (1327–77)
Richard II (1377–99)

LANCASTER
Henry IV (1399–1413)
Henry V (1413–22)
Henry VI (1422–61)
(Henry V was a brother of John of Bedford
and Humphrey of Gloucester)

YORK
Edward IV (1461–83, briefly interrupted by the
return of Henry VI from October 1470 to April 1471)
Edward V (king for two months)
Richard III (1483–85)
(Edward IV and Richard III were brothers of
Margaret of York, the wife of Charles the Bold)

TUDOR
Henry VII (1485–1509)
Henry VIII (1509–47)

HOLY ROMAN EMPIRE

Sigismund of Luxembourg (1411–37)
Albert II of Habsburg (1437–39)
Frederick III (1440–93)
Maximilian of Austria (1493–1519)
Charles V (1519–56)

SPAIN
Ferdinand of Aragon and Isabella of Castile (1474–1504)
Philip the Handsome and Joanna the Mad (1504–06)
Joanna the Mad until 1555, but not considered able to reign, so the regency
was assumed by Ferdinand II and then Charles I (who was Charles V as Holy
Roman Emperor, but the first King Charles in Spain)

POPES
Based in Rome until 1305. In Avignon from 1305 to 1378. In 1378
back in Rome, but with antipopes in Avignon until 1417. From
1409 to 1415 there were three popes, the third with his seat in
Pisa. From 1417 on a single pope in Rome once again.

HOUSE OF THE BURGUNDIAN DUKES

The time span shown in parentheses (such as 1404–19) refers to the person's full reign

Year of death is indicated by a dagger (†).

Philip the Bold
(son of King John the Good of France) ——————
Duke of Burgundy (1363–1404)

Margaret of Male
(daughter of Count Louis of Male of Flanders)
Countess of Flanders (†1405)

John the Fearless (1404–19)
× Margaret of Bavaria (†1424)

Philip the Good (1419–67)
× Michelle of France (†1422)
× Bonne of Artois (†1425)
× Isabella of Portugal (†1472)

Charles the Bold (1467–77)
× Catherine of France (†1446)
× Isabella of Bourbon (†1465)
× Margaret of York (†1503)

Mary of Burgundy (1477–82)
× Maximilian of Austria
Guardian and regent until 1493

Philip the Handsome (†1506)
Lord of the Low Countries from 1493
King of Castile from 1505/6
× Joanna of Castile (†1555) the Mad

Margaret of Austria (†1530)
Governor of the Habsburg
Netherlands
(1507–15 and 1517–30)
× John of Aragon (†1497)
× Philibert of Savoy (†1504)

Mary of Hungary
Governor of the Habsburg
Netherlands (1530–55)
× Louis II of Hungary (†1526)

Emperor Charles
Lord of the Low Countries (1515–55)
> Charles II of Burgundy
> Charles I of Spain
> Charles V of the Holy Roman Empire

ROYAL HOUSE OF FRANCE

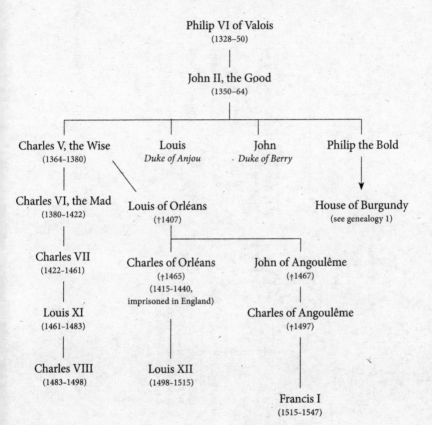

Philip VI of Valois
(1328–50)

John II, the Good
(1350–64)

Charles V, the Wise
(1364–1380)

Louis
Duke of Anjou

John
Duke of Berry

Philip the Bold

Charles VI, the Mad
(1380–1422)

Louis of Orléans
(†1407)

House of Burgundy
(see genealogy 1)

Charles VII
(1422–1461)

Charles of Orléans
(†1465)
(1415–1440,
imprisoned in England)

John of Angoulême
(†1467)

Louis XI
(1461–1483)

Charles of Angoulême
(†1497)

Charles VIII
(1483–1498)

Louis XII
(1498–1515)

Francis I
(1515–1547)

BAVARIA-BURGUNDY-FRANCE-BRABANT-LIMBURG-LUXEMBOURG ENTANGLEMENT

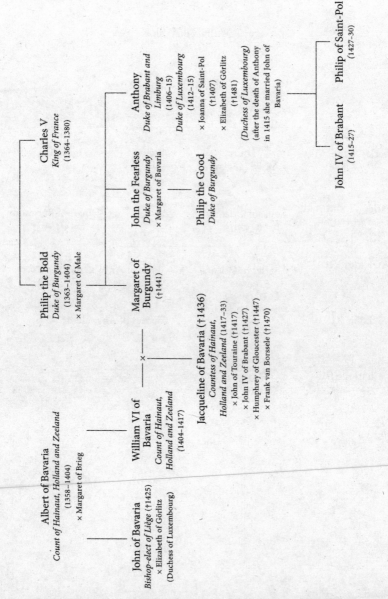

EUROPE around 500 AD

Cologne
Tournai
Tolbiac ⚔

Trier
Mainz
Worms

Soissons
Paris
Reims
Chartres
Catalaunian
Plains ⚔

ALEMANNI

**KINGDOM
OF THE FRANKS**

Strasbourg

**KINGDOM OF
BURGUNDY**

Vouillé ⚔
Poitiers

Dijon

ATLANTIC
OCEAN

Chalon-sur-Saône
Lausanne
Geneva

Clermont
Lyons
Aosta
Milan

Bordeaux
Grenoble
Turin

**OSTROGOTHIC
KINGDOM**

Bilbao
Genoa

Toulouse
Arles
Narbonne
Marseilles

MEDITERRANEAN SEA

**VISIGOTHIC
KINGDOM**

250 km

Bornholm /
Burgundarholmr
(BC)

Great Migration (1st – 5th century)

KINGDOM OF
BURGUNDY

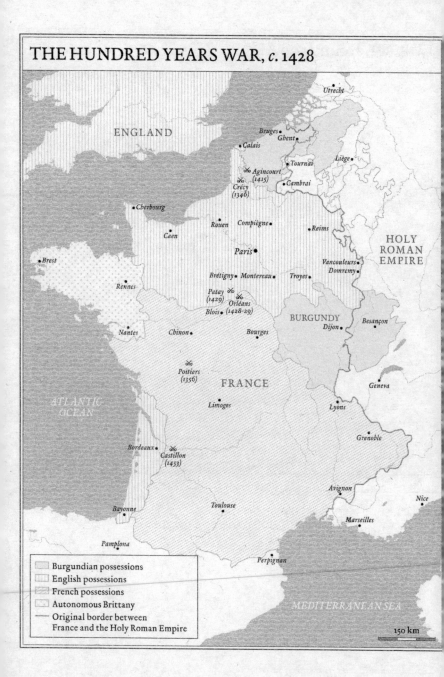

THE HUNDRED YEARS WAR, c. 1428

Utrecht

ENGLAND

Bruges • *Ghent*
• *Calais*
Tournai • *Liège* •
⚔ *Agincourt* (1415) • *Cambrai*
Crécy (1346)

HOLY ROMAN EMPIRE

• *Cherbourg*
Rouen • *Compiègne* • *Reims* •
Caen •
Paris •
Vancouleurs •
Brest • *Domremy* •
Brétigny • *Montereau* • *Troyes* •
Rennes •
Patay (1429) ⚔
⚔ *Orléans* (1428-29) BURGUNDY
Blois • *Dijon* • *Besançon*
Nantes • *Chinon* • *Bourges*
⚔ *Poitiers* (1356)
FRANCE
ATLANTIC OCEAN
Geneva
Limoges •
Lyons •
Bordeaux •
⚔ *Castillon* (1453)
Grenoble •
Bayonne •
Toulouse •
Avignon •
Nice
Pamplona •
Marseilles •
Perpignan •

▨ Burgundian possessions
▥ English possessions
▧ French possessions
▨ Autonomous Brittany
— Original border between France and the Holy Roman Empire

MEDITERRANEAN SEA

150 km

EUROPE in 1475

NORWAY

SWEDEN

NOVGOROD

SCOTLAND

NORTH SEA

Kalmar Union

LIVONIA

IRELAND

DENMARK

STATE OF THE
TEUTONIC
ORDER

LITHUANIA

ENGLAND

HOLY
ROMAN
EMPIRE

Calais
(English until 1558)

*ATLANTIC
OCEAN*

POLAND

BOHEMIA

BRITTANY

Konstanz

AUSTRIA

FRANCE

VENICE

HUNGARY

PORTUGAL

Nicopolis

CASTILE

ARAGON

PAPAL
STATES

Constantinople

NAPLES
(ARAGON)

OTTOMAN
EMPIRE

☐ Burgundy

500 km

MEDITERRANEAN SEA

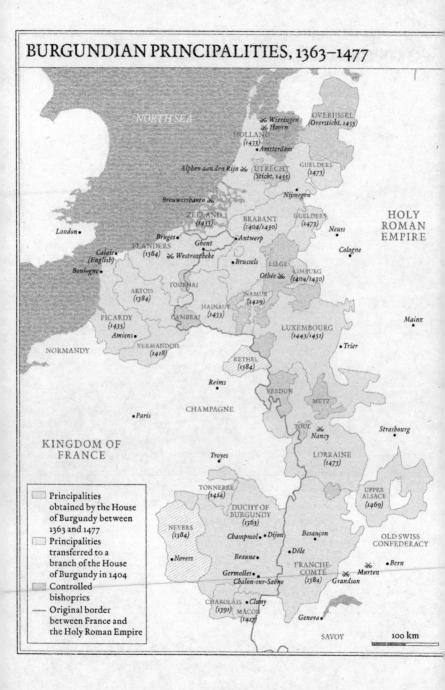

BURGUNDIAN PRINCIPALITIES, 1363–1477

NORTH SEA

✕ Wieringen
✕ Hoorn

OVERIJSSEL
(Oversticht, 1455)

HOLLAND
(1433)
• Amsterdam

Alphen aan den Rijn ✕

UTRECHT
(Sticht, 1455)

GUELDERS
(1473)

• Nijmegen

Brouwershaven ✕

ZEELAND
(1433)

BRABANT
(1404/1430)

GUELDERS
(1473)

• Neuss

HOLY
ROMAN
EMPIRE

• London

• Antwerp

Bruges •
✕ Westrozebeke

Gbent •

• Cologne

Calais
(English)

FLANDERS
(1384)

• Brussels

LIÈGE

LIMBURG
(1404/1430)

• Boulogne

Othée ✕

ARTOIS
(1384)

TOURNAI

NAMUR
(1429)

LUXEMBOURG
(1443/1451)

• Mainz

PICARDY
(1435)

CAMBRAI

HAINAUT
(1433)

• Amiens

VERMANDOIS
(1418)

• Trier

NORMANDY

RETHEL
(1384)

• Reims

VERDUN

METZ

CHAMPAGNE

TOUL
✕ Nancy

• Strasbourg

• Paris

LORRAINE
(1473)

KINGDOM OF
FRANCE

• Troyes

TONNERRE
(1414)

DUCHY OF
BURGUNDY
(1363)

UPPER
ALSACE
(1469)

NEVERS
(1384)

Chanpmol • • Dijon

Besançon •

OLD SWISS
CONFEDERACY

• Nevers

Beaune •

• Dôle

Germolles •

FRANCHE-
COMTÉ
(1384)

✕ Murten

• Bern

Chalon-sur-Saône •

Grandson •

CHAROLAIS
(1391)

Cluny •

MÂCON
(1417)

• Geneva

SAVOY

100 km

Principalities
obtained by the House
of Burgundy between
1363 and 1477

Principalities
transferred to a
branch of the House
of Burgundy in 1404

Controlled
bishoprics

Original border
between France and
the Holy Roman
Empire

SEVENTEEN PROVINCES around 1550

NORTH SEA

OMMELANDEN

Leeuwarden · *Groningen*

FRIESLAND

HOLLAND

OVERIJSSEL

ZUIDER-ZEE

Zwolle

Haarlem

Amsterdam · *Deventer*

Leiden · *Zutphen*

Utrecht

UTRECHT GUELDERS

Delft · *Gouda* *Arnhem*

Rotterdam

Nijmegen

Dordrecht · *'s-Hertogenbosch*

Zevenbergen

St.-Maartensdijk

Middelburg *Breda* *Geldern*

ZEELAND GEULDERS

BRABANT

HOLY
ROMAN
EMPIRE

Bruges *Antwerp*

FLANDERS

Sint-Winoksbergen *Ghent*

Mechelen

Cologne

Poperinge · *Ypres*

Kortrijk *Brussels* LIÈGE *Aachen*

Lille *Tournai* *Ath* LIMBURG

ARTOIS

Hesdin *Mons* NAMUR *Liège*

Douai HAINAUT *Namur*

Arras *Valenciennes*

Dinant

Cambrai

CAMBRAI

LUXEMBOURG

FRANCE

Luxembourg

☐ Autonomous prince-bishopric of Liège

50 km

'That white tablecloth with spots of grease, pure
Damask with Burgundy stains, sticks
To these fingers and slowly unfurls
Between two stanzas.'

Leonard Nolens: *Een dichter in Antwerpen en andere gedichten*
[*A Poet in Antwerp and Other Poems*], 2005

PROLOGUE

Jean-Léon Huens, print no. 182: Nancy, from 's Lands Glorie (1949–61).
Heirs of Jean-Léon Huens and Musée Royal de Mariemont.

THEY WEREN'T EXACTLY attractive. Their grey-green cloth covers looked dreary and dull. But once you opened the books, you found yourself in a world of excitement and adventure. By the time I was fourteen I had read them to pieces – all six volumes of 's Lands Glorie (1949–61). Along with Thea Beckman's famous fictional trilogy on the Hundred Years War, they were my 'open sesame' in 1987: the gateway to big history had been thrown open wide.

's Lands Glorie was the first work issued by the Historia Publishing Company. The idea was to cut out coupons that were printed on the packages of various food products. You then exchanged the coupons for little colour prints, each with a brief commentary on the back, so by eating the right products you could also acquire knowledge. You pasted the pictures into the green albums provided for this purpose. We weren't the only ones with such albums on our bookshelves. Two, maybe three generations of Belgians grew up with them. Their impact cannot be underestimated.

The author of the commentaries, Professor Jean Schoonjans, was not one to avoid clichés. In his terse summaries he spoke of 'hale and hearty soldiers',[1] called a lady dressed as a nun 'a cunning lady of the nobility',[2] and criticized 'the fearsome Duke of Alva'.[3] He viewed the past through a romantic filter and roused a sense of pride in us. It was no accident that the word 'glorie' appeared in the title. The spirit of the nineteenth century swept through every page.

Schoonjans was a dyed-in-the-wool Belgian nationalist, and in his uncompromising reading of history it was as if our country had always existed, as if the native population had been fully aware of their identity two thousand years ago. Didn't I learn from his books that in 57 BC 'the Belgians' were 'a happy people'?[4] But then came the Romans. That was on page nine, and I was already on the edge of my seat. Not long afterwards, Schoonjans claimed that 'the Belgians played a decisive role' in the conquering of Jerusalem.[5] I was so agitated that I even set Thea Beckman's novels aside. Forsaking her for the pedantic writings of Schoonjans is hard to explain, but 's Lands Glorie had another ace up its sleeve.

What made the series not only attractive but also unforgettable were the illustrations by Jean-Léon Huens. He often turned to the Old Masters for inspiration – I saw my first Van Eyck and Van der Weyden through his eyes – but he was just as happy to employ his own ideas. He tried out unexpected perspectives, played with surprising frames and painted the faces of the dying. His realistic style is firmly embedded in my memory. If someone happens to mention Charles Martel, Godfrey of Bouillon or William of Orange, their visages appear in my mind just as he once depicted them.

The pinnacle of his skill could be seen on page fifteen of volume III, identified as illustration no. 182: Nancy. Usually Huens served up some striking portrait, gripping scene or detail from a battle, but this time his illustration was conspicuous for its apparent emptiness.

Every time I see this picture, I'm fourteen again. I see that winter landscape just as I saw it back then: a tree, a snow-covered expanse, two armed men approaching in the distance. I was astonished by the bareness of that mainly snow-white illustration. The tree and the men were marginal details. Out of curiosity I read Schoonjans's commentary: 'In 1477 Charles the Bold laid siege to the city of Nancy. He met his death in battle, the circumstances of which remain unclear. His body was found beneath the snow half devoured by wolves.'[6] I looked again at the illustration, and only then did I see the dark outline barely visible in the shadow of the tree. You could just make out the contours of a dead body.

My eyes jumped from text to picture and back again, and the same questions cropped up. Who was Charles the Bold? Why was he given that name? What in the world happened to him in Nancy? And what about those wolves? No matter how much I was dragged along by the further course of history, I kept coming back to this illustration. To the wolves, the snow, the body... to the mystery of Nancy.

It would take thirty years for me to figure it all out. The tragic demise of Charles the Bold, Duke of Burgundy, became an important element in this book, in which I search not only for the facts surrounding this anecdote but also for what Huens and Schoonjans tried to dredge up in their own way in 's Lands Glorie: the origin of our whole region. And by that I do not mean Belgium, for despite Schoonjans's good intentions it was the Low Countries that emerged first, only later to be followed by Belgium and the Netherlands.

Finally, in 1987, I resumed my reading of Thea Beckman. After Geef me de ruimte! (Give Me Room, 1976) came Triomf van de verschroeide aarde (Triumph of the Scorched Earth, 1977) and Het rad van fortuin (The Wheel of Fortune, 1978). Countless Belgian and Dutch readers were gripped by the adventures of Marije, alias Marie-Claire, and her son Matthis. I regard their ordeals during the Hundred Years War as my first great reading experience. This was the real thing: reading great books that breathe new life into age-old events, getting inside someone else's skin, trembling with emotion and suspense. And learning something at the same time.

Beckman's trilogy covered the years 1346–69. She introduced characters who would haunt me for years to come: Bertrand du Guesclin, John the Good, The Black Prince, Charles V, Étienne Marcel. Not to mention the settings: the Battles of Crécy and Poitiers, the cities of Paris and Bruges in the fourteenth century. They all appear in the book you now hold in your hands. The period between the time depicted in her trilogy and the death of Charles the Bold constitutes its beating heart.

Some reading experiences are so powerful that they continue to ferment for decades. One day I could no longer resist the temptation, and I stepped into the breach that Beckman's trilogy and Huens's illustration no. 182 had opened in my imagination. Like the world around us, we ourselves are the fruit of the past.

*

I spent years peeking over the wall, and my eyes were invariably drawn to the south: to France, about which I've written several books. Feasting on that culture has made me who I am today. Only much later did I realize that in all that time my feet had never strayed far from home: first in the sandy soil of the Campine, then in the streets of Antwerp, and finally in the clay of West Flanders and, due to my increasingly frequent travels to the north, the polders of Holland. Suddenly my eyes abandoned the southern horizon and began looking down. The place occupied by my own feet began to intrigue me. How could I have been so neglectful of my roots for all those years?

Our historiography is full of book-length works explaining how the Low Countries broke up at the end of the sixteenth century, dividing the Northern Netherlands from the Southern Netherlands (and ultimately the Netherlands of today from Belgium). Historical research has paid so much attention to that painful division of property that we seldom ask ourselves what it had been like before the divorce. As if we had never been together at all.

I began to read and travel through time to Dijon, Paris, Lille, Bruges, Ghent, Brussels, Mechelen, Delft, Gouda, Nijmegen and 's-Hertogenbosch. I saw blossoming cities, incipient individualism and dying chivalric ideals. Schizophrenic kings, aggressive dukes and brilliant artists. Pyres and banquets, plague and jousting, Joan of Arc, Philip the Good and the Order of the Golden Fleece. This long search led me to the emergence of the Low Countries in the fifteenth century. And what did I learn? That the Low Countries are a Burgundian invention.

Naturally, the geographical fact of the '*lagen landen bi de zee*' (lowlands by the sea),[7] as an anonymous monk once put it, had existed for years, but the inhabitants of the principalities located there lived independent of each other for the most part. In feudal terms, they belonged either to the kingdom of France or to the Holy Roman Empire. Yet in the Late Middle Ages a number of these domains merged and, wedged as they were between these two great powers, a new entity was born. The Burgundian dukes Philip the Bold, John the Fearless, Philip the Good and Charles the Bold (who met his end at Nancy) played a leading role in this process and emerged as the founding fathers of the unified Netherlands. Philip the Bold laid the foundation, his descendants built on his legacy, and under the authority of his grandson Philip the Good the united lands on the lower reaches of the Rhine, the Meuse and the Scheldt would acquire a political dimension for the first time. These events certainly constitute the forgotten genesis of the Low Countries. But with the intense interconnectedness of those regions with France, England, the Holy Roman Empire and, finally, Spain, it's not too much of a stretch to also see them as European history of the highest order. Burgundy was the principal actor in history's last great crusade. It played a key role at the end of the Hundred Years War and was instrumental in the growing European power of the Habsburgs.

It all started when Philip the Bold, as Duke of Burgundy, married Margaret of Male, the daughter of the Flemish count. Their marriage in Ghent on 19 June 1369 seemed like the ideal opening for this book. The only problem was that after three pages I found I needed fifteen footnotes to keep from needlessly weighing down my text by identifying someone like Louis of Male or explaining a concept like feudalism. In short, I needed to back up a bit to keep the story from buckling under the weight of information that I could not assume every reader might have at hand.

Beginning half a century earlier might do the trick. Not far enough, as it turned out. A hundred years then? Eventually I cast my line almost a millennium earlier. My thinking went something like this: what if I were to begin the great story of the Middle Ages from the standpoint of the ancient Burgundians, the Germanic peoples who first appeared in the pages of history in 406, the royal predecessors of the dukes of the fourteenth and fifteenth centuries? It proved quite a challenge to find an alternative means of resurrecting an era that for the most part has been shrouded in mystery, but it was worth the effort. Not only did the ancient warriors point the way to a great many key historic moments, but they also solved the problem I was facing: now the reader would embark on the Burgundian journey with the proper luggage.

While the first part of the book spans almost a thousand years

(406–1369), the next part comprises a century (1369–1467). The third part covers a decade (1467–77), while parts four and five deal with exactly a year (1482) and a day.

The shape of the book is that of an inverted pyramid. It starts by spreading its wings and flying with rapid strokes high over the Middle Ages. Then it takes its time to observe events from a closer range. As its focus sharpens, it heads slowly but surely towards a carefully chosen destination: a forgotten day in Lier, a small city in the former duchy of Brabant, where on 20 October 1496 western history took a sharp turn.

*

Ten years ago, as if to thank me for services rendered, France sent one of its women my way – something no *Légion d'honneur* can top. She turned out to be a descendant of a Burgundian family and had spent her youth in the old duchy. Exactly 647 years after the wedding of Philip the Bold and Margaret of Male, we celebrated our Flemish-Burgundian nuptials. The dowry was less impressive, nor could our reception hold a candle to the lavish banquets of the Burgundian dukes, but the actual decision to get married occurred at approximately the same time as the plan to chronicle the historic bond between Burgundy and the Low Countries. My wife had to admit that despite her origins she knew little or nothing about the dukes, let alone Burgundy's connection with my native region. Burgundy has always been regarded as a poor relation in the history of France. Anyone who knows the story will understand why.

Our little daughter followed this entire process from close range. She was raised with an ear for both French and Dutch, and now she crosses the language border dozens of times a day without being aware of it. She also makes the actual journey to the south a couple of times a year – to the Burgundian motherland, to be exact. I decided to tell her about my new book by degrees. Could it be that I wrote it mainly for her? Wasn't she a French-Belgian child? Flemish-Burgundian? In short, the ideal reader of this book in progress?

After my last book she became quite skilled at chanting the names of all the Napoleonic campaigns, and now she's surprising museum visitors. On a recent trip to the Musée des Beaux-Arts (Museum of

Fine Arts) in Dijon I showed her the portrait of a man dressed in black, his gaze clear, with a black chaperon on his head and the chain of the Order of the Golden Fleece round his neck. When I asked her on the spur of the moment if she knew who this fellow was, this little girl – not yet four years old – promptly answered: Philip the Good!

At least there's one person who will recognize the man on the cover of my book, I thought: the most beautifully preserved portrait of the real founding father of the Low Countries, after a lost original by Rogier van der Weyden. While the dukes engaged in battles, entered into marriages and introduced reforms in order to forge a single entity from those fragmented lands, the unforgettable works by Claus Sluter, Jan van Eyck, Rogier van der Weyden and Hugo van der Goes were created under their impulse. Telling the story of the Burgundians is like opening a treasure chest full of masterpieces.

During the writing process, I realized I had no choice but to include large sections of French history as well. After all, Philip the Bold was the first of the four dukes, the youngest son of the French king John the Good, brother of Charles V and regent of the young Charles VI, and during the Hundred Years War he planned the most spectacular French-Burgundian invasion of England ever. The tension between France and Burgundy (and later, the Burgundian Netherlands) inevitably became a recurring theme in the narrative.

I have to admit that things didn't go quite as expected. In order to tell the story of the Low Countries properly, I would have to begin with what I had wanted to avoid all along: peeking over that wall. My gaze was once again drawn southward, towards France. Only gradually did my story make its way to the north. That happened step by step, little by little, a process that perfectly reflected the evolution that I myself had gone through.

The roots of the Low Countries run underground to the south. I never would have expected it, but my southward gaze and northern roots were destined to intersect.

Bart Van Loo
Druy-Parigny (Burgundy), summer 2015
– Moorsele (Flanders), autumn 2018

PROLOGUE

Along with the genealogies and maps I thought it necessary to provide in the front of the book, I have also included a series of miniatures, portraits and fragments from the works of art discussed in its pages, presented in chronological order. In the back of the book are a timeline of the main historical events and a list of the most important figures, each accompanied by a brief biographical sketch. These can prove quite useful in reading a book that necessarily involves a large number of actors and events.

PART I

'To us in olden story
are wonders many told
Of heroes rich in glory,
of trials manifold:
Of joy and festive greeting,
of weeping and of woe,
Of keenest warriors meeting,
shall ye now many a wonder know.'

Anon.: The *Nibelungenlied, c.*1200

THE FORGOTTEN MILLENNIUM

406–1369

---

*Or how you can take a fresh look at the first thousand years of
the Middle Ages from the perspective of the Burgundians, and
how these Romanized Germanic tribes always seem to have
been on the front line at great events such as the migration of
peoples, the fall of the Western Roman Empire, the emergence
of Christianity, the invasion of the barbarians from the
north and heretics from the south, the golden age of the great
monastic orders and the Hundred Years War between England
and France. In short, long before they emerged as the founding
fathers of the Low Countries thanks to Philip the Bold, John the
Fearless and Philip the Good, the Burgundians had already left
their mark on key moments in European history.*

FROM KINGDOM TO DUCHY

*Or how the Romans, Huns, Germans, Moors and Vikings
jostled one another on the way to an uncertain future, and how
Burgundy came into being.*

I N THE LAST month of the year of our Lord 406, temperatures
dropped to well below freezing. It was so cold that during the
Christmas holidays the Rhine froze solid in the area around the
city of Mainz. The seemingly untraversable river – the heavily
guarded border between Gaul, administered by the Romans, and
the obscure Germania, where countless tribes were always at each
other's throats – turned into a big and inviting bridge. Vandals,
Suebi and Alans wasted no time and soon overran Gaul.

Of course, there's no such thing as a watertight border. Just
imagining it was an exercise in futility. No matter how much
effort the Romans put into guarding the Rhine, the Danube and
the fortified wall defences between them during the first centuries
of the Common Era, border traffic had always been heavy, and the
main purpose of the so-called *limes* was to keep the numerous
passages under control. Some Germanic tribes were even given
permission by Rome to settle in the border region, forming a sort
of human buffer zone. Thus the Salian Franks fanned out between
the Meuse and the Scheldt, and held sway in large parts of what
today are the Netherlands and Flanders.

As the centuries passed, migration pressure intensified. Both
the prosperity on the other side of the border and their own growing
population made the Germanic tribes in the north-east and the
Goths in the east increasingly eager to trek westward. The second
and third centuries had seen a great many waves of migrants, but
by the end of the fourth and the beginning of the fifth there was no
stopping them. When the Huns from the steppes of Central Asia
commenced their rampage, they drove numerous Germanic tribes
from their homelands, and these groups subsequently propelled
each other westward, fighting all the way. The Romans refused

to grant asylum to this swarm, but before they knew what was happening to them a vast conglomeration of tribes was sweeping over them like a tornado. By the end of 406 the Germans were forced to break through the borders. The inundated Romans struggled against them for seventy more years, when they were finally swallowed up for good.

In this story of the Great Migration, as epic as it is complex, the Burgundians are often ignored altogether or mentioned in passing at the very most, if not whisked away in a footnote. Everyone knows their famous contemporaries Clovis and Attila, the Franks and the Huns, but who has ever heard of the Burgundians in this context? Yet this forgotten Germanic tribe also crossed the Rhine in 406–7 and made their contribution as a small cog in setting the gigantic wheel of time in motion and causing antiquity to tip into the Middle Ages.

When the Burgundians settled in the area of Worms after their crossing, they had centuries of wanderings behind them. If you reverse that journey and go further and further east, you end up in their ancestral homeland. Before Worms they had lived in the Mainz region; a century before that they populated the middle course of the Elbe, where they ended up after a sojourn near the Oder; and before that, in the first century AD, they lived on the banks of the Wisła in today's Poland. Rivers tell the story of peoples.

The Wisła empties into the Baltic Sea and points the way to their first home: the small island of Bornholm that lies in the Baltic Sea between Poland and Sweden 150 kilometres east of Denmark, of which it is now a part. At that time the old Norwegians called the island *Burgundarholmr*, which was echoed in the name the Burgundians claimed for themselves and smuggled all through Europe, across the Wisła, the Oder, the Elbe and finally the Rhine. They made their way valiantly but did not come out of the long journey unscathed. They fought numerous battles that have gone practically unnoticed and lost many of them, especially against the Alemanni, resulting in a steady decrease in their numbers.

In 406–7 King Gundahar led approximately 80,000 Burgundians

to the region around Worms; it is not clear whether this number refers to his soldiers alone or to the entire population. In exchange for guarding the border, the Romans gave him permission to establish a kingdom along the Rhine. But that was not enough for this ambitious monarch. In 435 he moved westward to Gallia Belgica, the area between the Rhineland and the Seine that would later lend its name to Belgium, in order to increase the size of his territory. Such audacity cost Gundahar dearly. In 436, with a mercenary army consisting of Huns under the command of a certain Attila, the Roman supreme commander Flavius Aetius crushed the Burgundians in a bloody battle.

Most of Gundahar's family were massacred. Only his son Gundioc managed to escape. Gundioc led what remained of his people to the south and saved the Burgundian royal house from extinction. The massacre must have been so overwhelming that it inspired Burgundian poets to create epic stories, which were passed on and embellished. Over the course of the centuries they would fuse into the German epic poem the *Nibelungenlied*, in which Gundahar appears as Gunther. The name of King Etzel could be seen as a nod to the Roman Aetius, but it probably refers to Attila. Whatever the case may be, Richard Wagner owed the inspiration for his operatic trilogy to a devastating defeat suffered by the Burgundians in the fifth century, and more specifically to their aborted desire to conquer what later became Belgium.

'The Fate of Western Civilization is Hanging by A Thread'

In 436 Attila had happily accepted payment from the Romans to teach the Burgundians a lesson, but in 447 he destroyed that lucrative alliance and made his way through Gallia Belgica, plundering and pillaging as he went. Although there's little to substantiate Attila's boast that the grass no longer grew wherever his horse left its hoofprint, his violent raids did inspire the Romans to undertake their last spectacular military operation in Western Europe. Unless they stopped Attila, Gaul would soon belong to the vast barbarian empire that stretched from the Rhine to the Caucasus and had initially been governed from present-day Hungary.

On 20 June 451, two motley armies crossed swords on the Catalaunian Plains near Troyes, in the north-east of today's France. On one side were the Huns and all the tribes they had managed to scrape together on their path of destruction, on the other was a bloc that the Romans had formed with Gallic and Germanic forces: the menacing horde from Central Asia against the western allies, the Scourge of God from the east against the most important man in the Western Roman Empire, Attila versus Aetius.

The composition of the armies says a great deal about the fragmentation that the various European migrations had brought about. The Huns themselves formed only a part of Attila's army, which consisted of Ostrogoths, Gepids, Thuringii and Rugii. Fighting on the other side along with the Romans and Burgundians were Visigoths, Alans and Salian Franks. Almost all the peoples who lived between the Atlantic Ocean and the Volga were present, and prepared to tear each other to shreds during the most important battle of late antiquity. According to the chroniclers, hundreds of thousands of warriors were involved, but modern estimates speak of around 60,000 troops, more or less evenly divided between the two camps.

For the Burgundians, Attila's arrival in Gaul was a signal for revenge. Driven by memories of the good times in Worms and the nightmare of a bitter defeat, they oiled their weapons and saddled their horses. Some of the older warriors among them had been present at the disastrous battle fifteen years earlier, and the youngest soldiers had replayed that defeat in their childhood games. Now the opportunity to get justice done was being handed to them on a silver platter. The fact that the Burgundians had been invited to join the fray by Aetius of all people, the commander who had unleashed the Huns on them in 436, didn't seem to bother them.

After a few skirmishes Aetius was able to take the high ground, enabling him to survey the Catalaunian Plains. Attila instructed his priests and diviners to hurriedly predict the battle's outcome.

After examining the shoulder blades of the sheep they had sacrificed, the priests announced that things looked far from rosy. The Hunnish leader saw only one way out. Offence was the best defence. 'I myself... will throw the first javelin, and the wretch who refuses to imitate the example of his sovereign, is devoted to inevitable death.'

Archers exchanged volleys for a short time, until suddenly the fearsome cavalry of the Huns made a great charge. These horsemen could twist their upper bodies while astride their galloping horses in order to attack their pursuers with bow and arrow. They opened a breach in the centre of Aetius's army. Theodoric, the King of the Visigoths, was killed in the chaos and then trampled by his own troops. In the face of total confusion and the danger of flight, Theodoric's son Thorismund drew his sword, set his father's crown on his head and drove the Huns back. Franks, Burgundians and Romans came to his aid, and Attila was forced to take cover behind an improvised fortress of saddles and wagons. The allies' advance was brought to a halt only by the coming of night.

Attila could not imagine himself leaving the field of battle alive. He set fire to his defensive enclosure and calmly prepared himself for death. During the allies' fatal final assault, he planned to cast himself into the flames as a martyr and thus avoid the humiliation of imprisonment. With that thought in mind, he went to sleep.

But the dreaded attack never materialized. Supreme commander Aetius put all his powers of persuasion on the line to convince his troops to let the Huns escape. With the skill of a master chess player, he had succeeded in getting all the tribes to join him while realizing that soon he would have to lock horns with them in a contest for the leadership of Gaul. The external threat of the Huns could come in very useful. The power of the Visigoths in particular was a thorn in his side. They occupied not only south-western Gaul but also part of the Iberian peninsula, so he was glad to trick Thorismund into returning home. He fooled Thorismund into thinking that his brothers had seized the throne in their capital city of Toulouse, now that their father Theodoric had perished. With the departure of the Visigoths the great army was deprived of its most effective force, and there were too few troops left to deal a death blow to the Huns. With his tactical cunning, Aetius had denied the Burgundians the chance to retaliate for all the pain they had suffered, but he would soon richly reward them.

When dawn broke, Attila was utterly astonished to see a practically empty plain stretched out before him. He quickly got over his astonishment, as well as his heroic suicidal intentions, and fled across the Rhine. Seeking revenge, he turned his attention to Rome. That campaign fizzled as well, although it did have important consequences. When the inhabitants of north-eastern Italy heard that Attila was on the march, they panicked and took cover on the islands in the lagoon of the Adriatic Sea. This precarious refuge would one day become Venice, the largest metropolis of the new age after Paris.

Attila was not the bloodthirsty tyrant legend makes him out to be. He was too clever and diplomatic for that. Nor was he the brilliant warrior that countless books have asserted. The meagre results of his western campaign of conquest give the lie to that claim. He did emerge as an exceptional leader who managed to forge one big empire out of the chaotic diversity of Hunnic tribes, and who forced the great power blocs of his age to face him down in one powerful alliance. But mainly he was the quintessential barbarian of his time, and he achieved this status when the up-and-coming barbarians were beyond counting. Because of the terrifying aura that surrounds him when he appears in the various chronicles, his most important conquest was posthumous: he now occupies a blood-drenched place in our collective memory. The small but sturdily built Attila (as he has been traditionally described) met his end during his wedding feast in 453 under less than heroic circumstances. One chronicler described him getting blind drunk and choking on his own blood as a result of a copious nosebleed; another cited his new wife, Ildico, as his unexpected murderer.

The claim that the fate of western civilization was hanging by a thread on 20 June 451 is romantic hyperbole. The end of the Western Roman Empire had already been written in the stars for quite some time. All the Romans did on the Catalaunian Plains was to ensure that the new driving force of the west would not be the Huns but the Germans, fighting it out among themselves: the Franks, the Visigoths – or perhaps the Burgundians?

In any case, halfway through the fifth century the Hunnish threat was defused for good, although Attila's ghost did come prowling round one last time a quarter of a century later. In 475, the successful politician Orestes manoeuvred his young son onto the Roman throne. This was only a diversionary tactic, for in fact the strong man in the capital was Orestes himself. When the Germanic Odoacer had the devious Orestes executed and then deposed the weak Romulus Augustulus – literally 'little emperor' – in 476, it meant the end of the moribund Western Roman Empire.

The Scourge of God must have had a good chuckle in the heathen hereafter. For this Orestes, who held in his hands the very last spark of Roman power, was none other than his former secretary. Attila could embrace eternity with a clear conscience.

'Rancid Butter, An Excess of Onions and Garlic'

Let's let the dust settle on the turbulent fifth century and turn our eyes to the Burgundians. After the defeat of the Huns, Aetius assented to what in reality was already a fact: the region of Savoy in today's France (with northern and southern offshoots) became the Burgundians' official territory. After a journey that took hundreds of years and covered thousands of kilometres, they found themselves nearing the endpoint of their adventurous trek, a hair's breadth from the French region that still bears their name. The Burgundians were almost home.

In the preceding centuries they had mixed so often with other tribes and adjusted so often to new climatological and geographical conditions that whether anything remained of their Scandinavian genes and customs is open to question. Scientists specialized in genography believe that based on recent research into human ancestry, the haplogroup Q – a particular group of genetically related individuals – occurs with greater frequency (> 4 per cent) in certain regions of Scandinavia, including Bornholm, and in the

French valleys of the Rhône and the Saône, with slight outliers running northward in the direction of Worms. Remarkably, this corresponds with the beginning and end points of the Burgundian wanderings.[2] However, similar research establishes with equal validity that the Vandals, the Suebi, the Franks and the Burgundians exchanged at least as many chromosomes as sword blows during their long journey towards Gaul. The genetic characteristics of the Germanic tribes that crossed the Rhine in the fifth century were acquired haphazardly for the most part, although it would appear that the story of the migrations can still be read to some extent in our genes.

Do we have any idea what the ancient Burgundians looked like? Sidonius Apollinaris, who later became Bishop of Clermont, encountered the tribe for the first time in 466 and described them as 'long-haired giants more than six feet in height who speak an incomprehensible babble'. On top of that 'they smear their hair with rancid butter... and their food stinks of an excess of onions and garlic'.[3] Quite colourful to be sure, but this was essentially the kind of cliché that refined Gallo-Romans would apply to any barbarian. It says just as much about the observer as the observed.

King Gundobad, son of Gundioc, profited from the disintegration of the Western Roman Empire and gradually expanded his kingdom, so that by the beginning of the sixth century it extended from Nevers to Basel, and in the south as far as Avignon. Yet that paled in comparison with what his Germanic rivals managed to pull off in Europe, and in around 500 there was every indication that Gundobad was in danger of being crushed from both sides. The almighty Visigoths and the fierce and ever advancing Franks were ready to eat the Burgundians alive. The challenge for Gundobad was not insignificant, but he proved himself a very capable administrator and politician. Not only did he manage to strengthen his international position, but a sense of Burgundian identity blossomed under his leadership. The latter in particular was quite a feat, given the fact that as Germans they were seriously outnumbered in their own kingdom, which was populated mostly by Gallo-Romans.

The Celts had been living in Gaul since time immemorial. The

Romans regarded them as a rather hot-tempered, macho people and mockingly called them *Galli* (roosters). In 52 BC, Julius Caesar put an end to the defiance of these Gauls by besieging Alesia for six weeks, after which the city surrendered and their leader Vercingetorix made a historic genuflection before the Roman commander. Caesar's triumph not only resulted in the birth of a mixed Gallo-Roman culture in the conquered areas, but it also gave him the self-confidence he needed to strive for supreme power in Rome. These events – the unfurling of Caesar's hubris and the official beginning of the Romanization of what would later become France – didn't happen just anywhere. Alesia lay in the region that soon would become known as Burgundy.

Like the Celts, who had been conquered by Caesar in bygone days, the Burgundians (and other Germanic peoples who arrived with them) would let themselves be intoxicated by Roman culture. This was evident not only in their adoption of Roman dress and gastronomic preferences but also in their tendency to soak their language and customs in a tub of Latinate herbs, of which the *Lex Burgundionum* (502), the statute book of King Gundobad, is a fine example. With this collection of laws, the Burgundians hoped to accommodate the local Gallo-Roman residents, who were now easily in the majority. Every trial had to be presided over by a Burgundian *and* a Gallo-Roman, and from then on the right of intermarriage was extended to both peoples. Germanic and Roman names were used interchangeably with greater frequency, and a new kind of aristocracy took shape, combining the large-scale land ownership of the Gallo-Romans with the militarism of the Burgundians – a forerunner of the feudal system. The incorporation of Germanic tribal customs into existing Roman law was rendered in Latin, interestingly enough. The Burgundians had already been living almost sixty years in Romanized territories, and most of them spoke East-Germanic as well as Late Latin. Thanks to the *Lex Burgundionum*, the Gallo-Romans did become a bit Germanized, but what the statute book mainly showed was how a Germanic people dropped their own language in official documents and opted for full Romanization.

Even during their Germanic period, the Burgundians had

a special craving for the alcoholic drink for which they would become world famous over the course of the next millennium. As the new statute book stated: 'If anyone enters a vineyard at night or during the harvest period and is killed by the guard, the family of the victim has no recourse to complaint.'[4] The Romans had introduced viniculture, and the vines seemed to thrive on the so-called Golden Slopes (Côte d'Or).

Some of the Germanic punishments must have surprised the local population. A man who had stolen a hunting dog was made to kiss the animal's backside in public. For stealing a falcon, the thief's head or chest would be covered with meat, after which the falcon would be released to satisfy its hunger. Clearly the legal texts did not rule out a certain macabre wit. But they also show how much importance the Burgundians attached to their animals, especially those that were used in hunting – another fact that would stand the test of time.

It was always possible to escape such ridiculous punishments by handing over a sum of money. First you paid the amount that the animal or victim was worth, then a financial penalty for the violation itself. The *Lex Burgundionum* contains a carefully compiled list of rates. To name but a few: killing a dog: 1 solidus (a Roman coin, from which the word 'soldier' was derived because that is how they were paid); raping a woman: 12 solidi; cutting off a woman's hair for no reason: 12 solidi; murdering a slave: 30 solidi; murdering a carpenter: 40 solidi; murdering a blacksmith: 50 solidi; murdering a silversmith: 100 solidi; murdering a goldsmith: 200 solidi.

Family honour was central to their culture, but in order to prevent clans from tearing each other apart in endless feuds the Burgundians worked out an ingenious system. Those whose honour had been defiled could simply be bought off. If the guilty family refused to pay, however, there was only one way out, and that was the so-called *faihitha*, or bloody vendetta. The vendettas in which the royal family became entangled over the course of the sixth century escalated to such a degree that it led to the end of the kingdom.

'Gaul Is Certainly Worth An Icy Bath'

On 25 December 506,[5] one hundred years to the day since the Germanic tribes had crossed the Rhine, a forty-year-old Frankish king waded through a vessel of holy water. When Clovis reached the other side of the large baptismal font in the cathedral at Reims, he looked round and nodded humbly, the sign for 3,000 Frankish warriors to do the same. The splashing of the sacred waves caused an undulation that would continue for centuries to come. The baptism of Clovis caused the wheel of time to click one notch further, but what a notch it was. The kingdom of the Franks, which would lend its name to *la douce France*, became 'the oldest daughter of the church' and would resolutely support Rome in the conquering of the west. Of course, this historic moment could never have taken place without the ruthless ambition of the Frankish king himself, but it was equally unthinkable without the persuasive powers of one particular Burgundian princess.

There had been little indication that one day Clovis would ensnare the Catholic Clotilde in his nets. Legend has it that his grandfather Merovich, after whom the Frankish Merovingian dynasty was named, had fought on the side of the Burgundians against the Huns, but little was left of that band of brothers. More than a century earlier, the Salian Franks had been given permission to live in present-day Belgium on the condition that they join in defending the borders against invaders. This small kingdom north of Gaul failed to satisfy Clovis's ambitions, however, and from his capital of Tournai he felt the south beckon. In 500 he marched on Dijon in Burgundy, where King Gundobad and his brother Godegisel were waiting for him.

The battle had just begun when Godegisel betrayed the Burgundian cause and defected to the Franks. Devastated, Gundobad fled to Avignon. Just as he was about to be overtaken by the enemy troops, they turned round and tore off to the north, having heard that the Visigoths, who controlled all of south-western Gaul, were threatening their land. Gundobad took advantage of Clovis's departure by personally killing his brother Godegisel, drowning his sister-in-law in the Rhône, beheading their sons and throwing them into a deep well. He spared his two grandchildren because they were too young, an impulse of human kindness that would have fateful consequences. He then formed an alliance with Clovis in order to guarantee the safety of the kingdom. As part of the negotiations, he thought it would be a good idea to marry his niece Clotilde, the Catholic daughter of a deceased brother, to the Frankish king.

And so it was that the two peoples who only recently had been at each other's throats were joined together in the bonds of matrimony in 501. At first the pagan Clovis would have nothing to do with the Christian faith, no matter how hard his pious wife tried to convert him. Nevertheless, Clotilde had their first child baptized without her husband's permission. When the child died in its baptismal garment, Clovis ranted that it was all the fault of that foreign religion. His rage was rekindled when their second child also succumbed to illness after having been baptized. Nevertheless, in the chill of Christmas night in the year 506 he would immerse his long, wavy locks (a Frankish sign of strength and regal dignity) in the holy water font. Just as the Huguenot Henry IV converted to Catholicism under the motto 'Paris is well worth a Mass' at the end of the sixteenth century, so Clovis might have thought: Gaul is certainly worth an icy bath. In his hunger for power, the leader had understood that he could make good use of the up-and-coming Catholic Church.

'Another Constantine advanced to the baptismal font, to terminate the disease of ancient leprosy and wash away with fresh water the foul spots that had long been borne,'[6] wrote Gregory of Tours. Even though his *Historia Francorum* (History of the Franks) dates to the end of the sixth century, Gregory described events as if he had been there himself. Thus he noted Clovis's promise to the bishop: 'the people who follow me cannot endure to abandon their gods; but I shall go and speak to them according to your words.' Clearly, Gregory was summoning every ounce of his rhetorical talent to make sure that Clovis, and by extension all of Francia (the kingdom of the Franks), was absorbed into the history of holy Rome. The reference to Constantine was not a gratuitous flourish. After the Holy Cross appeared to the Roman commander in 312, he ordered that every soldier's shield be adorned with this symbol. Constantine won the battle at the gates of Rome. Not only did he become the new emperor, but he also cleared the way for the Christianization of the Romans.

What happened to Clovis was strikingly similar. A few months before his baptism he had gone to war on the Tolbiac plain near Cologne against the Alemanni, the Germanic tribal confederation that controlled the southern part of today's Germany and was advancing westward. The Frankish troops were taken by surprise, and when the appeal to Wodan proved ineffective, Clovis, at his wits' end, was said to have cried out, 'Jesus Christ, whom Clotilda asserts to be the son of the living God, who art said to give aid to those in distress, and to bestow victory on those who hope in thee, I beseech the glory of thy aid, with the vow that if thou wilt grant me victory over these enemies, and I shall know that power which she says that people dedicated in thy name have had from thee, I will believe in thee and be baptized in thy name.'[7] The God of his Burgundian spouse must have sensed an opportunity, for He did what was asked of Him. The tide of the battle turned, and at the very last moment Clovis claimed victory. To show his gratitude to the benevolent Christian God, he solemnly swore that he would let himself be baptized.

Of course, his conversion was a masterly example of realpolitik more than anything else, but in France's national narrative this fable of insight and repentance, this story of Christian purification and divine intervention, sounded much better. It was hardly surprising when the Burgundian Clotilde was added to the growing list of saints almost immediately after her death, and that her intercession would henceforth be sought for the conversion of unbelieving spouses. Anyone who could prevail over the headstrong Clovis must have been cut from the right persuasive cloth. Interestingly enough, over the centuries she also became the patron saint of notaries, paralytics and light aircraft, the latter probably because the Frankish king crushed the Alemanni in Tolbiac 'thanks to fire from the sky', according to Gregory of Tours.

Legend has it that when Bishop Remigius – whose remains still lie in the abbey in Reims that is dedicated to him – discovered that he had forgotten to prepare the chrism on Christmas night of 506, a dove promptly flew in with a vial of oil. With this holy oil he was able to make the sign of the cross on the forehead of the Frankish leader in the name of the Father, the Son and the Holy Spirit. In Gregory's text we read that the king 'confessed all-powerful God in the Trinity'.[8] These innocuous words conceal an important medieval dispute: the internecine struggle between two different Christian beliefs, classical Catholics against the followers of Arianism, which the Catholic Church regarded as heretical. It was a power struggle in which the Burgundians again played an important role.

'The History Of France Starts Here'

According to the standard cliché, the freshly arrived barbarians did all they could to distinguish themselves from the local population. But what happened to the Burgundians is a good example of the opposite, and from it we can extrapolate what it was like throughout Western Europe. In any event, Gundobad did everything he could to eliminate the tense relationship between the Arian Burgundians (mainly aristocrats and soldiers) and the Catholic Gallo-Romans (the vast majority of the population).

Christianity didn't really take off until Emperor Constantine passed an edict in 313 in which the teachings of Jesus were officially tolerated, and the persecution of Christians gradually came to an end. At the end of the fourth century Emperor Theodosius went even further by prohibiting all other religions, and Christianity became the de facto religion of the state. By the early fifth century half the Roman population consisted of Christians. That growth was stimulated not only by the enthusiastic commitment of the emperor and the Bishop of Rome (the pope), but also by the growing riches of the church. The ecclesiastical authorities were only too glad to receive gifts from well-to-do aristocrats and citizens, who thereby hoped to secure their salvation. The faith thrived on the despair of the serfs and the riches of the aristocracy, like nettles and roses on a dungheap.

Not only did the followers of Christ come down firmly in their choice of Latin as the language of their cult, but their dioceses also adopted the late classical management structure, which benefited the spread and organization of early Christianity. The local establishment of the church progressed smoothly because the church had been clever enough to retain pagan shrines and convert them into Christian places of prayer. Monasteries began sprouting up here and there – a phenomenon that developed when the first ascetic hermits decided to give up their solitude and embrace community life. In these institutions, the monks kept classical culture alive thanks to their practice of teaching and copying manuscripts. Latin culture could have been entirely obliterated in the chaos of the migration of peoples, but partly thanks to the church the influence of Roman civilization would continue to make itself felt in the prevailing administrative language, liturgy, teaching and visual arts. The seeds of the great classical resurgence were sown in the Early Middle Ages.

By installing themselves in the still powerful structures of the Roman empire, feeding upon the spiritual inspiration of church fathers like Augustine, systematically winning over the allegiance of the barbarians, and thanks in no small part to their culture of hard-working synods and councils, the Christians succeeded in creating an inspiring administrative homogeneity. Probably the most dangerous problem the church had to deal with in that early period was that of heretics, people who espoused heterodox doctrines. One of the most important of these was Arianism, the teachings of Arius, a third-century Egyptian priest. He opposed the idea that the unique God of Christianity consisted of three equal manifestations: the Father, the Son (Christ) and the Holy Spirit, in which Jesus was the only one to possess both a divine and a human nature. Arius argued that Jesus was subordinate to the Father, having been begotten by Him, so he could not have a divine nature, while others professed that Jesus, the Father and the Holy Spirit were equals. This debate almost brought about a schism in the church. Who was right: the Catholic Trinitarians (three equal persons?) or the staunch Arians (Christ subordinate to the Father)? During the Council of Nicaea of 325, not only did the ecclesiastical officials decide what day Easter should fall on for the rest of eternity, but they also declared once and for all what orthodox teaching was, thereby branding the followers of Arius as heretics. It took a long time for that message to reach all the remote corners of Christendom. In the meantime, the Arian bishop Wulfila converted the Goths, which meant that the heresy was actually gaining followers. It was probably through the Goths that Arianism spread to the other barbarians of the east. The Burgundians had already converted during their Worms period, so they were heretics by definition when they landed in the valley of the Rhône and the Saône.

In order to integrate into Gaul successfully, there was little the Franks and Burgundians could do except join the Christianity of the Gallo-Romans. Gundobad himself equivocated for years when it came to converting, but he remained an Arian. He opted for a policy of tolerance and a gradual transition from one religion to the other. His wife, Caretene, was a Catholic, like Clotilde, and was given permission to build a large church in Lyon. The king even allowed Bishop Avitus of Vienne to dedicate an openly critical treatise on Arianism to him. This Avitus succeeded in convincing Gundobad's son Sigismund to convert only a few months before Clovis's baptism in 506. Because Sigismund was already a Christian (albeit of the wrong sort), he, unlike the Frankish leader, was spared a dip in cold water and had to make do with a simple laying on of hands. Thus the first Germanic leader to be received into the Catholic Church was a proper Burgundian king. This event quite probably hastened Clovis's religious turnaround.

Clovis and Sigismund were still well and truly converted when they left together for the war against the Visigoths, who ruled over an enormous kingdom that extended from the Loire to Andalusia. 'I take it very hard that these Arians hold part of the Gauls,' the brand-new ex-pagan Clovis piously exclaimed. 'Let us go with God's help and conquer them and bring the land under our control.'9 Sigismund didn't have to be told twice. What made this Frankish-Burgundian crusade against the heretical Arians a remarkable undertaking was that Sigismund's father was still a follower of that particular version of Christianity. Once again, and not for the last time, religion was a pretext for accumulating power, riches and territory.

Not far from Poitiers – in the village of Vouillé, to be precise – the Burgundian-Frankish forces stumbled upon the army of the Visigoth king Alaric II. The battle had been raging for about a day when Clovis suddenly came upon Alaric, and without hesitation he struck him with his battle axe. Just then, two strapping Goths jumped on the Frankish king. He managed to escape by hiding behind his shield and jerking sharply on his horse's reins, while Alaric, dead as a doornail, toppled off his grey stallion. After the death of their leader the Visigoths fled to the Iberian peninsula, where their kingdom held out for two more centuries before the Moors destroyed it. The news that the leader of that powerful barbarian tribe had been killed in battle, and by none other than Clovis, stunned half the continent and lent even more lustre to the Frankish victory. By the spring of 507, Clovis had occupied practically all of Gaul, with the exception of Burgundy and Provence. This makes it easier to understand why at the end of the twentieth century the inhabitants of Vouillé unveiled a commemorative plate with the somewhat bombastic but not entirely inaccurate words: 'The history of France starts here.'

In Latin texts, Chlodowig (as he was actually known) appeared as Clodovicus. The Germans call him Chlodwig (Ludwig, Lodewijk) and the French, like the Dutch, the Belgians and the English, refer to him as Clovis (the tribal name for Louis). Chlodowig is made up of the Germanic roots *hlod* ('fame') and *wig* ('combat'), and accordingly is taken to mean 'illustrious in battle'. Not only does his name summarize his career, but it also points the way to the French royal house, with its many kings named Louis. His aura of Frenchness only really began blazing at the end of his life, when the Frankish leader left the old capital of Tournai and chose Paris as the centre of his empire. Encouraged by his wife, Clotilde, he had a great church built, so that his life, which was characterized by bloodshed, ended in a semblance of peaceful piety. The king and his wife were interred in their church in 511 and 545 respectively. Today that place is graced by the Pantheon, where France buries its national heroes with all due ceremonial. French grandeur literally has its roots in a Frankish-Burgundian substratum.

'A Napkin Was Placed Under His Neck'

Whether by coincidence or not, the name *Burgundia* first cropped up in 506, the year of Sigismund's reception into the Catholic Church. When even the region's inhabitants began using this designation, local scholars decided it was time to start searching for a historic breeding ground. So they gathered stories of ancient saints who had died Catholic martyrs' deaths three or four hundred years earlier in what was not yet called *Burgundia* and combined them to form a kind of national creation myth. The resulting *Burgundian Cycle* presented a picture of Burgundy as a chosen land, with pious Christianizing heroes like Benignus of Dijon and Symphorianus of Autun. Suddenly the Burgundian kingdom, whose history had started less than a hundred years before, was shown to have existed for centuries.

In 516 Gundobad died, opening the way for his son Sigismund to let his subjects join the ranks of the orthodox Catholic peoples. Straightaway he built a cathedral in Geneva and asked the pope for a vast number of relics. Without batting an eye, the pope paid for the expansion of the Roman Catholic Church with a portion of holy remains, which were becoming increasingly minuscule the more they were divided and subdivided. The inexhaustible supply of Christian fossils and debris lent a lustre of holiness to the new churches.

Sigismund seemed to be on a winning streak: the Alemanni had been subjugated, the Visigoths driven out, and a strong link had been forged with the Franks. Yet within a short time the solid Burgundian empire collapsed like a house of cards.

After the death of his wife Ostrogotho, a daughter of the Ostrogoth king Theodoric the Great (as her name suggests), Sigismund remarried. This time it was to a charming servant of the queen, to the great irritation of his son Sigeric. One day, Sigeric noticed his stepmother dressed in the clothes of his deceased mother and striding through the halls of the palace. That was all the adolescent needed to bring his frustration to boiling point. 'You are not worthy to have on your back those garments which are known to have belonged to your mistress, that is, my mother,'[10] he shouted angrily. Insulted, the new wife complained to Sigismund. She blew the whole story into a conspiracy theory: his son was planning to overthrow him. The unstable Sigismund could not tolerate such a threat, and he had Sigeric killed during his afternoon nap. '...and while he slept a napkin was placed under his neck and tied under his chin, and he was strangled by two servants who drew in opposite directions,'[11] according to the account (quite sober for him) by Gregory of Tours.

That same evening, Sigismund had a change of heart and was racked with remorse. The broken king sought solace in the monastery of St Maurice, which he had founded in 515. There, nine teams of single-minded monks took turns singing psalms and canticles one after another, day and night, an eastern monastic tradition that entered the west via ancient Burgundy. The monks kept up their remarkable religious fervour until the beginning of the ninth century, good for almost 2.5 million hours of sung devotion.

Sigismund's deep distress and swift repentance, and his devotion to the Catholic faith, later earned him a saint's halo. Pious criminals honoured the unfortunate monarch as the patron saint of repentant murderers. In 1365, his skull and battle axe were sent to Prague at the request of Holy Roman Emperor Charles IV, who was ill at the time and was promptly healed, elevating the Burgundian Sigismund to the patron saint of the Bohemians.

But that triumph was posthumous. In 522 his situation was worrisome. As Burgundy looked nervously towards the Italy of the Ostrogoths, where Theodoric the Great was ready to take up arms and avenge the death of his grandson, Clovis's son Chlodomer did something that surprised both friend and foe alike. This Frankish leader had let himself be egged on by his Burgundian wife, Gundioca, the now-grown granddaughter of the Godegisel who had been beheaded twenty-two years earlier. For her, the hour of retribution had arrived. Traditionally, it was the duty of Germanic women to defend the family honour, and Gundioca demanded satisfaction for the murder of her parents and grandparents, all of them killed by King Gundobad. Gundobad himself was dead, but his son Sigismund, who had been weakened by these events, was the ideal victim for her vengeance. In 523, the army of the Franks crushed the demoralized Burgundian warriors of Sigismund, who himself managed a narrow escape. He fled to his monastery but was intercepted in sight of the gate. Just as the rules of the Germanic *faihitha* prescribed, Chlodomer killed him and his relatives in exactly the same way that Sigismund's father, Gundobad, had put Godegisel and his family to death: first by beheading them, then throwing their remains down a deep well.

Now that Gundobad's carefully wrought plans seemed doomed to go up in smoke, the Burgundians hurriedly crowned Sigismund's brother Gundomar as their new king. Surprisingly, Gundomar went on to give the Franks a drubbing one year later. Chlodomer's head ended up on a pike and Burgundy was once again alive and kicking. But this was no more than the last gasp for the royal house. In 534 the Merovingians crushed the Burgundian army once and for all, even though Gundomar managed to escape in the nick of time. He went into hiding and lived for years as a commoner in his own realm, which managed to preserve its identity even though it was now under the Frankish flag.

The Franks lived in an almost perpetual state of war. Because every male descendant had an equal right to the property of the head of the family, royal families tended to fight over every morsel of land. The kinsmen of the late lamented Chlodomer murdered his sons to avoid conceding any more territory to the Frankish-Burgundian branch. This attempt to purify the Frankish royal family of Burgundian blood was pointless from the start, for the simple reason that it would require the elimination of practically everyone, including the killers themselves. To understand the problem, all we have to do is climb up into Clovis's family tree. It may be tough going, but there's a minor revelation at the end. It's all contained in the following paragraph, which admittedly sounds like a Merovingian melodrama. Try reading it aloud.

Clovis married Gundobad's niece Clotilde, and their son Chlodomer had children with Gundioca, the granddaughter of Godegisel. After the death of Chlodomer, Gundioca was simply passed on to Clovis's third son, the notorious Clotharius. In addition to Clovis's oldest son, Theuderic – who, like his father, had bedded a Burgundian princess the second time round: Suavegotha, daughter of Sigismund – and with the exception of Theuderic's oldest son, Theudebert, child of the first marital union, all of Clovis's offspring had Burgundian blood flowing through their veins. Since Theudebert's branch consisted of only one son and one childless grandson, the non-Burgundian line quickly fizzled out. Consequently, the various genealogical twists and turns all point to one undeniable historical truth: the descendants of Clovis were as Burgundian as they were Frankish.

This may explain why the *Lex Burgondionum* remained applicable until well into the ninth century, and why, with the exception of a few rare Franks, most bishops, landowners and aristocrats could pride themselves on their Burgundian origins. The famous statute book had set a successful integration policy in motion, which in turn ensured that the population would continue to identify as genuine Burgundians. The mythical kingdom might dissolve in the mists of time, but the name of Burgundy would defy the centuries.

'Behold The Veil Of The Virgil Of The Lord'

The Merovingian kingdom soon split into three large sections: Austrasia (whose capital was Reims, then Metz), Neustria (whose capital was Soissons) and Burgundy (whose capital was Chalon-sur-Saône). After two or three centuries, the Merovingians lost their effective power and languished in idleness like bloated kings, while their major-domos, who took responsibility for all practical matters, gradually emerged as the real Frankish leaders. Under the feeble descendants of Clovis, the history of Burgundy plodded along until foreign invasions caused the somewhat sluggish wheel of history to turn once again.

By around 700 the Moors had conquered most of North Africa and ventured a successful crossing to the north, into Spain. In 711 they wiped the Visigoths off the map, and eight years later they invaded the land on the other side of the Pyrenees, where they immediately took Narbonne. The unstoppable Arabic leader Abd al-Rahman plundered the entire region. This new influx of foreigners threatened to gobble up all the main pillars of the previous migrations one by one.

One major-domo from the Meuse region would call a halt to the Arab invasion. Pictorial depictions of this early medieval hero are all quite similar. They show a Frankish leader fearlessly gazing into the distance, a band wrapped round his long hair, a shaggy walrus moustache beneath an oversized snout, his hauberk stretched tightly across his chest, shield at his feet. The most salient detail is the bloody battle axe in his right hand. Charles Martel is invariably depicted as the most valiant warrior of his time.

Martel's plan was to use the Moors' invasions to gain control of the fragmented territories of the Merovingians. In October 732, he and his warriors marched into the valley of the Clain, north of today's Poitiers. For the first time since their arrival on European soil, the Arabs were facing a disciplined military force that was armed to the teeth. It was the horsemen of Islam against Christian shock troops, Abd al-Rahman versus Charles Martel. As in the time of Aetius and Attila, the Burgundians formed an important division of the allied forces.

At first the Frankish elite contingent held back, letting the infantry fight the initial battle. Their many bodies, disembowelled and beheaded, covered the swampy, muddy ground. It was on that ghastly carpet that the battle was decided. Charles Martel fought like a madman, swinging his battle axe like a hammer – *martellus* in Latin. From the clash of two opposing cultures hacking away at each other, his name would illuminate the age after which he was named: the Carolingian.

The allies took heart. The Moors lost ground. Their army was more suited to large-scale raids than to a classical test of strength. When Abd al-Rahman was finally killed, his troops fled in panic. In his report of the battle, one chronicler accomplished two remarkable feats in one. Not only did he enrich the annals with his unforgettable name, Notker the Stammerer, but he also described the motley coalition of Christian troops as '*Europenses*'. For the first time, the word 'Europeans' flowed from a chronicler's pen.

During the whole Carolingian period, Burgundy was absorbed quasi-anonymously into the kingdom of Martel's grandson Charlemagne, and the old name was in danger of disappearing altogether. Only after the division of Charlemagne's empire in the Treaty of Verdun in 843 did the term *Burgundia* reappear in the writings of the chroniclers.

Charlemagne's immense kingdom was divided into three parts: West Francia, the area that would later come to be known as France; East Francia, the region that would develop into Germany – a Catholic kingdom next to an equally Catholic empire; and Middle Francia between them, which ran from Friesland to Italy but after a few decades became part of the eastern empire. In the division of Charlemagne's lands, old Burgundy was split down the middle. The eastern part soon separated from the Holy Roman Empire and began calling itself the Free County of Burgundy. The explicit reference to the old kingdom gradually disappeared, and in time this region would simply be called the Franche-Comté (the Free County), as it is today. Gradually, the name Burgundy came to be used for the western part alone, which had been ceded to West Francia, roughly the area between Nevers, Dijon and Mâcon.[12]

*

As if enough blood hadn't already been shed in the fiercely fought partitioning of the Carolingian kingdom, the Germanic and Arabic invasion of Europe was followed by the lightning incursions of Scandinavian warriors. At the end of the ninth century the Vikings snaked their way down the twists and turns of the Seine, the Loire, the Yonne and the Aube and deep into Burgundy, plundering the rich monasteries of the region as they went. The Count of Autun, a man named Richard, accepted the challenge to defend the threatened region. Richard was so effective in kicking the Vikings out of Burgundy that he soon became known as 'the Justiciar'. When word of his success spread, a great many monks left the north-eastern part of the kingdom and brought their relics to the relative safety of Burgundy, where new monasteries shot up like toadstools.

Richard may have pushed the Vikings back to the valley of the Seine, but that did little to make them less menacing. To say that the Viking leader Rollo and his troops made West Francia unsafe is an understatement. In 911 he set his sights on Chartres. As the siege went on, the town didn't seem to stand a chance. But suddenly a miracle occurred. The Bishop of Chartres, Gancelme, appeared in a diamond-encrusted chasuble. He knew that this was his moment, and he didn't hesitate. He dropped his crozier, thrust out his chest, tore his upper garment and pulled out a piece of cloth, which was immediately lit by a ray of sunlight from heaven. Then he cried out ecstatically, 'Behold the tunic of the Virgin of the Lord.' The garment that Mary had worn while giving birth to Jesus (according to tradition) must have worked like a kind of military aphrodisiac, for the heretical Norseman Rollo was mercilessly thrashed and by treaty was banished to a region that came to be known as Normandy because of his presence. There he would remain, consent to be baptized, and go on to defend France against the incursions of other Norsemen. A hundred and fifty years later, his great-great-great-grandson William would invade England from that very spot and would thereafter bear the epithet 'the Conqueror'.

The legend of Rollo's defeat is pleasant enough to read – the tunic of the Virgin is still preserved in the cathedral at Chartres – but the reality was a bit more prosaic. Gancelme had undoubtedly roused his troops with his flair for the theatrical gesture, but it was mainly the timely arrival of Richard the Justiciar, once again, that brought the Vikings down. After a siege lasting a hundred days, the Burgundian count liberated the town in July. The conclusion is as brief as it is important: no Normandy without Burgundy.

The man who performed so many feats of strength was given permission by the French king to style himself 'duke'. Richard chose Dijon as the capital of his duchy, which comprised only a modest part of Gundobad's legendary kingdom, but this does nothing to lessen its historic importance. Thanks to this victory over Scandinavian raiders, the seed of the illustrious Burgundian duchy took root at the beginning of the tenth century.

FROM BURGUNDY TO FLANDERS

*Or how the emergence of the feudal system also influenced
the evolution of the Burgundian duchy, how the church in the
eleventh and twelfth centuries could just as well have been
ruled from Burgundy as from Rome, but also how the plague
and the Hundred Years War were responsible for linking
Flanders with Burgundy after 1369.*

BECAUSE THE LAND was repeatedly partitioned among all the kings' sons, the Carolingian kingdom eventually fell apart due to an unstoppable process of fragmentation. After a while there was little territory left to partition. When Louis the Do-Nothing suffered a fatal fall from his horse in 987, the great lords of the kingdom were forced to choose a successor, and without delay. With his legendary penchant for *dolce far niente*, the deceased monarch had failed to leave any progeny. He would go down in history as the last Carolingian.

The counts and dukes cast their eye on the unremarkable Hugo Capet, whose very weakness made him look attractive. The uglier the king, the freer their hands. Capet's domain consisted of little more than the snippet of land between Senlis and Orléans, the region around Paris. His governing strategy was anything but ambitious, although he was clever enough to establish the policy of passing on territory in its entirety to the oldest son. This simple but brilliant idea of the 'crown prince' became the germ of his posthumous success. No one could have imagined that such a fragile king would be the first in a series of thirty-six monarchs. The Capetians would systematically enlarge their domain and occupy the French throne for 800 years. After 987, it became commonly accepted to speak of West Francia simply as France.

The once lean family tree produced a single robust twig whose foliage grew as far as Dijon and would cast its shadow over Burgundy for centuries to come. Capet's grandson Robert dreamed of toppling his older brother Henry I from the French throne, but in the end he had to content himself with Burgundy in 1032. The duchy was then passed down from father to son for the next 300 years. Duke Robert was the founding father of the Burgundian Capetians. In the eleventh century a close tie formed between the French crown and the region around Dijon, and the Duke of Burgundy became one of the most important authority figures in the kingdom after the king. While the French Capetians had great difficulty pulling their kingdom together, the Burgundian Capetians quietly gave shape to Burgundy. Slowly but surely they prepared themselves for a spectacular advance.

In the medieval feudal structure, the king occupied the top position. Beneath him were his vassals, who ruled a fiefdom in their sovereign's name, swore loyalty to him and pledged military support. These vassals did the same with the lords beneath them, and in this manner the waterfall of power cascaded down to the very bottom, where peasants worked for a lord in exchange for protection from outside danger. Because the arm of Hugo Capet did not reach very far, the actual power in still-young France lay with the counts and dukes of Aquitaine, Brittany, Normandy, Toulouse, Gascony, Anjou, Flanders and Burgundy. But even in those regions, power was pulverized into smaller and smaller units due to the absence of a balanced central authority.

During the raids of the Moors and the Vikings, local lords usually assumed the responsibility of defending their own villages, and walled fortresses were built. In these dark bastions, the local rural aristocracy imitated the king's royal household, but on a small scale. Peasants were treated like beasts, and in order to survive they often had to sell everything, sometimes even themselves, to the local baron, who enriched himself on the backs of his toiling serfs. To keep them obedient and submissive, the nobility recruited heavily armed horsemen. The English would later call these hauberk-clad servants 'knights', a boost in status that would never come to resonate in the Dutch word '*knecht*', which simply means 'servant' or 'farmhand'. The French word '*chevalier*' still retains the reference to horses, and the fact that these knights were horsemen, as does the Dutch word for knight: *ridder*, or rider.

This unfair division was part of a world order so unshakeable that no medieval person would even think of bringing it down: the *bellatores* (those who wage war), the *oratores* (those who pray) and the *laboratores* (those who work) formed a social structure that would hold firm roughly until the French Revolution. The churchmen prayed for everyone's salvation, the warriors fought on everyone's behalf, and the workers worked for the churchmen and the warriors. Not only was the system highly predictable, but so was daily reality. Hunger, war and sickness were the refrains of the average medieval existence. Most men never made it past thirty. This pitiful life expectancy was the result of a high infant mortality rate, a lack of nutritious food, and inadequate medical care. For women, twenty years of life was all they could hope for, since they began bearing children at around the age of fourteen and often died in childbirth. Yet there were quite a few old people. Once you passed twenty, you had a reasonably good chance of reaching a respectable age.

Slowly but surely the prestige of the praying folk began to rise, and early in the eleventh century the *oratores* made an attempt to curb the brutal rule of the aristocracy. By means of the so-called Peace of God movement, the church tried to erect a barrier against the waves of violence that were being stirred up by the local lords and knights. During heavily attended public ceremonies, knights would be required to take oaths promising not to harass any women or children, clerics or pilgrims, travellers or merchants – in short, anyone who was not participating in wars and battles. Bishops would raise their croziers in the air, and immediately thousands of hands would go up. It was a monumental gesture towards heaven. 'Peace! Peace! Peace!' came the cry, as if from a single mouth. Even the most merciless lords were impressed by these people's councils and literally dropped to their knees on pain of excommunication – a ticket straight to hell. Yet these efforts didn't always bear fruit. By the end of the eleventh century, the church decided to channel the violent excesses of feudalism in the direction of the Middle East, giving birth to the Crusades. Weren't the heretics there making life miserable for brothers in the faith? Wasn't it possible that they were defiling the grave of Christ? Weren't they even denying Christians entrance to the holy city of Jerusalem?

While the knights were expected to guard against physical threats in a way that was just and fair, a growing army of monks assumed responsibility for pleading for the world's salvation before the throne of the Creator. Since the king, who had been anointed by the church, often failed to fulfil this role, these monks were obliged to take on the job of tempering God's wrath and begging for his mercy. Countless individuals turned their backs on the world and embarked on a life void of sensual pleasures or riches. Alms came pouring in. Poor wretches as well as lords of the castle were eager to secure as comfortable a place in the hereafter as they could afford. Monasteries had long served as the spiritual playthings of the regional nobility, but a major reform movement brought that to an end. A vast number of abbeys emerged as the most important power centres of the eleventh century.

'A White Cloak Of Churches'

Not far from virgin forests, where rabbits, martens, wild boars, lynxes and bears roamed free (if they hadn't already been slaughtered during the tedious hunting parties organized by local potentates), lay the idyllic village of Cluny, which, aside from its hunting lodge, wooden chapel and a few shabby vineyards, had nothing to recommend it. This Burgundian hamlet, with its paradisiacal sweetness, was the ideal place to accommodate a new monastery. The hunters would have to satisfy their cravings elsewhere. The yelping of the hounds was replaced by the praying of monks. The new Benedictine abbey was consecrated on 11 September 910 as an independent institution. By the middle of the eleventh century it had grown into the centre of a religious network that numbered 1500 monasteries, one of first multinationals in history.

Ora et labora. Pray and work. Cluny bent the age-old Rule of St Benedict to its purposes. The accent shifted to the first aspect of the Rule, and not slightly but overwhelmingly. The monks may have had a symbolic encounter with a rake or a shovel, but it was serfs and tenant farmers who did most of the work. When it came to prayer and singing, however, they performed with gusto. As the Burgundian monk and chronicler Raoul Glaber wrote, 'I myself am witness that in this monastery it is a custom... that Masses be celebrated constantly from the earliest hour of the day until the hour assigned for rest.' At the height of their spiritual productivity, the brothers (who, thank God, could relieve each other owing to their sheer numbers) sang their way through 138 psalms in a single day, while St Benedict was quite happy if the monks could get through 150 a week. '...and they go about it with so much dignity and piety and veneration', Glaber continued, 'that one would think they were angels rather than men.'[1]

The monks of Cluny made it a point of honour to attend to the spiritual welfare of the dead. The order laid the basis for the celebration of All Souls' Day on 2 November. An ever-expanding cemetery grew up around the monastery, an undertaking as lucrative as it was pious. To pray for the salvation of all mortals, living and dead, the monastic community, with hundreds of daughter houses throughout Europe, released a boundless stream of prayers to the Heavenly Father. Otherwise, an impressive silence reigned in the monastery, and monks were forced to communicate in sometimes unfathomable sign language. The sign for a woman was the same as that for a trout: an almost sensual stroking of the forehead with the index finger from one eyebrow to the other.

The liturgical aesthetic was echoed in the increasingly beautiful design of Cluny's own abbey church. Three buildings followed each other in rapid succession, and the third remained the largest church in Europe until the construction of St Peter's Basilica in Rome. Artistic creativity and monastic religious expression went hand in hand, and thanks to the international network of daughter houses and pilgrim churches in eleventh-century Burgundy, these cultural forms spread across the continent. Europe embraced Romanesque architecture with enthusiasm. Older church buildings, the ceilings and roofs of which were usually made of wood and easily caught fire, made way for larger places of worship erected with massive stone walls and fitted with small windows. The pillars were connected by means of stone arches and ribbed vaults, thus allowing for larger interior spaces in which separate chapels could also be built – the success of the monastic life required more and more altars. For the first time, the exteriors of the churches were also ornamented, giving the facade in particular a most imposing vitality. As Glaber wrote, 'It looked as though the very world was shaking itself to take off its old age and to reclothe itself in all areas in a white cloak of churches.'[2]

It was mainly under the guidance of Abbot Hugo, who was elected in 1049 and led the order for sixty years, that Cluny made a name for itself and became known even in the far reaches of Portugal, Scotland and Italy. Hugo's intelligence and authority reflected on the entire monastic community. After King Philip I of France was excommunicated for adultery in the autumn of his years, he began to worry about his spiritual welfare and requested permission to enter the monastery. His only condition was that he be allowed to keep his crown. But Hugo was adamant: without distancing himself from worldly glory there would be no room for his royal cousin at Cluny. When William the Conqueror asked him for monks to staff his English monasteries, the abbot refused despite the handsome remuneration, and he did so because he feared his brothers would not be able to regulate their way of life in the same spirit of independence.

It would easily take as long to pray a couple of rosaries as it would to list all of Hugo's international achievements. The illustrious abbot wore out several popes in his long career, and he always maintained a direct line with Rome. He accompanied Bruno Egisheim, who had spent a night at Cluny as a pilgrim on his journey to the Vatican, and was present when Bruno donned the tiara for the first time as Leo IX. Pope Urban II was also steeped in the spirit of Cluny, and when he called for the First Crusade on 18 November 1095 during the Council of Clermont with the words 'Deo lo volt!' (God wills it), Hugo of Cluny stood approvingly at his side. Finally, Pope Paschal II, a former brother of the mother house, also aligned his policy with the great abbot's favourite themes.

Hugo's network supplied much-needed support for a thorough

reformation of the church. More than ever, celibacy for clerics and Christian marriage for the laity became two fundamental precepts. He also banned the sale of ecclesiastical offices, and laypeople were not allowed to interfere in religious affairs. The Peace of God movement, which first emerged in southern countries, only reached full bloom when Cluny agreed to support it. Soon, lords of the castle and knights from the northern Rhône valley, Burgundy, the Franche-Comté and even from the regions north of Paris – where the bloody tradition of the *faihitha* had never gone out of fashion – agreed to comply with the imposed rules for peace. The Holy See was firmly grounded in the *Ecclesia Cluniacensis*. In fact, over the course of the eleventh century the Catholic Church was being governed from Burgundy as much as it was from Rome. But that didn't stop the great Hugo from searching for his bed of straw every night to humbly sleep among his monks.

*

From 1100 on, the worldly success of the Benedictine order provoked growing criticism. Shouldn't the monks stick to their own affairs within the walls of their monasteries and leave the world to its own devices? Wasn't that how the Cluniac monks got started in the first place? Wasn't it the king's job to guarantee peace in his kingdom? Cluny's affluence and splendour also came under fire. Shouldn't modesty be a Catholic virtue? Could it be that the order had become far too rich?

The strongest opposition came from Burgundy itself. In Cîteaux, scarcely a hundred kilometres from Cluny, an abbey with even stricter observance was consecrated in 1098. Driven by Bernard of Clairvaux, a Burgundian born and bred, the Cistercian order would eventually unite more than seven hundred daughter houses within its fold. At a time when money and corruption were on the rise in church circles, the ascetic example of Cîteaux exerted ever greater fascination. Soon the Catholic world found that it could follow two opposing paths, two ways that led from and to Burgundy: a religiosity moved by beauty that was nourished by liturgical ceremony and dazzling churches, and a mystical passion that relied on the joys of poverty and asceticism, Cluny as opposed to Cîteaux, Hugo versus Bernard. More than ever before, Burgundy of the twelfth century had become the beating heart of the *Respublica Christiana*.

Bernard, unlike the followers of the great Hugo, honoured not only the *ora* but also the *labora* of Benedict's Rule. There were no serfs as there were in Cluny; the Cistercian brothers themselves put their hands to the plough. There was something particularly Burgundian about this physical doggedness, however. In 1110 the monks planted the first grapevines on the stony subsoil of a nearby slope, and they did their utmost to create as beatific a drink as possible. Was there a more perfect counterpart to spiritual labour than to harvest the blood of Christ by the sweat of one's brow? The Cistercians continued to plant their vines until thousands of acres were put into service. Gradually they improved their production methods, which had made little progress since the arrival of the Romans. It was a labour-intensive enterprise, but wasn't time something that the monks had in abundance?

They built a stone enclosure that served to defend their grapevines from the far too aggressive pigs, boars and deer. It also protected the early vines from the wind, and they thrived from the stored heat that the stones gave off at night. In 1212 this *Clausum de Vougeot* – the walled grove of Vougeot – was reported in a document, named after the adjoining village. And perhaps the abstinence-loving St Bernard once celebrated Mass with wine that would one day become the celebrated *grand crus* of Burgundy. 'Take this, all of you, and drink from it: for this *clos-de-vougeot* is my blood, the blood of the new and everlasting covenant, which will be poured out for you and for many for the forgiveness of sins.'

The Meursault and Clos de Tart wines, renowned for both their name and their finish, also came to full maturity thanks to the daughter houses of Cîteaux. The temptations of alcohol gave rise to the requisite moral dilemmas, and one of the monks once asked Bernard how the Rule of St Benedict could be reconciled with the love for Bacchus. 'By not drinking more than one hemina a day'[3] was the answer given by the spiritual leader. This ancient Roman measurement was the equivalent of 0.27 litres, one small carafe to get you through the day. In short, enough to modestly quench your thirst but not enough to cause you to nod off during the intoning of the psalms. And as an extra test of abstinence, the monks slept above the wine cellar at night.

Despite the severity of Bernard, who refused the position of archbishop when it was offered him in order to stay on as abbot, the order of Cîteaux ended up following the same path as Cluny and became one of the wealthiest religious organizations in Europe. Their inspiring power shrank as their treasuries filled and their administrative ambitions grew. The affluent Cistercians were a contradiction in terms. Few of their abbots were inclined to reject the bishop's mitre, and they built magnificent Gothic cathedrals that were a far cry from the sober, modest edifices their order had once so fervently promoted.

'Beware, Father, to the left! Beware, Father, to the right!'

To a great extent, the order of Cîteaux owed its very existence to Odo I of Burgundy. In 1098, the duke not only donated the land on which the abbey would be erected, but he also financed its construction. Three years later, the courageous and godly Odo took part in a final offshoot of the First Crusade. He died before reaching Jerusalem. The mortal remains of the worldly founder of Cîteaux were buried in the shadow of his abbey. For the next 250 years, all the Burgundian dukes would find their final resting place there (and all but three of them were named Odo or Hugo).

The prestige of the two mother houses outshone the dukes in life as well as in death, which had its advantages. Safe within that shelter, the dukes could work on steadily strengthening their central authority in Dijon. Compared with the spectacular advances of the French Capetians, who had retaken a large part of the former West Francia, the inheritance of their Burgundian relations looked much less impressive. But by taking advantage of the international appeal of Cluny and Cîteaux, they succeeded in breathing new life into the Burgundian sense of unity. The dukes achieved on a small scale what Gundobad had brought about on a larger one.

Because of its position on the border, the duchy was given the task of defending the kingdom, which strengthened its tie with the French crown. That assignment seasoned the early Burgundian consciousness with a pinch of French nationalism. But danger was lurking as well – not from across the nearby border with the Holy Roman Empire but from the other side of the Channel, where William the Conqueror and his descendants had been ruling since 1066. Henry Plantagenet, great-grandson of William and future King of England, married the clever and ravishingly beautiful Eleanor of Aquitaine in 1152. Scarcely eight weeks earlier she had been divorced from King Louis VII of France, with whom she had led a contentious married life for fifteen years. With relief she traded one crown for another, and overnight the great Aquitaine, the entire south-western region of the kingdom, fell into the hands of the English crown.

The tempestuous Henry, who was also Duke of Normandy (thanks to his great-grandfather) and Count of Anjou (through his father), was suddenly the most powerful vassal of the French king. That situation led to friction between the superpowers, which at the beginning of the fourteenth century would result in one of the bloodiest conflicts in western history, when periods of ceasefire would alternate with savage raids, invasions and epic battles. The conflict lasted so long that, for the sake of convenience, historians began calling the 116 years of misery the Hundred Years War.

*

In 1314 the French king, Philip the Fair, gave up the ghost. He left three sons, all of whom failed to produce heirs to the throne, and to make matters worse they all died young. Louis the Quarrelsome, Philip the Tall and Charles the Fair managed to occupy the throne for less than fourteen years altogether. The reign of the baby king, John the Posthumous, a mere five days, failed to resolve the problem. The stock of successors was exhausted, and a legitimate king had to be found without delay. Actually, the sister of the three late lamented monarchs, Isabella, could have claimed the throne, but the French found that idea very hard to swallow, since she was the widow of the recently deceased English king, Edward II. His son, Edward III, was barely fifteen and too weak to stand up to the French legal scholars, who were busy digging up apocryphal documents in order to prohibit succession via the female line. Now that the direct descendants of Hugo Capet had died off, the throne went to a cadet branch, an offshoot of a brother of Philip the Fair.

Ten years later, the new House of Valois – of which the Capetians were members, but which bore the name of their specific family branch – was forced to deal with the ambitions of Edward III, now age twenty-five. On 19 October 1337 he declared war on France and launched his long military escapade. From a purely genealogical standpoint, Edward was in the right: denying the throne on the basis of succession through the female line was nonsense, and as a grandson of Philip the Fair he was among the first in line, unlike the scions of the Valois cadet branch. In addition, he knew quite well what he was fighting for: the tempting prize of having an English king also sitting on the French throne.

In 1346 he crossed the Channel and pulverized the French for the first time near Crécy in Picardy. Then he began the siege of Calais that would drag on for a full year. The situation was hopeless. Six citizens, with nooses round their necks and the keys to the city in their hands, approached Edward III at a ponderous, shuffling gait to offer their lives if he would spare the town. Moved by this gesture, the English queen, Philippa of Hainaut, succeeded in convincing her husband to undertake an act of clemency – a romantic footnote in a sordid story. Auguste Rodin would depict the poignant scene in bronze half a millennium later. From then on, English troops had safe access to French soil at the port of Calais. With the fall of this strategic stronghold, the richest land in Europe stumbled into the darkest century of its history.

Three years later, Philip VI died – the first Valois king – and it was up to John the Good to defend France's honour. Why his countrymen called him 'the Good' is a mystery, since under his leadership the country went into a total decline.

In an effort to breathe new life into the old knightly ideals, John founded the Order of the Star. When the lords gathered together it wasn't just to brag about their heroic deeds. They also swore never to flee more than 600 metres from a battlefield, and to die or be taken prisoner rather than abandon their king. Such breathless valour would prove fatal to the French on more than one occasion.

In 1356 the English launched countless raids from Aquitaine. Now that the enemy was approaching the heart of France, the French king's call to mobilize met with a huge positive response. 'No knight and no squire remained at home,'[4] the chroniclers wrote. The king was so certain of victory that he even conscripted his four sons to fight. After a long pursuit, the French army came upon the enemy in the environs of Poitiers. On 19 September 1356, the king was given what he had so longed for: a second chance to make up for the defeat his father had suffered ten years earlier at Crécy. There they were, John the Good against the Prince of Wales; the French king, whose one desire was to become the greatest knight of his age, against the eldest son of Edward III, who wore a black cape over his armour: *le Bon* versus *The Black Prince*.

The English had chosen an ideal spot on high ground, which could only be reached by way of a road so thickly lined with hedges that even four adjacent riders had difficulty ascending it. This didn't keep the French king from throwing his principal forces into the fray. Blinded by the overconfidence he gleaned from ancient tales, the king sent his best horsemen up the hill even though he could just as well have chosen to starve the enemy into submission. But such a cowardly approach would have run counter to every ideal of chivalry.

A hail of English arrows descended on the cavalry and their horses, who tumbled over each other, collapsing and snorting. The horses that survived did an about-turn and, wild with panic, charged at the French ground troops. Suddenly John the Good realized what an exercise in folly it had been to send in all his sons. He quickly ordered the dauphin Charles and his two brothers to leave the battlefield in order to safeguard the line of succession. His youngest, and his favourite, the fourteen-year-old Philip, remained at his side.

The departure of the three princes looked so much like desertion that a large portion of the army decided to abandon the king. The 7,000 Englishmen, who had faced twice as many of the enemy when the battle began, suddenly took heart. John himself refused to leave. He insisted on defending his honour. 'Advance,' he cried, 'for I will recover the day or die on the field!'[5]

Fully aware that no cuirass would offer him better protection, John pulled over his armour a blue mantle embroidered with golden lilies, the symbol of the French monarchy. The enemy, who could thus easily recognize him, would do everything they could to take him alive and then demand an outrageously high ransom for him. When the English identified John the Good fighting in the melee, they rushed towards him. But the king wasn't going to give up that easily. Hacking away like a wild man at everyone around him, he seemed to have forgotten that he was clothed in fleurs-de-lis. In fact, he gave the distinct impression that he wanted to keep on fighting until his dying breath. Teeth were being broken, arms chopped off, entrails spilling from opened bellies. The group around the French king was shrinking by the minute.

'Ware, to the left!' shouted his son Philip, who was just able to block a sword's thrust. His father, one of the most feared old warriors in Europe, cut a path to the left despite the fact that his helmet had been knocked off. 'Beware, Father, to the right!'[6] screamed his son, and swinging his battle axe, John eliminated another approaching Englishman.

'Yield, yield, or you are a dead man!' someone shouted at the king.[7] It was Dennis of Moerbeke, a French-speaking nobleman from Flanders who had been banished to England for murder and was now serving in the army of the Black Prince. 'Yield yourself to me and I will lead you to the Prince of Wales.'

Exhausted and helmetless, John the Good handed his right glove to the nobleman from Moerbeke. His blue mantle was torn, the fleurs-de-lis drenched in blood. Philip followed his father's example.

*

As at Crécy, the strongest army of knights in Europe had bitten the dust. Even Francesco Petrarch, the poet and founder of humanism, who heard the news in Milan, could hardly believe it. The French had been undone by two major mistakes. Their troops still swore by the crossbow, admittedly robust but difficult to operate, while the English longbow was capable of shooting twelve arrows a minute, covering a distance of 300 metres and striking with devastating force. In addition, the French noblemen looked down on the infantry and preferred to fill their ranks with swaggering, drunken knights on horseback. The English weren't the least bit bothered by fighting alongside ordinary commoners who were skilled with the longbow, and they even put a premium on seamless cooperation between horsemen and archers.

In French history, 'The Battle of Poitiers' has the ring of a heroic thunderclap, a high point of military and national glory: Charles Martel beating the Moors and saving the country from the threat of an Arabic takeover. Not only was the actual situation a lot more nuanced, but patriotic historians kept cranking up the glory in order to divert attention from that other, doomed Battle of Poitiers. In the annals of French history, 25 October 732 has been successfully used to erase the blighted 19 September 1356. Anyone who evokes Poitiers today automatically thinks of Charles Martel, but not a living soul knows who John the Good was.

In the autumn of 1356, the deeply humiliated France had to find something to lean on, so the cry 'Beware, Father, to the left! Beware, Father, to the right!' became a heroic refrain that could be heard in every corner of the country. It provided the king's youngest son, Philip, with a nickname that the kingdom found warmly consoling. *Le Hardi!* The Bold! The Brave! An *epitheton ornans* that rang like a bell, a title of honour that would guarantee Philip the Bold a place in the history books. But the consequences of his bravado at Poitiers were especially important for the future of Burgundy.

'Voluntarily Risked Death'

After having descended into the snake pit of the Hundred Years War in the 1330s, France was forced to deal with one of the cruellest invasions in its history. At the beginning of 1348 the plague entered the country by way of Marseilles. By the summer, the bacilli had already overrun the capital. Half the population of Paris was mowed down, and then the epidemic swept northward.

In Flanders it was called the '*haestighe ziecte*' (the hasty disease),[8] or simply '*gadoot*' (sudden death).[9] Burgundy, too, was devastated. In the village of Rully only ten families survived. In Givry, with a population of just under 1,500 souls, 615 villagers died within fourteen weeks. In the town of Paray-le-Monial a mere 12 per cent escaped the grim reaper, and in Nuits-Saint-Georges this saying was making the rounds: '*En mil trois cent quarante et huit / A Nuits sur cent restèrent huit.*'[10] The phrase 'eight out of a hundred survived' may have been a bit of an exaggeration for the sake of the rhyme, but the famous chronicler Jean Froissart estimated that 'a third of the world' perished. This alarming figure would later be confirmed by historians.

While the plague raged more fiercely among the poor, the rich were not spared either. The Burgundian duke Odo IV was not the only one to succumb to the contagious disease in 1349. John the Good, then still the crown prince, lost his wife *and* his mother. His father, King Philip VI, ordered the medical faculty of Paris University to figure out where the infernal plague was coming from. The scientists pointed to the peculiar position of the planets. But most mortals firmly believed that the cause of the terrible malady was to be sought much further afield. What else could unleash a plague of such biblical proportions than the wrath of God?

Half-naked penitents began appearing in the streets. The best they could come up with was to drive out sin by flogging themselves with iron-tipped scourges, an exercise that provided very little relief to tormented humanity. A scapegoat, some thought, would be more effective. All fingers pointed in the same direction. Jews were accused of poisoning fountains and wells, and in Antwerp, Brussels, Basel, Strasbourg, Frankfurt, Cologne, Narbonne, Chinon – but also in the Burgundian city of Beaune – they were simply murdered or harshly driven out. The fact that they, too, were dying of the plague in droves was beside the point. After the Black Death had gone on its mad rampage – a process that took only a few days and involved pain in the chest, blood welling up in the throat, abscesses full of pus on arms and thighs, black spots on the skin, death agonies – it also made short work of common sense. Rats and fleas were such familiar companions that no one gave even half a moment's thought to the possibility that they might be the plague's carriers.

To make matters worse, after the retreat of the army of plague bacilli France was doomed to suffer the disaster of Poitiers in 1356. While King John the Good, now under lock and key in London, remained convinced that he had done his duty, riots broke out in France that drove the country to the brink of civil war. For the cunning Edward III, this was the signal that it was time to resurrect his claim to the French crown. In the autumn of 1359 he had 12,000 troops shipped to the harbour of Calais.

After the double fiasco of Crécy and Poitiers, the French refused to plunge into another reckless adventure. Everywhere they went the English encountered closed city gates. Not a single army was willing to take them on. When the city of Reims appeared impregnable, the peevish Edward decided to establish winter quarters in Burgundy. For the local inhabitants, the devastating raids throughout the duchy were their first real experience of the misery of war with England.

The sixteen-year-old Burgundian duke Philip of Rouvres – not to be confused with Philip the Bold, the king's son – was named after the castle in which he normally resided. He was glad to be able to conclude a three-year truce with Edward on 10 March 1360. The English king left Burgundy, but he found Paris a hard nut to crack. He cursed the French, who just didn't want to fight. The futile phoney war so affected his resolve that, when a hellish hailstorm put his exhausted army to the test, Edward said he was ready to talk peace.

On 8 May 1360, in the castle of Brétigny, not far from the place where Richard of Burgundy had crushed Edward's ancestor Rollo, a treaty was signed that gave the French a costly ceasefire. Edward acquired Aquitaine and Calais once and for all, giving him a third of the French kingdom, and in return he renounced his claim to the French throne. The French also had to cough up a fantastic sum of three million écus to purchase their king's freedom. In expectation of payment, John the Good was able to return to Paris, and his sons Louis and John took his place. One of the first orders of business undertaken by the released king was the horse-trading of his eleven-year-old daughter Isabella, who was transferred to Milan to marry the immensely rich Galeazzo Visconti for the record amount of 600,000 gold florins. John must have breathed a sigh of relief.

But the consequences of the treaty were catastrophic for the French population. The English soldiers and German mercenaries who were discharged from military service by Edward III did not all return to their homelands. A large number of them formed gangs, and for good measure they took on board a number of frustrated French knights who had been ruined by the high taxes. Like wasps roughly evicted from their nest, they swept across the countryside. The war had been going on for more than twenty years, and morals had not improved during that period. Wandering brigands organized themselves into self-sustaining companies whose ranks included not only bakers and butchers but also bankers and prostitutes. The mainly agrarian Burgundy, with its flourishing wine culture, was one of the regions most infested by bandits and mercenaries. Going on a journey without an armed escort became a suicidal venture.

One of the jobs of the duke was to stamp out these *routiers* (highwaymen), but Philip of Rouvres had something else to occupy his mind. While roaming criminals sucked the Burgundian region dry, a malicious illness was wearing away the young duke's vitality. The swellings in his armpits left no doubt: after twelve years' absence, the plague had returned. For ten days, fever, haematomas, boils and black spots heralded the death agonies to come. The duke died on 21 November 1361.

Burgundy was left without a successor, and Philip of Rouvres, the very last Capetian, was interred at the abbey of Cîteaux. It had been thirty-three years since the branch of the national Capetians had died off without issue, and now the Burgundian line had come to an end as well. In Paris, the crown had been passed on to the youngest Valois cadet branch. Now exactly the same thing would happen in Burgundy, as if Paris and Dijon were entangled in an inseparable brotherhood – an intertwining that would have bloody consequences.

In 1350, the French king, John the Good, had been remarried

to Joanna of Boulogne, the mother of the late lamented Philip of Rouvres. Like her son, she left this world during the second outbreak of the plague. As the closest living member of the Rouvres family, and in the absence of a legitimate vassal, John laid claim to the duchy.

He didn't keep Burgundy to himself for very long. On 6 September 1363 he gave the territory to his favourite son, Philip the Bold, to reward him for the courage with which he had 'voluntarily risked death' on the battlefield of Poitiers.[11] Twenty-four dukes had succeeded each other in Dijon since Richard the Justiciar, but from the perspective of eternity none of them would hold a candle to Philip the Bold.

A few months after John the Good had pleased his youngest son with this royal gift, he learned that his other son, Louis, had committed breach of promise and fled his golden cage in London. John's conscience dictated that he take his son's place and embrace imprisonment once more 'for the sake of his family's honour', so he sailed for England and was kept at the Savoy Palace in London. France had barely enough time to recover from its astonishment, for only a few months later their remarkable, chivalrous leader breathed his last on English soil.

'I Will Cut Off The Breasts That Fed You And Toss Them To The Dogs'

At that point the Hundred Years War came to resemble a common marital battle, at least for a short time. The new French king, Charles V, saw it as his responsibility as the oldest son of John the Good to choose a wife for his youngest brother, Philip the Bold, the equally new Duke of Burgundy. It was no surprise that his eye fell on Margaret, the daughter of the Flemish count Louis of Male. As heir to the richest principality in the north, she was a much coveted bride. Margaret had the additional attraction of already having been promised to a Burgundian leader in marriage as a young girl, the late Philip of Rouvres. Why not send her back to Dijon, reasoned Charles V?

Philip the Bold declared that he was quite willing to agree. However, the English king, Edward III, wanted Margaret to marry one of his sons and had even promised 175,000 pounds and a few strategic coastal areas to that end. At first Flanders was willing to consider the English proposal, even though Louis of Male knew that such an option would be unthinkable for his mother. Since losing her husband on the battlefield of Crécy, she had detested the English. Yet Louis tried to force the issue. The opposition that rose up against him can be felt across the plains of Flanders to this day.

'Because you refuse to obey your king or your mother, I will cut off the breasts that fed you and toss them to the dogs,'[12] Margaret of Artois ranted at her son. 'I will disinherit you,' she continued, 'so you can forget about Artois and the Franche-Comté.'

Louis chose France. Charles V even offered 25,000 pounds more, and threw the cities of Lille, Orchies and Douai into the bargain. So Margaret of Flanders ended up in a Burgundian bed after all, even after the plague had cancelled her earlier child marriage. Philip the Bold made his entrance on the world political stage in a way that would impart to Burgundy its characteristic lustre: with a wedding feast that was meant to astonish not only Flanders but half of Europe as well.

The duke, a big man with a dusky complexion, had a reputation for paying a great deal of attention to his personal hygiene. On 19 June 1369 he bathed in a tub of rose water and violet perfume that had been prepared by *le maître des déduits*, his personal 'master of diversion'. He was then dressed in a blue robe of great splendour. He had had it ostentatiously stitched with gold daisies (*margrietjes*) to honour his nineteen-year-old Margaret, without failing to include references to himself with embroidered Ps. Now he was ready to lead the Burgundian procession to the centre of Ghent.

All the bells of Ghent began ringing, but every eye was turned to the church of the St Bavo Abbey. A vindictive Edward of England had sent minor barons of the lowest rank as delegates of the crown, but the rest of Europe was represented by illustrious counts and dukes, who strutted across the church square like peacocks. As impressive as they were, they paled in comparison to the twenty-seven-year-old Philip the Bold. He had shaken the last cent out of his treasury in order to turn the journey to Ghent into a triumphal procession.

In almost all the Flemish cities along the way he stopped to chat with tradespeople, barge masters and aristocrats. He joined various bowmen's guilds, participated in tournaments and treated the prize winners to casks of Beaune, a collective name (which would soon become proverbial) for the better Burgundian wines, of the Gevrey and Marsannay type from near Dijon, and Pommard and Volnay from Beaune itself. He had saved the climax for Ghent, however. For days the city became the setting of sumptuous feasts, but when it came time for the final agreement to be signed the Burgundian duke blew his entire fortune. Without hesitation, he borrowed money from a few wealthy Ghent burghers and put several jewels up as collateral.

Repayment didn't worry him. Philip would never be a frugal man. On the contrary, he was one of the first princes in European history to realize that a good impression was at least as important as a full purse. In addition, the county whose thriving cloth trade made it one of the richest regions in Europe would soon be his. Compared with Flanders, the duchy of Burgundy, which was mainly known for its wine, amounted to very little in economic terms. But with his penchant for splendour, Philip seemed made to take charge of a county whose largest cities were bastions of luxury and wealth.

Thinking that he had won the hearts of his new subjects with a bit of macho exhibitionism would have been reckless indeed. For the moment, the Flemings saw him as a foreigner overflowing with ambition, a French king's son, a Burgundian. This generous opportunist would first have to demonstrate whose side he was on. Did he have what it took to keep Flanders out of the French-English hornets' nest? Was he a Frenchman first and foremost, or would he favour the interests of the Burgundians? And did he have sufficient empathy for the demanding people of Ghent and Bruges? Flanders had been the location of so many battles over the years that the population had learned to keep all their options open.

Philip was fully aware of this, but he was just as conscious of the fact that he had not miscalculated with his grand entrance into Flemish life. He simply had to be patient. The lavish dowry, which included not only Flanders but also the counties of the Franche-Comté, Artois, Nevers, Rethel, and the seigniories of Antwerp and Mechelen, was locked up tight as long as Louis of Male was still in the saddle. And there was no indication that his robust father-in-law was ready to call it a day. Philip would have plenty of time to get to know restless Flanders a bit better.

*

Burgundian history in the Low Countries began in 435 with King Gundahar's failed invasion of Gallia Belgica. The bloodletting that accompanied that event gave world literature the *Nibelungenlied*, and it also gave the Burgundians, who fled the scene, some land that would one day be theirs for good. Less than a millennium later, Philip the Bold was about to secure a considerable part of what later would become Belgium, thus realizing an ancient royal dream.

If you climb down Philip's family tree, you can see the roots shooting past the first French king, Hugo Capet, the man who was descended from Charlemagne via his grandmother. The emperor in turn was linked to the Frankish king Clovis via a small detour – the brother of his great-great-grandfather was a direct descendant – and to Clovis's spouse as well, of course, the Burgundian princess Clotilde. So Philip's genealogical odyssey ends in the illustrious family of Gundahar and Gundobad.

In short, there's a not-so-erratic arabesque running from the old kingdom to the new duchy, a line covering a thousand years of medieval history that was walked and/or trampled by Romans, Huns, Germans, Moors, Vikings and English, a span of time that was tested by plague, war and invasions, where residues of paganism, Islam, Arianism and Catholicism brewed and fermented, the nutrient-rich substrate from which another important turning point in European history would emerge, one in which Burgundy would proudly claim the leading role. Philip the Bold would not betray the honour of his illustrious forebears.

In fact, his arrival was the beginning of an improbable Burgundian ascent. The fame of the dukes would gradually come to rival that of the kings of old.

But without the sudden rise of the county of Flanders, this success story could never have been written.

PART II

'Hail fruitful mother! Holy name!
Your breasts that 'neath the linen boldly stand
still burst the bedclothes without shame;
and with good cheer you proudly claim
the body that gave birth to Burgundian land.'
Liliane Wouters: *Moeder Vlaanderen* [Mother Flanders]

THE BURGUNDIAN CENTURY

1369–1467

*Or how in an era of burgeoning cities, awakening
individualism and dying chivalric ideals, Philip the Bold,
John the Fearless and Philip the Good created a new dynasty
that was soon able to call itself the richest, most powerful
and most ostentatious in Europe. And how these Burgundian
dukes succeeded in forging the fragmented Low Countries into
a single entity by means of battles, marriages and reforms,
and, last but not least, how their impulse gave rise
to unforgettable works of art by Claus Sluter, Jan van Eyck
and Rogier van der Weyden.*

RISING FROM THE MUD

*Or how Flanders took root in boggy coastal soil and how
the early history of the county formed the blueprint for its
Burgundian future.*

FIVE WOMEN STEPPED forward, but none of them met the
requirements. They all returned home disappointed with a
payment for their trouble. In the spring of 1371, the doctors finally
selected a woman called Guyote, a strapping female from French
Flanders who had just what it took to serve as the perfect wet nurse
for the child of Philip the Bold and Margaret of Male.

The bedroom was filled with bottles, scales and flasks
containing infusions, vinegar, camphor oil and other potions to
alleviate the pain of the mother-to-be. Torches had been lit to
release a resin perfume, and although this considerably increased
the already high May temperatures, custom prevented anyone
from opening the windows to let in some fresh air before the
new mother had been churched. The layette consisted of two
cradles, one on wooden wheels for actual use and the other,
extremely luxurious and refined, for showing off. The duke didn't
want to cut any corners with his firstborn. Wet nurse Guyote,
who suffered under the burden of her colossal breasts, ate round
the clock, while Margaret of Flanders sighed and waited for the
ultimate moment.

On 28 May the hour finally arrived. The records from the
ducal palace in Dijon make note of the happy event with one
short sentence: 'Today *Jehan Monseigneur* was born.'[1] Rubbed
with honey and swaddled in linen, John, named after his late
grandfather John the Good, who had died in exile, wasted no
time letting himself be heard. Messengers spread the joyful news
throughout Burgundy, but they also headed for Flanders. The
Flemings applauded respectfully, while realizing that it would be
a long time before this baby became their count. At present, even
the father, Philip the Bold, would have to wait his turn, as Louis

of Male, John's maternal grandfather, remained the strong man in the north.

As a daughter of Flanders, Margaret made a sizeable donation to St Adrian's Abbey church in Geraardsbergen, a town that was also called Adrianopolis after this saint, who was often invoked by childless couples. Seven months after the birth, the duchess donated a small wax figure of her child weighing fourteen pounds to the Bèze monastery in Burgundy, an old custom that she was glad to honour and from which we can deduce that little John weighed about seven kilograms at that age. A large cow was brought in to supplement the milk produced by Guyote the wet nurse, and one year after John's birth a herdsman was even hired to guard the cows assigned to rounding out his milk consumption. A minstrel reported for duty to give the little boy music lessons, and a personal jester to stimulate good humour. With the appointment of a personal physician, chamberlains and a father confessor, his household gradually began to take shape. John was five when his huntsman initiated him into the art of the hunt, and six when he rode a horse for the first time. The youngest scion of the House of Burgundy spent his youth in the company of carefully selected young friends, all chosen from the better noble families.

Unlike his father, who grew up a French prince and whose dealings with Flanders began later in his life, the young John had it drummed into him from a very early age that one day he would hold sway over both Burgundy and Flanders. It was no accident that on 13 March 1378, Philip the Bold appointed one Baldwin van der Nieppe as tutor. This priest had a degree in law and came from a family of Flemish noblemen, so he was in a position to teach John the Dutch language. Philip the Bold would always regard his own inability to speak *la langue thioise*, or *Diets* – commonly referred to as Middle Dutch in English usage – as a drawback, which is why the future Count of Flanders wanted his son to become bilingual. It is doubtful whether this plan was entirely successful. Even so, John could just about manage in Middle Dutch, which he mangled into a peculiar sort of gibberish – a harbinger of how a number of Belgian kings would later perform.

Of course, Baldwin van der Nieppe also taught him the rich

history of Flanders. A good leader not only spoke the language of the people, but he was equally familiar with their past.

'In A Fit Of Monstrous Frenzy'

Flauma. It was with this Germanic word that Flanders crawled up onto the land – quite literally. Flauma means flood. In the Early Middle Ages the coastal region flooded twice a day, and the sea encroached deep into the interior. As a result, islands were created, the largest and most well-known of which was Testerep (also corrupted into Terstreep). On the western and eastern ends of the island, towns such as Westende and Oostende arose, with a church right in the middle where the town of Middelkerke would later stake its claim. Veurne was also located on an island, with Sint-Winoksbergen and Oudenburg right on the sea, while today you have to travel ten kilometres by land to reach the coastline from these three towns.

The first inhabitants settled in an area that was always dry owing to slight elevations in the landscape. These people were called *Flaumung*, a name that mutated into *Flâming*. It was on this sodden land on the North Sea, which extended as far as Bruges via an estuary, that the first Frisians and Saxons washed ashore. The Franks didn't appear until later, and there was little in the swampy region to interest them. Under the leadership of Clovis in the sixth century they would push southward, to Tournai and then to Paris, until they finally overran Aquitaine and Burgundy. During their advance through Belgica Secunda they drove the Gallo-Romans past the Boulogne-Bavay-Cologne military road. North of this axis, Latin was only moderately successful in taking root, allowing the Germanic language to develop into Middle Dutch. What later became French germinated further south, while the military road itself evolved into the language border. Despite this there was never a watertight division, for in a few enclaves on either side of the barrier both languages survived.

In 52 BC, Julius Caesar never got any further than Boulogne, from which he took the boat to England. Charlemagne was in

Ghent only once, where he went to inspect the defence line against the Vikings. Little is known of what happened in between, as if the thinly populated and constantly flooded region had disappeared under water. After the division of Charlemagne's lands at his death, the Flemish coastal region ended up in the hands of what soon would be called France, marking the beginning of a centuries-long controversy between the northern vassal and the southern feudal lord. In their written accounts, which were all in Latin, the Carolingians referred to the *pagus Flandrensis* – the shire of Flanders – which Charles the Bald, very much against his will, granted to Baldwin Iron Arm in 863. The first Count of Flanders had forced the hand of Charlemagne's grandson by running off with his daughter, although it must be said that Judith didn't put up much of a fight. The abduction of noblewomen was a tried and tested medieval tactic for forcing a marriage, and it provided the diligent Baldwin with both a wife and a shire.

At this point, tutor Van der Nieppe probably paused for a moment to tally up his list one more time. Satisfied with the result, he told John that twenty-five counts would have to come and go before the honour finally fell to his father, Philip the Bold.

Bruges as a city name was first mentioned in the mid-ninth century, after which it blossomed into the historic centre of Flanders. With the arrival of a count, this settlement on the banks of the Reie was transformed into an important stop for itinerant traders, merchants who often came from the north. They moored their boats to what they called a *bryggja* (a landing stage), thus supplying the city's name with its Scandinavian roots. With his iron arm, not only was Baldwin said to have been relatively successful in confronting the attacks of the less mercantile Vikings, but one day he also slew a bear who had been menacing Bruges and its surroundings. With a stroke of the same sword he swept the poor beast onto the city's coat of arms, where it stands guard to this day.

Ultimately, Baldwin was awarded other lands in addition to the coastal shire, and he ruled over areas in the Waasland, the Ghent region and the district of Saint-Omer. This unstable area, with its jagged outline, would gradually be expanded by his descendants. Baldwin had coins minted in Bruges, which (with a bit of goodwill) you might call the first official capital of Flanders – except for the fact that Flanders did not yet exist, of course, nor did the modern concept of a capital city. The most important places tended to be court cities that housed the county or royal administrative authorities. Sometimes the counts resided mainly in Bruges, at other times in Ghent (where Baldwin's heart and intestines were finally interred in St Peter's Abbey), and occasionally in Lille.

So the Flemish patriarch may literally have stolen his position, and like his successors he earned his fame, his power and his nickname mainly by dint of his struggle with the Vikings. There's a historic irony in that trial of strength. After the final defeat of Rollo at Chartres in 911, the Viking leader was first offered Flanders, but he couldn't bear the thought of wasting away in a bog for the rest of his life. In the end, the French king ordered him to withdraw to the region that was subsequently named after Rollo's own people: Normandy. Had he chosen the soggy marshlands instead, Normandy might be the name of what we now call Flanders.

Rollo's son, William Longsword, was undeterred by the damp north, where he attacked the county so ruthlessly that the Flemish leader, Arnulf the Great, had to pull out all the stops to resist him. During a peace conference in 942 at Picquigny, the count literally cut him down to size 'in a fit of monstrous frenzy and inflamed by a devilish spirit',[2] in the words of the chronicler Dudo of Saint-Quentin. William's son Richard succeeded in breathing new life into Normandy against all expectations, and he would be the first to sign his documents with the title *dux*. All of France took note: in addition to the prestigious Burgundy and the vast Aquitaine, a third duchy had suddenly been added to the kingdom.

There was nothing trivial about Richard's feat, but the greatest star in the ducal line of Normans – as they gradually came to be known, and not Norsemen or Vikings – would not arise for three generations and would seize the English crown at the Battle of Hastings. This William the Bastard, also called the Conqueror, married Matilda of Flanders. She was the daughter of Count Baldwin V, who devoted himself to the development of new market towns such as Torhout, Ypres, Cassel and especially Lille, for which he came to be called Baldwin de Lille, the city that still sees him as its founder. 'Love at first sight' is hardly how you would describe the budding liaison between his daughter and William. Matilda swore that she would sooner be a nun than lie in the bed of a bastard. Concealing his dubious origins was just as difficult for William as containing his violent tendencies. According to legend, he dragged Matilda by her plaits from her home in Lille and thereby wrested her affections. Surprisingly enough, this turbulent beginning led to a good mutual rapport. William's marriage was also a clever military investment, for the contribution made by the seamen of Flanders in the conquest of England in 1066 was considerable. Two years later, the Flemish Matilda was crowned Queen of England.

This minor miracle did not make the relationship between the Flemish count and his liege lord, the French king, any easier. In the centuries that followed, Flanders would remain stuck between a rock and a hard place: increasingly dependent on England for the much-needed wool for its growing textile industry, and tied to France by the principle of feudal loyalty. At the same time, the reverse reasoning also held true. As its prosperity increased over the next two to three centuries, Flanders began exerting a force that the two gluttonous superpowers found impossible to resist. With mutual marriages between members of the nobility, the presence of Flemish students in French universities, and the rapid spread of the French language, it made perfect sense that Flanders would maintain ties with France, while the connection with England was mainly of a commercial nature. Except that from now on, the importance of trade would start increasing dramatically, and Flanders's relations with France would thereby be affected.

This was something that tutor Van der Nieppe could not emphasize strongly enough. This evolution would have a significant impact on the Flemish future of Burgundy.

'I Thought I Would Be The Only Queen Here'

For many years, the sea continued to batter the Flemish coastline, forcing breaches and shoving the land aside. But in the early ninth century, the power of the North Sea seems to have subsided. Occasionally there were still spring tides, but the sea level stopped rising. Creeks and gullies stayed dry for longer periods, and the vegetation that grew there was found to be an ideal subsoil for raising sheep. To protect themselves from flooding, the local inhabitants built primitive dikes, a technique that proved so successful that hectares of land were easily snatched from the sea. In 300 years' time, the coastline would come to lie some fifteen kilometres seaward in places, a feat of strength that made the annals of world literature in the early fourteenth century. 'As the Flemings, living with the constant threat / of flood tides rushing in between Wissant / and Bruges, build their dikes to force the sea back,'[3] wrote Dante about half a century before John's birth, in the fifteenth *Inferno* canto of his *Divine Comedy*. The fact that every advantage has its downside was evident even then. Now that mud and salt marshes were being transformed into fields, the space for the salt-tolerant plants that supported the grazing of sheep declined dramatically, so that the textile industry was forced to buy even more English wool.

Because trees were being chopped down on a grand scale, new arable land was constantly being created inland as well as on the coast. Settlements arose everywhere, but mainly on the banks of watercourses. Even the young John of Burgundy could see the logic in that. Transporting goods by water was much cheaper. When his father, Philip the Bold, transported his vats of wine from Beaune to Avignon, it cost just as much to carry them the 25-kilometre distance to the Saône by horse and cart as it did to ship them the remaining 300 kilometres by water. Beaune and Dijon were built along Roman military roads and dated from the age of a centralized empire with a fully developed road network. By contrast, the emergence of medieval villages and cities was mainly fostered by the presence of navigable waterways.

Rivers were also the economic arteries of the new county that had evolved from the small district around Bruges. Etymologists and place name experts might start their investigations by pulling on their boots and wading through the soggy Flemish primordial mud. In the beginning, Lille was a dry bit of land in the middle of the Deûle River, a place where it was easy to cross. It was an island, in other words – *Insula* in Latin, *Isle* in French, which evolved into *Lille*, or (quite literally) The Island. The Dutch name for Lille, Rijsel, can be explained in the same way. First Lissele, then Rissele, then Rijsel. And there's a lot more water flowing through Flemish atlases. It's no accident that the Celtic word *Ganda* (confluence) forms the etymological heart of Ghent, where the Leie and the Scheldt embrace, just as the word *poorter* (city dweller) is derived from the Latin *portus* (harbour), or as Bruges was born on a Scandinavian wharf. An ancient Flanders without water is as inconceivable as a Belgian cafe without beer. The famous 'waterish Burgundy' from *King Lear* (written in 1606, set in around 1500)[4] is doubtless a nod to the boggy county that, as Shakespeare so beautifully put it, was mentioned in the same breath as Burgundy in the Late Middle Ages.

Thanks to deforestation and land reclamation, the county became urbanized at breakneck speed and developed into the most densely populated region in Western Europe. By around 1200 a quarter of the population lived in cities, which were separated from each other by less than a day's march – about five hours on foot. No other region of Europe was so urbanized. Over the course of the next century, the population of Ypres grew to 40,000, and that of Bruges to 45,000. In Ghent, the figure leaped to over 60,000. These were the largest centres by far. Of the cities north of the Alps only Paris was larger, reaching the magical number of 100,000 citizens (as did Venice).

As soon as barons and abbots got wise to the fact that water could be turned into gold, they tempted farmers and labourers with attractive conditions and let them do all the hard work that land reclamation and dike-building required. The classical medieval picture of penniless serfs working the land was transformed in Flanders faster than anywhere else. Half-free servants were soon transformed into tenants or free farmers, although an exploited proletariat emerged as a result. This need for a workforce drove the labour-intensive cloth-weaving industry from the villages to the cities, which grew into textile centres. The cities were also a source of capital, which was needed for the development of increasingly ingenious weaving techniques. Big cities were given permission by the count to draw up their own municipal laws, and they exacted certain benefits such as the reduction or abolition of tolls. As more and more Flemings moved to the cities, the cities became richer and more powerful. The emigration from countryside to city that started in the tenth century was one of the most important developments in medieval Europe, and Flanders, along with northern Italy, was a leader in this evolution.

By the eleventh century, defensive walls had already been erected around Ghent and Bruges. Such a fortification, usually with towers, was called a *burg* or *burcht* and would later lend its name to the city's free inhabitants: the *burghers* within the city walls. Ghent's walls were the most expansive, requiring about thirteen kilometres of masonry. The benefits, which had been negotiated with the count, were laid down in charters and were valid up to a mile beyond the walls of the city. This was the so-called *banlieue* (*ban* stood for the charter and *lieue* for a mile), the French name that would later be given to suburbs. Anyone who lived within the walls for a year and a day could share in the city's rights and responsibilities.

City dwellers were not ashamed of their wealth. In Ypres the first stone was laid for the monumental Cloth Hall in 1230, and not long afterwards Bruges astonished its rivals with an imposing bell tower that soared above the covered market. In this reinforced watchtower hung the alarm bells, which rang in the event of emergencies or for festivities. It was also the place where the charters were kept. Such monumental buildings were erected on the initiative of the city councils, which mainly consisted of wealthy patricians, merchants and businessmen. Gradually, the cities became detached from the influence of the counts and kings.

Arras, Douai, Lille, Saint-Omer, Bruges, Ypres and Ghent grew into textile centres that were famous far beyond their borders and served as a harbinger of what the industrial revolution of the eighteenth century had in store, but on a much grander scale: vast numbers of labourers working cheek by jowl in relatively small spaces, increasing human exploitation, ever-expanding technological possibilities. It produced much poverty and misery, but also great opulence. 'I thought I would be the only queen here,' said the wife of the French king Philip the Fair as she strode through the streets of Bruges in 1301, 'but I find six hundred others.'[5] No other city could match Flanders's historic centre. Interestingly enough, Bruges reached its zenith after the city council had largely turned its back on the textile industry. It was also in this city that the steward Van der Nieppe enjoyed a magnificent *fin de carrière*, and where the last great Burgundians and offspring of his pupil John would find their final resting place.

*

The textile that was produced and traded on such a grand scale had nothing to do with bedding or table linen. It was a highly processed and very supple felted wool from which durable clothing was made. 'All the nations of the world are kept warm by the wool of England woven into cloth by the men of Flanders,' we read in the thirteenth-century *Chronica Majora*,[6] written by the English Benedictine monk Matthew Paris. While the widely praised textile industry, which brought international fame to Flemish cities, may have been the most eye-catching aspect of the economy, the greatest source of income for the county was trade. Bruges became the commercial nerve centre of Flanders and welcomed traders not only from England and France but also from Germany, Italy and Spain. From then on, a substantial portion of Flemish capital was pumped into the development of Bruges. Next to the bell tower the immense 'Waterhalle' was erected in 1294, an architectural tour de force that made it possible to unload French wine, Portuguese grapes, Maghreb dates, Hungarian gold, Polish amber, Bulgarian ermine, Russian sable, Tatar silk, Armenian cotton and, of course, English wool from incoming ships in the typically rainy Flemish weather without any of these goods getting wet.

International commerce embraced Bruges with its tentacles and swallowed it whole. The annual fair officially set up its booths in

May, but now it seemed like a restless monster, chewing up goods all year long. Brothels, gambling houses and bathhouses rubbed up against the world of trade and high finance like greedy parasites. When John's father treated the people of Bruges to a tournament in 1369 to celebrate his marriage to Margaret of Flanders, there were 140 houses of ill repute in the city, approximately six times more than at the beginning of the century. The respected Italian rabbi Judah Minz explained Bruges's transformation into the tawdriest city on the continent with this witticism: 'It seems to the gentiles that it is a good thing to place prostitutes in the marketplace and town squares and in all the corners of their houses so as to save them from a graver sin, that is, from relations with married women.'[7]

At least as impressive as the increase in the number of prostitutes was the decline in the number of textile workers. At the beginning of the century they constituted half the population of Bruges, while after 1400 that portion would drop to 25 per cent. In Ghent, on the other hand, more than half the inhabitants were craftsmen, a number that never changed. Bruges had become a city of merchants, brokers and money changers. At the currency exchange offices you could deposit your money for a time and later withdraw it. Gradually, these shops grew into the predecessors of our modern banks. The inn that was run by the Van der Beurze family, built in around 1285, became the most important place for brokers to purchase securities and sell them at a later date. Going 'to Beurze' was a distinctly Bruges aphorism with a meaning all its own. When financial marketplaces in Antwerp and Amsterdam also came to be known by the name *beurs*, the family found itself in the dictionary. The name also migrated to other countries, such as Italy (*borsa*), France (*bourse*) and Russia (*birža*), the words we translate as 'stock market' in English.

Flanders had transformed itself from a swampy backwater to the Silicon Valley of the Middle Ages, a region that set the tone for industrial, technological and commercial innovation. While Ghent emerged as the rebellious centre of political power in the county, Bruges would grow into the largest money market in Europe. With little exaggeration, you could make the argument that Bruges was the cradle of capitalism in Western Europe.

'We Will Remain Flemings, No Matter What Language We Speak'

Jehan Monseigneur hung on the lips of his tutor, a man who could never have suspected that his pupil would go down in the annals of history as 'the murderous prince' and 'John the Fearless'. These two nicknames became the ideal vehicle for transporting his bloody reputation through the centuries and up to the present day. Unlike his father, John preferred the sword to the word. He would become a warlord, not a diplomat. Perhaps that's why the old stories of grievance and combat went down so well with him.

The sabre-rattling in those stories was also reverberating in his own world. Flanders, as rich as it was fractious, was feeling restless, and his father was seriously worried. John was not yet twelve years old, and for now he was being kept in the dark, but the air was thick with rumours. Yet life went on as usual, the home schooling continued as it always had, and the boy tried to focus on his lessons. He had to, for in two years' time he would be taking his first steps into public life.

He was certainly curious, and for a bright mind there was a lot to be learned from his tutor's stories of the past. John was quick to grasp that the internal disputes (city versus count) and external tensions (Flemish count versus French king) that were constantly overheating in the past were still matters of great sensitivity in the Flanders of his own time.

Young John often listened with his eyes half shut. No matter how much he tried to focus his attention on his teacher's long lessons, it was obvious that he was no scholar. He much preferred to train for the other aspect of his duties: not only was he expected to become a good ruler, but he also had to excel as a knight. For Baldwin van der Nieppe, imagining that his pupil would one day be confronted with threats and violence must have been the most logical thing in the world.

All he could do was pump as much knowledge and wisdom as he could into John's head, which was easier when his lessons were spiced with tales of epic heroism. His story of the Battle of the Golden Spurs was just the ticket: a story that introduced the burning timeliness of what John and his father had to deal with, a historic event that would colour the history of Flanders like no other.

*

At the end of the thirteenth century, the tension between the count and his cities became more complex when major conflicts also arose within those cities between the rich French-speaking patricians (the *Leliaards*, or the Lilies) and the plebs who toiled for subsistence wages and spoke Middle Dutch (the *Klauwaards*, or the Claws). The Claws appealed to the sympathetic count Guy of Dampierre, but when he made an attempt to improve their working conditions he was turned away by the city authorities, who were supported by the French king, Philip the Fair.

In despair, John's ancestor Guy of Dampierre forged an alliance with the English, but Philip immediately countered by placing the five largest cities directly under his authority. The count and his successor disappeared behind bars. The county's fate seemed sealed. But the high taxes that were imposed to pay for Philip's 'Joyous Entries' ignited a spark of discontent within the population.

On 18 May 1302, a group of dissatisfied Bruges locals slit the throats of the French soldiers stationed in their city and did the same to the prosperous burghers who had made common cause with the French crown. About 120 men lost their lives that night, which would come to be known as the Matins of Bruges. A furious Philip the Fair sent an army of knights to teach those bloody Flemish a lesson, but on 11 July, against all odds, the craftsmen-militias and peasant warriors cut the king's army to ribbons at Kortrijk. The *'volc de voet'* – foot soldiers – triumphed over the cavalry, who got bogged down in the ancestral swamps; the fleurs-de-lis literally sank in the Flemish *flauma*. From then on, the golden spurs plundered from the battlefield would hang as glittering war trophies in the Church of Our Lady in Kortrijk.

There are some Flemings today who are still proud of this tour de force. From a military standpoint, that's exactly what it was. Highly trained chargers bearing knights in well-oiled armour, with lances piercing the air, could no longer guarantee triumph and glory. But when author Hendrik Conscience salvaged the battle from oblivion following the independence of Belgium, the attention was focused elsewhere. The romance of his novel *The Lion of Flanders* (1838) echoed throughout the nineteenth century and established the myth of the victory of the Flemish language over French. When 11 July was elevated to a day of celebration for the Flemish community in 1973, however, there was never any mention of a revolutionary linguistic war. Dutch-speaking knights from Brabant had fought on the French side, and the imprisoned Flemish count spoke French. In the run-up to the battle, the residents of Doway (today's Douai) passionately declared their Flemish identity in their French mother tongue: '*Tos Flamens, tos Flamens estons! Par Dieu... por nient en parleis, car tos summes et serons Flamens!*'[8] – We are all Flemings and we will remain Flemings, no matter what language we speak!

Essentially, the Battle of the Golden Spurs was an opportunistic alliance of parties who challenged unjust feudal taxes and opposed the collaborating French-speaking patricians. The main lesson learned on 11 July 1302 was that in the absence of the count, the townspeople would take matters into their own hands. From then on, they insisted on managing their own affairs and were prepared to fight the king and his accomplices to the death in defence of this right.

Philip the Fair was not about to give in. He decided to put the squeeze on Flanders once again and presented it with the bill. The county was made to cede its French-speaking areas to France. This concerned the region around Lille and Douai; in the more westerly region of Dunkirk-Cassel-Sint-Winoksbergen (Bergues)-Hazebrouck – the so-called French Westhoek – Flemish had always been spoken. But the king could not bend everything to his will. He had to tolerate Flanders's right to exist, ruled, as before, by a dynasty of counts. At the same time, he allowed the craft guilds to resume their socio-economic role, and he gave them a political voice in the city councils.

The smell of change had been in the air for quite some time. In 1176, city militias had prevailed over the great German emperor

Frederick I before the gates of Milan. The seemingly unshakeable aura of Barbarossa had not been able to prevent the northern Italian cities from going their own way under the leadership of a local dictator. That possibility had tidily hamstrung Philip the Fair for the time being, but because of his blindness to the new power of the cities, France and Burgundy would be drawn into another series of military conflicts with the Flemish city militias in the fourteenth century.

Naturally, John of Burgundy was told by his tutor that his father, by marrying wisely, had managed to annex the lost regions of French Flanders in addition to acquiring the county. And that he had lied to his brother, Charles V, about ever giving these regions back to the French crown. In fact, the opposite was true. It was Philip's sacred intention to embrace these lands for all eternity. The duke was proud that thanks to him – and therefore thanks to Burgundy – the county could once again look upon such French-speaking cities as Lille, Douai and Cassel as Flemish property.

The message he gave his son John was clear.

We're never giving this up.

'The Shoe Restorer Cleaved His Head With An Axe'

The closer his tutor came to the present day, the greater John's concentration and attention. This was his own era, the doomed fourteenth century, the century in which the plague was waiting to pay a call, and above all the age of the Hundred Years War. That international conflict, which through John's doing would increase in intensity a few decades later, was also felt in Flanders. When King Edward III of England prepared to seize the French crown in 1337, there was only one question being raised in the north: what side should Flanders choose?

Count Louis of Nevers, John's maternal great-grandfather, did more than his duty to his French lord and took a group of English merchants prisoner in an act of provocation. The English king responded as if he had been stung by a wasp and brought all wool exports to a standstill. Now that the Flemish looms had shut down, the Flemish economy seemed destined to suffer the same fate. For the cities the choice was crystal clear. Despite all their feudal obligations to France, English wool remained the cornerstone of their wealth. The duchies of Brabant and Guelders took the same view, so that for the first time a small alliance of Low Countries was formed that committed itself to placating England. As it so often did, Ghent took the initiative, and during a popular assembly held at the beginning of 1338 it chose a new city council: five prominent men, led by one Jacob van Artevelde. Louis of Nevers was grudgingly forced to recognize Van Artevelde as his superior. Now it wasn't the count but a rich textile merchant who was lord and master in Flanders. Even the French king backed down and allowed the county to follow a neutral course. Edward III accepted this solution and the export of wool was resumed.

The Flemish count saw little point in putting up with this humiliating situation, so he fled to Paris. Van Artevelde now had everything going for him, and he decided to hold a magnificent masked procession. On 26 January 1340, Jacob van Artevelde was standing in the first row when Edward III was crowned King of France on Ghent's Friday Market Square. With this symbolic ceremony, the textile merchant created just the right legal basis for his rule – Flanders was still loyal to the 'French king', after all – which put French-English relations during the early days of the Hundred Years War on high alert.

Despite, or perhaps thanks to, all the English support, Van Artevelde didn't last long. France announced a grain embargo, thus exposing an important sore point. Economically, Flanders was dependent on English wool, but feeding the steadily increasing population required French grain, which was now in short supply. This was a problem that even the all-powerful Van Artevelde couldn't solve. His position became untenable when it was found that he had used Flemish money to sponsor Edward's war and was planning on appointing the Black Prince as the new Count of Flanders. Even the Anglophile Ghent was outraged.

On 24 July 1345, a crowd stormed Van Artevelde's home. According to an anonymous chronicler, the masses shouted threats that left little to the imagination. 'And they forced their way into the house, and Jacob had to try to escape through his stable, but the shoe restorer ran after him and cleaved his head with an axe.[9] And so the decade in which Flanders was being governed as a strange sort of republic came to a bloody end. All that time, the count sat sulking in his Paris hideaway. John's great-grandfather Louis of Nevers didn't even have a chance to enjoy a happy comeback. One year later he was killed on the battlefield of Crécy.

John of Burgundy listened with bated breath. In 1346 his grandfather Louis of Male came to power in Flanders, and the history lessons became much more tangible. He proudly learned that Louis, who ruled over the north with great skill, had initially managed to steer a middle course between France and England like a tightrope walker. He had been able to contain the overweening power of Ghent and other large cities like Bruges and Ypres. He had also succeeded in adding the Brabant seigniories of Antwerp and Mechelen to the county of Flanders by force of arms, thus blocking the use of the Scheldt as a transport artery and making sure that the Antwerp harbour was overshadowed by Bruges, at least for the time being. But that was the end of John's grandfather's success. The war with Brabant proved extremely costly, and it was the townspeople for the most part who had to foot the bill. Once again, the Ghentenars protested the loudest, an omen of greater disaster.

When it rained in Ghent back then, a few drops always fell in Paris. The fate of Van Artevelde spoke to the imagination. Étienne Marcel, master of the Paris merchants' guild and, like Van Artevelde, a dealer in textiles, organized a revolt in 1358 against Charles, the oldest brother of Philip the Bold. In the absence of their father – King John the Good was behind bars in England at the time – Marcel aimed his arrows at the dauphin. While egging the populace on with the cry 'Ghent!', Marcel managed to force his way into Charles's chambers and had two of his closest associates murdered before his very eyes. In addition, the dauphin was made to don a red-and-blue hat, the colours of the people of Paris.

When recalling this event, it's difficult not to think ahead to 20 June 1792, when the Tuileries Palace was stormed by the sans-culottes. They made Louis XVI pin a blue, white and red cockade onto his clothes, once again the colours of Paris but now with the royal white in between, which later became the tricolour of the nation. That hot June day in 1792 was almost like a re-enactment of the scene of 22 February 1358, as if the collective memory of the nation had unconsciously chosen to recall certain actions from the past.

With his tail between his legs the dauphin left the palace of the Conciergerie, which was transformed into a prison, and turned the Louvre into the royal residence in Paris. Marcel, like Van Artevelde, would ultimately be killed by his own townspeople. Even so, it had become patently obvious that the power of princes was no longer regarded as a legally binding gift of God. From then on, power would be either shared or disputed.

After Ghent and Paris, several other hotbeds of civil protest caught fire elsewhere in Europe. The name of the Flemish city could be heard everywhere. 'Ghent' had become a revolutionary battle cry.

GHENT THE FEARLESS

*Or how Ghent grew into the most stout-hearted city in
the west, how the Western Schism tore both the church
and the Flemish-Burgundian civil marriage asunder, and
how the Burgundian dukes nevertheless managed to confess
their faith with great sincerity.*

WITHIN THE SPACE of three centuries, the appearance of
Flanders underwent a total change. Ancestral lagoons
and creeks disappeared, forests from the time of the Celts were
chopped down, counts looked for ways to reduce their dependence
on the French but often ended up with just the opposite, new cities
sprang up and the textile industry transformed Flanders into one
of the richest regions in the world. To maintain it, the county had
to rely on the continuous delivery of English wool and hordes of
former serfs, who were absorbed into the battalions of overworked
labourers and craftsmen.

To say that it couldn't have been easy for John of Burgundy
to grasp this complex history would be an understatement. Just
trying to fathom current events must have made the boy's head
spin. Naturally, his primary concern was to find out what was
going on in rebellious Flanders at the present moment. In order
to explain that, tutor Baldwin van der Nieppe had no choice but
to make a detour to the Western Schism that tore the Catholic
Church apart. But how do you make a youngster understand that
in 1378 there were suddenly two different popes claiming to be
the ultimate representative of God on earth, one in Rome and the
other in Avignon? And that each of them had his own crowd of
followers? And that Burgundy, like France, had chosen Avignon,
while Flanders had chosen Rome?

First Van der Nieppe had to go back to 1305, the year the newly
elected Pope Clement V made it known that he was disinclined
to live in Rome, which was plagued by extreme violence. King
Philip the Fair of France may have been defeated by the Flemings

in 1302, but his real power was revealed four years later when he managed to move this pope across the European chessboard in the direction of Avignon. Politically the city belonged to the Holy Roman Empire, but it did lie right on the border. On the other side of the Rhône, which you could reach by means of a celebrated bridge, lay the kingdom of France. The popes knew that such a move would offer them protection, but they also knew that they would be closely monitored.

A colossal palace was built in Avignon, where the church worked to create greater centralization by channelling more power to the pope, the curia and the chancery. The dream of a return to Rome was never extinguished, but it wasn't until 1376 that another pope could travel to the Holy City. Just before the announced departure of Gregory XI, Charles V sent a diplomat with an impressive-sounding name to the south, none other than Philip the Bold, the king's most decisive and energetic brother. His mission was plain in its simplicity: to convince the pope to stay in Avignon. John was five years old when his father set out on that important southern journey.

As his boat glided down the Rhône, Philip could look back at the pleasant years he spent in his duchy. He had freed Burgundy from wandering gangs, improved the system of the annual fairs and was fully occupied with the modernization of winemaking. After a period of success and prestige, the production of that famous export had fallen into decline. Carelessness and laziness reigned. Philip the Bold woke the Burgundian winegrowers from their beauty sleep with a cluster of detailed measures from which he would craft a major wine law in 1395. His most important intervention was perhaps the banning of the Gamay grape, which, according to the duke, was only good for 'bitter wine in great quantities' and therefore 'must be torn out, root and branch'.[1] Gamay put up a good fight, but in the end it fled to the south and became the chosen grape used in the production of Beaujolais. Pinot noir, which fared better on the characteristic clay and limestone soil, began to increase in popularity and would become the quintessential Burgundian grape. The duke, who owned his own vineyards in Beaune, Pommard and Volnay, served his best Burgundies to placate Flemish and French patricians and noblemen. He also sold his wine by the vat at the gates of his ducal palace in Dijon. The arrival of his *nouveau vin* each autumn was a great event.

Philip knew that a vat of Beaune could smooth even the bumpiest negotiations, and he tried to put the Avignon pope in a good mood by offering him a large shipment of quality wines. Hadn't the poet Petrarch, who had grown up while his father was working at the papal court, complained that the only reason the curia insisted on staying in Avignon was to keep the wines of Beaune within reach? Yet God's chosen son Gregory XI was unrelenting, and he began his journey to Rome. Philip stayed behind with his brimming vats. That was the end of France's iron grip on Christianity. Apart from making the move, the pontiff didn't accomplish very much. Less than a year later he was dead. And then something happened that no one could have predicted.

Even though the French cardinals were in the vast majority at the conclave, an aggressive Roman mob forced them to elect an Italian pope, which they did for safety's sake. Who would it be? The young, inexperienced Urban VI would be someone they could keep in line. But power went to the new prelate's head, and in the confusion that followed he began railing against his cardinals day and night. He then withdrew his promise to return to Avignon. In the face of so much recalcitrance, the French quickly moved to elect an antipope. This French pope, Clement VII, was no soft touch either. To clear the way to Rome for Gregory XI, he had given the order the year before to kill thousands of rebels in the Italian city of Cesena. This dreadful bloodbath was still fresh in everyone's memory. 'Death to the Antichrist!' people shouted in the streets of Rome, and 'the butcher of Cesena' beat a hasty retreat to Avignon. Back in that little Provençal town, Clement VII announced that he was the only rightful pope. Urban VI was not impressed, and he stubbornly remained seated on the throne in Rome. Suddenly the Christian world was saddled with a towering dilemma: which pope to follow?

King Charles V of France wanted to keep the power of the church as close to Paris as possible, so he drew the Clement card.

England, France's traditional enemy, almost automatically opted for the rival candidate. Philip the Bold's Burgundy blindly followed the French crown. Entirely in keeping with his reputation as an Anglophile, and to the satisfaction of the cities, the Flemish count Louis of Male opted for the English camp, which meant that the French fief remained under Roman rule. His son-in-law, Philip of Burgundy, was forced to look on passively and accept the choice of his future subjects with much gnashing of teeth, but his brother Charles V was downright furious and called the Flemings traitors.

'Like A Prostitute At An Orgy'

So here we are. Since the autumn of 1378 we have had two popes, one illegitimate (the one in Rome) and one legitimate (the one in Avignon). That is approximately what Baldwin van der Nieppe must have said to his pupil, bringing him and his history lessons to the heart of current affairs.

These most recent developments didn't sound strange at all to John the Fearless. Thanks to the lessons of Baldwin van der Nieppe – who, after all, was a priest – and to the religious instruction of his pious mother, he was familiar with Bible stories and very knowledgeable when it came to church intrigue. Catholicism had anchored itself in his mind from an early age, and it never left his doomed body until four decades later, when his enemies brutally murdered him. On that occasion, as noted by the ducal records, scrupulously kept as usual, John was carrying 'an especially beautiful and richly decorated breviary'.[2]

He was eighteen months old when he went to church for the first time, or rather was taken to church by his mother, Margaret of Flanders. The education of a duke's son could not start soon enough, and his lessons began at the age of three, when he was taught to read from the *Sept Psaumes* book of psalms – in French. Dutch followed a few years later. In March 1378, just before the church was split in two by Catholic schismatics, the six-year-old was given his first prayer book from the hands of Guillaume de Vallan, Philip the Bold's confessor.

Like his father, he took a Dominican as his own confessor. The Dominicans owed their fame to itinerant preachers who magnetized huge crowds with their spectacular performances. The dukes were not insensitive to rhetorical feats of strength, but they were less scrupulous about the Dominican summons to sobriety. Confessors held an important position in court life. They heard the confessions of the duke and gave him absolution. As Dominicans they preached, of course, and on a regular schedule, and they published religious essays addressed to the attention of their employer. Like his father, John was a pious mortal who not only spent considerable sums of money on acts of charity but also set an example by devoting himself to religious practices. He attended daily Mass, as his parents did, and during major feasts he observed all the hours, from matins to compline, even occasionally spending an entire night in prayerful vigil. Whenever he travelled, John had a course mapped out that ran past churches and abbeys. The most insignificant trip was transformed into a glorified pilgrimage.

Like your average medieval man or woman, the Burgundian dukes had a deep faith in the power of the mortal remains of the saints: the touching of a toenail or a shinbone, a fragment of a coat or a splinter of a walking stick was believed to have miraculous effects. When Philip and John stopped at churches and monasteries, it wasn't just to attend Mass but it was also an opportunity to touch the local relics. It is known that John was the proud owner of a fragment of the skull of one of the 11,000 virgins who accompanied St Ursula, and who were invoked by believers to grant them good fortune in war and in marriage. His father Philip prided himself on having a handful of the ribs of St Louis, their illustrious forefather, which he kept in a display cabinet.

After counting up their religious fetishes and praying their rosaries, the dukes devoted themselves to the pleasures of realpolitik. Philip the Bold remained true to Avignon as long as it was politically expedient, and his son would have it no other way. It was more a question of international politics than piety. In their heart of hearts they must have wondered what they were supposed to do about the whole mess. For the average French, Burgundian,

English and Flemish Catholic, the Western Schism remained an entirely inextricable tangle. If it hadn't been Avignon that excommunicated Rome, then it was the other way round. When it came to dividing up the church's income, both popes were guilty of gross corruption and simony.

As addicted as they were to relics, saints and indulgences (by which you could earn a reduced sentence in purgatory), the people were terrified that the Schism might prevent them from ever reaching Paradise. Which choice would guarantee that you were on the right path? One chronicler said that Rome and Avignon took turns coaxing the church on 'like a prostitute at an orgy'.[3] But in the fourteenth century, not even the greatest visionary could predict that this schism would grow into a rift in the Catholic Church that held within it the seeds of the Reformation.

'Take Them Off As Speedily As You Can'

This history didn't really hit home for John until his grandfather, Louis of Male, came crawling to John's father to beg for help: the people of Ghent were in rebellion again. Was John reminded of his great-grandfather, Louis of Nevers, who tried to dampen the zeal of the Ghent textile merchant Jacob van Artevelde? Or his distant forefather, Philip of Alsace, who dealt with the haughty patricians from the city on the Leie?

For John, the best history lesson was the present day, while the past was his most revealing news bulletin. The big difference between now and then was that now there was an extra player in the game: his father, the powerful Duke of Burgundy, who – no matter how much he wanted to – was unable to escape from the ancient friction between France and Flanders.

*

The sun shone, the larks warbled, and in the imagination of the workmen the water was already gliding through the countryside. With their shovels as their only weapons, the day labourers tackled *le plat pays* and dug a canal from Bruges to Deinze. The sluggish

Leie River stank to high heaven, and this new waterway was meant to flush out the polluted sewers of Bruges. At least, that was the sales pitch that the people of Bruges were using to pull the wool over the eyes of the Ghentenars. But Ghent's good citizens wouldn't let themselves be taken in that easily. Naturally, they realized that the sole purpose of the project was to create a direct connection between Bruges and the Leie in Deinze, so that grain from France could reach their city without the costly detour through Ghent, and textiles from West Flanders could travel in the opposite direction more economically. A large portion of the staple rights by which Ghent had traditionally lined its coffers was now at risk of going up in smoke. And things were going downhill anyway.

After the death of Jacob van Artevelde in 1345, his political allies had been banished by Louis of Male. Many of them, with all their savoir-faire and experience, had gone to England to resume work as textile merchants. Contemporary Geoffrey Chaucer referred to this new trend with a playful reference in his *Canterbury Tales*. 'She bettered those of Ypres and of Ghent,'[*] he wrote of the skill of the Wife of Bath in the weaving of cloth. In due course, not only did the big textile producers suffer from the consequences of Flemish competition on the other side of the Channel, but cheaper textile products of considerably inferior quality were also being sold from smaller cities in the countryside.

In cities like Ghent, economic growth began to stagnate. Workers could only dream of less punishing wages. And just when things started looking especially precarious, the count saw fit to organize a great tournament, a feast that was to be paid for mainly by the people of Ghent and Bruges. Always the count's spoiled child, Bruges opened its purse with a smile – on the condition that the city be allowed to dig that canal. In typical Flanders fashion, Ghent grumbled in opposition. Count and city folk squabbled, the Ghentenars argued with the people of Bruges, and, as usual, the shadow of France and England hung over the local fray. It was typical of Ghent as well, although the top dog didn't stop with just a few barks.

In May 1379, the navvies of Bruges were halfway done with their canal when the White Hoods – the *Witte Kaproenen* – the dreaded Ghent city militia, appeared on the horizon. The canal diggers abandoned their wharves, and Jan Yoens, the leader of the White Hoods, returned in triumph with his gang to his home city. Nothing ever came of the canal. The count's bailiff wasn't going to take this lying down, and he arrested one member of the city militia. This apparently insignificant arrest was the falling domino that dragged down all of Flanders and would ultimately trigger a war with France.

The arrest was interpreted as an attack on city rights because the count's official had not consulted the aldermen and had acted purely on his own initiative. The indignant Ghentenars killed the bailiff and burned the count's new castle at Wondelgem to the ground. A long repressed sense of dissatisfaction bubbled to the surface: from wage slave to weaving supervisor, everyone had some frustration that had been festering in their hearts or their wallets.

Jan Yoens wasted no time. He and his troops had travelled throughout Flanders and managed to convince all the cities, with the exception of Dendermonde and Oudenaarde, to conspire against the count. The count's son-in-law, Philip the Bold, cobbled together a fragile truce, but he was unable to prevent the outraged count from seeking redress. Louis of Male knew what kind of people he was dealing with, and he managed to benefit from the Flemish disunity. He placated the nobility and the rich patricians, won their favour, and drove a wedge between Ghent and Bruges. Finally even Ypres abandoned the rebels, and Ghent was left isolated.

*

While the Ghentenars mobilized their forces and Philip the Bold waited to see which way the wind was blowing, an unexpected piece of news arrived that would be of vital importance to both Flanders and Burgundy. In 1380, King Charles V of France lay dying of tuberculosis.

Along with Bertrand du Guesclin, the notorious supreme commander of the French army, the king had succeeded in retaking his country city by city and came within an inch of leading France out of the hell of the Hundred Years War. On the day of his death, the English were still occupying the seaport towns of Brest, Calais and Cherbourg and a narrow strip of land between Bayonne and Bordeaux. If the king had lived a little less than ten years longer, the Hundred Years War might have been called the Fifty Years War.

During his sixteen-year reign, Charles V had strengthened countless cities and built scores of impregnable fortresses. One of these was the menacing bulwark that appeared above the streets of Paris. (The so-called Bastille would become world famous on 14 July 1789 and was immediately razed to the ground.) In addition to conducting a successful war policy, this oldest brother of Philip the Bold was also a patron of the arts and an art lover, a man who collected hundreds of precious manuscripts and books in a tower of the Louvre. Charles V was the first king to give shape to what later became the archetype of the great French leader: the politician-tactician who not only made the right decisions but could also quote from the right books.

And yet the great king was on the point of dying with a nagging conscience. He was all too aware that his support of the antipope in Avignon had plunged the church into its greatest crisis since its inception. If it hadn't been for his stubbornness, there would now be just one Holy See. How in God's name was Charles to face the Almighty? Of course he had almost rid France of the perfidious Albion, but he had financed that military undertaking by levying heavy taxes and sucking the ordinary Frenchman dry. His kingdom had become safer, but also poorer.

The cold breath of the Grim Reaper had moved countless medieval rulers to contrition and remorse. The king humbly declared that he had done wrong and that the *fouage* – a hefty property tax – would be cancelled immediately so that 'from now on our said people and subjects shall not pay any of them but shall be quit and discharged'.[5] His brothers scowled and wondered how the young dauphin would be able to accumulate the necessary means to carry out policy after his father's death. 'Take them off as speedily as you can,'[6] Charles murmured with his last ounce of strength, referring to the taxes.

On 16 September 1380, the forty-two-year-old Charles V passed away. The people found themselves with tax relief and a new king. The Parisians welcomed the young Charles VI with enthusiasm. But they cheered too soon, for his regent uncles would soon render the wish of the dying man a dead letter. The French king was barely twelve years old and had very little influence. The fate of the Hundred Years War now lay in the hands of two easily manipulated adolescents, for King Richard II of England was only thirteen. Both countries fell prey to the power games of greedy regents.

All this was more than obvious at the solemn coronation of Charles VI in the cathedral at Reims. Philip the Bold literally pushed his older brother Louis, the Duke of Anjou, from his chair, and calmly took his place beside the king. The coronation almost degenerated into hand-to-hand combat, but Charles VI soothed tempers and gave the Burgundian duke the much coveted place of honour.

John's father, who was gearing up to take control of Flanders, was the strong man in Paris from the start. He played the underage king like a marionette, and not only for the prestige that came with power. By having direct access to the treasury he could increase his ambitions considerably, and perhaps solve his father-in-law's problems at the same time. Weren't they by definition his problems as well? Why not settle the Flemish crisis with the help of the French army? And by cleverly hiding behind Charles VI, he could shift the resentment of his future subjects onto the crown. Once Philip the Bold recognized how rosily the future could unfold for him, he sprang into the French power vacuum like a tiger.

'The Worms Of The Earth Will Devour All The Lions'

Three times the Flemish count Louis of Male tried to starve out the rebellious Ghentenars by laying siege. Each siege ended in failure, but the fighting spirit within the ramparts was severely tested. 'If only Jacob van Artevelde were still alive,' sighed the famished burghers, who had lost most of their bravado. A majority of them supported a truce, but in late 1381 the extremists seized power and all hope of peace was lost.

To lend weight to their plans and to get all the Ghentenars on the same page, they rolled out their old artillery. It came in the form of a short man with small, piercing eyes, a voluble fellow with a vindictive disposition, owing to the death of his father. It was none other than Philip van Artevelde, the son of the legendary Jacob. He was given all the power, and he swore that he would lead Ghent to victory. First he dressed himself as if he were the King of France, then he eliminated the oldest sons of his father's murderers. Once that was taken care of, the little peacock could begin his bloody campaign against the Flemish count, invariably announced with a flourish of trumpets.

Louis of Male was not impressed. Now that he had reconquered practically all of Flanders, he decided to play hardball and demanded that Ghent surrender without delay. And not by placing a few signatures at the bottom of a sheet of parchment. No, Louis demanded that all the men of Ghent between the ages of fifteen and sixty appear before him in one long procession, and that they do it in a special way: without any head covering, barefoot, and with a noose round their necks. The count would then decide whom he would and would not pardon. Van Artevelde must have had a good laugh. For two decades he had been receiving an annuity from the English. So like his father he fixed his eyes on the other side of the Channel, where the promise of military support awaited him, giving a boost to his well-developed haughtiness.

On 5 May 1382, the starving Ghentenars – the three sieges had been a terrible ordeal – ambushed the count's troops at Bruges during the Procession of the Holy Blood. Their attack, or rather their act of desperation, caught the soldiers unawares, many of whom were unsteady on their feet on account of the festivities. The Ghentenars drove Louis's warriors to the centre of the city, where they carried out a bloodbath with axes and maces. The proud Count of Flanders fell off his horse and barely escaped with his life. 'If he hadn't run away he'd be dead,'[7] wrote the poet-chronicler Eustache Deschamps.

Night fell over the city like a dark blanket. As torches were being lit, the count fled through the streets of Bruges wearing his servant's clothes. Van Artevelde knew that Louis had to be somewhere, and he put a large price on his head. The hunt was on. The cry 'Ghent! Ghent!' resounded everywhere, as if the attackers were increasing by the minute. In despair, the terrified Louis knocked on a door. 'Let me in, madam, please. I am the Count of Flanders.'[8]

Whether it was from a sense of duty, fear or promises of gold, the door swung open. The proud Don Juan and begetter of eighteen bastards spent that night trembling in a child's cot. He got up at the crack of dawn and swam across the city's main canal, and two days later he reached Lille on the back of a farmer's bony nag.

There he learned that his mother, Margaret, had died, and that on the fateful day that he was being forced to abandon Flanders he had become Count of the Franche-Comté and Artois. Louis had nowhere to run, so he begged his Burgundian son-in-law for help.

*

Philip the Bold didn't hesitate for a moment. He harnessed his best horses and spurred them to action, doing full credit to his motto '*Il me tarde*' (I'm in a hurry, I wait for no one). Because of his importance, the motto was often corrupted into '*Moult me tarde*' (many wait for me). Both slogans were typical of his impulsive personality. The treasury had a special column in its books for 'horses worn out or killed in the service of Monseigneur'.[9] More than once he covered the 300 kilometres between Dijon and Paris in five days, spending from ten to eleven hours in the saddle. During the hot month of May in 1382 he galloped down the roads of France, oblivious to the dust his horse kicked up. A seasoned traveller, he had had gold and crystal eyeglasses made 'for the dust that blows in your eyes during horse riding'.[10]

In Senlis, the new French king went to meet him with a falcon on his fist. Above his large lower jaw and equally impressive nose glistened two powerful eyes. The Burgundian duke knew he had to deploy all his powers of persuasion to win the king over. The Flemings had thrown out their count, he told the king. His patrimony was in danger. The son of the rebellious cloth merchant had appointed brand-new mayors in many places and was now considering new laws. But worse than that, this same man was steering the county into English waters. That was all it took to convince the fourteen-year-old French monarch.

With the enthusiasm of adolescence, Charles VI dreamed of more heroic adventures than carrying a falcon around. 'There's nothing I would rather do than go into battle, for I have never handled a weapon, which is essential if I am to rule in a strong and honourable way.'[11] He immediately imposed a heavy tax to mobilize his war machine.

Before the fourteenth century, feudal armies were made up of vassals who quickly dispensed with their duties in order to see to their own local affairs. Now armies were reinforced by mercenaries who fought for whoever would pay them. Kings could no longer afford the exorbitant costs that this practice involved. They sought to borrow from bankers if necessary, and in time from rich cities. The complex financing of wars was still in its infancy and resulted in countless unpaid debts. The havoc wreaked by military action was bad enough, but such emergency taxation was a drain on resources that brought medieval states to the brink of collapse. In addition, French soldiers destroyed or devoured a large portion of the harvests, rendering the starving population an easy prey to infectious disease.

Charles VI, with his love of sword play, couldn't care less. The brothers of Philip the Bold, the quarrelsome regent uncles Anjou and Berry, and the Duke of Bourbon, brother-in-law of Charles V and member of the regency council, promised their assistance. All the Burgundian duke had to do was to let it be known that, like Ghent, the residents of Blois, Chalon, Orléans, Reims and Rouen were also rising up in revolt. If they failed to crush the spider in the web of insurrection, the future of their own class could be jeopardized. The aristocracy were shaking in their boots. The words of the Franciscan monk John of Rupescissa, who was repeatedly imprisoned for his writings and had died an invalid fifteen years earlier, had sent many Europeans into raptures. Now there was a danger that his words would become reality: 'First, the worms of the earth will take up such strength and boldness that they will cruelly devour all the lions, bears, leopards, and wolves. [...] the justice of the people will rise up and devour the traitorous noble tyrants in the mouth of twice-sharpened swords.'[12]

Popular uprisings broke out in Italy and England almost simultaneously with those in France and Flanders. Peasants and craftsmen were sick and tired of the endless taxes and refused to bear the burden of their lords' wartime expenses any longer. That unrest gave rise to a longing for more rights. Now that Christian charity was no longer enough to placate the indigent, who were tormented by plague, war and economic crisis, the established order was at a loss as to how to deal with the growing self-awareness of the lower class. At first the nobility and clergy were willing to wait and see, but when they realized that their position was being seriously threatened, they drew their swords.

The city of Ghent, which was gradually becoming famous throughout Europe, embodied the spirit of impending change more vigorously than anywhere else. Of course, the metropolis wasn't just an association of workers but a city that stood up for its rights as a body, and in doing so represented both the big merchants and the modest day labourers. They had plenty to squabble over among themselves, but all of them were fervently committed in their stand against the counts, dukes and kings.

'We Will Teach Him To Speak Flemish'

In the autumn of 1382, Charles VI convened a gathering in Arras. John's father could count himself lucky. He had managed to get the French kingdom to straighten out his Flemish mess. Not bad for someone who in fact possessed only a few territories around Dijon, which together amounted to a modest region between the Saône and the Morvan, only a fraction of Gundobad's old kingdom. If he really wanted to join in the game, he would have to save Flanders, no matter what the cost.

Van Artevelde's best tactic was obvious: to let the French stew in the dampness of the Flemish autumn until they left, staggering and shivering all over. The coldest season had started, and tradition prescribed a kind of military winter break. Everyone would go home to rest and warm up, after which the game of warfare could begin anew in the spring. But waiting was a waste of time for the impatient Van Artevelde, who did everything he could to trounce the French-Burgundian army. It was as if he had made the heraldic motto of Philip the Bold his own.

Then 10,000 Frenchmen – a fifth of whom were Burgundian soldiers – entered Flanders by way of the town of Komen, which had been conquered with great difficulty. Van Artevelde went out to meet them on 26 November, and near a swamp in Westrozebeke, a little village between Ypres and Roeselare, he saw the French banners and lances appear on the horizon. The two armies set up camp and got ready for the impending battle. For the time being, the general din and tapping of weapons were all they noticed of each other.

That evening round the campfire, the poet-chronicler Eustache Deschamps, whom the king had ordered to accompany the army to the clammy north, put into words his own unease and that of almost the entire army: 'The root of all this malicious baseness and betrayal of chivalric values is Ghent, which fancies itself above the law.'[13] The French-Burgundian warriors had developed a deep-seated loathing of the Ghentenars. Wasn't it their fault that the French had to grease their weapons every day in the drizzling rain?

Deschamps called on his fellow countrymen to 'impale the Flemings with their lances'.[14] All they had to fight with anyway were 'wheelbarrows and carts'. At the same time, he wondered aloud why he as a diplomatic courier was wasting his time in the Flemish mud. Yet for someone who sought to pack his poetry with worldly events, it must have been a chance of a lifetime to follow this hot news from close range. Deschamps, who came from the Champagne district, would remain a grouser till the end of his days and would shriek his profound dissatisfaction with the world in countless verses. In that sense, he was just the man to put into words the hatred being directed at the Ghentenars.

The very evening that Deschamps committed his indignation to paper, the Ghent leader addressed his captains. He was quite formal in conveying the bad news that in the end the English hadn't shown up: 'They would rob us of our fame before our very eyes.'[15] After all, having the French king descend on Flanders along with the flower of his nobility would be a golden opportunity, the ideal chance to deal with their arrogant southern neighbour. The fact that his remarks were preserved for posterity was not thanks to the grumbling Deschamps but to Jean Froissart.

The forty-five-year-old Froissart was three years older than his fellow chronicler Deschamps. Fearing that the tyranny of rhyming might tempt him to introduce inaccuracies or meaningless repetition, he decided not to write in rhymed verse. Chroniclers tell the story of their patrons, of course, but Froissart's patient way of gathering information, as well as his empathy, resulted in reports that are still worth quoting.

Like Deschamps, he was stationed in the camp of Charles VI. Froissart seemed to have a warmer spot in his heart for Flanders than Deschamps did. Naturally he condemned the Ghentenars, who were shaking up the feudal structures ordained by God, but the tone of his stories does betray a certain respect for the courage of the Ghent city militia. On the other hand, the more 'journalistically' inclined Froissart made no effort to gloss over the frivolity and megalomania of the Ghent leader.

'Tell your soldiers to show no mercy and to slaughter the lot. Spare no one but the French king. He is still a child, and he bears no blame. We will take him to Ghent, and there we will teach him to speak Flemish.'[16] After making this pronouncement, Philip van Artevelde withdrew into his tent. While he sought diversion in the arms of a Ghent beauty, the French boy king consulted his war council. The council expressed some dissatisfaction with Philip the Bold, who had taken a great risk by dragging the young Charles VI into this battle.

The Duke of Burgundy realized that he had to nip this doubt in the bud. The best swordsmen in the kingdom were told not to stray an inch from Charles's side, and the knight Guillaume des Bordes was ordered to hold tight to the reins of the king's horse. Officially, Philip placed the king within the heart of his troops, but in reality the fourteen-year-old monarch was kept somewhere safe in the rear.

For John's grandfather, Louis of Male, preparations for the Battle of Westrozebeke must have been difficult and humiliating. Not only did the French look down on him for his support of the pope in Rome, but in their eyes he was the idiot count who had to be rescued from the claws of the Flemish lion. To embarrass him, they placed him in the rear guard.

And so it happened, Baldwin van der Nieppe must have told young John, the son of Philip the Bold – so it happened that both the Flemish count and the French king found themselves at a safe distance from the place where all hell broke loose.

1789 AVANT LA LETTRE

*Or how a precursor of the French Revolution was nipped
in the bud on Flemish soil, and how time changed, both
figuratively and literally.*

A STONE'S THROW from the site where the terrible Battle of Passchendaele erupted 534 years later, two armies prepared for a totally forgotten showdown. Yet the Battle of Westrozebeke is of anecdotal and especially historical value and deserves to be snatched from the jaws of oblivion. This confrontation not only epitomized Philip the Bold's turbulent era, but it was also a prelude to another uprising – a successful one – that would take place some four centuries later.

To understand this, we have to go back to the foggy morning of 27 November 1382. Let us train our historical telescope on the two warring parties: Flemish arrogance face to face with French-Burgundian suspicion, commoners against nobility, Van Artevelde versus Philip the Bold (who shrewdly hid himself behind Charles VI), a greatly expanded city militia against half as many knights, but knights who were better equipped and fully experienced. Before dawn, the French unfurled the legendary *Oriflamme*, the main banner of Charlemagne, an orange-and-red battle standard decorated with golden flames that was only raised in holy combat. Because the Flemings had taken the side of the Roman pope, Urban VI, the campaign also took on the allure of a crusade. Avignon against Rome!

Philip of Artevelde could not restrain his impatience. He gave the order to attack and thereby lost his advantageous position on higher ground. With their lances, spears, sticks and clubs, the Flemings plunged into the wisps of morning fog that hovered before them. Their leader ran with them, taking his place in the front ranks of his fearsome White Hoods, and they all hooked arms to keep from getting lost in the mist. The French quaked with fear as a raging roar rolled down the facing slope.

At that very moment, the sun broke through. 'The spectacle was wondrous to behold: gleaming helmets, glittering weaponry, dazzling lances of steel,' wrote Froissart. The banners of Flanders's cities and trade guilds approached at full speed. 'There were so many of them that it looked like a forest.'[1] Van Artevelde strode beside a black flag bearing a silver lion, the great city banner of Ghent. The French commander Olivier de Clisson shouted himself hoarse in an effort to calm his troops.

The blow was enormous. The Flemings trampled the first French ranks 'like rampaging wild boars', driving deep into the opposing forces. De Clisson kept one eye on the king, the other on the two wings of his army. At first he didn't know how to react, but he was rescued by the alertness of the Duke of Bourbon and Ingelram de Coucy, the commanders of France's left and right flanks. Calmly seated on their horses, they carried on a dialogue amid the tumult of the Flemish attack that you can read about in the chronicles. Their conversation ended with Bourbon's remarkably sober words, 'That, my dear cousin, is good advice.'

It's not likely that there was time for such a polite conclusion to a tactical discussion in the heat of the battle, but we do know for certain that De Coucy ordered his infantry to attack the wild Flemings with such ferocity that it seemed 'as if all the bladesmiths of Paris and Brussels together were bearing down on them'.[2] For their part, the French knights cornered Van Artevelde's troops with a flanking manoeuvre.

Suddenly the Flemish rearguard found themselves cut off from their leader. While most of the attacking army was being held in an immense, living dungeon – thick walls of French soldiers – the remainder took to their heels. Faced with superior strength, the boxed-in Flemings had no choice but to retreat, but now that was impossible. The Ghent freedom fighters just stood there, pressed together in desperation. 'The mighty lances of Bordeaux cracked the hauberks open and sank into the flesh... They cowered, for never does a man give himself over to being impaled, not even if victory is at stake,'[3] wrote Froissart matter-of-factly.

The blood flowed only on the outside of the writhing circle. On the inside, the unstoppable process of suffocation caused a different kind of slaughter. The sound of hand-to-hand combat that had so fiercely characterized the beginning of the battle had turned into the groaning of men gasping for air, the cracking of imploding ribcages, and gradually the inaudible begging for air and light. Afterwards, the battlefield was littered with a vast number of bodies and hardly any traces of blood. They had been crushed and shattered by their own brothers-in-arms.

Van Artevelde was struck on the head, then trampled underfoot by his own troops. A captured Fleming later identified his mortal remains in a pile of bodies. 'And his stockings were padded at the knee with fur', we read in the *Bouck van Memorien der stadt Gent* (*Book of the Writings of the City of Ghent*). Charles VI must have laughed with pity. In his eyes, Philip van Artevelde was no more than a weakling if he had to wear fur knee pads to ease the chafing of his armour. He kicked the stripped body 'as if it were that of a serf' and had it hung from a tree on the battlefield.

To the surprise of the French, the battle lasted less than two hours. It induced Deschamps to write a victory poem in which every stanza ended in '*qui desconfiz furent en pou de temps*', which means that the Flemings were cut to pieces in the twinkling of an eye. It was sweet revenge for the time that the French, exactly eighty years earlier and fewer than twenty-five kilometres away, had been slaughtered by the Flemings on the Groeningekouter in Kortrijk.

While the crows feasted on the body of the protector of Flanders, the French, hungry for booty, rushed on to Kortrijk. As is so often the case, the war had to pay for itself. Funnelling tax revenues was a slow and inaccurate undertaking, and unpaid wages forced the mercenaries to collect their salary on the battlefield.

Before burning the plundered city to the ground – 'they set fire to Kortrijk on every side'[4] – they turned their attention to a much favoured and lucrative business of war: taking wealthy burghers captive and demanding ransom. Like a vulture, Commerce descended wherever War had broken camp.

'From Which She Still Hears Terce And Nones Ring Out'

To settle old scores, the French removed from the vaulting of the Church of Our Lady 'the five hundred golden spurs', which had been hanging there for eight decades as a relic of the miracle of 1302. The fifty-two-year-old Louis of Male could beg and plead all he wanted to save his beloved Kortrijk, but the fourteen-year-old Charles VI was unrelenting. Under the delusion that he, a wunderkind, had decided the Battle of Westrozebeke all by himself, the young monarch swore that the town's inhabitants would long remember that the King of France had been there. The plundering and burning of Kortrijk was the umpteenth blot on the escutcheon of the Flemish count, who was gradually wearing himself out with fighting.

For his part, Philip the Bold, always cleverly hidden behind fleurs-de-lis, just let it go. He knew you couldn't make an omelette without breaking eggs, and he let his Burgundian warriors serve themselves. He himself pinched a remarkable war trophy. The careful dismantling of the lovely bell tower was an act with at least as much symbolism as the removal of the golden spurs. From then on, the Duke of Burgundy would determine how the hours passed in Flanders. A procession of ox-carts transported the technical wonder to Dijon, where the so-called *Jacquemart* – the name of the mechanical figure that struck the hour – still manages the time from the Church of Our Lady.

*

For the Romans, the year began on 1 March. This explains the names of some of the other months, like September, October, November and December, which originally were months number seven (*septem*), eight (*octo*), nine (*novem*) and ten (*decem*). February was the last and twelfth month in the series and was assigned the number of days that remained – twenty-eight – sometimes supplemented with an extra leap day. In most of medieval Europe, the calendar still began with the coming of spring, determined more by Easter. Only in the course of the sixteenth century would the entire continent swap the

Resurrection for the Circumcision of Christ and establish the first of January as the beginning of the year.

In the Middle Ages, the notion of time was anything but precise and concrete. Scholars set their minds to unravelling spans of time in the Bible. It seems that Christ was dead for exactly forty hours, and Adam stuck it out for only seven hours in the Garden of Eden. But when it came to the here and now, timekeeping was a vague business. There was nothing remarkable about that, since the available technology allowed for little precision. Sundials only worked when it was sunny, and hourglasses varied in accordance with the grains of sand being used; 'the duration of three candles' differed greatly from church to kitchen. In the famous *Viandier* (*c.*1380), the first culinary masterpiece in French history, the writer-cook Guillaume Tirel said very little about the preparation time required for various dishes, unless it was based on religious inducements: letting a dish simmer while reeling off eighteen Our Fathers or twenty-three Hail Marys.

As even the cookbooks demonstrate, there was a thread of religion running through the age. Monasteries and abbeys were the nerve centres of this system. The day itself was divided into periods of three hours, each preceded by a prayer service, beginning with matins at around midnight, lauds around sunrise, followed by prime, terce and sext (around midday, the sixth hour after sunrise, *sexta hora*, from which siesta is derived), none, vespers and compline (which completes the day at around nine in the evening). The Matins of Bruges, referring to the massacre of the French garrison in 1302, was named after the first prayer of the day, the sounding of which was the signal for knives to be drawn.

The time between the various services was filled with clear-cut tasks, and an objective observer could tell what time it was depending on whether he encountered the brothers in the garden, the refectory, the church, the laundry room or the dormitory. Monks appeared like the hands of an imaginary clock. The monastery became a living timepiece, a mechanism entirely driven by God. Urban and rural environments could also organize the working day along the same lines. One of the monastics was charged with monitoring the time; this '*sorghvuldigen broeder*' – careful brother

– would ring the bells so his colleagues would have enough time to get to the proper prayer services. The reference points, of course, were sunrise and sunset, but mastering time was mainly a matter of observing the stars and checking the sundials.

In around 1300, this centuries-old way of life came under threat. Urbanization and industrialization required well-defined working hours. Wage labour didn't get very far with the marking of lauds and vespers. Thanks to the invention of what is known as escapement, in which the balance wheel of a timepiece is turned by means of gradual jumps, the first mechanical clocks soon graced the bell towers in all the major cities. At first the hours were struck by automatons, and it wasn't until later on that hands were introduced to literally indicate the changing time. Because peasants, labourers and burghers often made mistakes in counting the strokes and weren't sure whether it was roughly nine or ten o'clock, it soon became fashionable to ring four preliminary chimes. A brief melody announced that the hour would soon be struck, which gave everyone enough time to focus their concentration. This forerunner of the carillon was called a *quadrillon* in French (literally a foursome), which was corrupted into *carillon*, the name that would be adopted by other languages, English and Dutch among them.

Along with the urban areas of northern Italy, Flemish cities such as Kortrijk, Ghent and Bruges once again played a leading role in this development. The new age of the laity was subject to the whims of technology. Different cities had different times, a situation that continued for centuries. It wasn't until the coming of the railways in the nineteenth century that a standardized national time would be introduced.

'Florence, enclosed within her ancient walls / from which she still hears terce and nones ring out, / once lived in peace, a pure and temperate town.' The poet Dante Alighieri placed these words in the mouth of his great-grandfather, Cacciaguida, who addresses him in three *Paradise* cantos from his *Divine Comedy* (early fourteenth century).[5] These verses reveal that the writer is looking back nostalgically to the olden days, when people worked according to 'terce and nones' and weren't oppressed by the new age of the laity. The workers in the Dijon vineyards were none too enthusiastic about the innovations either. For employers, the system was a useful tool for increasing working hours and productivity. Workers and craftsmen, who were already being exploited, were forced into a tight-fitting temporal corset.

The Duke of Burgundy was less nostalgic than Dante. Philip the Bold bought twenty 'wearable' *orloges* in Arras so he would always know the correct time while travelling. Along with his special dust spectacles, Philip's appearance at the end of the fourteenth century became more and more futuristic. His wife, Margaret of Flanders, who was just as keen on travelling as her husband, never went anywhere without her own personal timepiece. This wonder of technology was almost as precious to her as her ever-present rosary. But while the prayer beads fit perfectly in the hand, the *orloge* was far too cumbersome to wrap neatly around the wrist. So from then on, her retinue consisted of an extra cart for lugging the immense object around and a Flemish or Dutch specialist whose job it was to keep the thing adjusted, since it was constantly losing time.

In the meantime, back in their capital of Dijon, the Jacquemart, which had been stolen from Kortrijk, was still tirelessly striking the hours throughout the day. Soon the duke ordered a similar city clock for Beaune. The complicated construction, the wages for the man who wound the clock, and the frequent overhauls made it an expensive undertaking, but the Burgundians were determined not to miss the wave of innovation.

'Serfs You Are And Serfs You Will Remain'

'All of you, from small to great, shall be wiped out one by one / Your name shall be effaced, sown with salt, choked / Wicked city of Ghent, bear this in mind.'[6] The pen of Eustache Deschamps spouted poison, not least in order to convey a sense of urgency to his own camp. According to Deschamps, Charles VI was wrong to waste too much time in Kortrijk. 'If he had immediately given chase, Ghent would have been his,'[7] wrote his Flemish colleague

Olivier van Dixmude. But the king was already back in France, where he had other things on his mind. Otherwise he might have ridden straight on to Ghent to subdue the city himself.

Paris had descended into pandemonium in recent months. Labourers, peasants and craftsmen had stormed the city hall and stolen the 3,000 war hammers that the government was keeping on hand to subdue civil disorder. Thus armed, the rioters themselves went on the rampage. The city council threw in their lot with the agitators. While the king was on his way to Westrozebeke, the capital was tearing itself loose from the kingdom. After the battle, he hurried back to Paris. Flanders had now become occupied territory, with French-Burgundian garrisons everywhere. Only Ghent was off limits. His advisors must have advised the king that the city, with its kilometres of walls and its position between the Leie and the Scheldt, was as good as impregnable. In addition, winter was coming and the French capital was in need of urgent relief.

Charles's troops arrived at the gates of Paris in early January. A battle was out of the question. The insurgents had been so demoralized by the defeat at Westrozebeke that the king reached his palace without a hitch, but that didn't make his repression any less merciless. Everyone involved in the uprising was either put under lock and key or killed outright. Workers hurried to complete the Bastille, and the Louvre was soon enhanced by a gigantic castle tower. That imposing house of torture would keep Paris in line, or so the king thought.

After the fall of Paris, Philip the Bold used a portion of the revenue to finally pay his troops. Almost half the Burgundian forces at Westrozebeke came from Dijon. Upon his return to the ducal capital, Philip gave the city a special gift: permission to adopt the duke's motto. Mayor Jean Poissonnet was so proud that he used the motto as an advertising slogan. He was a mustard maker by trade, and soon the '*Moult me tarde*' came to adorn every mustard pot from Dijon. Legend has it that the local speciality owes its French name to Philip's gift.

In any case, we do know for certain that the duke was mad for *moutarde*. In addition to improving the viniculture, he also devoted himself to modernizing the manufacture of that condiment. Eight years after Westrozebeke, Philip poured all his findings into a government decree which stated that mustard 'must be made from high-quality seeds... seeds that should be soaked in good wine vinegar'.[8] To lessen the bitterness of the cracked seeds, the product could not be sold until twelve days after being prepared. Perhaps it was due to Philip's passion for rules that it became customary in Burgundy to replace the commonly used grape must with vinegar in the production process, which gave the mustard a sharper taste and longer storage life.

It's far more likely that mustard took its name from the use of grape must: *'mustum'* (must) and *'ardens'* (burning). The *'Moult me tarde'* from Westrozebeke-Dijon sounds a bit less credible than the 'burning must' from the dictionary, but the more imaginative neologism nicely illustrates how condiment and city were almost synonymous as early as the fourteenth century.

*

Flemings today only remember the Battle of the Golden Spurs of 1302, and in French history, Westrozebeke has disappeared between the cracks of the Hundred Years War. Nevertheless, the clash of Ghent and other sympathetic cities with count, duke and king is the most salient example of an international revolutionary movement. The third estate – a collective term comprising both well-to-do burghers and indigent weavers – put a knife to the throat of the leading feudal class. In the final analysis, the total commitment at Westrozebeke was much more significant than battles such as Crécy and Poitiers, which appealed more to the imagination. It wasn't a question of English knights taking a stand against their French counterparts. It didn't have to do with the possible loss of territory. It was all about the potential demise of a worldview.

If the Ghentenars had won, wrote the brash chroniclers, they would have crowned Van Artevelde king in Paris. But it wouldn't have been easy for Charles VI to smother revolt in the cities of France. Froissart didn't hold back in his analysis: 'The third estate would have unleashed a revolution in other lands that was aimed at wiping out the entire aristocracy.'[9]

That possible upheaval should not be painted in overly democratic colours. Just look at Ghent. More and more people of humble origins were occupying seats on the city council, but the real power still lay in the hands of whoever could gather the largest militia behind him. Van Artevelde was a local tyrant who brought his opponents to ruin and indulged his friends. It would be too easy to regard the cities of the Late Middle Ages as the cradle of our modern democracy, even though that's where the traditional power dynamics did begin to shift. If Ghent had won the battle, then the Battle of Westrozebeke probably would have had the same impact as the Battle of Valmy in 1792, where French revolutionaries defeated a coalition of aristocrats. That victory not only put a decisive end to the Ancien Régime, but it also guaranteed the survival of the French Revolution, which was then under threat, just as a victory at Westrozebeke might have given the power of change an unseen impetus.

Ghent's defeat was now echoed in other attempts to incite government upheaval. The capitulation of Paris was followed by Rouen, Blois, Orléans and other cities. From then on, all public officials would be royalists. All that commoners' blood, shed for nothing. According to Deschamps, who had not calmed down by any means, it was only 'lawless, traitorous, spiteful, deceitful, disgraced, hated, monstrous' Ghent that was still standing up to the feudal power structures.[10]

This fiasco made people far less eager to launch a revolution of that nature and on that scale for quite some time, but it did put the leaders of the great Revolution of four centuries later in perspective: the revolutionaries of 1789 were the fortunate descendants of the failed fourteenth-century upheaval. Desmoulins, Robespierre and Danton sat on the shoulders of figures such as Étienne Marcel and the two Van Arteveldes. The Bastille arose in 1383 as the patron saint of the monarchy and would be razed in 1789 to lend symbolic force to the ending of the Ancien Régime.

And the cities? They would keep making waves, with Ghent in the lead, as usual. But despite their strength and vitality, the greater part of Europe evolved into an absolutist form of government led by strong monarchs. The people of the Late Middle Ages, unlike those of the eighteenth century, maintained an unswerving faith and trust in their duly anointed Catholic king, no matter what. During the English Peasants' Revolt of 1381, the only one who was able to inspire calm and order was the angelic figure of fourteen-year-old King Richard II. The ever popular Charles VI of France enjoyed a similar appeal. The divine aura of protector was a bonus that Charles's distant descendant, Louis XVI, could no longer count on in 1789.

Enjoying the favour of the people didn't keep the young Richard from speaking the truth: 'Serfs you are and serfs you will remain.' Charles VI would be the last to contradict him. Louis XVI, on the other hand, hardly dared to even think those words after 1789, and he ended up on the guillotine anyway, despite his willingness to please. He paid the price for centuries of monarchy and oppression. The legacy of Westrozebeke lay fermenting in the soil that held the blood of his decapitated body.

On a smaller scale, the battle was primarily a big success for Philip the Bold, who now seemed more than ready to succeed the washed-up Louis of Male as the Count of Flanders. By way of celebration, he had a wall tapestry woven on which the battle was illustrated. He didn't hang it up, however, but used it as a carpet so that every day he could tread on the defeated third estate with the soles of his feet. The widely acclaimed work of art, which unfortunately was lost in the course of time, made a big impression on everyone who walked through the ducal palace, doubtless including the twelve-year-old John of Burgundy. It's not even inconceivable that Baldwin van der Nieppe used it to tell him the story of his father's victory down to the smallest details, while standing on the likeness of the fallen Van Artevelde.

'Nowhere Do You Find Such Bad People'

Out on their island, the English had also anxiously awaited the outcome of Westrozebeke. With an instinctive sense of self-preservation, the king and his retinue hoped that the riff-raff would get the worst of it. Once they had shared their relief among themselves, they realized what a mistake it would be for the French to let success go to their heads because they had beaten a horde of city militias. The future of the aristocracy was an important consideration when counting up the pros and cons of war, but so was the economy. There was an urgent need to regularize the wool export to Flanders, which so often had been blockaded. The appeal issued by Pope Urban VI to attack France, Avignon's patron, and to organize a crusade 'against the schismatics' in Flanders did not go unheeded on the other side of the Channel. The fact that the English would then loot and pillage their way through Flanders, which actually had taken Rome's side, was wilfully overlooked: the county that was so important to England had to be liberated from those French schismatics – at least, that's how they saw it.

After all his good fortune, King Charles VI of France was optimistic as he headed into the spring of 1383. So he was all the more shocked when his Uncle Philip showed up in early May looking despondent. It was more bad news from the north. The Duke of Burgundy spat the truth in his face. That an English army, under the command of Bishop Henry Despenser, had landed in Calais. That he had taken Grevelingen, Dunkirk, Broekburg and Cassel by storm. That Sint-Winoksbergen, Veurne, Nieuwpoort and Diksmuide had surrendered without a fight. That the English, with assistance of troops from Ghent, had just laid siege to the great Ypres. That they seemed determined to reverse the French-Burgundian domination of Flanders. That there was no time to lose.

Then another miracle happened. For the second time in a year, Charles VI, his honour impugned, gathered an impressive army together to get his uncle out of trouble. Antipope Clement VII, who earlier had blessed the Westrozebeke campaign, got wind of the French mobilization and responded by christening this expedition his very own crusade. In effect, the Catholic schismatics were giving France and England the ideal pretext for fighting out their political vendettas.

In the meantime, the people of Ypres had made a sober assessment. Their city was too big. Because of the success of the textile industry, a collection of new districts had arisen over the course of the thirteenth century and attached themselves to the old city like piglets to a sow. A rampart was also built to enclose this suburb. But the fortification proved too large to defend, and the people of Ypres quickly decided to retreat into the old centre.

The English immediately razed the suburb to the ground. How optimistic they were! Three days! That's all the time they thought they would need to bring Ypres to its knees. But despite support from Ghent, despite bombardment with countless cannonballs, attacks with battering rams and the continuous efforts to starve out the populace, Ypres wouldn't budge. And by the time the French-Burgundian troops appeared in early August 1383, the English-Ghent coalition had come to the end of their tether. Not a day too soon, either, for the hunger the people were suffering inside the city walls was threatening to break their morale. In desperation, the people of Ypres had offered up prayers to the Virgin Mary. Now that the enemy had been driven off and was headed towards the coast, the townspeople attributed the deliverance of their city to the aid of the Holy Virgin. Even today, a procession of thanksgiving is held every first Saturday of August to commemorate the time when the Mother of God rescued the city from the English and the Ghentenars.

For all that, Our Lady was not able to prevent the siege from dealing a death blow to the once prosperous city of Ypres. At the beginning of the century there were 30,000 people living in the shadow of the new Cloth Hall, but after the economic crisis, the plague and the English campaign, only a little more than 10,000 remained. The former metropolis would never completely recover from the decline of the fourteenth century.

*

For its part, Ghent could pray as much as it liked to Our Lady, but after the flight of the English it found itself alone again in its struggle against count, duke and king. For the umpteenth time, the City of Artevelde demonstrated its resilience. On the day of the English surrender, the Ghentenars captured the city of Oudenaarde and took control of the Scheldt. Count, duke and king were amazed by their extreme stubbornness, but they had their hands full with the English. The peace negotiations dragged on and on, and to kill time the French and the English knights fought the battle all over again by organizing jousts.

For the last time, Louis of Male joined in the deliberations and firmly stood his ground. Peace was one thing, but not with the Ghentenars. The city would have to pay for all the misery the county had suffered at its hands. The count refused to back down.

But once again he was forced to give in. Ghent, too, was able to benefit from the truce that was signed on 26 January 1384. Remarkably, the French-Burgundian troops left it at that. Calais, the important port city that had been in English hands since the beginning of the Hundred Years War, was there for the taking like never before, in view of the troops assembled there following the English defeat, but the French let it go. Calais remained English. And Ghent remained Ghent.

Louis of Male bit his tongue. He gnashed his teeth with rage. He must have worn out his chin tugging on his goatee. The great realization was undeniable: he no longer counted. His time was passed. The broken count bowed and disappeared, never to return. Three days later he dictated his last will and testament in Saint-Omer, and on 30 January he died.

In a sense, the fifty-three-year-old Louis was the last Count of Flanders. From then on, foreign rulers would decide the fate of the county, beginning with his son-in-law Philip the Bold, uncle of the King of France, Duke of Burgundy and Count of Artois, Nevers, the Franche-Comté, Rethel and now Flanders itself. He seized his father-in-law's funeral as an opportunity to focus attention on his new status.

Striding slowly among the almost 2,000 candles that illuminated the Sint-Pieterskerk in Lille was Philip's wife, Margaret. Everyone had a chance to thoroughly admire her mourning cloak. No fewer than two hundred squirrels had been worked into the cloak's design, a feature that was not lost on the assembled guests. The Burgundian duke knew what he was doing: pulling out all the stops in an effort to win allegiance.

The colourful banners of all the counties and seigniories that belonged to the count-duke hung over the bier. Beside it stood ten knights in dazzling regalia, five Flemings and five Burgundians. They symbolized the most significant implication of this funeral: Flanders and Burgundy would be shackled together from now on. Philip had a detailed report written of the extravagant solemnities and saw to it that many copies were made and widely distributed. Having power is one thing, a clever display of power is another.

John of Burgundy was now the second in line. If anything should happen to his father, the power would fall to him. Under the guidance of Baldwin van der Nieppe, he steeped himself for the next three years in language and history. Philip the Bold gave John the countship of Nevers and decided his son was gradually becoming ready to make his entrance into public life. On 28 May 1384, his thirteenth birthday, John was officially presented to the fifteen-year-old King Charles VI.

There stood the two cousins, face to face in the royal chambers. John knelt reverently. Charles nodded. Even then it was clear that the gaze of the former was livelier and more alert. His facial expression radiated cunning. He came across as a bit more reserved than his father. More furtive, his enemies would later say.

It is not known whether they said anything to each other during that first meeting that went beyond the requirements of mere protocol, but from then on their lives would be closely knit. They had no idea what lay ahead of them, a complex era in which both would be at the forefront, the young Burgundian even more so than the king himself.

The one became John the Fearless, the other Charles the Mad. The future, as intrepid as it was deranged, could hardly be better summarized.

LOW COUNTRIES IN THE MAKING

Or how Philip the Bold used clever marriage politics to plant the first seed of what would later grow into the Low Countries, and also why the Burgundians would go down in history as ambassadors of theatrical displays of power and gastronomic pleasure.

P HILIP THE BOLD had to keep his mind fully concentrated in the winter cold of Cambrai. The tension was mounting, the outcome crucial, and there were so many details to remember. Should he enlist his son, John of Nevers, to join him in the fray? He considered the enemy and assessed his chances. This trial of strength would take place without helmets and weaponry, nor would there be any cavalrymen crushing an army of foot soldiers on the misty slopes. Blood-drenched soil wasn't the only way to initiate change. The outcome of marriage negotiations often had greater consequences than the most important battles, and that was particularly true of the discussions being held in Cambrai. They were so pivotal to the history of the Low Countries that the story deserves to be told in full.

It was as much horse-trading as it was a chess game. Philip loved it. As patriarch, he always stood firm. After all, the future of the new Burgundian dynasty was at stake. His position as influential regent with direct access to the French treasury would not last forever. Philip was all too aware that the young king would one day act on his own. Now that it was still possible, he wanted to apply his influence to arrange the best marriages for his offspring, beginning with his two oldest children. He had travelled to Cambrai especially for this purpose. The fact that John was not yet fourteen, and his sister Margaret barely ten, was a trifling detail. His dearly beloved children were investments that had to be made at the highest possible interest.

Sitting opposite Philip the Bold was the forty-nine-year-old Albert of Wittelsbach, Duke of Bavaria and Count of Hainaut,

Holland and Zeeland, all three territories feudally tied to the Holy Roman Empire and, except for Holland, bordering on Flanders. In Albert Philip saw the opportunity to expand the French sphere of influence to the detriment of the English, although what was closest to his heart, of course, was the steady progress of his own Burgundy. It was a two-sided game, and he played it with subtlety. While his descendants would later be able to proudly identify with their own duchy, Philip presented himself everywhere as a prince of French blood. That didn't alter the fact that he saw in Hainaut, Zeeland and Holland a beautiful necklace draped around Flanders, an elegant buffer around the Burgundian crown jewel. He realized better than anyone that the man sitting across from him, this Albert of Bavaria, was a walking synthesis of hundreds of years of European history. As a monk lets the beads of his rosary slip through his fingers, so Philip's mind explored Albert's family tree from branch to branch until he had a clear view of all its ramifications.

The patriarch of Holland was Count Gerulf, who was given a region near Kennemerland as a fiefdom by the East Frankish King Arnulf of Carinthia in 889. It wasn't until 1101 that his descendant, Floris II, began actually calling himself Count 'of Holland', a toponym derived from 'Holtland', most probably the name of the heavily forested lands on either side of the place where the Oude Rijn flowed into the North Sea. The name Holland would become the umbrella term for the whole region, which, like the soggy *pagus Flandrensis*, was gradually overrun by the sea and the swamps. Zeeland, which was already as sodden as its neighbour, remained a bone of contention between Flanders and Holland for years. But after countless skirmishes, a battle and devious negotiations, it would come to be linked to Holland via a dynastic union in 1256. Lastly, Hainaut, the shire through which the Haine flows, had belonged to the Avesnes family since 1246. They succeeded in joining the county with Holland and Zeeland by means of a personal union. From 1299 on, Hainaut, Holland and Zeeland would all be mentioned in the same breath. Due to the lack of male descendants, the Avesnes family tree continued to grow via the Wittelsbach family, and one day the entire inheritance fell into the lap of Albert of Bavaria.

By one of the whims of history, the man who sat across from Philip the Bold in Cambrai combined within himself a most desirable triple union. The fact that Albert was actually present at this table was owing to an unfortunate genetic accident. He hadn't come to power until 1358, when his older brother William in '*zijnre sinnen bijstr was geraakt*'[1] (he lost his mind), and Albert was obliged to lock him up in Hainaut castle, Le Quesnoy, where the poor wretch would spend thirty-one years in a haze of insanity before breathing his last.

Philip and Albert knew these political, genealogical and matrimonial twists and turns inside and out. Their regions were historically linked. But the past was the past, and now it was all about the future, which stretched before them far beyond the limits of their own lives. Both Philip and Albert would pass away in 1404, the one after forty years as Duke of Burgundy and twenty years as Count of Flanders, and the other after at least fifty years as ruler of Hainaut, Holland and Zeeland.

But in January 1385 they had to look beyond death.

'I Require The Counsel Of My Wife'

The English, too, had their eyes on the House of Wittelsbach. The threat of English influence on his borderlands was the last thing Philip the Bold needed. Thanks to a major charm offensive, he had lured Albert to Cambrai to listen to his proposal. The offer: according to Philip, the ten-year-old Margaret of Burgundy was the ideal partner for the nineteen-year-old William of Bavaria. Albert, who had both England and Burgundy to choose from, said he would have to discuss it. 'I require the counsel of my wife. Without her I do nothing when it concerns my children.'[2] Some spouses did indeed have something to contribute when it came to administrative affairs, but Albert probably just wanted to win time in order to drive the price up.

At the end of the month, his consort, Margaret of Brieg, joined him at the table in Cambrai, as did the wife of Philip the Bold, who also had a thing or two to say when it came to her children. 'The ceremonies were numerous,' Froissart learned, 'for the two dukes wished to treat each other as honourably as possible.'³ It was Margaret of Brieg who took matters into her own hands.

She would agree if the duke was prepared to marry off his eldest son, John. As the ultimate pawn, Margaret pushed her daughter Margaret of Bavaria across the negotiating chessboard. It was clear that Bavaria wanted a powerful union and demanded no less than a double wedding. So this is how the future looked: John the Fearless, the future Duke of Burgundy, would marry Margaret of Bavaria, and his sister Margaret would end up in bed with William of Bavaria, the next Count of Hainaut, Holland and Zeeland.

The duke was shocked. This was a move he hadn't expected, wasting two arrows to bag one fat pheasant. But like the experienced diplomat he was, Philip said not a word and probably made a movement with his head that lay somewhere between nodding yes and shaking his head no. He thought of his other plans: how he had always dreamed of joining his son John in holy matrimony with a sister of Charles VI, thus strengthening the age-old tie between the duchy and the kingdom of France. He couldn't just give away his successor for nothing, could he?

But Margaret of Brieg was adamant. It was take it or leave it. When the negotiations seemed to have reached a stalemate, a solution fell from the sky in the person of a woman of advanced years. Her name was Joanna of Brabant.

The idea of having a conversation in Cambrai was actually her brainchild. It went something like this. The duchy of Brabant had always been a powerful neighbour of Flanders. It was the region of great annual fairs and of course of the textile industry, but it was also famous for its breweries and for such thriving cities as Brussels, Leuven and 's-Hertogenbosch. Duchess Joanna had been married twice, but each time she had been left a childless widow. Now that she had rounded the cape of sixty years, the storm of her succession broke in all its fury. She was the aunt of Margaret of Flanders, with whom she got along very well. At the same time, she felt a connection with the house on the other side of the table.

Indeed, her first husband was an Avesnes, Count William IV of Holland, Zeeland and Hainaut. When this extremely volatile warhorse died without issue in a battle against the Frisians, the tripartite dynasty passed on to his sister Margaret of Hainaut, who was married to a Wittelsbach, the house that Albert of Bavaria was representing in Cambrai. Joanna formed the missing link between the negotiating partners, not only geographically but also politically and in terms of family.

Her participation wasn't just a matter of jovial camaraderie, of course, but of hard-nosed politics. For years, Joanna had been in conflict with the Duke of Guelders, who wanted to annex the border regions and openly fraternized with the King of England. If Hainaut, Holland and Zeeland were in danger of falling under English influence, Brabant would find itself cornered. Joanna was horrified by all the misery that she believed the English had caused in Flanders in past years. This is why in recent months she had been gently nudging the House of Wittelsbach towards a Burgundian wedding, and why she had hurried to Cambrai to convince Philip the Bold to involve his son John in the negotiations. Philip wanted cash on the barrelhead, so the childless duchess promised him that upon her death Brabant would go to Burgundy. It was Brabant for which the glutton was willing to risk his two oldest children.

And so the Duke of Burgundy, alias the Count of Flanders, finally said 'I will' – twice. An utterance that his two children were to repeat three months later in the same Cambrai, where preparations for the wedding immediately commenced. This was to be a feast without precedent: a double wedding that could be counted on to forge an alliance between the two most important dynasties in the Low Countries, a union that bridged the gap between the German and the French spheres of influence, a pact that over time granted Philip the Bold and his children access to Hainaut, Holland, Zeeland *and* Brabant. The wines of Beaune had been rolled out for far less than this.

The table at which all this was arranged has been lost, but it is doubtless one of the most important pieces of furniture in the history of the Low Countries.

'An Abundance Of Knights'

Charlemagne put an end to the sedentary existence of the Merovingian princes at the beginning of the ninth century. His kingdom became too big to be ruled from a throne. If he wanted to inspect any local matters, he had to travel thousands of kilometres to do so. Since then, important court events had become travelling affairs. Even in the Late Middle Ages, a monarch would insist on showing himself to his people, meeting local leaders and hearing grievances – in short, imparting a sense of proximity to himself and his country. In addition, since the average palace lacked running water, plumbing and other sanitary amenities, it was in need of a good scrubbing after a few weeks. So clearing the place out was also a matter of hygiene.

In the south, the duchy of Burgundy extended out from Dijon, its hub. In the north was the Flanders of Ghent and Bruges. In between was Paris, where Philip the Bold defended his interests as regent and where he usually stayed. The duke left his wife in the north to serve as his representative, but in reality both were constantly on the road. Those incessant journeys developed into extravagant processions that charmed the populace. The duke laid the basis for the theatrical display of power that is still associated with Burgundy. It was consistent with his love of beauty and luxury, but it was also a question of symbolism and propaganda.

While the discussions in Cambrai were taking place, there was no danger that Philip and Margaret would pine away from loneliness. Their retinue numbered 248 servants, whose work consisted of far more than dragging along the famous *orloge*. First came the *fourrière* division, which was split into two teams. The first team travelled in advance of the rest in order to make sure that all the furniture, wall hangings and bedding were unloaded in timely fashion, the water jugs were filled, hearth fires stoked, rooms scrubbed, straw spread over the floors, and a simple meal prepared for the group's arrival. They were also charged with finding good lodgings for those who could not be accommodated in the local castle. The second team stayed behind to pack everything carefully and tidy the place up. Jesters and minstrels also rode along with the *fourrière* division, as did falcons and hunting dogs.

An indispensable member of the retinue was the *maréchal*, the equerry who took care of the large group of horses: 232 animals in all, because almost every man travelled on horseback. The word *maréchal* was originally Germanic and dates from the Frankish period (*marha* = horse, mare; *skalka* = servant). At the royal court this equerry was eventually given the task of guarding the monarch's army train during battles, a function that would evolve into the highest military title of field marshal. Thus the first definition, that of 'groom', was relegated to the archives.

The duke-count could also rely on the chief baker with his battalion of bakers and patissiers, the chef with his horde of cooks, and of course the master of wine, alias the *échanson*, also a term from Frankish days. This 'cup-bearer' was not only responsible for the stocks of wine, but he also filled the glasses in the order prescribed by the rules of etiquette, and every day he was charged with washing the ducal tableware. As immediate assistant to the great cup-bearer, the *sommelier de vin* was responsible for transporting the wine. Ultimately his name would replace that of the *échanson*. Finally, the *fruitenier* not only supplied his employer with apples, quinces, medlars, nuts and chestnuts, but he also had the job of providing lighting and spent hours making candles and torches.

Wherever this travelling circus made a stop, the local lords would organize drinking bouts and archery contests. If this was the normal practice on an ordinary progress, one can imagine how exceptional the Burgundian festivities must have been in Cambrai on the day of the double wedding, 12 April 1385, where the cream of Europe would be present.

Weeks beforehand, an army of stonemasons and carpenters descended on the city to turn townhouses into luxury hotels. Ducal *fourrières* laid in tremendous amounts of food, cup-bearers tasted their wines, *fruiteniers* cast hundreds of wax candles. When it came time to send out invitations, heralds announced the news that the duke was organizing a tournament on the occasion of the double wedding at which the best knights could compete against each other. Charles VI immediately had his armour oiled and his best horses harnessed. 'You can and must believe that wherever the French king and so many high and noble princes were present,' Froissart noted, 'an abundance of knights would come pouring in.'[4]

The people who lived in war-ravaged regions, who scarcely had enough to eat and were still struggling with a sense of insecurity, must have watched with mixed feelings as the elite of France, Flanders, Hainaut, Zeeland, Holland and the Holy Roman Empire filed past their doors. The cavalry units, armed to the teeth, must have attracted particular attention. Bumping along among the cavalrymen was a mysterious cart carrying chests that were secured with chains. In those trunks, fashioned from a rare variety of wood, were the crown jewels that Charles VI had lent to his uncle to adorn the three Margarets: Philip's wife, daughter and daughter-in-law.

While all this was going on, the marriage contract was signed. Half the dowry went to John, and the remaining amount, which actually was intended for John's wife, was used by John's father, Philip the Bold, to purchase the county of Charolais, south of Burgundy. The pact with Brabant did cost him the city of Mechelen, which reverted to the Duchess of Brabant, but chances were not inconsiderable that the entire area would one day turn completely Burgundian. Filled with confidence, he worked his way through the crowd of guests, who respectfully stepped aside for him. After all, this was the man who had one leg firmly planted in the kingdom of France and the other in the German empire, and thus could effortlessly oversee all of Flanders, Hainaut, Zeeland and Holland.

In honour of the occasion, the duke had had twenty vermilion robes woven for himself, his son and the most important knights in their retinue. He insisted that cochineal be used in the dyeing of the robes in order to produce a pure cherry red tint, an extremely costly procedure. He also ordered 247 liveries for his servants, squires, musicians and falconers, and dressed all the ladies-in-waiting in cloth-of-gold before draping them in jewels. Philip decorated the Cathedral of Our Lady with luxurious wall tapestries, which he intended to bequeath to the church. But since these works of art traditionally belonged to his chamberlains, he was obliged to buy the gifts back from them in order to leave them in Cambrai as a sign of Burgundy's presence.

Chancellor Johannes Canard must have chewed on his beard in anxiety. He had to scrape together everything that was left in the treasury in order to pay for this extravaganza. But the only thought in the minds of the assembled guests was that the man who managed to respect such priceless decorum had to be fabulously rich and above petty concerns.

'Sitting Astride A Roasted Suckling Pig'

After the solemn Mass, the wedding feast commenced in the bishop's palace. The two newly married couples were seated at table with the French king and were served by aristocratic celebrities. The Burgundian lord chamberlain, Guy de la Trémoille, and even the sixty-one-year-old Count of Namur, mounted their chargers for the privilege of serving at the table of honour.

Liquid dishes were served in bowls, but the rest of the meal came to the table on thick slices of bread, as the custom had been since the time of Charlemagne. The cutting of the bread (*tailler* or *trancher*) gave this primitive plate its name: *tailloir* or *tranchoir*, 'trencher' in English. In the *Ménagier de Paris* (Landlord of Paris, 1393) we read that for a wedding meal, brown bread was used 'that had been baked four days earlier', thus forming a sturdy base for the meat and its copious sauce. In Cambrai, a wooden or metal cutting board was slid under the bread, as had become customary within the wealthier class. This was also called a *tailloir* or *tranchoir*. Only in the sixteenth century did this object gradually acquire a raised edge, looking in every respect like what would commonly come to be known as a 'plate'. The old term '*tailloir*' has easily stood the test of time: many Flemings still call a plate a *teljoor* or *telloor*.

At the wedding feast, most of the boards, each with a slice of bread, were shared by two adjacent table companions, who addressed each other as *copain*, literally 'bread partner', a name that continues to demonstrate how friendship and eating are intertwined in French. Bread played an important role in Cambrai. The potato would not appear on the tables of Europe until the discovery of America. The same was true for turkey, tomatoes, beans, chocolate and coffee. But the feast did offer the gastronomic harvest of the Crusades: cinnamon, cloves, ginger, sugar, bananas, oranges, lemons, dates, peaches, figs and apricots.

Philip the Bold did it, as did his son John and the king – and all the other guests as well, for that matter: everyone ate with their fingers. Etiquette dictated that one ate in a refined manner, which meant using the first three fingers including the thumb, never the entire hand – a rule that remained in fashion until after 1600. Each guest had a napkin, and after the meal, servants would come round with water jugs and towels. The spoon was the most commonly used eating implement. Pilgrims and travellers always carried one in their pockets. The spoon was made of wood, silver or gold, depending on the person's social status. For a long time the fork was regarded as the instrument of the devil and was therefore avoided; it did not appear on French tables until 150 years later. Knights and members of the nobility did carry knives and used them to spear food from the platters and transfer it to their *tailloir*. The king, the duke and the two bridegrooms, John of Burgundy and William of Holland, each had a personal *écuyer tranchant*, a nobleman who carved their meat for them and were permitted to eat the scraps that the high lords left behind. John and William served their newly minted wives, who were constrained by etiquette from exhibiting any excessive show of gluttony, thereby demonstrating that they could control their lusts.

The exact menu has been lost, but we need only look at the coronation feast of King Philip VI of France, grandfather of Philip the Bold, to get an idea of what was consumed by the guests in Cambrai. For his feast in Reims on 29 May 1328, Philip VI laid in huge numbers of livestock (82 oxen, 85 calves, 289 sheep, 78 pigs and 13 horses), plundered several dozen poultry yards (824 rabbits, 10,700 chickens and 850 capons) and had 345 bitterns and herons shot from the sky. With 40,350 eggs, 736 pikes, 3,150 eels, 2,279 carp, 4,000 crayfish and 243 salmon, the appetites of any non-carnivores were satisfied as well. The tables were already groaning when the servants hauled in 3,342 meat pies, 492 eel terrines and 2,000 cheeses.

The stomach capacity of medieval aristocrats was no greater than that of ordinary mortals, of course. It wasn't as if they could work their way through two dozen dishes in a single sitting. Rather, they chose whatever appealed to them from the culinary profusion. The Cambrai feast was not served in courses, which was entirely in keeping with the mores of the day. The meal was more like a buffet, or better still, like a sequence of buffets. New platters of food were brought to the tables several times in succession. This avalanche of dishes came in waves, a stream that first carried the most delicious fare to the king and the newly-weds. Then it was every man for himself. Two centuries earlier, this gluttony had already aroused the indignation of Bernard of Clairvaux, who exclaimed that 'though thou hast swallowed four or five dishes, the first are no hindrance to the last, nor doth satiety lessen thine appetite'.[5]

Naturally, the wine at a Burgundian feast flowed in rivers. It was poured in the ordinary way, but it also streamed from ingenious table fountains. There were casks brought in from Burgundy, but Saint-Pourçain, a wine from the Loire region that lost its popularity in later centuries, was also highly regarded. The feast was an exciting event for the *échanson*. He was expected to present his best wine, and although it already contained less alcohol than later wines would, he diluted it with water. Wine was never drunk straight. The fact that it was less strong to begin with, and then diluted, may explain the vast quantities that were drunk in the Middle Ages.

The great cup-bearer served the most high-ranking guests and tasted their wine for them. His purpose was not only to determine whether the wine was drinkable but also to dispel any fear of poison, which was considerable in that age of uncertainty. To this end, he resorted to a unicorn's horn – actually the tusk of a narwhal – as a means of detecting poison. If the wine in the horn began to seethe or give off fumes, he would know it had been poisoned.

Bottles didn't exist yet, and cork wouldn't be developed until the eighteenth century. Once it had left the cask, the wine soured rapidly. The obvious message was to drink fast. Cup-bearers tried to solve this problem by adding honey and an array of herbs. The sauces served with the meal, as well as the meat and fish, were heavily peppered. The eastern origin of most of these herbs made the average medieval man or woman dream of an exotic paradise, while doctors ascribed to them certain digestive qualities.

Sugar didn't feature at the end of the meal until the Renaissance. At the time of the double wedding it was used as a kind of spice in sauces, or in the preparation of roasted sturgeon or capon. But of course there were also tarts and waffles at the Cambrai party, as well as nuts and fruits, both fresh and candied. These desserts (from '*desservir*', which means to clear away) were served with hippocras, which the *échanson* prepared by adding a tablespoon of ground cinnamon, ginger, cardamom, nutmeg, galangal and a generous portion of sugar to two litres of wine. Philip's wife, Margaret of Flanders, loved this popular spiced beverage.

*

The powerful crackling of the gigantic hearth fires turned the kitchens of Cambrai into human-sized ovens, from which sweating servants in livery brought food to the dining room. The clatter of tableware, the cutting and chopping at the *tranchoir* boards, the singing of minstrels as they broke into the verses made popular by troubadours, the smouldering of torches and candles that were constantly being replaced by pages, the growling of dogs gnawing on bones under the tables, the sensual whispers of tipsy noblemen, the drunken cursing in various languages: these typical sounds of the festive meal reached the ears of the servants, but from a distance. They carried in great silver platters on which pieces of roasted veal, roebuck, venison, wild boar, goose, partridge and moorcocks, as well as bird varieties such as peacocks, herons, swans, thrushes and blackbirds, were mounded up in impressive pyramids. In the Middle Ages, dishes had to delight the nose and eyes as well as caress the tongue. To put table companions in the right mood, servants burned herbs and incense, and scattered violets and fresh herbs across the floor.

The cooks did their very best to surprise the guests with original presentations. They stuffed pork bellies with strings of sausages that spurted onto the table like grandiose rosary beads when the belly was cut open; they decorated bustards with precious stones; dressed hazel grouses in golden habits; served pork in the shape of a fish; fixed a cat's ears on a hare; attached a chicken's head to a rabbit's body; or cooked a dozen gigantic eggs in pork bladders. The Burgundians were wild about such extravagance. In the fourteenth-century cookbook *Le Viandier*, there are instructions for dressing a capon in armour for festive events, 'sitting astride a roasted suckling pig'.

But things got really spectacular when the peacock was placed on the table in all its glory. This was a classic of the genre, and there's no doubt that it made its appearance in Cambrai. First a master skinner would rid the beast of its jacket of feathers and skin. Then cooks would stuff the remains with strongly seasoned minced meat. A wet cloth would be stretched across the eyes to protect the head, which later would be on dazzling display, and the chef would impale the whole thing on a spit. When the bird was done, the cooks would dress it again in its ceremonial robe, gild the beak and legs, and work its tail feathers back into a fan. A kitchen boy would stuff a piece of cloth soaked in brandy into the bird's beak and then set the cloth on fire. Accompanied by the sound of horns, the fire-breathing peacock would finally be carried into the dining room in triumph.

Obviously, these ingeniously modelled intermediate courses – the so-called *entremets* – were meant to appeal more to the eye than the stomach. In the most refined cases, the *entremets* were not only examples of the desire for inventive spectacle, but they were also meant to tell a story. Epic portrayals of heroic deeds, battles or abductions went down very well. Jugglers, minstrels, musicians and actors poured into the hall as back-up to this gastronomic parade.

Poet and speaker Jan van Mechelen presented a memorable *entremets* that sent the assembled guests of Cambrai into raptures. Four wild beasts defended a castle from attackers, who had the appearance of Moors. Gracing the castle tower were two virgins.

One wore a crown, the other the fleur-de-lis. Finally, a white hart with silver wings came to hover above the tableau. This work of art, which consisted mostly of foodstuffs, was meant as an allusion to the advancing danger of the Turks in Eastern Europe and also as a stunning preview of the adventures that awaited bridegroom John of Burgundy as a future crusader. The Burgundians were masters of this humorous and poetic architecture of gluttony, and the double wedding was a striking episode in that evolution. John's son and successor, Philip the Good, whose birth was still eleven years off, would raise this Burgundian speciality to the heights of enchanting perfection in the course of the fifteenth century.

The price tag for this monumental gorge-a-thon was 150,000 pounds all told. To get an idea of what that might mean: a cask of Beaune (365 litres) cost 20 to 30 pounds at that time, a good horse 40 to 100 pounds, and for 1,000 pounds you could purchase a very nice house in Paris. A master bricklayer in the north of France earned about one pound a day. Since becoming Count of Flanders, Philip had been raking in 300,000 pounds a year, a sum that would increase to half a million in the years to come; the Flanders share of that amount varied from 35 to 48 per cent. His party in 1385 cost him practically half his annual income. Albert's share of the costs was much more modest – roughly a quarter of the Burgundian portion – but even that required him to borrow money, since the amount exceeded the annual income from Holland alone.

Philip had dug down deep, but it didn't keep him awake at night. He saw the feast as one big marketing coup. Displays like this had become a Burgundian way of doing business. In Froissart we read that in that regard Philip had succeeded many times over: 'Never in the past five hundred years had there been so solemn and resplendent a feast in Cambrai as there was in that period of which I write.'[6]

'Monstrous Error And Unbearable Urge'

The number of people who came out to celebrate the double wedding was far larger than the official guest list. The abbot of the local Augustinian monastery guessed that 20,000 had shown up, for whom more than 5,000 tents were pitched in the neighbouring villages. Whether all those people were treated to the leftovers of the wedding feast is unknown, but that wasn't their only reason for going to Cambrai. After the feast, the celebration continued for the best part of a week, and to the joy of many those days were filled with tournaments.

During the Hundred Years War, such contests usually took place in the big cities of Brabant, Hainaut, Artois and Picardy, but especially in Flanders, with Lille and Bruges in the lead. When truces or semi-truces were called, the English would also travel to these districts for an opportunity to cross swords with the French. In April 1385 the English were not present, of course, frustrated as they were by the fact that the Bavarian cornucopia had fallen into Burgundian hands. The French might lose one battle after another to the English, but at tournaments they put on quite a show, and when it came to cooking up a good marriage they were one step ahead of their hereditary enemy. Philip the Bold had already proved that in 1369 by swiping Margaret of Flanders from under the nose of the son of King Edward III of England, and now he had performed the same feat on behalf of his son John.

Knights who had been looking forward to these tournaments for weeks hardly considered the possibility that they might lose their lives. Church leaders were scandalized, even within the inner sanctums of Rome: so much senseless bloodshed! At the Second Lateran Council of 1139 it had been decided that any tournament fanatic who was killed in a joust would not be granted a Christian burial. In 1146, St Bernard of Clairvaux preached a Crusade in order to channel 'this monstrous error and... unbearable urge'[7] towards the Middle East. He also said that the soul of anyone who died in a tournament would go straight to hell. But there was no stopping the practice. The aristocracy was not about to let anyone take their contest away from them. In Cambrai, too, the tournament was the high point of the feast.

The first day looked like a fashion show. Parading on the field of honour were fine horses draped in colourful blankets, and if they could have laughed they would have revealed the golden bits in their mouths. These magnificent animals, who would be replaced the next day by trained chargers, bore the weight of suits of armour, be it gilded or painted, that concealed doublet-clad warriors. Some of the warriors' helmets were decorated with fire-breathing dragons, others with growling wolves' heads or protrusions that resembled the antlers of a stag. Seated on the grandstand were the guests, gleaming in their priceless apparel. The ladies held their scarves in anticipation of the outcome, ready to give them as tokens to their favourite champions. Standing around the field were a mishmash of high- and low-born commoners, merchants and craftsmen, farmers, labourers, whores, quacks, tooth-extractors, acrobats and clowns, all of them rubbing their eyes with astonishment.

Chain mail, which was made of interwoven iron rings and could weigh up to twenty kilograms, was replaced in the thirteenth century by the iron-plated suit of armour. Not only was armour lighter – it took a mere five kilograms of iron to protect the torso – but it also offered better protection from crossbow bolts. Because armour gave knights a certain invulnerability, there were fewer fatalities on the battlefield at first, and opponents were more frequently taken prisoner for ransom money. The disadvantage was that a knight who tumbled from his horse in full armour had great difficulty getting back on his feet, especially if the ground was as muddy as it was during the Battle of the Golden Spurs. Compared with fast-moving and lightly armoured infantry, these fallen supermen had little chance of surviving.

This sartorial earthquake caused great confusion, since no one was able to recognize a knight clad in iron. To remedy this situation, knights had their military equipment marked with special distinguishing emblems. In this way, armour sowed the seeds of heraldry. The Burgundian family coat of arms contained elements that referred to France (golden fleurs-de-lis) and to Burgundy itself (diagonal blue and yellow bars). John the Fearless would later add the black lion rampant of Flanders, which devolved upon him through his mother. Before long, the new status symbol was featured on tombs as well as on stained-glass windows.

As the years passed, coats of arms became increasingly spectacular and complex. By the time of the double wedding, what had been intended as a means of identification had degenerated into an impenetrable jungle of symbols. To clarify the situation, the House of Burgundy in Cambrai called on the services of a herald. This person announced the impending tournament far and wide, and during the festivities he helped the nobility deal with their heraldic confusion. As a medieval nerd, he had memorized all the coats of arms and could give a perfect account of, say, which knight had fallen over backwards. The most well-known herald of his day was Claes Heynensoon, a much sought-after heraldic consultant who had worked for John's father-in-law, Albert of Bavaria, for a few years. He wrote two books on coats of arms that have survived, as well as countless tournament reports, now lost, that became short-lived bestsellers in the aftermath of these knightly competitions.

After the rules and regulations had been read aloud, the participants had to swear that they had not hidden any magical talisman or incantation in their suit of armour, and that they were relying on nothing but their own abilities and God's support. What came next was a succession of tests. During the melee, two teams of up to a hundred knights imitated a classical battle situation. First they charged each other and tried to throw their opponents to the ground. Then they turned round (*tourner* in French, which gave us our English word 'tournament') and repeated the charge until the remaining warriors were left to fight it out in hand-to-hand combat. Participants could take each other prisoner and demand a ransom, just as in a real wartime situation. In the early years, this discipline was not only seen as a lively training exercise for military combat, but it was also misused as a way of settling feuds. The disordered melee had its origins in the eleventh century, the early days of the medieval tournament, and emphasized chivalry mainly as collective power. Due to the growing individualization of fame and glory, this discipline fell out of fashion with the passing of time, and it probably wasn't even on the programme at Cambrai. What was still quite popular was the *béhourd*, a test in which two teams of up to forty men in full armour competed against each other, with one team defending a 'castle' against a gang of raiders. In Cambrai, Philip the Bold did himself great credit during this test.

The joust involved two competing knights on horseback. Right from the start, this most famous part of the tournament was as popular as it was deadly. Stricter rules were always being introduced, but even at the time of the Cambrai festivities it was still the custom for the two riders to charge each other with lances extended, thereby risking a head-on collision. It wasn't until the fifteenth century that a protective wooden barrier a metre and a half high was added – each combatant being assigned a side – along which the two participants would bear down on each other until the expected blow knocked them off balance. Each knight would sit firmly in his tall saddle and charge to the right of his opponent, which meant that in order to strike he would have to angle his lance to the left above the neck of his horse. In the late fourteenth century, the aim of the joust was no longer to unhorse the oncoming opponent and take him prisoner but to smash as many lances as possible against him, a lance being a long wooden shaft with an iron point. The winner was the one with the most points. In the case of a draw, the referees based their final judgement on who had managed to break off the longest piece of lance. This heroic breaking of a lance would eventually become a figure of speech.

King Charles VI didn't do too badly during the Cambrai joust either. Chroniclers declared their respect for the valiant monarch, who mounted his horse nine times, but they disapproved of him exposing himself to such dangers. It was incompatible with royal dignity, wasn't it? That didn't keep Charles's descendants from engaging in this discipline – until King Henry II was critically wounded during a joust in 1559. Despite the helmet he was wearing, a lance penetrated his eye, dealing a death blow to both the French king and to jousting itself, which by the sixteenth century had become hopelessly old-fashioned. Firearms had long replaced lances and bullets could easily tear through armour, which came to assume a mainly ceremonial function. After 1559, the military techniques that had been practised during tournaments were relegated to the history books for good. The duel would soon eclipse the joust. Actually, this evolution had already begun in the fourteenth century, as was demonstrated by the battles of Crécy (1346) and Poitiers (1356), which were decided by archers and infantry.

In Cambrai there wasn't a single participant who could imagine that the uncommonly popular tournaments would one day disappear from the earth. The participants fought each other for days on end to their hearts' content. It was sport *avant la lettre*, a kind of knightly athletics that bathed in the glow of a courtly lifestyle, and the Burgundians were more than happy to lend it some lustre. With a broad smile, Philip's wife, Margaret, presented a diamond-studded gold buckle, which she had been wearing on her breast since the festivities began, to the winner, John of Donstiennes, a knight from Hainaut.

'Crushed Armoured Gloves'

Philip the Bold beamed all week long. This event may have been the wedding of his two oldest children, but it was *his* feast first and foremost, *he* was the real celebrity. The duke and his wife weren't anything to write home about as far as looks were concerned, but the elegance of luxurious garments certainly made up for that. Everything seemed to indicate that their marriage was a success, not only politically but also in human terms. They had brought ten children into the world, seven of whom would reach adulthood. Philip was frequently on the road and mistresses were part of his life, but he did not engage in excessive carnal activity. He acknowledged two illegitimate children, which was nothing compared to the almost twenty offspring sired by his father-in-law, Louis of Male.

The bridegroom, John the Fearless, was at least as ambitious as his father, and he also inherited Philip's ability to act decisively. But when it came to outward appearance, he didn't hold a candle to the old man. John's gait evinced a degree of awkwardness. He paid little attention to his dress, and wagging tongues claimed that he sometimes showed up looking downright scruffy. But on grand occasions he was able to show off the Burgundian splendour with dignity. Unlike his tall father, he was small of stature and blessed with a large head graced by a sharp nose. Despite his inherent ugliness, he did make an impression with his heavily lidded eyes. He was surprisingly severe, perhaps the first intimations of his future policy as duke. The fear that legend says was totally alien to him was something he did arouse in others.

The reader should not forget that in Cambrai he was still only thirteen years old. Seated in the grandstand, the youngster looked out at the wild goings-on on the battlefield. All around him people were discussing, pointing and laughing. The connoisseurs fired off comparisons with illustrious fights from the past. Clever manoeuvres evoked memories of legendary champions like Richard the Lionheart or Philip of Alsace. Only the most brilliant displays got the seal of approval of William Marshal – the Eddy Merckx of tournament history – who took 500 knights prisoner at the end of the twelfth century and was regarded as the greatest knight of all time.

John the Fearless, who himself was in training at the time but was thought too young to join in, knew the achievements of these heroes like the back of his hand and dreamed of his own future military glory. Two years later he was allowed to take part for the first time, and he showed himself to be a skilled player. As duke, he paid talented champions to defend the colours of Burgundy. He imported satin from Lucca and velvet from Florence to drape over his gem-encrusted suits of armour. He hired the best masters-at-arms, specialists who could effortlessly 'patch up suits of armour … clean helmets, rings and hooks, mend torn surcoats, repair crushed armoured gloves, replace iron and leather coverings and secure the vulnerable spots'.[8] After John's death, the ever scrupulous ducal bookkeeper listed in the 'jousting armour' category a collection of nine helmets, eight suits of armour complete with plates for legs and arms, special saddles, various head- and breastplates for horses, ten brass bells and two belts with little bells that were fastened to the equipment to add a bit of jingling to the visual spectacle. In April 1385, the thirteen-year-old John could only dream of such opulence. Until then all he had been given was a meagre allowance from his father, and he had to patiently wait his turn.

Duke Philip watched the wildly gesticulating characters on the grandstand like a politician calculating his chances, while his son John gaped at the scene of action. His bride, eight years his senior, sat beside him. She would bear him eight children: seven daughters and, thank God, one son. Later, John would emerge as a frequent visitor to the bathhouses, most of them places of carnal corruption. He would eventually sire four illegitimate children. The son he begot with Lady Agnès de Croy was also named John. As Bishop of Cambrai, this bastard became one of the most famous scions of the Croy family, who acquired a position of great power in the Burgundian establishment and almost succeeded in destroying the ducal dynasty in the years after 1450.

John learned to play the flute and the bagpipe at an early age, and his wife, Margaret of Bavaria, was a harpist of not inconsiderable talent. Music proved to be a unifying force in their arranged marriage. They engaged the services of writers and composers, who performed special pieces at birthday and New Year festivities, and they paid musicians to add lustre to ceremonial moments. Their bookkeeping records list seven minstrels, six trumpet players and a harpist on the payroll; remarkably, there was no jester, while his father had at least four in his retinue.

Despite his fondness for music and theatre, John the Fearless would never feel entirely comfortable at parties that were dominated by gallant gestures and trenchant bon mots. He did not possess a quick wit and he lacked the diplomatic nature of his father, who knew better than most that the right smile could prove exceptionally profitable. Philip, who owed his prestige to his image as a rich and decisive politician, managed to hold his ground with flair in the world of calculation and hypocrisy. But the master of the life of refinement was John's cousin, Louis of Orléans, the younger brother of the king, a sophisticated youth who moved among the guests in Cambrai with courtly elegance and would leave a lasting mark on John's life in particular and that of Burgundy in general.

Louis of Orléans was always one step ahead when it came to plays on words, compliments and banter. Even the dominant Charles VI was forced to yield to his little brother in that regard.

Louis was the kind of man who could dance tastefully, crack a joke with a bow and impress the ladies with a single glance. But he could also be extremely melancholy. His outlook on the world alternated between sombre and sensual. His pious disposition regularly compelled him to seek solace at the monastery of the Celestines in Paris for prayer and contemplation. As a God-fearing merrymaker with a sense of humour and an air of despondency, Louis perfectly incarnated the extremes of the Late Middle Ages.

John and Louis were made to be compared with each other. The two cousins were one year apart in age and held similar positions, Louis as the younger brother of the reigning king, John as the eldest son of the man who was actually the kingdom's leading figure. Orléans was number two in the kingdom, John number two in Burgundy-Flanders. Together they embodied the future. Their comradeship, which grew by fits and starts, was marked from the beginning by the unpleasant affliction known as rivalry. Louis's social successes, his jests and the astonishing ease with which worldly things went his way, offended John's taciturn soul.

Gradually, John developed an aversion to the man who, in his eyes, was a fashionably dressed good-for-nothing who bent reality to his will without giving it a moment's thought. Even the way Orléans treated him, extremely polite but with a touch of irony, rubbed him up the wrong way. But John held his tongue. He even tried to play along, but it always seemed forced. Yet he must have felt early on that one day his jealousy, masked as irritation, would crystallize into hatred. It would take the death of his father to really bring their discord to a head, although the seed of animosity had been planted much earlier. While knights in Cambrai noisily competed for their honour, an incipient hostility was silently germinating on the grandstand.

FRANCE AS THE DRAUGHT HORSE
OF BURGUNDY

Or how the one technological feat of the fourteenth century
was really a shot in the dark, but also how Philip the Bold
once again got the French king to do his Flemish heavy lifting
for him, and how all the military adventures came to benefit
the Burgundian duke alone and strengthened the foundations
of the Low Countries.

———————————————

THERE WAS NO stopping him. He was omnipresent and he knew it. Scarcely had Philip the Bold married off his two oldest children than he could pat himself on the back as the royal matchmaker. When he had shown Charles VI of France a portrait of Isabeau of Bavaria a few weeks earlier (Isabeau being the niece of John's wife, Margaret), the sparks began to fly. The king wanted to meet her as soon as possible.

On 14 July 1385, Isabeau knelt before Charles in Amiens. Froissart witnessed the meeting. 'The king… looked at her wide-eyed, a look that opened the floodgates of his heart to love and passion. He saw how young and beautiful she was, and he felt a growing desire to possess her.'[1] Charles withdrew and called immediately for a messenger: 'Go to my good uncle Burgundy and tell him to proceed with haste.' As had been the tradition for centuries, energetic matrons were called in to examine the future queen in order to determine whether she was physically capable of childbearing. Isabeau got through the ancestral entrance exam without difficulty and was declared fertile. She would go on to bring twelve children into the world. Number eleven, who was named Charles after his father, would be crowned King of France, and in 1429 he would meet the most remarkable woman in all of French history. But before the Almighty sent the angel Joan of Arc to deliver France, the country would have to get through another forty-four years of calamity.

Philip the Bold couldn't believe his luck. By linking the

French royal house to Bavaria as well, he argued, he would be strengthening his own connection with the family that ruled Hainaut, Holland and Zeeland. But to accommodate the king, he was willing to compromise when it came to protocol. He himself had dreamed of a gigantic feast in Arras, but the sixteen-year-old Charles was so feverishly obsessed with his imminent wedding night that he insisted on combining the pledging of his marital vows with the marital act itself. 'In that case,' Philip responded, 'we'll just have to put you out of your misery.'[2] Scarcely three days later, the fourteen-year-old Isabeau of Bavaria was married to the King of France.

During the festivities, Philip dreamed of his plans for an invasion, which at that point were well advanced. He felt confident enough to invade England by sea and thereby put an end to the war that had already lasted almost fifty years. The king had promised his help, of course. The French and Flemish fleet lay anchored at Sluis, ready to set sail. In fact, a small French army had already landed in Scotland in May with the intention of joining the rebellious Scots to invade northern England. On 1 August, two weeks away, the landing from Flanders would complete the scheme. First sweat out this little wedding feast and then bring England to its knees.

If his plan seemed like a certainty on 17 July, Philip was forced to file it away one day later. A killjoy of the worst sort made his appearance at the eleventh hour.

'O Proud, Proud City'

The French king, who had planned on relishing the afterglow of his wedding night, was rudely awakened from his reveries. No sooner had he exchanged his vows with his slender German in the Cathedral of Our Lady of Amiens than the 'depraved city' of Ghent awoke from its winter sleep and released its devils yet again. Frans Ackerman, Ghent's populist leader, had captured the city of Damme. At least, that was what his uncle Philip reported. The Burgundian seemed to have a franchise on bad news from Flanders.

It needs to be said that Jean de Jumont, Philip the Bold's grand bailiff in Flanders, had been wreaking incredible havoc in recent months. Even Froissart couldn't deny it. 'Once he laid his hands on people from Ghent, he didn't just demand a ransom; he put them to death, put out their eyes or cut off their hands, ears or feet, after which he sent them home as edifying examples.'[3] Jumont was the bellows that brought the smouldering coals to life.

Two centuries earlier, the Flemish count Philip of Alsace had founded the seaport town of Damme to enable seagoing ships to moor closer to Bruges. Because of the silting of the Zwin, however, they never got further than this new harbour, where the goods were transferred to smaller vessels that continued on to Bruges. The silting continued unabated, and finally the town of Sluis further north-east was also designated an outport.

Damme was located right between Sluis and Bruges, and because of Ackerman's seizure of the town the French-Flemish-Burgundian army was cut off from its fleet from one day to the next. 'Thou wicked city of Ghent,' orated Eustache Deschamps, the court poet, who took it upon himself to gladden the world's heart with even more woeful elegies. Charles, now wide awake, had no choice but to put out to sea with Philip the Bold.

It was a blessing in disguise: because of the planned invasion of England the army was already in a state of readiness, and two weeks later Charles VI and Philip found themselves at the gates of Damme. For the third time in less than four years, the army blazed a trail of destruction through Flanders. The sorely tested populace were at their wits' end, but for Philip the entire enterprise was an urgent necessity. He had no choice. Invasion plans and wedding merriment aside, as long as the town was in the hands of Ghent the duke could forget his English dream. But perhaps he could kill two birds with one stone and lead his county into calmer waters once and for all?

Despite the numerical superiority of the French-Burgundian troops, Ackerman put up a good fight in Damme, partly thanks to the archers who had been sent by England. Philip and his troops were practically freezing in the wet summer cold. They couldn't make any progress and incurred many losses because they hadn't counted on a siege. The Burgundian sent for artillery from Lille, but the days of waiting were difficult to get through. 'I sleep outdoors,' Deschamps wrote, 'I'm stiff from the cold and lie armed in the sand / what a lovely gift from Ghent and this cruel Flemish land.[4]

With the persistent damp, the mildewed clothing, the piles of horse manure and animal offal, the French-Burgundian troops stank to high heaven. 'Buckets of lice had come to call / They cause my very skin to crawl,'[5] rhymed Deschamps, who served as a guard and was forced to stay in the field while the king lay resting in Male castle. But his pen turned acidic when he learned that Ackerman and his men were within the walls, imbibing the wine that Charles and Philip had stored there in anticipation of the English campaign. 'I'm lost if I can't drink wine,'[6] lamented our correspondent between watches.

The stench wafted over the walls and into the city, where the Ghentenars held out courageously in expectation of the promised reinforcements from London. But the English had their hands full with the Scottish-French coalition, which was pounding them from the north. They were able to hold off the first invasion, but it was no longer possible for their forces to reach Damme. After six weeks Ackerman was forced to admit defeat. He secretly shepherded his small force out of the city and left the inhabitants to their fate. On 30 August the French entered the city. The wine turned to blood. Damme went up in flames and the whole surrounding countryside was plundered.

While Deschamps rushed back to Paris with his king and, 'seated in front of a cosy fire' in Ertvelde, actually succeeded in writing his first cheerful verse in human memory, Philip the Bold turned his attention to smoothing ruffled Flemish feathers. He organized talks with the moderate party of Ghent and did everything he could to begin a process of reconciliation. He was even prepared to let the city keep its privileges, to authorize free trade and not to raise the subject of obedience to the pope of Rome.

Philip the Bold's honey worked better than Louis of Male's vinegar. Ghent was not insensitive to his charm offensive, and when they saw that the invitations to the peace conference had been written in Dutch, the representatives set off for Tournai in December.

Yet at the very last minute everything threatened to go wrong. By dressing themselves too lavishly, the Ghentenars denied the duke his precious privilege of standing out from all the rest. What's more, pig-headed and vain to a fault, they refused to make the customary genuflection. Philip bit his lip with rage. He considered calling off the whole event, but Margaret of Flanders begged her husband to abandon the pomp and circumstance just this once. Peace above all else! She thought of the stagnating trade, the collapsing Flemish textile industry, the spreading poverty.

Wavering between innate arrogance and compassion, between rage and love, Philip swallowed his irritation. He accepted the Ghent burghers' promise to abandon their alliance with the English. And he in turn swore to respect the city's privileges. All the parties signed the peace treaty on 18 December 1385.

More than five hundred years later, the poet Albrecht Rodenbach captured this moment in his turgid nineteenth-century Flemish, rendered here in translation:

Philip could take no more. 'O proud, proud city,'
He spake, 'go forth, and thank your peace to my dear spouse.'
And graciously saluting their count and their countess,
The noble Ghentenars quietly and calmly departed.

Rodenbach ended his poem 'Pride' with words that would become the cri de coeur of a Flemish national awakening: 'Alas, where has the pride of the Ancients gone!'[7] Where in God's name has the ancestral vigour hidden itself in our good and gentle land, Rodenbach wondered in 1876. Generations of Flemings would recite this poem. The words became a way of expressing the longing they felt for those epic days of yore. Many found it impossible to get through the last verse without a catch in their voice.

*

After almost seven years of war, a sigh of relief ran through the county. All attention was now turned to the reconstruction of such devastated cities as Bousbecque, Ypres, Oudenaarde, Bruges, Kortrijk and Damme. Philip the Bold set aside his plan for an English invasion for the time being and launched a large-scale programme to reinvigorate the stagnating Flemish economy and 'to revive the land that for so long had been prey to plundering'.[8]

Clever as he was, he added the Brugse Vrije (the region around Bruges, called 'the Franc of Bruges' in English) to the all-encompassing Flemish consultative organization comprising the 'Big Three', Ghent, Bruges and Ypres, which weakened their power position. From then on, the group would be called the Four Members of Flanders. Most of the mayors and aldermen of the Franc of Bruges were not knights but landowning gentlemen farmers, and their demands were considerably less radical than those of the townspeople. In making this addition, Philip created a kind of administrative margin within which he could operate more freely. At the same time, he implemented significant institutional reforms. The emphasis was on the centralization of ducal institutions. Two courts of auditors were created, one in the south in Dijon and another in the north in Lille, and in the same two places he installed a council chamber that functioned as a court of law. Why Lille? For political and linguistic reasons. Lille was located in Flanders, but in the French-speaking part that had never revolted. Having these two centres put an end to the countless judges and accountants who were either locally established or who always travelled with him. He also combined the functions of northern and southern chancellor in a single person. Johannes Canard became the highest Burgundian official and remained Philip's right-hand man until his death. His reshuffled Great Council followed him wherever he went, of course, and thanks to a clever network of horsemen and messengers they were always in close contact with the lords in Dijon and Lille.

One striking aspect of his programme was his decision to eradicate the *faihitha*, a centuries-old custom that his own Germanic ancestors had brought from eastern to western Europe. In Burgundy it had largely disappeared, but in Flanders this blood feud was still very much alive. It's enough to recall the death of Jacob van Artevelde, or the reprisals that Jacob's son Philip carried out as soon as he came to power. Frans Ackerman of Ghent, who became reconciled with Philip the Bold and was pardoned after the Peace of Tournai was signed, was murdered two years later by an avenger of blood.

Philip also left his mark at the ecclesiastical level. For centuries, religious life in Flanders had been dictated from French-speaking episcopal cities such as Cambrai, Thérouanne, Tournai and Arras. The absence of specifically Flemish dioceses had not kept the Flemish church from choosing Rome after the Schism, contrary to the choice of the French liege lord. After having appointed the right people to key positions, Philip thought he was strong enough in 1392 to force the people of Flanders to switch their allegiance to the pope in Avignon. Only Ghent remained untouched. This exceptional status appealed to a remarkably large number of churchgoers from outside the city, which chronicler Jan van Dixmude did not fail to notice. 'The churches in Bruges were empty on feast days and Sundays. Hardly anyone went to church.'[9] Up to a quarter of the population of Bruges celebrated Easter in Ghent at the end of the fourteenth century.

Philip the Bold did not hesitate to express his policy in terms of slogans. By using the catchphrase 'governing strictly and justly', he made it clear that he was striving for public peace and the protection of everyone's rights in the interest of the common good. He must have been one of the first rulers to employ this kind of rhetoric.

Good communication didn't smooth out all the wrinkles, of course. Flanders kept hammering away at normalizing trade with England, albeit under explicit conditions: committing to the free import of wool, but prohibiting the import of English textile products. It wasn't until 1396, when a long breathing space opened up in the Hundred Years War, that trade agreements were drawn up again between both sides of the Channel. By the end of the century, all foreign traders had finally come to settle in Bruges. Flemings were also annoyed by the predominant use of the French language in administrative affairs and the constant absence of the duke. The continuous presence of French troops worried them as well. In 1405, Bruges asked, without success, that certain garrisons be populated by 'armed men who were born in the land'.[10]

Although peace had finally come, the old conflicts didn't magically go away. On the one hand you had the duke-count whose power base was in Paris and who had great experience as a European diplomat to fall back on, and on the other hand you had the cities that had spent centuries acquiring skills in the autonomous exercise of power and had become masters in international trade. Peacefully ushering all those assets and areas of tension into the fifteenth century proved to be a real challenge. With his reforms and his peace treaty, Philip had already brought about something of a rapprochement between Flanders and Burgundy: his assemblage of separate parts could be seen as a first step towards a great fusion of federated states.

His wife, Margaret, did her bit and oversaw the cross-breeding of Flemish cattle with specimens from Cîteaux in Burgundy. The offspring grazed peacefully in the countryside surrounding her castle in Germolles sixty kilometres south of Dijon, a new breed languidly digesting the offerings of the new union. In 1393, in the gardens of the same castle, the duke and duchess installed a life-size sculpture depicting themselves as good shepherds, the peaceful herdsmen who had led Flanders and Burgundy into a single warm stable.

'If It Hadn't Been For You We'd Be In England By Now'

'IL ME TARDE.' The duke's motto was printed in huge letters on the mainsail of Burgundy's flagship. The words were encircled by lifelike daisies (*marguerites*), a tribute to his wife, Margaret. When wind filled the sail, the Burgundian letters and Flemish daisies tumbled over each other. The stern was upholstered with blue cloth adorned with the blazons of all the counties and dukedoms that Philip represented. Melchior Broederlam must have been satisfied. The former court painter of Louis of Male, who now wielded his brush on the orders of the duke, had produced work of great refinement. The ships of other royalty, knights and counts were a delight to the eyes, but this vessel outshone them all.

Sluis harbour was packed with cogs, carracks, galleons, hulks and scows, almost all of them (except the cargo ships) equipped with a cage around the central mast to position the crossbow archers. It was undoubtedly one of the largest fleets in the history of Christendom. The 1,200 vessels, decorated like reliquaries, were compressed into a single terrifying fist that was meant to crush the much-hated enemy. If it had been more than four centuries later, the chroniclers might have seen it as an immense pistol aimed at the heart of England.

In September 1386, Philip the Bold stood looking out from the quay, his son John beside him. John would have been glad to get things moving; he identified with his father's motto. *Il me tarde*? Yes, he was in a hurry, too. But he had to be patient. He had no choice. His father had only recently drawn up his last will and testament, and if anything should happen to him, the fifteen-year-old John of Nevers would be the next Duke of Burgundy. So his son stayed on the mainland and was given permission to call himself the lieutenant of monseigneur the duke. He never once entertained thoughts of wanting his father dead. Philip was in the prime of his life, at the top of his game. All John hoped for was a chance to show off his talent. But now all eyes were on Philip the Bold, who had to raise his voice to be heard above the flapping sails: 'We can make something of this that will be remembered for centuries.'[11]

On all the roads behind them carts were rolling up, bringing in so much food that it looked as if another great banquet was in the works: hundreds of sheep, cattle, chickens, capons and geese, 2,000 barrels of rusks, tons of salted pork, vast amounts of smoked salmon and mackerel, hundreds of pounds of barley, rice and almonds, along with 400 cheeses from Brie and no less than 4 million litres of wine. When Burgundians went to war, there had to be adequate provisions. And then there was all the wood that arrived in Sluis, which was intended for *the* technical feat of the fourteenth century, the masterpiece of the entire expedition: the famous wooden city. Essentially, it was a gigantic

IKEA flat-pack *avant la lettre* based on an idea of Charles VI, one of those brain flashes in which the brilliance of his madness was already in evidence. Calais gave the English a seaport in France, but the French had no such base of operations on the other side of the Channel. To rectify this imbalance, the decision was made to ship a kind of collapsible Calais to England. The enclosure, many kilometres in length and seven metres high, and with a lookout post every twenty metres or so, was easy to dismantle and just as easy to assemble. Once transported to England, the mobile citadel could safely screen off a 500-hectare area.

Five thousand woodcutters and carpenters had worked their fingers to the bone, chopping and sawing in the forests of Normandy to bring this mad city to life. Locksmiths and silversmiths produced the iron hinges that were needed to create seamless fits between all the wooden panels. But that was only the beginning. At the same time, workers were toiling round the clock on another do-it-yourself kit consisting of houses and barracks that were meant to fill the wooden city, and where the necessary amounts of food and animals would be stored. This ambitious design excited the fantasy and only served to inflame the bellicosity of Philip the Bold's troops. Thanks to this *ville en bois*, they felt safe from the outset. It was the English who ought to be worried. The megalomania in Sluis rolled in in waves.

Only the law-abiding Froissart had anything critical to say. 'The poor farmers, who had harvested all their cereal crops and were left with nothing but straw. If they dared to express any doubts they were beaten until they couldn't walk, or killed. Lakes and ponds were depleted of fish stocks, and houses were demolished for firewood. The English themselves couldn't have wreaked more havoc.' Even the ever grumbling Deschamps, who had gone back to Flanders very much against his will, delivered his own lament – but of a very different sort than that of Froissart. In his first poem about this campaign, he frankly stated that he needed 'juicy grapes and grain' in order to survive 'in a land without grain and wheat'.[12] The starving Flemish peasants who stood gaping at him as he made his way north would certainly have agreed with him.

Philip was the very picture of martial vigour. *Il me tarde*, I wait for no one. But his patience was being sorely tested. First there had been the delay at Damme the previous summer, then the task of raising an army, and now it seemed that it was taking an unusually long time for his brother, the Duke of Berry, to appear in Sluis. King Charles, who was practically faint with the desire for action, couldn't understand it either. So the king amused himself with pleasure boating and was glad to discover that apparently he was not prone to seasickness. This seemed like a very good sign. Consultations were held every few days, and the officers wondered when they were likely to hear the order to embark. The answer was always the same: tomorrow or next week. In the meantime, the nobility organized their usual festivities and boasted about the toilets and other conveniences on board their vessels. The lords also squabbled about whose ship had the longest peak.

Meanwhile, Philip the Bold cursed his brother to the pits of hell. Together they formed the core of the regency council, and now Berry was threatening to leave him in the lurch. John of Berry, a man whose pug nose only added to his hidden frustrations, was always busy with more important matters. He was not cut out for warfare. He preferred to fritter away his time tracking down curious rarities and relics. Nothing sent him into raptures as much as drops of milk from the Blessed Virgin or molars from Charlemagne, unless it was groping docile maidens. It has never been known whether he was too busy with his trinkets or was jealous of his brother, who set off on one wild expedition after another at France's expense. One thing is certain, however: in the autumn of 1386, John of Berry raised the art of procrastination to uncommon heights.

When the frivolous Berry arrived in mid-October with a broad smile on his face, the ideal departure time had passed. 'If it hadn't been for you we'd be in England by now,'[13] Philip snarled at his older brother. He couldn't very well tell him why he had waited for this silly curiosity-collector instead of leaving without him: that the great Duke of Burgundy found it impossible to leave the country in the hands of a satin-clad twit.

Berry got out of this awkward situation with a joke or two and immediately started inspecting the fleet. By this time, the great encampment had been transformed into a gigantic quagmire, and the stockpiled food had taken to fraternizing with the local mould and mildew. It made no sense to stay any longer. The only question was where this run-down army should set its course: towards home or towards London?

To his delight, Berry noticed that the westerly wind had begun releasing its devils. Was it wise to launch a fleet in such turbulent seas? After endless discussions, the king and Philip decided to cancel the invasion. While the duke was devastated, Deschamps was beside himself with joy. After returning to France, he was resolved never again to set foot in the miserable land of the Flemings. 'I never saw much celebration / In all their grim determination / And I'll curse them to my dying day / Now I've crossed the Leie and I'm far away.'[14]

Despite the capsizing of his monster project, Philip the Bold still managed to somehow acquire a certain reputation. His spectacular battle plans had been broadcast far and wide, a great bonus for him as the initiator. Bravado proved to be a powerful trademark, although the difficulties and stresses had worn Philip to a frazzle. His honour took more of a beating when it was learned that the crown jewel of the campaign, the marvellous wooden city, had been intercepted by the English on its way to Sluis. They managed to board two of the ships and transported a portion of the kit to London, where French joiners were given permission to assemble a number of the parts, much to the edification and mainly the amusement of the English. When the news reached them that the French-Flemish-Burgundian fleet had given up, there was round-the-clock celebrating within the walls of the wooden barracks. The fear had been considerable.

Philip was given the rest of the magical city as a gift from the French king, who set Berry straight in no uncertain terms. But his trust in the Burgundian duke never wavered. In addition, Philip was given the assurance that he could keep French Flanders permanently, despite all previous agreements. Charles VI, a true addict of glamour and wealth, was enchanted by Burgundian grandeur, although his entourage kept having to explain to him that the duke had not yet attained Olympian status.

Not without a feel for opportunism, Philip had his crippled pre-fab city brought to the region of Bruges, where it came to house his Burgundian arsenal. He then made a radical policy reversal and henceforth would come out as *the* champion of peace with England. Political animal that he was, Philip the Bold was not so miserable he couldn't switch directions once he realized that his desired path was solidly blocked.

'To Catch A Goose'

The duke tried once more to manipulate the French king, but it proved to be one manoeuvre too far. In 1388, the puppet Charles VI finally cut himself loose from the powerful Burgundian hand that had been pulling the strings for so many years.

It all started when Charles VI received a letter from one William of Guelders. The letter had been written on ordinary paper, not on parchment – the first insult. The king had to have it explained to him that his lordship was the young potentate of a modest duchy, of which Roermond, Nijmegen, Arnhem and Zutphen were the major cities. It was expected that the king would ignore the letter and let this odd bird screech away on his northern nest, but nothing could have been further from the truth. Here was a two-bit nobody who had the effrontery to address Charles VI as 'he who calls himself the King of France' – the second insult – and who was challenging him to a duel – the third sting, which Charles found difficult to stomach. And all because this William of Guelders, in exchange for a generous annual allowance, had become an ally of the English king – yet another slap – and had dared to describe Richard II as 'the King of England *and* France' – the final blow. The French monarch was so indignant that those near him feared for his health.

Once the first shock had passed, his shaky emotional state changed to happiness. Finally, he, the great hero of Westrozebeke, after the failed invasion of England, could strike his mortal enemy in the flank. He wanted to leave for Guelders straightaway, although his advisors were of the opinion than an elephant does not alter its stride for a mere vole. But Philip agreed with Charles wholeheartedly. Of course a monarch of his calibre could not let himself be insulted! If he himself had been king, Philip would have ignored this William of Guelders without giving it a moment's thought. But if the duke acted deftly now, he could manage to fill his pockets with French money once again. For years, William of Guelders had been involved in a war with Brabant, whose childless Duchess Joanna had promised her duchy to Burgundy. Earlier on, she had asked Philip to expel the Guelders upstart from her territory. This was the perfect opportunity not only to oblige her but also to convince the proud cities of Brabant of his goodwill.

The fact that the king was in a rage might be convenient for the duke, but a great deal of grumbling could be heard from behind the throne. It was the inevitable lamentation of Eustache Deschamps, who felt in his bones that he, the poetic conscience of the kingdom, would be ordered once again to hoist himself into his armour and mount a wheezing nag in pursuit of his master's glory. The logical route that the army would follow ran straight through Brabant, and the thought alone made the sixty-six-year-old Duchess Joanna blanch with anxiety. Knowing the terrible havoc that soldiers could wreak, she begged Philip the Bold to spare Brabant. Philip was prepared to do anything to placate the duchy, and he moved heaven and earth to talk Charles VI into making a wide detour. So Charles sent his troops via a very circuitous route through the Ardennes.

Now Deschamps was terror-struck. The notorious Ardennes! He had been preceded a half century earlier by his fellow poet Petrarch, whose travel account, written in Latin and one of the first tourist documents in history, was not exactly a glowing advertisement. 'I journeyed alone through the forests of the Ardennes. [...] It is so dark there that the soul freezes in one's breast. You will admire my courage, especially when you learn that war was raging at the time. But as the saying goes, God has a special providence for fools and drunkards.'[15] Deschamps clung to these words, especially the last ones, but after climbing a few hilltops in the unrelenting rain he penned a few shivering verses that were brimming with adjectives like 'cursed' and 'terrifying'.

The poet began wondering what on earth had possessed Charles VI to threaten this provincial tyrant with such a large force. Why didn't he save his best gunpowder for the English? 'They're letting an eagle go in order to catch a goose,'[16] he noted, as the French-Burgundian army waded into Guelders during a downpour.

They plodded past Roermond in the direction of Nijmegen, where William of Guelders was holing up. He was delighted. The probes and raids of his mercenaries had done considerable damage to the enemy army. Finally the news reached William's warrior father, the Duke of Jülich, who raced to Nijmegen at lightning speed and berated his son for a full week. William responded by getting angry and slamming doors. The insult that had escalated into an armed conflict ended as an ordinary family squabble. William the loudmouth finally gave in when his father threatened to disinherit him. He was also forced to admit that he had needlessly waited for English support and that fighting against such a large army was probably not such a good idea.

A surly William approached the French and petulantly begged the king for forgiveness. He said the letter had not been drafted by him but by the English chancery, and that they had made use of his ducal seal. It was an awkward pack of lies, and he presented it without apologizing for the letter's contents. He barely managed a bow. Yet Charles VI and Philip the Bold were satisfied with this clumsy justification because their soldiers, bone-weary from all the campaigns, were too tired to pick up their swords. King Charles VI found consolation in the arms of a Guelders beauty, and all the setbacks seemed to have been forgotten.

Philip was able to present Joanna with a report that was excellent on all counts, for when the forces returned home they once again passed the duchy by. It was then that the sky opened up and the summer rains poured down, turning the trip through the Ardennes into a death march.

As the water dripped from his helmet, it finally occurred to the French king: now that he was twenty, it was high time that he should be the one to call the shots. This longing for independence was inspired by Louis of Orléans, Charles's younger brother, the smooth-talking cousin of John of Burgundy, who saw his chance and seized it. Hadn't their uncles – Berry in Sluis and Burgundy in Guelders – lost all credibility? He worked unceasingly on the malleable Charles, trying to steer his brother, whose increasingly wild mood swings put him in danger of losing all perspective, back into the French fold. But his main objective was to squeeze out the two uncles, that damned Philip first of all, and ultimately to get a taste of power for himself.

On 2 November 1388, Charles called a special conference in Reims. All Souls' Day struck him as the appropriate moment to change course. It was the cardinal of Laon, the faithful advisor of his late father, Charles V, who raised the issue. First he delivered a long panegyric to the monarch. Then he proposed to the assembled guests that the twenty-year-old Charles finally be permitted to serve as ruler. The applause that followed was overwhelming. Philip and his brother Berry had scarcely recovered from their astonishment when they heard the king thanking them for services rendered.[17] His speech was so splendidly worded that it could only have been prepared beforehand. Louis sat gloating next to his brother Charles.

Philip the Bold nodded graciously but felt the hatred blazing up within him. This would be something the Orléans dandy would live to regret. His feelings were shared by his son John, who realized that the growing suspicion he had felt towards his cousin was completely justified. On All Souls' Day 1388, the suppressed enmity between the two houses was exposed for all to see. The first victim was the cardinal of Laon, who suddenly fell ill and died. The autopsy revealed that poison was involved.

The money tap, at which Berry and Burgundy had been quenching their thirst for years, was temporarily turned off, and along with the cessation of dubious annual allowances and taxes there came an end to the legal theft of government funds – although that wouldn't go on for long. But the time in which Philip was able to use the French army to solve his own problems was definitely over.

Philip did not despair, however. He considered himself indispensable and expected Charles to recall him presently. But the young king threw himself into his new role and surrounded himself with loyal friends. Finally, the duke resigned himself to the situation. He even seemed to prefer it. To survive was to adapt, and the political sidelines to which he had been involuntarily relegated gave him the opportunity to fully occupy himself with local concerns. First he had to get the Burgundian treasury back in order, for no matter how much he scrimped and scraped, he always spent more. He saddled Joanna with the 200,000 francs for the Guelders adventure that he had had to pay out of his own pocket, knowing that she was going broke. It was up to her to figure out how she was going to repay him. He was quite willing to wait for it, friendly as he was. A few years later, by way of compensation, she would give him Limburg, a small duchy between Verviers and Aachen whose main cities were Eupen and Limburg, which were also called the 'Lands of Overmaas'.

Philip tapped a cask of Brabant beer when Joanna also signed a contract giving Brabant to Burgundy after the Guelders expedition, although the aging duchess kept the usufruct until her death. This was bad luck for Philip, for the sixty-six-year-old Joanna may have been destitute, but she'd still have a good eighteen years ahead of her. It was another apple of discord that the duke found a clever way to swallow. He expressed total understanding when the cities of Brabant protested the arrival of someone who, in their eyes, was a power-hungry Burgundian. What they wanted was an independent duchy. By way of compromise, Philip put forward his second son, Anthony, as his heir. Joanna accepted the proposal and would personally prepare Anthony for his responsibilities.

Now that he had sucked the best marrow out of the French kingdom, the time had come to take stock. 'I remember when I was young they used to call you Landless Philip,' wrote the author and contemporary Honoré Bonet. 'Now the generous God has made you a great name, one that is featured beside the names of the giants of the earth.'[18] Gradually, there could be no more denying that the grandeur of old Burgundy had risen from its ashes, and that an energetic effort was being made in Dijon to cobble together a realm that deserved to be reckoned with.

The great Gundobad must have looked down with approval

from his cloud in Germanic heaven. And it cannot escape the historian from his observation post in the twenty-first century that thanks to the Burgundian embrace of Flanders, Brabant, Hainaut, Holland, Zeeland and Limburg, the blueprint of the Low Countries was gradually taking shape.

*

Much to his irritation, Eustache Deschamps was forced to endure the Guelders campaign in the wake of Louis of Orléans, to whom he instantly took a dislike. The way Louis's retinue tormented him along the way actually imparted an extra jolt to the elegiac content of his verses. After his death he fell into deep obscurity. Eustache, whose nom de plume was Deschamps but who in reality bore the name Morel, like his father, has lain buried among his tens of thousands of verses since 1404.

In the nineteenth century he would be dredged up again and interred in a dusty antechamber of French letters as the inventor of the ballade (a poem with three stanzas and an envoy) and as the author of L'Art de dictier, the first French discourse on poetry. Specialists occasionally quote some of his erotic verses, to which he gave a melancholic tint in his latter years: 'Many's the woman who has fled / from the selfsame cock her cunt once filled / when I was young and brisk in bed / now that my shaft is weak and chilled.'[19]

Not an unimpressive achievement, all in all. But history has done him a great disservice. This furious hater of Flemings also deserves to be remembered as one of the first war correspondents from his region of Europe. At the age of sixty, four years before his death, Deschamps took stock of his life with a heavy heart, the last spasm of his peevish temperament.

King after king, they come and go,
Four generations since my days began,
Philip, John, then Charles in tow,
Fifth of that name, all in one lifespan,
The next scion followed, and under his skill
The Flemish were defeated on Roosebeke's hill;

Twenty-six thousand were killed by his lances,
He was scarcely thirteen, and the triumph was France's.

...

Prince, I have seen times of chaos and pain,
No rights, no laws, countries left to expire
Injustice, catastrophes, towns set on fire,
I hope we will live to see concord again,
Though I wouldn't bet money on any such yearning
For the world's joys are hollow and beyond my discerning.[20]

BEAUTY AND MADNESS

*Or how Burgundy launched the last real Crusade of the
Middle Ages, but also how, thanks to the patronage of
Philip the Bold, the Low Countries would be the first to
bear fruit in the fine arts.*

TURKISH FIGHTERS TOSSED the captured Lazar Hrebeljanović,
the Serbian tsar, beside the dead body of their sultan, Murad
I, who had died earlier that day. The tsar barely had time to blink
before a scimitar was raised, glittering in the sun. With one stroke,
a Turkish warrior took vengeance for the death of his leader.
Sultan and tsar lay lifeless, side by side. Now that the two supreme
commanders had been killed, the Battle of Kosovo reached a
decisive phase.

On 28 June 1389, the army of Hungarians, Bulgarians,
Albanians, Bosnians and especially Serbians stood just outside
Pristina (in what is today Kosovo) opposite a massive Turkish
force: Europeans against Ottomans, Christians versus Muslims,
Lazar toe to toe with Murad. Without batting an eye, Murad's son
Bayezid assumed command from his father and decimated the
coalition of Eastern European Christians. As the new sultan, he
brought the fragmented emirates under his control, subjugated
part of the Balkans, threatened Constantinople and moved on to
Hungary by way of Bulgaria and Serbia. This great-grandson of the
famous Osman I – after whom the Osman or Ottoman empire was
named – dreamed of stabling his horses in Saint Peter's Basilica
in Rome. His Turkish horde resembled that of the ancient Huns,
a flash from the east shooting westward. Bayezid's nickname,
appropriately, was The Thunderbolt.

One by one the first rumours began dribbling into Paris, where
life was following its normal routine. It wasn't the Ottoman threat
that was the most important news of the summer but the coming of
Queen Isabeau to Paris. Although she had borne the title of Queen of
France for the past four years and had ridden into the capital dozens

of times, Charles VI thought she had a right to a Joyous Entry of her own, as tradition dictated. During her triumphal procession on 22 August, two angels descended from a vaulted imitation heaven studded with stars and placed a gold crown on Isabeau's head. On the city's street corners, brass bands put their best foot forward, one after another, and children organized mythical tableaux. Between times, the queen could gape at imitation castles, where devotional plays were performed. The procession advanced so slowly that it was growing dark by the time Notre-Dame finally came into view. The bridge that led to the cathedral was festooned with taffeta and decorated with golden fleurs-de-lis. To top it all off, an acrobat tottered across a rope that had been stretched between the massive church towers and a building on the Pont Saint-Michel. Everyone held their breath as the man continued his progress with a burning candle in each hand. In the darkness of the night, this human bat could be seen and admired far and wide.

In order to watch his ravishing wife take everyone's breath away, and to do it undisturbed, the king had to mingle incognito in the crowd. No one recognized him! On the evening of the festivities, he bragged that a guard had given him a smack because he had come too close to the queen's coach. He couldn't believe his luck, and looked at Philip the Bold with satisfaction, as if he had pulled the throne out from under the grand master of amusement for just one day.

Burgundy shrugged. His velvet doublet was attracting all the attention. The forty swans embroidered on his jacket were all adorned with pearl necklaces that, like the graceful birds themselves, seemed to float on the velvet. But why spoil the king's illusions? If Charles VI was happy, then he was happy too.

*

While Isabeau of Bavaria was spending her days beaming like a French fairy-tale queen, and the Ottomans were imagining themselves the new kings of Eastern Europe, Philip set out for Dijon. Jean de Marville of Hazebrouck, who had been his most important sculptor for years, had decided to lay down his chisel for good, and just when the duke needed him most. But one man's loss is another man's gain. Soon a Dutchman would be taking charge of one of the most important construction sites of the Late Middle Ages.

In 1377 the God-fearing duke had purchased a piece of land in Champmol with the intention of building a Carthusian monastery there. This was a remarkable decision, to say the least. Philip, a flirtatious man who would acquire 160 different head coverings between 1392 and 1394 alone, chose the most contemplative and ascetic monastic order of his time. The Carthusians wallowed in poverty, rejected possessions and renounced all forms of vanity and prestige. The duke was placing his salvation in good hands. After all, it was the prayers of the poorest of monks that received God's most ardent attention.

His Flemish wife, Margaret, and their son John, who was twelve at the time, had laid the first stone in 1383. Later he had it noted in his will that he wanted to be buried in this monastery. Indeed, Champmol was designated the mausoleum of a new dynasty, of which he saw himself as the founding father. In doing so he made sure that the political axis of his empire would be in the south, in Dijon, and not in Lille, which was still the administrative centre of prosperous Flanders. Under his successors, the interests of the north would gradually take priority and would ultimately outstrip the old duchy altogether.

The monastic buildings and the church were erected with relative speed, but by the end of the eighties virtually all the decorative finishing touches had yet to be completed, and that was where Philip's new court sculptor would play a crucial role. He was looking for an exceptionally talented man, someone who not only possessed great artistic gifts but who was also able to manage a large construction site, hire the right craftsmen, and purchase the better raw materials at the best prices. In the summer of 1389 his eye fell on the Haarlem-born Claus Sluter,[1] who had served as Marville's assistant for quite some time.

First the Dutchman installed himself in a manor house with an accompanying studio. It lay within walking distance of the ducal palace, so that Philip could easily drop in to discuss the progress of the work. Before the master began carving, he put together a team of '*ymagiers*', or image makers, who turned up from every corner of the Low Countries. Some of their names are listed here to show how much Middle Dutch (and Walloon to a lesser extent) influenced this French-Burgundian construction site. The names could easily have been abbreviated, but it is hoped that listing them in their relative entirety will speak volumes.

The first to be invited were Maes de Roek, Jan van Prindale, Willem Smout, Heine van Merchteren, Peter van Liekerke and Dirk Gherelex. Sluter knew them all well from Brussels, where he had mastered the sculptor's trade in his youth. Next came Nicolaas de Hane of Tournai, Gilles van Seneffe of Hainaut, Antoine Cotelle and Humbert Lambillon of Namur, Jacob van der Baerze of Dendermonde, and finally his cousin Claus van de Werve of Hattem in Guelders. Some of them stayed in Burgundy the entire time, others were merely temporary. Master Joseph Colart of Dinant was responsible for the iron foundry, and Jean de Liège, who came from the Meuse region near Liège, was in charge of carpentry. Their names are the only ones that have come down to us, but of course they did not do their work alone. They were assisted by more than two hundred anonymous stonemasons, bricklayers, labourers, iron founders, wood carvers and carpenters. Given the origin of the artists, it wasn't surprising to hear a bit of Dutch being spoken at the Champmol building site every now and then. So Henri Boucher, who as '*ouvrier de verrerie*' was responsible for the glasswork, began to turn up in the accounts of the Burgundian court of the early nineties as Henri *Glasemaker*.

With Sluter's choice of sculptors, a new wind began blowing in the Burgundian arts, a fierce north wind. It was no accident that this happened after the duke had become Count of Flanders in 1385 and had managed, with the marriages of his children, to open the Burgundian door a crack to Hainaut, Holland, Zeeland and Brabant. Philip's court painter, Jean de Beaumetz, may have been a Frenchman, but his assistants, Gerard van Nijvel and Torquin van Gent, were from Brabant and Flanders, as were the most important painters working at the Burgundian court from then on. Melchior Broederlam of Ypres completed a great many assignments, and Johan Maelwael was appointed the new official court painter after Beaumetz's death in 1397. His name was Gallicized to Jean Malouel. In Middle Dutch, Maelwael literally meant 'he who paints well', from the German word '*malen*'. Like Sluter's chief assistant, Claus van de Werve, Maelwael came from the duchy of Guelders – Nijmegen, to be precise. He would work under Philip and then under his son John, who would continue the completion of the monastery after his father's death.

It would be another seventy-five years before the official birth of the Burgundian Netherlands. In the meantime, in Champmol in the late fourteenth century, a carefully selected group of artists, most of them from Flanders, Hainaut, Namur, Guelders, Brabant and Holland, formed a laboratory of sorts that was a small-scale version of what would later develop on a much larger scale throughout the Burgundian empire: a new affiliation of regions under the aegis of a single duke-count. In the history of the Low Countries, art has always preceded politics. While this exceptional team of artists from the north was fulfilling the great dream of Philip the Bold, his son John was soon given the chance to realize his own dream deep in the heart of Eastern Europe.

'Monseigneur Wants To Kill You!'

In the summer of 1392, an irritable Charles VI left Paris at the head of a large army to teach the Duke of Brittany a lesson. This scoundrel was refusing to hand over the criminal who had carried out an attack on Olivier de Clisson, the supreme commander of the French forces and the man who, ten years earlier, had cut Philip van Artevelde down to size in Westrozebeke. Although the king had been feeling feverish for days and had taken to speaking gibberish on several occasions, he refused to follow the advice of his physicians. As far as he was concerned, staying home was no option. De Clisson had to be avenged.

John of Burgundy and his father, Philip, were part of the royal forces. John was twenty-one, and he couldn't care less about the king's fever. The only thing that occupied his mind was the fact that he was still a mere squire. He was bound and determined to be made a knight on the basis of a few blows he had dealt on the battlefield. Following behind him was his cousin, Louis of Orléans, the king's younger brother and now his right-hand man, who was so full of himself that his horse almost collapsed beneath him.

On 5 August, Charles VI led his troops into the forest of Le Mans and entered the territory of the insubordinate duke. Suddenly a strange figure popped up from the undergrowth and began screaming at the king to go no further: 'Go back, noble king! You are betrayed!'[2] Because this ragged recluse was apparently nothing but a poor beggar, he was not arrested and was kept a respectable distance from the French king. But the lunatic kept repeating the same words for several minutes, a mantra that took possession of the feverish brain of Charles VI like an evil spirit. The words 'You are betrayed!' seemed to strike a nerve. Rigid with terror, the king stared into the distance as if the shrieks of this woodland devil were tightening his inner mainspring.

When they left the forest, the sun began beating down on them. One of the pages, who had been nodding off for quite some time, finally fell asleep and let the king's lance fall against the helmet of one of his companions. The noise shook Charles VI out of his stupor. He began raving, 'Attack the traitors! They want to deliver me to the enemy!'[3] Then he drew his sword and lit into his own retinue, hacking away like a maniac.

'My God,' Philip shouted to his son John, 'the king has gone mad. Someone must restrain him!' The king killed a handful of his knights, who were caught completely off guard, and then turned on his brother, Louis of Orléans. 'Flee, dear nephew, flee,' Philip called to him. 'Monseigneur wants to kill you!'[4] Louis didn't have to be told twice. He spurred his horse and vanished.

Finally, Charles snapped out of it and was easily overpowered. Those standing nearby could see his eyes rolling back in their sockets. He was restrained, put in a cart and taken to Le Mans, where two days later he seemed to have recovered. His doctors tried to calm him by attributing the breakdown to the intense heat and suggesting that he regain his health by devoting himself to relaxing activities. But a few months later, when Charles almost went up in flames at a costume ball – he and a few friends had disguised themselves as shaggy forest dwellers, covering themselves with hemp and using flammable pitch to make the hemp stick – the spring seemed to snap. While his friends burned like torches and took three days to die, the king miraculously escaped death. His aunt, the fourteen-year-old second wife of the fifty-one-year-old Duke of Berry, threw her cloak over him and was able to extinguish the flames just in time. In his mind, however, the flame of madness had now been stoked.

Until his death in 1422, the French king would vacillate between lucidity and insanity. Every now and then he would participate in political life and attempt to leave his mark, only to have his mind stray into mist and darkness and stay there for months. Charles became estranged from his Isabeau and lived in darkened rooms, where a procession of physicians and quacks took him in hand. They prescribed an endless series of concoctions and conducted bloodletting by the bucketful. Sometimes he became so violent that he had to be tied down, babbling such blatant nonsense as 'I am George the Aggrieved'[5] or pointing to his stunningly beautiful wife with the words, 'Who is that woman the sight of whom torments me?'[6]

A few months before his death, during a stretch of relative health and stability, he took part in an archery contest. But for most of the remaining thirty long years in which he was shackled to the throne, Charles VI, the king with an unstable mind and a strapping body, would exist in a state of insanity. Surprisingly, that painful condition endeared him to his subjects all the more. They did not call him 'the Mad' – a nickname that cropped up later on – but invariably '*Charles le Bien-Aimé*', Charles the Beloved. Even that, however, could not keep the Catholic Church, the kingdom of France and French-English relations from becoming just as fragmented under his rule as his own befuddled mind.

'I Can Hardly Wait'

John of Burgundy cursed with disappointment when they turned back at the forest of Le Mans. Yet another missed opportunity to show off his skill! His father, Philip, viewed it through a different lens. Now that Charles was at times a mere shadow of his former self, Burgundy announced that the kingdom needed a powerful regent more than ever. He succeeded in dismissing Charles's advisors, branded Charles's brother Louis of Orléans as too young and inexperienced, and catapulted himself into the highest regions of power by assuming the position of regent once more. He immediately called a halt to the war against Brittany – what could possibly be gained from that engagement? – and arranged to have a large portion of the government revenues flow back into Burgundy. To revive the trade between England and Flanders once and for all, he then tried to make short work of the Hundred Years War.

In the spring of 1393, the village of Leulinghen, not far from Boulogne-sur-Mer, was the backdrop for the new peace talks. The border between France and England ran right through the parish church, which had both a French and an English entrance. Philip the Bold, who only a few years before had dreamed of a big military landing on the other side of the Channel, was now pulling out all the stops to achieve peace. It was already too absurd for words that the French and the English were upsetting the European balance of power while the Turks were intruding deeper and deeper into the continent in the east. So now he said that it made more sense to join forces in a new Crusade than to keep tormenting each other. In fact, peace did not come – the truce was only extended for four years – but the other idea did take root.

At the end of the Middle Ages there was a full revival of the old Crusading ideal, although the setting had shifted in the intervening years from Jerusalem – where Christian pilgrimages were welcome once again – to other places. In the fourteenth century, for example, western warriors went to North Africa and Spain to fight against advancing Muslims, or they took on heretics among the Baltic peoples in Prussia. Now that the French king was in the clutches of madness, and Burgundy was looking more and more like a superpower, Philip the Bold realized that supporting such undertakings had top priority. He had never been a crusader himself, but he had financed the journeys of countless knights from his regions. As usual, his motives were infused just as much with religious conviction as with propagandistic opportunism. Philip was eager to promote both his faith and the prestige of his house, and to do it on an international stage.

The thought that the great Burgundy had never led his own Crusade was a thorn in the duke's side. Wasn't it a stroke of fate that on 13 March 1393 he had been able to procure the sword of the legendary crusader Godfrey of Bouillon? In any case, when the Hungarian King Sigismund begged for European help to hold back the advancing Ottomans in the summer of 1395, Philip the Bold did not hesitate to claim the leadership of the international coalition. At the last minute, however, he decided not to go himself but to hand over the supreme command to his son. John left no room for doubt: 'I can hardly wait to prove myself.'[7] Philip stayed home because all the tedious sabre-rattling in Flanders had left him with little taste for battle and he was looking forward to developing his artistic legacy. He had already established his reputation as The Bold. Now he wanted to leave his mark as a patron of the arts as well.

To pull off the Turkish venture financially, the duke introduced extraordinary new taxes – women, children and the elderly were made to pay in lieu of participating, for example – and he borrowed large sums of money from the wealthy Flemish townsmen. He managed to rake in 520,000 francs and two tonnes of gold, which he almost instantly spent on magnificent trappings. His son's retinue were richly furnished with green satin tents, black satin doublets and velvet horse blankets. Those of John himself were made of silk interwoven with gold. Now that the Burgundians were in charge, the scene of battle had to be properly dazzling.

To assist his inexperienced son, Philip the Bold brought together a choice selection of knights that included the French field marshal Boucicaut, who had been knighted in Westrozebeke at the age of sixteen, and the seasoned Ingelram de Coucy, a man with many campaigns behind him. His two hundred bodyguards included almost forty Flemish knights. The richest region provided fewer than 20 per cent of the elite troops but reached deeper into its purse than any of the other domains. John's personal corps – all the squires, archers and grooms put together – amounted to about seven hundred men.

The future duke, almost twenty-five years old and still just a squire and count of the insignificant Nevers, would ultimately command an army consisting of both his own Flemish-Burgundian contingent and an almost equally large group of French knights. In addition there were adventurers from Scotland, Poland and Spain, a large detachment of Knights Hospitaller from Rhodes, troops under Humbert of Savoy and German princes from the Rhineland, Bavaria and Saxony. Soldiers of King Sigismund of Hungary would later join them, accounting for 10,000 men and 30,000 horses all told. And even though the English had finally decided to stay home, the clever Philip the Bold had succeeded in raising a fine army.

Before waving goodbye to John and his men, the duke arranged for the assurance of adequate indulgences and papal dispensations: plenary indulgences, permission to eat and sleep with non-believers, and permission to attend Mass before dawn. After being blessed with that carte blanche, the crusaders went to church, collectively and with much devotion, to beg for the aid of as many saints as they could pray to. At the last minute, Philip the Bold consulted two astrologers in order to assess the future. After receiving their blessing, John's army set off on 30 April 1396 from Dijon. In John's luggage was a roll of gold ribbon from Cyprus, with which the ambitious Burgundian planned to adorn his clothing on the day he was knighted.

While John was fighting his way into legend, the greatest artists from the Low Countries set to work in Dijon. It was a double-pronged offensive that united in one family the two poles that humanity had been travelling between for hundreds of years: the culture of chivalry and the world of spirit and faith, two worlds that increasingly clashed over the course of the fourteenth century. The longing to build a Carthusian monastery and to organize a Crusade made the Burgundians true representatives of their time, which they accomplished in a way that was as boastful as it was distinguished. They were like the best students in class, always wanting to astonish both their classmates and themselves.

'A Jewel To Hang Round The Neck Of A Cathedral'

For a long time, Catholicism had been mainly the business of priests and monks, but over the course of the fourteenth century it found its way into the hearts of ordinary people, and on a grand scale. Itinerant preachers managed to move great crowds with their gripping and spectacular stories. During these forerunners of our modern-day festivals, religion came down from its throne, and those in attendance were literally touched by the Word of God. They listened with open mouths, cried and laughed. There was singing, and plays were performed. Christianity shed its elitist garments and revealed itself as a folk religion that was confessed by cardinal and baker, monk and mercenary, priest and peasant. In the past, an order like the one in Cluny assumed the task of praying for all mankind. Now every mortal soul muttered his own prayers. Priests began preaching in the vernacular during Masses that were celebrated in Latin. This democratization of the contemplative life made Christianity less abstract and more tangible, more naive and simple. It was transformed into a recognizable story in which profound feelings like the fear of death were given an important place.

More and more believers also wanted a place at home where they could cross themselves in peace. Private chapels appeared in the castles and manor houses of counts, dukes and wealthy burghers. This was out of reach for most of the population, of course, but people began hanging crosses in corners of their homes, where they would occasionally pause and light a candle. This gave rise to an industry that specialized in the production of simple wooden crucifixes and rosaries, rough sketches of the saints or homely reproductions of certain stories from the Bible. Jesus, Mary, Moses and various saints left the churches and monasteries and came rushing into people's houses and huts.

The democratization of religion brought with it a vulgarization of Catholic art. Complex symbolism had to make way for straightforward realism; faith was meant to be experienced rather than confessed. People also wanted to carry signs of their faith on their person, at all times. Those who could afford it kept books of psalms or books of hours in their pockets. For others, it was a simple rosary. With people admitting religion to the privacy of their homes, carrying it with them wherever they went and beginning to experience it in their own way, the burgeoning individualization of western man took a small step forward.

Philip the Bold understood that evolution like no one else, and once again he wanted a front-row seat. Just as he always dragged his portable *orloge* wherever he went, so he never left home without his rosary and relics. He was unsurpassed in embodying the idea that time and religion had become portable. Naturally, the duke preferred extremely elegant psalm books and priceless relics, and twenty-five-kilogram candles were no exception. He also emerged as the chief promotor of a new kind of fashion among the super-rich. For his ingeniously crafted images of the saints and other expensive gifts, Philip often called on metalworkers Jan van Haarlem and Jan van Haacht, whose surnames were another reference to the north.

The church of the Carthusian monastery in Champmol was to be his personal court chapel as well as the place where he would be buried. It was obvious that everything revolved around Philip the Bold and not around Sluter and his team. On the threshold of the fifteenth century the commissioning authority was still much more important than the craftsman. Names such as Maelwael, Broederlam and Sluter are known to us because they appear so often in the Burgundian financial records, not because they signed their work. Yet within these tight strictures Sluter was still able to let his talent flourish, to contribute his ideas in discussions with the duke, and to add his own accents to the finishing touches. During the Renaissance, the ego of the artist didn't just come rolling down the slopes of Parnassus as if from nowhere. Its ascendance was one of gradual development and bursts of rapid growth.

Sluter's first big assignment was the decoration of the church porch. Philip insisted that the Blessed Virgin be featured on the central pillar of the entrance door. Could he imagine a better advocate to plead on his behalf for his sins? The Mother of God would surely show him the way to Paradise in the next life. Sluter rolled up his sleeves, reached for his chisel and went on to carve himself a path to eternity. The face of Mary suffused with emotion was something the people of France had never seen before.

Religious art had come a long way since the monks of Cluny had placed an image of God the Father at the entrance to their monastery church in the mid-eleventh century. Their fear of being found guilty of blasphemy had been unfounded: they had not been struck by lightning. By the fifteenth century, a self-assured Philip didn't even hesitate to have a likeness of himself placed in the church porch. Sluter made stone carvings not only of Philip but also of his wife: the duke as the seasoned warrior and diplomat, with his severe gaze and inseparable big nose, Margaret as the devoted mother of eight children, who, as a woman of fifty, could no longer hide her double chin. For good measure, Philip had himself flanked by John the Baptist and the duchess by Saint Catherine. The sculptor positioned the images in such a way that all four of them would be gazing at the Blessed Virgin until the Day of Judgement. The nineteenth-century writer Aloysius Bertrand called the porch 'a jewel to hang round the neck of a cathedral'.[8]

In the meantime, Philip urged his painters on to greater productivity. After the woodcarver Jacques de Baerze of Dendermonde had patiently carved scores of delightful little scenes for his *Retable of the Crucifixion*, Melchior Broederlam painted the whole series in gold tints. When the retable was shut, it was no longer an ingenious biblical puppet show that the faithful saw but painted tableaux from the New Testament. The outside panels exhibited the full force of Broederlam's talent. Specialists still scratch their heads over the extraordinary degree of perfection that he managed to demonstrate in the late fourteenth century in paintings whose magnificent colours still shimmer as much as they did hundreds of years ago.

In the Carthusian church, this retable had sparkled above the altar. Today, the oldest preserved altarpiece of Flemish workmanship hangs in the Museum of Fine Arts in Dijon. In the Louvre, the attentive visitor will come face to face with the *Large Round Pietà* by Johan Maelwael, one of the paintings that decorated the monastery walls. The duke had decreed that every monk should be able to indulge himself in God-fearing beauty.

In the 1390s, Champmol saw the production of one masterpiece after another. But in the spring of 1395, Claus Sluter began what can be regarded as an art historical high point, pure and simple. The artist from Haarlem carved a pedestal rising out of a well, the most beautiful pedestal ever to support a crucifix. Around it he posted six Old Testament prophets, the most famous of whom would give this *Well of Moses* its name. Sluter's Isaiah has parchment-like skin and an expression permeated with a sweet sadness. Jeremiah, shown reading a book, has slightly pursed lips to emphasize his concentration. These are no longer archetypes. They are figures that seem to come to life, thanks to their gestures, facial expressions and details such as wrinkled foreheads, folds in the skin, knitted brows and veins in the wrists. Hovering on the pillars between the prophets are sorrowful angels who drive the words of the prophets upward. Improbable as it seems, this was only the base of an enormous gilded cross that bore an almost life-size suffering Christ, with a weeping Mary, John and Mary Magdalene beneath him. To complete this titanic job, the sculptor was assisted by his cousin, Claus van de Werve. On orders from the duke, they chiselled the coats of arms of his domains at the very base of the pedestal, with those of Flanders and Burgundy gracing the crossbeam of the crucifix.

Philip got what he had so longed for. The suffering of Christ, foretold by the prophets and mourned by angels, a work of art that built a bridge between the two Testaments in a most ingenious way. No wonder it became an attraction for pilgrims, especially when in 1418 Cardinal Orsini granted each pilgrim up to a hundred indulgences. It was partly due to this success that Pope Julius II would begin refusing admission to female pilgrims in 1506, the argument being that their presence was a serious disturbance to the spiritual peace of the monks.

At the end of the Middle Ages, paintings were regarded as less important than alabaster and marble sculptures or metalwork. In terms of the materials involved, they were simply worth less (wood and a bit of paint), while the other objects could be lucratively recycled for another use. The most important assignment for Maelwael was not so much the making of panels as the painting of Sluter's figures. Stone and wood were too earthly in the eyes of medieval people, so a painter was required to apply colour to them. Maelwael's polychromy was so pleasing to Philip that he soon appointed him court painter.

Maelwael alerted the duke to the talent of his nephews, Paul, Herman and Johan van Limbourg. Like their uncle, these miniaturists came from Nijmegen, and in 1402 they would illustrate a Bible for Philip. His brother, the Duke of Berry, was so deeply impressed by the results that he asked the three Limbourgs to illuminate a book of hours for him, *Les Très Riches Heures du Duc de Berry*. The assignment not only resulted in dazzling miniatures but also made sure that Berry's flattened pug's nose, which he so despised, would go down in history. The Limbourg brothers' book of hours would become world famous for its depiction of an idealized Middle Ages: the age of beautiful castles, idyllic woodlands, fields and gardens, and the colourful figures who populated these fairy-tale settings.

*

The vulgarization of religious art proceeded at high speed in order to meet the demands of an ever-growing public, but in Champmol there was no question of rapid mass production. There, the greatest talents of the day collaborated for years under the impetus of the duke. As patron of the arts, Philip the Bold wanted to do more than keep the monastic tradition alive. He also dreamed of leaving behind a monumental work of art for which extraordinary artists had complied with his every wish, to which he had given his blessing for every stone and ornament – a work that featured both his likeness and his gleaming coat of arms, where even the statue of the Blessed Virgin was covered with his initials and those of his wife, where he could go to church when it suited him, and where he would ultimately be laid to rest. The miracle of Champmol was an edifice directed by him and dedicated to him, a manifestation of his assertive ego that demonstrated how the gradual individualization of humanity, which paved the way for the Renaissance, also ran through his ducal umbilicus.

His desire to immortalize his name was once again in evidence when Philip had his own coat of arms affixed to a silver-plated goblet that had once belonged to Julius Caesar. It would take quite a bit of eternity for the Carthusians to pray all that vanity away. But their task came to a premature end during the French Revolution, when the monastery was destroyed. Just as with Cluny, all you can do is curse the revolutionaries who, in their blind fury, or simply for the sake of cold cash, put an end to so much beauty. But there are still a few masterpieces in Champmol that survived the fire of the Revolution and cause your heart to leap for joy.

The porch of the old church is still standing, to which a neo-Gothic chapel was attached in the nineteenth century. Except for a few brilliant fragments, the Christ of Sluter's monumental crucifix bit the dust. But the *Well of Moses* is there to admire, thank God, and you can even catch a glimpse of Maelwael's polychrome. Because it's located just outside the city, Champmol itself remains a well-kept secret, even for the French. Along with a visit to the Museum of Fine Arts in Dijon – which is housed in the old ducal palace, restored by Philip and expanded by his successors – it's a required stop for anyone wishing to embrace the delicate beauty of the Late Middle Ages. The perfect place for hearing in one's imagination the tapping of Sluter's hammer and chisel and the sound of Philip's footsteps.

OSTENTATION AND PROPAGANDA

Or how a death that was anything but heroic,
as well as a tragic debacle, would impart to Burgundy
a small claim on immortality.

I N 1394 CLEMENT VII drew his last breath. The pope who had torn the church in two in 1378 was no more. Philip the Bold understood that the Schism was still a highly sensitive matter in Flanders, and that a union of the Burgundian state might only be possible in the bosom of a unified church. The fact that his enemy Louis of Orléans was clinging to the split only strengthened Philip in his conviction. Now that the papal throne in Avignon was unoccupied, he saw the opportunity to put an end to the accursed Schism. As a prominent member of a large French delegation he hurried to the south, to Avignon, but he arrived too late. The conclave had rushed through a new pope. Earlier on, this Benedict XIII had given his assurance that stepping down would be as easy for him as taking off his hat. But once he had ascended the papal throne, the lure of power proved irresistible. The Schism would fester for almost twenty-five more years at the foundation of an international political structure that was already in disarray.

This must have grieved King Charles VI of France during his more lucid periods, for enlightened minds had promised him that God would solve all his mental problems in exchange for bringing the Schism to an end. After all, hadn't he been struck by the lightning of madness because his forefather, Philip the Fair, had sent the popes to Avignon, and because his father, Charles V, had supported the Schism from the start? But look, all was not lost, for the other path to recovery undoubtedly lay in the ending of the Hundred Years War, another inherited sin – how many of his forefathers did not share in this guilt? – that had reached the point of explosion in his brain.

At the moment, the Schism seemed insoluble. But then King Richard II of England suddenly suggested that it was time to put an end to all this warfare. To make his words more convincing, he asked for the hand of Isabella of Valois, the six-year-old daughter of Charles VI. In France, the offer was initially met with suspicion. Richard II, who was born in Bordeaux, may have had a sincere love for France, but he was mainly an unstable monarch who had trouble controlling his anger. He had recently razed a castle to the ground, the one in which his first wife had died in 1394, and now he wanted to make peace with England's long-standing enemy, contrary to the wishes of his most important advisors. In reality, he was hoping to eliminate his domestic rivals, such as the Duke of Gloucester, by calling on French support. He was even prepared to return the cities of Brest and Cherbourg to achieve this goal. For him, the last six decades of misery couldn't end fast enough. As fishy as his proposal may have sounded to French ears, Paris was thoroughly fed up with fighting the conflict on French soil. Philip the Bold was a leading champion of peace, not least because he knew how much profit the Flemish textile industry would generate. In the spring of 1396, just before crusader John left for the east, Richard and Isabella exchanged their vows in Paris. The marriage was performed 'by the glove', which meant that the bride was marrying her groom by proxy. The absent English king had an envoy lay his glove on the altar as a sign of consent. At the same time, a twenty-eight-year truce was signed. The war seemed on the way to dying a quiet death.

The Burgundian duke, who as a youth had fought against the English on the side of the great Bertrand du Guesclin, felt that now he could die with a clear conscience. His son had recently left with the last real Crusade of the Middle Ages under his command, he had successfully married off his children, he had managed to remove the sting from the complex Flemish question, he had expanded his territory and explored the possibilities for expanding it even further, created a renewed Burgundian state apparatus, built the monastery of Champmol... and now, at the last moment, the end of the Hundred Years War seemed within reach. Yet all that peace of mind was soon to come to an end.

'Son Of The King Of Flanders'

Summer was coming to an end, and nothing had been heard from the crusaders who had left for the east in the spring. By autumn, when the marriage of the twenty-nine-year-old Richard II and the now seven-year-old Isabella had actually been solemnized in Calais, a few rumours reached Paris. The unfortunate bringers of bad news were immediately put behind bars. You can't banish the truth that way, of course, let alone the rampant anxiety that now seemed out of control. More bad news slowly dribbled in. After a while, Philip the Bold could no longer disguise how worried he was about the fate of his son. Processions were organized, Masses were said, the whole Catholic bag of tricks was opened to beg for a safe return.

On 24 December 1396 the crusader Jacques de Heilly arrived in Paris. Still wearing his tall leather gaiters and spurs, he related the account, in fits and starts, of a tragic campaign. Charles VI, Louis of Orléans, John of Berry and especially Philip the Bold listened to his report in a state of shock.

*

The story began on 9 May 1396, when the highly disciplined army arrived in the Swiss city of Laufenburg. John had issued strict orders. 'A nobleman who incites arguments and provokes conflicts will be deprived of his horse and armour. A squire who is found to be a knife fighter will lose his hand, and if he steals, his ear.'[1] The journey passed without incident, and no one impeded their progress. They heedlessly pillaged their way over hill and dale.

21 May: the vanguard arrived in Vienna. John of Burgundy didn't join them until 24 June. He had spent some time with his father-in-law, Albert of Bavaria, in Straubing in order to integrate the German troops into his army. His level-headed father-in-law received him with open arms but refused to allow his son William to take part in what he regarded as an arrogant undertaking 'against a people who never did us any harm'.[2] He looked on with distaste as the richly attired John had to borrow money to feed his troops. In early August, the French and Germans arrived in Buda and

joined King Sigismund's Hungarians and the other warriors who had pledged their support. The army was now practically complete.

15 August: the warriors left Buda and travelled southward. Supreme commanders John and Sigismund rode side by side most of the time. Their plan was to take Nicopolis (today's Nikopol), a fortified city on the banks of the Danube occupied by the Turks. This would give the crusaders free access to Bulgaria. On the way to Nicopolis, the army took the city of Vidin without much difficulty, an achievement that was sufficient to finally earn John of Burgundy his knighthood. Three hundred more youths underwent the coveted ritual with him, but he was the only one who could celebrate with a gold ribbon from Cyprus. The city of Rachowa was next to capitulate, although it put up more of a fight. The opposition was gradually growing.

12 September: the troops finally reached the strategically vital city of Nicopolis. After a few fierce but futile assaults, the crusaders prepared for a long siege and installed themselves as comfortably as they could outside the city walls. Owing to the distance from the motherland and to lack of social control, the siege quickly degenerated into an unrestrained carnival of gastronomic and sexual excess. The crusaders arranged for a shipment of luxury products to be brought in via the Danube, and a horde of ladies of easy virtue set up their tents in the camp. Dressed in their elegant, long-sleeved garments, the Burgundians strutted beneath the walls of Nicopolis. But it was their 'chaussures à la poulaine' that most amazed the Turkish prisoners. Known as 'Crakows' in England, these shoes were characterized by long, pointed toes. Sometimes the toes twisted out into an ornamental tendril of up to half a metre in length. The higher the rank, the longer the toe. Chronicler Michel Pintoin could not hide his disgust at such excessive vanity, especially because long-toed shoes made it difficult to kneel in prayer – and because they made it easier to lift ladies' skirts. At least Bayezid, the Turkish sultan, was a man who took his false religion seriously, according to Pintoin.

24 September: Tirnovo. Less than two days' march from Nicopolis, the scouts of King Sigismund ran into the vanguard of the Turkish army. The luxurious goings-on at Nicopolis had given

Sultan Bayezid enough time to suspend his siege of Constantinople and to move westward with all due haste. When the arrival of the 'Great Turk' was announced, the westerners were tucking into an elaborate dinner. A few of them brazenly cut the long toes off their shoes and then murdered the Turkish prisoners. It was a lynching for which they would pay a heavy price.

25 September: Nicopolis. King Sigismund would have liked to have put Transylvanian troops in the vanguard, but he found himself clashing with the old French chivalric culture. Only John of Burgundy and his men could be granted the honour of being first to engage the enemy. Such a delicate job must never be entrusted to the peasantry. Sigismund took a dim view of this idea. He thought it would be far more interesting to strike the final blow. But the great knights had already left the starting block. 'Forward, in the name of God and Saint Denis!' With jaunty confidence they took down the light cavalry that Bayezid had deliberately sent out. Convinced of an imminent victory, they recklessly forged ahead, even while many of them fell under a rain of arrows. It was as if they had learned nothing from the battles of Crécy and Poitiers. Soon the survivors came crashing into a barricade of sharpened poles that had been driven into the ground diagonally and were aimed right at them, ripping open the bellies of their horses. Once they were past that obstacle, the real battle began. Bayezid's strategy worked like a charm. The decimated French-Flemish-Burgundian troops came face to face with the Turkish infantry. The cries of *'Allahu akbar'* gradually drowned out those of *'Montjoie! Saint-Denis!'* John lived up to his reputation and hacked away courageously at the enemy surrounding him, but when Bayezid's cavalry mounted yet another attack he had to admit defeat. They took John prisoner, while Sigismund in the rearguard could do little more than flee. He survived the battle, but a considerable number of his German-Hungarian troops drowned in the Danube. When it was all over, the battlefield was awash with splendid colours and glistening jewels, but all that Burgundian glitter could not conceal the fact that the battle of Nicopolis had ended in a grandiose fiasco.

26 September: still in Nicopolis. Standing on a rise overlooking

the battlefield was a raging Bayezid. He had counted many of his troops among the dead, and had also learned how the Christian dogs had treated their prisoners. Chained together and stripped to their underwear, the French, Burgundians and Flemings appeared before the sultan. He gave the order to kill them all. A shudder ran through the ranks of the crusaders. The decision met with protest among the Turks because it meant far less ransom money. Only those of the highest rank were spared, since they were worth a great deal more. It was the messenger Jacques de Heilly who, because of his knowledge of the Turkish language, was given the unenviable job of indicating who would bring in a sufficient amount of cash. As 'son of the King of Flanders' John may have escaped death,[3] but not the scene in which his fellow combatants played their role with fear and trembling. Scimitars worked without interruption, chopping away at the crusaders who were made to queue up naked in groups of four or five. They knew what was awaiting them. Before them lay piles of heads and torsos spouting blood. Hasty Flemish prayers and French curses on one side, weary executioners and Turkish sighing on the other.

John of Burgundy, white as a sheet, was forced to stand there and watch. But when he saw Boucicaut in the queue he could no longer restrain himself. Falling to his knees, he begged the sultan to spare his good friend. It was the only other life that he was able to rescue. The Christian blood kept flowing for three hours until the sultan himself was sickened by it all. What remained of John's war contingent was almost entirely destroyed. Bayezid took thirty important seigneurs and princes into his custody, and most of the 300 other survivors were carried off as slaves. He had John and his men shipped off to Bursa in Anatolia.

The lord knights, who had spent most of the hours of their active lives on horseback, were forced to make the journey barefoot. Witnesses declared that John never lost his good humour during the humiliating death march and did all he could to comfort and cheer his companions. In reality, the ordeal must have affected each of them deeply, and those who survived would remember it for the rest of their days.

'Pride And Folly'

With heavy hearts, Charles VI, Louis of Orléans and John of Berry learned of the long list of faithful supporters and family members who were lost to them. Philip the Bold was also hard hit. The death of Guy de la Trémoille, marshal of Burgundy and one of his most loyal associates, grieved him deeply, while his wife, Margaret, mourned the loss of her Flemish half-brothers Louis de Haze, Louis de Fries and John van Vlaanderen, three bastard sons of Louis of Male. The very thought that her husband was languishing behind bars in faraway Anatolia almost sent John's wife, Margaret of Bavaria, into a nervous collapse. The Flemish admiral John of Cadzand had also departed this life on the battlefield. The Count of Eu and the great Ingelram de Coucy would soon die in captivity. The noble families who had no victims to mourn could be counted on the fingers of one hand. Nicopolis had robbed the French-Burgundian knighthood of its best and brightest. During the requiem Mass, those present in Notre-Dame Cathedral wept as much as they prayed. In the churches of Paris, Dijon and Ghent, the death knell rang without ceasing.

In the meantime, Jacques de Heilly had already begun his eastward journey to start discussing ransom money. Even in those brutal circumstances, there was no ceremonial detail that Philip the Bold failed to consider. Packed in Heilly's luggage were new clothes for his dear son, to help him retain his princely dignity. During the negotiations, Dino Rapondi, the duke's chief banker and purveyor, spoke words that would echo down the ages: 'There is nothing that cannot be fixed with gold and money.'[4]

As it turned out, Burgundy had to cough up 710 kilograms of gold to ransom John and his entourage. The entire Crusade ended up costing far more than all the expenses for the Champmol monastery put together. Barely two years after the imposition of heavy taxes to pay for the Crusade in the first place, Philip's lands were now expected to hand over even more piles of cash. The payments did have a striking side effect: for the first time, the discrete regions began to look like a single Burgundian entity.

*

In the company of only ten noblemen, John finally set foot again on French soil. On 22 February 1398 he could take his one-and-a-half-year-old son in his arms for the first time. The baby had come into the world on 31 July 1396, when his father was still on his way to Nicopolis. Deeply moved, John the Fearless stared into the eyes of the later Philip the Good, the duke who would do the most to brighten the sheen of Burgundy's glory. It would be another month before John could embrace his own father in Ghent. In Bruges the two were received by John's tutor, Baldwin van der Nieppe, who had now become chancellor of Flanders and provost of St Donatian's church, thanks to the intercession of his former disciple. It was the beginning of a triumphal procession that brought a grateful John the Fearless to all the major Flemish cities. After all, that's where most of his ransom money had come from.

In Kortrijk, Ypres, Bruges, Sluis and Ghent, crowds of people gathered to see the Burgundian parade. Remarkably, the atmosphere of mourning and funeral rites had turned into a mood of festivity and celebration. Philip the Bold did all he could to make his investment in the Crusade pay off. By constantly banging on about his son's heroic deeds, and by peddling him as a chivalric trophy, Philip succeeded in suppressing thoughts of the defeat. His long imprisonment in a Turkish cell conferred on John a kind of martyr's crown. In addition, the future Duke of Burgundy, otherwise known as the Count of Flanders, had shown himself a brave combatant, had refused to be pushed around in prison and had consistently demonstrated what a worthy leader he was. Far from tarnishing John's honour, the defeat at Nicopolis would actually enhance his reputation. In fact, it would leave him with the famous sobriquet John the Fearless, just as Philip owed his bold reputation to the defeat at Poitiers in 1356. That the biggest debacles of their time provided both father and son with such illustrious monikers shows how well the Burgundians understood the importance of propaganda.

A few of the Turks who travelled with John were baptized, and one of them even entered the Carthusian monastery of Champmol. Fashion inspired by Nicopolis was briefly all the rage. In the ducal palace at Dijon, Philip's little namesake walked around for a while dressed as an Ottoman prince. Twenty years later he would come across a great many Turkish weapons among the items inherited from his father. But the disastrous enterprise had far more significant repercussions. The survivors of the Nicopolis adventure would occupy key positions in John's personal household and would be instrumental in shaping policy for the next two decades.

While the Burgundian Crusade may have been born of Christian and propagandistic ambition, once it had been set in motion the whole enterprise quickly turned into an extravagant display of valour. Bravado proved to be more important than tactics and reconnaissance. Swaggering trumped pragmatism. This exaggerated cult of heroism had led to one disaster after another – from Crécy via Poitiers to the aborted landing in England – without bringing about a change in mentality. Despite the dishonourable debacle of Nicopolis, overconfidence remained persistently fashionable. The fact that John the Fearless was welcomed home as a hero, and that epic poetry was written in his honour, was not only the result of cleverly concocted propaganda. It also demonstrated a chronic lack of self-criticism.

Yet two chroniclers dared to address the cracks in the knightly escutcheon. In his last writings, Eustache Deschamps would report critically on the 'pride and folly' of the crusaders.[5] His colleague Jean Froissart reproached the Burgundians for their 'great desire to win honour'[6] and pointed out how their craving for ostentation was diametrically opposed to the virtue of Christian modesty. Vanity may be as human as hunger, thirst and sex, but on this point the Burgundians seemed more human than all the English and the Turks put together. Nicopolis proved to be the most opulent funeral that the ancient chivalric ideal had ever dreamed of organizing, except neither the participants nor the onlookers realized it at the time.

The Burgundian Crusade did have a positive military outcome that was quite unexpected. Bayezid may have won, but he lost so many troops that he emerged from the battle in a weakened state. In 1402 he was crushed by the Mongol-Turkish horde of Timur the Great, which reduced the fervour of Ottoman expansionism for quite some time. As a result, the death throes of the languishing Eastern Roman Empire and its last bastion, Constantinople, were prolonged for several more decades. Naturally, the Burgundians wasted no time claiming that Europe owed its renewed tranquillity to John the Fearless.

'We're Really Going To Miss The Good Duke Of Burgundy'

On 27 April 1404 a Burgundian officer knocked on the door of the Carthusian monastery of Herne in Hainaut. He insisted on seeing the prior. Philip the Bold, Duke of Burgundy and Count of Flanders, had unexpectedly succumbed to the effects of a flu. He was fifteen kilometres away in the small city of Halle near Brussels, and he was sixty-two years old. In compliance with the duke's wishes, the officer had come to ask for a Carthusian habit. The best-dressed man of his time had stipulated in writing that he wanted to be buried in the traditional costume of the most shabbily dressed monastic order.

The duke had come to Brussels for the Brabant transfer of power. Duchess Joanna, now eighty-one, realized that her time was up, which meant that Burgundy's had finally arrived. Strictly speaking, Joanna was ceding all her powers, something that naturally called for a big celebration. In order to avoid an excessive concentration of power, it had been agreed earlier that not Philip but his second son, Anthony, would become the new duke. For the time being, Brabant did not fall to the duke himself, and even though the councilmen were Brabantians and retained their own chancellor, the duchy gradually acquired a strong Burgundian flavour.

On 16 April, Philip arrived in Brussels in the company of his three sons: John, Anthony and Philip.[7] Ten days later, the Burgundian party caravan was transformed into a mobile hospital. Philip had suddenly been overcome by a fever, so he set his course for Arras, where his wife, Margaret, was staying. Peasants and ditch-diggers led the way, trying to flatten the road ahead of Philip's carriage, in which he was lying on a chaise. But soon it became apparent that he had the flu, which had already taken so many victims in that region, and his suffering became so severe that he could go no further. The procession stopped in the town of Halle. Right across from the church, in an inn known as Den Hert, he breathed his last on Sunday, 27 April.

The heart of the king's son was taken to the French necropolis in Saint-Denis near Paris, his intestines were given a place in the crypt of the basilica of Saint Martin in Halle, Hainaut,[8] and his embalmed body set out on its last journey to Burgundy. The division of his dead body perfectly summarized his career. Philip was born in 1342 in Pontoise, not far from Paris, where for years he would be the most powerful man in France. In 1369 he married Margaret of Flanders in Ghent, the city to which, after years of struggle, he would firmly commit himself. In 1385 in Cambrai he married his son John into the house of Bavaria, which ruled over Hainaut, Holland and Zeeland, and he reinforced that tie by marrying his daughter Margaret into the same house. In 1388 a military campaign took him to Nijmegen, which provided Philip with the duchy of Limburg and a formal promise of Brabant. During the festivities celebrating the crowning of his son Anthony as Duke of Brabant in 1404, he died surrounded by his loved ones. He was entombed in Champmol, Burgundy, where all the foregoing regions came together in one unprecedented artistic melting pot.

After marrying well himself, Philip spent a great deal of time developing a politics of marriage that was unequalled in the Late Middle Ages. Not only did he work on making interesting matches for John and Margaret, but he also saw to it that his other children enjoyed marital bliss, materially speaking.[9] In this way he succeeded in forcing the influence of Burgundy into the duchies of Savoy and Luxembourg, the Austria of the Habsburgs, and Picardy, which in the Late Middle Ages was the collective name for the seigniories north of Paris where Flemish was not spoken. At the same time, he was careful not to neglect the tie with the French royal house, and just before his death he arranged for the marriage of his grandson Philip the Good with Michelle of Valois, daughter of Charles VI. This same grandson would patiently assemble the pieces of the territorial puzzle that his grandfather had gathered until one day a Burgundy suddenly emerged that was universally feared and admired. Chronicler Jean Froissart was entirely correct when he wrote that Philip the Bold 'saw far into the future'.

On 27 April 1404 his sons had little time for historical musings. Not only were John, Anthony and Philip overcome with grief, but they were also confronted with acute financial problems. Their father, who spent more in his lifetime than his three sons put together would ever do, didn't have enough cash on hand to pay for his own funeral. Suddenly, silverware had to be pawned and money borrowed without delay. That small detail was typical of the pecuniary position of the former duke. Because of his inordinate spending he often found himself in financial trouble, but each time he reassured himself by remembering that rich Flanders was in his purse and everything would turn out well. Thanks to financier Dino Rapondi it did this time too, but it was quite a feat to get all 155 members of the funeral cortège dressed in black in five days' time. Finally, the journey to Dijon could commence, a trip that Philip had taken countless times. He was dressed as a simple Carthusian and carried in a lead-lined casket via Geraardsbergen, Oudenaarde, Kortrijk, Lille, Douai and six other cities. The caravan arrived in Champmol on 16 June.

*

Death was a matter of vital importance in the Late Middle Ages. You had to make sure you were thoroughly prepared by showing contrition for your sins and taking enough time to pray. Once you were six feet under, the work was far from over. Then your relatives had to pray for you. A great many years yawned between God's first verdict and the final weigh-in on Judgement Day, and once you landed in purgatory you would really be in need of sublunary assistance. That meant Masses for the dead, and even though the number of required Masses could sometimes bring a family to ruin, no better protection from hell had yet been discovered. But Philip was in good hands. His Carthusians had soundly discharged their duties and could easily carry on for a few more centuries. In addition, the closer the mortal remains were to the source of prayer, the more potent the spiritual effect. Here, too, the duke scored well. He could literally hear the monks praying from his tomb.

In the first centuries of its existence, Christianity did not allow ordinary people to be buried near churches. Such places were reserved for saints and prelates. Gradually this practice changed, and when Catholicism emerged as a national religion there was no turning back. Everyone wanted to be interred as close to the altar as possible. While the burials of rich people in the church's far-off early days were conducted in an atmosphere of restraint, such funerals would now blossom into prestigious affairs in which no expense was spared. In the fourteenth century it was the length of the funeral cortège that showed whether you had many 'friends' and whether you were important or not. Philip understood this quite well, as was clear from the spectacular funeral he organized to honour his father-in-law, Louis of Male, in 1384. Now he wanted to go even further and turn his own tomb into an everlasting spectacle, where he would be able to rest in peace throughout eternity. At the end of the eighteenth century the revolutionaries tried to destroy this work of art, of course, but thanks to skilful hands and well-executed restorations, everyone can gaze in admiration at this alabaster and marble miracle in Dijon's Museum of Fine Arts.

We must not forget that the mortal remains of the duke lay in a crypt beneath the monument, and that now all our attention is focused on the tomb above ground. We see Philip himself lying in state, life-size, his eyes open and his hands folded heavenward. Reclining at his feet is a lamenting lion, and at his head are two charming angels – a lovely reference to the status of man, a creature halfway between angel and beast. The winged beings grasp Philip's helmet as if they were about to slide it over his head. We have to imagine Sluter, stooping far over to carve the smallest details on the inside of the helmet. What we see emerging is no longer stone but real leather. The polychrome is again by Johan Maelwael. A recent restoration has revealed that both the striking detail of the seam and the extremely realistic padding of the helmet continue on to the furthest point, which you can't even see when the monument is in its normal position. But our eyes are drawn downward to the forty *pleurants*, the mourning figures beneath the recumbent duke, who re-enact his funeral cortège.

Philip's generous patronage gave Sluter the chance to shape the standard characteristics of the art of his time, but it also gave him the freedom to push its boundaries. Over the previous century, the sarcophagus of a monarch, which had started out as a rather sober affair, had become an art object that depicted not only the deceased but also his entire funeral. Sluter had not opted for the typical bas-relief, however, nor for the more adventurous high relief. Instead, he resolutely placed the *pleurants* in the space allotted to them as three-dimensional figures. The arrangement is not a haphazard one but a sophisticated mise-en-scène. Out from beneath the superbly carved arched vaults of a monastery corridor come the bishop and the priests who will celebrate the Mass,[10] followed by a few Carthusians, members of the family and royal household, and finally several servants. Sluter wanted to bring the entire procession theatrically to life as it moved from Halle to Champmol, with room for interaction between the mourners: a look of understanding here, a gesture of consolation there.

Has the author of this book mentioned that you really ought to visit Dijon? When you do, squat down and notice how each figure has been given its own pose and expression, how naturally the figures scratch the backs of their heads, brush away their tears or page through books, how beautifully details such as buttons, pages, rosaries, purses and belts are crafted, how the folds of the garments fall so realistically, how a few of the mourners are entirely hidden beneath their swaying monks' hoods, how authentic the glances of the others are, how correct the wrinkles... Feel how the alabaster begins to breathe. It's almost as if these mourning individuals, who are expected to grieve for Philip the Bold forever, had stopped what they were doing for a moment and will immediately start moving again.

Duke and artist both coloured outside the lines, each in his own way, and on the threshold of the fifteenth century they both advanced the wheel of time by a single cog. While Philip let the centuries-old feudal garments subtly slip from his shoulders with the founding of a new dynasty that would unite Burgundy in the south with a handful of northern counties and duchies, Sluter, with his profound realism, pointed the way to the meticulously detailed art of the Van Eyck brothers and other Flemish Primitives, who would give their figures the look of living statues à la Sluter.

No matter how skilfully the Haarlem-born artist managed to bring marble and alabaster to life, his name and fame have passed into oblivion in his own land. It's true that he can be seen strutting among the other art heroes on the south facade of the Rijksmuseum in Amsterdam, and he even pops up a second time in a stained-glass window in the entrance hall.[11] Yet almost no one in the Netherlands knows who he was. The one or two people whose eyes happen to fall on his likeness just walk away with a shrug.

*

Now that his master had been called to his eternal reward, it seemed to the weary Claus Sluter that all his hard labour would soon take its toll on him as well. Yet he continued to work with great discipline on the tomb of Philip the Bold, which was not yet ready by the summer of 1404. His new boss, John the Fearless, kept pressing him to hurry, but in that same year an exhausted Sluter withdrew to the abbey of Saint-Étienne and was seen less and less frequently at the construction site. All that is left of his last residence in Dijon is the fourteenth-century gate, through which the decrepit artist shuffled to get to his studio during the last months of his life. In 1406, the greatest sculptor of the Late Middle Ages passed away with the comforting thought that Claus van de Werve, whom he himself had trained and who had worked at his side for almost ten years, would continue his oeuvre.

It was a time of death and harvesting. In December 1404 Albert of Bavaria also traded the temporal for the eternal, making his son William count of Hainaut, Holland and Zeeland. Logically, William's wife, Margaret of Burgundy, the sister of John the Fearless, came to sit beside her husband on the throne. Their three-year-old daughter Jacqueline would grow into one of the most famous women in the history of the Low Countries, and two decades later would carry on a desperate struggle with Philip the Good, who was now only eight years old. Their common grandmother, Margaret of Flanders, left this life on 16 March 1405, so that John the Fearless, Duke of Burgundy, also became Count of Flanders in one fell swoop.

The seeds that progenitor Philip the Bold had so carefully planted in Burgundian soil would germinate and send up shoots in the year of his death. Without doubt, he and his grandson Philip the Good were the greatest of the four Burgundian dukes. Thanks to him, the new dynasty could spread its wings into the fifteenth century.

He himself had planned to travel to Paris as quickly as possible after the transfer of power in Brussels in order to thwart the plans of Louis of Orléans. Orléans was of the opinion that Burgundy's domination had gone on long enough. Every time Charles VI suffered a mental collapse, Louis took advantage of the situation by gaining a tighter hold on the reins of power, plunging his hand deeper into the treasury and provoking England. Five years earlier, the Francophile King Richard II had been overthrown and then murdered a year later under mysterious circumstances. The new English king, Henry IV, seemed ready to respect the peace, at least for the present, but the future would show how premature that notion was. If the duke didn't intervene, or so he thought, even bigger problems would arise. Three years earlier, Philip had raised a small army near Paris to intimidate Louis of Orléans. In that he was successful, but in 1404 the rebellious nephew began making more noise. Undoubtedly, the duke must have devoted his last lucid thoughts at Joanna's festivities to searching for a lasting solution.

Except now he was dead and the ball was in his son's court. Philip's diplomatic approach would clear the field for the aggressive politics of John the Fearless. 'I'm telling you, we're really going to miss the good Duke of Burgundy,'[12] noted the writer Christine de Pizan immediately after his death. Soon she would be proved right.

MURDER AND THE LANGUAGE WARS

*Or how a Burgundian assassination brought France
to the verge of collapse and how John the Fearless found
a safe haven in Flanders, which successfully championed
the use of the vernacular.*

'MONSEIGNEUR, THE KING requests that you come to him without delay. He urgently wishes to speak to you about a matter that concerns you both.'¹ The chamberlain of Charles VI had scarcely spoken these words than Louis of Orléans jumped to his feet. In recent years he had begun acting as his mad brother's deputy, more or less. On several occasions the king became so unhinged that he refused to shave or dress himself. Charles screamed that he was made of glass, that he could shatter into pieces at any moment. Eventually he became covered in scabies and pustules. Fleas leaped through the palace halls. Louis visited Charles less and less frequently. But occasionally the king was clear-headed and would try to participate in ruling the country. Had another such period of lucidity now arrived? Then Louis would have to hurry to Charles's side in order to maintain his influence. Or was he in great need? As the closest blood relative, it would be his responsibility to care for him.

The Duke of Orléans took leave of Queen Isabeau after having tried to lift her spirits. She had just given birth to a son, who had not survived the day of his birth. She and her husband had been spending most of their time apart since the madness struck, and she and Louis had become very intimate. The refined youth of earlier days had grown into a mature, attractive adult whom women found it very hard to resist. Evil tongues whispered that Isabeau's most recent children were not those of Charles VI, but that the future Charles VII was actually an Orléans. The queen could hardly be blamed if it were true. It must have been a source of great suffering having to share her life for the past fifteen years with a madman.

It was 23 November 1407 and Louis left the queen's chambers at about seven in the evening. It would be the last time the two saw each other.

*

In recent years, the tension between the Duke of Orléans and John the Fearless had reached a fever pitch. After the death of Philip the Bold, there was, unsurprisingly, no room for the new Burgundian duke in the regency council. His father had been an uncle of the sick king, but John was only one of many cousins. Now that the flow of state money had been blocked, the Burgundian court, with its love of ostentation, was forced to take a big drop in income, and the duke found himself in a tight spot. He did everything he could to secure a place for himself in the regency council. First he tried to justify his presence by manipulating public opinion. Wasn't Louis hoping to breathe new life into the war with England? Wasn't Orléans opposed to ending the Western Schism? Was he not bleeding the populace dry with excessive taxes? And had he not enriched himself by plundering the treasury? In other words, shouldn't John occupy a place in the inner circle in order to avoid a total calamity? His populist remarks – especially the promise to lower taxes – made John the Fearless well liked among the general population.

But Louis of Orléans would not let himself be browbeaten so easily. He may have been less of a crowd-pleaser, but he did have the legal right to chair the council and exclude his cousin. As a result, the Burgundian duke felt compelled to put on a show of military force. In the summer of 1405 he formally pledged himself to his brother Anthony and his brother-in-law William, creating an official alliance between the Flemish-Burgundian state and the strong blocs of Brabant-Limburg and Hainaut-Holland-Zeeland, another step towards a stronger tie between the various regions of the Low Countries. With that impressive military backing, he demanded a seat on the regency council. But he could not prevent Louis, as clever as he was charming, from winning over most of the members and continuing to have the most say. Orléans retained control over the keys to the treasury and did not hesitate to use that money to support the Burgundian's foreign enemies. He held the position that Philip the Bold had regarded as his own for so long, that of the most powerful man in the land.

So after taking leave of the queen on that November evening in 1407, Louis was in a particularly good mood. Astride his mule, he played nonchalantly with one of his gloves. The reins hung loose in his hands, and he was humming a tune. He regarded himself as lord and master, especially because more than six hundred knights and squires were quartered in Paris. Couldn't he summon them with just one snap of his fingers? Except that now he had no desire for a heavily armed escort. Why should he? He was only a few streets away from the Hôtel Saint-Pol, the immense palace complex in the Marais where his brother, Charles VI, had his residence. Was he not the all-powerful Duke of Orléans? Didn't everyone step aside when he passed by? Two squires on one horse were riding ahead of him, six servants lit the way with torches. They languidly continued down the Rue Vieille-du-Temple. The atmosphere was jovial.

John the Fearless was sick and tired of Orléans's hold on power. Although he had secured himself a place among the greats of the kingdom, he found it difficult to step away from the shadow of his rival. And to top it off, a few months earlier Louis had reorganized the king's Great Council, an advisory body consisting of legal experts, prelates and prominent citizens, while John was tending to business in Flanders. Louis profited from his absence by reducing the number of members by half, and as fate would have it, John's pawns were among those dismissed, leaving the Great Council entirely in Orléans's hands. When John returned he could barely contain his rage.

What also got under his skin was Louis's shameless skirt-chasing. Orléans was a Don Juan who openly bragged about his female conquests. He even collected their portraits! On one occasion, when the Burgundian happened to find himself in Orléans's amorous Valhalla, he felt his blood run cold. In one corner he saw a portrait of his own wife. That the successful dandy had also seduced his spouse has never been proved, but it was not beyond the realm of possibility. In any case, it gave a personal touch to the political feud that was about to erupt in 1407. Burgundian spies claimed that an attempt on John's life was in the works. Later, these proved to be very vague plans, but for the duke the situation was abundantly clear: it was either him or Louis. Orléans's 600 warriors hadn't come to the capital for nothing. John had convinced himself that simply being on his guard was not enough. He had to be proactive, and he had already hired a band of assassins.

When Orléans and his retinue passed through the Barbette gate on 23 November, a handful of masked men leaped out of the shadows. One of them cried, 'Kill him! Kill him!'[2] and struck Orléans with his axe. It wasn't enough to knock Louis from his mule. Indeed, he still had enough strength to call them to account by shouting, 'I am the Duke of Orléans!' as if he was sure the brigands would quickly change their minds. Their answer proved just the opposite: 'He's the one we're looking for!' After a second blow he fell from his mount. The thirty-five-year-old duke scrambled to his knees and cried, 'Who is that? Who is doing that?' They responded by bludgeoning him with sticks and axes and chopping off his clenched left hand.

His squire, Jacob van Mekeren, who came from Horssen near Nijmegen, threw himself upon his master like a living shield and thereby earned himself a certain death. 'Murder! Murder!' shrieked a woman from a nearby window. The men fired a few arrows at her and shouted at her to shut her mouth. She did, although later on she would recount everything in detail.

When the duke showed no more signs of life, the group of hirelings began to slink away. A deep wound ran from the duke's left ear to his right, a terrible fissure through which his brains protruded. One of the murderers delivered a final quick blow with his club, another threw a burning torch into one of the houses. 'Fire! Fire!' they cried, before disappearing into the night.

*

Hanging at the entrance to the Impasse des Arbalétriers in Paris there is still a sign that commemorates the murder: 'Dans ces parages, Jean-Sans-Peur, duc de Bourgogne, fit assassiner par des

spadassins, le 23 novembre 1407, son cousin Louis, le duc d'Orléans.'
His guilt has gone unquestioned for more than six centuries, but
at first no one suspected John the Fearless.

One day later, the royal family paid their last respects to the
body of Louis in a church near the place where the crime was
committed. Son Charles, who had just celebrated his thirteenth
birthday, was inconsolable. Orléans's left hand and part of his
brains had just been found lying in the street. They were placed
with his mortal remains. John the Fearless also came to express
his condolences. He looked distressed and seemed quite shocked.
'Never has a more malicious and treacherous murder been committed in this kingdom,'[3] he said bitterly. Everyone gathered
round the bier agreed with him. Interestingly, the atmosphere in
the streets of Paris was buoyant. Ordinary people seemed relieved
that Orléans the tax fiend had been put to the sword. 'Blessed be he
who cut him down to size,' they said, 'for if he had lived any longer
he would have sent the whole kingdom to perdition.'[4]

At first, suspicions were harboured against another enemy of
Louis of Orléans. But when it was discovered that the man had
skipped town more than a year before without leaving a forwarding
address, the investigation was dropped. John thought he had made
a lucky escape, until the provost of Paris decided to search the
palaces of the city's grandees. Water carriers claimed that on the
night of the attack they had seen the murderers flee in the direction
of the Hôtel d'Artois, the Burgundian duke's residence. Suddenly
John felt the net closing in around him, and on the evening after
the funeral, in a burst of contrition, he confessed to his uncle John
of Berry that, 'driven by the devil',[5] he had given orders to have
the murder committed. The sixty-seven-year-old Duke of Berry
was stunned. With tears in his eyes, he said, 'I am losing my two
nephews.'[6]

John the Fearless fled the French capital at breakneck speed.
In one day he covered 140 kilometres on horseback, stopped
to rest in Éclusier near the Somme, crossed the river the next
morning, and set his course for Lille. In his rich land of Flanders
he felt safe. His brothers Anthony and Philip, the four Members
of Flanders and the most important barons and counts assured

him of their complete support. That was a great relief. But the question remained: what should he do now? His craven display of bereavement, his remarkable confession and the inglorious flight had put him in an extremely awkward position.

The assassination constituted a definitive break with the cautious, intelligent and visionary politics of his father. From now on, John would always have to stay one step ahead of his enemies. Suspicion became the Burgundians' second nature. In fact, after 23 November 1407 suspicion would become endemic among the French for years to come.

'Anything Walloon Is Treacherous'

The fact that Flanders had received him with open arms was not so surprising. Two years earlier, during his Joyous Entry, the Four Members (Ghent, Bruges, Ypres and the Franc of Bruges) had served him with a list of substantial demands, and John the Fearless had complied with every one of them.

First of all, he promised to spend more time in Flanders and to do so on a regular basis – after all, here he was – and if that was not possible, to allow his wife, Margaret, to reside there. From that time on he would spend an average of two to six months a year in the north. He also assured the Flemings that he would get to work on a trade agreement with England. Orléans's sabre-rattling had caused the old wound to start festering again. The agreement would be quick in coming, thereby enabling the Flemish textile industry to run at full speed once more, thanks to imported English wool. John demonstrated that he, like his father, could speak with a forked tongue: using threatening language against England and laying siege to the English Calais, but just for show – to placate anti-English Paris and to reach a better agreement with Albion.

With all these efforts, John managed to gain the support of the Flemish cities. His purpose was not to weaken their power but to make himself indispensable as count and duke. By encouraging marriages that tied important families to the ducal clan, and by stimulating the appointment of abbots and bishops who were favourably disposed towards him, he succeeded in penetrating Flemish inner circles. The cities had to admit that since the Peace of Tournai was signed in 1385 the Burgundian dukes had acted as excellent counts of Flanders. John the Fearless was described as 'courtly, modest, amenable and even good-natured'.[7]

Finally, during his Joyous Entry, John had sworn that the ducal court of law, known as the Council of Flanders, would be moved from the French-speaking city of Lille to the Dutch-speaking region of the county, and that his subjects would be addressed in their own language. Only a few weeks later the court of law was officially moved to Oudenaarde, and two years later even to Ghent, which had been called the 'wicked city' thirty years before.

In answer to the quite provocative question put by the Flemish cities – whether the inhabitants of Dijon or Nevers would be happy if he spoke to them in Flemish – John was just as gracious. From now on, his correspondence with the Flemings would be written in Dutch. The Flemings, who were as self-confident as they were proud, were aware that they were a cash cow for Burgundy, and they acted accordingly. John donned velvet gloves in order to milk his Flemish cow as elegantly as possible.

The Four Members had also asked that officials who were not fluent in Dutch be simply dismissed. One thing was clear: the language question was proving to be extremely sensitive.

*

It would be a long time before any effort was made to standardize the local languages of the Low Countries. It just wasn't necessary. Most communication took place within the same small community, where everyone understood everyone else. So the term 'Dutch' (*Diets*) does not refer to a single standard language, which didn't even exist at the time. It is a collective term for all the local languages that were being spoken: Flemish, Brabantic, Hollandic, Limburgish, and so forth. For centuries, Latin had been the international lingua franca. Noblemen were usually a bit less literate, and they had clergymen write down their doings and dealings in the language of Virgil. Over the course of the twelfth century a change occurred, and the need arose in the Low Countries to write things down in the vernacular as well.

In past centuries, any cross-border contacts maintained by the county of Flanders were usually with France. As important vassals of the French king, the counts tended to speak very good French – if they weren't French-speaking already. There was little need for translations of treaties and agreements. The demand for texts in the vernacular would arise elsewhere. It began in the twelfth century, when the cities insisted that the rights they had wrung from the counts be enshrined in official documents. At the same time, the need arose within those same cities to lay down various agreements in writing. At first the new documents were still written in Latin – starting in 1147 in Ghent and in 1170 in Ypres – but over the course of the thirteenth century the vernacular seeped into the pens of clerks, aldermen and magistrates.

Latin fell from its official pedestal. What man on the street understood the language of the ancient Romans anyway? The demographic explosion that took place in the cities brought with it an avalanche of administrative documents written in the vernacular. It was a matter of dire necessity. 'There are cities where the rich families usurp the government and exclude the common people. The civil authorities require the lord to demand payments every year, in public, and in the presence of representatives of the lower orders,'[8] wrote a royal bailiff in 1281. Specialists regard the statutes of the Ghent leprosarium from 1236 as the first administrative text written in a vernacular of the Low Countries. This was followed in 1250 by the aldermen's deeds in that same city, and in 1262 Bruges joined in.

In most Flemish cities a bilingual system was in common use, simply because the nobility spoke French. In Brabant and in the northern regions of the Low Countries there was an evolution towards the exclusive use of Brabantic, Zeelandic or Hollandic: Middelburg in 1254, Lubbeek and Delft in 1267, Dordrecht in 1277 and Haarlem in 1280. If a document in Latin was issued, it was usually a translation of a Dutch draft text that was meant to be read aloud to the local authorities. Latin had become a dead language – a ceremonial language at the very most.

Of the 2,000 Middle Dutch texts from before 1300 that have been preserved, 70 per cent were drawn up in Flemish, 17 per cent in Hollandic and 11 per cent in Brabantic. The remaining 2 per cent concern regional languages from Utrecht, Limburg and Zeeland. Most of the Flemish texts came from Bruges, an international trade hub where commercial translations of transactions were more than welcome.

The vernacular also made its debut in literature. The first was Hendrik van Veldeke, who began writing in Maaslandic in 1170. Jan van Heelu followed one century later with his Brabantic *Rijnkroniek van de slag bij Woeringen* (1288). But it was mainly Jacob van Maerlant, who was born in the Franc of Bruges and, according to legend, could write with two hands at the same time. He would prove his literary skill in Middle Dutch over the course of the thirteenth century. At first he produced translations of French chivalric romances, but gradually he abandoned these models because he found that the frivolous southerners were more interested in rhyme and beauty than in historical accuracy. Van Maerlant summarized his course of action succinctly in an expression that is still being repeated, often wrenched out of context: '*Die scone Walsche valsche poeten*'[9] (Those beautiful, treacherous Walloon poets). Contrary to what later would be frequently claimed, this was not a political-linguistic statement. Van Maerlant was merely reproaching the French poets (by Walloon he meant French) for playing fast and loose with the facts in order to improve the style of their narrative. Hendrik Conscience later seized these words and ran off with them, dropping the context and twisting them to his own liking: '*Wat Walsch is, valsch is.*'[10] (Anything Walloon is treacherous.) Of course, the Flemish Movement preferred to quote the Conscience version of Van Maerlant's statement.

Van Maerlant was so successful that his strophic poem *Wapene Martijn* was the first Middle Dutch work to be translated into French. Not only did he pen a historic novel, a world history and an encyclopedia of biology, but this 'father of all Middle Dutch poetry'[11] also produced a retelling of the entire Bible in Middle Dutch – to the irritation of a great many clerics who were not happy that the plebs now had access to biblical wisdom. His books brought about a wide dissemination of beauty and truth in the vernacular. With his *Spiegel Historiael* (1288), Van Maerlant successfully transformed the Latin world history *Speculum Historiale* into a singular Middle Dutch work that was as readable as it was didactic. After the founding of the University of Leuven in 1425, academic research would mostly be conducted in Latin. The elitist character of such writings became highly pronounced once more, while the number of readers plummeted.

*

The linguistic evolution could not bring about change in the county administration. The counts pretended nothing was happening and continued to communicate in French. But in 1352 Louis of Male put a stop to it. He must have been the only Flemish count who resorted to Flemish as the working language in official documents, even though French was the language of his court, and did so for a solid thirty years. The arrival of the French-Burgundian Philip the Bold turned the clock back in this regard. After the difficult war years, Philip may have emerged as a good administrator, but when it came to language he was a failure. He neither understood nor spoke a single word of Flemish, and his son John the Fearless had to deal with that frustration. In view of the French politics of his father and of the predecessors of his grandfather, John's relaxed attitude was surprising, to say the least. But in the end, he was and remained a French prince. The fact that he responded to all language-related complaints was part of a carefully considered policy from which he benefited considerably in Flanders. Thanks to the duke's concessions, the Flemish language certainly did move forward, although that could only have happened as smoothly as it did because a great deal of administrative work in the cities had already been drawn up in the vernacular.

Ghent and Bruges, the latter in particular, were among the economic leaders of Europe, and those who wanted to do a brisk business there were at a distinct advantage if they had mastered the local vernacular and didn't have to bother working through a translator. Sometimes the Four Members even required foreigners to 'put their request into writing as close to the Flemish as they can'.[12] For their part, shrewd Flemish businessmen made sure they had several languages in their skill set. The stereotypical image of the Low Countries polyglot probably had its roots in the international trade establishments of Bruges.

The fact that John the Fearless tried to speak to his northern subjects in their own language – 'to the best of my ability'[13] – meant he could count on considerable sympathy among them. John emphasized his commitment to Flanders by choosing the Middle Dutch phrases *Ic zwijge* (I remain silent) and *Ic houd* (I persevere) as his personal mottos. He also saw to it that his son Philip learned to speak and write Flemish by the age of three, and Philip's son Charles the Bold would follow the same path. Yet none of this could prevent French from increasing in importance in Flanders during the Burgundian era.

John the Fearless must have attained a degree of proficiency in order to converse in Flemish, but like his court and his immediate staff he always spontaneously conversed in French. In addition, the court of auditors in Lille, which controlled Flemish finances, was French-speaking, as were the reports of the ducal court of law in Ghent. So if you really wanted to be included and to participate at the highest level, bilingualism was a must. Most Flemish careerists spoke French as well and as often as they could, and they sent their children to the south to practise the language, '*buten lands omme walsch te leren*'[14] (to foreign lands to learn *walsch* – French). In some cases they even Gallicized their all too Flemish-sounding names. With the steady centralization of power and the mechanism of ambition-driven upward mobility, French would only become more prestigious. Even the linguistic skills attributed to the Flemings emphasized the superiority of French. Flemish was acceptable and permissible, but French remained the language of the dukes and therefore of the elite and those in power.

On 9 December 1407, when John, through confidant Simon de Saulx, abbot of the Burgundian monastery in Moutiers-Saint-Jean, disclosed the sad fate of the Duke of Orléans in Lille, it was in French. The next day a translation was handed to the Four Members of Flanders.

'Such A Person Deserved To Be Burned At The Stake'

A month after the murder of Louis of Orléans, John the Fearless had yet to be officially convicted, despite the appeals of Valentine Visconti, Louis's inconsolable widow. Incredible, perhaps, but it was no mean feat to execute a prince of his calibre without triggering a civil war in the process. Negotiators sought a compromise, but the proposal to let Burgundy go scot-free on the condition that he hand the murderers over to the law courts did not go down well with John. He didn't want a solution that was as half-hearted as it was cowardly. On the contrary, he wanted his deeds to be justified.

At the head of 800 armed horsemen, John made his re-entry into Paris on 28 February 1408. He was met with cheers, much to the dismay of the Orléans supporters. The duke who had left the kingdom as a murderer under the cloak of night returned as the messiah who would rescue the French from a heavy tax burden. He had coaxed the theologian Jean Petit to ride along with him. Petit had written a scholarly treatise proving John's innocence.

On 8 March almost all the dignitaries and prominent men of learning were present in the Hôtel Saint-Pol, the palace that the late lamented Orléans had failed to reach two months earlier. The very last to enter the crowded hall was John the Fearless. His red flannel coat had long sleeves and was decorated with gold leaves. When he held up his arm, everyone could see that beneath all that glitter he was wearing a hauberk, a coat of mail that imparted a touch of the military to his ceremonial presence. Behind this man, who would yield to no one, the door slammed shut.

Theologian Jean Petit held forth for four long hours without once raising his voice. His words spoke for themselves. He accused Louis of using sorcery and devilish incantations to arouse the madness of his brother, to plunder the treasury, to promote the Schism, to attempt to have the king put to death on more than one occasion. Finally, Petit delivered his verdict, still at the same pitch: 'Such a person deserved to be burned at the stake.'[15] He meant to prove the innocence of John the Fearless by means of a syllogism: it was good to murder a tyrant; Louis of Orléans was a tyrant; therefore the fact that the duke had taken upon himself the disagreeable task of getting rid of the devil incarnate should be cause for jubilation. A great many of the people in the crowd were dumbfounded but didn't have the temerity to question his conclusion.

The next day, the Great Council of the King acquitted the Burgundian duke of any wrongdoing. Who could have dared to object? Less than a week later, Charles VI awoke from another fog of madness and, with a slightly trembling hand, signed the official pardon. As if nothing had happened, John once again assumed a place on the Council of Regents.

The family of the victim seethed with rage. On 11 September, Orléans's widow organized a counter-spectacle. In an equally long speech, an equally scholarly speaker declared that the duke should be punished for his crime, and that on the very spot where Louis's skull was bashed in he should openly do penance and ask for forgiveness on his knees. And that was only the beginning. All his houses in the capital should be razed to the ground, his duchies and counties should be ceded to the crown, and he should spend a million pounds on good works. John himself should be banished from the kingdom for twenty years.

Remarkably enough, the Great Council honoured this request. Suddenly Burgundy was saddled with the blame once again.

While the basis was being laid for an actual civil war in Paris, the accused was not even able to defend himself. On the contrary, John was conspicuous by his absence. How else could they have dared pass such a sentence? He was on his way to engage in a major campaign in the prince-bishopric of Liège. His brother-in-law, Prince-Bishop John of Bavaria, was having problems, and although the duke had other things on his mind, he took off.

Was it an exercise in mindless heroism to leave the capital to his enemies and help the brother of his wife, Margaret, out of a tight spot? At first sight it certainly seemed that way. But if he should succeed in assisting the prince-bishop in his hour of need and getting him back on his throne, then the Burgundian sphere of influence would be vastly upgraded. Liège, Tongeren, Hasselt, Dinant and Maastricht were not to be sneezed at. Who in Paris would do anything to obstruct the most powerful military leader in Europe? But then he would have to win. It was all or nothing.

In the summer of 1408, John the Fearless went for broke.

ARRANGED MARRIAGES,
UNCONTROLLABLE TUMULT

Or how John the Fearless succeeded in expanding Burgundy's
sphere of influence in the Low Countries by force of arms and
astute marriage arrangements, but also how he ended up on
French soil in an especially bloody conflict.

O N HIS WAY to Liège, John the Fearless stopped to light a few candles at St Adrian's Abbey church in Geraardsbergen. When he was born, his mother had offered thanks to St Adrian for answering her prayers, and now he in turn was making a stab at begging for protection. Thirty-eight years before, Margaret of Flanders had prayed for fertility; today her son was praying to avoid sudden death. How convenient that some saints could be called on for completely different things. As he rattled off his prayers, John had plenty of time to consider his situation.

The Bavarian connection was a thread that ran through his whole story. Not only did his wife come from Bavaria, but his sister had married someone from the same family back in Cambrai. And this William wasn't just anybody. He had now become Count of Hainaut, Holland and Zeeland. In addition to a number of bastard sons, William had one legitimate daughter, little Jacqueline, who was the apple of his eye. For her fifth birthday he had arranged a marriage for her to the second youngest son of King Charles VI of France. The half-Bavarian, half-Burgundian Jacqueline was preparing to assume control of her three principalities, and to that end she was being given a solid education: from botany through biblical history, mathematics and languages to the rules of etiquette. As a young girl she was just as good at analysing medicinal herbs as she was at knowing the correct way to wear a train. She was bright, inquisitive and not especially pretty at first glance. Yet in the coming years she would grow into the most desirable bride of Europe and would marry four times.

Her venerated father – John's brother-in-law and comrade-in-arms William – was more of an old warhorse than a great statesman, and he struggled to hold his ground in the conflict between the Hooks and the Cods in Holland, which had been going on for decades. It was a complex hostility that was tearing his land apart, and he probably couldn't even explain it to his daughter. He might have said that the Cods were open to change and were more interested in cooperating with cities and burghers, while the Hooks (from the hooks that catch the cod) were more conservative and adhered to the classical feudal structures. But the various members switched parties so often that what it boiled down to was an ordinary power struggle, sometimes even blood feuds between families, who passed the hatchet from one generation to the next until the dispute was cancelled (or not) by means of a procedure of 'kissing and making up'. The fact that William had chosen the Hooks side, while his father, Albert, became more and more closely aligned with the Cods over the course of his life and finally even took a Cod mistress, showed how inextricable the Holland tangle was. This struggle for influence and power would go on for about 150 years and claim thousands of victims. One day, John the Fearless and his son Philip would also become involved, but in 1408 the Burgundian duke had other family worries.

His wife's second brother now occupied the throne of the prince-bishopric of Liège, which comprised large areas on both sides of the Meuse and had been ruled by a prince-bishop since 985. As in Flanders, two languages were spoken there: French in the south and Dutch in the north. The Flemish counts weren't the only ones with a turbulent fourteenth century behind them. The prince-bishops of Liège also fell prey to unrest. It was John's brother-in-law John of Bavaria who succeeded in putting an end to the chain of rebellions with his accession in 1390, but in recent years both the townspeople and the nobility had become irritated by his authoritarian style of governance. They chose Diederik of Perwez as a counter-prince-bishop, thereby winning the support of the late Louis of Orléans and of the Avignon pope Benedict XIII, the most important players in the anti-Burgundian camp.

When John of Bavaria was forced to hole up in a besieged

Maastricht for a second time in a row, John the Fearless and William of Holland joined forces to keep the situation from 'degenerating into a universal rebellion'.[1] In short, John wanted to pull off a repeat performance of what his father had achieved in Westrozebeke, not only to enhance the prestige of Burgundy as a growing power bloc, but also to safeguard the centuries-old feudal relations: nobility and clergy at the top, the rest of humanity below. The thought of burghers rising up against their lawful lords was absolute anathema.

'Let Them All Die'

The rebels abandoned their siege of Maastricht and rushed to take on the Burgundian forces. Just outside the village of Othée, halfway between Tongeren and Liège, the troops discovered each other and decided to do battle. It was 23 September 1408, almost twelve years to the day since the battle of Nicopolis. The Hungarian debacle had left an indelible scar on his soul, but now John the Fearless was forcing a rematch.

He had learned his lesson. This time the infantry were given every opportunity to join in the fray, with Scottish archers hired with Flemish money taking up the slack. John also forbade his forces from simply attacking at random. On the contrary, he decided to wait. And he kept waiting. But the Liège rebels, who were looking down from a small hill, employed the same tactic. Not a single warrior left his hideaway. There was no noticeable movement, as if the universe were holding its breath.

Suddenly, John the Fearless's troops found themselves under attack. Not by archers – the distance was too great for that – but by portable field artillery, an innovation that constituted a cautious advance in the waging of war. It involved a rather modest collection of culverins and ribaudequins that took quite a long time to reload.[2] Only a few were wounded, but the troops still had no choice but to mount a frontal attack. First the duke quickly ordered 400 cavalrymen to execute an enveloping movement, which meant they would have to attack the enemy from the rear.

Seated on a small horse, John the Fearless led his troops and ordered them to annihilate the 'insane' and 'vicious' Liège rebels and to show them no quarter.[3] He trotted down the whole front line, as if to spur each one on personally. Burgundy's banner bore the emblem that had accompanied him for several years: a carpenter's plane. The symbolism was unmistakable: he would shave off anything that got in his way.

John raised his voice and gave the order to attack. Hundreds of horses shot from the starting block, bearing on their backs men of steel with their shields and lances. The thunder of horses' hoofs resounded in answer to the lightning of the artillery, a broad front of helmets and banners that were meant to prevent the Liège shooters from loading too often. Unlike what happened in Nicopolis, the assault was controlled. The captains even allowed for pauses, so the heavily steel-encased warriors and their horses could catch their breath.

When the cavalry was only 250 metres away, the Scottish archers let fly, leaving a trail of destruction throughout the Liège army. Then the horses thundered over the enemy lines. The knights knocked down everything in their path, hacking away as they went. The Liège infantry used their halberds to search out the small space between helmet and armour that was visible on every knight. Swinging with great strength, the halberdiers were sometimes able to penetrate the armour itself. If that failed, they tried to drag the riders from their horses by means of the special hook with which the halberds were fitted.

After the cavalry charge came hand-to-hand combat. It was especially frenzied around John the Fearless, who seemed to be the target of twice as many of the Liège warriors. According to chronicler Michel Pintoin he fought like a lion, parrying countless sword strokes and dealing several himself without being wounded. Despite his daring, for which he was later so highly commended, the battle didn't really begin to turn in his favour until the 400 knights reached the Liège rearguard, where they sowed panic and confusion. The Liège bakers, brewers, butchers, clog makers, rope makers, tanners, basket weavers, goose catchers, silversmiths, barbers and broom makers wanted to flee, but they were trapped. From one moment to the next the battle turned into a massacre.

William of Holland and John of Burgundy had agreed not to take any prisoners, despite the ransom possibilities. Even when his captains finally asked him if it wasn't time to bring the bloodshed to a close, John answered, 'Let them all die.'[4] Was it the intransigence of Bayezid the Thunderbolt that the duke was thinking of when he later examined the piles of bodies?

A relieved John of Bavaria had all suspicious burghers and noblemen beheaded in Liège or drowned in the Meuse. From then on he would go through life as 'John the Pitiless'. He was back in the saddle, but he was also indebted to John of Burgundy more than ever before. The prince-bishopric had basically become a Burgundian protectorate.

The news of the duke's victory resounded across the European mainland. Some sources even claim that it was this event that earned him the name 'John the Fearless'. Like his father after Westrozebeke, the duke commissioned the weaving of large wall tapestries in Arras to commemorate the victory. The battle itself was depicted on a tapestry measuring at least seventeen by five metres. Wall tapestries served an ornamental function, of course, but they were primarily used as insulation in the halls of palaces that were often difficult to heat. They could also be hung as partitions, to divide large rooms into various compartments. Very occasionally they became weapons of propaganda, as the two dukes demonstrated after Westrozebeke and Othée with great panache.

Heaven seemed to reward John's latest achievement with a eucharistic tribute as well. From then on, he could pray for the souls of the fallen at both Othée (23 September 1408) and Nicopolis (25 September 1396) during the same Mass of Remembrance. Whether Othée had wiped out the mistakes of Crécy, Poitiers and Nicopolis remained to be seen. But word spread from Liège to Maastricht, Brussels and Ghent, and all the way to Paris, that John the Fearless was not someone to be toyed with, especially with such a mighty national alliance behind him.

*

Just when a law was being drafted in Paris stipulating that if the duke dared to dispute his guilt in the murder of Orléans, violence would be used, the news came that Burgundy had won a resounding victory. His opponents, who were feeling very smug, found themselves slinking off with their tails between their legs and leaving Paris to the victor of Othée. On 25 November 1408, the duke made his entrance into the city to the sound of great public acclaim. For the people of Paris, the fact that he was officially persona non grata was like water off a duck's back.

After lengthy negotiations a settlement was reached, a compromise that managed to prevent a civil war just in the nick of time. On 9 March 1409, Charles of Orléans, the fifteen-year-old son of the victim, was made to publicly offer forgiveness to his arch-enemy John the Fearless in Chartres Cathedral. The young Charles burst into tears. Heaving with sobs, he forgave the man who had murdered his father. This illusory peace ushered in a period of deceptive calm. John wrote to his brother Anthony that now he could devote himself to 'the interests of the kingdom' once again.[5] His victory seemed complete, but it only served to fan the flames of revenge in the mind of Charles of Orléans.

John the Fearless realized he had to be on his guard. He had a twenty-seven-metre castle tower erected at the Hôtel de Bourgogne, the ducal residence in Paris. It was built right against the city wall, to enable him to make a hasty escape. John wanted every room to have a latrine. These oldest preserved toilets in the city were heated and had internal drains, which was quite exceptional. Usually, the waste disappeared through an opening onto the street or into the garden, and you simply had to put up with the filthy smears on the walls. John made sure his military tower was luxurious and beautiful. The vaulting over the long spiral staircase was of unparalleled splendour – an echo of Champmol in Paris – and because of the quality of the stone it would stand the test of time. Like a glorious, esoteric medieval relic, the Tour Jean-Sans-Peur is still a feature of the busy Rue Étienne Marcel. How many pedestrians would suspect that all by itself, this ancient tower should remind Paris of one of the bloodiest episodes in its history?

John could have walked his murderous path to its logical

conclusion by killing the weak-minded Charles VI and declaring himself king. But he didn't. The mystique of the anointed king was so deeply entrenched in France that even the fearless John of Burgundy would not take such an extreme step. The slowly greying forty-one-year-old wretch, who needed the active assistance of two or three servants to keep him clean, continued to serve as the steadfast embodiment of royal authority.

Although he never laid violent hands on the king, John would wade through blood for years. It wasn't long before Charles of Orléans, who was consumed by revenge, declared war on Burgundy. There remained only one way for the duke to save his skin: to win this civil war. From now on he would focus almost all his attention on France.

In Flanders he installed his fifteen-year-old son Philip as his permanent representative. Philip would move into the Prinsenhof in Ghent in 1411, and three years later he would become the official governor of Flanders – literally the *lieu-tenant*, the 'place-holder', a function that would be given the name 'stadtholder' in the regions of Holland. In collaboration with the Four Members, the young Philip (who officially was still only the Count of Charolais) drew up a balanced international policy and breathed new life into the trade relations with the French liege lord, local partners such as Brabant and Holland, the English wool industry and the German Hanseatic League. During the dark years of the French civil war, any further centralization of the Flemish-Burgundian state was put on hold. But Burgundy's centre of gravity had begun its imperceptible journey to the north.

'The True Account Of Bitter Grief'

At first, all the power during the civil war lay in the hands of the Burgundians, although Orléans's followers put up a good fight. But since becoming the father-in-law of Charles of Orléans in 1410, the cruel count Bernard of Armagnac assumed the role of leader of the opposition against Burgundy, and with great success. His name sounded a sharp clarion call, and made immediately clear that the unyielding and untrustworthy Armagnac was not to be mocked. After a while, no one spoke of Orléans any more; it was the conflict between the *Armagnacs et Bourguignons*. The key was Paris. Whoever got his hands on the capital would be master of the kingdom.

John the Fearless had hoped to deal with the Armagnacs in one big battle near Montdidier in 1411. He left the capital in an optimistic frame of mind, but just as the fighting was about to break out his Flemish mercenaries abandoned him. No matter how humbly he pleaded with his 'most loyal friends', they insisted on going home because they still hadn't been paid. The duke, who saw an ideal opportunity to destroy his enemies go up in smoke, would think twice from now on before recruiting Flemish soldiers for further engagements.

One year later, John made another attempt just outside Paris. He besieged Bourges, where the Armagnacs had recently entered into a treaty with the English. Being rather clever, the English worked out which party had the most to offer, thereby sabotaging the skewed French political system. King Charles VI, who appeared in public every now and then like the mechanical bird in a cuckoo clock, only to creep back into the darkness of his madness, took the side of the duke when the siege began. The walls of Bourges didn't flinch. In the end the two parties declared a truce for the umpteenth time.

In the summer of 1413, circumstances turned against John the Fearless. 'Long live Burgundy!' could be heard on the streets of the capital, but the undertone was grim. The skinner Simon Caboche was head of the main butchers' guild. His followers, known as the *Cabochiens,* would leave their chopping blocks with cleavers in hand to assert their rights if the situation called for it. They stood as one man behind John the Fearless, who did his best to introduce financial reforms. The *Cabochiens* had come to his aid in previous crises, but they were frustrated by how long it took to get anything done. So they took matters into their own hands and demanded the surrender of sixty dignitaries, who in their estimation were too lavish in the spending of government money. Enraged, they stormed the Hôtel Saint-Pol and forced their way into the royal chambers, just as Étienne Marcel had done in 1357. John the Fearless, who barely managed to save the life of the dauphin, felt himself losing control of his own popular shock troops.

The Armagnacs demanded the right to restore order. After all, somebody had to rescue the king and the dauphin from the clutches of these rampaging butchers. After the *Cabochiens* were driven out, new slogans were instantly adopted. Now all that could be heard was 'Long live Armagnac! Long live Orléans!' John the Fearless, outstripped by his own populism, fled to Flanders once again with all the Burgundians in his wake. Nothing became of the reforms in France. On the contrary, new high taxes were levied to finance the war. Bernard of Armagnac drained the city dry. His reign of terror suffocated every glimmer of hope.

Armagnac wanted to strike while the iron was hot. Hoping to drive the Burgundians not only out of Paris but out of the whole kingdom, he laid siege to Arras in the summer of 1414. Arras was the last big fortified city before Flanders. This time, Charles VI, who again had taken temporary leave of the royal cuckoo clock, fought on the side of the Armagnacs. John the Fearless waited in Lille, biting his nails to the quick, but his enemies failed to break Arras's defence. Neither party was able to stifle the power of the other.

After yet another false peace, John withdrew to Burgundy for the first time in years and spent a few months there. It gave him a chance to catch his breath and turn his attention to hunting. In the company of his falcons, goshawks, sparrowhawks and vultures, he was able to take his mind off the recent disasters. There was also time for romping with his favourite dog, *Martelé* (Spot). Among the most unusual members of John's animal collection were a leopard, a talking linnet, a porcupine, a camel, a handful of apes and a pair of aurochs. In his aviaries tweeted turtle doves and goldfinches. When evening came, he would take the time to listen to their singing.

*

In the meantime, the internecine struggle in France continued during the Council of Constance (1414–18), where the Western

Schism was finally brought to an end. After two years of bickering, Martin V became the one and only pope, with his seat in Rome. That intervention was of the utmost necessity. While the two active popes had been deposed in 1409 and a new one elected, the first two had not accepted their dismissal. For the past five years, Christianity had been blessed with at least three popes, all of them squawking to be heard.

Now that that agony was out of the way, the church officials could turn their attention to the heresy of Jan Hus, who had denounced the corruption fuelled by the Schism. The Bohemian theologian, later regarded as a forerunner of the Reformation, went to the German city of Constance to defend himself. Despite earlier promises, he was immediately thrown into prison and was burned at the stake a few months later.

Among the matters of heresy on the agenda, besides that of Hus, was a discussion of the treatise of Jean Petit. The duke's enemies seized the opportunity of the Council to attack him on theological grounds. The honour and church membership of John the Fearless lay in the balance. He did escape excommunication, but only by the skin of his teeth. The duke would go on to dedicate himself to the new pope with such enthusiasm that Martin V would respond by praising him as the champion of united Christianity.

While the future of the church was being debated at the Council of Constance, the Armagnacs and the Burgundians were engaged in spying on each other in France. John the Fearless had not resigned himself to the situation, and he was determined to reconquer Paris. Indeed, the time to seize the upper hand was gradually approaching, for at that very moment the Hundred Years War between England and France was being rekindled. In all that chaos, who had a grasp of the big picture?

In 1415, after several vain attempts to win one of the warring factions to his side, King Henry V[6] of England chose to throw caution to the winds and try to conquer France, which had been weakened by civil war. He landed on 13 August, and on 22 September Harfleur fell. Suddenly in France it was all hands on deck. The dauphin even asked John the Fearless to help out. Could he send 500 soldiers and 300 archers? His request was modest because he didn't want the Burgundian duke to mobilize a large army under the pretext of dealing with the English threat. He had also asked Charles of Orléans the same question. Orléans showed up with much greater numbers, although he left the Count of Armagnac at home. Somebody had to keep an eye on the furniture and the mad king.

For his part, John the Fearless decided not to get involved. He also forbade his nineteen-year-old son Philip from taking part in the fighting. He couldn't risk endangering his successor, and charged him to stay in Flanders. Philip 'withdrew to his room and shed bitter tears', and until the day he died he would complain of 'not having been in Agincourt, to triumph or to die', according to the chronicler Monstrelet.[7] On the other hand, John did nothing to prevent his own brothers from running off to one of the most important battles of the Hundred Years War. As grandsons of John the Good, Anthony and Philip insisted on upholding their honour.

In rain-soaked Agincourt, two long-standing enemies, neither of which had forgotten Crécy or Poitiers, prepared for the third great encounter of the war. France against England, 18,000 well-equipped warriors against 10,000 wind- and dysentery-tormented Englishmen, the French without a real leader versus the canny Henry V. It's hard to have to say it, so unlikely is the stupidity of the same thing happening twice, but on 25 October 1415 the French shot themselves in the foot once more. The terrain was much too narrow, which meant they couldn't even consider a flanking manoeuvre, the obvious move in view of their numerical strength. To compensate for the lack of space, their chivalrous egos insisted on moving the archers to the rear. The lord knights were packed so tightly together that each step to the left or the right caused an entire battalion to come apart at the seams.

As the morning sun rose in the sky, the heavily laden animals sank more and more deeply into the brown-yellow mud. The French glittered in the light, and the plumes of their helmets danced elegantly in the wind. Waiting across from them was a sombre conglomerate of archers and infantry clad in leather and wool, some of them barefoot. Far behind them were the knights on horseback. 'Attack! Attack!' came the order, but the French steeds stood motionless, as if they had been nailed to the ground. As they struggled to pull one leg after another out of the boggy mire, thousands of English arrows came raining down on them. Were the Frenchmen still sleeping? Henry V asked himself in astonishment. Why didn't they move? Fifteen minutes later, half the aristocracy of France lay floundering beside their horses, and the English infantry simply walked among them, finishing them off with axes and spears.

The battle was as good as over when Anthony of Brabant came racing up. Much too late, but just in time to be killed in action. He commandeered his chamberlain's armour, improvised a tunic from a trumpet banner and stormed onto the battlefield incognito. Six minutes later he was dead. John's youngest brother, Philip, also lost his life, along with 6,000 others.

Charles of Orléans was dragged alive from a pile of bodies by the English. The man who for years had sought revenge for his murdered father would have to spend the next quarter of a century languishing in prison on the other side of the Channel. He would find consolation in poetry and would emerge as one of the most important poets of the French Middle Ages. 'While writing in my book of woe / I found my heart, to my relief; / the true account of bitter grief / all bright with endless tears that flow.'[8]

John the Fearless took the time to mourn for his two brothers and made his way to Brabant. On 5 November 1416 in Dendermonde, the States of Brabant and the Burgundian duke signed a compromise concerning the succession of the fallen Anthony. Despite the resistance of Sigismund, the Holy Roman Emperor, John the Fearless succeeded in securing the Burgundian succession by steering Anthony's son onto the Brabant throne as John IV. Yet all did not go according to plan. Leuven, Brussels and other cities prevented John from assuming the guardianship of his twelve-year-old nephew, which he had much desired. The cities thought it safer to put together their own regency council and to hold the great duke at arm's length. In 1408 he had brought the people of Liège to their knees by force of arms, and now he was too weakened to give Brabant the same treatment. So while the result may not have been the personal union of Flanders and Brabant he had hoped for, there still remained a separate Burgundian-Brabant duchy.

The manpower that John had built up over the years was immense, and despite all the pressure he had been under he succeeded in maintaining control. He rushed from Dendermonde to France to work on the recapturing of Paris. For the moment there was nothing he could do, but as a cunning diplomat he smelled an opportunity when France's Queen Isabeau of Bavaria was cast out of the French court by the Count of Armagnac. John made every effort to meet with her in secret, and on 2 November 1417 the hour had come. The queen had left her isolation in Tours incognito in order to speak the following words to the Duke of Burgundy at the Abbey of Marmoutiers: 'I have no choice but to trust you, more than any other man in the kingdom. At my request you have left everything to come and free me.'[9]

Isabeau, who had a soft spot for luxury, found she had no choice. If she ever wanted to be queen again, she would have to put her fate in the hands of her lover's murderer. The only mortal who could still stand in the way of John's struggle for power in France was the Count of Armagnac. But John had to hurry up, strike now and recapture Paris, because Henry V was making headway with his conquest of Normandy. After his glorious victory at Agincourt, the English king was steadily advancing on the French capital. His progress was accompanied by much violence, but for Henry that was only normal: 'War without fire is like sausages without mustard.'[10]

*

As if the Duke of Burgundy didn't have enough on his plate, another piece of news came in that he could not ignore. While both he and the English monarch were making their way to Paris, Count William of Hainaut, Holland and Zeeland died at the age of twenty-five as a result of a dog bite. John's sister Margaret of Burgundy was left an inconsolable widow.

Once again, John the Fearless found he had yet another ball to juggle. Recalling his earlier experience in Brabant, he could not allow Burgundy to lose influence in these important regions. So he went to great lengths to arrange a marriage between William's daughter, Jacqueline, and John IV of Brabant, even though they were cousins. Sigismund, the King of the Romans, was willing to do whatever it took to thwart the marriage, but once again he backed away. Against his better judgement, the German leader failed to see that his power as a feudal lord in the Low Countries was shrinking. Burgundy was tightening his grip on a large part of his fiefdom. All Sigismund could do was stand there and watch, gnashing his teeth and pondering revenge.

And so it was that a few months before undertaking his raid on Paris, John the Fearless pulled off his masterstroke in Holland. Jacqueline of Bavaria and John IV of Brabant swore their eternal devotion to each other in The Hague. His niece Jacqueline, daughter of his sister Margaret, placed Hainaut, Holland and Zeeland in the wedding basket. Her husband, John IV, son of his brother Anthony who had been killed in action, did the same with Brabant and Limburg. The duke forged five not inconsiderable power blocs into one. The marriage that he pulled out of his diplomatic hat would have elicited a proud smile from his father, Philip the Bold.

The Burgundification of the Low Countries continued apace, but soon it would encounter great opposition. Jacqueline took up her tasks as Countess of Hainaut without much trouble, but in Holland and Zeeland things proved a bit more difficult. There she had to navigate between the Hooks and the Cods. The former rallied round Jacqueline, while the Cods fell in behind the German emperor Sigismund, who was still bent on getting back at Burgundy. He had urged John the Pitiless to leave the prince-bishopric of Liège for what it was and, as brother of the late Count William, to make sure that Holland and Zeeland were removed from the Burgundian sphere of influence. Would the man who had been saved by John the Fearless ten years earlier, thanks to the victory at Othée, now suddenly oppose Burgundy's plans?

It didn't take long for such an opportunist to make up his mind. These counties had more ships at sea than England and France put together, so compared with the prince-bishopric of Liège they were far more important. To the irritation of Jacqueline, John the Pitiless let himself be celebrated in Dordrecht, Holland's richest city, as its governor. Since he had never been ordained, he was still technically bishop-elect. Now he made grateful use of the fact that he could always return to the status of layman, and he launched a fierce struggle against his niece Jacqueline.

In the spring of 1418, with the situation in the Low Countries growing more explosive by the day, John the Fearless and his troops gathered once again at the seemingly impregnable gates of Paris. The English king was in the distance and moving closer. Behind the walls were the Armagnacs, taking it all in. The Parisians were in their houses, longing for peace and freedom.

SEVERED HAND, CLEFT SKULL

Or how John the Fearless met the same terrible fate as Louis of Orléans, and how his son Philip sold out France to England in revenge, but also how the new duke began focusing more and more of his attention on the Low Countries.

O N 28 MAY 1418, a conspirator opened one of the city gates, and the banished Burgundians streamed into the French capital once again. Suddenly, the two hostile groups found themselves occupying the same city. The tensions between the followers of John the Fearless and of Armagnac were running high, and two weeks later all hell broke loose. At first the Burgundians had restrained themselves and kept their opponents locked up, but now they roamed through the streets of Paris, murdering and setting fires as they went. Finally, on 12 June 1418, they seized the Count of Armagnac and skinned him alive. His bloodcurdling screams summed up the entire past decade: years of violence, furtive betrayal and chaos.

It had cost rivers of blood, but John was lord and master once again. He had been making progress over the past few months, in Paris and elsewhere throughout the country. Yet the end of the misery was not in sight. One enormous problem remained: a few of Armagnac's supporters had succeeded in smuggling Charles, the fifteen-year-old dauphin, out of Paris, and he was now holding court on a small scale in Bourges. From there, this hesitant adolescent would still manage to shake a powerful fist.

What was John to do? To leave Paris and do battle with the English would mean virtually handing the capital over to the dauphin. An attack on the dauphin would give Henry V the opportunity to plant the English flag in Paris. So back to the bargaining table.

In the summer of 1419, John and the dauphin Charles arrived at an agreement: together they would take a stand against England and finally settle this interminable war. The news was met with great relief across the capital, where the townspeople celebrated for days. In his response, Henry V mockingly called the Duke of Burgundy 'Little Johnny of Flanders'. This frustrated swipe barely masked the agitation that the news generated in England. Who but this experienced scoundrel would be able to knock out the English in battle?

To wrap up the final details, the dauphin invited John the Fearless for a talk, to be held on the bridge of Montereau-Fault-Yonne. Enclosures had been built on either side of the bridge to ensure the safety of the encounter. The meeting would take place in the middle. Each party was allowed to bring ten men-at-arms. It was risky to be sure, since the dauphin had surrounded himself with Armagnacs. But did John have a choice? He wanted to end the war, get France back on its feet and safeguard his rich county of Flanders.

God-fearing man that he was, would John have crossed himself before stepping onto the bridge on 10 September 1419? Was John truly Fearless at that crucial moment? Did he hope that all his prayers, his pilgrimages, and even his failed Crusade would protect him? Or did he think of his successful Liège campaign, the overhauling of the tax system and other plans for reorganization in Flanders? Of his dearly beloved son, who spoke much better Flemish than he did and ran the county so skilfully? Of his handsome wife, who always stood firmly behind him? Of his bodyguards, who had never strayed from his side in recent years? Or simply of his dog, Spot? Did he look at his hands and the blood that clung to them? Or was it beauty that fluttered through his mind, all the lovely manuscripts he had had illuminated, the court painters he continued to support, in imitation of his father? Perhaps his main thought was of his direct form of diplomacy, which had borne so much fruit. Even now, here he was. Perhaps he was speaking to himself in Flemish? 'Ic houd.' I persevere.

The doors at each end of the enclosure were opened. The dauphin Charles entered from the town side, the side of Montereau, and John from the side that gave access to the local castle and the countryside. Flowing beneath the two approaching groups was the

When the Rhine froze over at the end of 406, the so-called barbarians didn't hesitate. They crossed the river and overran Gaul. Among them were the Vandals, the Suebi and the Alans, as well as the Burgundians.

The baptism of Clovis (around 500). The Musée de Picardie in Amiens has a book in its collection from the eleventh century that is dedicated to the life of St Remigius. On the lower panel of the beautiful ivory binding we see him making the sign of the cross with holy oil on Clovis's forehead. On the far right, Clovis's Catholic Burgundian wife is closely watching the proceedings.

King Sigismund of Burgundy was the first Germanic leader to enter the Catholic Church. His conversion may have hastened Clovis's religious turnabout. Years later, Sigismund was the victim of the *faihitha*, a Germanic form of vendetta. His enemy Chlodomer had him beheaded and thrown into a well.

On 11 July 1302, the Flemish *volc te voet* – foot soldiers – prevailed over the French cavalry. This legendary conflict got its name from the golden spurs plundered from the battlefield. In this miniature we see the French leader Robert d'Artois being dragged from his horse. The foot soldiers are waving the greatly feared *goedendags* – maces: cudgels with iron tips. The silver helmets have discoloured over the years.

On 24 July 1345, a mob stormed the house of the leader of the Ghent rebellion, Jacob van Artevelde. 'And they forced their way into the house, and Jacob had to try to escape through his stable,' wrote an anonymous chronicler, 'but the shoe restorer ran after him and cleaved his head with an axe.' That last detail has not been omitted from this miniature (right).

Anonymous portrait of King John the Good
of France (father of Philip the Bold) from the
late 1350s. It is regarded as the oldest preserved
portrait since the Age of Antiquity.

During the Battle of Poitiers (1356), France suffered a terrible defeat at the hands of the English. In this miniature we see King John the Good of France being taken prisoner. The man at his side, also cloaked in fleurs-de-lis, is his youngest son, Philip the Bold, who owes his epithet to the courage he showed that day. The importance of this battle to the future of Burgundy (and therefore to the Low Countries as well) cannot be underestimated.

King Edward III of England, who started the Hundred Years War, is giving Aquitaine to his son Edward of Woodstock, the Black Prince, in 1362. Edward decimated the French at Poitiers (1356). Note the emblems of the fleur-de-lis (France) and the leopard (England) on their armour: Edward saw himself as king of both England and France.

In an effort to stamp out the *haestighe ziecte* – the hasty disease – half-naked penitents began appearing in the streets in 1348. They believed that such a wrath of God had to be driven out with the right kind of scourging. This miniature shows a group of flagellants from Bruges reaching the city of Tournai.

Anonymous portrait of Duke Philip the Bold, richly attired in keeping with his reputation. He doesn't seem to have skimped on the jewellery. The large nose and strong chin are characteristic features. Seventeenth-century copy of a lost original from *c*.1400.

Portrait of Margaret of Male, Countess of Flanders, Duchess of Burgundy, consort of Philip the Bold, mother of John the Fearless. Oil painting from the sixteenth century.

On 19 June 1369, Philip the Bold married Margaret of Male and the fate of Flanders was riveted to that of Burgundy. Notice the daisies (*margrietjes* – a nod to Margaret) and the Ps (for Philippe) on the robe of the Burgundian duke.

Louis of Male.

Humphrey of Gloucester.

John IV of Brabant and his
brother, Philip of Saint-Pol.

In 1382, a forerunner of the French Revolution was nipped in the bud on Flemish soil. Led by Philip the Bold, a French-Burgundian army crushed the warriors of Philip van Artevelde, taking resounding revenge for the Battle of the Golden Spurs eighty years earlier.

The peerless *Well of Moses* by Claus Sluter, with traces of the polychrome applied by Johan Maelwael still visible. On display in Champmol, near Dijon. Here we see Daniel and Isaiah, with a fragment of Moses's beard on the right.

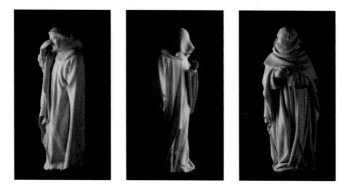

The *pleurants* surrounding the tomb of Philip the Bold are among the most beautiful ever created. A masterpiece by Claus Sluter, completed by his cousin and assistant Claus van de Werve. It's almost as if these mourning figures, who were meant to support the recumbent duke indefinitely, had momentarily suspended their activities and are about to start moving again.

The attentive visitor to the Louvre is bound to come face to face with the *Large Round Pietà* by Johan Maelwael (*c.*1400), one of the paintings that graced the walls of the monastery in Champmol. Duke Philip the Bold decreed that every monk should be able to indulge in pious beauty.

The Dendermonde woodcarver Jacob van der Baerze carved scores of magnificent little scenes with utmost patience. Melchior Broederlam then painted the entire work in gold tints. This detail from the *Altar of Saints and Martyrs* shows the beheading of John the Baptist.

Portrait in profile of John the Fearless, a copy (*c*.1500) of an original from 1404, perhaps by Burgundian court painter Johan Maelwael. Here we see a proud John the Fearless, who became the next Duke of Burgundy after the death of his father.

Anonymous portrait of Margaret of Bavaria, consort of John the Fearless, sixteenth-century oil painting. She was the sister of Count William of Hainaut, Holland and Zeeland, who in turn married a sister of John the Fearless.

In a joust, the aim was to shatter as many lances as possible against the oncoming opponent. The winner was the one who collected the most points. In the event of a tie, the referee determined who had broken off the longest piece. In this miniature from 1342, we see John of Beaumont taking a direct hit. He was lucky to survive. King Edward III of England is watching from the balcony.

On 5 August 1392, the French king was stricken by madness. Charles VI drew his sword and turned on his own retinue, hacking away like a maniac. Until his death in 1422, the king would hover between lucidity and insanity.

After the disastrous Battle of Nicopolis (1396), Sultan Bayezid commanded that the French, Burgundian and Flemish crusaders be paraded before him in their undergarments. He then ordered them to be killed one by one. John the Fearless was forced to stand by and watch, but he himself was spared.

On 23 November 1407, John the Fearless had his arch-enemy Louis of Orléans murdered at the Barbette gate in Paris. In this miniature, we see that Louis's hand has been chopped off and his head cleft by an axe. His last words were, 'Who is that? Who is doing that?'

Yonne, which emptied into the Seine a few hectometres further on and then set course for Paris, its strength doubled.

'Please come here.' Monseigneur the dauphin is waiting for you,' said Tanguy du Châtel, the right-hand man of the murdered Count of Armagnac, the man who had succeeded in fleeing Paris with the dauphin. A warrior of the hardest sort, one whom John hoped to take into his service at a later date.

'This is someone I trust,' said the duke, genially placing a hand on the shoulder of Tanguy du Châtel. The dauphin was leaning against the railing of the bridge. John knelt before him, took off his head covering and spoke words of loyalty. 'Monseigneur, I swear obedience to you and to the king, and I promise that I shall do all I can to save the kingdom. Do not believe those who say I will do you harm.'

'*Beau cousin*,' said the dauphin, 'you say it better than I could have done myself. Stand up and put your hat back on.' He reached his hand out and helped the duke to his feet.

At exactly that moment, Tanguy du Châtel cried out, 'Monseigneur of Burgundy, take that!' and struck him between the shoulder blades with his axe. Terrified, the duke looked at Tanguy and heard the shout 'Kill him! Kill him!' resounding across the bridge.[1] Armed men came running from the city side. The door on the Burgundian side was locked.

A man dressed in black raised his sword and brought it down with full force. The blade severed John's tightened fist and struck him in the face. He was still standing, but only for a moment. Now he lay on the ground, the hero of Nicopolis, his eyes fixed on the dauphin who just stood there, motionless. It all happened so quickly that only three of John's companions were able to draw their swords. They were either killed or imprisoned, along with the other seven. As they were being carried away, they had just enough time to see a soldier kneel beside their fallen leader and stab him with his sword. The forty-eight-year-old John the Fearless was able to straighten his back, but that was all. His death rattle was the last thing they heard from him.

John was buried in the Church of Notre-Dame-et-San-Loup in Montereau, which in the twenty-first century is the only witness to what took place on that bridge on 10 September 1419. Later on his severed hand, his cleft skull and the rest of his mortal remains would be transported to Champmol, where they would have to wait a few decades for the completion of a tomb. A monumental double tomb was built by Claus van de Werve, Juan de la Huerta and Antoine le Moiturier respectively, giving John's wife, Margaret, a resting place as well. It wasn't until 1470, three years after the death of his son Philip the Good, that the tomb would be officially consecrated.

Scrupulously as ever, all the costs involved in the journey to Montereau were noted in the ducal records. Every detail, from horse feed to midday meal; nothing was left out. On 10 September, the bookkeeper in service at the time could not contain himself, and wrote in large letters across all the columns of figures: 'Today great dismay at the death of Monseigneur.'[2]

'The Opening Through Which The English Entered France'

The twenty-two-year-old Philip of Charolais was not yet aware that on 10 September he had become the new Duke of Burgundy and at the same time the latest Count of Flanders. At that particular moment he was staying at the Prinsenhof in Ghent, a castle that his great-grandfather Louis of Male had rebuilt to serve as a residential palace. The Gravensteen, or the Castle of the Counts, a grey colossus with thick walls and gloomy chambers, was built in 1180 by Philip of Alsace but was found to be too uncomfortable and now functioned as a court of law and a prison.

One day later, Bishop Jean de Thoisy of Tournai arrived at the Prinsenhof. How on earth was he to communicate the sorrowful tidings? Unlike his father, who was short of stature and of a reserved disposition, the man whom the bishop had come to see was a lanky, high-spirited fellow. No matter how much Thoisy prevaricated, he finally was forced to share the terrible news.

The new duke dropped to his knees. He screamed like a wild beast. Overcome by panic, he ran to his wife and shouted at her, 'Michelle, your brother has murdered my father!'[3] Trembling and powerless, they stood there together, the sister of the dauphin Charles and the son of John the Fearless. The two had been paired by the late Philip the Bold in the hope of creating a firm tie between Burgundy and the French crown. They wept until they dropped from exhaustion. 'They lay there in the room like two corpses,' wrote the chronicler Georges Chastellain.[4]

The murdered duke had always had a great deal of respect for his father, even though he was very strict and didn't entrust him with any noteworthy responsibilities until he was much older. Despite his admiration for Philip the Bold, John chose a different approach when it came to his own son. The boy was barely fifteen when he was allowed to assume the role of Count of Flanders. Philip would never forget how he always felt the armour under his father's clothes whenever he hugged him. For him, John the Fearless incarnated the cruelty of uncertain times as well as the security of human warmth. He was a schemer, to be sure – impulsive one day, aggressive the next – but he had always been patient with his son. Philip had known a side of his father that few others had ever seen. He had told him lengthy stories about his grandfather, Philip the Bold: about what it was like to be a statesman, and that there had never been a leader who could wash his hands in innocence. The murderer of Orléans had been a loving father.

Like any self-respecting Burgundian, Philip the Good (as we will now call Philip of Charolais) loved flashy attire. But from now on he would wear only sombre or even black clothes as a sign of mourning. At first glance there was little evidence of the goodness for which he was later renowned. He forgot how much he had wanted to fight the English king at Agincourt, and on 21 May 1420 he concluded a momentous treaty with him at Troyes. In his blind thirst for revenge, the Burgundian duke handed France over to England.

Although it was legally impossible to break the male line of succession, Philip managed to convince poor Charles VI (who, like a hungry little bird, would swallow anything) to marry his daughter Catharine to Henry V. Charles and his wife, Isabeau, also agreed to let the English king occupy the French throne after Charles's death. And the dauphin? Queen Isabeau managed to announce that he was illegitimate. The so-called bastard was simply struck from the succession list.

With tears in her eyes, the eighteen-year-old princess exchanged marital vows with France's arch-enemy in the Church of St John in Troyes. Henry V laughed up his sleeve. He had spent three years conquering Normandy, and now France was being dropped in his lap in a single day. Philip the Good, stiff as a poker, dressed in black from head to toe, looked on from the first row. He had just buried his father, and he seemed to be doing the same to his country. But was France still his country? Did he still have his eye on the north?

Recently, Philip, the international adjudicator, had forced his cousin Jacqueline to agree to let her husband John of Brabant share power with her uncle John the Pitiless in Hainaut, Holland and Zeeland, thus avoiding war at the last minute. She would still receive income from her domains, but it wasn't an agreement that made her especially happy. How could it? She was a woman for one thing, and not a very accommodating one at that. Philip could well understand why his cousin John so detested his enterprising wife. At the same time he could see that the young duke was an insipid layabout, and that it was difficult to live and govern with him. Well, so be it! Perhaps this was a situation he could benefit from.

So when John IV abandoned his energetic Jacqueline during the siege of Dordrecht and deeply insulted her during a recent Easter celebration by failing to attend to her ladies-in-waiting, the Burgundian duke smoothed it over and let it slide. Even so, it had not been very chivalrous of him to humiliate her like that. The headstrong Jacqueline had left the banquet table and run weeping through the streets of Brussels to De Spiegel inn, where her mother was staying. That was not so worrisome, although he had found her reaction somewhat hysterical. But after that she managed to flee to England, where she fell head over heels in love with the brother of King Henry V. According to all reports, she couldn't wait to marry for the third time. The fact was that Jacqueline was unexpectedly emerging as a political animal. This Humphrey of Gloucester was cut from quite different cloth than the lethargic

John, so Philip had to do everything in his power to keep the dangerous wedding of 'Dame Jake' from taking place. Imagine an English prince resisting his plans by force of arms, just after he had handed France to England on a silver platter.

The times were so terribly chaotic that it was difficult for him to grieve for his father in a calm fashion. Perhaps Philip suspected that the murder of Louis of Orléans would forever sully his father's good name. In his eyes, John the Fearless had been the capable leader of a Flemish-Burgundian state, a statesman who accepted his responsibility in the French crisis for mainly pecuniary reasons and who, like every other fourteenth-century ruler, had aspired to expand his kingdom, influence and territory. Burgundy had also been enlarged. The county of Tonnerre and the city of Mâcon in the south, the county of Boulogne and the county of Vermandois in the north would now fall under the authority of the duke, who had also set his seal on the prince-bishopric of Liège and was keeping a firm finger on the pulse in the regions of Holland and Brabant.

Would Philip the Good have wondered whether the curious marriage of Jacqueline with John of Brabant, arranged by his father, had not been deliberately intended to fail? Was the union of the headstrong Jacqueline and the flawed John simply a recipe for failure? Had the cynicism of John the Fearless been so great that he actually counted on it, so that Burgundy could benefit from the weakening of power in the north?

*

History, great glutton that it is, could hardly get enough to satisfy its hunger in those days. On 31 August 1422, Henry V died of dysentery. He was not granted the pleasure of plucking the fruits of his success. The rights to the French crown were passed on to his eight-month-old son, Henry VI. The apparently indestructible Charles VI lived on as before, sometimes lucid, mostly raving mad. But his subjects were soon to mourn their beloved king, for two months later, on 22 October, his body gave out along with his mind.

It was as if all hope in France had died with the departure of

Charles's soul. The winter that followed was especially severe. The Seine froze solid. Food provisions vanished. In their despair, gangs of wandering children sought one last spark of warmth in the piles of manure that lay in the streets. There was no bread, no grain, no firewood. People died of cold, of hunger. Wolves invaded Paris and dined on the dead.

In Holland and Zeeland, too, the apocalypse seemed imminent. A great north-wester brought with it such tidal waves that winter that the dikes, which had been neglected due to the continuing tension between the Hooks and the Cods, gave way one by one. Coastal areas were flooded with millions of litres of brown sludge; people fled to their roofs and begged the Almighty to come to their aid. The flood devoured dozens of villages. Thousands of people, dogs and cows drowned. The storm persisted so long that rescue operations became exceedingly laborious. In such a divided country, it was no easy task to get the restoration work underway.

But neither the freezing cold nor the breaches in the dikes could change the way the cards had been dealt. A Hainaut-Holland princess was planning an English wedding while still being married to the Duke of Brabant, and Henry VI was King of England *and* France before the end of his first year. The baby had fulfilled the dream of the late Edward III. In the year of our Lord 1340, the instigator of the Hundred Years War, standing at the side of Jacob van Artevelde, appropriated this double title as a means of provocation at the Friday Market in Ghent. Eighty-two years later, the throne was actually in English hands.

Another century later, in 1521, King Francis I of France would visit the Burgundian mausoleum in Champmol. The great Renaissance monarch, who lured Leonardo da Vinci to France and ordered the building of the castle of Chambord, looked in admiration at the works of art by Claus Sluter. A Carthusian monk led the king around. In the crypt he showed Francis I the shattered skull of John the Fearless. The words that the monk is said to have spoken perfectly summarize the tragedy: 'Sire, this is the opening through which the English entered France.'[5]

Owing to his steady perseverance, Philip the Good would

finally succeed in forcing a crack in the resistance of Jacqueline of Bavaria. And through that opening he would enter Hainaut, Holland and Zeeland once and for all.

THREE COUNTIES, ONE DUKE

*Or how Philip the Good's insatiable appetite, both
amorous and political, was there for all to see, and how he
struggled with one of the most remarkable women in the
history of the Low Countries in order to conquer Hainaut,
Holland and Zeeland.*

IT WAS AS if a gladiator had stumbled into the Middle Ages, but
the fellow who carried on with such fervour was actually Philip
the Good. In April 1425, the Burgundian duke began preparing
himself for an unprecedented contest. Each morning he practised
as if everything was at stake. And it was. He had challenged none
other than Humphrey of Gloucester to a duel to the death.

This younger brother of the recently deceased Henry V had
become Lord Protector of England and had managed to marry
Philip's cousin, Jacqueline of Bavaria, even though she was still
wedded to John IV of Brabant. Being a scandalous flirt was one
thing, but to Philip's astonishment the countess had violated the
sacrament of holy matrimony without giving it a second thought.
Jacqueline was now married to two men! And like John IV,
Humphrey was now calling himself Count of Hainaut, Holland
and Zeeland. The question was not *whether* a fight would erupt
but *when*.

The Burgundian duke had to do his duty. After all, he was the
heir of John IV of Brabant... at least, if John's more quick-witted
brother, the morbidly withdrawn eccentric Philip of Saint-Pol,
were to leave the world childless. On the other hand, the opposite
was also true. If he, Philip the Good, were to die without issue, the
Flemish-Burgundian state would go to the Duke of Brabant. The
fact that the idiot son of his Uncle Anthony (who had perished at
Agincourt) was his next of kin was enough to make Philip's blood
run cold.

He knew what he had to do, but the marital bed was proving
uncooperative. He himself couldn't possibly be the problem, as

his many illegitimate children clearly demonstrated. It wasn't that the duke was lacking in opportunities to show off his fertility. Philip's rather lean but statuesque figure, his straight posture, red lips and shaggy eyebrows did not leave the ladies cold. He sat stylishly in the saddle, played a mean game of fives, danced exceedingly well and was quite a talented archer. Tradition has probably exaggerated his elegant appearance somewhat, but the combination of talent, power and appetite made the duke a successful erotomaniac. According to chronicler Olivier de la Marche, that voluptuary lifestyle resulted in 'a very fine company of bastards of both sexes'.[1] Historians have never agreed on the exact number, but it is certainly true that Philip's performance in this regard easily eclipsed that of his father and his grandfather. Realistic estimates speak of around twenty-five mistresses, with whom he fathered twenty-six children. The most skilled *bâtards de Bourgogne* were given important functions, but when it came to inheritance they were beyond consideration, of course.

His first wife, Michelle, had died of grief after the murder of John the Fearless. Philip didn't deign to go to her funeral. She was, after all, the sister of the man who had ordered John's death. He then married Bonne of Artois, the wife of his Uncle Philip, who had also been killed at Agincourt. The union with his aunt was not a very joyous one, and barely six months later she, too, passed away on her sickbed. It was five years before he gave a thought to marrying again. During those years, the duke was driven by another, equally uncontrollable desire to conquer.

When Jacqueline's newly wedded husband Humphrey accused him in a letter of being overly concerned about the fate of Brabant, Philip exploded in one of his typical outbursts of rage. Marrying a married woman *and* getting up on his high horse: it was the proverbial last straw. He also had another bone to pick with this Humphrey. On one occasion the Englishman had dared to ignore him for several minutes in order to continue a conversation with a subordinate. The memory of that indignity came bubbling to the surface. His normally calculating outlook had been so clouded by anger that he challenged the English regent to a duel. It was extremely uncommon for two leaders of this calibre to take each other on, but the purchase of a diamond-studded suit of armour showed that Philip was deadly serious.

He tried to get into perfect physical shape 'both by restraining his eating and by taking pains to improve his stamina'.[2] Experienced swordsmen poured into his castle at Hesdin. They put his ability to parry blows to the test, and prescribed a series of practice drills. Every day, more and more people came to watch *monseigneur de Bourgogne* work up a sweat. His sheer daring, wrapped in priceless luxury, excited their fantasy. It was top-class sport wrapped in the robes of state. An attraction without equal.

'Incredibly Oversexed'

Yet some people began asking questions. How on earth could anyone make sense of the fact that the man who had just sold France to England was now hell-bent on running the English Lord Protector through with his sword? Philip believed that the outcome of the royal duel would save thousands of soldiers' lives. In addition, a trial by combat like this would bring the truth to light. Yes, the Almighty would show who had the most right to Hainaut, Holland and Zeeland. The duke had long stopped taking the rights of poor John of Brabant and his younger brother Philip into account.

At the same time, it was a kind of advertisement. Half of Europe was talking about his valiant initiative. What a hero! But there was also this: was the new duke as impetuous as his father? Was this man of the new generation really just a man of the old school, someone who still blindly believed in the threadbare ideals of chivalry? In the spring of 1425, many people wondered whether Philip hadn't taken leave of his senses. The opposite was actually the case.

Whenever the duke went to visit the unfinished tomb of his father in Champmol, he would stretch himself out beside it, stricken with grief, and this was no theatre. Nor was it all for show when he dragged himself to the *Well of Moses*, like one of Sluter's *pleurants* come to life. There he would kneel before the figure of

Jeremiah while reading the words that the prophet held in his hands: 'Is it nothing to you, all you who pass by? Look and see if there is any sorrow like my sorrow.' Then he would swallow his grief and carry on his negotiations with the burghers of Dijon. He had spent the better part of his young life in Ghent, and now he had to work on making himself popular in his own Burgundy. The fact that he could be deeply emotional and exceptionally rational at the same time made him a formidable opponent.

Of course Philip felt both offended and insulted, but he was clever enough to make as much political hay as possible out of that perilous position. The Treaty of Troyes, so treacherous for France, and the evocative prospect of a duel underscored the image of a man who was prepared to risk everything. A knight who would run roughshod over corpses and countries. A big shot who entertained with boundless extravagance. An attention-seeker who was willing to bring a competitor in line by means of an old-fashioned trial by combat. But Philip was also the negotiator who could patiently bide his time. The Burgundian who could show great moderation at table. The dinner partner who was more drawn to 'a slice of salted beef than to a partridge'.[3] The pious churchgoer who could pray till he dropped. The ascetic who wore a hairshirt under his clothing. He was also the man who gave himself over to boundless passion and deep feelings. The son who was consumed by grief and malice. The 'incredibly oversexed' Casanova who seduced women by the score.[4] The courtier who was as proud as he was easily offended. The hot-tempered ego-tripper who could be appeased by a simple word.

Lewd and abstemious, sentimental and tactical, vindictive and forgiving, eager and brooding: the man who would become known as the actual founding father of the Low Countries was not easily categorized. Like his grandfather, he was unequalled when it came to realpolitik, but the turbulent blood of his father also flowed through his veins. Energetic as a tactician, fearless as a knight, Philip possessed the great qualities of the first two dukes of the Burgundian Valois line and combined them in unpredictable ways. It would take him far. Very far.

However much his enemies put him to the test or plotted

assassination attempts, he would reign for almost fifty years with a flair that knew no equal. Contemporaries called him *Philippe L'Asseuré*, Philip the Confident, and for very good reason. He became more easy-going with the passing years, and occasionally put state matters on hold in order to enjoy more of the good life, but even then he was fully aware of what was going on in his realm. Naturally he was not alone in this effort. Of all the talented figures who assisted him, chancellor Nicolas Rolin was the most important. Rolin emerged as the Richelieu of Burgundy, the man who guided his master past the most dangerous of obstacles. It's fair to wonder how Philip could have managed without him. In any case, this born and bred Burgundian helped set out the guiding principles right from the beginning. For forty years, Rolin shared the throne with his sovereign as a sort of prime minister. Nicolas and Philip were two sides of the same Burgundian coin. The fact that his senior official, in whom he had total confidence, was greatly enriching himself in the meantime was something the duke accepted as perfectly normal.

Although it certainly didn't look that way, the pact with England was much more than an expression of rancour and grief resulting from the death of his father. Everyone close to him had called for revenge: the associates of John the Fearless of course, his mother first and foremost, and also the burghers of Paris. It couldn't come fast enough. Yet Philip thought about it for weeks. A whole month passed before he was prepared to start negotiations with his long-standing enemy. He remained a French prince, and it was certainly not his fondest wish to bring down the kingdom. Perhaps he sensed that the French would be talking about 'the shameless Treaty of Troyes' for centuries to come, a thought he was not eager to entertain. But neither pure revenge nor worries about eternity would be the deciding factor. Philip just wanted the best for Burgundy itself.

Even his vow to dress himself in black forever is deserving of some nuance. Black was not only the colour of mourning and penance, but in the early fifteenth century it was also the favourite fashion colour in all the courts of Europe. In fact, under certain circumstances he did not hesitate to wear more colourful attire over his basic black. The clichés with which Philip is associated do contain a grain of truth, but they are shattered just as easily. If the black treaty with Albion now seemed like the best option, as an adherent of realpolitik he would not hesitate to show his true colours years later and burn his proverbial bridges over the Channel.

In England, a little boy was now sitting on the throne who was too young to rule, the four-year-old Henry VI. Nor was the English regent in Paris able to govern without difficulty. This John of Bedford, another brother of the late lamented Henry V, had his hands full with the French dauphin. Charles VII, as he called himself, may not have been crowned yet, but he had not given up hope. The Treaty of Troyes had not put an end to the French-English conflict. Even the pope deemed it necessary to express his disapproval. Two men claiming to be King of France was a situation that had to end without delay, cried Martin V, who seemed to have forgotten how long the church had had two popes.

Philip the Good also had a great deal to gain from the discord, so he was careful to maintain a low profile whenever he went to the English Paris. He definitely did not want to become an involved party, so he kept the door open a crack for any way out that might present itself. To keep up appearances, he lent a helping hand to the English and gave his own sister Anne to Bedford as collateral. But in secret, Philip and his powerful chancellor, Rolin, carried on exploratory peace talks with the party of the dauphin. The essence of his politics was to prevent either of the two parties from gaining the upper hand. As long as the power in France remained divided, he was free to indulge his northern expansionism. This also explains why he ostentatiously ignored the French capital: the power centre of Burgundy lay less and less in Paris or Dijon and more and more in the Low Countries. But in order to build up a prosperous state in the north, Philip the high-wire artist would have to maintain a neutral neighbourly relationship with both France and England.

But then Jacqueline of Bavaria threw everything into confusion. Her husband Humphrey had recently led an army in an attack on Hainaut, which was nothing short of a nightmare for Philip. Cities such as Valenciennes, Ath and Mons were not exactly eager for the English to arrive, but in the face of such superior numbers all they could do was open their gates. As soon as he arrived in the capital city of Mons, Humphrey announced that as the Count of Hainaut, Holland and Zeeland he was accepting the challenge and taking up the gauntlet.

The duel with Philip would take place on 23 April 1425.

'The Most Wickedly Betrayed Woman In The World'

In the meantime, John of Bavaria had joined the choir invisible. The fifty-year-old prince-bishop-elect of Liège, who had exercised authority over the north with John of Brabant for quite some time – in actual practice, he had assumed full governance – died as the result of poisoning. In all probability it was Jacqueline, or at least her followers, who was behind this protracted murder. The perpetrator, Jan van Vliet, who was married to one of Jacqueline's illegitimate sisters, was first beheaded and then quartered: four horses, each tied to a different limb, were driven in four different directions, thereby tearing Van Vliet's body to shreds. The body parts were then nailed to the gates of several of Holland's large cities. His head ended up at the entrance gate to the count's court in The Hague.

For her part, Jacqueline was enormously relieved that John the Pitiless was out of the way, but she soon discovered that his demise cleared the path for an even more dangerous opponent. Just before his death, John of Bavaria had turned over all his private property to Philip the Good. It was a modest beginning, but now that Voorne, Gooiland and Woerden were his, the Burgundian advance to the north could begin in earnest.

A decision quickly had to be made as to who the rightful Count of Holland and Zeeland actually was. Duke John of Brabant wasted no time and travelled by coach from city to city. The administrators of Dordrecht and Zierikzee let it be known that they preferred to await the definitive clarification of the marital mystery before welcoming him; those of Gouda and Schoonhoven simply refused to receive John and decided forthwith to take the side of Jacqueline, and therefore of Humphrey of Gloucester. The long battle for Hainaut, Holland and Zeeland could begin. First in line was Hainaut.

The question of who Jacqueline's true husband was still had not been resolved, and the pope was dragging his feet. In the meantime, the Duke of Brabant began raising an army. This was not something John IV did lightly, but he was being pushed hard by his cousin Philip the Good. John himself had no desire to lead troops into battle, so he sent his more energetic brother, Philip of Saint-Pol, to the south. Saint-Pol advanced on Hainaut, along with Burgundian troops. Their mission was simple: to get rid of Humphrey the Englishman. Once Humphrey was gone, Philip the Good would look after Jacqueline.

During the siege of 's Gravenbrakel, a town halfway between Brussels and Mons, Humphrey came rushing in to drive away the enemy troops. His arrival made for a rather surrealistic scene. The battle was announced to the sound of trumpets. The two armies took up their positions. Each man held his breath – and kept holding it – until the signal was given to retreat. The hundreds of banners that had just been proudly raised were pulled down. In a little while this remarkable spectacle was repeated. Finally, both armies slunk away.

Neither Saint-Pol nor Gloucester felt confident of victory and refused to risk a pointless bloodbath. The battlefield was muddy and it was also too small – in short, a second Agincourt in the making. In addition, both Philip the Good and Philip of Saint-Pol had learned their lesson. The former had cooperated militarily with the English after the signing of the Treaty of Troyes in France and was keeping his eyes peeled. The latter had lost his father at Agincourt. The Brabant-Burgundian army had hired plenty of archers and was clearly a match for the English.

Jacqueline was furious that her third husband had not thrown himself manfully into the fray. Now she was forced to look on as Saint-Pol calmly continued the siege of 's Gravenbrakel. Fortunately, there was no way for him to get through… until the English unexpectedly surrendered. The Brabantians and the Burgundians couldn't believe their eyes. Why give up a city that was so easy to defend? The English said they had seen Saint George, their patron saint, fighting along with the enemy. Saint-Pol discovered that they were talking about Daniel van Boechout, a Brabantian whose coat of arms looked exactly like that of Saint George and who, like the saint, was riding a white horse.

After the curious events at 's Gravenbrakel the two armies declared a ceasefire, and all attention was turned once more to the duel between Philip and Humphrey. Aside from Philip, no one was looking forward to such a trial by ordeal. Bedford, the English regent in Paris, begged the Burgundian duke to give up the idea. Philip gallantly submitted. Then Bedford turned to his own brother. Would he really squander the pact with Burgundy for a woman? Did he have to jeopardize the future of England in France for the northern counties? Humphrey's answer was a wholehearted yes, and yes again. Bedford was able to get his brother's agreement on only one point: that he would temporarily return to London. At the moment, his uncle, the Bishop of Winchester, was ruling a bit too enthusiastically in his place. If Humphrey were to leave immediately, he would be able to reprimand his opportunist uncle and be back in time for the duel on 23 April.

It was a sorrowful Jacqueline who watched her husband set sail for England. Humphrey took a woman named Eleonora Cobham along with him for good measure, a ravishingly beautiful lady-in-waiting from Jacqueline's retinue. The countess stayed behind in Mons and must have wondered whether this didn't mean the end of her marriage. She had little time to grieve, however. Philip argued that he had only entered into a ceasefire with Humphrey, who was now on the other side of the Channel.

With the help of the Brabantians, Burgundy took one Hainaut city after another. This time the two parties wouldn't do things by halves. By the end of May 1425, the troops arrived at the gates of Mons, the last Hainaut stronghold.

*

Jacqueline was standing on the city wall with a few faithful supporters. Beyond the enemy army, with its trebuchets, cannon, horses, carriages, banners and tents, she saw her county. This was where she grew up. Thirty kilometres further on, at the castle of Le Quesnoy, she had learned to write, dance and ride horses. You could hardly have called her a charming little princess. She had studied swordsmanship, she knew how to hunt, and she spoke fluent French and English – Dutch was apparently one language too many. All she needed was a suit of armour and she'd be ready for battle, in a manner of speaking. The only thing now was to convince the Hainaut nobility of Mons not to abandon her. The hours she spent on the city walls must have been gloomy indeed.

Of her three counties, the French-speaking Hainaut was dearest to her heart. She knew its history, she knew that Hainaut had once formed a single entity with Flanders, and that by way of the vicissitudes of dynasty and the battlefield it had finally ended up in her Bavarian family. As in Flanders, her distant county predecessors had tried to stimulate the area's economic growth by granting advantageous charters and toll exemptions to the cities, especially new, strategically placed seigniories such as Binche, Soignies and Lessines.

In the distance lay a handful of small cities. They were typical of her county. Mons itself numbered a good 6,000 souls. Larger cities of more than 10,000 inhabitants were few and far between. What you did find every 25 kilometres or so were towns of 2,000 inhabitants at the most that bravely took on the task of local government and administration of justice. The efforts of the old counts were less successful than in Flanders. Outside of Tournai – which was a French enclave feudally speaking but was located in Hainaut – and Valenciennes, not a single city would develop a sphere of influence that went beyond the county borders. Valenciennes and Tournai profited from their situation on the Scheldt and could therefore to some extent ride on Flanders's economic success story.

In past centuries, the Flemings had fashioned most of their monumental buildings – from the Cloth Hall in Ypres to Gravensteen castle in Ghent – out of Tournai stone, which was transported by boat in vast amounts. In that city, and the periphery of villages around it, the stones were roughly dressed and later turned into finished products such as baptismal fonts and memorial tablets. The most beautiful example of what humanity had managed to do with Tournai limestone was in the city itself, the Notre-Dame cathedral with its five magnificent towers, all of which were over eighty metres in height. Jacqueline had also learned first-hand that the people of Hainaut exported both coal and fur, and she was taught that along with Artois in France, the county had become the breadbasket of Flanders and Brabant thanks to its vast stretches of loamy soil. All she could do was sigh, for the leaders of the regions that were fed by her county were ready and waiting, armed to the teeth, to take the last city of Hainaut that had not yet been conquered. Would the patricians and nobility of Mons and its surroundings still want to support her? And where was the handsome Humphrey, her agile lover, with whom she could converse so freely about art and science? Due to his absence, the long-awaited duel with Philip the Good was finally cancelled.

The truth was that two compelling reasons were keeping Humphrey in England: sex and politics. His uncle, the Bishop of Winchester, was a tough customer who had such control over Parliament that any financing of a military sortie was out of the question. And Humphrey had also become entangled in the nets of Eleonora Cobham, who would bear him two children in the coming years and would make his life exceedingly difficult on account of her fondness for water dowsers and alchemy. Jacqueline was aware of none of this. She emphatically defended her husband to all the assembled dignitaries of Mons. He would come back and set everything to rights! But no one believed her any more.

The siege had been going on for two days. Cannonballs and burning arrows had already wreaked havoc. Everyone feared that Mons would be totally annihilated. A written declaration from Philip the Good was greeted with widespread approval. He promised to convince John of Brabant to raise the siege, spare the city and take Jacqueline under his care until the pope made his ruling on the marriage. She protested vehemently and appealed to her feudal rights, apparently unable to understand that her battle was over. A few hotheads grasped at other arguments. While

Jacqueline was inciting the troops to fight on, the people of Mons beheaded Humphrey's henchman, who had remained behind, before her very eyes. Only then did she fall silent, realizing that Hainaut was lost. Philip gave the county back to John of Brabant, although John himself was more inclined to return to Brussels as soon as possible. A Burgundian straw man was installed in Mons as stadtholder.

That night, Jacqueline wrote a heartbreaking letter to her English husband. 'You must know that I am writing as the most desolate and the most wickedly betrayed woman in the world... I have good hopes that you will come, since that is my perfect right. For as long as I live I will do nothing to displease you; I am even prepared to die for love of you and your noble person, so much does your noble lordship please me... even though it appears that you have forgotten me... Written with a very sorrowful heart, on the sixth day of June.'[5]

Of course, Humphrey did not come, but Philip's envoys did. One week later, a dejected Jacqueline left her city of Mons escorted by Louis, Prince of Orange. In Ghent she was given shelter in the Posteerne, a city palace that had been used by Louis of Male, who happened to be the forefather of both Jacqueline and the Duke of Burgundy. Not only that, but they both had the same grandfather, Philip the Bold, who had frequently put up at the same castle.

Jacqueline of Bavaria, who would never set foot in Bavaria, was destined to play a leading role in the Low Countries simply by virtue of her origins. Her father was Count of Hainaut, Holland and Zeeland, one grandmother was from Hainaut and the other from Flanders. She had a stronger tie to the Low Countries than Philip, and for that very reason he would use her to become their lord and master. Now that she was a prisoner, he really got down to business. On 19 July 1426 he was given control of the government of Holland and Zeeland. John of Brabant, who was effortlessly manipulated by Burgundy, declared that he could not satisfactorily carry out that function himself. On the other hand, he added, his good cousin Philip would do an outstanding job.

That meant the end of John's career, which had actually started looking quite promising. Thanks to his marriage to Jacqueline of Bavaria, he was given authority over Hainaut, Holland, Zeeland, Brabant and Limburg. As lord and master of these five principalities, he could have made things exceedingly difficult for Philip the Good. But just the opposite happened. John surrounded himself with the wrong noblemen and succeeded in hurting Jacqueline very deeply, losing her, and then incurring the wrath of a number of Brabant cities. Gradually he lost all the ammunition that might have made him a powerful statesman.

The Burgundian duke, on the other hand, realized he had all the keys he needed to make the northern regions his own: not only was he regent for the incompetent John, but he was also his heir as long as the imprisoned Jacqueline had no legitimate children. With a rejected husband in Brussels and a separated spouse in London, that situation didn't seem likely to change.

*

While the twenty-five-year-old Jacqueline was wasting away in her prison, a thirteen-year-old girl from the French village of Domrémy heard a voice in her head. 'It seemed like a worthy voice', she would later say, 'that was sent by God. When I had heard it for the third time, I knew it was the voice of an angel.'[6] The voice soon identified itself as that of the archangel Michael. He told her that she was destined to free France from the English, that she must lead the troops into battle and wear a suit of armour. At first she was just afraid. But then Saints Catherine and Margaret began talking to her. The young girl was completely bewildered by what was happening to her, but she felt that she was part of something greater than herself. For four years she would struggle with the voices in her head. Finally, she stopped resisting and realized there was no way back.

The house in which she was born was 100 metres from the Meuse in the heart of Lorraine, almost 300 kilometres east of Paris. 'Where I was born I was called Jeannette, but later on they called me Jeanne.'[7]

THE BATTLE FOR HOLLAND
AND ZEELAND

*Or how Holland and Zeeland grew into prosperous counties
for which Philip the Good was prepared to fight to his very last
breath, but also how Jacqueline of Bavaria, who seemed utterly
exhausted, surprised friend and foe alike by holding
the Burgundian duke's feet to the fire.*

EVERYONE THOUGHT THAT Jacqueline didn't stand a chance.
The whole case hung on the pope's ruling, but Rome was
in no hurry to come to a decision. Both John of Brabant – read
Philip the Good – and Humphrey of Gloucester had sent their own
mediators, who kept digging deeper into their pockets in search
of increasingly abstruse arguments for and against. The Duke of
Gloucester may have grown tired of Jacqueline, but he certainly
hadn't lost interest in her territories. For a short time, the battle for
the Low Countries was fought in the back rooms of the Vatican.
Jacqueline, for her part, was tired of waiting. Working in secret, she
devised a stunt that would turn the whole case on its head.

On 31 August, she made it known that she did not want to
be disturbed. She was going to take a bath, she said, and then go
straight to bed. While the courtiers and guards ate their meal, she
undressed – not for her evening ablutions, however, but to change
into men's clothing. As if it were the most normal thing in the
world, she strolled outside, parading through the streets of Ghent,
before leaving the city by way of the closest gate. Two men with
horses were waiting for her. The three of them galloped northward,
reaching the ferry at Antwerp 60 kilometres further on. There, a
carriage drawn by several horses carried Jacqueline another 100
kilometres northward to Asperen, where she stopped to rest. On 2
September 1425, at about nine in the morning, she reached the city
of Vianen, where she finally was able to take off her *manscleder*
(men's clothing). She continued on by boat to Schoonhoven, a

town between Rotterdam and Utrecht, where she was welcomed by friendly nobles of the Hook party.

When she disembarked at Schoonhoven she must have pinched herself in disbelief. Suddenly, the story she thought had reached a dead end still had a few chapters to go. From here she would take a stand against Philip the Good! Meanwhile, back in Ghent, the Burgundian duke was at his wits' end, gravitating between shame and fury. How in God's name could he have let Jacqueline escape? He sent out agents to block all the roads to England, but to no avail. Only then did it finally get through to him that she had had the audacity to flee to her counties in Holland.

No matter how decisively she had wanted to act, Jacqueline's life up until then had mainly been dictated by the laws of marriage. First she came to occupy the bed of the French dauphin. When he died, she found herself between the sheets with John IV of Brabant, a bleak situation that she would abandon with disgust. The flight through the streets of Brussels that would bring her to England was an act of considerable resistance, but the only way she could survive after that was to assume another subservient role, that of the wife of the English Humphrey of Gloucester. Without all those men, none of whom made her happy, her political clout would have been considerably lighter. After her escape from Ghent, the situation looked quite different. Now she had every reason to believe that her fate was finally in her own hands and that she was in charge of events, at least for the time being. Yet even that should not be viewed too romantically. The noblemen of the Hook contingent could make extremely good use of her as a figurehead in their confrontation with the Cods. And the opposite was also true, of course. The puzzle pieces were falling into place for both parties.

Jacqueline's escape forced the Burgundian duke to act boldly. Armed to the teeth, he travelled north: Philip against Jacqueline, Burgundy versus Holland and Zeeland, Cods toe to toe with the Hooks, a war of conquest that was also a civil war. Philip donned the diamond-encrusted armour that he had planned to wear in his duel with Humphrey, took his place at the head of 3,000 warriors, and conducted a series of Joyous Entries in Holland. The people there weren't exactly eager to get a look at a half-Frenchman who was intent on using their taxes to cover his personal expenses. The frugal merchants of Holland were willing to let Philip organize banquets and play the patron of the arts, but not with their money.

Although the situation looked favourable enough for the duke to dream of far-reaching Burgundification, he was not looking for a quick profit. His aim was to win hearts and minds. He adopted an attitude of leniency, just as he had done in old Burgundy, and was generous with privileges. The burghers of Amsterdam, Haarlem, Rotterdam, Leiden and Dordrecht had expected Philip to come barging in with iron fists, and they were happily surprised. The immensely rich Burgundian promised to launch major dike-building projects (Dordrecht, for example, had been completely surrounded by water since the Saint Elizabeth's flood), to assist them in the struggle against English pirates, and to offer support in the commercial battle with the Hanseatic League. In short, this was a man you could do business with.

Philip's approach worked. Jacqueline's advance stalled. If she had hoped that her presence would serve as the spark that would set all of Holland ablaze, she was sadly mistaken. The Hooks poured in from miles around, although they were careful to remain hidden, and important noblemen such as Lord van Montfoort, Willem van Brederode and Jan van Vianen threw in their lot with her in order to strengthen the leadership of the anti-Burgundian resistance, but apart from the cities of Schoonhoven, Gouda, Oudewater, Montfoort and Vianen, the rest of the land remained in the hands of the Cods.

From her Holland bulwark in Gouda, Jacqueline sent her men to Alphen aan den Rijn, some fifteen kilometres further north. There, Philip's Cod allies cobbled together a wooden fort near the Gouda lock, giving them perfect control over the confluence of the Gouwe and the Oude Rijn. The local population were on Jacqueline's side, and on 22 October they provocatively began herding their cattle round the fort. This irritated the Cods no end. Such a small group of peasants could be driven off just as easily as the peasants themselves had driven their cows, or so they thought. But when they called on them to clear out, Jacqueline's armed

Hooks came out from hiding and made short shrift of the fort's occupiers. Thanks to their ambush they were able to capture the city banners of Amsterdam, Leiden and Haarlem.

This prestigious catch was given a place of honour during the festive Te Deum in Gouda's Great Church. 'The blessed countess thanked the Lord our God and her friends, who had thrown themselves into battle with ferocity.'[1] There wasn't much Jacqueline could do, but she did make things quite difficult for the Burgundian duke with her little guerrilla war. Upon hearing the bad news, Philip cursed up a storm. From then on he travelled with the greatest caution, fearing an attack. Every time he left the Binnenhof in The Hague he made sure he had his army behind him.

In late December, Philip was dragged out of bed in the middle of the night. He was still half asleep when the facts were thrown in his face. That Humphrey had complied with Jacqueline's appeals. That the English had crossed the Channel. That they had already reached Sluis. That urgent action was called for. It was almost like a repetition of his grandfather's Flemish campaign. Back then it was the Ghentenars or the English that made life miserable for Philip the Bold. Despite the pact signed in France, Albion was once again the enemy. Now the Ghentenars had turned into Hooks.

The duke had only one option. He had to strike, just as his grandfather had done. He could not let the chance to secure full control of the northern counties slip away from him. Surely Holland was well on its way to becoming as enticing as Flanders was back then, and that justified all his efforts.

'All Our Prosperity… Is Bound Up With Holland And Zeeland'

In Holland, the Great Reclamation of the past centuries had ground to a halt a long time ago. Everything that could be done had been done, within the technical possibilities of the time. Almost all the reclaimed land, as well as countless forests and peat bogs, had been converted into agricultural areas and pastures. Peasants dug deeper and deeper into their peat beds in order to use or sell the valuable peat as fuel. Their digging caused the land to sink, sometimes to below sea level, which threatened the solidity of the dikes. Every now and then the water would take back the land, despite all the defences thrown up against the sea.

This phenomenon had taken place repeatedly in the Low Countries: people loading half their village or their entire church onto carts, to save it from the rising tides. After the storm surge of 1394, the Flemish city of Oostende had to be pushed inland several hectometres, where the new Oostende arose with the support of Philip the Bold. In order to keep this from happening again, all the existing Flemish dikes were joined together after the great flood of 1404. Whether John the Fearless actively supported these efforts, or was even well disposed towards them, remains food for discussion, but the continuous Graaf Jansdijk – the Count John's Dike – which ran from Dunkirk to Terneuzen, was named after him in any case.

The northern counties were even more heavily burdened than Flanders by dangerous attacks from the sea. Zeeland in particular would long remain the demographically weak link. First the name *Maritima Loca*, literally 'Places on the Sea', was used to refer to *Zeelandia*, with its criss-crossing of creeks and gullies. In 1375 the sea wiped Koudekerke and Elmare off the map, and two years later a storm surge destroyed the greater part of the island of Wulpen. After the terrible Saint Elizabeth's flood of 1421, dozens of villages in Holland and Zeeland disappeared beneath the waves forever.

Starting in the early fifteenth century, draining mills were used to carry off excess water by means of an ingenious system of brooks and canals. The first such mills made their appearance in the area around Alkmaar and Leiden in around 1408, but it would be another century before they evolved into what we today would call the typical postcard view of Holland. The maintenance of ditches, canals, sluices and windmills was so expensive that local inhabitants and land users developed a rational and common-sense approach out of sheer necessity. They drew up rules and regulations and followed them to the letter, and they agreed to apportion the workload and financial contribution based on the scale of land use. That mentality would later come to be regarded as typically Dutch and would form an important aspect of the capitalistic spirit with which the country's inhabitants came to be associated over the course of the centuries. These qualities, which obviously cannot be attributed to Protestantism alone, were completely at odds with the extravagance and ostentation of the Burgundian character, and more than once made for sharp confrontations.

While the sea and the great rivers kept proving themselves enemies to be feared, a final evolution was taking place: that of the transformation of farmland into pasturage. Pastures do much better on peaty soil, which is not an ideal substrate for cereal crops. The resulting lack of bread made famine a real possibility, but the cows that soon began grazing there triggered a boom in dairy production. This led to a rise in cheesemaking, which required a great deal of salt. Clever entrepreneurs from the town of Biervliet saw a hole in the market and began specializing in the digging of salt-laden peat, from which they extracted salt by means of drying and burning. Cattle breeding required less manpower, but the workers who were now available quickly found employment in other sectors. Most of them ended up in the fishing industry or in merchant shipping. Workers were retrained not only as boatmen or fishermen, but there was also a need for shipbuilders, rope makers, coopers, sailmakers and, of course, dike workers. The hostile sea had grown into a source of economic prosperity. In Dordrecht, millions of herring passed through the tollgates, after which the fish were shipped far and wide, some of them all the way to Novgorod. The fish were first gutted and then pickled with Biervliet salt, which meant they could be preserved much longer.

The flexible Hollanders made a virtue of necessity and managed to capitalize on the situation. Their fishing and preservation technologies were innovations, and they also were ahead of their time when it came to engineering: their ships were not only bigger but also faster and easier to control. By improving their skills as sea carriers and shipbuilders in the Late Middle Ages, they laid the basis for their domination of the oceans in the seventeenth century.

Despite their nose for renovation, they didn't always have a patent on originality. In Leiden they imitated Flemish textile techniques. By aiming for mediocre quality, this new industry reached a large public that was happy to make do with less refined but cheaper products. The herring fishermen copied their Danish and Scandinavian counterparts at the Skanör annual fairs. The same thing had already happened with hops beer from Bremen and Hamburg. For a long time, beer had been flavoured with a special herbal mixture called *gruit*, but that ended when successful experiments were carried out in these two German cities using hops as the additive. The Land of Heusden became the new hops district, and in 1370 brewers from Delft, Gouda and Haarlem produced almost eleven million litres of the beverage. Production was steadily increased, and most of it would disappear down the throats of Flanders and Brabant. But the Flemings and Brabantians hadn't been lagging behind either. Over the course of the fifteenth century, plenty of high-quality hops beer was produced in cities such as Lier, Kortrijk and Lille.

To make sure all these new products reached their destination, the distribution system had to run like a well-oiled machine. The vast number of interior waterways proved to be of huge monetary significance. Economic networks emerged along the Meuse and the Rhine, as they did on the Scheldt in Flanders, and over time they became increasingly cooperative. Ships transported their cargo effortlessly from Lübeck in northern Germany to Flanders by way of the Dutch rivers, lakes and canals. Cities that lay on the confluence of two rivers were at a great economic advantage. In Flanders, Ghent was able to benefit from the confluence of the Leie and the Scheldt, while in Holland central toll points such as Gouda and especially Dordrecht could profit economically thanks to their location at bifurcations of the Rhine and the Meuse. Philip the Good was quick to understand that the counts of Holland obtained more than a quarter of their income from tolls.

★

As more and more farmers were retrained as workers they flocked to the cities, which consequently had to be expanded. Gradually, the population figures increased as well, although hunger, war and the plague kept them from rising in a straight line. Observing this from our cloud in the twenty-first century, the medieval population numbers appeal to the imagination.

There were no official counts, so any census figures we have are guesses from later centuries based on fiscal data such as taxes that were paid 'by hearth'. In each case, an average number of persons per family is determined, and this number can then be multiplied by the number of 'hearths'.[2] Added to this are vagrants without goods and chattels (there were quite a few of these, but it's impossible to know just how many), as well as nobility and the clergy, who were exempt from paying taxes (about 2.5 per cent of the population). In short, a combination of pure guesswork, scientific research and common sense.

The population of Europe doubled over the course of three centuries – from 38 million in the year 1000 to 75 million in 1300 – but suffered a decline of 30 per cent in the terrible fourteenth century due to plague, famine and armed conflict. The population of France was approximately 14 million in around 1400, which was 5 million fewer than before the plague struck. By way of comparison, England, which had held the great France in a chokehold for decades, had to make do with only 2 million souls in the same year.

By the end of the fifteenth century, the Low Countries numbered at least 2.5 million inhabitants. Leading by a mile was the county of Flanders (740,000 in 1469), followed by the duchy of Brabant (415,000 in 1473), the county of Holland (270,000 in 1514) and the county of Hainaut (210,000 in 1458). At the very bottom of the list was the duchy of Limburg (16,000 in 1489) and the county of Zeeland (11,000 in 1389, the only figure taken from right after the greatest plague outbreak, hence the strikingly low number).

Holland had begun a very decent recovery, but for the time being that was nothing compared with Flanders, which by the end of the fifteenth century made up a third of the population of the Low Countries. That lag is also striking when you look at the figures per city. Ghent (65,000), Bruges (45,000), Ypres and Lille (both about 30,000) had already made their greatest advance by around 1350. In around 1400, Leiden had 6,000 inhabitants, Gouda 5,000, Delft 6,500 and Amsterdam 3,000 – up from only 1,000 burghers in 1300 – so that these cities could be compared with Kortrijk in Flanders or Mons in Hainaut in terms of size. Haarlem and Dordrecht were gradually advancing towards 10,000 burghers.

At the end of the fifteenth century, Utrecht was perhaps the largest city in the north with close to 20,000 souls, within the same range as Liège and Leuven but smaller than Brussels, where the threshold of 30,000 inhabitants had been exceeded. That rise continued. The populations of Gouda and Amsterdam would double and triple respectively in less than a hundred years. Amsterdam soon surpassed Utrecht, and about halfway through the sixteenth century it topped 30,000. That was only the beginning, for over the course of the seventeenth century the new metropolis came to comprise more than 200,000 inhabitants. Before that phenomenal explosion was reached, the city of Antwerp in the duchy of Brabant would leave the Flemish cities of Ghent and Bruges far behind: from 6,000 in 1373 to almost 40,000 in 1526, after which it would head for 100,000.

By way of comparison, in around 1300 Paris was the only city north of the Alps with more than 100,000 inhabitants, while the number of townspeople in the old Burgundian capital of Dijon never went beyond 10,000 during the Late Middle Ages. The population of the French capital rose to half a million in 1700. It wasn't until the nineteenth century that London and Paris passed the million mark. We will close this enumeration, patient reader, with the thought that Rome may already have reached this magic number in ancient times. Following the great migrations, countless sieges, sackings and plunderings, floods and especially a few horrible waves of plague in the sixth and seventh centuries, the Eternal City would shrink to a population in the low tens of thousands. *Sic transit gloria mundi.* It would have to wait until the sixteenth century before any change came in that figure.

In around 1500, Holland, like Flanders and Brabant, was one

of the most urbanized regions in Europe. In the Burgundian Netherlands, 'only' two out of three people (about 65 per cent) lived in the countryside. Elsewhere in Europe that figure was much higher. Farmers and labourers were drawn in because the cities offered the prospect of work, better pay and well-organized poor relief. Often reality fell short of expectations, so that burghers would look for a better life in other cities, giving rise to a lot of comings and goings between the various cities of the Low Countries. That intensified the inter-city dynamic, which was already quite active.

*

Thanks to their nose for trade, innovation and imitation, their flexible and rational mentality, countless navigable internal waterways, rapidly growing shipbuilding and fishing industries, and the quality of their dairy products, beer and turf, Holland and (to a lesser degree) Zeeland experienced enormous economic and demographic growth. What was remarkable was the trade dynamic that came into play between Flanders and Brabant, the same way that Hainaut and Flanders were linked together. For a long time the Low Countries may have been nothing but a geographic designation – the area surrounding the lower reaches of the Meuse, the Rhine and the Scheldt – but gradually they also formed an economic entity. Cheese was transported southward by ship, and the same ships were then loaded with grain and sent back home. 'All our prosperity... is bound up with Holland and Zeeland,' noted the Antwerp city council in 1399.[3] The fact that Dordrecht always lost out to Bruges as a trade centre, but kept trying to improve itself nevertheless, was a fine example of how prosperous Flanders stimulated the commercial development of Holland.

Naturally, such cross-pollinations would have reached a higher level of development if the Low Countries had formed a political unit at some point. If Philip the Good were to triumph over Jacqueline of Bavaria, then enterprising merchants might allow themselves to dream of such a thing. So it's not surprising that in the struggle that was now erupting, the merchants and cities tended to side with Burgundy, while the old nobility gravitated towards Jacqueline.

'Hunted Me Down From One Land To Another, All Of Them Mine'

Jacqueline's prayers were heard. At the end of December, Humphrey sent a battle fleet across the Channel with 24 ships and 2,000 warriors. He had convinced a friendly faction in England to foot the bill for this campaign. Their hope was that by backing Humphrey they would be able to demand part of the Burgundian pie, which was what had happened in France thanks to his brother Bedford. Gloucester himself did not dare accompany the troops, not because he was afraid of fighting, but because he no longer trusted the Bishop of Winchester and felt compelled to stay behind. Jacqueline's territories were most welcome, but giving up his power position in England was out of the question. Lord FitzWalter served as the commander in his place.

After having been locked out of the Zierikzee harbour, the English fleet was finally able to dock in Brouwershaven. Now that the enemy army had landed, Philip had to act fast. In just a few days, he succeeded in readying 120 ships carrying both Burgundian troops and mercenaries from Picardy, as well as Cods from Dordrecht, Delft and The Hague. Mercifully, he had been tipped off by Bedford (who may have been Humphrey's brother but was mainly Philip's inside man in France) that an English invasion was about to take place, giving him plenty of time to hire a sufficient number of flat-bottomed boats. This would make it easier for him to travel through the sandbank-riddled waterways of Holland. The English, whose boats lay deeper in the water, did not have that advantage.

He left Schiedam, to which he had travelled in great haste on 5 January 1426, and brought his army to the outskirts of Brouwershaven. In the meantime, most of the Hooks of Zeeland had arrived at Brouwershaven and joined the English army. On 12 January, the Burgundian fleet appeared off the coast. The wind was too strong to go ashore, but the trumpeters blew their hearts out to let it be known that Philip the Good was raring to go.

One day later the wind died down, the sign for the Burgundians and Hollanders to land. About two-thirds of the troops reached the coast before the English archers could begin their dreaded ballet. The first row drew their bows, released their arrows and dropped to their knees, and while these bowmen were pulling new arrows from their quivers a second row behind them repeated the same action, ducking down and letting a third row shoot their lethal darts. Then the military dance started all over again. The arrows flew from man-sized longbows, haphazardly seeking the holes and chinks in the enemy's armour. Burgundy recoiled when the front line was shattered.

Philip, who had remained on board, saw that general destruction was looming. Without a moment's hesitation, he jumped in the water in order to join his men. The duke reacted with such ferocity that he risked being surrounded by the English. Thanks to the intervention of Jan Vilain, a Flemish giant from Ghent, he was rescued just in time.

The Burgundian elite were advancing behind him, hardened warriors who fought their way through enemy lines. The English and the Hooks were driven back across the shifting sands and past a dike, where they were trapped. Lord FitzWalter and a few others were able to flee, but a great many of their comrades in arms were killed or driven into the sea and drowned. By sunset, Philip was able to claim victory. 'By the grace of God they were defeated,' he wrote with obvious relief in a letter to the ducal council in Dijon.[4]

Jacqueline's disappointment was immense. This was supposed to have been the great breakthrough. Her spirits sank even lower when she learned that part of the English fleet, which had set its course for Gouda, had been pushed back to Calais by the wind. Once again, she was completely isolated. Philip, for his part, stayed two more months in Middelburg and was delighted to learn that almost the entire county of Zeeland had crossed over to his side. Except for Gouda-Oudewater-Schoonhoven, Jacqueline's triangular stronghold, practically the entire county of Holland was now his. Such was his self-confidence that he took a bit of time off to catch his breath in Flanders, a respite that the remarkably persistent Jacqueline seized upon in order to play one of her last cards. It was a trump card that even she hadn't counted on.

*

She had never taken much interest in the peasants of Kennemerland and West Friesland. But when these same farmers rose up in revolt against the high taxes being levied by the Burgundian duke, she couldn't let the chance slip by. Leading this army of peasants from northern Holland, she first laid siege to Haarlem, a Cod stronghold. The city would quickly surrender, or so she thought. But the Flemish knight Roland van Uutkerke, who skilfully led the defending forces, refused to be intimidated. In response, Jacqueline gave the order to set fire to eighteen windmills. The gigantic torches blazed in the wind and could be seen for dozens of kilometres – a fitting symbol for a land in flames. Her tactic seemed to work. The city council, who looked on from the walls, began to have misgivings. Why hold out against this apparently God-sent superwoman? But Van Uutkerke, who had fought in the Battle of Othée on the side of John the Fearless almost twenty years before, did not flinch. 'Jacqueline is in no position to resist so powerful a lord as Duke Philip,'[5] he insisted. The Fleming managed to convince the council not to open the gates. They would wait for help from the south.

Because of her peasant alliance, Jacqueline had dared to leave Gouda. But when an army of Flemings, on Philip's orders, began advancing towards Alphen aan den Rijn with the intention of taking the city by storm, she was forced to rush back to defend the area around her home base. She succeeded in crushing the Flemings, who were under the command of Van Uutkerke's son Jan, but a possible capture of Haarlem backfired. As if she didn't have enough on her hands with the opposition of the Cods and the Burgundians, now it was Flemings who were putting her on the spot. It was almost as if Philip had mobilized all his territories against her. Yet the minor victory at Alphen was enough to rekindle the spirits within her ranks.

Meanwhile, the Kennemer peasants stubbornly refused to

yield to Burgundian supremacy. When Philip had had enough, he and a large army marched on the peasants, most of them armed with pikes, axes and scythes, and obliterated them near Hoorn, about 20 miles north of Amsterdam. His verdict was harsh. The Kennemer peasants and West Frisians, who had taken up the sword because they found the tax system unjust, were now forced to pay a gigantic fine. From then on, they could forget about any former privileges having to do with the administration of justice. They were also obliged to hand in their weapons; the only ones they were allowed to carry were 'dull bread knives without pointed tips'.[6] This time Philip felt obliged to play the severe father, which was against his nature. The duke no longer trusted the peasants; the only people he was willing to deal with were the city-dwellers. He filled Holland and Zeeland with Burgundian garrisons and launched reinforced defensive works at strategic river junctions. This approach made one thing clear: it didn't make him feel any safer.

The guerrilla war in the countryside raged on. Small skirmishes caused enormous local damage: livestock were slaughtered, farms set on fire, travellers attacked, trade routes blocked. There was still no sign of a definitive victory, although Burgundy gradually strangled Jacqueline's Hook opponents with the help of the Cods. Slowly but surely, this tangled mix of international conflict and civil war seemed to be heading towards a climax. Philip was determined to crush the last pockets of resistance. He fought on relentlessly. In April of 1427 he captured the Hook city of Zevenbergen in southern Holland after a month-long siege. And by winning the sea battle at Wieringen in northern Holland in September 1427, he kept Jacqueline's fleet from freely sailing the Zuiderzee. Only then did he feel strong enough to lay siege to Gouda, her last bulwark. Unlike his son Charles, Philip would never let himself get caught up in rash military actions.

Would Jacqueline have been reminded of the siege of Mons, her last bastion in Hainaut, three years before? Would she have peered over the heads of the Burgundian army at her county of Holland once again, scanning the horizon, hoping for the arrival of her husband Humphrey? Jacqueline was no fool. She realized that complete control over her domains had become impossible. Yet she did not lose heart. In her letters she kept applying pressure to the entourage of the six-year-old English king, Henry VI. 'In an attempt to cheat me out of my inheritance, my cousin Burgundy has hunted me down from one land to another, all of them mine. This has caused a great shedding of blood among my poor and faithful subjects.'[7] The message was clear. Didn't England's knightly honour demand that they come to her aid? The tone of her letters became more and more pathetic. 'I have now been abandoned, and despised and rejected by all the world, like a repudiated wife without comfort and counsel... without seigniories, without treasury, personal property, money or strong friends. Because of my marriage, my closest family members have become my greatest enemies and opponents.'[8]

It came to her attention that England was going to send one last fleet. The assault was being led by the Earl of Salisbury, who was all too eager to give Philip a good thrashing. Three years earlier, during a ball in Paris, the Burgundian had not only openly flirted with his wife but had seduced her into having a little fling with him. Jacqueline's hope was momentarily rekindled. But in the spring of 1428, three messages demolished her mental resistance for good.

The first bombshell was the news that Gloucester was having an affair with Eleonora Cobham, her former lady-in-waiting, *and* had become the father of a daughter with this woman. Politically speaking, the second piece of news was a disaster of even greater proportions. Pope Martin V had finally disentangled the marital knot. Her union with Humphrey of Gloucester was declared invalid. After the crack in her heart left by the Cobham affair, this denial of her legitimacy was an enormous blow. Humphrey could now marry Jacqueline's lady-in-waiting with a clear conscience, and he cancelled a final English support payment to his ex-wife. Last but not least, she was told that the English fleet that had embarked from London had turned away from Holland at the last minute and set course for France. Her self-confidence lay in tatters.

Naturally, Jacqueline lost to the all-powerful Philip the Good, and it was also true that she had no choice but to submit to the papal ruling. But her greatest defeat had to do with the fact that English interests in France were incommensurate with those in the Low Countries. The French crown far outweighed the struggles in Holland and Zeeland. Regent John of Bedford had done everything he could from Paris to restrict the manoeuvring room of his brother Humphrey of Gloucester, and Burgundy had deftly worked this to his own advantage. Philip's diplomatic efforts had gently pushed Bedford in the right direction, of course. It was a victory of both the word *and* the sword.

Jacqueline surrendered without further opposition. The war of attrition had left large swathes of the counties in ruins. Wilderness areas had emerged here and there, disordered conglomerates of plundered, torched villages, neglected dikes and flooded fields. It was high time to set the warring aside and to restore the houses and dikes. Everyone, including Jacqueline, was hungry for peace.

*

In order to seal the agreement officially, the duke had ordered a large dais to be built on the Delft market square. Philip the Good and Jacqueline of Bavaria did not kiss each other on the mouth, as had long been the custom, but they did sign the peace treaty with the requisite sense of the ceremonial before the gathered crowd. Despite the absence of the kiss, the agreement was called the Kiss – *Zoen* – of Delft. The first definition of the verb 'to kiss' – *zoenen* – was not what we understand today as kissing, but '*verzoenen*', or reconciliation, although that often went hand in hand with a Kiss of Peace.

They had not seen each other for at least three years, and now here were the two cousins, standing face to face. The chroniclers are silent on the emotions that this encounter must have aroused in these two sensitive individuals, but we can be assured that they both felt relief. Finally, peace had come. Purportedly, the two walked amiably through the streets of Delft. Placating the supporters of the Cods and the Hooks had required three months of negotiations. In the text that was read aloud on 3 July 1428 in both French and Dutch, it was emphasized that Philip recognized the said Jacqueline of Bavaria as the Countess of Hainaut, Holland and Zeeland, but that she appointed her cousin regent of these territories. Should she set sail for the fourth time on the ship of matrimony without Philip's permission, then the three counties would become Burgundian property – this to avoid a repetition of the Humphrey scenario. The same would happen if Jacqueline were to die without issue. If Philip were to die childless then everything would go to Jacqueline.

Together they formed a *Landsraad*, a State Council, consisting of nine members who were favourably disposed towards maintaining peace:[9] six to be appointed by Philip, three by Jacqueline, and with the Fleming Roland van Uutkerke as governor. It wasn't an altogether disadvantageous arrangement for the conquered countess, because she divided the net income from her territories with Philip. To make sure the treaty found broad acceptance, the Hookish exiles were allowed to return to their domains, and a total ban on the use of the names 'Hooks' and 'Cods' was instituted. The Burgundian wanted to finally close the gap that had divided Holland society for decades.

After the feast in Delft, Philip and Jacqueline journeyed through their three counties 'like brother and sister'. For these Joyous Entries they went to Gouda, Leiden, Haarlem, Alkmaar and Amsterdam, followed by the most important cities of Zeeland. In Goes, Jacqueline was crowned queen for winning the archery prize. The cry 'long live the queen!' must have had a slightly odd ring to it, at least for her. She couldn't count on any more power and influence than that, but there would be plenty of parties.

In Hainaut, too, the city visits alternated with the festivities. Everyone seemed at peace with the fact that Philip held the actual power, while Jacqueline was allowed to retain her titles. After a tournament and a Burgundian dinner party, the cousins said their goodbyes in Mons. With three years of fighting behind him, Philip finally was free to devote his days to other concerns, and Jacqueline had all the time in the world to enjoy the forests of her youth, just as she had in the old days.

AS A WOMAN OR AS A MAN?

*Or how the spouses of Flemish counts and Burgundian dukes,
as well as Jacqueline of Bavaria and writer Christine de Pizan,
were ladies with powerful personalities, but especially how Joan
of Arc would write history with her 'male' accomplishments.*

READERS OF THE twenty-first century might ask themselves whether things would have been different if William VI of Holland had had a son. Would Jacqueline have achieved more as Jacques? Did the fact that she was a woman get in the way of any real success?

Women in the Middle Ages carried very little clout. Within the aristocracy, members of the female sex were mainly seen as the easiest way to secure a piece of land. Often they were married off to someone at an early age. The Burgundians had mastered the finest points of this discipline, and even Humphrey must have been interested in more than Jacqueline's charming personality. She was born into a phallocracy, a society in which the highest good that a ruler could accomplish was to beget a male heir, a world in which misogyny was common practice.

The medieval church openly emphasized its difficult relationship with women, and even took a long time to credit them with having a soul. During the council held in the Burgundian city of Mâcon in 585, the assembled bishops addressed this thorny question. According to legend, which is admittedly disputed, women were granted souls by a majority of three votes. True or not, it was grist for the mill of the already misogynistic medieval culture.

'You're all, or were, or will be whores / By deed, or wish which is the cause,' wrote Jean de Meung in the second part of *Le roman de la rose* (1275, *The Romance of the Rose*).[1] In the early fifteenth century, this medieval bestseller par excellence was still one of the most widely read books in Western Europe. It was generally assumed that a creature as driven by sensuality as a woman had absolutely no aptitude for exercising worldly power. In order to underline this gem of wisdom, the Franciscan Alvaro Pelayo wrote an essay in 1330 at the request of Pope John XXII in which he listed the 102 (!) defects of the female individual: unable to keep secrets, profligate in her spending due to her ceaseless longing for luxury, weakened by limited mental and physical abilities…

Yet in reality life wasn't always so misogynistic. The Middle Ages saw the flourishing of courtly love, which was basically a guide to subtle forms of adultery. Infatuation, and particularly seduction, were raised to the level of true virtue, equal to the feudal loyalty from a vassal to his lord. In this sophisticated erotic diplomacy, every form of sexuality was delayed as long as possible, because it was feared that afterwards the beautiful song of male attention would be played out. The woman was placed on a pedestal, rather like a Virgin Mary. You could look, you could invoke, and you might even touch, but only after having been patient for a very long time. It was no coincidence that the Gregorian Reform of the eleventh century, which contrasted the symbol of the immaculate Virgin with the diabolical voluptuousness of the earthly woman, happened at almost the same time as the emergence of courtly love.

When Jacqueline's adventures took place, courtly love was still held in high regard. In January 1400, for example, Philip the Bold, under the watchful eye of the schizophrenic Charles VI, took the initiative to form a *Cour amoureuse*, a poetic society in which members sang the praises of woman with as much originality as they could muster.

How all these precepts and good intentions could be reconciled in practice with a misogynistic society remains a mystery. In all probability, such prostrations before the female sex amounted to little more than a few expressions of frivolous rhetoric and light-hearted banter. It was a contemporary of Jacqueline of Bavaria who exposed this contradiction for what it was.

In 1390 the well-read Christine de Pizan found herself suddenly alone. Her husband had died unexpectedly, leaving her with three children to feed. She decided to support the family on her own, but not in any typical way: she was going to write. This made her one of the first women to live by her pen. Philip the Bold and John the Fearless both took her on as court writer, and the fact that her father served as physician to Charles V, their brother and uncle respectively, certainly didn't hurt. From one day to the next she became *homme de lettres*, or to put it in her own words: '*De femelle devins masle*' – I changed from a woman to a man. For writing, like the exercise of power, was a male domain. Jacqueline of Bavaria also tried to rule as if she were a man.

Pizan was rowing against the tide. First she screamed out her grief in a series of poems. Then she risked more serious work. She wrote philosophical and political essays and took on the misogynistic legacy of Jean de Meung. If ladies were really as perverse as he claimed, Pizan wondered, why did the author provide so many tips on how to approach and seduce them? 'Remember, dear ladies, how these men call you frail, unserious, and easily influenced but yet try hard, using all kinds of strange and deceptive tricks, to catch you, just as one lays traps for wild animals.'[2]

She also made a bold case for women on the throne. 'I assure you that the same can be said of a great many women, whether from the upper, middle, or lower class, who, as anyone who wishes to pay attention can clearly see, have maintained and maintain their dominions in as good condition as did their husbands during their lifetime and who are as well-loved by their subjects… although there are ignorant women, there are many women who have better minds and a more active sense of prudence and judgment than most men.'[3] Her reward for sticking her neck out like this was to bring the entire academic and ecclesiastical world down on her head. But not on the basis of rational arguments. No, the assembled intellectuals wondered what in the world gave a woman the right to express an opinion about such things, and they were most surprised by the fact that she wanted to defend her opinion in writing.

Yet Pizan's viewpoint was borne out by evidence. There were indeed a great many women who, upon the early death of a spouse, had successfully carried out a wise policy as mother and regent. And how many ladies didn't end up managing the family estate while their other half busied himself with more glorious undertakings, such as crusading and warfare? Women were quite obviously able to exercise power, even if it was mostly in the shadows, by order or in place of the lord of the manor.

During almost two-thirds of the thirteenth century, women ran the show in Flanders: from 1214 to 1278, the power lay in the hands of two sisters, Joanna and Margaret of Constantinople, while their husbands languished in prison or died before their time. During their reign they consolidated the complex peace with France, so the cities of Flanders were able to blossom both economically and demographically. And with great self-confidence they stimulated the formation of women's monasteries and béguinages, and founded numerous hospitals and leprosariums. The famous Hospice Comtesse, founded in 1237 by Jeanne de Flandre, as the French call Joanna, can still be found in the centre of Lille. Today, the medieval complex is a museum with beautifully panelled vaulting that is well worth a visit, a reminder of the improbable thirteenth-century ascendance of a Flanders that was governed by women. Also on display are a number of fine portraits of the Burgundian dukes.

The wives of the dukes had the right to make decisions. Think of the wife of Philip the Bold, who represented the duke in Flanders, her patrimony, or the spouse of John the Fearless, who governed the old Burgundian duchy in the south. Philip the Good would invest his third wife, Isabella of Portugal, with considerable diplomatic power. The Burgundian duchesses saw to the needs of the personnel, monitored the organization of all the magnificent banquets and maintained important contacts with other rulers. Joanna of Brabant also knew how to get things done. She would be instrumental in bringing about the double wedding in Cambrai, and would allow Brabant to begin a process of Burgundification. And how about Isabeau of Bavaria? Was she not brilliant at steering a middle course between the various parties? Was it not partly thanks to her that France fell into English hands in 1420?

In purely legal terms, there was quite a difference between France and the Holy Roman Empire as far as leadership roles were concerned. According to Salic law, which was laid down in 1327, it was impossible for a woman to rule the kingdom of France, which is why the mother of Edward III was denied the throne, even though she had every right to it, and her son would launch the Hundred Years War a few years later out of revenge. You might even call this French-English conflict the first feminist struggle in history – with a certain sense of anachronism and hyperbole – even though the woman in question died in 1358.

In the German hereditary domains, women did have the right to succession, just as long as there were no male candidates available. In the eleventh century, Richilde von Egisheim laid the basis for the county of Hainaut, which was a fief that could be inherited by a woman and consequently could be governed by a countess. Before Jacqueline came to power, three women would be elevated to the title of Countess of Hainaut.

There is no doubt that Jacqueline belonged to a small circle of extraordinary women, despite the fact that our national historiographers have rather eagerly catapulted her to the status of superwoman. In reality, she remained a pawn on the chessboard of England and Burgundy, albeit a very unruly one. She was also subject to the iron law of her age: that when a female heir inherited the title of countess, the authority that went with it was to be exercised by her husband. Now, John was a notorious fool and Humphrey an impulsive scoundrel. So the question of whether Jacqueline would have performed better as Jacques can only be answered by saying that it would depend on the character and the talent of the said Jacques.

In any case, there are two myths that must be dispelled. Jacqueline is all too often accused of having had an extraordinarily cruel disposition, while the offences that she is often charged with were standard fare in times of war, civil or otherwise. In this respect her behaviour was no different than that of many other leaders, and there's no question that she was less bloodthirsty than her uncle, John the Fearless. The claim that Jacqueline repeatedly went into battle like a knight on horseback belongs to the realm of fantasy. Only once did she find herself in a battle situation, and that was completely unintentional. It would never happen again.

Examples of women wielding great military force simply didn't exist. And it was precisely because they never commanded an army or played an essential role in the tumult of battle that female leaders were rarely taken seriously. But in this age of turbulence there was one exception to the rule: a French village girl would realize the legend that was ascribed to her, including military success, and she would do it all by herself.

You can ask yourself what might have happened if Joan of Arc had had blue blood, as Jacqueline did. Her lack of aristocratic origins did make things difficult for the village daughter from Domrémy, but it was that very drawback that enhanced the fairy-tale quality of her story.

'She Fully Renounced Her Female Appearance'

The voices that Joan heard became more and more urgent over the course of 1428. No matter how much pain it might cost her, she had to leave. Abandoning the village of Domrémy, her parents and her friends was not as simple as many thought, but after three years she was ready to make the sacrifice. 'Even if I had had a hundred fathers and a hundred mothers... I would have left,[4] she said later on during her trial. The voices told her that she would lead the troops to liberate Orléans. Although she had never wielded a sword, she did not hesitate. Some well-documented historical facts never lose their patina of mystery.

On 14 October, the English regent Bedford had put an end to the relative tranquillity of the previous years. Now that peace had returned to the Low Countries and his brother Humphrey was focusing all his attention on England, Bedford decided to crush Charles VII. However much the so-called King of Bourges doubted his own legitimacy, he had eliminated John the Fearless and succeeded in organizing his own court. So his plan to drive the English from the throne had to be taken quite seriously. Not much happened after the Treaty of Troyes, but the tension was palpable. When would the bomb burst?

The Hundred Years War and the civil war had torn the country into three large segments: the region around Bourges and the south belonged to Charles VII; the north and Burgundy to Philip the Good; the centre, Aquitaine and Normandy to the English toddler king Henry VI and his regent, Bedford. Only the Bretons were left tottering on their own legs, sometimes leaning on the shoulders of the French king, sometimes gazing longingly at England.

The past years had been a period of skirmishes, but mainly a long quest for money. Both Bedford and Charles had soldiers to pay, and to do that they drained the plundered and burnt-out France even further in order to survive. To pay for his wars in the Low Countries, Philip the Good applied a cunning manoeuvre. He secretly devalued the local currency, put inferior gold pieces into circulation and financed the battles with the profit, which he managed to slip into his own pocket.

The way to win wars was to be creative in imposing your so-called benevolences and taxes, but naturally you had to cash those investments in on the battlefield. In 1424 the claimant to the French throne lost an important battle to the English, and the end seemed nigh. Bedford had the power for the taking, but France was saved by Jacqueline of Bavaria. Her marriage to Humphrey diverted attention to the north. Bedford's brother wanted to capture Hainaut, Holland and Zeeland, which confused not only Bedford himself but also his ally Philip the Good. At approximately the same time, a minor palace revolution was taking place in London, where the Bishop of Winchester was profiting from Humphrey's absence and advancing his own interests. In short, just when France had presented itself to England like an apple ripe for the picking, Bedford had to go to London to calm Winchester down and frustrate his brother's plans for Holland.

He spent fifteen months on the other side of the Channel. In March 1427 Bedford returned, more determined than ever to eliminate the would-be King Charles VII for good. The English had succeeded in expanding the borders of their French domain practically everywhere, and in the summer of 1428, when Salisbury's fleet docked in Calais (with Jacqueline waiting in vain in Gouda), Bedford felt he was ready for the final raid.

At about the same time, Joan of Arc left her native village. Durand Laxart, her cousin by marriage, took her to Vaucouleurs, twenty kilometres north of Domrémy. This unknown Laxart deserves a proper place in the history books: he was the first to be convinced by Joan of her holy mission. Upon arriving at Vaucouleurs, Joan said she wanted to speak to Captain Robert Baudricourt, who was in charge of the king's last bastion in the north-east. Without beating about the bush, the sixteen-year-old virgin told him that God had sent her to relieve Orléans, crown the king at Reims and toss the English out of the country. The man burst out laughing and ordered Laxart to give her a couple of cuffs on the ear and send the child back to her parents. Joan walked away in tears.

The city of Orléans that Joan was referring to was located on the Loire and was the ideal gateway from Paris to the France of Charles VII. On 12 October, Salisbury began what would become perhaps the most famous siege in the history of France. If Orléans fell, the war would be over. Charles knew that the fate of France was at stake, and he improvised a meeting of the States-General in Chinon. There it was decided to break through the English supply lines, since without food it would be impossible for them to maintain the siege. Charles emptied his treasury. In January he sent troops to Orléans, which bravely held out under the attacks of the English.

Joan refused to give up, and she went back to Baudricourt again and again to argue her case. Although she made not a single inch of progress, she did succeed in gaining support within the captain's entourage. Who was this strange young girl with her remarkable story? Was her arrival a sign from God? Now that France was on the point of losing everything, wasn't it time to take some risks? Baudricourt felt the mood change within the ranks. Even the inhabitants of Vaucouleurs had taken Joan's side. In these dreadful times, they were willing to clutch at any available straw, certainly if that straw was the convincingly prophetic appearance of the maid from Domrémy. They went ahead and fashioned men's clothing to fit her so she could ride a horse more easily. Joan also had them cut off her long locks so the helmet would stay put. I changed from a woman to a man, as Christine de Pizan would have said in her place.

'Joan fully renounced her female appearance,' we read in the closing statement of her trial from 1431. 'Her hair was cut in a pageboy style, she wore a shirt, braies, doublet, hose, tall laced shoes, a short, knee-length tunic and a cut-out hood.' She also had her own 'boots with tall leather gaiters, stirrups, a sword...'[5] Almost three years earlier, on 31 August 1425, Jacqueline of Bavaria had also dressed herself in *manscleder*, but three days later she took it all off. Joan of Arc would never wear women's clothing again.

No other person in France would be enshrined in so many statues. Joan is invariably shown as a man, boldly mounted on a charger or looking austere in her suit of armour. These sculptures seem to proclaim one big message: if a lady wanted to set herself apart from the rest of her sex and do it in a spectacular way, all she needed was an air of masculinity. Is Joan of Arc, the woman who wrote history as a man, a proto-feminist? Centuries later she would serve as the poster girl for the suffragettes. At the same time, the heroic adventures of the Maid of Orléans would supply the raw materials for the figure of the warrior woman so often featured in films, comic strips and TV series.

Captain Baudricourt, who naturally was not in possession of a crystal ball, continued to have his doubts. He was afraid that this was all a joke, that he was being made to look ridiculous. An unknown virgin who would save France from ruin? On 13 February 1429, Joan barged in on him once more. 'In God's name, you're taking far too much time to send me off. Today the dear dauphin [as long as Charles was not yet crowned she would invariably refer to him as the dauphin] suffered a defeat at Orléans. If you continue to delay, a much greater defeat will follow.'[6]

Baudricourt was at a loss. What was he to do with this strange female creature? Many historians would later wonder how on earth she could have known that the French troops had just carried out their biggest orchestrated assault on the English supply convoys. And that the entire plan had been a monumental failure. Or was she just bluffing, hoping for the best? In the light of what was to come, the beginning of Joan's adventure proved to be so prophetic that the neutral observer hardly knows what to think.

Soon the event would mockingly be referred to as 'The Battle of the Herrings' because the English happened to be transporting fish that day. Cod, pork, whatever – the French were massacred. When Charles VII, still in Chinon, was informed of the debacle, he was sure the end was coming. Weeping, he withdrew to his private chapel and prayed for assistance. He implored the Almighty to give him a sign that somehow everything would turn out all right.

As if he were enacting a highly implausible scenario, Captain Baudricourt decided that then was the time to send in Joan of Arc. 'Come what may,'[7] he said. He looked with amazement as she mounted her horse, dug in her spurs and galloped off. Was this creature really a woman?

GOLDEN GLITTER

*Or how Joan of Arc first appeared in the life of Philip the Good,
how Jan van Eyck simplified his search for a marriage partner,
but especially how the duke combined his territorial expansion
with increasing splendour and decorum.*

_____

A T EXACTLY THE same spot where the pagan Clovis converted
to Christianity a cool 923 years earlier, Charles VII had himself
crowned King of France. The cathedral of Reims was flooded with
people. Everyone wanted to witness the miracle. After all, wasn't it
a miracle that the dauphin had been able to reverse a lost cause in
just a few months? He had succeeded in lifting the English siege of
Orléans, conquering one occupied city after another, wiping out
the humiliating defeat at Agincourt with a resounding victory at
Patay – and, to top it all off, successfully travelling the risky route
to Reims through enemy territory. Chroniclers ran out of words
in their efforts to glorify this unexpected resurrection of French
resourcefulness.

You weren't really king until you had gone through the ancient
rites in the Coronation City and been anointed with Holy Oil, but
for years the English and the Burgundians had blocked Charles's
way. So entering Reims must have made a deep impression on the
dauphin. Here, his mythical predecessors such as St Louis and
Philip Augustus had sworn their loyalty to God and to France.
Against all predictions, he would also be included in the list of
illustrious forefathers.

The inhabitants of Reims quickly decorated their city and
brought the cathedral to a state of ceremonial readiness. The
dauphin had stretched himself out on the ice-cold church floor to
thank God for hearing his prayers. Hadn't the Almighty sent him
a ministering angel? When a procession led him through the city
the following day, the crowds lining the streets took up the ancient
cry 'Noël! Noël!' Under normal circumstances, preparations for
the anointing of a king would take a whole week, but in this case

only a few hours were necessary. The most celebrated coronation in French history took place in a setting of papier mâché and half-polished jewellery.

Thankfully, standing beside Charles VII on 17 July 1429 was the personification of French victory. She was glowing. Everyone in the cathedral was pointing at her. Look! Joan of Arc, the miracle incarnate who has taken away the sins of France! The comparison with the Lamb of God didn't become obvious until later on; now she was shining in all her invincibility. Without her, Charles VII could have kissed his crown, sceptre and ring goodbye. Each and every time, she had convinced the wavering prince and the grumbling army leadership to throw themselves into the fray. Onward! God is with us! Have faith! While she was never put in charge of a military mission, she could always be found in the front ranks. Her presence electrified the French troops. Joan's white banner proved to be a more powerful stimulant than the *Oriflamme*, the ancient fabled battle standard of Charlemagne.

According to legend, Joan was an attractive woman. She slept among hardened, coarse soldiers who never laid a finger on her. At the king's request, a committee of matrons was formed to confirm the purity of the Maid of Orléans by means of empirical evidence. If she hadn't been a *pucelle*, her meteoric rise would have been impossible. Virginity gave women a halo of inviolability. At first the English tried to make a mockery of the 'whore of the Armagnacs', but gradually their scorn turned to fear.

Undaunted, Joan climbed ladders in the storming of fortresses. She once took a serious fall, and she bounced right back up. She received several blows to the helmet and was hit in the shoulder with an arrow. Nothing could stop her. She invariably wanted to be the first on the battlefield and the last to leave it. Although she saw countless soldiers perish, her fighting spirit never dwindled. She herself fought with the flat of her sword and by her own account she never killed anyone. Joan was merciful and uncompromising, ravishingly beautiful and beyond sensual lust, illiterate and clever, God-fearing but more manly than three generals put together.

Periods of war and misery were an ideal breeding ground for the emergence of self-proclaimed emissaries of God, but this daughter of a well-to-do peasant family couldn't have timed things better. Charles's initial reaction was lukewarm: she's harmless, so what do we have to lose? But soon he too became convinced that heaven had sent him a beacon in dark times. Seated on her charger, the maid drove the reborn land from victory to victory. The faint-hearted dauphin had mustered up all his courage and followed her to Reims, the city overladen with royal symbolism.

After the five-hour ceremony, Joan knelt before Charles VII, clasped him round the legs, and spoke these words in tears: 'Good king, the wish of God is now fulfilled. It was His will that I break the siege of Orléans and conduct you to Reims. So that you might receive Holy Unction. So that it would be perfectly clear to everyone that you are the true king.'[1]

*

The coronation was a turning point in the Hundred Years War. The English flag was still flying in Paris and Normandy, but from now on the enemy had to bear in mind that they were dealing with an officially anointed French monarch. Despite this unmistakable triumph, Charles VII soon began feeling a degree of ambivalence towards Joan.

Occasionally she had gone too far in her doggedness, and she had dared to rebuke him for his indecisiveness. Such bravado made his Valois blood boil. After all, he was the descendant of great kings and she an unlettered shepherdess. Whether a talent for diplomacy would have made her position stronger is doubtful. Her headstrong swagger was the very key to her success. And it was galling to Charles that her name was on everyone's lips. With reluctance he had to admit that he was not being seen as the long-awaited saviour, while she was regarded as the divine liberator.

During the coronation, Joan was caught a few times exhibiting a certain arrogance. Charles thought that bragging was a privilege reserved for him alone. Now that he had been officially crowned king, he gradually came to feel strong enough to stand up to her. It was a slow realization, however. Everything this king did happened at a sluggish pace. But it was based on a calm steadfastness that would lead him to bring about the total liberation of France. Until the very end he would wrap his irritation with Joan in courtly mannerisms. And she devoted herself tirelessly to her king.

Immediately after the coronation, still on 17 July 1429, the illiterate Joan dictated a letter to Philip the Good. Philip had kept remarkably aloof during the past months; he had sent only a handful of troops to Paris, barely enough to maintain order. The English had expected more. Regent John of Bedford, who had been exercising power in the French capital on behalf of the very young Henry VI, responded with disappointment. Why were the Burgundians being so restrained? Joan, too, could not hide her disappointment. Three weeks earlier she had sent the Burgundian duke an invitation to the coronation in Reims, but Philip did not deign to answer her. This time, the farmer's daughter from Domrémy approached him as if she were a statesman of the same calibre. She asked him to 'stop fighting against the holy kingdom of France', and let him know 'on behalf of the good King of France' that he was prepared 'to make peace'. If it pleased the great Philip to fight, 'he should aim his arrows at the Saracens',[2] words that prophetically anticipated the older duke's dream of launching a Crusade.

Philip read her missive, gave it some thought, but again refused to reply. The curious phenomenon that answered to the name of Joan of Arc was difficult for him to assess. What he as a realistic tactician did understand was that Charles VII, after so many triumphs, was still in need of Burgundian support and terrified of the English. As European arbitrator, he decided to let the situation simmer for a while, but mentally he began to prepare himself. One day he would have to make peace with Charles, even though the king had had a hand in his father's murder.

Joan may well have had the most triumphant spring and summer in French history, but the autumn and winter that followed were bleak. Her king seemed war weary. Charles VII was no great warrior. He was more a diplomat who had let her provoke him to action. He always believed that the ultimate solution was a matter of negotiation. Even after his coronation he refused to follow through. He did give Joan permission to besiege Paris, looking on suspiciously from a distance, but his heart wasn't in it.

Perhaps he secretly hoped that this nuisance would be killed. For the Maid of Orléans, sent with a small detachment in the company of the Duke of Alençon, it was fighting a losing battle.

Not that she just gave up. Until the bitter end she kept shouting at the Parisians, telling them to surrender. The future was French! Not English! And certainly not Burgundian! But at long last, after having been hit in the thigh, the indefatigable Joan was carried off the battlefield by her companions. When the king ordered her to end the siege, she made her way to the basilica of Saint-Denis. Deeply discouraged, she prayed over the mortal remains of all the warrior kings who were buried there. She did not understand that Charles VII had let himself be taken in by Philip the Good, who claimed to be preparing for peace talks, while according to her he was trying to gain an advantage by sowing discord.

Doubt began to grow among the king's acquaintances. Had Joan's voices deceived her? After all, she had failed to cut Paris down to size. The fact that Charles VII had hardly offered her any support recently was swept under the rug. Her military career had come to an end, to all intents and purposes. Although she had been admitted to the royal court, frustration overtook her. The French had locked their ministering angel in a golden cage. Common sense told her to get married and lead the life of a prosperous civilian. She was famous and beautiful; there would be no lack of candidates. The only problem was that she had pledged her virginity to God and sworn to liberate all of France from the English. So while her momentum may have passed, she kept looking for a way to be of service.

In January 1430 she was treated to a festive reception in Orléans, the city she had liberated six months earlier. She dined with old friends, former warriors who had returned to their work as bakers and butchers. The banquet that the city council proffered was quite impressive, but it paled in comparison with the festivities being held in Bruges that same month. Philip the Good was marrying for the third time, and this wedding, he decided, would rival that of his parents', the tour de force in Cambrai that had become the stuff of legend.

'The Skill And Virtuosity Of Jehan De Heick'

Suddenly, the duke became concerned with the question of progeny. The idea had been convincingly put to him in September 1428 by the Four Members of Flanders. It was high time, said the delegates from Ghent, Bruges, Ypres and the Franc of Bruges, that Philip turned his efforts to producing an heir, especially now that the Kiss of Delft had made him the de facto ruler of Hainaut, Holland and Zeeland. The men reminded him that these very territories had fallen to him because John IV had not succeeded in begetting a child by Jacqueline of Bavaria. In short, he was not to make the same mistake.

While the English were laying siege to Orléans in October 1428, Philip sent a delegation to the King of Portugal. Just as the most illustrious Frenchwoman of all time was setting out on her perilous journey through the English-Burgundian part of France in February 1429, destination Chinon, the most important painter of the Late Middle Ages was applying the finishing touches to his portrait of Isabella of Portugal in Avis. As Joan of Arc, having reached Chinon, was trying to convince the dauphin Charles of her holy mission, Jan van Eyck sent his two portraits northward from Portugal – one by land, the other by sea. When Charles, after much deliberation, gave Joan his blessing so her remarkable series of heroic deeds could commence, Jan the painter travelled to Santiago de Compostela for a bit of rest and to make some sketches. The spider in this web of stories was Philip the Good. He held the fate of France and England in his hands, had dictated the doings and dealings of Jan van Eyck since appointing him court painter in 1425, and would soon decide the fate of Joan of Arc.

The artist was part of a secret mission. Except for the negotiators – Jan van Herzele, Andreas van Toulengeon, Boudewijn van Lannoy, Gillis van Schorisse and Van Eyck himself – few had been informed of the actual circumstances. It was not the first time that he would be dispatched by the duke, nor would it be the last. Like Rubens after him, Van Eyck would be responsible for producing paintings and carrying out diplomatic missions.

Little is known about the painter in any event, and nothing

at all about his childhood. How he ended up working for John of Bavaria in The Hague is a mystery, nor do we know what brought him there. His name first appears on 19 May 1425 on a Burgundian document confirming the appointment of 'Jehan de Heick' as court painter for Philip the Good on account of his 'skill and virtuosity... which the duke had heard about from a few of his own people, and who knew some of his works and had actually seen them'.[3] In the Burgundian court records he appears variously as 'Deick', 'Deecke' and 'de Heecq'. Apparently, Philip the Good's strictly French-speaking acquaintances rarely talked about 'van' Eyck. The painter moved from The Hague to Lille, where he lived for five years. After returning from Portugal, he settled in Bruges.

Although no works have been preserved from the first period of his life aside from a few miniatures,[4] the fame of 'Iohannes de Heecq' must have been sufficiently impressive to serve as the basis for his appointment as chamberlain *and* court painter to the most influential duke of his time. Like Claus Sluter, he didn't actually serve as chamberlain, but he did enjoy the honorary fee attached to that position. His appointment brought other advantages as well. Unlike ordinary painters, he was free to disregard the rules of the painters' guild of Lille (and later of Bruges) and thus escaped the taxes imposed on guild members. His annual salary was supplemented by allowances for various travel costs.

Jan must have spent hours sitting across from the future Duchess Isabella. She was the daughter of John of Portugal and the sister of Henry the Navigator, who himself was not a great traveller but who had sent out countless adventurers and thereby laid the foundation for the Portuguese empire. A not unimportant detail: her mother, Philippa of Lancaster, was a granddaughter of Edward III, the English king who struck the match that kindled the Hundred Years War. While Philip's first two marriages were deeply French, now they took on a distinctly English lustre, which the Flemish and the Hollanders certainly appreciated from an economic standpoint. As a great-grandchild of the great Edward, Isabella's Albion content was within reasonable limits, all things considered, and Philip's choice of a Portuguese princess mainly showed that he was gradually feeling strong enough to demonstrate a certain neutrality, even in his married life. He seemed to be saying: I can do without France, and despite the validity of the Treaty of Troyes I'm only willing to toss England the occasional bone – a bone that might prove useful to me if negotiations over English wool were to start again.

On 13 January 1429, Jan looked on as Gillis van Schorisse, professor in canon law, discussed the subject of marriage with King John of Portugal. He did this in Latin. A Portuguese scholar translated the words into John's mother tongue. And so the communication continued, back and forth. The king was flattered, and Jan was given permission to begin his portrait.

Unfortunately, the fruits of his labour have been lost, although we do have a drawn copy made in the seventeenth century. Isabella looks us straight in the eye, like the figure in *Portrait of a Man in a Red Turban* (1433). The claim that the turban painting, which is believed to be one of the first self-portraits in history, is also the first example of a sitter looking directly into the eyes of the viewer, can be tossed aside – unless you qualify it as the 'oldest preserved' work of this kind.

There are several known examples of portraits from antiquity, but the practice practically vanished with the emergence of Christianity, which maintained a long and troubled relationship with human representations in general and representations of Christ in particular. Gradually, that association loosened up, although human facial features continued to be rendered schematically for quite some time. The profiles of princes on coins also lacked individual characteristics. It wasn't until the fourteenth century that an art of portraiture developed that was worthy of the name, often used in connection with marriage negotiations or simply to keep a dead or imprisoned prince symbolically present. It was an evolution that was consistent with the increased attention being paid to the individual in the run-up to the Renaissance.

Because so few panels from the pre-Eyck period have survived the vicissitudes of history, experts will probably never agree on how innovative Philip's court painter really was. At any rate, the portrait of John the Fearless attributed to Johan Maelwael from c.1405 proves that experiments in portraiture were being carried out before Van Eyck. The anonymous portrait of his grandfather, John the Good, from the late 1350s, is sometimes regarded as the oldest preserved painted portrait since the age of antiquity. The king was in prison in London at the time, and in this small painting he is shown as an ordinary man, far removed from the majestic figures shown in the miniatures that were inlaid with gold leaf. Others claim that because of that simplicity, the work must date from before his reign. Be that as it may, should you ever find yourself standing before this portrait of John the Good in the Louvre, remember that this is the man with whom this entire book originated. If he had not given Burgundy as a gift to his son Philip the Bold, you would be reading a very different history.

Labelling Van Eyck as the grand master of the portrait is a truth difficult to dispute, but to see him as an artistic extraterrestrial who simply fell out of the sky is an exaggeration. Even on the basis of the few available examples, it is obvious that he was following in the footsteps of Burgundian painters such as Maelwael and Broederlam, although he far outshone them with his eye for detail and incidence of light from an unseen source. We need only cast a glance at his so-called self-portrait from 1433. The head and the turban stand out in sharp detail while the background is black, vastly different from the rather flat and stylized faces of Broederlam and Maelwael. The drawn copy of Isabella's portrait shows that he had already mastered these techniques in 1429. The trompe l'oeil technique that he employed later on is also in evidence here. The left hand of the future Duchess of Burgundy is resting on a stone alcove, a kind of window sill over which her fingers appear to be hanging.

Philip was quite willing to do whatever was necessary to satisfy the wish for future descendants as long as he had some guarantee of the desirability of his bride, another reason for hiring the best portraitist of his time. If the painter from The Hague were to send him a rendering of a fine woman, he could depend on its accuracy: the lady was sure to be a *beauté* in the flesh. On 4 June, the Burgundian delegation received a message in which the duke expressed his enthusiasm for Isabella. Like his daughter, the King of Portugal was in seventh heaven.

In early autumn the delegation began their homeward journey. The small group had now grown to a whole fleet of 2,000 knights, soldiers and courtiers. There's no doubt that Van Eyck was relieved. Now he'd finally have the time to finish the monumental *Ghent Altarpiece* (also known as the *Adoration of the Mystic Lamb*) started by his late brother Hubert. But he'd have to be patient. A series of storms drove the fleet apart, and some even feared that the new duchess's life was in danger. Finally, the missing princess was able to go ashore in Sluis on Christmas Day. The journey had been one long ordeal, and for Philip the wait was equally arduous, but when he saw her the duke immediately recognized her fresh appearance from Jan's portraits. The Burgundian womanizer was not too timid to adopt the words *'Aultre n'auray'* as his motto. 'I will have no other.'

'It Is With Such Baubles That Men Are Led'

After the official solemnization of their marriage in the main church of Sluis on 7 January, a procession led the new duchess to Bruges. A band of seventy-six trumpeters welcomed Isabella, who didn't know where to look first. Red and white wine spouted from the hoofs of a lion. A stag pissed spiced wine in an endless stream. A squirrel held up a jug from which rose water flowed. The three creatures were cut from wood and so beautifully painted that they looked real. No matter where her eyes came to rest, there were no empty spaces to be seen. The Burgundian *horror vacui* reigned supreme. Full, fuller, fullest. Bruges had become a festival of triumphal arches, decorations and tableaux vivants.

Guests from all points of the compass arrived in the most diverse assortment of outfits. Even the palette that Jan van Eyck had used in painting the new bride's portraits must have paled in comparison with the vividly coloured masses who strode through the streets of Bruges on 8 January. Afterwards, chroniclers worked flat out serving up descriptions of the most prominent guests, which read like a 'Who's Who of 1430'. One enthusiastic chronicler counted 5,000 participants, another wrote of 150,000 spectators

– although the triumphant juggling of figures in the chronicles should always be taken with a pinch of salt. A great many houses were hidden behind specially erected viewing stands, where local residents rented places to those who wanted to watch the wedding procession. The new duchess was far from alone in her amazement. Philip had had his economic capital transformed into one big theatre.

The *entrements*, both edible and inedible, filled the guests with awe. The biggest surprise was a blue ram, who cleared a path out of an immense pie with his gilded horns. Also hidden within this oversized pastry construction was a giant, who began romping with a frolicking female dwarf, much to everyone's delight. The duke beamed. He had snapped up this little lady in Hungary for a small fortune. And look, there was someone sitting astride a roasted pig! Further on was a stuffed wild boar, who would defaecate radishes when you tugged on its curly tail. Need it be said that the amount of gorging and guzzling that went on was colossal? That for days Bruges was overflowing with knights who risked their lives jousting each other, just as in Cambrai in 1385? That everyone who was there would never forget it, and would talk about it non-stop?

The reader may rest assured: this is not going to be a repeat of the detailed description of the Cambrai wedding feast. Just try to imagine, if you will: bigger, more luxurious and richer. Imagine in terms of superlatives. Imagine an ultimate show of peaceful power. It was no accident that the coats of arms of all Philip's principalities were part of the table decorations. What seemed like ingenious formality was really clever marketing. Philip used gastronomy and the fine arts to showcase his power, and to imprint in everyone's mind the obvious superiority of grandson Philip the Good over grandfather Philip the Bold. His wife might stand with him on the dais, but this marriage was primarily a coronation of the duke as king of Burgundian theatricality.

*

Where did Philip the Good get his predilection for theatrical glitz? First of all, he was standing on the shoulders of his grandfather, the king's son who had observed the French court first-hand and had turned every feast and funeral into a ceremonial opportunity to put Burgundy on the map of Europe. But when it came to the dukes' marketing of spectacle, there was one fairy-tale castle that had been inherited by Margaret of Flanders and that played at least as important a role. The domain of Hesdin had captured the imagination of Margaret's husband, Philip the Bold, but it would excite the fantasy of his grandson even more. To tell the story of this famous theatrical monarchy without mentioning Hesdin would be like sitting down to a banquet where no casks of Beaune were being tapped.

Robert of Artois, one of the most famous knights of the thirteenth century, had started collecting curious automatons and decorative inventions in Hesdin in 1288. The man best known in the annals of Belgian history as the French leader who was cut down by a Flemish weapon known as a *goedendag* – a long-handled spike – on 11 July 1302 was a visionary as well as a great warrior.

In the chaos of his relatively short life, John the Fearless had had little time to let himself be captivated by the wonders of Hesdin, but his son Philip fell under their spell early on: the spouting statues, the distorting mirrors, the traps that landed visitors on sacks of feathers, or the bridge that would sag under the weight of the people who crossed it and dump them in the local moat. The funhouse quality of such stunts was very popular. In one of the rooms you would be sprinkled with flour, in another you'd find yourself in the midst of an indoor rainstorm. Over there was a wooden hermit, and here was an owl – all of them devices that could speak. Balanced on a lectern was a book of ballads so beautifully illuminated that guests would spontaneously leaf through it, only to be sprayed with water. Another automaton ordered the guests to leave the room, but as soon as they attempted to do so a second mechanism would strike them down. Those who remained would be treated to yet another shower. Water was the main feature of this interactive experience *avant la lettre*. Philip, with his soft spot for female beauty, must have been especially pleased by the ingenious installations that blew up women's skirts and then sprayed their legs with water. Hesdin's other attractions included fake apes and lions outfitted with an ingenious mechanism that enabled them to walk backwards and forwards. It was all highly artificial, but it worked, and the invited guests were apparently wild about the remarkable combination of practical jokes and illusionism.

To pull this all off, Robert of Artois made use of the latest advances in military and agricultural technology from the late thirteenth century. The newest developments in chronometry and clockmaking also came in handy. Hesdin was not far from Arras, the first successful centre of the textile industry before the rise of Ypres and Ghent. Only later would wealth and innovation begin their journey to the north.

As a passionate reader of chivalric romances, Robert had noticed how mysterious trumpet blasts would warn his beloved heroes of danger, and how they would then be rescued by hovering wooden horses or shown the way by talking owls. The magic derived from fiction became the inspiration for the marvellous place that made such an impression on Philip the Good, who himself was busy organizing reality into a story that he had contrived.

The duke spent a great deal of money restoring the dilapidated Hesdin castle, making a few improvements here and there and hiring a 'master of amusement machines' to maintain all the 'engins d'esbattement'. He would make full use of the technology of automatons, with their hidden mechanisms, bellows and feathers, during the famous *entremets* at his feasts and banquets.

*

Appearing on the mobile presentation tables in Bruges, which can best be compared with today's parade floats, were not only innovative dishes but also mechanically driven fountains, fish with rolling eyes and other creatures that would excrete titbits on command. Everyone saw it was a trick, but as with any sleight of hand, the secret behind the trick remained secret. After taking a few turns round the room the great engines would disappear as if by magic, and the guests would wonder how in the world their originator had pulled it off!

The rich of the earth sat in a fairylike decor, designed and painted by the team of Jan van Eyck, and watched mechanically driven figures that would spit water in their faces if they weren't careful. High art, ingenious inventions and silly hijinks went hand in hand. As long as the guests were left flabbergasted.

After three days, when everyone had gradually been exhausted by admiration, too much drink and far too much food, Philip ratcheted things up a notch. At a solemn gathering, he presented the Order of the Golden Fleece. In Philip's territories the textile industry was very important, hence the use of the word 'fleece' in reference to the wool taken from shorn sheep. In the context of Philip's order, it referred of course to the ram with the golden fleece of classical mythology, the booty that Jason and his unforgettable Argonauts had their eyes on. Immediately, the guests understood that the ram with the gilded horns that had escaped from a pie a few days earlier had been a spectacularly decorated herald.

Philip the Good was eager to associate his brand-new knightly order with Jason's tried and tested heroism, not least because the ancient tale was something he had grown up with. Philip's grandfather, Philip the Bold, had asked Melchior Broederlam to work the story into monumental wall paintings, and as a small boy the duke had deciphered the fate of the Argonauts on the walls of his grandfather's the castle in Hesdin. The marvellous *engins* in this fairy-tale palace created the illusion of thunder, lightning and rain, and as a youngster Philip must have imagined himself one of Jason's travelling companions. Later on, he'd be able to scrutinize the story's most minute details in *History of the Destruction of Troy*, a medieval bestseller by Guido delle Colonne that he found in the library of his father, John the Fearless. The version contained in this work differed slightly from the ancient tale, but it was one that everyone in Philip's time knew backwards and forwards. With the help of Medea's magical arts, Jason was finally able to catch the ram, which was being defended by snakes and dragons. He killed the beast, skinned it and came back with the golden pelt – the so-called golden fleece – from which the head and legs were still hanging. That image formed the inspiration for the pendant hanging from the chain that members of the new order of knights received and were expected to wear at all times. Why would the talisman that protected Jason and his men from all adversity fail to protect Philip the Good and his followers?

The duke saw his order as a religious brotherhood whose mission was to defend the honour of Christianity and serve as the driving force behind any future Crusade. A few pious members of the order made a fuss over the association with the pagan Jason. Fortunately, a scholar soon dug up the figure of Gideon, an Old Testament hero who had also had miraculous adventures with a sheep's fleece. That made it possible for every member to choose whatever source of inspiration satisfied him, although Philip, in his heart of hearts, would always remain an Argonaut. Besides, the Burgundian dukes were convinced that they had descended from the mythological Trojans. As far as they were concerned, the Greco-Latin and the Judeo-Christian traditions blended together seamlessly.

Membership in the Order of the Golden Fleece quickly became the greatest honour to be awarded in Philip's empire. 'You call these baubles,' Napoleon would say of his *Légion d'honneur* almost four centuries later, 'well, it is with such baubles that men are led. You call it vanity, but vanity is a human weakness.'[5] Philip the Good would not have disagreed with him. In addition to the golden bauble, which contrasted nicely with their scarlet robes, members also enjoyed legal immunity. They were expected to stand up to 'brotherly admonition', however. The purpose of this ritualistic custom was to help maintain a high level of moral authority within the group and to create an opportunity to settle private conflicts. During the annual chapters, members were allowed to openly accuse each other of unpaid debts, exaggerated curses or excessive adultery – although whether a member dared to raise the subject in the company of the order's sovereign remained to be seen. In the seventeenth century, however, the obscure writer André Favyn insinuated that the Golden Fleece was a tribute to the golden pelt of Philip's former mistress, Marie van Crombrugghe.

Like the knights of the Order of the Star, founded by his great-grandfather John the Good, members swore knightly loyalty to Philip on the battlefield and beyond. But the duke did not see the Order of the Golden Fleece as a mere nostalgia club for military daredevils. By getting top members of the Burgundian aristocracy to pledge their fealty to him in a way that was both prestigious and personal, he created a network at the highest level and a presumption of political unity. At the same time, it was a way of obtaining the commitment of the high nobility of the recently acquired principalities.

By establishing his Order of the Golden Fleece, Philip was also sending out an international message. It was a message laden with brocade, velvet and jewels, but that made it no less a heartfelt thumbing of the Burgundian nose at France and England. The fact that the two largest kingdoms had chivalric orders of their own, The Star and The Garter, was part of the normal course of things. But here was a duke who, without batting an eye, took his place beside the kings of England and France.

His gesture spoke volumes. Take a good look. I'm right here beside you. And even if I'm not a king, just the splendour of my wedding is enough to put you in the shade. I can even afford to marry outside your great houses. In the presence of the economic and aristocratic elite of Europe, Philip revealed himself in Bruges on 10 January 1430 as a sovereign prince who would not be lectured in humility by anyone. Whether the assembled guests, blinded by glitter and glamour, had understood this message of non-alignment was another question. Somehow, reality would soon enlighten them.

THE BURIAL PIT AND THE STAKE

Or how the ancient duchy of Brabant was carried to its grave and how Philip the Good and Joan of Arc suddenly found themselves face to face, but mainly how the Maid of Orléans would leave a blackened mark on the history of France that would last forever.

JOAN WAS STILL sitting in her golden cage. She had enough money to improve the life of her family, which seemed to give her some degree of pleasure, but otherwise she was bored to tears. Her frustration hit boiling point when Charles VII sent his army home. It was impossible to maintain all those soldiers, he claimed, especially now that peace was around the corner. Philip the Good had promised!

But Joan was right. The Burgundian duke wasn't at all interested in peace, at least not for now. To placate him, the English regent Bedford, who realized that Philip was soft-soaping the French, had made a few territorial concessions. Philip could take total control of the Champagne and Brie regions – if he could recapture them from the French, that is. It was a smart move on Bedford's part, for Philip wanted nothing more than to expand his territory. After the wedding feast in Bruges, he ordered John of Luxembourg, one of the first generation of Golden Fleece knights, to raise an army and take the city of Compiègne. The siege turned out to be an expensive failure, but it would make its way into the history books for another, quite unexpected reason.

To protect Compiègne from the Burgundian traitors, Joan of Arc left her golden cage, even though the king himself had already abandoned the city. She then recruited an army of mercenaries at her own expense. On the way, heavenly voices told her that before the summer the Maid of Orléans would fall into the hands of the enemy, all the more reason for Joan to quicken her pace. She cunningly managed to steer her modest army past the Burgundian lines and lead them into Compiègne. On 23 May 1430, at the head of a small troop of soldiers, she attempted an attack that was soon routed by the Burgundians. When her warriors realized that they had been cut off from Compiègne, they all took to their heels. 'The Maid, who forgot she was a woman, carried on courageously and did all she could to save her company. As leader, as the most courageous of them all, she stayed behind,' wrote the Burgundian chronicler Chastellain with great admiration. Thanks to her, some of her troops were able to gain access to the city, but Joan herself watched the drawbridge close before her very eyes. The governor of Compiègne didn't dare risk waiting any longer.

The golden tabard she wore over her armour was what brought her down. An archer grabbed Joan by the embroidered tunic and effortlessly pulled her from her snorting horse. The bastard of Vendôme, whose name has long been forgotten, took her prisoner. Proud as a peacock, he brought his famous detainee to his commander, John of Luxembourg. John then notified Philip the Good, who was encamped nearby. That same evening, Joan and Philip met for the first time.

There they were: the two most celebrated figures of their time standing face to face, the seemingly all-powerful duke and the seemingly unassailable Maid of Orléans. These are the moments when a writer is glad that the Burgundian chroniclers always described events down to the most trivial details. How many times did the gentlemen and ladies change clothes at the Bruges wedding feast? Check. How did Philip react to the murder of his father? Check. What were John the Fearless's last words? Check. The writer asks, the chroniclers get to work. And so this author, full of expectation, leafed through the writings of Georges Chastellain from the land of Aalst and Enguerrand de Monstrelet of Picardy, scrutinizing the momentous encounter between the two key figures in this book.

Both commentators were tireless in their descriptions of how *la Pucelle* was taken prisoner, but afterwards they cloaked themselves in surprising silence. Chastellain mentioned that the duke met her 'and spoke to her, but none of their conversation was conveyed to him'.[2] Monstrelet, who did witness the meeting, insisted 'that he no longer remembers what the duke said to her'.[3] How could the man who spent hundreds of pages proving he had the memory of an elephant fall prey to an inexplicable form of amnesia?

Could it be that Philip, who found it perfectly normal for anyone in his presence to shrivel into a little mound of reverential goodwill, had suppressed all reports of his having been confronted by a woman who stood up to his gaze? Who made him out to be a traitor? Who predicted that soon he would be compelled to make peace with France? For all we know, he may have wanted to present her to his wife Isabella as a sort of curiosity. She was known to have been fascinated by the stories about Joan that were making the rounds. In any case, they must have said *something*. Historians have often scratched their heads, while writers of fiction have been only too glad to fill in the colourful blanks. All we know for certain is that the duke released the glorious tidings that very evening. Soon everyone from Dijon to Bruges, and then to Leiden and Amsterdam, knew that Joan of Arc was in Burgundian hands.

England let Philip know how much they wanted Joan for themselves, a woman they regarded as being endowed with diabolical powers. For her part, this was what she feared the most. She would 'rather surrender her soul to God', as she would later say during her trial, 'than fall into the hands of the English'.[4] While she anxiously waited, the duke was not quick to give his consent, if only because he felt how much sympathy the Maid of Orléans was able to extract from Duchess Isabella, from the wife of John of Luxembourg, and yes, even from the wife of Bedford. Or did he hope to drive up the price with his procrastination? He was as rich as Croesus, so that couldn't have been the reason. Perhaps he was just weighing up all the advantages and disadvantages, as he always did. In the end, the anti-feminist camp would win. After repeated and increasing pressure from Bedford, the council of the University of Paris and the Inquisition, the duke washed his hands of Joan and let John of Luxembourg have his way. John heard the jingling of money and immediately started negotiating. It would take six months, but finally she was sold to the English for 10,000 pounds, the going rate for ransoming a prince of royal blood.

With Philip's crude horse-trading, Joan's fame would take on mythic proportions. Yet the duke was unconcerned about her possible martyr's image. He still had no comprehension of the Joan of Arc phenomenon – and who did? – but he certainly didn't see her as a witch. Although he knew that the English would try her for heresy, he put little stock in such charges. Thirty years later he would rescue from the stake eighteen dignitaries who were rumoured to have taken part in a witches' sabbath. For him, Joan was just a political problem, which he therefore approached as such. As a power broker, he decided (in consultation with Chancellor Rolin) that placating the English was his wisest move. After all, they had suggested that wool exports to Flanders might be scaled back. Philip used Joan as a bargaining chip in his international relations. And she could brace herself for a trial in which she didn't stand a ghost of a chance.

And the French king? The spineless Charles VII didn't lift a finger to free his saviour and defender.

'I Would Rather Be Beheaded Ten Times Over'

Even without Joan and without the king, Compiègne stubbornly held out against Philip the Good. But thankfully the irritated duke also received good news during the hopeless siege, news that even ten Compiègnes couldn't match. On 4 August, Philip of Saint-Pol, Duke of Brabant, drew his last breath. Philip knew he couldn't hesitate. He abandoned the siege and set out for Brussels.

Saint-Pol had been a much stronger personality than his helpless brother John, who had passed away three years earlier. If he had died first, there's no doubt the story would have been quite different. The lack of leadership on the part of John IV of Brabant demonstrates that the sharp ascendance of Philip the Good was not by any means based on his own merits alone.

As John's successor, Saint-Pol had signed the Treaty of Lier, thereby making it clear that in the absence of heirs, Brabant would go to his cousin Philip the Good. Burgundy's other claims left him cold. Certainly, his father had been a brother of John the Fearless, and he himself was a grandson of Philip the Bold and a full cousin of Philip the Good, but in Brabant he wanted to set a different course and start his own dynasty. Saint-Pol actively began looking for a fertile consort of rank. He hired Jan van Eyck to paint his portrait, and with this trinket he stormed the marriage market. According to some art historians, Van Eyck's *Portrait of a Man with a Blue Chaperon* (1429–30) is none other than Philip of Saint-Pol, based on a similar portrait. It's a relatively small and therefore portable picture of a man ostentatiously holding a diamond ring, implying that as a marriage candidate he is not to be undervalued. In the summer of 1430 his search came to an end. He had found the mother of his heirs in the person of Yolande of Anjou.

Saint-Pol marrying a French princess irritated Philip the Good immensely. A cousin and sister-in-law of the king? A close family member of the man who had ordered his father's death? The Burgundian duke was fit to be tied. The fact that he himself had carried on secret negotiations with France was one thing – but a marriage? Saint-Pol couldn't care less. He had heirs to think of. Unlike his impotent fool of a brother, this was something he would certainly succeed at. Hadn't he already sired a whole slew of bastards? Just look at the children he had fathered by the charming Barbara Fierens, a beauty he had met in the ducal palace. Her father worked as winegrower at Coudenberg. Saint-Pol was fully convinced that the French princess would become pregnant even faster than his mistress. Barbara Fierens was paid a handsome amount by the Brabant auditor's office for having been 'deprived of her maidenhead'.[5] Her sons attained the position of chamberlain of the Burgundian duke, but of course they had no place in the line of succession.

On the way to Reims, where he was to meet his future wife, Saint-Pol fell prey to stomach cramps. They had been afflicting him for months, but now the internal ulcers that were causing them seemed to be gaining the upper hand. Groaning with pain, he ordered the marriage caravan to turn back. It was forced to stop in Leuven, where a critically ill Philip of Saint-Pol passed away on 4 August 1430.

His unexpected demise proved extremely convenient for Philip the Good. Fingers were pointed at the Burgundian, but the autopsy confirmed that the Duke of Brabant had been suffering from stomach problems for quite some time, so murder was officially ruled out. Philip could thank his lucky stars. This was a Burgundian windfall of gigantic proportions. Now all the duke had to do was capitalize on the opportunity. But there was a competitor in the wings. Sigismund, who, as King of the Romans, had feudal rights to Brabant, presented himself as usual. He could never swallow the fact that Philip had become the strong man in Hainaut, Holland and Zeeland, and he would blame the Burgundians to his very last breath for botching the expedition to Nicopolis with their stupid bravado. As King of the Romans, however, he was an empty colossus. He may have had a highfalutin title, but he had little power or means to make things difficult for Philip.

Cunning as he was, the duke discussed the transfer of power at length with the States of Brabant. He had no choice. A tradition of civic participation had developed in Brabant that was stronger than anywhere else in the Low Countries. Without the support of Antwerp, Brussels, Leuven, Bergen op Zoom and 's-Hertogenbosch, Philip would find himself caught up in endless disputes. Indeed, the same tactic had served him well earlier on in Hainaut, Holland and Zeeland. The negotiations dragged on for weeks, but the Burgundian duke had all the time in the world. In the meantime, the embalmed body of Philip of Saint-Pol lay in state in the castle chapel in Leuven. That somewhat macabre presence symbolized the continuity of his ducal power.

As soon as Philip the Good, after a few concessions, was accepted as successor by the States of Brabant, the dead duke could be committed to the earth, ulcers and all. An immense dark spot accompanied him on his final journey. More than 250 black-clad men – from high nobility to chamberlain, from falconer to kitchen boy – gathered round their master for the last time and then disappeared into obscurity. The entire Brabant court was buried with Saint-Pol. For them, there was no room in the Burgundian inn.

In the autumn of 1430, the sovereign of the Golden Fleece began yet another series of Joyous Entries, this time as Duke of Brabant and Limburg – now the southernmost province of the

Netherlands – a principality linked to Brabant that was thrown in for free. The inhabitants of the cities of Brabant were told that the county of Namur had also recently fallen into his lap. John III of Namur had found himself so desperate for cash that he sold his county in 1421 for 132,000 crowns. A man with a penchant for luxury, the count did retain the usufruct on the property. He would hold out for another eight years, but after 13 March 1429 Philip was able to call himself Count of Namur as well.

His impressive territorial triumphs compelled the duke to work on producing an heir as soon as possible. As his own successes had taught him, the lack of an heir could quickly turn against him.

*

Two decades later, Charles VII claimed he wanted to know the full truth about Joan of Arc, and a posthumous retrial was conducted. It would be a mistake to be excessive in complimenting the king. The Catholic monarch only wanted to prove that he had not been assisted by a heretic. Full of reverence and respect, scores of witnesses told of her adventures as they themselves had observed them. On 7 July 1456, the jury declared her conviction of 1431 'null and void', and she and her family were rehabilitated. The idea of the poor shepherdess took shape with the passing of time, although in reality Joan had tended very few sheep and had come from a relatively wealthy family. What also emerged was the legend of the strong woman who had almost single-handedly changed the course of the losing battle with the English. The memory of poor Joan continued to smoulder, but it would not burst into flames until after the nineteenth century.

Shakespeare presented her as an indomitable virago in *Henry VI, part I* (1590–91), while Voltaire, in the burlesque *La Pucelle d'Orléans* (1762), made fun of her and inveighed against the people's shallow superstitions. It took another French myth to turn the tide. 'The famous Joan has demonstrated that there is no miracle that French ingenuity cannot bring about when national independence is in jeopardy.'[6] In 1803 this kind of voluntarism could only have issued from the mouth of Napoleon Bonaparte, who was not yet an emperor but was fully engaged in a conflict with the English (again). One legend paved the way for another, but it would take a historian to bring about the real reversal.

In 1841, the great historian Jules Michelet successfully catapulted Joan into the incarnation of the French people. He did this in a way that was both lyrical and bombastic, in a style that today would be called typically French: 'Never forget, people of France, that the fatherland was born in the heart of a woman, that it rose out of her tenderness, out of her tears and out of the blood that she shed for us.'[7] After Napoleon and Michelet, the path to eternal glory was open wide.

Yet in his *Grand dictionnaire du XIXe siècle* (1870), Pierre Larousse was more critical and refused to attach any credence to her 'voices', although he did see her as an example of someone with 'an exalted patriotism' that was curtailed by both the king and the church. By rehabilitating her, he said, the national and the ecclesiastical authorities could wrap her in legendary stories and appropriate her to their own ends. In 1920, Joan, who in 1430 was sentenced to death by an ecclesiastical court, was declared a saint by the same church. Twelve years earlier, Nobel Prize winner Anatole France declared her the victim of a clerical conspiracy. He insisted that her famous 'voices' were no more than hallucinations, and that the miraculous liberation of Orléans could easily be explained as the result of weak military action on the part of the English.

For the left, she would always be the victim of church and king, for the right the absolute heroine of the 'national romance'. And after France was humiliated by the Germans in 1870, right-wing nationalists were all too eager to make her their poster child. Six years later, the equestrian statue, gilded from head to toe, was erected at the old Louvre Palace in Paris. In 1904, a meeting of reactionary groups ended with the cry 'Down with the Jews! Down with the Republic of Freemasons! Long Live Joan of Arc!'[8] Jean-Marie Le Pen, founder of the Front National, did not hesitate to use her as his party's historic standard bearer, as the symbol of the fight against outsiders who endangered the security of the fatherland. In his eyes, those invaders were no longer the English, of course.

In 2015 at least 426 French schools bore her name, and with that number she bested such luminaries as Victor Hugo and Antoine de Saint-Exupéry. For most of the French she has always been the anchor of their history, but also the woman who is inextricably bound with her terrible fate, her annihilation in the flames, as Leonard Cohen poignantly sang in his 'Joan of Arc' (1971).

*

Alone in her cell, Joan could hardly have suspected what kind of illustrious life her memory would lead, of course. Abandoned by God and everyone else, she fearfully awaited her end. 'Oh, I would rather be beheaded ten times over than burned at the hands of men,'[9] she said on 30 May 1431. It was seven o'clock in the morning. She was in the prison of Rouen and had just been awakened. The fear trembled in her eyes. She was terrified by leaping flames. A few days before, that sense of desperate constriction had induced her to give in on all points. She had even started dressing like a woman again.

Soon her cowardice made her feel so miserable that she retracted her renunciation. She went back to wearing men's clothing. It was impossible for her to pretend to be someone else. Bishop Cauchon, who had done everything he could to sentence her to the stake, rubbed his hands with satisfaction. He described Joan as 'a dog who returns to its own vomit'.[10] Later, the French would brand this Cauchon as '*cochon*' (pig) and, in that capacity, confine him symbolically to the genus of traitors to the country.

In the capital of Normandy, where the English were more sure of themselves than in Paris, Joan had been given an unfair trial over the past few months. Her fate was sealed from the beginning. The clerics, almost all of whom were church scholars hand-picked by the English, and many of them affiliated with the University of Paris, convicted her of heresy because she judged the authority of dubious voices from heaven to be higher than that of the church. She was also sent to the stake because she, as a woman, had appeared in public in men's clothing. For the English, it was also a means of weakening Charles VII by demonstrating that he owed his crown to someone who was guilty of idolatry and the invocation of the devil.

A great multitude of burghers and beggars flocked to the Place du Vieux Marché. The cart on which Joan was transported had to clear a path through a restless sea of humanity. Hundreds of soldiers formed a barrier between the crowd and the solitary Joan. The English had mobilized an incredible show of force. They still feared that the thankless Charles VII would attempt a spectacular rescue operation. Philip the Good followed the trial closely. He kept himself informed of its progress and knew without a doubt that Joan was on the road to her death on that next-to-the-last day of May 1431.

Towering several metres over the centre of the square was a stake. What was about to happen to this apostate was meant to be seen by everyone. Once she arrived, Joan fell to her knees. Sobbing, she asked for a crucifix. One of the English soldiers, deeply moved, knocked a simple cross together from pieces of firewood, which he thrust into her hands. The executioner was given the order not to shorten her suffering. No wet wood for her, which would result in suffocation by smoke inhalation. Nor was the customary death by strangling permitted. The flames shot through the bone-dry wood like one vast sea of fire. Everyone heard her cry for Jesus at the top of her voice. One great howl for help. For minutes on end she called to Him. That unrelenting faith in God made the churchmen who had condemned her turn pale. When she fell silent, the executioner pulled down her burning shirt so everyone could see her naked, black, burned female body.

One month earlier, at her trial, she had spoken her last prophetic words. 'I am convinced that the English will be driven out of France, except for those who will die here.'[11]

BEAUTY AND PEACE

Or how Jan van Eyck incarnated the spirit of the times in pictures, how Philip the Good snatched up more and more of the Low Countries, how he made peace with his father's murderer, and how, despite the arrival of a long-awaited son, in the end he could only dream of dynastic succession.

WHY COMMISSION SUCH a gigantic painting? Was Joos Vijd trying to erase the memory of his father's infamy? Vijd's father had shamelessly embezzled funds from the treasury of Philip the Bold and was unceremoniously dismissed from the duke's accounting office in 1390. Or was he attempting to mask the minor frustration he felt as a rich landowner with aristocratic allure, who unfortunately was not descended from an old noble family?

Ah, perhaps it was just a matter of Vijd wanting to leave something behind that contained within it a presumption of eternity. He was going on seventy, he was childless and he knew there was no one to carry the family name forward. For a man without heirs, it wasn't such a mad idea to invest his fortune in an ambitious art project. By asking Hubert van Eyck, Jan's older brother, to paint the *Ghent Altarpiece* for the family chapel in the Church of St John the Baptist, at least he would be stealing a march on the certain extinction of his name. Had he not done so, no writer centuries later would have even considered opening a new chapter in his book with the name of Vijd.

In around 1420, he and his wife, Elisabeth, scion of the prominent Borluut family of Ghent, began to mull over the idea of actively contributing to the beautification of the old Church of St John, which was renamed the St Bavo Cathedral in the sixteenth century. This twelfth-century edifice dedicated to John the Baptist had become too small due to Ghent's rapid demographic development. Enlarging the church took a great deal of time. Slowly but surely, the church cast off its Romanesque apparel. The final transformation to Gothic, culminating in the famous bell tower, was something that Vijd and his wife would not live to see, but they were able to finance one of the five new radiating chapels. What would make their chapel so important was not only the decision to adorn it with the largest polyptych in the Low Countries, but also the idea of awarding the commission to one of the most talented masters of their time. Unfortunately, Hubert van Eyck died in 1426 and work on the *Ghent Altarpiece* was halted for a period of time. Hubert's brother Jan then took over, but he was so busy working for Philip the Good that it wasn't until his return from Portugal that he was able to carry out his brother's initiative.

Generations of historians, loupe and microscope in hand, have tried to figure out exactly which of the two brothers painted what, but so far no one has been able to detect two separate hands at work. Even less clear is to what extent Hubert was his brother Jan's teacher. In any case, the inscription on the outside of the *Ghent Altarpiece* reads as follows: 'Painter Hubert van Eyck, whom no one has ever surpassed, began (the work), and his brother Jan, ranking second in art, completed the heavy task at the request of Joos Vijd. With this verse he invites you to come and see the completed work on 6 May.' Such a panegyric to a predecessor was not unusual, although the words 'heavy task' seem to imply that the younger brother was responsible for the greater part of the work. Jan certainly did not do it all on his own. Knowing that he could only paint if the daylight was sufficient, and that the sceptre of Christ alone would take a month to complete (according to the sixteenth-century painter and art expert Karel van Mander), Van Eyck must have been assisted by a team of talented painters who adopted their master's style. In any case, when the Bruges city council paid a visit to his studio on 17 July 1432, they left a tip for twelve assistants.

The fact that the duke gave him enough personal leave to bring the colossal *Ghent Altarpiece* to a satisfactory conclusion shows how highly Philip the Good thought of his court painter. Claus Sluter, who spent the last twenty years of his life in Champmol, fared quite differently. No private commissions for him. Until his death, the master sculptor remained the brilliant hireling of Philip the Bold. Soon after the death of Sluter's employer, civil war broke out between the Armagnacs and the Burgundians, and Philip's successor, John the Fearless, had less and less time to concern himself with art. His son, Philip the Good, would breathe new life into Burgundian patronage. Even though the duke himself was not the commissioning authority, in all likelihood he was present at the solemn installation of the *Ghent Altarpiece*.

'Johannes De Eyck Fuit Hic'

Joos Vijd was certainly no stranger to Philip. In the summer of 1425 he was part of the ducal retinue that would plead for peace between Philip and Jacqueline of Bavaria in The Hague, more specifically 'to speak for the benefit of peace between our fearsome Lord and my Lady of Holland'.[1] Except the delegation never arrived. Jacqueline's escape, and the eruption of hostilities, put a definite stop to it.

His father may have fallen into disgrace with Philip's grandfather, but the burgher of Ghent had done very well for himself. Yet there must have been a feeling of unease that he could not shake. Without his father's indiscretion, he might have become part of Philip's court. That was a level he would never attain, even though the success of the *Ghent Altarpiece* put him entirely back on the map. One year after the installation he was appointed chief alderman of the metropolis of Ghent, a position more or less equivalent to that of mayor.

Joos Vijd had played his cards right. By throwing in his lot with Jan van Eyck, he was sure of attracting the duke's attention. And another bit of unexpected fortune also came his way. The day of the installation, 6 May 1432, was not only a lovely day for Joos Vijd himself, but it was an even more memorable feast for Philip the Good and his wife, if such a thing were possible. To their great sorrow they had lost their first son, Anthony, two months earlier when he was barely a toddler. But God be praised, a second infant soon followed, and coincidentally – or maybe not – the baby was baptized on 6 May. To top it off, the new son was named Joos (Josse in French), just like the patron of the great work, although that was purely by chance: Isabella had a great devotion to St Jodoc, or Josse, as he was also known. Yet it was an unusual name in a family in which almost all the male members were called Philip, John or Anthony.

Although it has never become clear exactly how the baptismal ceremony and the installation were interwoven, everything indicates that Philip the Good was present when the altarpiece was officially opened for the first time. A minor debate has raged on this subject between historians and art historians,[2] but it seems logical to us that the duke would not have been absent when his possible successor was being received into the bosom of the Catholic Church.

Of course, the *Ghent Altarpiece* – the *Adoration of the Mystic Lamb* – was a symbol for the passion of Christ. But Van Eyck's ingenious decision to place the holy animal in the centre of the composition must have made Duke Philip reach for his chest in an involuntary reflex, seeing a reflection of the golden ram he wore around his own neck in the image of the sheep. Not only was the painter paying tribute to the recently established Order of the Golden Fleece, but he was also serving up an allegory of the Flemish commercial adoration of wool. Wool was a subject of topical interest because at that very moment the Burgundians and the English were involved in an economic conflict on this very point.

Nor could it have escaped the duke's attention that life-size portraits of the two patrons of the work were featured on the outside panels. If Joos Vijd and his wife had been wearing the same traditional dress that they wore in the *Ghent Altarpiece*, the assembled guests would have sworn that the two of them were standing in front of a mirror. Just as Philip the Bold and Margaret of Flanders had had themselves carved in stone by Sluter in Champmol, here were Joos Vijd and Elisabeth Borluut appealing for their eternal salvation on the altarpiece beneath the approving gaze of two beloved saints.

It's tempting to see the *Ghent Altarpiece* as a symbol of the growing importance of self-confident citizenship. But the truth is a bit more complex than that. To begin with, Vijd himself had probably been raised to the peerage by this time, an honour that was still seen as an ultimate boost in status, even among the extremely wealthy burghers. In addition, he took great pains to emulate the Burgundian dukes. He chose Philip the Good's favourite artist and did exactly what that duke's grandfather Philip the Bold had done: had an image of himself displayed in a chapel that he himself had built. While The Bold had brought an entire monastery, church and mausoleum into being, Vijd was satisfied with a chapel and two priests to celebrate a daily requiem Mass. But it would always be an imitation of the great Burgundian example. So the *Ghent Altarpiece* is indicative of an increasing entanglement of the urban and the aristocratic elites, an evolution that the Burgundians had done everything they could to stimulate since their arrival in the northern regions. Patronage and artistic snobbery were no longer the privilege of kings or dukes, but they were still the role models. Now that the royal houses of England and France had hit rock bottom financially on account of the never-ending Hundred Years War, the fabulously wealthy Burgundians were the only ones left to take on the role of pacesetter.

Van Eyck's portrait of the patrons was fully consistent with the greater picture of growing individualism. The fact that the painter was all too eager to warm himself at this gently building bonfire of the vanities could be seen two years later in the completion of *The Arnolfini Portrait*. Right in the middle of that work he wrote '*Johannes de eyck fuit hic*'. And in the mirror hanging beneath that inscription we can just make out his own silhouette. We only know the name of Sluter thanks to Burgundian record-keeping, but Van Eyck made a leap that the Haarlem sculptor had never dared attempt: to that of self-confident artist. So walking among the high-ranking company that made its way to the Church of St John on 6 May 1432 we have to imagine Jan van Eyck himself, prominently in view, somewhere between Vijd and Philip the Good. The artist as bridge-builder between the elites of his age.

It is nothing short of miraculous that the *Ghent Altarpiece* has not only withstood the perils of history, but that its location has not changed since 1432, with the minor difference that a copy is now hanging in the Vijd Chapel and the original has been housed under high security in the cathedral's baptistry for the last few decades. Thankfully, during the Iconoclastic Fury of the Protestant Reformation in 1566, the monumental altarpiece was taken down at the very last minute and hidden. If the authorities had hesitated for even two days, we might have had to imagine the Late Middle Ages without this masterpiece. 'It would have been an unbearable pity', wrote the historian Marcus van Vaernewyck in 1568, 'if such a piece... had been ruined at the hands of those filthy swine.'[3]

★

Painting was considered a trade like any other, although in Van Eyck's time a change seemed to be happening in this regard: no furniture maker in 1432 would have got it into his head to sign one of his cabinets. Above *Portrait of a Man in a Red Turban* (1433), alleged to be his self-portrait, Van Eyck wrote '*als ich can*', which means that he completed this work 'as well as I am able' given his devotion and ability – a sardonic quip from an artist who knew perfectly well what he was capable of. He wrote his name at the bottom of the frame. Nine of his preserved works are signed, amounting to almost half the paintings we have from him.

Yet it's important to point out that although Van Eyck could move with relative freedom and confidence within Philip's court and beyond, this is far from the romantic image of the free-spirited artist we have today. Even under the Burgundian dukes, painters were mainly talented craftsmen who could be called in to perform a vast array of jobs. As the artistic jack-of-all-trades, Van Eyck was responsible for the decors of Philip's wedding feast, for painting sculptures in polychrome, making wall paintings, small portraits of marital candidates and a world map (now unfortunately lost) that he gradually modified on the basis of his many journeys. The painter probably even travelled to Jerusalem in order to colour in the map's geographic features for Philip's crusader ambitions.

In most cases, Jan's ducal assignments were thus of a perishable nature. Party decorations and wall paintings were more or less destined to disappear over time, which explains to some extent why not one of his ducal works has survived, and why all his known masterpieces were private commissions. This is no more than a partial explanation, however, and at the very least we can ask ourselves what kinds of important paintings he must have made for Philip. The records of the Burgundian court have nothing to offer in this regard: there are lists of payments, but no details. Yet historical research has uncovered something else.

As was customary, Van Eyck as court painter made a series of dynastic portraits. We know this thanks to seventeenth-century engravings of Philip the Good and Jacqueline of Bavaria, among others. The engravers added the words '*Ian van Eyck pinxit*', thereby indicating that they based their portraits on his work. The originals were probably destroyed when Coudenberg Palace in Brussels went up in flames in 1731; later, the palace of the Belgian king would be built on this spot. Whether it was the cooks who approached the preparation of jam with too much enthusiasm or a carelessly extinguished fire in governor Marie-Elisabeth's fireplace, the blaze spread too quickly for firefighting efforts, which were hampered by the icy temperatures. We can only imagine what that conflagration took from us: the magnificent castle to begin with, where Duke Philip the Good and Emperor Charles V both strode through the corridors. The known portraits of Philip are copies of original work by Rogier van der Weyden, who did not succeed Van Eyck as court painter but was frequently hired by the duke.

Van Eyck's predecessors were also given the most diverse assignments. Melchior Broederlam painted the sails of the Burgundian ships that were being made ready for the unsuccessful attempt to conquer England in 1386, and he also decorated the coach of Margaret of Flanders and the walls of Hesdin castle. Johan Maelwael of Nijmegen had a similar career.

Maelwael and Broederlam joined forces in 1401 to paint countless suits of armour for the wedding of John the Fearless's brother Anthony one year later. This may have been the most typical assignment for the average court painter, one that formed the etymological basis for the modern Dutch verb *schilderen*, to paint, which has its roots in the word *schild*, meaning shield or coat of arms. To impart an individual and recognizable character to the knight behind the helmet and armour, a great many shields and related objects were given a heraldic lick of paint. The Middle Dutch verb describing this practice was *scilden*.

Maelwael died in 1415 and was succeeded by someone else from the north: Hendrik Bellechose of Breda. Bellechose continued to work in Dijon after the death of John the Fearless. He carried on until 1430, but gradually fell from grace. It was difficult for the Brabantian to compete with the Maaseik-born bruiser who had won the heart of Philip the Good. Like Maelwael, Broederlam and Bellechose, Van Eyck painted heraldic emblems on an enormous number of shields. Although their paintings are what attract our attention, they probably constituted only a small portion of their work.

The Large Round Pietà (Maelwael, *c.*1400), the outsides of the wings of the *Retable of the Crucifixion* (Broederlam, *c.*1390–1400) and the *Saint Denis Altarpiece* (Bellechose, 1415–16) are still magnificent works of art of Flemish and Netherlandish workmanship. But the fact remains that a museum visitor from the twenty-first century who comes face to face with a Maelwael or a Bellechose will spontaneously and without hesitation think 'medieval', while he is much less likely to have the same immediate reaction upon seeing a Van Eyck a few metres further on. Maelwael, Broederlam and Bellechose were among the artists who worked in the International Gothic style, and although they gradually abandoned the idealization of the human figure and opted for a more realistic, natural approach, they were more disposed to the work of the Limbourg brothers, Conrad von Soest or Pisanello than to that of Van Eyck. In Italy, Spain and France, artists continued to follow the International Gothic as a mode of painting until the beginning of the Renaissance, while in the Burgundian Netherlands Van Eyck would bring about an earlier break.

The differences between the work of Van Eyck and that of his predecessors are immediately evident. First of all, he departed from the kind of background that was so characteristic of their work: polished gold leaf and shining aureoles and halos as well as the abundance of gilded details. He also flattened the pathos that was so typical of the characters depicted by the first generation of Burgundian painters. But it was mainly his revolutionary approach to the incidence of light that set him apart from Maelwael and the others. Combined with his extraordinary mastery of the cast shadow, Van Eyck was able to suggest volume as no one before him had ever done, almost as if he could rival reality. He wanted to present reality as it really was, and not idealize it: a wart was a wart, a double chin a double chin. His seemingly photographic rendering of body hair, folds of the skin, flower buds, the lettering of books, etc. heightened the illusionistic effect and made the difference between his work and that of Broederlam and Maelwael that much greater. Even we, who after several centuries of realistic art are used to a trick or two, find ourselves enchanted by Van Eyck's technical genius. We are as stunned as the doctors who studied *Virgin and Child with Canon van der Paele* (1436) and were able to diagnose the clergyman's arteriosclerosis. So how fascinated the group of Burgundians must have been in 1432 as they gazed at the *Ghent Altarpiece*. They probably had never beheld such flagrant realism before.

Yet it hadn't come out of nowhere. Van Eyck's realistic rendering owes a great deal to the work of sculptor Claus Sluter. With all the travelling he had done for the duke, he certainly must have had the opportunity to scrutinize Sluter's three-dimensional flesh-and-blood figures, who seem to have stepped right into the room. Compare the drapery of his figures' clothing with that of the Haarlem artist. Look at the wrinkles here and there, the eyebrows, the frowns. On the closed back panels of the *Ghent Altarpiece* Van Eyck presents the ultimate homage. Didn't he paint two statues between the portraits of Vijd and Borluut, John the Baptist and John the Evangelist? Strikingly, they are not polychromed, as statuary usually was at that time. Otherwise, of course, we wouldn't have seen the difference between them and the other figures. No, here we have a chance to admire the pure plasticity of the sculptor/painter. It's as if Van Eyck had wanted to fling the truth in our faces: take a good look, this is the essence, I've seen it in his work in Champmol, where I came to understand how the artist must observe things, it's Sluter – *sleuteldrager* in

Dutch, the key bearer – who handed me the key with which I was able to unlock the new age of art.

'Duke By The Grace Of God'

However happy 6 May 1432 had been for Philip and his wife, disaster struck once more only a few months later. Little Josse died. 'The Lion of Flanders', as Philip was commonly called, suffered a breakdown. Weeping, he wondered what heaven had against him. His two young sons had died in infancy within the space of a year. Why did fate not grant him an heir? The inconsolable duke, who fathered so many bastards that historians have stopped counting, asked himself if his thirty-five-year-old wife was even capable of giving him a son.

For two long years, Philip stifled his frustration. Then on 11 November 1433 the Long-Awaited One finally came into the world. The expectations placed on his delicate shoulders were not insignificant: from day one, the tiny Charles seemed destined to let the Burgundian world shine as never before. The prophecy that this child of the gods would run his father's empire into the ground forty-four years later was anathema.

After Charles's death, historians would give him what they regarded as an appropriate nickname, *Le Téméraire*. The English translation of *Charles le Téméraire*, Charles the Bold, is unfortunate, not least because it suggests that he had inherited the epithet from his great-grandfather, who actually was called *Philippe le Hardi*. 'Hardi' can indeed be translated as 'bold', while '*téméraire*' is closer to 'reckless' or 'foolhardy'. It would have been better, certainly in view of the tragic end to his life, to have called him Charles the Reckless or Charles the Daredevil. Unfortunately, it's too late now to change well-entrenched names.

For the present, there was little evidence of daredevilry. The little baby lay innocently crowing in a cradle that naturally had been made by the very best craftsmen. Charles was the last child that Philip would beget with Isabella, but this time the Chosen One survived infancy. Usually the ducal couple spent most of their time in the Low Countries, but during the autumn of 1433 they settled in Burgundy so that Charles, like his father Philip and grandfather John, could enjoy the light in the ducal palace of Dijon. He himself would be a prince of the north for the most part and would stay in the original duchy fewer than thirty months, half of them as an infant.

At about that time, the Burgundian part of the duchy was falling prey to countless attacks from the French. The defiance of the impregnable Compiègne had already proved it: Joan of Arc's death was stirring up fierce nationalist sentiment. While Rolin, Philip's right-hand man, formulated the military and diplomatic course in the south, Philip himself stayed in the north for a time after his Brabant Entries. Chancellor Rolin had to pull out all the stops. The French encirclement was making Burgundy gasp for breath. Thanks to a few quick decisions, Rolin was able to wrest a much-needed truce and win an important battle. At long last, the anxious duke went south to Dijon to size up the situation. That's how his son came to be born there, and it's why his great joy went hand in hand with a sense of uneasiness. More than ever, Rolin emerged as the champion of a major peace treaty.

The infant's parents showered him with honours, and in the stupor of their happiness they even dubbed him a knight. How different from the experience of grandfather John the Fearless, who had had to travel all the way to Nicopolis thirty-seven years earlier to receive the chivalric accolade. With a snap of his fingers, the brand-new father catapulted his baby to the rank of Count of Charolais, a title Philip the Good himself, as heir to the throne, had not been given until his fourteenth year. Lastly, three weeks after his birth Charles was admitted to the Order of the Golden Fleece, which gathered in the ducal chapel of the Dijon palace for the only time in its existence. Yes, this son, who was named after Charlemagne, was going to amaze the universe. In the midst of all the commotion, Philip the Good seemed to be releasing a subtle message for all the world to hear. Was it accidental that the last three French kings were also called Charles? Was this his way of making it known that the end of the shaky English-Burgundian pact was in the offing?

As a child, Charles was educated in the 'practice of nobility'.[4] Entirely in accordance with tradition, his training couldn't start early enough: history, languages, law and a bit of the art of warfare, of course. No flea market hobby horse for the second birthday of Sir Charles of the Golden Fleece. A celebrated Brussels saddler made a toy steed for him so the toddler could master certain riding techniques. In addition to his total immersion in old knights' tales, the two-year-old Charles was immediately plunged into the marriage market, and as a fledgling prince he was present at the most important international meeting of his time.

★

The discussions that France and Burgundy had been carrying on for years in secret began to bear fruit when Philip the Good realized that he had more to win from an alliance with France than by stubbornly clinging to his pact with a weakened England. The fact that Charles VII was now supporting opponents of Burgundy in the Holy Roman Empire in addition to ramping up his own military actions helped clear away Philip's last doubts. After the death of his sister Anna, the wife of the English regent Bedford, there was nothing to stop him from breaking the promise he had made at Troyes. Yet the duke wasn't about to drop the English just like that. The aim of a new meeting was total peace, no more and no less.

In early August 1435, representatives of the three concerned parties, along with Cardinals Niccolò Albergati and Hugo van Lusignan, made their way to Arras, the former as papal nuncio of Eugene VI and the latter as sent by the conciliar fathers. Their presence was evidence of a new conflict within the church – who had the last word, the pope or the council? – but it lent prestige to the meeting as well, which could also boast of the arrival of observers from Aragon, Bohemia, Brittany, Castile, Cyprus, Denmark, the Holy Roman Empire, Genoa, Naples, Navarre, Poland, Portugal and Venice. No one wanted to miss the first international peace conference in history. Everyone wondered whether the three great powers, after having fought a life and death struggle, would really fall into each other's arms.

Need it be said that the procession of the Burgundian delegation attracted the most attention? That the other envoys looked on with a slight sense of resentment as Philip's 500 archers and 300 attendants, all of them dressed to the nines, turned the centre of Arras into a magnificent display of red and green? That the prominent guests were especially looking forward to the parties being organized by Duchess Isabella? Dozens of carts laden with Burgundian wines, Brabant beers, Holland cheeses and other specialities were driven into the astonished Arras.

King Henry VI of England, now thirteen years old, who had only seen Paris for the first time in 1431 where he was immediately crowned King of France, was represented by high-ranking aristocrats, as was Charles VII, also King of France since 1429. Philip the Good insisted on showing himself off. Thousands of flower petals were thrown from countless windows, all of them contrasting beautifully with his black attire. His two-year-old son met with even greater acclaim, as if that were possible. A show horse carried a litter draped in Flemish lace and inlaid with gold and silver, from which the Burgundian heir apparent gazed with astonishment at the equally astonished spectators.

On 6 September the English torpedoed the negotiations and went back home. After their endless war on the continent, they found it impossible to recognize Charles VII as the rightful King of France. In their eyes, that would always be their own Henry VI. Nor were they eager to tear up the Treaty of Troyes. Without the support of Burgundy, they would never triumph over France.

The ailing Duke of Bedford, who as regent for the young English monarch had spent years making every effort to maintain good relations with Philip the Good, was so upset by the failure that on 14 September 1435 he suddenly died. Ten days later, another leading player left the stage. Isabeau of Bavaria, now fifty-five years old, the widow of the mad Charles VI, who, along with Philip, had delivered France into the hands of the English in 1420, lived just long enough to see the Treaty of Troyes relegated to the archives. As if suddenly aware of the senselessness of her promising life, she too cashed in her chips.

The negotiators at the Arras conference did not succeed in administering the last rites to the Hundred Years War, but they did bring about reconciliation between France and Burgundy. It was by no means a smooth operation, with the Burgundian duke himself slowing down the process. Philip could not easily erase the memory of his father's death, and Rolin had to spend days persuading him. Even though he would have preferred a general peace treaty, Philip gradually came round. In what might be called a morbid coincidence, it was on 10 September, exactly sixteen years after the drama on the Montereau bridge, that he gave permission to discuss the details of the treaty.

Even then he wondered whether he could simply renounce his sworn loyalty to England. The papal nuncio and the conciliar legates hastily gave the duke their approval to revoke his sacred oath, based on the fact that England itself had quashed the general negotiations. Now Philip could in good conscience reconcile himself with the man who had given the order to murder his father. Of course he demanded a few things as compensation. His signature brought him not only the counties of Mâcon, Auxerre and Boulogne, but also the seigniory of Bar-sur-Seine and the viscounties of Roye, Péronne and Montdidier, not to mention the most important cities of the Somme (Saint-Quentin, Amiens, Abbeville…), although Charles VII did retain the right to buy them back at some point.

All in all it was a limited territorial expansion, but Philip could now add Picardy to his long list of possessions, which meant that his northern domains extended southward to about 100 kilometres north of Paris. More important was that he was released from paying homage to Charles VII. He was no longer compelled to literally kneel before the king, nor was he obliged to recruit soldiers for him in the event of war. That was all well and good, but a peace with both England *and* France would have been a much greater triumph. Now the partial peace was forced to mask the congress's partial failure. His envoys could have achieved more, but the French king had bribed a number of the negotiators. For Charles VII, the crucial goal was not peace with England but a French-Burgundian agreement, to be attained at all costs. The Burgundian chancellor Rolin raked in a sum equal to five hundred times the annual salary of a skilled labourer in Bruges.

To compensate for the murder of his father, Philip managed to pull a handful of moral concessions out of the fire. But none of them would keep the crucial northern Burgundian domains from being very displeased with the agreement. What did Holland, Flanders and Zeeland have to gain from the building of a monastery in Montereau, where Carthusian monks would pray for the soul of John the Fearless? All they cared about were trade relations with England, which now came under enormous pressure. Not even a hundred commemorative crosses on the Montereau bridge could mask the threat of economic calamity that this agreement represented. When news of the Treaty of Arras crossed the Channel, it was Flemish negotiators in London who were immediately made to suffer for it.

That didn't keep the ambitious Philip from enjoying French kowtowing, not by any means. Bishop Jean Tudert knelt before him and asked his forgiveness for the murder of Philip's father in the name of Charles VII. The king himself was not present, and with good reason: he would never openly demonstrate remorse to the Burgundian duke, not for all the money in the world. In French historiography, where Burgundy is rather negatively depicted as a rebel, it is often suggested that Charles actually had very little to do with the murder. But the facts speak otherwise. Not only was he present when the crime was committed and calmly let the perpetrators do as they pleased, but he never distanced himself from the murderers and would even award their leader, Tanguy du Châtel, with a generous pension. The man who in 1419 was still the dauphin not only wanted to avenge the death of Orléans, but he also saw the murder of John the Fearless as the only way out for his civil-war-ravaged country. That proved to be a big mistake.

In 1435, Philip couldn't resist the temptation to badger the French king one last time, and he signed the treaty that ended the civil war as 'duke by the grace of God'. Tradition dictated that he sign as 'duke by the grace of the king', but he wanted to make clear once and for all that he refused to tolerate any prince above himself. It's not surprising that Philip and Charles would never meet. For the next twenty-five years, any communication between the two gamecocks would be the responsibility of Duchess Isabella of Portugal. Charles VII was willing to swallow the humiliation because he had won his battle. Not only did Burgundy recognize him as the rightful King of France, but the duchy would no longer provide assistance to England and would simply stand by and watch as the Hundred Years War dragged on.

Philip insisted that the two-year-old Charles the Bold be present at the solemn signing of the treaty on 21 September 1435. In order to strengthen the ties between France and Burgundy, it was agreed that the boy would marry Catherine, daughter of the French king. Five years later, a seven-year-old Charles and a twelve-year-old Catherine pledged their undying troth in Cambrai, the place where the House of Burgundy had concluded earlier successful marriages. Charles was able to enjoy a relatively carefree childhood in Coudenberg Palace in Brussels in the company of a few of his father's bastards and his wife, Catherine, who would die childless in 1446.

'The Greatest Master In The Art Of Painting'

His son was not the only one whose presence the duke explicitly required at Arras. He also summoned his beloved court painter. 'To Johannes the painter, whom monseigneur ordered to be paid an honorarium to cover the expenses he recently incurred for travelling from Bruges to Arras,' we read in the Burgundian bookkeeping, whose dry precision points the way to a tangible reality. During the peace conference, Van Eyck made a drawing of Niccolò Albergati, the churchman who had spent years promoting French-Burgundian reconciliation. It is not clear whether the portrait was commissioned by the duke or by the legate himself, or whether Van Eyck produced any other portraits. The drawing from 1435 is the only work of art to come to us from Arras.

Three years later, the painter reworked the magnificent sketch into a fully fledged colour portrait. On his draft, Jan kept a written reminder of the colours he would have to use for certain passages: indications such as 'ash-grey, with ochre overtones' for the hair on Albergati's head, or 'very pale, whitish purple' for the lips. His comments for the painting of the eyes alone show how important colouration was for Van Eyck. He left himself instructions to apply a 'yellowish brown' tone around 'the black' of the pupil, he saw a 'bluish' glow around the white, and he called the white of the eye itself 'yellowish'.[6] In making the definitive portrait of 1438, he clearly did not let his own advice go unheeded.

The opulent colours that have continued to astonish the minds of so many observers, contemporaries and generations of Van Eyck fans cannot be blindly attributed to his invention of oil paint. Research has shown that the method had already been used by earlier artists, although Van Eyck did introduce improvements to the process and can therefore be seen as one of its originators. The use of linseed oil instead of egg yolk as a medium enabled painters to impart a far more shimmering quality to their colours than they had ever had before. No one experimented with the new achievements like Van Eyck. He mixed his pigments with a refinement that was quite unprecedented, and thanks to the technique of glazing he was able to superimpose transparent layers of paint in an innovative way. He excelled in this practice due to the addition of siccatives, which made the oil paint dry more quickly. As a result, he succeeded in creating the illusion of real depth and in giving more lustre to the colours. The blue of the sky was more luminous than ever, the grass was greener, and the gold was no longer the shiny effect that his predecessors had achieved by using gold leaf; his looked like real gold.

By unravelling his scribbled colour suggestions from 1435, language historians have concluded that Van Eyck must have spoken a Maasland dialect. This confirms the theory, assumed but never convincingly advanced, that the Burgundian court painter was born in Maaseik in today's eastern Belgium. His name itself seems to support this line of reasoning. Nor can it be a coincidence that Jan's daughter Lievine entered the St Agnes convent in Maaseik in around 1450. It is partly thanks to the Congress of Arras that little doubt exists concerning the origins of the greatest painter of the Late Middle Ages.

Chancellor Rolin regarded the successfully concluded treaty as the masterpiece of his diplomatic career. The fact that he had actively contributed to the end of the civil war between the Burgundians and the Armagnacs filled him with so much pride that he looked for a spectacular way to reward himself. A knighthood was out of the question – the aristocratic antecedents of this self-made man were far too meagre – but he had money in abundance. So Philip's right-hand man called on Van Eyck. His request inspired the painter to produce one of his greatest masterpieces. In *The Madonna of Chancellor Rolin* (1435–6), the second most powerful man in the duchy appears in a mink-trimmed, gold brocade robe. He may be kneeling at a prie-dieu, but the humility with which Joos Vijd had himself depicted on the outer panel of the *Ghent Altarpiece* is nowhere to be seen. Unlike Vijd, Rolin doesn't even appeal to a patron saint to mediate with the Almighty on his behalf. The chancellor focuses directly on Jesus, and Christ blesses him approvingly from the lap of his Holy Mother. Rolin doubtless saw the work as a portrayal of religious meditation, but the man kneeling here seems well aware of his own greatness. Even contemporaries wondered whether the balance here hadn't tipped from piety to pride.

As master of the portrait, the well-considered composition and the landscape painting, Van Eyck reached the apex of his art in this work. Opening up behind the main figures is a panorama in which researchers have discovered elements of Bruges, Ghent, Liège and Rolin's own Aymeries. In the far distance are the snow-capped peaks of a mountain range, a first in the history of art. In all probability the landscape constitutes a blend of Jan's travel recollections and is symbolic of the heavenly Jerusalem.

In the centre of the background is a man in a red turban, a nod to his own supposed self-portrait. It is tempting to see in him the painter himself, propelling the gaze of the viewer along a central watercourse and into the glorious distance. The careful observer will notice that on the bridge crossing the river Van Eyck has painted a large crucifix: it was exactly what the French king had promised, a commemorative cross on the cursed Montereau bridge.

In the year of the Treaty of Arras, Van Eyck found himself in the midst of a minor financial controversy. The duke had converted his annual salary of a hundred pounds into a lifetime pension, a fourfold increase. The responsible official at the Lille accounting office thought a huge mistake had been made, and he refused to make the payments. The artist summoned up his courage and protested to Philip the Good, who immediately took up his pen and gave the official a dressing-down. He ordered that the injustice be rectified immediately, 'or our painter Jehan van Eyck' (here the duke used his Middle Dutch name) 'will be forced to leave our service'. That would be a nightmare, because Philip wanted 'presently to call on him to take on certain large works', and he would 'never find anyone so excellent in his art and skilfully adept'.[7] One year later, the same official chose a petty way to have his revenge. Because Van Eyck could not verify his travel costs with the necessary receipts, the man claimed that it was impossible to pay out the last few cents. Whether Philip intervened again is unknown.

Clearly, the relatively intimate relationship between duke and artist was no pose: Philip stood godfather to Jan's first child, and after Jan's death he paid a handsome pension to his widow. The painter was buried in the prestigious necropolis of St Donatian's church in Bruges, another token of great honour, where John the Fearless's tutor Baldwin van der Nieppe was also given a final resting place, along with Canon Joris van der Paele, who became world famous thanks to Van Eyck.

In 1799 the church was demolished, but shortly before 1603 someone had taken the trouble to copy out the words chiselled on his tombstone: '[Here] lies Jan van Eyck, the greatest master in the art of painting who ever lived in the Netherlands.'[8] Even by then, the footsteps of countless churchgoers had worn away the date of his death. It wasn't until the twentieth century that a document was found in the Burgundian bookkeeping records providing a decisive answer. The payment for the funeral and the ringing of the bells was entered on 23 June 1441,[9] so we can say with certainty that Jan van Eyck laid down his brush for good when the summer began. He must have counted off about fifty springs in all.

THE BURGUNDIAN DREAM

*Or how Philip the Good, at the risk of his own life, imposed
restraints on rebellious cities like Ghent and Bruges, but also
how he tried to merge the various principalities of the Low
Countries at the judicial, financial and administrative levels,
and how this imposed Burgundification laid the foundations
for the modern state in that part of the world.*

O N 23 MAY 1430, when one of the city gates of Compiègne came
crashing down before her, Joan of Arc was like a rat in a trap.
Seven years later almost to the day, the same fate awaited Philip the
Good in Bruges, the difference being while Joan was locked out,
Philip could no longer leave. The Maid of Orléans fought like a lion,
but she was taken prisoner. The Duke of Burgundy also furiously
resisted. Now that he was cut off from his own troops, who were
outside the city walls on 22 May 1437, it looked as if his hour had
come. The circle tightened, but like the fierce warrior that he was
Philip refused to let himself be led to slaughter.

An objective observer would not have believed his eyes. Was
it true that the Burgundian bodyguards had been backed into
a corner? The facts certainly spoke for themselves. This was no
military exercise; it was a fight to the death. Was the knight in black
velvet really Philip the Good? Indeed it was. The golden pendant
of the Order of the Golden Fleece removed all doubt. Only one
question remained: how did the almighty 'Lion of Flanders', who
seven years earlier had given the most dazzling wedding feast of
all time in this very city, end up in such a precarious situation?

'Terrible Whitsun Wednesday'

There is no doubt that the Treaty of Arras eventually turned out
well for the Burgundian cause, but it was a bitter pill at first,
especially for Flanders. Not only were the Flemish merchants in

London brutally treated, but the Flemish ships started running into obstacles in the Channel from one day to the next. In addition, after the death of Bedford, the English sent his brother Gloucester to serve as the strong man on the continent. The ex-husband of Jacqueline of Bavaria had a bone to pick with Philip after his pernicious adventures in Hainaut and Holland, and he whipped up his international friends to turn against Burgundy.

The duke was not one to sit back and watch. First he extended a helping hand to the French in retaking Paris. On 13 April 1436, his marshal, Villiers de L'Isle-Adam, planted the French flag in the capital and he opened the city gates for Charles VII, who finally returned to the Louvre Palace after an absence of nineteen years. With that triumph behind him, and in high spirits, Philip then moved on to Calais, the English staple town in France and a key position for the enemy that he was eager to lay hands on. Remarkably enough, he planned on using mainly Flemish city militias to lay siege to Calais, and he knew what sensitivities he had to play on in order to bring it off. Resentment had been building in recent years concerning the raising of taxes on English wool that came into Flanders via Calais. With that argument he was able to coax the cities to mobilize more or less en masse, giving the Burgundian attack the semblance of a Flemish war against England.

It was madness, of course, to take up arms against one's most important economic partner. First of all, he should have known that the Flemings were not the most highly motivated of soldiers. Hadn't they deserted his father in 1411 at Montdidier? John the Fearless had learned his lesson, and from then on he had used them only to sponsor his military ventures. This time, too, the whole operation backfired. Besides building a wooden tower, the city militias did little else. One sortie was all the English needed and the tower was theirs. The Holland-Zeeland fleet, which had sailed from Sluis, took much too long to be of any use to the land troops. When it became clear that the promised support from the sea would arrive too late, the Flemings packed it in.

And there was Philip the Good, reduced to inordinate begging. He was very close to falling on his knees. It was a repetition of how his father had grovelled at Montdidier over twenty-five years earlier. Van Eyck could have made a beautiful double portrait of them both: two dukes begging for help, not from Christ but from the Flemings. It made no difference. The surly Flemings left for home. It had been a serious error of judgement not only to mobilize them but also to saddle them with the financial consequences of the operation. Had Philip really thought they'd be eager to strangle their own wool supplier? That the Flemish got cold feet was quite understandable.

In any event, the Flemings had to foot the bill. The failed siege became the prelude to more misery. Gloucester, who first had entrenched himself in Calais, set his course for Flanders. He laid waste to such picturesque towns as Drincham, Quaëdypre, Bambecque, Haringe and Reningelst, and razed the important city of Poperinge to the ground. There, among the blackened stones and charred ruins, he proclaimed himself Count of Flanders on 15 August. As terrible as his raid had been, there was something ludicrous about the scene itself. The man who earlier had longed to be the Count of Hainaut, Holland and Zeeland, but had failed, now took grotesque revenge among the ruins of Poperinge. As soon as he heard rumours of a Burgundian mobilization, he fled with his tail between his legs. Like a madman, he brutalized Belle, Hazebrouck, Moerbeke and Wallon-Cappel, but after having smoked out southern Flanders he withdraw to safety behind the walls of Calais.

At the same time, Albion also struck in the north. To facilitate the landing of the English fleet, supporters built huge fires in the Scheldt estuary. Holland and Zeeland didn't lift a finger. They wouldn't lose their English trading partner for all the money in the world. It was a lively example of realpolitik. The fleet was given permission to moor in Middelburg, the city of the Anglophile Frank van Borssele, thus enabling the English to sail along the banks of the Zwin, plundering and destroying villages in northern Flanders. Finally, they withdrew to the harbour of Calais, just as Gloucester had done. England wasn't so stupid as to beat the living daylights out of a privileged partner like Flanders, even if they had been able to do so. But they let it count as a warning – and to humiliate the great Philip of Burgundy.

To say that the matter had knocked the bottom out of his authority is an understatement. After returning from Calais, the Bruges city militia were not about to behave themselves. Now that they had come back empty-handed they refused to disarm, as was the custom after a military campaign. First they demanded their wages. They had pulled the same stunt on his father in 1411, a dust-up that Philip himself had been allowed to resolve. In addition, Bruges insisted on regaining authority over the nearby city of Sluis, which had been passed on to the duke.

To make it clear that they meant business, members of the militia cut the duke's bailiff's throat. After that they sentenced the captain of Sluis, Roland van Uutkerke, to death in absentia for high treason, in other words because he served the duke more than the city. Van Uutkerke was not just anybody. He was a veteran who had fought on the side of John the Fearless in Othée in 1408. In the mid-twenties he had been one of Philip's strong men in the Holland war, and in 1430 he belonged to the first generation of Golden Fleece knights. *Voilà*, thought the men of Bruges. Now the duke would have to come up with a good answer.

★

On 22 May, Philip the Good and a troop of armed soldiers stood before the gates of Bruges. He swore that he only wanted to pass through the city, that he was on his way to Holland. The Bruggians had a bad feeling about this, and word that 'the duke has come to destroy the city'[1] began to make the rounds.

After a lot of palaver, one of the gates was opened. Even though his marshal, Villiers de L'Isle-Adam, found it anything but wise to enter Bruges under those circumstances, the duke couldn't wait to put spurs to his horse. He reached the Great Market without any problems. But long before all his soldiers were within the city walls, the gates were slammed shut. Encircled by only a few hundred Picardy soldiers, the duke suddenly had the enraged city militia all over him, at least according to Burgundian sources. Chronicler Jan van Dixmude contended that it was the duke's soldiers who attacked the Bruggians, to teach them a lesson. In any event, one thing was certain: on the other side of the wall the

2,500 remaining members of Philip's army began to hear shouting and howling. They stood there helpless, unable to see what was going on.

Arrows were flying thick and fast. The first dead fell. Philip and his small detachment fought their way to the Boeverie gate. On the way, Marshal Villiers de L'Isle-Adam became separated from the rest. The Bruges mob tore off his Golden Fleece chain and unceremoniously lynched him. The naked body of the man who, not very long before, had kicked the English out of the French capital was dragged through the streets of Bruges like a war trophy. In the meantime, Philip managed to force open the Boeverie gate, and the 'Lion of Flanders' galloped all the way to Lille. Once again, history seemed to be taking pleasure in restaging old scenarios. Hadn't it been fifty-five years since Philip's great-grandfather, Louis of Male, also fled from a hostile Bruges on a scrawny nag in the month of May?

After this 'terrible Whitsun Wednesday',[2] the city began a long series of beheadings, since, aside from the duke, only a few of his companions had been able to run for cover. We might say that the Matins of Bruges of 1302 thereby acquired a lesser-known successor 135 years later. We might even call it the Vespers of Bruges, given the time of day. Yet the revolt was soon quelled. An economic blockade, increasing hunger, a plague epidemic, a fundamental lack of support from the other Flemish cities and a severe winter finally brought Bruges to its knees in 1438.

The 280,000-pound fine that Philip imposed on the city was far more than the city was able to pay. It was almost twice what the entire county of Flanders had turned over to the duke as tribute in 1440, of which Bruges usually accounted for just under 16 per cent. An expiatory chapel was also set up, where hundreds of Bruggians, barefooted and bareheaded, were required to beg the duke for forgiveness. In French, of course. Ten locals were executed – by none other than the hated Van Uutkerke.

It was Hugo van Lannoy, knight of the Order of the Golden Fleece and stadtholder of Holland and Zeeland, who told the duke that from now on he should strive for a comprehensive peace; that a lasting ceasefire would have favoured economic consequences; that only as preserver of the peace could he make himself popular in his northern domains. Otherwise the people of Flanders, Holland and Brabant would regard him as nothing but a treacherous foreigner. After all the suffering, this political lesson did not fall on deaf ears.

In this pursuit of peace, Duchess Isabella would play a leading role in the years to come. First she smoothed things out with the English. She turned out to be a shrewd diplomat and drew on her ancestral roots during the lengthy negotiations in Grevelingen. In the summer of 1439, she presented her husband with a Flemish-English *and* Holland-English trade agreement: free movement of traders and goods!

A strong wind blew over the Low Countries that autumn. It was a monumental sigh of relief. Isabella's popularity in Flanders and Holland knew no bounds. A comprehensive peace seemed somewhat more difficult, but Isabella persisted, and five years later a great armistice between Burgundy and England was the result.

During the long discussions that had taken place in past years, the duchess also succeeded in negotiating the release of the most important prisoners from the Hundred Years War. After twenty-five years in English confinement, the forty-five-year-old Charles of Orléans, knight-turned-poet, set foot on French soil once more. In 1440 he married the fourteen-year-old Marie of Cleves, a niece of Philip the Good. Little by little, the son of the murdered Louis of Orléans would seek reconciliation with the son of the man who had ordered that murder. In 1445, Charles was even received into the Order of the Golden Fleece.

'Et Cetera'

Now that Burgundy was breathing peace and reconciliation, Philip the Good could reflect on all the things he had achieved – and take the time to pass on the history of the House of Burgundy to his son, Charles the Bold.

Charles's great-grandfather, Philip the Bold, was given the duchy in 1363 as a gift from his father for his feats of heroism during the debacle of Poitiers seven years earlier. In addition to realizing the most beautiful artistic dream of the Late Middle Ages in Champmol, the older Philip had established an exemplary standard when it came to better dynastic marriages. He himself had snagged Margaret of Male, the richest heiress on the continent. He had not hesitated to use French money and military means to teach the rebellious Flemings a lesson, but even so he succeeded in building a good partnership with their powerful cities. He then catapulted his son John into bed with Margaret of Bavaria, scion of the dynasty that held sway in Hainaut, Holland and Zeeland, and manoeuvred his second son into the duchy of Brabant. He swung open the door to the north. The opening he created was without guarantees – it would cost blood, sweat and tears to steer those lands into Burgundian waters – but nevertheless it became the foundation of the Burgundian Netherlands. Philip the Bold made himself master of the pieces with which his grandson, Philip the Good, would win the territorial chess game.

The chivalrous nature of grandfather John the Fearless was something the young Charles found particularly appealing. Leading a failed but heroic Crusade, murdering his own cousin without a moment's hesitation, crushing the people of Liège while being driven into a corner in Paris, tirelessly struggling against the diabolical Armagnacs and being horribly massacred – many of these elements would mark Charles's life as well. Lastly, his father, Philip, elevated the pageantry of the Burgundian theatre state to unprecedented heights and brought the chess game of his predecessors to a vigorous end.

Just before Charles's birth, another piece of the puzzle had fallen into place, and Holland and Zeeland had come under his father's protection. After the Kiss of Delft, Philip had handed the management of Holland and Zeeland over to Frank van Borssele, who was assisted in this work by his cousins Philip and Floris. He had also asked Frank to keep an eye on Jacqueline of Bavaria. Since the Delft pact, she was entitled to half the net proceeds from her domains, but clever stewards had figured out a way to profit from this arrangement. She was also a spendthrift. She was always in financial difficulties, and gallant as Van Borssele was, he helped solve her problems.

Legend had it that the two were lovers and had been married in secret. In the war that had only just ended, Jacqueline the Hook and Frank the Cod had been foes, but now they were in bed together. Besides that, their marriage was a violation of what Jacqueline had promised: that she would consult Philip the Good first before marrying for the fourth time. It also came out that Frank van Borssele had his hands in the till, and not for trifling amounts. He had pocketed a small fortune at the duke's expense.

Whether on account of financial misdoings or the secret marriage, Frank van Borssele ended up in prison and Philip seized the opportunity to put the thumbscrews on Jacqueline. If she refused to relinquish Holland and Zeeland, her lover/husband would never be released. It was more pressure than she could bear. Now that she had finally found happiness in love, she didn't want to lose it. In April 1433 she renounced her worldly ambitions for good. Unfortunately, the lady who had made life so difficult for Philip the Good was not granted time enough to enjoy her new-found love. Three years later she died of consumption at age thirty-five.

Philip's hunger was still not satisfied. He had long had his eye on Luxembourg. Hadn't his Uncle Anthony married the heiress Elizabeth of Görlitz? And hadn't their children died without issue? In 1441 the duke paid her an annuity of 7,000 gold florins, and in exchange Elizabeth appointed him governor. But money was not enough. Once again, a campaign was necessary to convince the local inhabitants. After her death in 1451 Philip coughed up another 40,000 gold florins to secure the rights of succession in Luxembourg. He went to a lot of trouble for the vast, thinly populated Luxembourg, which wasn't even rich. But he saw it as an important tactical move to acquire a third ducal title within the Holy Roman Empire. It was also a first attempt to close the large gap between the northern and southern domains. From now on, Philip the Good would go by way of Luxembourg whenever his travels took him from Dijon to Brussels.

The court tutors charged with teaching the young Charles the

Bold which principalities fell under his father's authority gradually came to need a crib sheet and plenty of stamina: Philip Duke of Burgundy, Lower Lorraine, Brabant, Limburg and Luxembourg; Count of Flanders, Artois, the Franche-Comté, Hainaut, Holland, Zeeland, Namur, Boulogne, Charolais, Guînes, Ponthieu, Saint-Pol; Margrave of Antwerp; Lord of West-Friesland, Mechelen and Salins. Chroniclers couldn't be bothered to write out the entire list for every official ceremony they covered, so sometimes they took the risk of mentioning a handful of properties followed by a revealing 'et cetera'. From then on they referred to Philip as 'the Grand Duke of the West'.

Founding father Philip the Bold, as regent to the mentally ill Charles VI, had the great advantage of having direct access to the French treasury. That fairy tale had ended long before, but thanks to the acquisition of about a dozen principalities, grandson Philip the Good made an even stronger showing than his grandfather. There were only two active dynasties in the Low Countries: the House of Guelders and his own, but even that valiant survivor would soon be swallowed up by the Burgundian moloch. The illustrious counts of Holland and dukes of Brabant were gone without a trace.

Whether or not by means of the sword, thanks to disputable or indisputable hereditary claims and owing to trickery, bribery, bargaining, the purchase of a principality or just plain luck: by around 1440 Philip the Good was the ruler of a large portion of the Low Countries. Any balance in his Burgundian empire gradually disappeared. Most of the regions, *and* the most important ones, now lay in the north and contrasted sharply with the original Burgundy and the Franche-Comté. What did Dijon, Dole and Chalon amount to in comparison with Bruges, Ghent, Brussels, Dordrecht or The Hague? The fact that the centre of gravity lay in the north was also apparent from the way Philip referred to his domains. He called the south, the old Burgundy, 'the lands thither', which essentially meant the lands far from me, while the north was 'the lands hither', the lands close to me, the Burgundian Netherlands. This designation (the lands here, the lands there) automatically changed whenever he moved from the north to the south, or vice versa, except he spent so much time in the north that the south became 'the lands thither' in point of fact.

The next quarter of a century was a period of peace and prosperity for Philip's domains. This stability, negotiated by himself and his wife Isabella, finally made it possible for Philip to realize his dream: to work on a thorough Burgundification of the Low Countries. The personal union that he had put together from various principalities slowly began to assume the air of a state.

'Others Get To Skim Off The Cream'

In the historiography of the Low Countries, the Burgundian dukes were long regarded as foreign oppressors who were out to destroy the individual character of the people of Brabant, Flanders and Holland. Only later did historians raise them up as miraculous founding fathers who, with an unprecedented display of ostentation, transformed a group of highly diverse regions into pearls that shone in the Burgundian crown. It was the Belgian historians in particular who went in search of the young nation's ancient roots. They dug up the long-forgotten Burgundians, and in the process they stumbled on the figure of Philip the Good.

At first, Philip the Good was just as much of a tyrant as the later Spanish ruler Philip II, but now, as *conditor Belgii* – unifier of the Low Countries – he was more or less smothered with affection.[3] In the Netherlands, by contrast, he was long seen as the aggressive duke who so stimulated the innate longing for autonomy in the northern Low Countries that he essentially pointed the way to the revolt of the 1570s against the Spanish Habsburgs. Healing unifier or prophet of division? It all depended on which big story you as a historian wanted to write.

Whichever view historians supported, the emphasis was almost always on the centralized power of the duke: he was the indispensable linchpin in the process of unification. Only much later would researchers conclude that this interpretation failed to recognize the influence of economic factors, and in further research the emphasis would be placed on the role of the duke's subjects themselves in this process, which should not be underestimated. The truth probably lies nowhere in its entirety but everywhere in small amounts. There's no denying the centralizing energy brought to bear by Philip the Bold, and especially by Philip the Good, but the reader of this book must have noticed how often and to what extent cities played a corrective role. At the same time, it was clear that even during the thirteenth century a number of principalities had become part of the same economic network and would therefore benefit from political unity to a certain extent. So the correct questions are not: duke or cities? Politics or economy? The formation of the Burgundian state is not a chicken-or-egg story but the result of continuous interaction between the duke and his subjects, an interplay between centralizing forces and economic patterns.

★

It's too easy to insist that Philip the Good conquered the Low Countries with the sword. It would be more correct to say that he fought a path to the best place at the negotiating table. He appeared there with a real sense of urgency – and even more than that, as a possible saviour.

The fact that Philip occupied such a comfortable position there was partially owing to the misrule of the regional sovereigns. We need only glance at the way the finances were handled by the old counts and dukes of Holland, Brabant and Hainaut to understand what was going on. What we see – or better, what we don't see – is simply inconceivable: the towering mountains of debt hiding everything from view. Today the media would discuss the insolvency of the old royal houses in minute detail. What seemingly caused their ruination was an overly luxurious life at court. But no matter how profligate their habits, the cost of frivolous feasts was always a fraction of the sums they spent on warfare. The Brabant campaigns in the Meuse-Rhine basin, the involvement of Hainaut in the French civil war, the county of Namur that lived in constant conflict with the prince-bishopric of Liège, the continual flare-ups between the Hooks and the Cods in Holland...

Not one of the royal houses was able to come up with the money needed to fund these exorbitant wars. In order to survive, the counts and dukes put up pieces of land as collateral (which they were almost never able to buy back), made stabs at currency devaluation, were guilty of issuing endless annuities... all of them measures that led directly to financial ruin. 'The land and the borders of Brabant are withered, violated, pawned and disfigured, in all sorts of areas and aspects, in the villages as well as in the interest rates, in seigniories and in many other ways,'[4] stated the members of the States of Brabant in 1407. It wasn't much better elsewhere, but Namur beat the lot. Acting out of pure necessity, the count put his principality on the auction block. It was a bargain for someone like Philip the Good. An all too familiar scenario, but that's the way it was: what the leaders in the Low Countries lacked in the early years of the fourteenth century was... a long-term vision. The ultimate consequence of that failure has just as familiar a ring to it: unmanageable indebtedness.

But now the old principalities were nowhere to be seen. They had been shoved aside by Philip the Good, the man whom the city officials were staring down on the other side of the negotiating table. Did the Burgundian have rightful claims on his side? The fact that some of the dynastic lines had petered out due to insufficient fertility made the arrival of a new leader necessary, of course, certainly if he came equipped with persuasive military power. But other than that, the Burgundian had few actual arguments going for him. Whether it had to do with the transfer of power in Hainaut, Holland, Zeeland, Brabant, Namur or Luxembourg, the duke had never been the most obvious party, let alone the most legitimate. There were always others who had more rights than he did.

But the city representatives could not afford to vet Philip by scrutinizing the rules of succession. Who would be the best person to do business with? A powerless aunt or moderately wealthy female cousin who, according to the uncompromising law of dynastic lineage, had legitimacy on their side, or the fabulously rich Duke of Burgundy? After all, he stood at the head of a state apparatus that was beaming with health. He had

Flanders under his Burgundian bonnet, still the front runner of the West European economy. Philip also managed to pull out all the stops during times of financial crisis by throwing wild parties and banquets. He seemed to be the best guarantee for peace, at least within the borders of the Burgundian Netherlands, so that the economic network that had been created there could calmly continue to develop. And finally, he was prepared to buy out the rightful claimants with large sums of money.

Naturally, the city elites chose the irresistible Duke of Burgundy. On the other hand, these separate transfers of power were not simply unilateral decisions made by the duke alone. Philip and his representatives had to talk long and hard about the stipulations of each transfer. Many of the cities in the Burgundian Netherlands had a strong tradition of advocacy on behalf of special interests. In each city there were craft guilds, corporations of traders and religious brotherhoods that defended the interests of their members. When dissatisfaction arose, they joined forces. This sometimes led to spectacular uprisings, as we saw in the time of the two Van Arteveldes in Ghent, but it could also mean that the brewers might turn off the taps for a few days. It's important to note that the vast majority of the urban proletariat did not belong to any umbrella organization, let alone be represented in the city council. That role was reserved for the grand masters of the various trades. Real democracy was nowhere in evidence, except for representation of the richest members of society, a top layer that determined city policy.

Towards the end of the Middle Ages, the rulers of the Low Countries had no choice but to let themselves be advised by the increasingly wealthy townspeople. The influence of the clergy and the nobility shrank noticeably beside that of cities like Ghent, Bruges, Antwerp, Leuven, The Hague, Dordrecht... In Brabant an actual league of cities emerged, Flanders had the Four Members, and elsewhere there were urban alliances that outweighed the policies of their prince.

Philip the Good had no plans to ignore these new forces. He was all too aware that that's where the money was. Without their support he'd find himself back in troubled waters, which was something he was not eager to see happen. The disabling of the old principalities had been very demanding, so during the negotiations with the townspeople he was quite willing to make certain concessions. The weight of the clergy in this debate had been reduced to almost nothing. A select group of noblemen still kept a finger on the pulse. But Philip's most important interlocutors in the Low Countries were undoubtedly the city elite.

He did everything he could to encourage the mixing of the ducal and the city elite. The old feudal tie between liege lord and vassal took on middle-class ramifications. The duke held on to the rich burghers by pampering them with gifts, top functions and donations. In exchange, they represented and defended the duke's rule. This system formed the cement of Burgundification in the Low Countries, and of course it played right into the hands of what we today would call fraudulent practices and outright nepotism. After all, the Burgundian web could not be allowed to extend too far; the club of power players had to be limited to a number of wealthy families. During the first quarter of Philip's reign, three-quarters of the brewers of Ghent who attained the coveted status of master brewer were the sons of master brewers, after which that figure rose to 95 per cent. Admittance to the club of the rich became more difficult, and the frustration of those who fell by the wayside subsequently increased. At the request of the patricians of Ghent, Philip signed a harsh measure into law in 1437 directed against gentlemen of lower rank who thought they could work their way to the top by raping or abducting gentlewomen.

As time passed, the richest members of the commercial bourgeoisie were the local clients of the duke. This ever-growing conflict of interest boiled over into resentment among the common people on more than one occasion and was partly the cause of the Bruges revolt of 1437. Van Uutkerke, favourite of Philip the Good and symbol of the system, became a target for their ire. In the meantime, the members of the power network began modelling themselves after the duke. From their choice of clothing to their etiquette, everything was imitated – even Philip's Joan of Arc hairstyle: very short and neatly trimmed above the ears. Occasionally, even his art patronage was mimicked. A good example of this was the *Ghent*

Altarpiece, essentially the imitation of a ducal pattern of behaviour that was executed by the official court painter at the behest of a very rich burgher. While the Burgundification of the Low Countries happened at cruising speed, Philip's preference for grandeur and decorum was increasingly imitated, confirming Burgundy's reputation as a 'theatre state'.

*

The old dynastic houses may have disappeared one by one, but the regional policy bodies didn't suddenly dissolve into thin air. Gradually, Philip would reform the old administrative structures and try to erase the disparities between them.

First and foremost, the Burgundian court came to take the place of the various regional courts. The relentless overhauling of these courts was an unmitigated disaster for countless equerries, chamberlains, secretaries, quartermasters, bakers, soup chefs, bellows boys, barbers and other cup-bearers who found themselves out of a job from one day to the next. Someone who had only recently been enjoying the view from his 'high horse' was now reduced to 'sitting in the mud in full livery' and 'walking the streets like a poor wretch with a runny nose', wrote the Brabant chronicler Wein van Cotthem. Now that Philip the Good had come to power as the central Burgundian duke, 'there were others who got to skim off the cream'.[5]

In 1371 the Burgundian duke had approximately a hundred courtiers and servants in his employ. This number climbed to 300 in 1445–50, and peaked in the seventies at 900. Like his predecessors, Philip the Good refused to choose a fixed location for his court. Cities fought to host him, since naturally the arrival of his household was good for business. And the duke profited by having his palaces freshened up at their expense. He divided his time mainly between Brussels (Coudenberg Palace, 22 per cent of the time), Lille (Palais de la Salle and Rihour Palace, 11 per cent), Bruges (Prinsenhof, 10 per cent), Dijon (Palace of the Dukes, 6 per cent), Ghent (Prinsenhof or Hof ten Walle, 4 per cent), Mechelen (the later Hof van Savoye, 0.5 per cent), and other locations (46.5 per cent). A quick tally shows that the duke spent almost one out of every two days in Flanders or Brabant. Hainaut, Holland and Zeeland got the worst of it, and the old Burgundy seems to have disappeared almost entirely from the radar. Obviously, the power centre lay in the southern Low Countries.

The hours and days that the duke spent on the road – in the company of personnel, kitchen equipment, household furnishings, stalls and library – must have been almost innumerable. Philip ruled over more than a hundred thousand square kilometres, an empire with almost three million subjects. He had to let himself be seen. Back then, the giants of the earth couldn't provide evidence of their lives by opening a Twitter account. His subjects wanted to gaze upon the duke with their own eyes so they could believe he was still alive. Time after time, Philip apologized to his people. 'In view of the fact that we have to govern and watch over many other regions, we have no choice but to be in as many different towns and lands as possible.'[6] Because of his scant presence in the northern Low Countries, a rumour made the rounds in Holland in around 1464 that he had been missing for the past ten years.

Like the impressive battalion of pots and pans, the duke's Privy Council also followed him around. It was the heart of the Burgundian system, about forty-five men who had responsibility for the day-to-day administration. At the head of this ambulatory Privy Council was the chancellor, the duke's right-hand man, a function held by Nicolas Rolin for more than forty years. At the end of the 1430s, when the great unification was in full swing, the Great Council split off from the Privy Council. This Great Council functioned as a central supreme court where important cases having to do with the ducal government could be heard, but also where sentences rendered locally could be appealed. The local and regional common law continued to exist, and collided on more than one occasion with the centralized organ. Philip also created regional financial antennae. These courts of auditors were located in Lille, Brussels and The Hague, and in Dijon in the south. They exercised effective control over the income and expenses of the bailiffs, stewards and tax collectors. At the head of these bodies was a general governor for financial flows, a kind of permanent minister of finances.

This evolution marked the beginning of professional management in the Low Countries. Indeed, as time went by the councils came to be staffed less frequently by nobles. Experts who had been properly educated and had a solid background in jurisprudence and bookkeeping took the reins. Pieter de Leestmaker, also known as Bladelin, made a deep impression on the duke during the years 1436–8. This merchant's son, who had been retrained as a financial expert, did all he could to solve the runaway conflict that had developed between Bruges and the duke. His efforts went down well with Philip, who soon appointed him the first governor-general of finances. Bladelin benefited very nicely from the new job. In around 1440 he had a sumptuous palace built that you can still admire today on the Naaldenstraat in Bruges. His position made him so self-confident that, like Joos Vijd, he had himself immortalized as the patron of a painting. He asked Rogier van der Weyden to make a *Nativity Triptych*. On the right side of the central panel Bladelin is prominently shown kneeling, his eyes piously downcast. Rising behind him are the towers of the Flemish town of Middelburg, which he founded.

In order to train financial experts and specialists in canon and Roman law, the right kinds of schools were required. These also took shape under Philip the Good. In 1423 the University of Dole emerged as the intellectual centre of southern Burgundy. The choice of Dole was no accident. After the murder of his father, Philip had only just come to power and Nicolas Rolin was his recently appointed chancellor. One year later, Rolin married Guigone de Salins, a prosperous lady from the Franche-Comté, as you might expect, of which Dole was one of the more important cities. It was obvious that Philip was going to found his own university in Dijon, but the French king, as the rightful liege lord, had put a stop to it, even though he had no authority over the Franche-Comté. So the founding of the University of Dole was essentially Philip's way of giving Paris the middle finger.

Three years later, the Alma Mater of Leuven was established. Brabant, like the Franche-Comté, had traditionally been attached to the Holy Roman Empire, which once again did not interfere. Officially, John IV was behind the founding of the University of

Leuven, but in reality it was an initiative of the city councillors. They hoped to counter the slow decline of the cloth industry by injecting their city with a new intellectual spirit. These interests extended far beyond Brabant, of course, because the target audience comprised all the inhabitants of the Burgundian Netherlands. The fact that Philip the Good had a soft spot for the university became apparent when he asked the pope to add a theological faculty in 1426–7.

It was essential that two fully fledged universities be quickly established in the Burgundian hereditary lands. Because of the continuing wars, wealthy parents were no longer willing to send their children to Paris, Bologna or Montpellier by way of unsafe routes.

'As If All The Devils Of Hell Were On Their Way'

Bladelin, Vijd and Rolin were symbols of what, with a bit of goodwill, you might call the Burgundian dream: well-to-do burghers who belonged to the right circles could accumulate a great deal of power and wealth, as long as they had some talent and training. The time was past when all you had to do was produce aristocratic bona fides to make a career for yourself in a prince's household and administration.

The nobility had missed the modernization train. Flemish nobleman Jean de Lannoy, a beloved courtier of Philip the Good, admitted to his son Louis in a letter from 1465 that because of his lack of education he was incapable of exercising any administrative influence. Although he had been active for years at the highest level, he felt that the finer points of policy kept slipping through his fingers. His letter is the testimony of an aristocrat who realized that if the nobility didn't watch out, they would simply be replaced by a horde of scholars. That evolution seemed difficult to stop. Since it was obvious that they didn't know the first thing about the technical aspects of good governance, more and more noblemen fell by the wayside. Men whose great role models had once conquered Jerusalem were now being pushed to the margins.

In its slow descent into insignificance, the centuries-old rank of knight clung to epic stories in which Lancelot, Parsifal and Arthur were still able to wield the sword with authority. As ivy overran their castle walls, the knights themselves sought refuge in literary fictions from bygone days. The worse it got for the knightly rank, the greater the success of those stories, as demonstrated by the collection of the Burgundian Librije. That ducal library, which grew from 150 books at the time of Philip the Bold to almost one thousand items over the course of the fifteenth century, contained many such popular stories of chivalry. Literature proved to be the world in which the knight would live the longest – until a century and a half after the death of Philip the Good, when even there he gave up the ghost and would survive in the collective memory as Cervantes' befuddled hero from La Mancha. At that point, it was a matter of waiting for Sir Walter Scott and his *Ivanhoe* (1819) before the knight would finally be presented again as a credible hero.

While knighthood as an institution seemed doomed, the nobles themselves remained firmly in place and would occupy front-row seats until the French Revolution. But increasingly the knightly dimension of their lives took on all the glamour of an honorary title whose value had more to do with nostalgia than with the reality of heroic warriors on horseback. While the knights' painful decline gradually entered its last phase during the days of Philip the Good, the old estate went out with a bang. It died in a setting of tournaments and banquets that were among the greatest and most luxurious in history. The Burgundian Knight of the Golden Fleece Jacques de Lalaing was one of the last swordsmen to incarnate the aura of Charlemagne and Arthur. An enemy cannonball robbed the famous knight of his head and his life in 1453. What was the power of the sword in the face of such fire?

Besides the impressive increase in the proportion of archers – from 12 per cent during the Battle of Westrozebeke in 1382 to 70 per cent under Philip the Good – the use of artillery also intensified. Philip the Bold had 80 pieces of ordnance at his disposal, while his grandson would deploy 575 during the siege of Calais in 1436 and would purchase more than 300 in the years that followed. The most practical weapon was the blunderbuss or arquebus, a kind of handheld cannon that was mounted on a hook-like stand and could be operated with relative ease by a single individual.

The medieval cannon, also called a bombard, grew bigger and bigger in size and involved entirely new logistics. You need only think of 'Dulle Griet' (named after a Flemish folklore figure), which peacefully adorns the Friday Market in Ghent today, to realize how much extra manpower and horsepower such a super cannon required. This monster of more than twelve tons, sister of the famous Mons Meg that today resides in Scotland at Edinburgh Castle, dates from the time of Philip the Good and could fire a 300-kilogram cannonball. When this 'stone cannon of marvellous size [...] was fired, it could be heard from five hours' walking distance during the day and ten hours' distance at night,' a chronicler stated, 'and at the firing, the thunderous roar was so great that it was as if all the devils of hell were on their way.'[7]

Dulle Griet involved a fairly complicated bit of assemblage. The barrel alone required thirty-two separate pieces that were welded together and then girded with sixty-one hoops. Aiming the cannon to hit a target was simply out of the question. Monsters like this could not easily be turned to the left or the right, and directional mechanisms wouldn't be invented until the beginning of the sixteenth century. But when it came to the razing of city walls, they were of inestimable value.

As far as the knighthood of yore was concerned, the 'devils of hell' really had been unleashed. Not only were the knights forced to relinquish their decisive role on the battlefield and in sieges to the archers and cannoneers, but in the ducal administration they were also swept away by the writers of bills of exchange. Philip, who admittedly had a weakness for the old-fashioned chivalric ideals, surrounded himself more and more with legal scholars and retrained merchants. Countless aristocrats missed the boat and could no longer be assured of a place in political or administrative councils.

Eventually, the decreasing number of noblemen in the Burgundian government was conveniently dealt with. The duke would simply elevate dozens of members of the new elite to the peerage. Not only was this a way of honouring them, but the certificate of blue blood they received was necessary for expediting communication with the remaining aristocratic officials. Bladelin may have been minister of finance, but as a commoner he could not openly communicate with lords and viscounts, according to tradition. Philip handily solved this problem by creating a new kind of nobleman, while at the same time giving an extra boost to the typically Burgundian entanglement of elites.

Despite the downward spiral that affected mainly the local nobility, the upper echelons of the old nobility managed to hold their own. The duke invariably needed experienced nobles when it came to diplomatic missions. In that context, the proper knowledge of etiquette and the aura of old family trees always made an impression. Even the army commanders had blue blood. Moreover, the upper crust of the aristocracy always managed to scoop up the top jobs in the Burgundian civil service, if they hadn't already been conscripted into the Order of the Golden Fleece or appointed stadtholder.

The stadtholder was the substitute for the duke in his various domains. Philip could hardly be everywhere at once. The members of the council chambers, who helped the stadtholders in their tasks, were given permanent positions, usually in the old royal palaces. High-ranking aristocrats and knights of the Golden Fleece like Roland van Uutkerke and Louis de Gruuthuse were so honoured. The duke had learned that appointing local notables could end badly – take the corruption of Frank van Borssele, for example – and in a rather modern move he would appoint more and more outsiders. The chance of better leadership seemed greater, the danger of local conflicts of interest smaller. In any event, the two aforementioned Flemings did rise to the position of stadtholder in Holland and Zeeland.

'Faithful Friends'

The phenomenon that finally brought about a real sense of solidarity in the Low Countries was the result of pressure from the cities of Brabant and Holland. They successfully appealed to the duke to introduce a common currency, which Philip himself agreed would be quite useful. The language he used at the time of the launching seems very modern to us today. He characterized 'a stable currency' as 'the most important driving force' behind 'the prosperity of people and prince'.

The coin known as the *'vierlander'* (or 'four lands') was issued in 1433 and was so named because it was originally put into circulation only in the four most important economies of the Low Countries: Flanders, Brabant, Holland and Hainaut. In practice it also came to be used in Limburg, Luxembourg, Namur, Artois and Zeeland, so that, from 1443 on, all of Philip's subjects in the Low Countries could make payments with the same currency. The alloy (proportion of pure gold or silver) was based on the most widely used coin at the time, the Flemish groat. The fact that the depreciation of the currency was practically nil for decades is indicative of remarkable economic stability.

Now that everyone was using the same coinage, was it simply coincidental that there was also an increase in interregional consultations? Whether it had to do with the setting of tolls, competition with the cities of the Hanseatic League or the endless vicissitudes of the wool trade with England, the various regions of the Burgundian Netherlands were more and more inclined to coordinate their positions as a whole. This resulted in an economic front in which it was difficult for other lands or trading partners to play the regions against each other.

*

The classical taxes were collected largely in the form of tithes, leases, fishing rights, duties on logging, fines, tolls, import duties and excise taxes. Collection was a chaotic affair in most of the regions, but Philip the Good tried to regulate it by means of his courts of auditors. His Burgundian state was costing him more and more money, and in addition to the normal taxes he also regularly demanded additional financial support – except it was getting harder and harder for him to get away with it. From now on he had to produce a solid explanation every time he came round asking for what was known as a 'benevolence'. Gradually, a connection arose between paying taxes and having a say in things. Quid pro quo.

The classical reasons for imposing benevolences were the payment of ransom money if the prince had been imprisoned (John the Fearless in Nicopolis), a wedding (Philip in Bruges) or the waging of war (without Flemish funds, John the Fearless could never have taken Paris in 1418). The delegates of the cities rightfully argued that they could never be sure whether all the funds were actually being used for the alleged purpose. Was it government money well spent or a brazen shakedown? Discussions on this point became increasingly arduous.

To remedy the situation, Philip the Good pulled a rabbit out of his hat in 1447. At least, he thought he had come up with a magical solution by levying taxes on salt, the so-called *gabelle*. It would guarantee regular revenue and prevent him from having to negotiate with the cities every time he needed some extra cash. Salt was extracted only in Salins (the Franche-Comté) and Biervliet, so checking these two sources would be relatively easy. Yet he didn't want to put his proposal on the table everywhere at once. First he went to Ghent, his largest city – and his most obstinate. If he could make headway with those tough customers, he would undoubtedly succeed everywhere else.

He stirred so much honey into his discourse that the councilmen of Ghent knew right away that caution was called for. 'Good people, faithful friends. You all know that I have lived here since early childhood, and that I grew up here. That is why I love this city, far more than any of my other cities.'[8] Of course he loved it. He was desperate for money. His latest exploits and the acquisition of Luxembourg had cost him bucketfuls of cash. But, he said, and not without exaggeration, the duchy was the perfect buffer for the defence of Flanders and Brabant. He even presented the military conquest of Holland and Zeeland as important protection for his Flemish crown jewel. Philip spoke in terms of a just war; he had 'God and justice' on his side.[9]

While he was at it, the duke praised the possible salt tax as an act of good governance. And that's how it looked at first. Salt was something that everyone made use of, not only in the preparation of food but even more so in its preservation. So this tax would affect all the duke's subjects – the rich possibly more than the poor, he said. That was a misrepresentation of the facts, for in proportion to their general budget it would be the least affluent who would be most burdened by a salt tax. But the duke carried on undeterred. Hadn't his previous benevolence been a blow to the farmers? Hadn't they been 'milked so dry' that the poor wretches had hit rock bottom? This tax was the solution! Everything would be more fairly distributed.

What was so repellent to the people of Ghent was the permanent character of such a tax. To agree to such a thing would mean there would never be anything more to negotiate, whereas up until now they had always had a say in what extra amount they would contribute. So Philip's proposal to eliminate the annual benevolence in exchange for the new salt tax was rejected. Perhaps social motives would be the deciding factor, but nothing in the world would persuade Ghent to give up its influence.

Now that his 'faithful friends' had let him down, Philip was boiling with rage. The two heads of the craft guilds had assured him that his salt tax would go down well. Their word and their lobbying proved worthless. The city of Van Artevelde had made him look ridiculous. And to make matters worse, the people of Bruges, apparently in lockstep with Ghent, had taken the Ghent point of view, and the idea of a salt tax died a silent death. What a difference with France. The subjects there regarded the *gabelle* as normal. That kind of widespread docility was something Philip could only dream of.

Unlike Leiden, or Besançon, where rebellion also broke out during those years, Ghent refused to back down. In most cities, the people realized that it was better to form a unified front with the duke, and in exchange they succeeded in extracting certain privileges. Philip was also capable of being sincerely well disposed towards his cities. In 1452, three-quarters of Amsterdam went up in flames, but thanks to a tax exemption granted by Philip the city was able to pull through. The duke was convinced that this Dutch commercial city was a source of great potential. But cooperation with the recalcitrant people of Ghent was disheartening. The constant friction produced heat that could ignite at any moment. It had long been a source of indignation to Philip that Ghent's jurisdiction went far beyond the city walls, that everyone in that region could easily become a burgher and thereby escape ducal adjudication. In his rage, he tried to have deans of guilds appointed who were favourably disposed towards him, he gave his own bailiff more authority and he challenged the vast Ghent jurisdiction any way he could. Philip then recalled his bailiff and thereby blocked the normal judicial process. He used these kinds of provocations to exert pressure.

The Ghent populace forced the duke's city council to take action against him, and they spread pamphlets with texts that left little to the imagination. 'You gutless weaklings of Ghent, / Who now hold the government, / We'll no longer report it to you, / But will take our complaint to a new Artevelde.'[10] After the duke's supporters were publicly beheaded, Philip declared war on the city.

More than seventy years after his grandfather had shown how it was done in Westrozebeke, Philip cut the Ghentenars to ribbons on 23 July 1453 at Gavere. The unfortunate explosion of a shipment of gunpowder gave rise to panic among the ranks in Ghent. Philip profited from this by ordering a full attack. The duke, now fifty-seven years old, fought bravely with his men and dragged his son Charles along with him, just as his great-grandfather John the Good had done with his grandfather Philip the Bold at Poitiers. This was not without danger. He broke his lance and was injured, but he survived the battle.

Yet the victory was far from a joyous occasion for him. During preliminary fighting he had lost both his beloved bastard son Corneille and his highly respected knight Jacques de Lalaing. Almost every military success went hand in hand with loss of life, which would certainly have given a sensitive person like the duke something to reflect on.

*

After the suppression of the rebellious Bruges in 1436–8, Philip had curtailed the judicial power of the metropolis in the western part of the county by appointing as many of his own judges and officials as he could. Now he would do the same in Ghent, which had an even greater sphere of judicial influence that covered almost half the county. He also imposed a fine of 840,000 pounds, almost double the astronomical amount that Bruges had had to pay. Even after he had rounded it down at some point later on, the sum was enough to make the duke quickly forget the salt tax fiasco.

He also demanded a moral penance, of course. On a miniature from 1458 we see Philip the Good on a white horse, observing the Ghentenars, stripped down to their underwear, barefooted, bareheaded and kneeling, as they beg him for forgiveness. And he granted it too. Ghent was neither plundered nor destroyed. In that respect, Philip more than lived up to his epithet 'the Good'. 'The Ghentenars are my people; the city is mine. If I should burn it to the ground, I do not know any living creature who could build its like for me.'[11]

The duke was shown this incredibly beautiful miniature during his progress of 1458. Such a Joyous Entry basically amounted to a festive introduction to a new sovereign, who promised to respect the privileges of the city in exchange for the recognition of his authority. But very occasionally, as in this instance, the ritual assumed the form of a great ceremony of reconciliation. A born-again Ghent offered its duke a 'joyous and lavish' salute.[12] In addition to brass bands and theatrical performances, the city served him a monumental tableau vivant: a living depiction of Hubert and Jan van Eyck's *Ghent Altarpiece*, spread out across three levels. At the very top of the scaffolding was Christ enthroned, exactly as he was shown in the original painting. Philip must have felt like a messiah himself. Wasn't he the ruler of the Low Countries, now more than ever? His successes in Ghent and Bruges, the two biggest and richest cities of his dominion, inspired other cities into submissiveness. He was even able to scale back a number of city privileges in the powerful Brabant.

A century earlier, Ghent was at least as rich as the Count of Flanders, and Leuven could easily match the Duke of Brabant in terms of wealth. But by acquiring so many principalities Philip was able to bolster his war chest on a much greater scale than his regional predecessors. The cities experienced that first-hand, but the lack of solidarity and the competitive struggles there also played into Philip's hands. However much the Burgundian duke was intent on sharing his power with the urban elites, when push came to shove he always managed to gain the upper hand. So his era was an important step in the direction of the monarchical state.

'Lands Of Promise'

Surprisingly enough, outside Philip's court there was no over-arching organ that bridged the gap with old Burgundy. The south played no part in the pursuit of centralization, making the Low Countries in fact an entity unto themselves. Beside this structural conversion to a state of unity there was the great renewal taking place in the professionalization of the civil service. For the first time, not only did the legal and financial experts receive a fixed salary but so did the councilmen, and they were all engaged on the basis of their skills. Feudal customs were discarded in favour of concepts like bureaucracy, salary and personnel. Words like prosecutor, lawyer and cassation were introduced and would survive the centuries.

Naturally, the implementation of this whole system was very time-consuming, and there were plenty of bumps along the way. The clientelism by which the duke placated the elite and won them over to his side opened the door to corruption. Philip's courts of auditors were entirely incapable of channelling the problem of informal flows of money. Much to his exasperation, he himself was in it up to his neck. Although the expenses in this regard were astronomical, it was evidently difficult for him to say no when friends, or friends of friends, came to him for favours. The difference between public and private monies was virtually non-existent at almost every level.

When the duke was no longer able to alleviate his need for large sums of money by means of regular taxes or benevolences, he began leasing public offices. He would demand an advance on the money that high-level officials would earn. But if the functionary in question later proved incompetent, Philip couldn't just rap his knuckles, let alone dismiss him, unless he came up with the sum he had been paid earlier. This leasing of offices considerably weakened Philip's position as ruler. Another problem in the unification of the Burgundian Netherlands was the vastly unequal geographical distribution of both courtiers and knights as councilmen. A majority of them came from French-speaking Flanders, Picardy, Artois or Burgundy itself. French was and remained the administrative language. Gradually, the shortage of members from Brabant, Zeeland and Holland was redressed, but the proportions remained unbalanced.

Despite all these shortcomings, the duke did succeed in creating an image of a good ruler. At the end of the fifteenth century, the French chronicler Philippe de Commynes even looked back with longing to the reign of Philip the Good. Either all the abuses and failings seemed to have dissolved in the patina of his nostalgia, or the misery of the present situation made the past look good by comparison. 'In those days, the subjects of the House of Burgundy enjoyed great abundance because of the long-lasting peace they lived through and the goodness of their sovereign, who levied few taxes on them. It seems to me that his lands, more than any other seigniory on earth, can be called lands of promise. They were inundated with riches and were places of great tranquillity, which was not the case afterwards. People spent a great deal of money, the clothing of both men and women was sumptuous, the meals and banquets grander and more lavish than in any other place I know of.'[13]

While the proverbial pinch of salt is called for in reading these overblown words, the scales really did tip in a positive direction, especially in the Burgundian Netherlands. Purchasing power rose and remained high, the currency was stable, the economy grew, the tax burden stayed within reasonable limits, and above all Philip made sure there was peace at the borders. From 1440 until just after his death in 1467, there lived a generation in the Low Countries that had it significantly better for the most part than the generations that preceded and succeeded it. The southern Low Countries would have to wait until the nineteenth century to reach that level again. This success did not alter the fact, however, that for the lowest strata of the population, poverty remained structural. The chance is small that Philippe de Commynes had farmers, labourers and minor craftsmen in mind when he wrote his remarks. But he could observe with his own eyes that the elite here were more widespread than in the neighbouring lands.

*

Of course, the Burgundian Netherlands was a far cry from the image we have of a modern state, but it was in those regions that the first far-reaching steps were taken in that direction: courts of law that had to respect certain rules and procedures; a form of financial control, thanks to the courts of auditors; a successful currency that was in circulation everywhere; an impressive coordinating royal court; and naturally an army, which barely resembled that of Philip the Bold owing to the increase in archers and artillery, although the days of Charles the Bold, when Burgundy finally had a permanent army at its command, would still be a long time coming. Philip had to recruit anew for every campaign he planned. Apart from the vassals – aristocrats who could be called up for no more than a month and preferred to operate within their own borders – the mercenaries who fought in Philip's military actions in the Low Countries were mostly from Picardy and Hainaut.

Despite the considerable success of the reforms, you could hardly call the Burgundian Netherlands an organic whole. They were more like a fused entity of independent lands, a construct that in a way is comparable to the European Union. Just as in Europe today, the separate lands back then were governed by centrally controlled regional organs and rulers. While the *vierlander* might be considered a distant precursor of the euro, a single currency does not a union make. The Burgundian coin could not keep the various inhabitants from thinking of themselves as Flemings, Zeeuws, Hollanders or Brabantians – and perhaps Ghentenars or Amsterdammers first of all – rather than Burgundians, just as the people of Europe today think of themselves more as Belgians, Dutch or French than Europeans. Despite all attempts at centralization, the parts were and are more important than the whole.

In Flanders, Burgundification had already begun in the 1380s, in Brabant around the turn of the century and in Holland not until half a century after Flanders. In most of the northern regions there was much more resistance to the practically monolingual French administration, so the legacy of the Burgundian era is greater in modern Belgium. The painters and composers from the Late Middle Ages whom we venerate today were almost all from the southern Low Countries. The architectural and museological remains are also much more numerous in, say, Ghent or Bruges than in the north. You also notice it in the way the inhabitants see themselves today. In the Netherlands, only the inhabitants of the provinces of Noord-Brabant and Limburg regard themselves as 'real Burgundians', by which they mean they like to 'dine heartily', as the Van Dale Dutch-English dictionary defines it, a quality that Flemings and Belgian Brabantians fully identify with. So gushing about the good life is a direct legacy of the Burgundian era, a period of gastronomic excess and political reforms, which is still something the Belgians seem more fond of than the Dutch.

Between his banquets and his reforms, the duke also spent his time working on a process of popular representation by introducing the French idea of 'States' to his empire: a gathering of clergy, nobility and burghers that usually took place during moments of crisis. His first step was to organize it at the regional level. Such an advisory organ already existed in Brabant, where his grandfather Philip the Bold had launched 'the States of the lands of Flanders' in 1400. In Holland, the phenomenon first appeared at the Kiss of Delft in 1428. Philip would gradually create the same system in Namur and Luxembourg. These States would meet every now and then, occasionally with representatives from several regions at the same time, but they were far from a real States General that represented the entire nation, as there was in France.

Yet it did happen, and just before his death. The duke could credit this institutional breakthrough to the most spectacular plan of his life: Philip had made up his mind to go on Crusade.

PHEASANT AND FOX

*Or how a palace of an infirmary for the indigent sick arose
in the village of Beaune in Burgundy, how the Hundred
Years War finally came to an end, and how at exactly the
same moment another event shook the old world to its
foundations and tempted Philip the Good to undertake an
unprecedented spectacle.*

A NAKED CHRIST, draped in a luxurious vermilion robe edged in gold, is seated on a rainbow with a globe beneath his feet. The message is clear: this is the ruler of the universe, as human as he is unassailable. Below him is the archangel Michael, weighing souls on the Day of Judgement. With his right hand Jesus blesses the good sons of men, and with his left he consigns the bad to hell. This masterpiece of composition and colouration, which the sick people in the brand-new hospital of Beaune would be shown on Sundays and feast days, was finished in good time. Rogier van der Weyden had worked himself to the bone. Now his *Last Judgement* hung in the great infirmary, folded shut and waiting for the first group of patients.

On 31 December 1451, Chancellor Nicolas Rolin, without whom none of this would have come about, strolled through the corridors of his immense hospital just before the solemn opening. This was a satisfied man. At the age of seventy-five, he had every right to call himself a privileged witness to a troubled era. He had grown up during the Flemish-Burgundian crisis of the 1370s and 1380s, learning to live with the fact that there were two popes and that England and France had already been at each other's throats for decades. He was still a young man when John the Fearless returned from his failed expedition to Nicopolis, twenty-five when he distinguished himself as legal advisor to Philip the Bold, thirty-two when the French-Burgundian civil war broke out and he was given a permanent position as lawyer for Burgundy, forty-three when Duke John was murdered, and forty-five when he took the greatest step of his career and was appointed chancellor and right-hand man for Philip the Good. At the age of fifty-nine he reached what he regarded as the pinnacle of his career: negotiating the Treaty of Arras and having himself painted by Jan van Eyck.

In all those years, he served his duke faithfully and cunningly, led Philip to great triumphs, assisted him in the Burgundification of the northern domains, and accumulated great wealth while doing so. With death now among the looming possibilities, Rolin wanted to give something back to the world. And so he did, in full Burgundian fashion: with great ceremony, driven by an insatiable appetite for splendour and not without a hefty dose of arrogance. But the result was magnificent. Whether the project was motivated by piety and the desire to secure his salvation was something his contemporaries openly doubted. 'The chancellor was called one of the wisest men in the empire, at least on the worldly plane. As for the spiritual, I would rather not say',[1] in the words of the Flemish chronicler Jacques du Clercq. The chronicles contain quite a few of these negative, if not jealous comments about Rolin. Perhaps the chancellor wanted just one more opportunity to show off his brilliance, this time in the widely cherished glow of Christian charity, and maybe in this case he was sincere. Who can say? Naturally, he had Van der Weyden immortalize himself and his wife, Guigone de Salins, on the outer panels of the painting, and the initials of both their Christian names were scattered throughout the building.

Guigone had told her husband more than once that the war with England had inflicted untold misery, and that the profusion of sick, poor and infirm people were often forced to go without any form of care. So it was his wife who gave him the idea for his final dream. Under the impulse of this couple, and in the placid town of Beaune, rose one of the high points of late medieval architecture. The plans were drawn by the Flemish architect Jacques Wiscrère, possibly a Gallicized form of 'Visscher', or Fisher. The work began in 1443, and to the exasperation of the impatient Nicolas and Guigone it would take almost ten years. But their hospital would be built. And what a hospital!

The Hôtel-Dieu in Beaune is still the showpiece of the

Flemish-Burgundian building style, an architectural jewellery box containing a pearl of fifteenth-century art. If you haven't yet beheld the most beautiful hospital in Western Europe, then make your way to the old duchy and see for yourself. The spectacle of multicoloured roof tiles, chimneys, pinnacles, dormers and weathercocks transports the eye to a world where Flanders and Burgundy are once again intertwined. Gaze upon the wall paintings in which the Ns (for Nicolas) and the Gs (for Guigone) elegantly embrace. Walk attentively through the Salle des Pôvres. Imagine how the rows of beds on either side, neatly divided from each other by red curtains, became the backdrop for fever and disease in early 1452. Look up at the monumental chestnut ceiling that hangs from the sky like an upside-down ship. Slowly count the crossbeams that are spewed forth by dragons. And hold your breath at the *Last Judgement* by the Tournai-born Rogier van der Weyden.

What makes the depiction of the Last Judgement so special is the absence of devils and other monsters. Usually, the evildoers are pushed into the flames of hell by grotesque creatures armed with spikes and pickaxes. Probably Van der Weyden or Rolin were of the opinion that reality had flooded humanity with enough images of damnation in recent years.

'How Sweet It Is To Sit In Solitude And Speak With God'

A year and a half later, westerners were forced to take yet another threat on board. On 29 May 1453, Mehmed II succeeded in conquering Constantinople. The news of the end of the Eastern Roman Empire came like a thunderclap. The Hagia Sophia basilica had become a mosque! After the debacle of Nicopolis, the advance of the Mongols under the leadership of Tamerlane had halted Ottoman expansion, but since the 1420s the Ottomans had made enormous progress. Thanks to powerful cannon made available by the Hungarian iron founder Orban (after having been refused by the Byzantines), the last barrier had fallen. The path to Europe was wide open. In Rome, Pope Nicholas V felt the Antichrist breathing down his neck. Deeply anxious, he called on all of Europe to rise up in response.

There was a lot of shouting over the next few months, but little in the way of action. Then an opening occurred: a tacit armistice that made new military operations possible, at least in theory. On 17 July 1453, the French army, with more than three hundred cannon at its disposal, defeated the English troops at Castillon, fifty kilometres east of Bordeaux. France having real field artillery was an important innovation. Until then, such ordnance had mainly been deployed in the besieging of cities. The English commander Talbot was killed by a cannonball, symbolically enough. Was the shooting of that cannon the last military action of the Hundred Years War, a conflict that had been dragging on for 116 years? Had the prophecy of Joan of Arc finally come to pass?

By all appearances it looked as if the English had been knocked out for good, although it was always possible that at some point they would rise from their ashes. How many supposedly decisive battles and treaties had been followed by even more of the same? Despite all the rancour, this time the sworn enemies would no longer cross swords, although it would take until 1475 for the two countries to officially acknowledge that the summer battle of more than twenty years earlier had really been the final chord of a terrible symphony. Calais, however, remained in English hands until 1558. Until the eve of the nineteenth century, Albion would continue to call its monarchs 'King of England and France'.

Steady improvements in the equipping of the troops in both south-western France and the Bosphorus sealed the end of an era. In the year of our Lord 1453, the battle of Castillon seemed at first like just another horror show. All eyes were focused on the fall of Constantinople. This historic event immediately grew into an outrage without precedent, except that everyone just stood there watching. Only the Duke of Burgundy felt called to great deeds, an impulse that was revealed in typical Philipian fashion.

What was the response of Philip the Good to the news of the century? He would give the feast of the century.

★

While there may have been doubts regarding Rolin's piety, everyone agreed that Philip showed authentic religious zeal. In 1443, after having decided to subjugate Luxembourg by force of arms (even though it had already been bequeathed to him), he was drummed out of bed at two o'clock in the morning. His troops had successfully taken the Saxon garrison in the capital city, and now it was up to him to capitalize on this triumph with all due speed. He jumped into his armour, but while his officers were getting ready to spur their horses, he insisted on praying first. 'Monseigneur could easily wait until later to say his rosary,' his commanding officers said with a smirk. Philip shrugged and spoke words that revealed his deep piety. 'God has given me victory. He will certainly keep it for me.'[2] He then closed his eyes and serenely worked his way through his prayers.

It will not surprise anyone that the library of the duke, who made use of a lantern and eyeglasses when he read, contained several copies of the ever popular *Imitatio Christi* by Thomas à Kempis. The four volumes of this *Imitation of Christ* were published separately starting in 1424, the oldest manuscript with the complete work dating from 1441. The writings of Thomas à Kempis, an Augustinian monk who worked in Zwolle, would become the greatest bestseller of the Low Countries and possibly the whole world after the Bible, with more than eight hundred manuscripts and a hundred incunabula in the fifteenth century alone, and countless printed editions in myriad languages right up to the present day. In 1447 Philip the Good ordered a French translation of the original Latin text for his own personal use.

'I have sought everywhere for peace, but I have found it not, save in nooks and in books' is a quote that is invariably attributed to Thomas. Not only did those words suit him to a T, but they were also a sign of the times. They also reflected an evolution in which his *Imitatio* played an important role. At about the same time as the invention of the printing press, literature underwent another important breakthrough: the private reading of texts in the vernacular. It was a minor revolution for mankind, whose knowledge of literature had long been almost exclusively confined to oral forms: from the performance of farces and passion plays, the telling of fabliaux and the singing of poems or tales of chivalry to the reading aloud of passages from the Bible. Monks, of course, had been gobbling their way through Latin texts on their own for centuries, but *The Imitation of Christ* was the first book that ordinary readers read on the same scale, in their own language and 'in nooks'. That practice was perfect for a work that demanded a deep confrontation with oneself. After the success of the *Imitatio*, reading would never be the same. Another important hurdle was cleared on the way to growing individualization. People became solitary word processors.

Thomas belonged to the spiritual movement known as the Devotio Moderna, whose aim was to reform religious life by emphasizing personal engagement and the prayer lives of the faithful. *The Imitation of Christ* was not a complex treatise but a readable spiritual guide in which every form of theological hair-splitting was avoided. Not mystical contemplation but tips for actual religious practice. The titles of the chapters speak volumes: 'Of the Profit of Adversity', 'Of the Joy of a Good Conscience', or 'Of avoiding Superfluity in Words'. The simple and practical dimension of the work undoubtedly explained part of its success. This little book had everything necessary to make it a practical vade mecum for any believer who could read. 'How wholesome it is, how pleasant and sweet it is, to sit silently in solitude and to speak with God,'³ declared Thomas à Kempis, with which countless readers could agree.

Completely in line with the philosophy of life described by Thomas, Philip wanted nothing more than to stand personally before Christ in his prayers. To a great extent, the whole rhythm of his life was dictated by Christian acts. Philip was strict in performing his religious exercises, which he did with deep devotion. He attended daily Mass, often arriving late to keep from being accosted by other believers. He didn't fail to pray before, during and after battles, thought nothing of fasting on bread and water for a few days at a time, sometimes wore a hairshirt, donated a great many stained-glass windows to places of worship – from the Great Church in Dordrecht to the Hôtel-Dieu in Beaune – was constant in his almsgiving, went on pilgrimages, possessed a number of enviable relics such as the sword of Saint George (whether there was still dried dragon's blood clinging to it is unknown), had a long list of annual Masses said for his ancestors and other important deceased persons, celebrated the name days of several saints by having special Masses said – Saint Andrew in particular, the patron saint of Burgundy and of the Order of the Golden Fleece – and every year on Holy Thursday washed the feet of twelve paupers, to whom he also offered a hot meal.

That the customs of the time demanded a degree of religious zeal was taken for granted, but Philip's religious devotion surpassed the normal bounds. He spent a great deal of time in prayer, as Thomas à Kempis dictated. While those solitary prayer sessions were times of ascesis, his daily attendance at Mass took place in an atmosphere of beauty and mental exaltation. He was the first Burgundian duke to maintain a twenty-member court chapel. He regularly presided over the auditions for new choir members and his standards were extremely high. In 1447 he rejected the services of Johannes Pullois of Pulle in Kempen, who had been the highly esteemed choirmaster of the Church of Our Lady in Antwerp.

The Burgundian's good taste was attested to by his employment of Guillaume Dufay and especially the Mons-born Gilles Binchois as composers for his court chapel. Later, these two would become known as the founders of Flemish polyphony, whose most important exponents were from the Walloon districts. It must have pleased Philip that Dufay and Binchois wrote both religious and worldly music, that they were the first to close the gap between the sacred and the mundane, between the cerebral-intellectual and the physical-sensual, and do it with such elegance. One need only listen to Dufay's *Messe de l'homme armé* or to a handful of Binchois's profane songs to realize how relatively accessible and breathtakingly beautiful their late medieval compositions were, how smoothly the voices or instruments went their own way while at the same time creating melodious harmonies. In this respect Philip clearly distanced himself from Thomas à Kempis, who resolutely chose austerity, and even ugliness if necessary, as long as the music came from the heart. 'If you cannot sing like the lark and the nightingale, sing then like the raven and the frog in the pond, who sing as God gave them to sing.[4]

However devout he may have been, it is by no means certain that Philip the Good strove to imitate the 'life and manners' of Jesus in every possible aspect, to 'be truly enlightened, and be delivered from all blindness of heart', as Thomas wrote on the first page of his book. At any rate, Thomas's aversion to outward show and decorum was difficult to reconcile with Philip's lifestyle. We might also wonder how the deeply religious but incorrigibly lascivious duke dealt with the sensual defilement of his conscience. At least we can be sure that the content of the chapter 'Of the Growth of Patience in the Soul, and of striving against Concupiscence' did not inspire him to change his behaviour. How often must Philip have read the words 'The flesh will murmur against thee' and sighed as he continued: 'but with fervency of spirit thou shalt bridle it.' Perhaps he blamed sexual excess on his alter ego and was able to take refuge in the chapter 'Of bearing with the Defects of Others'?[5]

In any case, Philip was living proof that a person hooked on luxury and sensuality could still be a deeply religious and practising Christian. Evidently, no one even called this contradiction into question.

*

Besides his fondness for devotional practices and Christian love of neighbour, Philip had been entertaining a dream of going on Crusade. The fact that his father had been crushed at Nicopolis didn't stop him from believing that a great army from the west could wipe out the heretics in the Middle East. Hadn't he commissioned Jan van Eyck to make a map of the world? Hadn't he sent a number of Burgundian explorers eastward, sent ships across the billows to protect the Knights Hospitallers of Rhodes from barbarian invasions? Hadn't he had the church of Bethlehem restored at his own expense? Wasn't the Burgundian court a welcoming sanctuary for Byzantine refugees? For Philip, there could be no mistake: the fall of Constantinople was a sign that he should convert all his preparations and plans into great deeds.

The smaller expeditions that he had supported in past years paled in comparison with what he had in mind: an internationally supported Crusade, with himself as the great source of inspiration. Old-fashioned chivalric ideals certainly played a role, although Philip was equally driven by political and religious concerns.

But he was virtually alone. Almost none of his fellow rulers or knights would let themselves get caught up in his enthusiasm. The tenor of their argument was clear: we're no longer in the twelfth or thirteenth century, we have enough to worry about in our own countries, why in God's name sacrifice our money and lives for a victory in Constantinople that would be difficult to secure? But Philip was clever. He knew more than anyone that you could influence minds by providing the appropriate context.

First he had to look for the right place, and he found it in his beloved Lille. Even though his new Rihour Palace was still under construction, the great event he was planning could serve as an ideal swansong for the old Palais de la Salle. The engagement of his niece Elizabeth of Burgundy to John of Cleves seemed to him the perfect occasion. John of Cleves, also known as 'the Baby Maker', was said to have fathered six official and thirty-six illegitimate children, easily outdoing the prolific skirt-chaser Philip the Good. In any event, now that a few hundred nobles would be gathering in Lille, the duke saw the engagement feast as the starting signal for a whole series of banquets and tournaments that would culminate in the widely announced feast of all feasts on 17 February 1454.

'I Will Not Sleep In A Bed On Saturday'

The age of antiquity seemed to be pointing the Burgundians to new horizons. Twenty-five years earlier, Jason had inspired the duke to found the Order of the Golden Fleece, but it didn't stop there. Philip the Good commissioned translators to produce French versions of ancient Latin writings and asked makers of tapestries to weave mythological tales into their work. Historians place the arrival of the Renaissance in the Low Countries in the sixteenth century, but the Burgundians had been digging deep into the culture of classical antiquity well before that.

On 17 February the walls of the great hall of the Palais de la Salle were hidden behind immense wall tapestries depicting the Twelve Labours of Hercules. Once again, Philip used a theme from pagan classical culture to inspire his contemporaries to deeds of Christian heroism. After all, wasn't Hercules the forefather of Gundobad, the fabled Burgundian king from almost a thousand years before – at least, according to legend? On this day, every detail was fitted into a greater whole.

Between the various courses being served, each featuring forty-eight dishes, the guests were treated to a variety of tableaux. As usual, these famous and inimitable *entremets* veered between culture and kitsch. These 'in-between courses' were still partly edible at the time of the Cambrai double wedding in 1385, but now they had become pure spectacle.

Right in the middle was a statue of a naked woman. Her right breast produced a continuous stream of spiced wine, while a real (!) lion lay chained to her feet. Written on a small shield were the words 'Do not touch the lady'. The guests trickled in, held their glasses beneath her breast, and winked at each other. Before taking their seats, they all took the time to admire the decor of the hall.

Gracing the first table was a cruciform church, fitted with artistically styled stained-glass windows and with four singers hidden in the bell tower. This somewhat exalted construction was flanked by a naked little boy on a rock, peeing rose water: the Burgundian version of Manneken Pis, the oldest mention of which, according to later historians, was dug out of a Brussels archive and dated two years before this banquet. Another table had been turned into a gigantic pie. The invitees pointed to it and counted. And yes, there were twenty-eight musicians sitting in the immense construction. Beneath them was a handful of blind people who reportedly were unsurpassed in the playing of the hurdy-gurdy.

The guests moved from one wonder to the next: here an ogre on a camel, there a castle from which orange drink flowed, and over there a Portuguese ship with sailors busily working on their sails. And so it went. You couldn't take it all in. At the end of the tour a magic forest appeared with all sorts of strange beasts: ingenious ambulatory automatons. It couldn't have been easy for the guests to actually sit down at the table, for the precious dinnerware and the diamond-encrusted crystal table fountains were also laid out in great numbers. Chronicler Olivier de la Marche needed so many words to describe it all that he never got around to writing about the food, and had to make do with 'astonishing dishes'.[6]

During the feasting, a musical conversation took place between the singers in the church tower and the pie musicians that consisted of intermezzos written by court composer Gilles Binchois. Sacred songs wafted from the church, the pie was a source of profane melodies, and sometimes the two blended together. Each of Binchois's strains announced new, mobile tableaux.

The duke's painters, sculptors, carpenters, cooks, composers and automaton builders had bent over backwards in staging these flawlessly orchestrated performances. A gnome with animal-like legs and feet rode a wild boar decked out in green silk; the one and only Jason from the original Golden Fleece fought a grim battle with a giant snake; a singing stag carried a child, who gripped the antlers with both hands; and falconers released their birds in an attempt to catch a flying heron. In the meantime, a fire-breathing dragon flew over the heads of the diners like a flash of lightning. Finally, all these profane wonders gave way to what was billed as the religious climax.

Slowly but surely, a giant strode into the hall. The older guests whose memories were still sound recognized Hans, the colossus who had played a starring role during the festivities at Philip's wedding in Bruges twenty-four years earlier. This time he appeared as a Saracen from Granada, one of the few Spanish cities still in the hands of the Moors. He was leading an elephant, a gigantic automaton with a palanquin on its back in which sat a most marvellous figure. This was no ordinary pious female. The lady was the personification of Holy Church, who addressed the public with a long lament. 'My domain is being trampled underfoot [...] It is in the hands of unbelievers. [...] Do not forget the divine mission, you knights of the Golden Fleece [...] he who rescues me will reap fame, his soul will attain glory.'[7] Everyone understood that the high point was imminent. Would a mysterious messenger fall from the sky? They all looked around, breathless with expectation.

In stepped Golden Fleece, a man in flashing armour. He carried in his hands a live pheasant. Around the neck of the bird was a golden chain studded with precious stones. Following him was a procession of warriors and maidens. Golden Fleece knelt before the Grand Duke of the West. It was an ancestral custom, when making spectacular plans, to swear on a peacock, swan or pheasant.

Philip the Good didn't have to be told twice. Slowly, the fifty-seven-year-old rose to his feet and swore that he was more determined than ever to go on Crusade, and that he was ready to challenge the Grand Turk to a duel to the death. He then produced a document on parchment with more chapter and verse and handed it to Golden Fleece, who read out the ducal message in a stentorian voice. Everyone nodded enthusiastically and with great reverence. This did seem like just the right thing to do.

The words of Holy Mother Church and the duke's oath were so effective in moving hearts that one lord after another leaped up in the heat of the moment to make bold pronouncements. Stretching an arm out over the pheasant, Charles the Bold set the example, after which there was no holding back. The lord knights, who until quite recently had not shown the slightest enthusiasm for unleashing a holy war, whipped each other up with their resolutions, which rose to grandiose proportions. 'Until I have skewered a Saracen on my sword, I will not sleep in a bed on Saturdays,' cried the lord of Pons. 'And I will no longer eat meat on Fridays,' vowed the bailiff of Cassel, 'until I have engaged an enemy of our faith in combat.'[8] The seventy-seven-year-old Rolin was the only one to admit that he was not able to make the journey, but he promised to send one of his sons in his place, in the company of twenty-four noblemen. No sooner had this met with sympathetic nods than someone else stepped forward.

Up until then the guests had been sitting like spectators watching a marvellous show, but now, during the dénouement, they found themselves assuming the leading role. There they were, dressed to the nines in the midst of the most outrageous decor they would ever lay eyes on. They looked at each other, thrilled with excitement, glad that they had been given the chance to lend colour to this historic moment. In their midst was the beaming duke. His plan had succeeded beyond his wildest dreams. He had managed to coax all these stubborn souls to do an about-turn. With his head for propaganda, he had also ordered the building of four grandstands so that hundreds of nobles and wealthy burghers who had not been invited to the actual feast could witness this miraculous reversal. Filled with awe, they gazed at the uncrowned king of the Burgundian theatrical monarchy, a radiant Philip the Good at the peak of his powers.

In the meantime, the knights, now transformed into actors, could no longer be restrained and became completely absorbed in the role assigned to them. Before leaving, Philippe Pot promised never to dine on Tuesdays, Hugues de Longueval would drink no more wine until he had spilled the blood of a heretic and Guillaume de Montigny actually swore that, in anticipation of the great event, he would don part of his armour every night before going to bed. The heroes began to speak with such passion that Philip eventually ordered them to stop and asked his guests to put their oaths down in writing. When it was time to leave, everyone seemed ready to mount his horse and ride on to Constantinople in a single stretch.

Montigny would probably have regretted his pious resolution if he had known how many awkward nights in armour awaited him. The bedless Saturdays of the lord of Pons must have started weighing heavily on his mind as well. And after a while Longueval probably wondered whether he would ever drink another glass of wine.

In short, the preparations dragged on.

★

However implausible this 'Feast of the Pheasant' may seem, it's totally consistent with the dukes' tradition of propagandistic feasts. Furthermore, it was described by several chroniclers.

They couldn't all have suffered from mythomania. The few scenes reported here are only the tip of the iceberg. Enthusiasts can consult the chronicles and immerse themselves in the long accounts, where no feature is left unmentioned.

The most important description of Philip's feast in Lille was the work of Olivier de la Marche, a confidant of Philip the Good and a man who really was a jack of all trades. Not only was he a diplomat and writer, but he served as the scenarist and director of the 1454 feast, organizing the event down to the smallest detail, paying all the artists and craftsmen who were involved and even taking part in the spectacle itself. The woman on the elephant, the incarnation of Holy Mother Church, was none other than a brightly made-up and ingeniously costumed Olivier de la Marche.

Although he never hid his enthusiasm for the feast, he did venture a few observations several decades later. La Marche found the staggering amount of cash that the feast had cost 'an excessive and unreasonable expense'. The only thing he found meaningful was the *entremets* of the church – in which he himself played the title role – because it led to so many solemn proposals. But was all the rest really necessary?

The people of the Middle Ages were willing to be a lot more histrionic than we are today. Furthermore, on 17 February 1454 they were more than a little tipsy. Yet the sudden reversal from opponents to enthusiasts for Philip's Crusade is still quite remarkable, although it remained to be seen what the value was of such promises at a time when ceasefires and other agreements were constantly being violated.

In any event, Philip did not despair. He organized meetings in Arras, Bruges and Lille to discuss the practical preparations for the Crusade. Between meetings, he travelled as vassal of the Holy Roman Emperor to the Imperial Diet in Regensburg because Brabant, Hainaut, Holland, Zeeland, Namur and Luxembourg were feudally bound to the Holy Roman Empire. There, too, Constantinople would come up for discussion. But although Philip was received with the utmost courtesy, Frederick III would not commit himself. In fact, the successor to Emperor Sigismund[9] only sent his secretary because he was busy settling a conflict with the Hungarians. Not that he refused Philip his cooperation, but the promises came to nothing.

The duke had secretly dreamed of again asking the emperor for a king's crown for his 'German' domains in the Low Countries. It was that old longing to breathe new life into the legendary Burgundian kingdom of Gundobad. Seven years earlier, Frederick had promised him the title of King of Brabant or Friesland, but that wasn't enough for the proud Philip the Good. He dreamed of merging all his domains into one great kingdom. But in 1454, reality proved as painful as it was indisputable: the weak emperor feared a strong Burgundian duke in the west. So he made the best of a bad job and veiled himself in invisibility. To make matters worse, Philip fell seriously ill for the first time in his life. He had to abandon his dream of leaving for Constantinople in May. That didn't keep him from taking advantage of this long journey to build up a German network, however, which meant that going to Regensburg had not been a total waste of time.

While his propaganda machine spread the news of the Turkish threat, the Burgundian accountants started planning the mobilization of 12,000 warriors and the building of 36 ships. Flags and banners were painted, but a portion of the court personnel were also sacked. The Feast of the Pheasant had left a hole in the treasury. At the same time, the duke was worried about the future of his son Charles. Charles's wife, Catherine, had died eight years earlier at the age of fifteen. It was time to start looking for a new bride.

To keep Charles from marrying the wrong woman during his stay in the east, Philip gave the nod to Isabella of Bourbon as the next consort. This was his way of bringing the Bourbon power bloc over to his side as a kind of counterweight to the increasing domination of King Charles VII of Valois, now aged fifty-two. Perhaps this would make it easier to gain the king's support for his Crusade?

Charles the Bold himself had little enthusiasm for the wedding being imposed on him. An English union would have been more to his liking. Not only that, but Isabella was a full cousin. After considerable effort on his father's part, however, the pope gladly gave his consent. In late October 1454, the two were discreetly married in a very un-Burgundian ceremony in Lille, an event that just so happened to provide his father with the small county of Château-Chinon. Any extra expansion of his territory was always a welcome bonus.

Although the wedding had more or less been shoved down Charles's throat, it did result in a good relationship, even to the extent that he would never cheat on his wife. That was certainly not among his father's demands! For Philip, marital fidelity was an anomaly and infidelity the most normal thing in the world. In Charles's case, it was tenacity that marked his personality: single-minded, faithful and stubborn. If he got an idea in his head, he never wavered. His wedding also marked his coming of age. The next time, his father wouldn't be able to dictate the rules so easily.

In July 1455 Philip sent Chancellor Rolin to the French king, but Charles VII turned up his nose at the old crusader ideals. Drive the Turks out of Constantinople? What nonsense! He'd much rather throw the English out of Calais. He also made it clear to Rolin that after the defeat at Castillon the old enemy would soon strike back, and he had to be ready. It was no more than an excuse, for at that very moment a bitter power struggle was erupting on the other side of the Channel. No sooner had an end come to the Hundred Years War than the first stirrings occurred of the Wars of the Roses, the bloody fight for power between the Houses of York and Lancaster that would so capture Shakespeare's imagination. The English civil war finally ended in 1485 with the rise of Henry VII of the House of Tudor, father of the famous Henry VIII and grandfather of the Virgin Queen Elizabeth. The fact that the current king, Henry VI of the House of Lancaster, had begun to display signs of madness did little to improve the political balance. The French knew all about that from first-hand experience.

So although his hands were relatively free, there wasn't a hair on the head of the King of France that thought it was a good idea to liberate Constantinople: nothing but outdated chivalric ideals! Rolin went home empty-handed. And under the circumstances, Philip had even less reason to count on the English. When his supporter Pope Nicholas V fell asleep in the Lord in 1455, the matter was dropped.

For the time being, that is, until Nicholas's successor, Callixtus III – the first church leader from the illustrious Borgia family – jumped on the Burgundian bandwagon. When he was elected, the year 1456 suddenly became *the* year of the Crusade. But just when Philip could start dreaming again, Rudolf van Diepholt died.

'A Fox Who Will Eat Up All His Chickens'

As bishop of the Sticht Utrecht (a *sticht* was any piece of land governed by a bishop or abbot), Van Diepholt always wore two hats. He was spiritual ruler of Holland, Zeeland, the Sticht, the Oversticht and part of Flanders, but he also occupied the secular throne of the Sticht Utrecht itself, roughly corresponding to today's province of Utrecht, and of the Oversticht, comprising today's provinces of Overijssel, Drenthe and a small part of Groningen. Philip's political antennae were on high alert. This was a death he had to profit from. He would have to fill the position with one of his straw men, which would allow him to parachute friends and clients into countless ecclesiastical offices and to greatly enlarge the Burgundian sphere of influence once again. The noble Crusade would have to wait.

But the Utrecht chapters nominated Gijsbrecht van Brederode, a fervent anti-Burgundian and eminent Hook. Over my dead body, thought Philip, who responded by fishing his bastard son David out of his hatchery of illegitimate children. According to Philip, David was the ideal candidate because, as Bishop of Thérouanne, he was a man with much experience. Philip's episcopal network had many branches, by the way. He had given seats to family members and friends in Amiens, Tournai, Arras, Cambrai and Liège as well as in the southern bishoprics of Mâcon, Autun, Nevers and Besançon. Philip's deep devotion went hand in hand with his religious imperialism. The fact that Utrecht rejected his candidate meant nothing to him. After all, the pope himself had sided with the driving force behind the new Crusade.

The duke moved his court to temporary quarters in The Hague, where he asked the States of Holland for financial help to save Constantinople. While he was there, he used the opportunity to exert pressure on Utrecht, which refused to budge. So Philip raised a large army and began to march resolutely on the city. Utrecht quickly surrendered. Of course, it didn't hurt that he had promised his opponent, Gijsbrecht van Brederode, another top position as well as a remuneration equal to 900 times the annual salary of a trained artisan *and* an annuity 75 times that amount. With his sword in one hand and his treasure chest under his other arm, he rode into the capital of the Sticht on 5 August 1456. That evening, a 'wondrous infinity of lanterns' hung from the windows of Utrecht, while the inhabitants, 'packed together like ants', threw a wild party.[10]

Philip then travelled across the richly forested Veluwe region, in the eastern part of today's Netherlands, until he reached the Deventer city walls. His aim was to win the Oversticht to his side, as he had done with Sticht. But the siege wasn't easy. The IJssel River had burst its banks, forcing the Burgundian troops to make their way through the mud, grumbling and cursing as they went. After a month-long slog, Deventer also gave in.

Saying that the duke was able to add the Sticht and the Oversticht to his possessions is a bit of a stretch, but thanks to the presence of David of Burgundy his influence now extended from south of Dijon to north of Deventer. In the north, only Guelders was still standing on its own two feet. But for how long? Somewhere in between, Alsace and Lorraine now beckoned.

While the awareness of so much glory was awakening his longing to establish the fame of Burgundy in Constantinople, Philip heard some surprising news – tidings that saddled him with a great moral dilemma. The fact that the French dauphin, Louis, was at odds with his father, Charles VII, was an open secret, but the situation seemed to have got completely out of control. Louis had fled his father's kingdom and was now asking the Grand Duke of the West for political asylum.

★

He had always been restless, unscrupulous, callous and author-itarian. He accused his father of being a weasel, a perpetual waffler. The fact that Charles had managed to resolve the Hundred Years War in his favour and had pulled France out of the vale of misery only made his son more restless. Charles VII was no cream puff who could easily be crushed. Louis found that out when he was sixteen and took part in the *Praguerie*, an easily suppressed revolt of unruly nobles who had deluded the young dauphin with visions of a rapid accession to the throne. Charles forgave him, but not without qualification: 'You are my son. You may not ally yourself with anyone without my permission. If you want to go, then go! We'll find other members of our family who serve our kingdom and our honour better than you have done so far.'[11] Since then, they had always found something to quarrel about.

Louis's participation in the last fighting of the Hundred Years War revealed him as a man of great cruelty, but at least he served his country. As soon as he exchanged the battlefield for the court, the run-ins with his father intensified. Charles had fallen under the spell of a certain Agnès Sorel, which his son found deeply disturbing. It was an unheard-of situation. For the first time in history, a woman had attained the status of acknowledged mistress. That the illustrious predecessor of Gabrielle d'Estrées (Henry IV), Madame de Maintenon (Louis XIV) and Madame de Pompadour (Louis XV) could stride elegantly and sensually through the corridors of the royal palace was what Louis liked least of all. Gowns with endless trains, bare shoulders, plucked eyebrows and elaborate, towering hairdos: Agnès's majestic forehead came at you like the erotic prow of a ship. When all the ladies-in-waiting began dressing and behaving à la Sorel, it struck the dauphin as particularly distasteful.

What irritated him even more was that she had influence on his father's policy and personality. Charles was basically a gloomy man. Sorel knew how to cheer him up and instil in him the courage he needed for the home stretch in the fight against the English. After the chaste Joan of Arc, the sensual Agnès would inspire him to acts of decisiveness. On top of that, Charles VII, who was physically rather staid, underwent a tremendous erotic awakening. That, too, was abhorrent to his son. Didn't his father care at all about his mother the queen, poor Marie of Anjou?

On 1 January 1447 the situation finally came to a head, and Louis threatened his father's lover with a sword. Sorel fled to the bedroom of the French king. Beside himself with rage, Charles ostracized his son from the court. He sent him to Dauphiné, the region that would fall to him as dauphin, where Louis was allowed to play governor. Father and son would never see each other again.

Three years later, Agnès Sorel died in childbirth. The official cause was puerperal fever, but many suspected the dauphin of having poisoned her. As the first official royal mistress, she achieved a fame that has endured to the present day. Less well-known is that she was the model for *Virgin and Child Surrounded by Angels* by Jean Fouquet, the French court painter who also made an intriguing portrait of Charles VII. But this masterpiece, now in the Royal Museum of Fine Arts Antwerp, is more than a portrait. We see a fifteenth-century Mary with piously downcast eyes, surrounded by red angels and dressed in blue and white attire while exposing one impressive breast. The high forehead, small mouth and very modern colour combination make Sorel the most enigmatic Mother of God in art history.

Soon Dauphiné had become an independent province to all intents and purposes, where Louis wasn't the least bit concerned about paternal directives. Spies at court kept him informed of the king's wavering health. With the perennial Alpine snows in view, he waited impatiently for the death of his progenitor. In the meantime, he hatched all sorts of conspiracies and intrigues, which have proved a nightmare for his biographers; he did his best to catch royal mercenaries in his nets; set cities such as Venice, Genoa and Florence against each other for his own benefit; and, much to his father's horror, married the eleven-year-old Charlotte of Savoy. Louis and his father-in-law then entered into a military defence pact against the French king.

The correspondence between father and son was no more than a rhetorical game of polite but sweet-and-sour platitudes. In reality it seemed as if the country was once again on the verge of an internal war. Charles summoned Louis back to court. The king's patience was being regally tested. Finally, he sent an army to the snow-capped peaks of Dauphiné.

Despite all his big talk, Louis didn't have the means to stand up to his father. He was afraid that royal henchmen would stuff him into a sack, sew it shut and dump him in the Rhône. The man who later was referred to in the annals as 'the big spider' and 'the most terrible French king ever' decided to play it safe. During an innocent hunting party, he took off with a handful of companions and made for Burgundy. On the way he wrote his father a respectful letter. 'I have learned that my good Uncle Burgundy is planning on undertaking a Crusade, and I would very much like to offer him my services [...] so that I might contribute to the defence of the Catholic faith.'¹² He might just as well have spat in his father's face.

*

Wiping the Deventer mud from his armour, Philip didn't know what position to take. At times it seemed as if he were being chased by a nest of hornets on horseback, and at other times he saw it as the greatest political opportunity of his life. If he embraced Louis, the French king would immediately denounce him. And the power of Charles VII had now reached impressive proportions. But could he easily refuse hospitality, with its code of honour? Incur the wrath of the next King of France? Charles VII seemed to be nearing the end of his life. If he treated Louis well, it would create immense possibilities.

He journeyed southward via Dordrecht, his mind constantly weighing the two extremes. Finally, he made a decision. His political instinct told him to take the side of the rebel son. If he could make the dauphin beholden to him, Burgundy would be all the better for it – or so he thought. In the meantime, he wrote to the French king, explaining that he had had nothing to do with his son's arrival, but that the laws of hospitality demanded that he take him in.

On 15 October 1456 the two men met in the courtyard of Coudenberg Palace in Brussels. As a destitute refugee, Louis pulled out all the stops. He refused to let Duchess Isabella pay the customary homage to him, and he also implored Philip to drop all

The murder of Louis of Orléans was followed by a bloody civil war. On 10 September 1419, Dauphin Charles (the later Charles VII) avenged the death of his uncle. He was present when John the Fearless was killed before his eyes on the bridge of Montereau.

Portrait of Jacqueline of Bavaria (*c*.1500), copy of a portrait from 1432 by Lambert van Eyck, the lesser-known brother of Jan and Hubert. The Countess of Hainaut, Holland and Zeeland was a granddaughter of Philip the Bold and a cousin of enemy Philip the Good.

In *The Madonna of Chancellor Rolin* (1435–6), the second most powerful man in the duchy appears in a mink-trimmed, gold brocade robe. As a master of the portrait, the carefully planned composition and the landscape, Van Eyck attained the pinnacle of his art in this work.

With his flair for detail and mastery of the indirect light source, Van Eyck far outshone his predecessors at the Burgundian court. One need only glance at his *Portrait of a Man in a Red Turban*, thought to be a self-portrait, from 1433. The head and the turban are moved to the foreground and shown in sharp detail while the background is black, quite different from the still relatively flat and stylized faces of Broederlam and Maelwael.

After having illustrated a Bible for Philip the Bold, Paul, Herman and Johan van Limburg were asked by Philip's brother John of Berry to illuminate the book of hours (*Les Très Riches Heures du Duc de Berry*) in 1410. Their dazzling miniatures became world famous. Shown here is a festive depiction of New Year's Day. The man in blue with the pug nose is John of Berry.

On 23 May 1430, Joan of Arc was taken prisoner at Compiègne by the troops of Philip the Good. The drawbridge of the city gate closed before her very eyes. The Maid of Orléans had nowhere to run.

In this magnificent miniature from 1458, we see Philip the Good mounted on a white horse and looking on as the Ghentenars, in their undergarments, beg for forgiveness after their revolt. 'The Ghentenars are my people; the city is mine. If I should burn it to the ground, I do not know any living creature who could build its like for me.'

Portrait of Isabella of Portugal, consort of Philip the Good. Most probably a copy from *c.*1500 of a lost original by Rogier van der Weyden.

Famous miniature by Rogier van der Weyden (*c.*1447). The man in black is Philip the Good. Standing beside him in blue is Chancellor Nicolas Rolin. The young lad in yellow is Charles the Bold. The duke is being presented with *Chroniques de Hainaut*, translated from the Latin by Jean Wauquelin.

During the legendary Feast of the Pheasant (1454), Philip the Good called for the liberation of Constantinople. This gave rise to the production of literary works that breathed even more life into the idea of a Crusade. This miniature features a battle scene from *Renaut de Montauban*, an Old French heroic poem that Philip had copied and illuminated.

In 1473, Charles the Bold established the Parlement of Mechelen, the highest judicial body in the Low Countries. The opening session followed in 1474, and the first painted representation of that event a year later. Today we have only later copies, such as this colour drawing from the seventeenth century.

In this portrait from 1461–2, Rogier van der Weyden gives us a glimpse into the soul of Charles the Bold. We see a self-confident man in a dark velvet doublet. Hanging round his neck is the chain of the Order of the Golden Fleece. The black-green eyes of the future duke stare straight ahead. Those eyes – and there lies Van der Weyden's true bravura – radiate both strength and vulnerability.

Opposite: A naked Christ is draped in a luxurious vermilion robe edged in gold. He's seated on a rainbow with a globe beneath his feet. The message is unmistakable: this is the ruler of the universe, and he's both human and inviolable. Below him is the archangel Michael, weighing souls on the Day of Judgement. Fragment from *The Last Judgement* (1451) by Rogier van der Weyden, which is still hanging in the *Hospices de Beaune.*

Never had children been given such a prominent and realistic role to play in a painting. It was a first, and what a first: the children's portraits that Hugo van der Goes made for the *Portinari Altarpiece* (1473–7) evince a poignant beauty that call to mind the mastery of Rubens and Van Dyck.

Coudenberg Palace in
Brussels, seen through the
eyes of Jan Brueghel the
Younger, *c.*1627.

Anonymous portrait of
Margaret of York (*c.*1470), the
third wife of Charles the Bold.
The roses on her necklace refer
to the House of York, the letter
C to her husband, Charles.

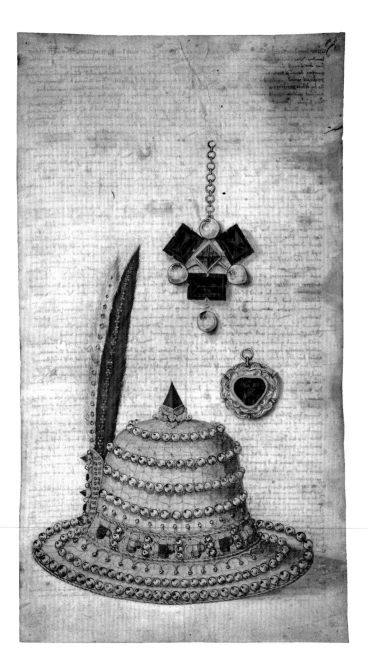

Portrait of King Charles VII of France by Jean Fouquet (*c*.1445–50). The influence of Van Eyck is noticeable in the precision with which the painter has rendered the royal garment.

Below: Portrait of King Louis XI of France, a sixteenth-century copy of an original by Jean Fouquet.

Opposite: Drawing (watercolour on parchment, 1545) of the legendary hat of Charles the Bold, studded with diamonds, pearls and rubies. His seven-tiered headpiece left no doubt as to his royal ambitions. In the upper right we see 'The Three Brothers', the famous jewel belonging to his grandfather John the Fearless. All were seized by the Swiss after the Battle of Grandson (1476).

Family portrait by Bernhard Strigel (c.1515). From left to right, top row: Maximilian of Austria, his son, Philip the Handsome, and his wife, Mary of Burgundy. Bottom row: grandson Ferdinand I, his older brother, Charles V, and Louis II of Hungary, the husband of Maximilian's granddaughter Mary.

Anonymous portrait of Philip the Handsome (c.1500).

Portrait of the young Charles V by Bernard van Orley (1515–20).

civilities. Yet the duke insisted on making a number of prostrations. After the second prostration, Philip remained on his knees so long that Louis cried out with embarrassment, 'Upon my word, good uncle, if you don't stand up now I shall leave and let you lie there.'[13] The first hour was thus spent on a courtesy contest that Louis won on points. Although Philip tried to restrain himself, the etiquette-bound duke would never allow his horse to venture beyond the tail of the dauphin's steed during the hunt. Noblesse oblige – but then in all respects. Louis led a very comfortable life in Genappe Castle, at Philip's expense. For Philip, it was an investment that he believed would easily pay for itself.

When King Charles VII heard that Philip the Good had taken his son in, he cursed both his ungrateful heir and the meddling grand duke. It led him to utter this remarkable statement: 'My cousin Burgundy is feeding a fox who will eat up all his chickens.' Naturally, the king was driven by frustration. Of course he was hoping to ward off misfortune by means of a bit of hyperbole. And he was probably engaging in wishful thinking. But Charles VII knew the dauphin through and through. He knew the kinds of sly tricks this wily Reynard was capable of.

For his part, Philip the Good was pleased as Punch and thought he was facing a rosy future. In his wildest dreams he couldn't have suspected that within one year all this would lead to a break with Chancellor Rolin as well as with his wife Isabella *and* his son Charles the Bold. The arrival of dauphin Louis heralded the bleakest period of his life. It was the twilight of the patriarch.

FATHERS AND SONS

*Or how the buried resentment between Philip the Good
and Charles the Bold ended in an Old Testament-like fury that
heralded the end of Philip's rule, how the Burgundian court in
Brussels changed for a time into a remarkable
literary laboratory, and how, thanks to the resurgence
of Philip's crusader ambitions, the Low Countries were
given an official christening.*

SINCE THE COMING of dauphin Louis, Charles the Bold was only third in rank at the Burgundian court. His father's will was law. Gritting his teeth, he resigned himself to the situation and even maintained polite contact with Louis, but it never amounted to a warm relationship. Louis's verbal humour, his disregard for etiquette, his loose morals, overly familiar dealings with subordinates, penchant for simple clothing and, worst of all, his sheer inscrutability got on Charles's nerves. The fact that the dauphin thought nothing of meddling in family affairs, under the pretence of profound gratitude, was more than the heir to the Burgundian throne could stand.

Even Philip the Good had to set clear boundaries: no Golden Fleece for Louis, no willingness to lend a sympathetic ear when the dauphin came to whine about his father, Charles VII. The duke placed great value on hospitality, but he could not allow himself to get involved in anti-French agitation. Secretly, Philip was pleased that his son didn't fall for Louis's dangerous charms. Louis had broken with his own father, and this less than edifying example was Philip's nightmare. A similar feud with his own son would be extremely troubling to the sensitive, irascible duke.

Charles the Bold looked with deep suspicion at Louis's overly familiar relationship with the members of the House of Croy. This family of Picardy aristocrats had attained a privileged position at the court of Philip the Good in recent decades. The rise of the Croys was really boosted when Charles's grandfather, John the Fearless, embarked on an extramarital affair with Agnès de Croy, whose father was in on the plot to murder Louis of Orléans. Their bastard son would serve as Bishop of Cambrai for forty years. Agnès's brothers, Antoine and Jean de Croy, also captured key positions within the Burgundian establishment. Both were dubbed knights of the Order of the Golden Fleece, and Antoine became governor of Luxembourg, Namur and Boulogne, while Jean was appointed grand bailiff of Hainaut.

Ranged against the Croys were the followers of the iron chancellor, Nicolas Rolin. A few members of the Rolin clan had also made their way into the Burgundian inner circles, of course. Nicolas's oldest offspring, Jean, held sway over Autun and Chalon as bishop, and his brother William was the chamberlain of Philip the Good.

The power blocs of Rolin and Croy had been living side by side in relative peace for years, but as Rolin approached the age of eighty his influence began to wane. The Croys smelled blood. They accused the chancellor of extensive corruption and talked the duke into conducting a massive investigation into possible irregularities. It was an open secret that Rolin had enriched himself on a grand scale. No one had ever dared put this on the agenda, mainly because most of the highly placed officials also had their hands in the till. Yet because of the lobbying carried on by the Croy faction, old Rolin, who had meant so much to Philip, was eventually sidelined.

Powerless to do anything, Charles was forced to look on as his usually wise father dealt with the whole affair in a very surprising fashion. What the heir to the Burgundian throne really wanted was to clamp down on the Croys' power grab.

'Forced To Bow Down To Trees'

On Monday, 17 January 1457, Duke Philip went to Mass at the chapel of Coudenberg Palace in Brussels. As the place of worship emptied out, he remained absorbed in pious meditation. Then he called for his son Charles. Charles had just appointed Antoine, the youngest son of Chancellor Rolin, as chamberlain. The duke wanted to give the function to Philip, son of Jean de Croy. He hoped that the serene setting would make for a quiet discussion, but he was in for a disappointment. When Mass was over, all the unspoken irritations between them came to the surface.

'Charles, about the position of chamberlain, I want you to cancel the contract with Rolin and appoint Lord de Croy,' the duke blurted out. As etiquette demanded, he addressed his successor using the formal pronoun.

Charles the Bold remained friendly, but this time he refused to bend to his father's will. 'Monseigneur, I ask you to retain Antoine Rolin.'

The duke was surprised by Charles's attitude. He saw the request as a mere formality. He raised his voice. 'Appointing and dismissing people is my prerogative!' Then somewhat softer: 'I want the Lord de Croy on your side.'

'As unpleasant as it may seem, monseigneur,' responded his son, 'I ask you to forgive me, but I cannot do what you ask.' Then came the fatal words. 'It is the Croys who have turned you against me. I see that all too well.'

'Is it possible that you will not obey me? Will you not do what I require?' cried Philip.

'Monseigneur, there is nothing I would rather do than comply with your orders, but this time I must refuse,' insisted Charles firmly. It wasn't just because his grandfather had once had a romp with a lady from the House of Croy. No, he had to accept the fact that the driving forces behind a palace revolution were calling the shots for him as well. Charles had logic on his side, but his resistance was uncommonly hard for his father to swallow.

'You good-for-nothing!' screamed Philip. 'Do you insist on defying me? Get out of my sight!' The blood drained from his face and his heart filled with malice. Philip the Good always failed to live up to his epithet when he became enraged. Chronicler Georges Chastellain, who described the affair as if he had been looking over the duke's shoulder the whole time, said that Philip was on the verge of drawing his dagger. Duchess Isabella was witness to this sharp exchange, and she pulled her son out of the chapel in panic.

The priest standing at the door refused to let them leave unless Charles asked his father for forgiveness, fearing the consequences. The son would not relent. The three of them could hear the duke shouting his displeasure in the distance.

'Quickly, my friend,' begged the duchess. 'Open the door or we are lost!'

The duchess and her son escaped by way of a spiral staircase. Isabella went straight to the dauphin and begged him to mediate. But when Louis appeared before Philip, he only made things worse. The very idea: that his wife had revealed this thorny family matter to the son of the French king! Now the duke seemed to be drowning in rage. He showed the dauphin the door. Louis fell to his knees, but Philip's anger was such that he, too, fled in terror. In tears, he told Isabella of his failed intervention.

Philip would soon calm down and reconcile with the dauphin, but a deep rift had opened up between himself and his son. The fact that Charles had turned against him caused a crack to form in the duke's cast-iron mental armour. Later that afternoon, a still furious Philip mounted his horse. It was drizzling, the thaw had just set in and the roads were thick with sludge, but nothing could convince him to stay a minute longer in Brussels. With an icy gesture he sent a courier to the Croÿs to announce that he was waiting for them in Halle. Then he sped away, dressed in plain clothing so that no one could recognize him.

The solitary rider traversed fields and paths, now making a U-turn, then veering left or right, often looking over his shoulder. The only purpose of this extremely curious route was to shake off possible pursuers. He feared that his son would send someone after him, a worry that turned out to be quite unjustified. Before anyone in Brussels noticed that the duke had bolted and fled the palace in panic, Philip had left all the fields and roadways far behind. His tempestuous flight had caused him to lose his bearings. Although he had never before ridden his horse so far from the palace, the experienced commander finally had to admit that he had lost his way.

When night fell, he hadn't the slightest idea where he was. His horse's legs sank into the soil, which had been softened by the thaw. But the old warrior refused to give up. On the contrary, he persisted in his anger and rode into a pitch-black forest. There wasn't a path to be seen. He steered his horse between endless rows of trees, up hill and down, cutting himself on briars, then dismounting to explore the undergrowth. 'The man before whom countless others had bent the knee only a few hours before was now forced to bow down to trees,' wrote Chastellain with a touch of wit.

The duke almost disappeared into a river he had mistaken for a snow-covered path. His horse's refusal to keep on going protected him from further injury. But the desolate wilderness was too much for the animal, who fell several times. The saddle broke, and Philip the Good had to continue on foot. He led his horse by the reins through the Sonian Forest. Dazed, the duke began to call for help. There was no answer, not even an echo.

Finally, he saw a light in the distance. He hurried up to it. Smoke was rising from the earth. 'The fire twisted out of more than a thousand holes.' Was he on the road to hell? Was he seeing the spectacle of a soul searching for the path to purgatory? Philip's imagination went wild. It proved to be no more than an innocent charcoal burner. 'The consolation he had hoped to find turned into melancholy, and the clarity he had seen into dark listlessness. It was about midnight.'

It is a pleasure to read how Georges Chastellain unravels every detail of the adventure. Although there had been a great many chroniclers in the previous decades who had shone their light on the trials and tribulations of the dukes, he was the first to be declared the official Burgundian court writer. Johan Huizinga is not wrong when he says that his chronicles, written in French, contain both an 'evocative vigour' and a 'succulent colourfulness'.[2] Today, the writing style of Chastellain, who came from Aalst in Belgium, would be described as typically Flemish. His tinsel-clad realism makes him the ideal writer to record Burgundian pomp and glory.

After wandering around for quite some time, Philip reached the hut of some poor devil living in the woods. Full of expectation, the most well-to-do ruler in the west knocked on the rickety door.

Speaking in Dutch, he begged to be let in. Without knowing exactly who he was helping, the host served him a few slices of coarse bread and some simple monastery cheese. No carver, no cup-bearer and no taster, but the duke eagerly tucked in to his frugal meal.

The next day the Grand Duke of the West was back, and after a frantic night the Burgundian court could breathe a sigh of relief. The tears and embraces failed to hide the fact that father and son barely trusted each other. Inspired by Louis, Charles even considered applying to the French court for political asylum, but the reshuffling never took place. As the family discord increased, dauphin Louis emerged as the duke's darling and the lesser gods paid the price. Both Antoine Rolin and Philip de Croy could kiss the job of chamberlain goodbye.

In the Museum of Fine Arts in Antwerp there's a portrait of the man behind this rift between father and son. It's worth taking the time to contemplate this work. Rogier van der Weyden depicted him in 1464 as a God-fearing man with a rather substantial nose. Yet the painter must surely have modified the truth, as he often did in his portraits of aristocrats, for according to witnesses Philip de Croy had an even more impressive nose, a feature that was reportedly typical of the family. The De Croys would stick their noses ever more deeply into the duke's affairs.

'The Finest, Biggest And Thickest Cock For Miles Around'

Nevertheless, scarcely one month later there was again reason to rejoice. While the birth of a crown princess would normally have been regarded as the cause for lavish festivities, now the court celebrated the happy news in a somewhat minor key. Mary of Burgundy, who would play such an important role in the Low Countries, uttered her first cry on 13 February 1457. She was a link between two major eras. Her grandfather was the imposing Philip the Good, and her grandson would grow up to be one of the greatest rulers of the world in the first half of the following century.

Four days later, exactly one month after the falling out between Philip and Charles, little Mary was baptized in the chapel of Coudenberg Palace. Philip did not deign to attend, ostensibly because the child was only a girl and he had his heart set on a boy, but actually because he wanted to avoid seeing his son. The baby's father, Charles, stayed away for exactly the same reasons. The event was conducted with typical Burgundian splendour. The newly baptized infant lay in an ermine-lined cradle, her back supported by gold brocade pillows. A green velvet canopy was hung above the silver baptismal font, where light glistened from the hundreds of torches carried by the attending guests. Dauphin Louis stole the show. While the court chapel performed compositions by Gilles Binchois, it was Louis as godfather who held little Mary over the baptismal font. Chroniclers were surprised by the choice, but Charles really couldn't bring himself to ask his father to fulfil this role. In doing so, however, was he essentially placing a snake in his daughter's cradle, as chroniclers suggested?

While father and son drifted further and further apart, Louis couldn't believe his luck. He spent five years in Genappe organizing a succession of bacchanals and hunting parties. Still seeing it all in terms of investment, Philip remained undisturbed and footed the bill without batting an eye. At some point all this would amply pay for itself. All Charles could do was shake his head. But the dauphin didn't stop at playing the party boy. He looked with admiration at the way the local merchants conducted their business and chose to hang out with them rather than with the preening peacocks of the aristocracy. The modestly dressed son of the French king had had quite enough of the Burgundians and their excessive luxury.

What he later as king would ask of his broad network of spies was something he was now doing himself. He took a good long look and forged friendships with important figures whom he would come to use as straw men. As cunning as he was charming, he moved through the Low Countries in Philip's wake for five long years, giving shape to his already complex personality. A fox in a party hat. A snake with a pleasing hiss.

Charles couldn't take it any more. One day he decided to part company with the court, as hard as it was to leave Burgundy to his unstable father, to the Croy bloodsuckers and to Louis, whom he regarded as untrustworthy. After quite some wandering he finally settled in the city of Gorinchem in Holland, where he devoted himself to falconry and fishing, but where he also became acquainted with the rulers of Holland and Zeeland.

The man who had made his way to the north was handsome, with a proud gleam in his eye. He looked very much like his father, although shorter and more muscular, and with his Portuguese mother's dark locks. The Hollanders found his powerful personality rather frightening. He was as authoritarian and short-tempered as his father, but at least Philip managed to adopt a generous and accommodating attitude. Charles was inflexible and did not hesitate to use violence when dealing with relatively insignificant matters. In that regard he was the polar opposite of dauphin Louis of France. Louis hated bloodshed and would achieve his greatest victories by provoking hostilities that worked to his advantage. The personalities that would colour the next tragic decade gradually began to reveal their most prominent features. Louis, the sly schemer. Charles, the audacious commander.

The heir to the Burgundian throne was always welcome at knightly tournaments. He had devoted his early years to swordplay and to reading chivalric epics. From Lancelot and Arthur to Alexander the Great and Caesar, reality and legend became intermingled in the feats of strength that populated his dream world. If Thomas à Kempis had written *The Imitation of Caesar*, it would have been Charles's closest companion. But despite his propensity for violence, he was anything but a barbarian. He read Latin, spoke fluent French, English, Portuguese and Dutch, and loved to be read to from weighty tomes. He peppered his speech with classical references.

This armoured man of learning also had an artistic bent. Charles played creditable harp and wrote a number of compositions, among them *Madame, trop vous mesprenes* (*Madam, you are quite mistaken*), which is still being played today. Despite his musical aptitude, however, the music lover simply could not carry a tune. That didn't alter the fact that for him a day without a sung Mass could not be called successful. His court chapel was so dear to him that he even took the singers along with him on military expeditions.

In the late 1450s he began going to Brussels at least every six months to see his father. But the family agonies of Philip the Good didn't end with the voluntary exile of his son. Duchess Isabella could no longer endure all the suppressed tension. Philip barely deigned to look at her because she had sided with her son during the conflict. His cold hatred sent chills down her spine. What a terrible man he had become! A little gratitude would have done him credit. Hadn't her diplomatic efforts brought about economic peace? Hadn't she done her duty as a woman and given him an heir to the throne? And hadn't she passively accepted his serial infidelities all those years? Deeply unhappy, she too shut the door of the Brussels palace behind her.

First she found a place in the Nieuwpoort monastery, then she relocated permanently to the castle of Motte-aux-Bois in Nieppe. Only occasionally did she appear beside her husband for ceremonial events. Philip withered into a petulant old man whose clear gaze was visibly deteriorating. Without the support of his son, wife and chancellor, he was completely at the mercy of the Croy family.

It eased Philip's personal distress that the crown prince occasionally regaled him with suitable words of praise. The spectacular Joyous Entry to which the tamed Ghent treated him in 1458 was also balm to his tormented soul. The Burgundian duke had been dealt a nasty blow, but for the time being he was able to hold his head high.

*

In an effort to brighten up the lonely winter evenings, Philip the Good often summoned enthusiastic storytellers to Coudenberg Palace in Brussels. These were not professional artists but ordinary people from his retinue, like Louis of Luxembourg, Jean d'Enghien and Antoine de la Salle. Even the long-nosed Philip de Croy and the crown prince signed the guest book. A total of thirty-six storytellers put in an appearance, among them Golden Fleece knight Baldwin of Lannoy, who apparently was able to assume a merrier expression than the one we see in the funereal portrait by Van Eyck from 1435.

In the years 1457–61, the duke required everyone to take turns dishing up a surprising story, a hundred in all, and he would do the same. Philip wasn't angling for tales of courtly love or examples of knightly derring-do. What he thirsted after were adventures full of deceit, adultery and off-colour jokes. The jolly company were only too happy to comply with his request and cheerfully poked fun at both women and priests. Christine de Pizan and Thomas à Kempis, both prominently represented in the ducal library, would not have been amused, to say the least. The model for this frame narrative was obviously Boccaccio's *Decameron* (1353), the collection of risqué tales with which a group of travellers fleeing the plague attempted to pass the time in the hills of Florence.

In France, Boccaccio's masterpiece was known simply as *Les cent nouvelles* because the collection actually contained a hundred episodes. As a way of describing these Italian stories, the French word *nouvelle* (short story) was coined in the sense of 'made-up tales'. It seemed a good idea to Philip the Good to build on Boccaccio's popular classic, of which he owned three copies. The bawdy stories with which his companions entertained each other were later compiled in a book titled *Les cent nouvelles nouvelles* (*The Hundred New Short Stories*). In 1462 Philip was given the completed manuscript, and he found a place for this Burgundian frame narrative in his library. Philip's library was one of the most impressive of the Late Middle Ages. His collection of books can be read not only as a symbol of Philip's ambivalent personality but also as a symbol of an entire era that gave rise to courtly texts, noble knights' tales and pious bestsellers, as well as farces and fabliaux that were as misogynistic as they were riotous.

The collection provides a striking picture of the suggestive comedy that was in vogue among Philip the Good and his retinue. The colourful language used by the storytellers is the most charming aspect of these roguish tales, but to summarize them is to run the risk of reducing them to vulgar jokes. For example: there once was an innkeeper on Mont-Saint-Michel who was said to have 'the finest, biggest and thickest cock for miles around'. A high-spirited lady decided to test his reputation by means of an experiment, so she claimed to be going on pilgrimage. Smelling trouble, her husband switched places with the innkeeper that night. The next day the woman was deeply frustrated because she had failed to find what she was looking for. 'Irate and fuming, without having eaten breakfast, without having gone to Mass or having knelt before Saint Michael, she took leave of her innkeeper and hurried home.'[3] We have to imagine Philip and his friends shaking with laughter.

The tenth story from the series was tailor-made for the duke. It was the product of the imagination of Philippe Pot, Lord of La Roche, the first man Philip the Good encountered after his mysterious disappearance on 17 January 1457. Even then, he had been able to conjure up a smile on the face of the flustered grand duke by greeting him with a good joke. 'Good day, My Lord, good day, what is this? Are you playing King Arthur now or Sir Lancelot?'[4] It is quite likely that the well-spoken Pot had a hand in the general editing of the collection.

In his much appreciated contribution, Pot told of the adventures of a rich English nobleman who had a hearty sexual appetite. A young knight was charged with arranging casual meetings for him. But once the nobleman got married, the knight refused to continue serving as his agent. Marital fidelity comes first! The newly wedded Englishman was bent on revenge, and ordered his kitchen staff to serve the knight nothing but eel pie from then on. His accomplice eagerly tucked into his favourite dish. But after eight days, he had eels coming out of his ears, and he complained to the nobleman. 'I cannot face another meal of eel pie. Anyone in my place would come to resent it. My stomach literally turns over at just the smell of those eels.'[5] The nobleman came right back at him. 'And don't you think I've had enough of the body of my wife? That after a while I'll be as sick of her as you are of your pie?' The knight could only nod and resume his coupling activities with renewed enthusiasm.

Duchess Isabella of Portugal, who was tired of being Philip's eel pie, had already left the court and fortunately was spared these rarefied narrative evenings. As the father of twenty-six bastards, the duke must have split his sides upon hearing Pot's edifying marital fable. The implausible romanticism of his motto – 'I will have no other as long as I live' – was already obsolete in the very first year of his marriage.

The lewd shenanigans from *Les cent nouvelles nouvelles* aptly reflected the atmosphere of virile swaggering at the Burgundian court, but today the work is mainly regarded as a small milestone in the rich tradition of French eroticism and as one of the colourful precursors of the oeuvre of François Rabelais. The collection also resonated in the world of Dutch letters, and far more than the well-known model of Boccaccio himself. Boccaccio wasn't even translated until 1564 (and then only partially) as *Vijftigh Lustighe Historiën* (*Fifty Lusty Histories*). Philip the Good's Burgundian *Decameron*, however, was the direct inspiration for the highly successful *Dat bedroch der vrouwen* (*The Deception of Women*, before 1530) by the printer-writer Jan van Doesborch, who picked out a few of his favourites and published adapted versions of them in translation.

In addition to supporting the work of Flemish Primitives such as Van Eyck and Van der Weyden, the duke actively stimulated Flemish polyphony; appointed a skilled writer like Chastellain as official court chronicler; commissioned the translation, copying, compilation and writing of didactic texts, travel stories, biographies, chronicles, chivalric novels, breviaries and books of hours; asked miniaturists, calligraphers, bookbinders and printers to issue these works as beautifully illuminated books; and inspired wealthy friends to do the same. This network of well-educated bibliophiles included figures such as Louis de Gruuthuse, to whom we owe the transmission of the most famous poem in Middle Dutch, *Egidius waer bestu bleven* (*Egidius, where have you gone*, c.1400). Finally, Philip's sorely tested temper also explains why one of the first collections of stories in all of French literature had its inception in Brussels.

It is inspiring to think that the actual founder of the Low Countries made the fine arts one of his priorities. This close interconnection and affinity between the ruler and his artists took shape in the mind of Philip the Bold, came to fruition thanks to

Philip the Good and would be taken over by the French court after the decline of the Burgundian empire. It then travelled through the centuries, from Francis I to François Mitterrand, as a typical French hallmark. But the truth has its rights: the development of this tradition on such an intense scale is a Burgundian invention.

'As The Wind Varies, Blown From Side To Side'

King Charles VII of France had long suffered from a wound on his leg that would not heal. Afraid of being poisoned by the confederates of his son Louis, the sick and suspicious king began refusing almost all food in July 1461. It was this pointless diet that eventually killed him. He was so weakened that in the end he was no longer able to take in nourishment, or at least that's how legend has it. Other sources speak of a persistent tooth abscess that kept him from eating. In any event, the man who had led France out of the Hundred Years War, partly thanks to Joan of Arc, starved to death at the age of fifty-nine. Upon hearing the news, dauphin Louis danced through Genappe castle. That his father had finally given up the ghost elicited a cry of joy from him that brought a blush of shame to even his own royal household.

In his new capacity as Louis XI he set his course for Reims, where Philip the Good personally placed the crown on his head on 31 August. Just for a moment, the Burgundian duke felt like the most important man in the universe. For five long years he had protected the banished dauphin and thereby risked a major crisis with France. In addition, he did everything he could to transform the coronation into a spectacle. Now it was time to reap what he had sown. The new king would certainly defer to him, not out of mere courtesy but because Philip was convinced that Louis simply needed him. Finally, Burgundy would be able to relax with his French neighbour.

Of course, Philip also demanded a bit of glory for himself. The gleaming of the pearls, rubies and diamonds on his robe literally left Louis in the shade. Even the people of Reims paid more attention to the Grand Duke of the West. When Philip and his retinue set off for the capital, the Parisians acted the same way. 'How we have longed for you!' cried a butcher in the crowd. Everyone wanted to touch him. And yes, the Burgundian enjoyed every minute of it. Did he have a premonition that this was his last visit to Paris?

He must have known that the giants of the earth don't like being taught lessons in humility or being urged to show their gratitude. In fact, all that Burgundian bluster left the new king cold. Half amused and half irritated, he gazed out from under his small black hat and his white damask doublet. Even Philip's horse was more regally decked out than he was. But what of it? At long last he was in control.

That this clever but uncouth monarch was taking a stand in the world quite different from that of Philip became immediately clear during the coronation feast. Like any common vagabond, he offhandedly removed his crown and set it down between the salt tub and his silver drinking goblet – the ultimate symbol of imperial power that the duke had just so solemnly placed on his ward's head! Philip almost choked to see this shocking lack of ceremonial. At the final Burgundian feast in Paris in honour of the new king, Louis even refused to dignify the occasion with his presence. The message could not have been clearer. He amiably refused all the tips and help that the experienced duke offered to him. If Philip had hoped to tuck the new French king into his back pocket as his grandfather Philip the Bold had done three-quarters of a century earlier, he was sadly mistaken.

It is highly doubtful whether Louis could have made it to Reims without Philip, just as Charles VII could not have been crowned without his guardian angel Joan of Arc. The same comparison also extends to the way things turned out. Ingratitude was Joan's reward, as it was Philip's. Except that in the end, the Maid of Orléans had nowhere to run. The exceedingly wealthy Philip still had his vast duchy. Yet the Flemish Lion was somewhat crestfallen upon his return to Brussels. He had crowned Reynard king.

*

The poet-thief François Montcorbier was in Meung-sur-Loire prison, doing time for robbery, when Louis XI released a number of criminals (as was the custom) during his Joyous Entry on 2 October. Montcorbier jumped for joy. He was one of the lucky ones. With great relief he travelled to Paris to write his masterpiece, *Testament*, ageless poetic meditations on great themes such as time and death.

Montcorbier was born in 1431, the year Joan of Arc died screaming in English flames. '*Et Jeanne la bonne Loraine / Qu'Anglais brulèrent à Rouen*' ('And Joan the Maid from fair Lorraine / Burned by the English in Rouen'), as the poet would write in his '*Ballade des dames du temps jadis*' ('A Ballade of Ladies of Former Times'), which was later sung by George Brassens. Nothing is known of his father, but a virtuous curate took responsibility for raising the young François. This Guillaume de Villon discharged his duties with such excellence that the boy took his name as a pseudonym by way of tribute. The name François Villon would resonate throughout literary history.

In 1455, the twenty-four-year-old poet murdered a priest. It being a case of lawful self-defence, he was pardoned. The experience did not inspire Villon to adopt an attitude of caution, however; a poet has to eat, too. After committing grand larceny, he fled to Paris in March 1457 when one of his companions was arrested. While Philip the Good was recovering from his strange and erratic journey through the Sonian Forest, Villon was racing through France to put as much distance as he could between himself and the capital. Before leaving, he quickly dashed off a poem that he predated Christmas Eve 1456, the evening of the break-in. It must be the first and perhaps the only time that someone used poetry as an alibi. If he were apprehended, he could innocently say he was working on a poem.

His adventurous life formed a perfect counterpart to the uncertain times that Philip the Good was going through, trying to hold on with his last ounce of strength. On the way, Villon took up with one of the many bands of thieves that were menacing France and Burgundy in the last days of the Hundred Years War. What better place for unemployed hirelings to get started? That school of hard knocks yielded unforgettable verses.

I know how a doublet's collar lies,
A monk by the gown he wears at home,
I know the servant from master wise,
A nun by her veil when she does roam.
I know what slang will a thief become.
I know fools live on custards, too,
And wine by its barrel's size and room –
    All things – except myself – I know![6]

Yet for a brief time he found himself in the company of the higher nobility. Charles of Orléans, the unhappy hero of Agincourt, who kept on writing after his return from an English prison, had tried to restore the soured relationship between Charles VII and Philip the Good. When that didn't work, and with no meaningful role reserved for him, he devoted himself entirely to poetry and sought the company of itinerant poets. Among them was the poet-thief, whom the poet-prince received at his court with open arms. If the prince had known that without Villon he would have become the most famous poet of the French Middle Ages, he might have acted differently. But the fact was that Orléans genuinely loved beauty.

Villon dazzled at the poetry contests the prince organized but failed to make a career as court poet. On the contrary, the Bishop of Orléans had him locked up in the dreadful dungeons of Meung-sur-Loire for robbing the church. Thanks to Louis's generous pardon in 1461 he was able to take to the highway again. Sometimes free as a bird, sometimes behind bars, the life of a wanderer and petty criminal was more to his liking than that of an officially employed writer. The combination of poetry and wretched vagrancy made him one of history's first *poètes maudits*, the archetype for other 'cursed poets' like Nerval, Baudelaire, Rimbaud and Verlaine.

After a disorderly brawl, Villon landed behind bars once more. To his great misfortune, the statute of limitations on the old break-in had not run out and this time he was really sentenced to death. While facing execution in 1463 he wrote 'La ballade des pendus' ('Ballade of the Hanged'), the most anthologized poem from the French Middle Ages and still sure to leave poetry lovers with a lump in their throats. The fate that awaited him – bodies swinging back and forth – was seared into his memory. He imagined the hanged speaking to him, and through him to all of humanity.

> You see us hanging here, some two or three –
> As for the flesh we too much satisfied,
> Now it's all eaten away and putrefied; […]
> We cannot sit, but swing perpetually,
> As the wind varies, blown from side to side.
> At the wind's pleasure, constantly we ride,
> Pricked by birds' beaks, like a tailor's fingerstall.
> Don't join our brotherhood whate'er betide,
> But pray to God that he'll absolve us all.[7]

But by some miracle he was rescued from death. The Paris Parlement, the highest court in the land, unexpectedly commuted his death sentence to exile. With that, the most notorious medieval poet vanished into the mists of time, while his writings embraced eternity.

Immediately after his presumed death, Villon's tumultuous life became food for the imagination. An apocryphal work attributed to him that appeared in 1480, *Recueil des repues franches* (*The Free Meals of Master Villon and his Companions*), features a master crook who reveals the tricks of the better sort of vagabond's life. In the mid-sixteenth century this book enjoyed some success in the Low Countries with the title *Die conste ende maniere om broot ende vleesch, visch, wyn, gebraet, spijs, dranc, ende den vryen kost te kryghen sonder ghelt* (*The Art and Methods for Obtaining Bread and Meat, Fish, Wine, Sausage, Food, Drink and Sex Without Money*). The fact that his name improved the sale of such fabrications, even among modern readers, shows how quickly Villon evolved into a legend in France and beyond. By mysteriously stepping out of the picture, he enhanced the appeal of his reputation.

Villon's adventurous fortunes are deeply ingrained in the soul of this era. Yet despite his poverty, the poet's last exploits, his floundering about and rising again, also have a great deal in common with the end of the Burgundian empire, years that were characterized by alternating splendour and adversity and ended in sudden collapse.

The memory of those remarkable Burgundian dukes was equally enduring. But time flies. '*Où sont les neiges d'antan*,'[8] Villon wrote, wondering with gentle wistfulness 'where are the snows of last year gone?'. It's a question that Duke Philip the Good asked himself with increasing frequency.

*

The cool attitude of Louis XI deeply affected Philip. Suddenly he felt old. He struggled with asthma, suffered from gout and plodded along from one day to the next. In January 1462, a high fever confined him to his bed, and it was feared that his days were numbered. His son Charles hurried to Brussels and kept watch over his father's sickbed for days. Processions for the healing of the beloved Philip were held throughout the Burgundian empire. Even Edward IV of York, who had only recently driven Henry VI of Lancaster from the throne, instructed his subjects to pray for Philip. As far as Edward was concerned, this was an ally worth a few English rosaries.

The first one to die was not the duke, although the death of the eighty-five-year-old Chancellor Rolin on 18 January clearly heralded the end of an era. In Rolin's birthplace of Autun, the people respectfully shuffled past the body for three days and nights as it lay in state. Philip, feeling a bit anxious since the management of the entire Burgundian regime had been taken over by the Croÿs, had secretly consulted with his old comrade in arms on more than one occasion. Could the weakened Philip bear this unfortunate news?

The announcement caused the duke's fever to flare up. Delirious, he imagined that Death was coming to get him. Louis XI chose that moment to place a ban in France on Burgundian salt from Salins. He quickly reversed the decision, but it was enough to deal the critically ill duke an extra blow. That was the signal for Duchess Isabella of Portugal, who was passing her days in the countryside as a quasi-nun, to return to the court and care for her dying husband.

To everyone's astonishment, Philip pulled through. The family reunion proved to be the best medicine. Husband and wife, father and son – they all fell into each other's arms. Remarkably, it was the failing duke who was worried about Charles. 'I urge you not to trouble yourself about me,' he said with trembling voice. 'I could infect you, and that would distress me deeply. It is God's will that I am sick. Let it be something I suffer alone, and not the two of us.' Charles pretended to leave, but he moved into the next room. Although Philip would be declared completely recovered by the summer of 1463, he was never the same. When he visited his beloved Lille, everyone hid their shock behind a facade of courtesy. The duke was a shadow of his former self. Every now and then he fell prey to attacks of senility.

The Croys hoped to profit from that weakness in order to be of service to their second employer. In recent years they had accepted money from Philip with one hand and from the French king with the other. They urged the duke to listen sympathetically to Louis XI, who wanted to delete a clause from the Treaty of Arras (1435) and to buy back the cities of the Somme for the immense amount of 400,000 gold écus. Despite strong resistance from Charles, the transaction was completed. For the heir to the Burgundian throne, this was definite proof that his father no longer had his wits about him. Why in God's name sacrifice that southern buffer? In cities like Saint-Quentin, Abbeville, Amiens, Péronne and Montdidier, he had a perfect view of what was going on in France.

Was it a last gasp of greed that led Philip to make this tactical blunder? Or had the king promised his support for the Crusade against the Turks? Now that he was recovered – or thought he was – the old idée-fixe came to dominate his thoughts. During their encounter in September 1463, Louis XI did not refrain from speaking ill of Philip's disloyal son, and to tell him that he would guarantee Burgundy's safety if the duke decided to journey to Constantinople. Perhaps, the king suggested, he should divide the large duchy into pieces during his absence: here a Croy, there Louis himself, over there another Croy – and why not entrust a portion to King Edward IV of England?

Given the duke's mental condition, everyone held their breath, but Philip politely declined the proposals. He did, however, collect the money and relinquish his Somme towns with a smile. Although Louis had promised to retain the local Burgundian rulers, he immediately sent them packing. Once again Philip felt cheated, but it was too late now. It was beyond comprehension that this was the same man who had so vigorously captured Hainaut, Holland and Zeeland.

Charles the Bold, who had ostentatiously left for Gorinchem, was tearing his hair out, but he said nothing in view of his renewed filial affection. Nevertheless, he deeply resented his father's renunciation of the cities. Philip would have been glad to have his son at his side during the negotiations, but Charles preferred to amuse himself in long hunting expeditions rather than listen to the untrustworthy Louis. His melancholy nature and the flat landscape of Holland went well together.

It wasn't easy for him to indulge his penchant for luxurious attire in Gorinchem. As punishment for his absence, the duke had frozen his allowance. So Charles called his household together. He told them that he could no longer pay for their services and asked them to seek employment elsewhere. All his servants swore one by one that they were willing to serve him even when times were tight. Their decision to stay is proof that Charles must have had a hypnotic sort of personality, that he was able to command their admiration and trust even though he could be an irritating tyrant.

'The Foundation For Our Parliament'

Remarkably enough, while the thirty-year-old Charles was afraid of what his father would come up with next, the sixty-seven-year-old duke, enfeebled as he was, felt the need to launch a Crusade more than ever before. Rumour had it that he had sold the towns of the Somme so he could afford to breathe new life into his old dream project. Once the Turks pushed their way into Bosnia, he reacted with horror and called together the men who had sworn their allegiance at the Feast of the Pheasant. This inspired Jean

Molinet, secretary to Chastellain and tipped to be his successor, to pen a few stirring verses in January 1464.

Shout it out in town and glade
Your duke is going on Crusade.
Support him now, come to his aid
And never let your gladness fade.[9]

The threat of a Crusade was a cause of great unrest in the Burgundian Netherlands. Who would exercise authority over Philip's domains during his absence? He was constantly at loggerheads with his son Charles. The cunning French king would not be a welcome sight in the north. And they had just as little trust in the Croys. Suddenly, old Philip's Crusade was on everyone's lips. Who in the world could rule in his place? This crisis became the basis for what can be regarded as the official birth certificate of the Low Countries. It would be the last important achievement of Philip the Good.

Rulers of the cities of Holland and Zeeland asked Bruges to invite the municipal representatives of the northern domains to come together in order to solve this thorny problem. Bruges took action and presented Philip with a fait accompli. But Philip wasn't about to let himself be taken in that easily, and with the energy of the elderly he organized a similar meeting at exactly the same time. He summoned the three estates of the Burgundian Netherlands to Bruges. As a result of his action the two initiatives came to coincide, and Philip, as initiator and organizer, was able to conduct the solemn opening of these 'states of the land of our fearsome lord of hither', that is, his northern lands.[10] Essentially, then, the birth of the Low Countries was initiated from both the bottom up and from the top down. The happy spiritual father was Philip of Burgundy, and the cities played the role of godfather.

On 9 January 1464, the States General of the Low Countries gathered for the first time in history.[11] Representatives from Artois, Flanders, French Flanders, Brabant, Hainaut, Holland, Zeeland, Namur, Boulogne and Mechelen signed the attendance list.[12] In his opening speech, Philip expressed his irritation at the audacity of the cities: convening the States General could only be done on his initiative. He also lambasted his son for allegedly spreading the news that the duke was going to transfer power in Holland and Zeeland to the King of England in his absence. The atmosphere was tense. The States would keep their tents pitched at Bruges city hall until mid-February. There was no sign whatsoever of Burgundy and the Franche-Comté. This was a matter for the north alone, with Artois and French Flanders included.

Thanks to the mediation of the States General, Philip the Good and Charles the Bold were reconciled, effectively eliminating the question of a possible power vacuum. On 12 February, Charles knelt before his father to officially beg his forgiveness. Afterwards, the duke and his son thanked everyone in attendance for their efforts, and all the representatives were able to return home.

From then on, not a single monarch would be able to rule in the Low Countries without the States General, which met once a year on average between 1464 and 1576. The Burgundian power structure was more and more clearly dividing into three parts. At the bottom were the cities and local authorities, followed by the various domains with their council chambers and courts of auditors, and their state and city assemblies. At the top were not only the duke with his councils and chambers but, from 1464 onward, the States General as well.

In the *Polygoon-journal* (cinema newsreel) of 9 January 1964, Dutch moviegoers were shown coverage of the solemn commemoration held in the stately Ridderzaal of The Hague. Flanked by Queen Juliana and Princess Beatrix, Jan Jonkman, chairman of the Senate, spoke the following words: 'Our Chambers have decided to commemorate this day as the day on which, five hundred years ago, an assembly of the States General was held in the Low Countries that can be regarded as having laid the foundation for our parliament of 1964.' Understandably, he said this with a certain reservation. The Burgundian States General was not a democratically chosen organ, nor was it a place where permanent policymaking was carried out, as would later be the case. On the other hand, it was a symbolic date that cannot be ignored: the first time that an interregional consultation was held on such a scale, and the first time that the idea of the Low

Countries was concretely and officially being implemented. In the Netherlands, the parliament is still called the States General.

It is not surprising that the chairmen of the Belgian Chamber of Representatives and Senate, and those of the Luxembourg parliament, also took part in the 1964 festivities. 'The history of our regions belongs in part to that of the Belgian and Luxembourg parliaments,' Chairman Jonkman rightly added.

*

Louis XI watched the reconciliation between father and son with suspicion. He was afraid that in the absence of Philip, Charles would try to seize the Somme towns by force of arms. So the French king did everything he could to convince the Burgundian duke to put off his Crusade for a year. Did old Philip really believe he could reach Constantinople on horseback? The fact that he had again postponed his plans suggests not. Yet Philip didn't want to leave Pope Pius II completely in the cold. He sent a small fleet to the south under the command of his bastard sons Anthony and Baldwin, but when they arrived in Marseilles they learned that the pope, exhausted by all the preparations for the holy war, had gone to meet his Maker. That was the end of the Crusade. A new pope was elected, but a Crusade was no longer of interest to him, and suddenly Philip's lights went out. His declining mind had already showed signs of dotage, but now the poor duke had become completely senile. In the end, the west simply left Constantinople to its fate.

And so it was that the last glorious achievement in the history of the Crusades was a Burgundian feast in Lille in 1454, an ingenious banquet full of unforgettable images and impassioned words, a brilliant masquerade centred on a pheasant. Never again would a Crusade worthy of the name make the journey eastward. What remained was the memory of the debacle of John the Fearless at Nicopolis, although nostalgic warriors preferred to think back to the expeditions of Saint Louis, the adventures of Philip Augustus, Richard the Lionheart, Philip of Alsace, and above all the conquest of Jerusalem by Godfrey of Bouillon in 1099. But, as even the most obstinate knights had to admit, that was getting to be a very long time ago.

The Ottomans would systematically press on with their advance. It wasn't until they were attacked by the Persians that they suspended their activities on the western front. Only in 1683 would they call a halt to their campaign of conquest at the gates of Vienna, although they would occupy the Balkans until the First World War and leave their traces there.

Charles assumed power from his infirm father and immediately put the Croÿs under pressure. When they complained of their fate to their beloved duke, the decrepit Philip became so overwrought that he threatened Charles with a stick and cried that 'he just wanted to see if his son would kill his own people'.[13] It was Philip's last spasm of willpower. In April 1465 he suffered yet another relapse. During one of his few lucid moments, Philip and Charles made up once again. 'My son, I forgive you all the mistakes you have made. Be a good son, and I shall be a good father.'[14]

Scarcely ten days later, the States General, this time meeting in Brussels, would invest Philip's successor with full power. As '*lieutenant général*', Charles the Bold had in a sense become regent for his helpless father. The Croÿs fought back, but soon they were presented with the bill.

Because of their considerable responsibilities in the southern Low Countries, the Croÿs, as immediate neighbours, had built up good relations with the French king. This meant they were eating from the plate of both the French and the Burgundians, which greatly displeased Charles the Bold. It was a game of doubles that he quickly put an end to. A good move, he thought – even a deed of knightly justice – but in fact he couldn't see past the end of his nose. He ended up shattering the much-needed buffer between his empire and that of King Louis XI.

'The Year Lays Down His Mantle Cold'

Disoriented, sluggish and increasingly resigned, Philip the Good spent the last years of his life in Coudenberg Palace. The memories there must have been lurking in every nook and cranny. The more his empire expanded, the more this enchanting palace also increased in size. Coudenberg symbolized the vast immensity of Burgundian ambition. The sovereign who lived in this imposing complex could only be the Grand Duke of the West, the uncrowned king of the Low Countries. His ever-expanding household performed a strictly regulated ballet of etiquette and grace. But after his dream of a Crusade collapsed, poor Philip was barely aware of the remarkable solar system revolving around him. The Burgundian sun was burning out.

The mobile court had frequently stopped in Brussels – an average of one day in five between 1419 and 1467 – but that number increased sharply with the passing of the years. The city stepped in and did all it could to make the duke comfortable. Sizeable investments were made in the renovation of the palace, followed by alterations in the city itself. The nearby Warandepark and the Sonian Forest, rich with game, were great favourites of the Burgundians with their passion for hunting. Bruges had made a name for itself as a centre of trade and money, and Ghent was constantly throwing itself into daring revolts, but Brussels seemed to have all the ingredients necessary to make it a pleasant place to live.

In 1435, the city council had appointed the already famous Rogier van der Weyden as city painter, a position that was created especially for him. He left Tournai, where he had long been working in the studio of Robert Campin and had earned a mastership three years earlier. The frequent presence of the duke must have made it much easier to decide to move to Brussels. Jan van Eyck may have had a good word to say on Rogier's behalf to both Philip and the city council. The Low Countries' two best-known fifteenth-century painters had met each other before.

Van der Weyden was immediately commissioned to paint four gigantic justice scenes for the city hall, the first wing of which had just been completed. With this ambitious structure, Brussels hoped to compete with the city hall of Bruges, erected under Philip the Bold and John the Fearless. It would in turn challenge the old Brabant capital of Leuven to build an even more delicately chiselled Gothic city hall. The names of master bricklayer Jan Roegiers (Bruges), stonemason-builder Jacob van

Tienen (Brussels) and architect Sulpitius van Vorst (Leuven) also deserve to be snatched from the jaws of oblivion.

In 1444, an eleven-year-old Charles the Bold laid the first stone for the second wing, which would be considerably smaller than the section in which the Van der Weydens had been hanging since 1439. The painter's interpretations of the justice of Trajan, Gregory and Herkinbald (a legendary eleventh-century magistrate from Brabant) must have inspired the aldermen of Brussels to carry out their task properly. The completion of the spectacular tableau attracted a great deal of attention. The city even appointed someone to provide visitors with appropriate commentary, just as Ghent had done with the *Ghent Altarpiece*. The most popular anecdote had to do with the self-portrait that Van der Weyden had worked into the painting: his eyes were said to follow you around wherever you went! No visit to Brussels was complete without having beheld 'the city tableau'. The city's inhabitants so identified with the exclusivity of the work that when a copy turned up in 1499 the order was given to burn it.

The tableau made such an impression on the Bruges humanist and painter Dominicus Lampsonius in the second half of the sixteenth century that 'he could hardly keep his eyes from staring at it endlessly'. While viewing it, all he could do was to keep repeating, 'O Master Rogier, what a man you were.'[15] Van der Weyden's fame spread throughout Europe, thanks to such witnesses. Sadly, these paintings that were declared absolute masterpieces by countless visitors were lost in the bombardment that Louis XIV unleashed over Brussels in 1695.

Bishop Georges de Saluces of Switzerland had a wall tapestry made in 1442 that was based on the four panels, and he insisted that it include the self-portrait of the master. So it's still possible to look Rogier in the eye in the Bern Historical Museum and to come away with an idea of how majestic his Brussels justice cycle must have been.

The painter found a house a stone's throw from Coudenberg, and after having made an official portrait of Philip the Good – which we only know through copies – he found himself besieged by feverish requests from courtiers who wanted the same thing for themselves. Eventually, Van der Weyden could no longer meet the great demand, and every now and then his studio would supply paintings that were mostly the work of the master himself, but in which certain figures had been created by assistants, a practice that Rubens would carry to extremes in the early seventeenth century.

On 18 June 1464, Rogier van der Weyden passed away, yet another esteemed mortal from whom Philip the Good was forced to take his leave. The city painter, who must have been about sixty-four at the time of his death, was actually named Rogier de la Pasture, but in Brussels he was called by the Dutch equivalent, 'Weyden' being the Middle Dutch word for 'pasture'. The name carved on his tombstone in the Church of St Gudula – which only much later became a cathedral – was 'Master Rogier', all that was needed to identify him. The city also added a tribute in Latin: 'Brussels mourns your death and fears that it will never find anyone of your skill.'

As 'portraitist of the city of Brussels'[16] and favourite painter of the Burgundian court, he had managed to set himself up as successor to the great Jan van Eyck. His compositions and imagery may have been less complex than those of the man from Maaseik, but they would be frequently imitated. He created scenes so lifelike that the viewer can easily believe they actually happened. But what made his work truly remarkable was the depth of emotion in his figures. Van Eyck was famous as the master of observation and static harmony, Van der Weyden as maestro of the sensitive expression. The streaming tears in his *Descent from the Cross* (c.1432–5) are nowhere to be seen in Van Eyck. In the work of Van der Weyden, the folds in a garment or cloak are an extension of the wearer's state of mind. The sublime pathos of Maelwael and Broederlam, which Van Eyck did away with, reappeared in the art of the Low Countries thanks to Van der Weyden.

In 1461–2, a good two years before his death, he painted an intriguing portrait of Charles the Bold. In this work, Van der Weyden grants us a glimpse into the soul of the Burgundian heir apparent. We see a wealthy, self-confident man in a dark velvet doublet. Hanging round his neck is the chain of the Order of the

Golden Fleece. It's as if Chastellain had based his description of Charles's thick red lips and dark brown, unruly head of hair on this particular painting and not on the real thing. The black-green eyes of the future duke are staring straight ahead. Those eyes – and this is where Van der Weyden's true mastery lies – radiate both strength and vulnerability.

Charles understood that the tide was turning, that at long last an end was coming to the trembling final chord of his father's leadership, and that the gods were smiling on him. He felt as elated as Winter in that magnificent poem by Charles d'Orléans, the harsh winter that had now prevailed over both the old poet and Van der Weyden himself. And soon he would wind the good duke in his mantle as well.

Once again, the wheel of eternity had turned one cog further. It seemed to Charles that he was the one pushing the lever. But it wasn't the 'laughing suns and seasons fair' that were awaiting him. It was the fatal 'bitter air' of hubris.

The year has changed his mantle cold
Of wind, of rain, of bitter air;
And he goes clad in cloth of gold,
Of laughing suns and season fair;
No bird or beast of wood or wold
But doth with cry or song declare
The year lays down his mantle cold.
All founts, all rivers, seaward rolled,
The pleasant summer livery wear,
With silver studs on broidered vair;
The world puts off its raiment old,
The year lays down his mantle cold.[17]

PART III

'Magistrates, soldiers, beflagged city, beflowered gibbet
Charles the Bold is coming to Ghent,
the people gasp at the scenes of the Passion,
at the majesty of the duke,
at his all-embracing gaze.'

Hugo Claus: beginning of 'De Ziekte van Van der Goes' ['Van der Goes's Malady'] from *Heer everzwijn* [*Mr Everzwijn*], 1970

THE FATAL DECADE

1467–77

Or how Charles the Bold strengthened the unity of the Low Countries, further enlarged his Burgundian empire, and even – for a moment – seemed to rival old Gundobad, but mainly how he met his tragic end.

JOYOUS ENTRY, SOMBRE RECEPTION

Or how Charles the Bold laid his father to rest, learned a lesson in humility from Ghent, reduced Dinant to ashes, married and hardly ever saw his wife, but also how, thanks to him, the glory days dawned of the painter Hugo van der Goes.

L IKE A MAN seemingly determined to deserve his own resounding epithet, the heir to the Burgundian throne tore across the battlefield of Montlhéry. Charles was thirty-two and hopping mad. The fact that Burgundy had lost the Somme towns because of his ailing father's decision was a thorn in his side. In recent years he had gathered around himself a group of dissatisfied French vassals, who were greatly displeased that the authoritarian Louis XI was giving the aristocracy less and less of a say in government. As head of this motley coalition, Charles then declared war on the French king.

Charles did not make a particularly bold impression during the turmoil at Montlhéry. With grim determination he had set off in pursuit of one small enemy troop, who seemed to be fleeing. He imagined that the horsemen who spurred their animals so suddenly were doing so out of fear of him. That foolhardy sortie gave him the name 'the reckless', *le Téméraire*, watered down to The Bold in English.

Unfortunately, the soldiers he was chasing had turned on the French king and were abandoning the battlefield. When Charles realized he had turned his back on the real fighting, he had no choice but to foolishly reverse his steps. It was a struggle just to remain upright. The battle ended in a draw, but because Louis thought it made more sense to defend the capital he decided to leave the battlefield by night. According to the old rules of combat, the man who was left on the field of honour was automatically proclaimed the winner, but you could hardly call it more than a pyrrhic victory.

It did result in the return of the Somme towns, a restitution that was mainly a tactical concession on the part of the king. Louis wanted to calm the bloodthirsty heir to Burgundy by tossing him a few bits of red meat. The king then did all he could to bring the old duchy down, slowly and stealthily. He began by stationing his men in the towns he had just relinquished. Solemnly promising something and then fulfilling his promise only partly, or too late, or not at all: that would become his trademark. Now he had to keep the Burgundians occupied somewhere else in order to free his hands again. Scarcely a year later, he made sure that Charles was almost entirely focused on the prince-bishopric of Liège.

With its flourishing metal and coal industries, the prince-bishopric had developed into an important economic region and had always attracted the interest of the dukes, especially John the Fearless. Liège was too closely connected to the pope to simply annex it, but Philip the Good had turned it into a kind of protectorate by installing a bishop there in 1457 who was sympathetic to him. In 1465, mayor Raes van Heers succeeded in driving the Burgundian bishop out of the city. Louis XI wasted no time in throwing his support behind Van Heers in order to keep the dangerous Burgundians as far from his country's borders as possible. The tactic worked: Charles the Bold began marching eastward without delay. He easily defeated Liège at Montenaken and concluded a treaty that for the rebels was particularly humiliating: their city autonomy was curtailed, their privileges cut to ribbons, and of course they had to submit to a collective underwear-clad prostration. The Perron, the bronze pillar that stood on the market and served as the city's signboard, was moved to Bruges.

In August 1466 he showed even less mercy to Dinant. The inhabitants had called him a bastard and accused his mother of adultery. And to top it off they had burned him in effigy. The deeply offended Charles bombarded the city in the presence of his sick old father, whom he had brought in on a sedan chair to observe the spectacle.

After the surrender he was said to have drowned 800 locals by tying them hand and foot and throwing them in the Meuse. Countless others were hanged. Then Dinant was literally levelled and everything that remained was set ablaze. The whole event was so devastating that afterwards 'the city looked as if it had already been a ruin for a hundred years'.[1]

'What Is It That Has So Excited You, You Wicked People!'

It can hardly be imagined that a healthy Philip the Good would have approved of so much destruction. His clear vision had been impaired by several strokes, but his body remained strong. The death struggle could go on for quite some time, as Charles was also aware – until pneumonia struck, and suddenly the end became a question of days. A final cerebral haemorrhage triggered vomiting, which drove the last spark of life from the duke's body. His mouth was still thick with foam when Charles arrived. He had ridden as if the devil was at his heels. Powerless, the son sat at his father's deathbed. Theirs had not been the closest of relationships, but at least they had reconciled on several occasions.

When Philip the Good departed this life with a final death rattle on 15 June 1467, the son gave way to a grief that came as a surprise to the Burgundian court. A certain amount of public emotion was typical of this era, but Charles was unable to control himself. He shook, trembled, fell on the floor wringing his hands, tore at his hair, shouted and cried until half the Prinsenhof of Bruges were alerted. 'We could hardly have imagined that he would exhibit a quarter of this distress,'[2] noted Chastellain, who wondered out loud whether Philip's pride and joy wasn't overdoing it a bit.

Charles's feelings lay just below the surface. He was far more likely than his father to give in to fits of anger, and much more easily offended than the old duke whenever he was wronged. Clearly he had inherited these passionate characteristics from Philip the Good, but Charles possessed them in spades. His extreme prudishness, his strong work ethic and his pathological need to control made him just the opposite of his father. What most marked Charles's character was a deep and ever-present sadness. It was a kind of rancour that he couldn't get a handle on and compensated for by means of superhuman energy and by striving for unrealistic goals. On two or three occasions he would pay for his manic single-mindedness with a breakdown.

Philip the Good had more than once aroused anger among his subjects, but on the whole his relations with them were positive. In any event, he seems to have been widely mourned. Anyone who couldn't afford the appropriate clothing could obtain black cloth from the Prinsenhof. Bruges gave a worthy send-off to the duke whom the chroniclers sometimes called 'the Lion of Flanders', a leader who felt so strongly about this nickname that he took in a lion at his Bruges residence in addition to the camels. Each week, the city magistrate was instructed to supply three sheep for the animal to feast on. The gluttony of the king of the beasts was a fine symbol for the energetic fervour with which the king of the dukes had expanded his empire.

On the day of the funeral, summer burst forth in all its glory. Not only did the temperatures rise sharply, but with 1,400 candles St Donatian's church was transformed into a greenhouse. The mourners surrounding the coffin of Philip the Good were panting in their funeral attire. The ceremony took four hours from beginning to end. At one point openings had to be made in the windows or no one would have survived. Finally, Charles was handed his father's sword, the weapon he would raise in triumph two weeks later in Ghent.

*

Scarcely fourteen days after Philip's death, Charles the Bold beamed as never before. No longer was he the Count of Charolais; now he was officially the Duke of Burgundy, which he celebrated with a spectacular entry into his largest city. The ignorant hero of Montlhéry who had behaved like a war criminal in Dinant now thought he was invincible and saw himself as the new Caesar. And that's how he appeared before the people of Ghent. On 28 June 1467, the brand-new duke glistened from poleyn to cuirass. Over his ruby-encrusted armour he wore a long cloak. A golden feather was stuck on his black velvet hat. The whole point was to arouse admiration, and it worked.

Once again, Ghent served as his test case. Charles's father had punished the city severely fourteen years earlier following a revolt that got out of hand and ended on the battlefield of Gavere: guilds were no longer allowed to carry banners, four of the city gates were bricked up, extra taxes were levied and a monstrous fine was imposed. It was not inconceivable that a sense of resentment was still smouldering in many hearts. Remarkably, the Ghentenars had invited him to honour their city with his first visit. The aldermen promised Charles a flawless tour. On Saturday, the guilds carried the reliquary of St Livinus to Sint-Lievens-Houtem, where the Christian martyr was said to have died. The pilgrims didn't return until Monday. On Sunday Ghent would be a haven of peace, and the duke could sleep soundly.

From Zwijnaarde, Charles the Bold travelled down to the Arteveldes' city. A delegation of burghers and aldermen presented him with the keys, after which he rode past a line of young orphans arrayed with flowers and into the city. Trumpets played with great gusto, and the bells of Ghent merrily chased the clouds away. On the Kouter, a square in the city centre, he nodded to everyone approvingly. The Nine Worthies greeted him with enthusiasm: from Hector, Alexander and Caesar to Arthur, Charlemagne and Godfrey of Bouillon, the old heroes beckoned to him as if to say: come stand with us, here is your place, honourable duke! It was a big display of moving mechanical automatons, but to Charles it was magnificent.

Hanging from the bell tower was a gigantic black cloth emblazoned with the words 'Je lay emprins', the duke's motto, which meant something like 'I took action'. Roland, the bell that over the centuries would become one of the city's main symbols, underscored the duke's decisiveness by filling the air with its bold ringing. From tableau to orchestra, the procession advanced to the Church of St John, where Charles swore to respect the city's privileges. This was thirty-five years after his father had had his older brother Josse baptized there (Josse had died in infancy), and where he had admired the Ghent Altarpiece for the first time. Now that Van Eyck and Van der Weyden were gone, there were other artistic giants coming to the fore. In Bruges, Petrus Christus was the first to fill the great void left in the city by the man from

Maaseik, but after the death of Philip the Good it was mainly Hans Memling who would reap success. Dirk Bouts made a big impression in Leuven, and in Ghent the era of Hugo van der Goes had dawned. The wealth of Flanders and Brabant as well as the prestige and patronage of the Burgundians continued to provide a breeding ground for artistic talent.

The inauguration went off without a hitch, although there was a minor snag on the Korenmarkt. Charles was chosen to represent Paris of Greek legend – the Ghentenars knew how much the Burgundian loved classical antiquity – and was kindly requested to decide which of three ladies was the most beautiful. It turned out to be a tasteless joke. When the ladies displayed their nakedness to the duke, he was expected to choose between an obscenely fat female, a hunchbacked dwarf and a skinny beanpole. His father would have slapped his thighs and howled, but the new duke didn't move a muscle. While everyone else roared with laughter, he icily averted his gaze. The exuberant Ghent had made its acquaintance with Charles's legendary lack of humour. There would never be a follow-up to *Les cent nouvelles nouvelles* in his court, that much was certain. As Chastellain put it, 'No doctor, nor anyone else, could ever bring joy to the duke, let alone peace of mind.'[3]

Nevertheless, the Joyous Entry was a rousing success and the duke spent an untroubled night in Ghent's Prinsenhof. Waking up would be another story.

The next day, the tipsy pilgrims left Sint-Lievens-Houtem on unsteady feet. The pilgrimage had become a travelling funfair. The reliquary bounced on the shoulders of guild members singing bawdy songs but made it past the walls of Ghent unscathed. There the group, who by this time had drowned all their piety, stumbled upon the customs house where the so-called *cueillotte* was collected. In order to pay the monstrous fine imposed by Philip the Good, an extra tax had to be paid on the sale of all merchandise. 'Down with the *cueillotte*!' someone shouted. The cry was taken up by the rest of the crowd, and the procession degenerated into a chaotic protest march. No one could push St Livinus around. The little custom house was crushed to bits.

'Kill them, kill them, those shameless bloodsuckers!' arose

the cry. 'Where are they? Where are they?'[4] The noise resonated through to the Prinsenhof. Charles the Bold straightened his back. He'd give those wretches what they had coming. Wasn't it his boldness of action that had brought the rebellious cities of Liège and Dinant to their knees the year before?

Although the Ghentenars knew that their new duke was capable of horrific atrocities, they once again stood up for their rights. They bravely clung together when Charles came rushing towards them. The duke couldn't believe his eyes. The guilds had gathered on the Friday Market and were waving their banners, a right that had been denied them by his father at the battle of Gavere. By forbidding this important instrument for group assembly, the old duke had hoped to undermine their collective identity. The fact that this symbol was now being displayed in large numbers made Charles furious. Brandishing a stick, he cleared a path through the crowd while roaring, 'What is it that has so excited you, you wicked people!'[5]

Fortunately, Louis de Gruuthuse was able to defuse the explosive situation. Louis came from a family that had made its fortune trading in *gruit* (*gruut*), a herbal mixture that for a long time was an essential ingredient in the brewing of beer. This enabled his grandfather to build a house (*huse*) to be proud of at the beginning of the fifteenth century, the palatial mansion on the Dijver canal in Bruges that invariably causes tourists' jaws to drop. Louis wanted to use the family capital to build an oratory that would connect the building with the Church of Our Lady. But what he mainly pumped his money into was the creation of an impressive manuscript collection. It's a heartening thought that without the Flemish consumption of beer and the Burgundian craving for beauty we might never have known about the Song of Egidius.[6]

Gruuthuse had fought at both Gavere and Montlhéry, had sworn along with the others at the Feast of the Pheasant, and now, on 28 June 1467, he hauled his own duke over the coals. 'What in God's name are you up to? Are you going to have us butchered here like sitting ducks because of your volatile temperament? [...] Don't you see that you alone can calm everyone down with just one peacefully spoken word?'[7] That outburst had a calming effect on Charles. Reasonably composed, he walked to the house where the dukes customarily addressed the people.

The crowd fell silent when he appeared at the window. The duke spoke in Dutch. How different from the prostration that the Ghentenars had made ten years earlier before his father, followed by excusing themselves profusely in French. The language that was spoken revealed the balance of power, and this time Charles said politely in his best Flemish, 'My children, may God be merciful to you! I am your prince and your natural lord, whose desire is to bring you peace with his presence. [...] If you act graciously, I will do everything I can for you that lies within my power.'8 Gruuthuse was right. The people applauded enthusiastically. 'Willecome! Willecome!' could be heard from thousands of mouths, although a few muttered that his Dutch had sounded rather wooden. Gruuthuse quickly took over and expressed the duke's good intentions from the bottom of his heart.

At that very moment, a ruffian climbed up to the window and slapped an iron gauntlet on the windowsill. Gruuthuse and the duke looked on, stupefied. Before they could recover from their surprise, the man turned to face the crowd like a genuine rabble-rouser. What did the people want? The abolition of the cueillotte? The opening of the bricked-up gates? Permission to use their banners again? With each question, the populace answered with an increasingly passionate 'ja, ja, ja!'. Finally, the man, whose name was Bruneel Hoste, turned to the duke. 'Look, monseigneur, this is what the people want.' Gruuthuse was able to convince the man to clamber back down, and once he reached the bottom he disappeared into the crowd like an apparition.

The next day, a stunned Charles acceded to a number of their demands, and on 1 July he left the city in the company of his daughter – the now ten-year-old Mary of Burgundy – along with the fortune that his father had kept at the Prinsenhof. He dared not leave his two greatest treasures in unpredictable Ghent.

*

It seemed like the same vicious cycle: the rebellious Liège, the recalcitrant Ghent, the duke's arrogance, the retribution. Two years later he would reverse his concessions and even reintroduce the *cueillotte*. Ghent was a source of endless problems. It kept cropping up in Burgundian history like an odious but inevitable refrain. There was always a final showdown, invariably to the duke's advantage, which served as the seed of further discontent. It was as if a kind of powerlessness lay hidden within the duke's domination.

His reception in Antwerp, Brussels and Mechelen also ran from tepid to hostile, although the dissatisfaction there never degenerated into true rebellion. Right from the start, Charles had a difficult relationship with the urban elite, who nevertheless were an essential part of the Burgundian state organization. The cities of Flanders and Brabant were rich, so they could easily foot the bill for his military campaigns. Of course, it wasn't quite that simple. He wasn't interested in going to great lengths to make himself popular, as is evident from a letter he wrote to the Flemings in 1470. 'You scorned my predecessors and you hate me. Well, I would rather be hated than scorned.'[9] Charles the Bold didn't even try to curry favour with his people. He preferred to inspire fear in them.

His attitude also worried his colleagues in the Order of the Golden Fleece. During the so-called brotherly admonition, each member was given the opportunity to criticize the other knights. During their meeting in Bruges on 10 May 1468 they lectured their leader, politely but firmly. They said Charles worked too hard, 'addressed his servants too brusquely' and occasionally 'was too short-tempered with other princes'. They also advised him to 'give a benevolent and temperate impression' and 'only to resort to war as a last resort'.[10]

After a while everyone began to miss the good old duke who, because of the stark contrast, began to look better and better by comparison. Even in Holland, where Charles had built up a relatively positive reputation during his long stay in Gorinchem, dissatisfaction began bubbling to the surface. In the coming years there was almost universal indignation over his administrative reforms, his military campaigns and the tax burdens that went along with them.

Philip the Good had made many changes during his reign and

had acquired a great deal of land as well. Charles forgot that his father had been in power for almost half a century, and that that long reign had been one of Philip's greatest assets. Charles's tendency to do everything at lightning speed proved counterproductive, certainly because the day-to-day management of Burgundy, which was as vast as it was heterogeneous, was already a colossal job. He simply didn't have the political instincts necessary to grasp that fact. No matter how talented he was as an organizer or how hard he worked, he lived too much in the world of his own infallibility. In daily life he was constantly making compromises, but at the political level that unfortunately was something he would rarely consider.

On the other hand, a bit of distrust was understandable at a time when leaders systematically flouted the peace accords they signed. Not much later, chronicler and confidant Philippe de Commynes didn't hesitate to abandon the duke in order to work for the King of France. That betrayal hit Charles hard. His necessary dose of caution turned into paranoia. After a while he trusted no one but himself.

'A Worm Wrapped In A Sheath'

Hugo van der Goes was born in Ghent, and there he would achieve the status of master painter in 1467. He was immediately given the job of artistic director for Philip's funeral, although he was essentially working at the behest of the city council. He was both a painter of monumental works and a maker of tableaux, and he also spent a great deal of time polychroming coats of arms and sculptures.

Van der Goes is another artist who forces us, with our twenty-first-century eyes, to consider the difference between handicraft and art. The ornamentation that was specific to that time strikes us as inferior when compared with portraits or triptychs, but Van der Goes's contemporaries didn't see it that way. The city of Bruges would not have asked the great Van Eyck to paint the niche figures in the facade of the city hall if they had considered it a trivial little job. Any visitor to the St Salvator Cathedral in Bruges has to admit that the coat of arms of the Golden Fleece made by Pieter Coustens for Anthony of Burgundy in 1478 is truly a work of art. Without a doubt, the men who agreed to take responsibility for what in our eyes are mere decorations were the greatest artists of their time. When Duke Charles needed someone to enliven a vast array of banners and sculptures, he went straight to Van der Goes. The duke was marrying for the third time, and after the modest celebrations of 1439 and 1454 he wanted to pull out all the stops.

Duchess Isabella of Bourbon had died of tuberculosis after the battle of Montlhéry. The duke wanted to remarry shrewdly, so he chose Margaret of York, the sister of King Edward IV of England, in order to strengthen the ties with Albion. This union was the crown of the recently concluded treaty with England, which secured economic peace and opened the way for a possible reconquest of France. And Charles in turn would be bringing a trustworthy ally on board in his struggle with Louis XI. Marriage as a higher form of cross-border politics: all problems seemed resolved.

Hugo van der Goes joined seventy-five other artists and craftsmen in the large-scale wedding activities. According to some sources, he even took charge of the entire operation. Statues, triumphal arches, theatre props, table decorations, flags and coats of arms had to be both designed and painted. Practically all the Guilds of St Luke from the southern Low Countries descended on Bruges in the spring of 1468. That collaboration became the basis for an annual conference for which painters from Tournai, Ghent, Valenciennes, Lille, Ypres and Brussels took turns inviting each other, concrete proof of how ducal assignments influenced painting in those regions.

The colourful wedding procession also included the guilds of foreign merchants. At the head of the Florentine delegation was Tommaso Portinari, representative of the Medici banking family. Not coincidentally, he bore the same surname as Beatrice, Dante's famous muse; they belonged to the same family branch. Like her, he was said to have inspired artists to heights of great beauty. He commissioned his own portrait from Hans Memling, who was working in Bruges, and he would also call on Van der Goes.

Business in Bruges went so well that Portinari was soon able to purchase the famous palatial mansion of the Burgundian governor-general of finances, Pieter Bladelin, as a branch for his employer. The banker enjoyed being part of the duke's entourage. Although his employer, Piero de' Medici – sovereign ruler of Florence and father of Lorenzo il Magnifico – had warned him to watch out for the grandiose ambitions of the Burgundians, Portinari rose to the position of Charles's advisor. He loaned the duke a large sum for the dowry of Margaret of York.

Perhaps it was during the wedding festivities that he became aware of the talent of Hugo van der Goes. In any event, a few years later Tommaso would commission him to paint an *Adoration of the Shepherds* (c.1473–7). 'Hughe de scildre' (Hugh the painter) worked on this pinnacle of his powers in his house on Sint-Pietersnieuwstraat in Ghent.[11]

There's something special about the palette of this triptych. The sumptuous colours that we're used to seeing in the work of other Flemish Primitives do leap off the canvas, but they're tempered by the presence of pallid and cool blue hues, making it seem as if Van der Goes had laid an intangible film of sorrow over this joyful scene. The expression of Mary, the central figure, suggests that beyond the miracle of this birth she can already discern the suffering of her son.

This work, known as the *Portinari Altarpiece* or *Portinari Triptych*, is in the tradition of Van Eyck's *Ghent Altarpiece* and Van der Weyden's *Descent from the Cross*. In this work, monumental as it is masterful, Van der Goes combined the feel for detail and composition found in the former with the emotional power of expression in the latter. Look at the still life in the foreground with its sheaf of wheat and vase of flowers. Then take a closer look. Note that this is no optical illusion based on a few clever brushstrokes, and realize that here the lifelike reproduction of reality has reached a new high point. In all likelihood, the Flemish mastery of detail can be traced to the art of the miniature that was flourishing at the time: if you can capture certain subtleties on small surfaces, you can work magic on larger ones, and that is what Van der Goes has done in this magnificent still life in the manner of Van Eyck.

Then turn your gaze to the shepherds, who apparently have just arrived and come bounding in when they're stopped short. Feel the sense of joy in one, the surprise in the other. What rhythm, what emotion. The ghost of Van der Weyden is haunting this work.

Portinari had his triptych shipped to Italy, where it ended up in the chapel of the hospital of Santa Maria Nuova in Florence. The quintessence of fifteenth-century Flemish painting was thus exported to the cradle of the Renaissance. But that also meant that for a long time the altarpiece was unknown in Flanders, unlike the tableau of Van der Weyden, which remained in Leuven for a century and, after much wandering, came to rest in the Spain of Philip II. The *Ghent Altarpiece* is still in Ghent. The Portinari triptych would not be attributed to Van der Goes until some time in the nineteenth century, a problem that also affected the oeuvre of Van der Weyden. Unlike Van Eyck, these two artists did not sign any of their surviving panels, so that over the course of time their works could only be properly catalogued on the basis of archival documents, contemporary witnesses, invoices and stylistic studies.[12]

Van der Goes did not have a large studio like his illustrious predecessors, and for years he laboured alone on the immense triptych, which measures twenty-two square metres. That approach drove him to develop a highly personal style. Unlike other painters, he rarely resorted to standard heads but created an original character for every figure he depicted, with a look that speaks to us alone. And his Christ? He looks so vulnerably newborn. The viewer's eyes rest on the little Jesus, and along with Hugo Claus we can only think of what we all once were: 'A child like the one painted by Van der Goes: / a worm wrapped in a sheath, / in dirty snow that melts in the hay.'[13]

Portinari asked Van der Goes to immortalize himself and his wife on his triptych, just as Joos Vijd and Elisabeth Borluut had required of Van Eyck. Yet there was one important difference. In the case of Vijd and Borluut, their childlessness was the motivation behind the commissioning of the *Ghent Altarpiece*, while here Portinari's family was the source of inspiration. The Florentine financier also insisted on including his daughter and two sons in the tableau. Never before had children been given such a prominent and realistic place in a painting. It was a first, and what a first: children's portraits of poignant beauty that evoke the mastery of Rubens and Van Dyck. Any art lover would gladly go to Florence just to see little Margherita, Antonio and Pigello, where they are now on display at the Uffizi.

*

It was hoped that Charles and Margaret would bring a few children into the world. But no matter how fabulous their Bruges wedding feast may have been in July 1468, that was an expectation that would not be met.

A detailed description of this last pinnacle of the Burgundian banquet culture might be more than readers can stomach after having waded through so many already. And Charles wanted to outdo them all. His plan was to rival the Feast of the Pheasant by organizing not one but nine such receptions, each preceded by a jousting match. The chroniclers went wild, of course, but the insane accumulation of dishes, tableaux and fandangles probably had exactly the opposite effect: his father's Crusade dinner was *not* driven from the annals of history. There is such a thing as too much.

Philip had been right to work towards one extraordinary event in order to connect the right symbolism and splendour with a single powerful message. In 1430 he paired the pomp and circumstance of his wedding to Isabella of Portugal with the founding of the Golden Fleece. In 1454 he profited from the presence of the flower of the Lille aristocracy in order to sell his dream of a Constantinople Crusade with a lavish and costly display. But to repeat such a spectacle for days on end for the sake of a 'mere' third marriage… it's enough to send even an enthusiastic historian to sleep. This one secretly wonders whether there weren't a few guests who also found that the limits of overwrought power display had finally been reached.

Once again, between courses the guests were treated to kidnappings, sieges and shipwrecks, with the high point being the entrance of a flawlessly replicated whale at least eighteen metres long. The sea monster had moveable fins and tail with large mirrors for eyes, and out of its mouth came mermaids and sea knights who danced and sang songs composed especially for the newly-weds. Then a gilded lion, who was able to utter marital wishes, conducted the inevitable female dwarf to the stage, while Hans the giant (now quite elderly) looked on with a mischievous grin. Hans can safely be called the old warrior of the Burgundian banquet culture. Especially notable was the unicorn carrying a leopard on its back. The animal held a daisy (*marguerite*) in its left paw. This remarkable combination was meant to suggest that the English princess, Margaret, had arrived in Bruges in a state of unquestionable virginity.

The new duchess was twenty-two springs young, and according to witnesses she was an attractive woman. But that wasn't enough to hold Charles's interest. In 1468 they spent fewer than three weeks together, scarcely two months the following year, and in 1470 at least five months – a record – although the number dropped dramatically in 1471 and 1472 to one to two months, and in 1473 and 1474 to only two weeks a year. They saw each other for the last time in July 1475, just a year and a half before Charles's death. The words 'spent time together' are not to be understood literally, by the way, for when the ducal couple were on the road Charles always had his wife stay elsewhere, as if he were taking pains to avoid having to sleep with her. They didn't even spend their wedding night together following the church ceremony in Damme. 'He wanted to catch up on his sleep, as if he were expected to stand guard the next day,'[14] noted Olivier de la Marche. The hard-partying knights at the Bruges celebrations never got to bed before morning. La Marche added with a less than subtle wink that he wasn't sure whether the 'naughty bits' of those naughty knights had actually slept at all. Such risqué ambiguity certainly didn't apply to Charles.

Is it any wonder then that this marriage produced no children? All he had was one daughter, not even a male to succeed him. One infant by three wives – although the first union was a child marriage – is almost incomprehensible in view of the enormous dynastic interests involved. No mistresses, of course no bastards, and an almost non-existent sex life with his lawful spouses... why did Charles differ so radically from his self-indulgent father? Most of his contemporaries attributed his remarkable behaviour to overly developed piety, and a few dared to portray him as a homosexual. Sodomy was a mortal sin, so everyone was understandably tight-lipped about it. Only his half-brother Baldwin openly accused him of such acts, but not until he had defected to the French king. He did so, in his own words, because Charles had asked him to do 'loathsome and indecent things'.[15] The chronicles of Chastellain confirm that the duke dearly loved his half-brother and that for a long time the two were inseparable, but this can scarcely be called conclusive proof. Another hypothesis that made the rounds had to do with a disorder of his reproductive organ. After his death, traces of a fistula were found on his right testicle. This may explain his failure to induce pregnancies at an advanced age – he was a young man when he fathered Mary by his second wife – but that still doesn't address the mystery of his weak sexual appetite.

Margaret of York spent most of her time with her stepdaughter Mary, who was only eleven years younger than herself. Usually the two stayed at the Hof ten Walle in Ghent. She also got on well with her mother-in-law, Isabella of Portugal. Otherwise, all the duchess could do was obediently suffer the absence of her husband, although her devotional preferences indicate that she venerated saints who were known to stimulate fertility and to save unhappy marriages from collapse.

Although the duke was descended from the House of Lancaster on his mother's side, he supported his wife's family during the English civil war. Margaret appreciated it immensely, but that was the only marital solicitude she would ever be able to count on. Intimacy was out of the question. And hoping that life at Charles's side would be more peaceful than in chaotic England was futile. She had been right to choose an optimistic motto. Her '*Bien en advienne...*' would soon become the catchphrase for the entire duchy: 'May it all end well...'

THE CROWN FOR THE TAKING

Or how Charles the Bold took the King of France on a horrifying punitive expedition to Liège, how he worked tirelessly on the further expansion of the Burgundian dominions, and how he thereby came in contact for the first time with the Habsburgs.

H E PACED THE room, greatly agitated. He ranted – no, Charles the Bold roared like a lion. If he could claw, he would have done so. In the middle of the room stood a stony-faced Louis XI. In Péronne, the French king was going through the most perilous hour of his life. He was at the mercy of the Burgundian duke, who could no longer contain his anger. The hero of Montlhéry was now kicking over all the tables and chairs.

He had rushed from The Hague when he heard that Louis was mobilizing his army. The King of France wanted to put an end to the coalition of rebellious vassals, of whom Charles had emerged as the undisputed leader. The armies had faced off with weapons drawn, but the battle was suspended just in the nick of time. First the duke and the king would talk.

Commynes, Charles's chamberlain and diplomat, describes the talks in great detail in his memoirs. His dissatisfaction is considerable. This was his worst nightmare. Why were the two princes bargaining with each other one-on-one? It was madness, pure and simple. After all, wasn't that what diplomats and senior officials were for?

The talks got off to an auspicious start. Their reunion was more cordial than anyone could have expected. While everyone knew that the two men absolutely loathed each other, they kissed, slapped each other on the back and embraced like old friends. The negotiators looked on in disbelief as the two men engaged in comradely chuckling that went on for quite some time.

A few hours later, Louis was already ill at ease. He had ventured into the lion's den with a relatively modest escort. He trusted

Charles, but Charles's entourage were looking on with a mean glint in their eyes. So he asked the duke if he could spend the night in the castle. Charles immediately opened his doors and assured the king that he had nothing to fear.

Now the peace talks could proceed undisturbed. Little by little, the group hacked away at a tough agreement. Charles would leave the French alliance he led, the so-called League of the Public Weal. In addition, his intimate tie with England would be severed. In exchange, Louis would reduce the influence of the Parlement of Paris in Flanders and Artois. This French supreme court had always been the most important court of appeal, while the duke was very keen on an autonomous administration of justice. Charles also wanted to force the promised transfer of the Somme towns. On top of that, a general peace would be concluded.

The needle was long, the eye was narrow. But in three days' time, remarkable progress had been made. An improbable accord seemed close at hand. But just then, messengers arrived with the news that would turn the summit into a nightmare.

'The Chaste Duke With His Beard On Fire'

A revolt had once again broken out in Liège and the prince-bishop had been taken prisoner (even murdered, was the rumour). The Burgundians had been thrown out of Tongeren and several priests had been killed – 'chopped up in pieces that were tossed about for fun',[1] as we read in Commynes. Spies of the French king had been detected among the rebels. That was quite possible, for Louis had long supported the resistance. The unavoidable conclusion was explosive: the king was soft-soaping Charles while plotting behind his back. The timing couldn't have been worse, nor Charles's rage more extreme.

On 12 October 1468 in the city of Péronne in Picardy, the Burgundian duke resorted to the inevitable. He clapped the French king in irons. The king was choked with fear. An unhinged Charles the Bold was capable of anything. Louis's father, Charles VII, had had John the Fearless killed on the Montereau bridge in 1419. Why wouldn't the Burgundian take advantage of this situation and exact revenge once and for all?

Despite his anger, Charles didn't have it in him to go that far. The duke was still a knight with French roots – a knight, moreover, who had given the king his word. Besides, his interests lay mainly in the east, where the possibilities for expansion were most promising. But his councillors saw opportunities and urged him to go ahead and annex France! Commynes, who would soon defect to Louis, served as mediator and succeeded in keeping everyone's feet on the ground.

Finally, the duke demanded that the king dissolve what was almost the last real tie between the French crown and Flanders and Artois: from now on, the jurisdiction of the Paris Parlement would end at the borders. And Picardy would fall into Burgundian hands once more. Louis conceded. He had little choice. Charles then forced the king to accompany him to Liège to quell the revolt that he himself had provoked. Louis looked on as an unleashed Charles let loose his army on the people of Liège. Six hundred Franchimontois, men from Franchimont, had plotted an attack against the Burgundian leader, which proved unsuccessful. He had every one of them killed. How Louis, who couldn't stand the sight of blood or violence, got through those days is a mystery, but there's no doubt that it would inspire him to revenge. And the worst was yet to come.

Neighbourhood after neighbourhood, house after house, church after church… in the winter of 1468, Liège was systematically plundered. Amid the plundering there were summary executions, even in the places of worship. Five thousand locals were murdered, about a fifth of the population. Finally, the duke had the city burned down just as systematically. Only the church towers were spared. Seven weeks later, Liège looked like a bombed-out twentieth-century city. Here and there a stone finger could be seen pointing accusingly at heaven. The Burgundian fury was the talk of Europe. According to an Austrian chronicler, the prince-bishopric was covered by a blanket of red snow.

The survivors of Liège were forced to flee into the woods and forests. Nowhere were they welcome. Aachen hastily offered

Charles the keys to the city but shut its doors on the Liège refugees. In Maastricht and Hoei they were simply tossed into the Meuse. Cologne apologized profusely to the duke for having accepted a handful of them. Powerful city councils cowered out of fear of the dreadful duke's reprisals. Only much later were the people of Liège allowed to come down from the trees and return to their charred city, where they began reconstruction. In exchange they were made to provide Charles with a large number of archers for his interminable military campaigns.

To wash the stain from his escutcheon, Charles presented the Church of St Lambert in Liège with a golden reliquary in 1471. Of course it features an image of himself, but he's shown kneeling before St George, who is trampling on his inevitable dragon. In large letters on the pedestal are the words '*Je lay emprins*'. It was traditional when designing such trophies to include the ducal motto, but his 'I took action' in this context was extremely cynical. It is open to question whether Charles's purpose in donating this votive object was to wash away his sins, as is usually assumed. Perhaps it was a self-conscious desire to claim responsibility for what he had done.

From then on, not a single Burgundian city did anything to thwart Charles's intentions. Even the headstrong Ghentenars made their way to Brussels in fear and trembling to ask forgiveness for their moral support of Liège, while the consequences of the wretched Joyous Entry of a year and a half earlier still had to be settled. As if they weren't shuddering enough, the duke made them wait in the snow for an hour and a half on 15 January 1469, after which he humiliated them in his inimitable fashion in front of a group of European diplomats, who didn't know where to look for the vicarious embarrassment they felt.

The proud men of Ghent had to kneel and grovel until they dropped, listen to a reading of their privileges one more time, and then watch with their own eyes as their rights were symbolically scratched out with a knife on the parchment on which they were written. Seated on his high throne, the duke nodded with satisfaction as the city, in the person of Baldwin Goethals, bowed low before him and described him as 'someone who is not only a man' but who also 'occupies the place of God'.[2] To drive his point home, Charles had poor Bruneel Hoste hanged, the man who had so bravely voiced the feelings of the Ghentenars on 29 June 1468.

In less than two years, the duke of Burgundy had grown into the most powerful ruler in the west, but also the most brutal. His maxim 'I would rather be hated than scorned' had become reality. In the light of what was to come, it's certainly fair to wonder about the state of Charles's mental health. In any case, his confidant, Philippe de Commynes, could no longer bear to witness his master's derangement, and in the summer of 1472 he defected to the French king, approximately two months after Charles had dealt with the inhabitants of the small French town of Nesle just as mercilessly as he had treated the people of Liège. 'Those who were taken prisoner were hanged, many had their hands chopped off… It appals me to write about these cruelties, but I was there and it is my duty to report them,'[3] he wrote years later in his memoirs. Charles's vanity and intransigence could only lead to his demise, Commynes argued.

Historians like to play the French king off against the Burgundian duke, and rightly so. But in his eyes, the various city councils, whom he regarded as far too powerful, were opponents of equal importance. The man who had set Dinant and Liège alight would be led to ruin ten years later by an alliance of cities that included Strasbourg, Basel, Sélestat, Colmar, Zürich, Lucerne and Bern, although the group was secretly egged on by the cunning French king.

Under Charles's reign of terror, the hatred continued to smoulder. When he had a handful of men from Liège led away to Coudenberg Palace in Brussels in order to offer them forgiveness on the condition that they swear fealty to him, they refused. They would rather die as men of Liège than have to live as Burgundians. The prince-bishopric itself had little choice and was conquered by the duke.

The hatred and fear that Charles aroused among his subjects would appeal to the imagination for centuries to come. The Belgian poet and novelist Hugo Claus captured the heinous deeds of the beardless Charles in a handful of verses.

Remember instead how the chaste duke
rode through his blazing cities
   – with his beard on fire –

the war was a theatre then too,
and most things burned down,
   except for the churches and the tax returns.[4]

'Predestined To Rule The World'

Taxes had little to do with poetry. It was daily bread of the toughest sort, and Charles the Bold wanted more and more of it – certainly now that he had decided to establish a standing army. France had already introduced a permanent fighting force in 1445, just when the Hundred Years War was winding down, oddly enough. Charles VII had used his standing army mainly as a way of giving wandering unemployed mercenaries a steady job and a place to live, which cut down on the plundering problem. France used this army to throw England, their mortal enemy, out of the country in 1453. And fifteen years later it provided Louis XI, heir to the throne, with an iron fist to defend France against Charles the Bold.

Even with his aura of invincibility, the Burgundian duke was forced to conclude that mobilizing mercenaries was extremely time-consuming. In an effort to speed things up, he began working out the composition of a standing army down to the smallest details. This was essential, not only in order to take more land but also to maintain control over the existing heterogeneous Burgundian domains.

In 1469 he purchased Upper Alsace, roughly the region on both sides of the Rhine between Strasbourg and Basel. Sigismund of the House of Habsburg was eager to get rid of it because he was in desperate financial straits. Swiss forces had occupied Waldshut and demanded only a modest sum for their withdrawal, but even that was more than poor Sigismund could afford. In previous years he had poured far too much money into his castles in Tirol, not only Sigmundsburg but also Sigmundlust and – yes – even

Sigmundsfreud, as he had christened one of his castles according to the *Panorama der Österreichischen Monarchie* (1846). Whether this particular Habsburg had had problems with his mother is not known, but in any case the transfer of property came as an enormous relief to this compulsive squanderer.

Charles the Bold saw Upper Alsace mainly as an expansion of his influence on the eastern border of his empire. Three years later he would expand it even further by taking the duchy of Guelders (part of which now comprises the eastern Dutch province of Gelderland), with his standing army on the front line for the first time. The old duke, Arnold of Egmond, had been occupying the throne there since 1423. His son Adolf had been frantic with impatience as he waited for his father to breathe his last. Finally Adolf could think of nothing better than to force his father into retirement after forty-two years of faithful service. By 1465, Arnold was under lock and key.

The tragedy of estranged fathers and sons is ageless, but in the 1450s and '60s it went way over the top. Charles the Bold clashed with his father Philip the Good, and the dauphin Louis despised King Charles VII. But throwing their fathers in prison? Neither of them had even considered it. The scandal of Guelders resonated as far as Rome. The Christian world asked the pope to appoint an international arbiter, so the Holy Father began looking for a wise man who could intercede between father and son. The fact that Charles the Bold was assigned this role certainly had nothing to do with his sense of justice, nor with his decisive diplomacy. He was simply the only one whom the pope thought would be able to confront the ever-advancing Turks. Charles couldn't care less about the Ottomans, but he took the task of mediator to heart, and in his own way.

The old Duke of Guelders was released and the conflict between father and son was reignited. Charles felt compelled to put the energetic son under constant guard. When Adolf defied his house arrest, he ended up behind bars. His liberated father was too weakened to keep his restless son under control. In a state of total exhaustion, he decided to bequeath everything to his saviour, Charles the Bold. Charles paid him a peace offering of 300,000 guilders and pulled out in order to lay siege to a few rebellious cities, Venlo, Roermond and Nijmegen among them. Resisting the Burgundian artillery was hopeless.

Arnold soon passed away. Adolf, his rightful heir, was in jail for life. At the start of 1473, Charles was able to add the duchy of Guelders *and* the neighbouring county of Zutphen to Burgundy. These new possessions ran from near Masseik in the south to the Zuiderzee in the north, more new puzzle pieces that were meant to complete the Burgundian edifice. Little by little, people began to wonder whether Charles's greed would ever be sated.

More than half of the Burgundian lands now lay within the Holy Roman Empire, and Charles the Bold began to dream aloud of a king's crown. Before his marriage he had ordered a wall tapestry that featured King Gundobad of ancient legend radiant in all his glory, not an incidental addition. Who or what could stop Charles now? Not only did his military and financial reputations speak for themselves, but so did the ever-expanding Burgundian empire. Moreover, Emperor Frederick III was prepared to discuss a possible marriage between Mary of Burgundy and his son Maximilian. Frederick's ruined cousin Sigismund, with whom Charles had recently signed an agreement, brought the two closer together. The cards had never been more auspicious.

The emperor had agreed to meet him in Trier. Charles prepared himself for what would have to be an audience of critical significance. He left as duke and would return as king. Nothing less would do.

*

To understand what was at stake, we should first take a look at the Holy Roman Empire, a gigantic patchwork quilt of hundreds of regions, many of them minuscule – a bishopric here and a sort of city-state there – plus counties and duchies. At the head was the Holy Roman Emperor, a title that commanded respect but whose significance gradually came to have more in common with the Legion of Honour than with any effective power. Since 1356 the emperor had been chosen by seven electors (three archbishops and four secular rulers), who were unscrupulously susceptible to bribery and rarely chose the best candidate. The actual power lay as much with the seven electors as with the emperor himself, which only increased the fragmentation of power. It was with good reason that the great Belgian historian Henri Pirenne called this construction 'anarchy in the form of a monarchy'.[5]

The chosen one was first given the title King of the Romans, and only after the papal consecration could he call himself emperor of the unwieldy *Heiliges Römisches Reich*. The greatest emperor, the one who most appeals to the imagination, had also been the first: Charlemagne (crowned 25 December 800). The connection between King of the Romans and emperor was only institutionalized when Otto the Great, as King of the Germans, was crowned emperor by the pope in 962.

Charlemagne's legacy gave rise to the two most important power blocs on the Western European continent. Traditionally, the regions of the Low Countries were dependent on either the French crown or the German empire, in accordance with feudal law. The border ran along the Scheldt through eastern Flanders, which meant that the greater part of the Low Countries had to orient itself eastward in order to comply with its feudal obligations, although the German emperor would always have less influence there than the French king did in Flanders. That limited power prevented the emperors from interfering in the Burgundian successions in the Low Countries. Philip the Good had turned the old order upside down by adding the most important part of the fragmented Low Countries to his own domain. Charles the Bold had practically eviscerated the tie with France and then wanted to radically reduce his dependence on Germany, preferably by becoming King of the Romans himself and eventually even emperor. In any event, that was the motivation behind his journey to Trier: personal glory, and an official confirmation of Burgundy's international standing.

Since the mid-fifteenth century, the emperorship had been in the hands of the Austrian Habsburg Frederick III. The first to assume the title of count of *Habsburg* was Otto II (1057–1111). The name itself was taken from the *Schloss Habsburg*, earlier known as *Habichtsburg*. You can still visit the ruins of this ancestral fortress in the village of Habsburg in Switzerland, which was named after the castle. The Habsburgs had been ruling the duchy (later the archduchy) of Austria since 1278. In the fifteenth century they formed a dynastic family who were powerful enough to land the title of emperor but otherwise had little influence in German affairs. In the eyes of the seven electors, the introverted and indecisive Frederick III seemed the ideal candidate. As emperor he adopted the presumptuous A.E.I.O.U. as his motto, but in reality he had to pull out all the stops to get anyone in Germany to listen to him. That made *Austriae Est Imperare Orbi Universo* – 'Austria is predestined to rule the whole world' – seem more like a joke.

It's reminiscent of how the weak Hugo Capet was chosen King of France in 987. No one gave a tuppence for his chances, yet the Capetians would occupy the French throne for eight centuries (first by direct descent, then via the Houses of Valois and later Bourbon). Similarly, no one in the fifteenth century could have suspected that the Austrian Habsburgs would supply emperors for almost five centuries and would soon grow into the most powerful of Europe's royal houses. The unforeseeable fulfilment of A.E.I.O.U. would never have happened without Charles the Bold.

'King Of Burgundy'

Naturally, the deal that lay on the table in Trier in the autumn of 1473 had to be attractive to both parties. If the emperor could arrange for Charles to be elected King of the Romans, the Burgundian was prepared to slip his daughter, Mary, into bed with Frederick's son Maximilian – provided, of course, that the forty-year-old Burgundian became the new Holy Roman Emperor after the death of the fifty-eight-year-old Frederick. Charles solemnly promised that his son-in-law, Maximilian, would then be elected King of the Romans as his successor. But why should Frederick III agree to this? Simply because the chance was minute that Charles would beget another child by a woman he rarely saw, and Maximilian would consequently inherit the impressive Burgundian domains. Later on, his son as emperor would reign over an empire that would have to be capable of stopping the Ottoman advance, a prospect that would greatly appeal to the pope of Rome.

On 14 August, Charles left Nijmegen as Duke of Guelders and Count of Zutphen, two additional patents of nobility that he proudly flaunted. Charles made a detour through Aachen to visit the grave of his namesake, Charlemagne. Wasn't he on his way to walking in the great emperor's footsteps? After that he stopped in Luxembourg to quickly respond to the death of the Duke of Lorraine. There he agreed to join the new twenty-two-year-old Duke René II in forming a front to oppose the King of France. Charles also demanded that his troops be given free passage through Lorraine to enable him to travel from Dijon to Brussels without having to enter French territory. Icing on the cake: he was also permitted to appoint Burgundian captains to important fortifications in Lorraine. A success across the board.

It was Charles all over: first take Guelders, then make a quick and symbolic prostration at a historic spot, rapidly turn Lorraine into a half-Burgundian protectorate, and finally race on to Trier to scoop up the title of king. His energy was inexhaustible, his ambition insatiable. Louis XI feared the worst. It seemed as if Charles got everything he set his mind to. Setbacks had no impact on him. The only thing the French monarch had to cling to was the thought that hubris had been fatal to many a mortal before him. And the more rarefied the height, the more crushing the fall.

On 30 September 1473, the duke finally met the Holy Roman Emperor in Trier. Frederick had not come alone. He was travelling with a company of 2,500 princes, knights and other dignitaries. Charles, for his part, appeared at the head of 15,000 soldiers, with fewer nobles and more frills. Over his gilded armour he wore a cloak bedecked with 1,400 pearls and 23 rubies. Although it was raining when he rode into Trier, he refused to don any protection against the elements. Under no account was the splendour of his appearance to be concealed. It was immediately clear that this international summit was also meant to be a fashion show. The hats that Charles would wear when appearing in public in the coming weeks would certainly challenge the limits of good taste, especially when he strutted about in a headdress adorned by a gigantic stork feather decorated with precious stones.

The first talk between the two was mainly concerned with etiquette: should Charles accompany the emperor to his lodgings, or vice versa? The search for an answer easily filled half an hour, a long, drawn-out ode to the pleasures of protocol. They simply were unable to agree. A few days later they would once again agonize over whether Charles should sit to the left or the right of Frederick. At this conference, there would be no lack of ceremony. The question was whether any results would follow.

While getting acquainted on 30 September, the duke saw for the first time the man who might very well become his son-in-law: Maximilian, a scrawny lad of fourteen with long blond locks and a remarkable protruding jaw. This was the notorious Habsburg jaw that Strigel, Dürer, Titian and Rubens would never fail to capture in their portraits of Maximilian and his descendants over the coming centuries. While Charles the Bold in his glittering armour beheld the most frequently depicted jaw articulation in European history, he continued to rack his brains over the burning courtesy question. Wasn't it up to him as duke to accompany the emperor to his lodgings?

Frederick III was a bit disgruntled that Charles had left his daughter at home. Could it be true that Mary of Burgundy was ill, or mad? Of course, these were absurd rumours, but the emperor would have liked to have scrutinized his future daughter-in-law up close. He did see hundreds of wagons pass by that were filled with furniture, jewels, clothing, wall tapestries, dinnerware... as if Charles had brought all his belongings along with him, except for his heir.

Finally, it was decided that each man would return to his residence on his own. These promised to be lengthy negotiations.

*

After a month and a half of feasting, parading, breaking lances and negotiating, things finally seemed to be moving forward. That was urgently needed, for the Austrians were gradually losing patience with all the Burgundian dandies decked out in gold brocade, velvet and ermine. The duke in particular dressed and acted like a demi-god and didn't seem to realize that he was only irritating the German lords with his exaggerated display of wealth. What had once been a formula for bonding with and impressing people began having the opposite effect. The glamour didn't work with the Germans, or maybe it was the applied dosage. To make matters worse, the emperor began to realize that he was never going to convince a majority of the electors to vote for Charles.

An attractive alternative eventually began to take shape. Charles would be crowned King of Burgundy. Lorraine would also be included, so that a new kingdom would emerge between France and Germany that extended from Dijon to Amsterdam. The old empire of Gundobad would rise from its ashes, or at least a more northern variant of the same. Although he seemed to have lost his bid for the post of imperial coxcomb, in the end the ostentatious Charles found the proposal quite appealing.

The ceremony was planned down to the smallest detail. Trier Cathedral became a beehive of activity, with workers and artists coming and going both inside and out. Grandstands were built, banners painted. Charles, who had developed something of an affection for the young Maximilian, taught him popinjay shooting in expectation of the event. The hard-working duke even showed him the latest elaborate plan he had devised to make his Burgundian army more efficient. The Austrian prince looked up to Charles as the great knight he was, at least in his young eyes. Then the golden throne appeared. Goldsmiths had completed the sceptre and crown in advance. The Bishop of Metz had come to Trier especially to perform Charles's consecration. The clergyman held a dress rehearsal. The final date was announced: 25 November 1473.

Yet the coronation was a washout.

RENEWAL AND INNOVATION

Or how the dreaded Charles the Bold was far ahead of his time, judicially, financially and organizationally, and how the greatest innovation in centuries came to full fruition during his rule.

Emperor Frederick III had slipped away like a thief in the night. The sun hadn't even come up before he secretly made his way to the river Mosel. He embarked at dawn. It couldn't happen fast enough. In the meantime, Charles was told of his hasty departure, and the man he sent to pursue the emperor was none other than Peter von Hagenbach, whom he had appointed governor of Upper Alsace. As a loyal lieutenant of the duke, he acquitted himself of his duties with an iron hand. It hadn't taken long for the Alsatians to come to despise him. In Trier it was now up to this enforcer to save the coronation of Charles the Bold.

When he reached the Mosel, Hagenbach and a few followers scrambled into a rowing boat. They rowed as if their lives depended on it and managed to overtake the emperor's ship. Hagenbach, who was fluent in both French and German, could address Frederick III in his own language and asked whether His Majesty wouldn't wait a bit for the Burgundian duke. Hagenbach said Charles felt wretched because the emperor had risen so early. If it pleased Frederick to exercise patience, the duke would be able to say farewell in a dignified manner. Even in delicate circumstances, courtesy remained an important consideration.

Frederick III agreed on the condition that it did not take too long. When half an hour passed and the vessels were still bobbing idly on the current, a frown appeared on the emperor's face. Hagenbach declared that he would fetch his master. He couldn't be far away. Frederick nodded. The governor of Upper Alsace then jumped into his boat, but he was barely out of sight before the sovereign of the Holy Roman Empire gave the order to continue their journey. By the time Hagenbach reached his duke, the bird had flown.

Charles fell prey to the greatest tantrum of his life. He locked himself in his room and smashed all the furniture to smithereens. To make matters worse, the emperor had stuck him with the bill. The day – 25 November 1473 – was supposed to be one of glory and triumph, but it became one of fury and shame. All that trouble, all that money, and for nothing.

Historians disagree over the motives of Frederick III. Trying to discern the workings of his mind is pure guesswork. What is clear is that Charles, with his posturing in gold brocade, had made himself anything but popular with the emperor and his entourage. Nor was the duke's initially arrogant attitude towards the electors a particularly clever move. His decision to boastfully court them when he realized how much he needed their support was even less well received. In addition, he had dug in his heels when it came to such petty matters as the county of Moers. After his conquest of Guelders he had removed the local count, and Frederick wanted him rehabilitated. Charles was not prepared to throw the emperor that particular bone. Gradually, the emperor had to conclude that establishing a kingdom with this pompous glutton of a Burgundian was something he could not square with his conscience.

Frederick was not a terribly effective communicator. He was vague and indecisive, and he kept changing the subject. He didn't dare show his hand, or just didn't want to. But he was not a stupid man by any means. He finally secured the engagement of his son Maximilian to Mary of Burgundy, the richest heiress in Europe. Once he had his hands on the prize, however, he rudely took off, leaving Charles with the vague hope that the crown would somehow fall out of the sky. Despite his anger, the duke did not rescind his daughter's engagement. He hoped that when the marriage contract was discussed he would be able to raise the question of kingship once again.

It remains unclear whether Frederick's feeble self-confidence wasn't a deliberate pose. Perhaps we ought to regard the weak personality that almost every book attributes to him as his ultimate trump. Befuddled age as strategy. In any event, the indecisive emperor had led the unyielding duke down the garden path. At the end of this long intrigue, the Habsburgs would come out on top. The foundations of that triumph were laid in the autumn of 1473 in Trier.

'A Prince Of Justice'

As soon as his anger cooled, Duke Charles of Burgundy again began to display his irrepressible voluntarism. Boldly move forward, that was his maxim. He travelled to Lorraine to consult with his ally the duke, the young lord who so unfailingly danced to Charles's tune. Crown or no crown, he was received in Thionville as the greatest leader of his age. Diplomats poured in from all over to pay their respects, request his advice and ask him to serve as arbiter in international conflicts. Everyone regarded him as the ruler you couldn't ignore. After Trier, his already restless existence would spiral into a whirling roller coaster ride.

The toughest job he faced: Ruprecht, Archbishop of Cologne, who had asked him for assistance. Just as in Liège a few years earlier, the townspeople and burghers from the surrounding area had risen up in revolt against the bishop's temporal power. As Duke of Guelders, which bordered on the Electorate of Cologne, Charles felt he had to choose sides. At first he sent the energetic Bernhard von Ramstein to Cologne, a fellow cut from the same cloth as Hagenbach. Charles promised to finish the job personally, but first he wanted to turn his full attention to a major restructuring of Burgundian institutions.

*

Despite all the criticism that a controversial warrior and arrogant fop like Charles the Bold would arouse centuries later, he also deserves positive appraisal. Not only did he do everything he could to maintain his father's existing policies, but he also entertained big plans as a reformer and hoped to go much further than his progenitor had done. For ten years after enjoying his own rich career, Philip had denied Charles any authority, and in that last period he had made a fine mess of things. He entrusted all real governance to the Croys. As his senility progressed, Philip the Good succumbed to a childish form of tinkering 'by threading needles, making clogs, soldering broken knives, repairing damaged eyeglasses, and so on'.[1] The Grand Duke of the West had become an incoherent hobbyist. His son had been right to seize the upper hand, or the Croys and Louis XI would not have hesitated to divide Burgundy between them after the old duke's death.

Philip had let the French problem fester during the last years of his life. The Treaty of Arras was more than thirty years old at his death, and in all that time he hadn't really done more than placate Louis XI. Indeed, it was a courtship that culminated in a great fiasco; he should have listened to his son. On the other hand, how could the French problem ever be solved? Both Charles VII and Louis XI saw the Burgundians as violent arrivistes who flouted the old feudal rules. The bigger Burgundy became, the more evident the stalemate. At some point the French and the Burgundians would have to reach an agreement. If they didn't, one of them was certain to destroy the other. On top of that, the greater part of Burgundy lay in the Holy Roman Empire, and there too people were beginning to revolt against their imperialist neighbour, who had never been willing to pay feudal homage for Brabant, Limburg, Hainaut, Holland, Zeeland, Luxembourg, Namur and the small part of Flanders east of the Scheldt. Yet this old ceremony, in which a vassal confirmed his pledge to a principality, made little sense because the power of the emperor in those regions had practically vanished.

Charles wanted to install a third entity between the two great powers, a kingdom that had just as much right to lay claim to eternal significance. With that idea in mind, it was rather impractical that the northern and southern regions of his realm were just short of 200 kilometres distant from each other. Philip had improved that situation somewhat by taking Luxembourg, but that annexation dated back to 1443. Charles also did his best to abolish the division. The purchase of Upper Alsace and the agreement on the semi-protectorate of Lorraine were steps in the right direction. In the north almost all the Low Countries fell under his rule, and thanks to Bishop David of Burgundy his influence also extended to the prince-bishopric of Utrecht and to the Oversticht (Overijssel and Drenthe). Only Friesland (in the north of today's Netherlands) escaped his grasp. These were sensible enterprises in themselves, and he would firmly press ahead with them to the bitter end – too firmly, unfortunately.

He also continued his father's work within the judicial realm. While it's true that the establishment of the Great Council amounted to a kind of all-inclusive travelling court of justice, in practice it could not compete with the Paris Parlement. Large institutions or individual cities often called on the French supreme court if they wanted to challenge a legal decision. Essentially, this meant that the dukes of Burgundy never had control of the highest judicial powers in their own domains.

This weakness had always been a source of great irritation to them. One day during a meeting of a chapter of the Golden Fleece, Philip the Good had to listen to a French bailiff call him up as a witness for a lawsuit initiated in the French capital, and that was the last straw. He would do all he could to put an end to this practice. He only succeeded with cases in Flanders, and then only for a period of nine years. His son would go further.

In the aftermath of his meeting with Louis XI in Péronne, Charles had summarily dealt with the old duty and custom of always turning to the Paris Parlement as the highest court of appeal. It was another example of Burgundy thumbing its nose at old France. In other words: whatever we do ourselves, we do better. At the same time, he introduced a major legal reform that seamlessly followed upon the earlier agreement: he scaled down the Great Council, which always travelled with him, to a Parlement, and gave this supreme court a permanent home in Mechelen, more specifically in the Schepenhuis, which today still proudly reflects its Gothic heritage between IJzerenleen and the Great Market.

It cannot be a coincidence that Charles gave his tribunal the same name as the Paris Parlement. His aim in doing so was to accord Burgundy the same status as France. Clearly he had counted on becoming the sovereign of a kingdom in the meantime. Of course, that would have crowned his reforms with a golden halo, but even now he stormed ahead. The Mechelen Parlement only had authority in the northern regions – in the south he installed a counterpart whose headquarters alternated between Beaune and Dole – so that Mechelen became the de facto capital of the Low Countries, and the creation of the Parlement reinforced its unification. Remarkably, the duke made the audacious move of populating his supreme court with largely French-speaking magistrates from Burgundy and the Franche-Comté. Only six of the twenty-one were Dutch speakers. His subjects immediately began harbouring suspicions against this '*walsche* [Walloon, i.e. French] *parlement*'.

The judges and magistrates settled in Mechelen, which would grow into an elite collection of luxurious mansions and small city palaces, some of which are still an intrinsic part of Mechelen's beautiful city centre. Mechelen was chosen because, along with the surrounding villages, it constituted a seigniory that lay within the geographical limits of Brabant but had always been a separate entity, with its own judicial system and institutions. This explains why it was always mentioned separately in the list of ducal titles. In this way, Charles cleverly avoided having to choose between the strong-willed Brabant, Flanders or Holland, and thereby tabled a *compromis belge* – a 'Belgian compromise' – *avant la lettre*: settling an issue in such a way that no one can really object to it. Even so, there was plenty of protest. The Flemings were unwilling to give up their age-old relationship with the Paris Parlement. But Charles wouldn't listen and insisted on getting his way.

The Mechelen Parlement was mainly famous as a court of appeal. In the overly fragmented judicial system that existed in the Low Countries, cases were often contested, so Mechelen was the ultimate recourse. Even when the Parlement was temporarily suspended after Charles's death, it would return fairly soon and continue as the 'Great Council of Mechelen' until the end of the Ancien Régime. In the Luxembourg dialect the expression '*mir ginn op mecheln*' (I'll go to Mechelen) still exists, a linguistic relic from days long past that fully resonates with threats that are sometimes made today: 'If we have to, we'll go to Strasbourg!' In principle, any resident could take his case to Mechelen, but in practice only rich burghers, nobility or higher authorities such as cities or monastic orders ever made such a move. Simple burghers, artisans and farmers remained loyal to the local courts.

So Charles tried to tighten his grip on the local aldermen, whose authority was much broader than that of today's mayors and councillors. In addition to maintaining roads and waterways, having control over health care and education, collecting certain taxes and supervising craft guild regulations, they adjudicated on financial crimes and civil disputes in their city or seigniory. This was done on the basis of unwritten, orally communicated common law that could differ from village to village, which accounts for the large number of conflicts.

Charles already had the aldermen of Mechelen, Ghent, Bruges and Liège in his back pocket, but now he wanted to post his straw men to seats of justice in other locations as well. The drawback was that he sold such positions to the highest bidder, and eventually the jobs came to be held by wealthier subjects who were not always competent. The Rotterdam clerk Jan Allertszoon summed it up in a pithy rhyme: 'Since e'er they were sold / For silver and gold / The offices here, / Our justice is shaken / And all but forsaken / That once was so dear.'² Yet Charles thought he could kill two birds with one stone: strengthen his hold on the local law courts and beef up his war chest. Concern about the war chest was increasing, and in the last five years of his reign taxes would triple. The result of this effort was mixed. More money in the chest, but much more resentment among his subjects.

This does not alter the fact that Charles the Bold deserves to be remembered as the first sovereign who made intensive efforts to bring *pax et justitia* to the Low Countries. Andreas van Heule called him 'a prince of justice'³ in the *Memorieboek der stad Ghent* a century later, and for good reason. The number of legal ordinances he left behind was truly impressive. He assembled an important library on the subject and surrounded himself with legal scholars, which wasn't just a way of showing off. They were always lurking in the shadows when his own self-esteem was at stake. In the so-called *Montpellier Parchment*, Charles appears as an Atlas figure who carries on his shoulders the jurisprudence he modernized – indeed, he is presented as the incarnation of divine justice. It's tempting to imagine the Parchment hanging over his head when he administered justice in Mechelen.

He tried to make improvements in the area of finances, too. He combined the courts of auditors in Lille, Brussels and The Hague into one big institution that, like the Parlement, was located in Mechelen. From that point on, he wanted all benevolences – requests from the duke for extra financial support in special circumstances – to be presented to the States General of the Low Countries and not to the individual cities or regions, another clear attempt at more centralization. He also tried to introduce a general method of taxation throughout all of Burgundy, something that the big cities invariably managed to prevent. They simply wanted to maintain control over their own tax systems. Here too his own ideas clashed with the heterogeneous structure of the highly urbanized Low Countries. In fact, in this respect he was ahead of his time.

In Thionville, he issued a military policy paper in addition to the financial and juridical reforms, the text of which he had presented to Maximilian a few weeks earlier. As a relentless manager, he issued ordinances that documented the organization of his corps of 11,250 professional soldiers and almost 2,000 members of his personal guard down to the minutest details. This kind of staffing plan was new and would influence the make-up of armies in the early Renaissance, although it would not save Charles himself from disaster.

His interference was far-reaching: from the detailed description of soldiers' equipment and the selection of military exercises – which was unprecedented – to the ban on marching that was either too fast or too slow. Nor did he refrain from dictating specific military instructions. For example, archers had to learn to 'fight back-to-back by way of double defence, or in a square, or in a circle, but always with the pikemen on the outside in order to repel the attack of enemy horsemen'.[4] He also issued a completely unrealistic rule against soldiers cursing and playing dice. On the other hand, he did realize that his warriors had need of women, and he was willing to turn a blind eye to the traditional custom of prostitutes following the army around, as long as the numbers were limited. He had calculated that 3 per cent was a good average, thus 30 ladies per company of 900 soldiers, with the extra rule that no personal relationships were to be formed. The women belonged to everyone.

Charles expected that his captains would pound these new regulations and tips into the heads of all his professional soldiers. But his troops were far from ready for such a modern approach. Perhaps it would have been different if he had allowed for a calm, slow implementation. No matter how detailed his decrees were, he went right ahead and issued new rules a year later even though the old ones hadn't yet been adopted.

As Napoleon would later do on a much larger scale, Charles emerged as a leader who combined micro- with macromanagement. *Charles le Travaillant* – the Worker, as Olivier de la Marche called him – governed on the basis of rapid decisions and with a maniacal control over details large and small. His need to control was so great that in 1471 he changed his signature so that his secretaries would have more difficulty forging it. We have to imagine the duke bent over his papers, working out his legal, military and financial policy measures, but also trying to make sense of his bills and invoices. Undoubtedly he was a tireless administrator and a talented manager, but neither his army nor his domains could follow his frenetic pace and impatience.

Charles the Bold was blinded by his own energy and ambition. On the battlefield he failed to measure up to the Corsican, who would succeed in scoring an imperial title three centuries later and would combine all the local rules (many of which dated back centuries to before the arrival of the Burgundian dukes) into his notorious *Code Civil*, something Charles the Bold could only dream of.

Finally, there was the big problem of nomenclature. As powerful as he was, Charles was still a walking amalgam of titles. Despite the fact that he is consistently referred to as 'the Burgundian duke', even in this book, that title only refers in the strictest sense to Dijon and Beaune. In Brussels he was the Duke of Brabant, in Ypres the Count of Flanders, in Nijmegen the Duke of Guelders, and so on... To put an end to this tangle of titles, he had done all he could in Trier to be crowned King of Burgundy, a title he could assert wherever he went. But even then, there still remained the question of what was to be done with Flanders, most of which belonged to France, feudally speaking.[5] Would Flanders be part of the Burgundian kingdom? In other words, in the scenario of a possible coronation there were always territorial and institutional knots to untangle.

★

From Thionville Charles travelled to Dijon, where he had not set foot since becoming duke. Although he hadn't made his entrance as king, his seven-tiered headpiece, encrusted with diamonds and rubies, left no doubt as to his ambitions. Nor did the words he spoke to the assembled States of Burgundy. He specifically promised to breathe new life into 'the old Burgundian kingdom that the French had unjustly appropriated for so long and had reduced to a duchy'. Of course he mentioned the name of the legendary Gundobad, the old king and lawmaker whose *Lex Burgundonium* of 502 had played an important role in his imagination. Charles gave this illustrious 'Dijon speech' in the great hall of the palace, where tourists today gape at the sepulchres and *pleurants* of Claus Sluter. On 25 January 1474 his words reverberated as never before, but in practice he had come to Dijon mainly to conscript soldiers and levy taxes to keep his army on its feet.

A few days later, a macabre caravan arrived with cargo from the north: the mortal remains of Charles's father, Philip, and his mother, Isabella (she had died two years earlier). The two were solemnly interred in the crypt of the Carthusian monastery in Champmol. While the glorious future of Burgundy was unfolding in the duke's head, his eyes were confronted with the remains of his ancestors. Of course they would need a mausoleum as well, but Charles would never be given the time to search for a new Claus Sluter for his parents.

'Printing Converted It Into A Revolution'

Besides the innovative restructuring of the legal system and the army corps, the renewal that took place under Charles the Bold was also manifested in an entirely different area. Just before the death of Philip the Good, the Frenchman Colard Mansion, who had made his home in Bruges, completed an order for the old duke. Not without pride, he handed the doddering Philip his *Romuléon*, a manuscript of the history of Rome written by Benvenuto da Imola. A copyist and calligrapher, Mansion had gone to great lengths to provide the Grand Duke of the West with a unique copy. Apparently he was successful, for he was then commissioned by Louis de Gruuthuse to transcribe the full text of *Pénitence d'Adam* (*Penitence of Adam*, anonymous). These projects were completed in 1467 and 1472 respectively, just before a brand-new invention was about to reach the Low Countries. The same Mansion would play a pioneering role in its distribution.

*

In addition to painting and polyphony, the market for illustrated manuscripts flourished under the Burgundians. They were avidly sought as luxury products by the circle of bibliophiles that had gathered around Philip the Good and Charles the Bold. Only the very wealthiest could afford the price tag – up to a hundred times the annual salary of a professional artisan – that such luxury manuscripts commanded. As an international hub between the mercantile cities of northern Europe and the Italian city-states, Bruges was the place from which countless manuscripts travelled to the furthest corners of Europe. The results can only be imagined. Many bookbinders and copyists set up shop in the shadow of the most famous bell tower in the Low Countries. These so-called stationers joined forces in the Guild of Saint John the Evangelist in Bruges, the only association of its kind outside Paris, of which Mansion was leader for a time. At one point the guild had more than a hundred members. In the 1470s they were all confronted by a new technique that had been developed by Johannes Gutenberg.

Gutenberg of Mainz hadn't invented the art of book printing;

he had developed the use of moveable metal type, a finding that sparked a small revolution. Before moveable type, the only technique for book reproduction was woodcutting, in which an entire text was cut into an easily worn-out woodblock. It was an extremely time-consuming method, and it was only of practical use in the printing of prayer cards and pamphlets. This was about to change with Gutenberg's invention of around 1453. Thanks to reusable lead type, not only could thick books be printed much faster and more cheaply, but they could also circulate in higher print runs – Gutenberg printed no fewer than 180 copies of his Bible. Rapid duplication suddenly gave rise to the idea of *editions*, and the number of book owners increased sharply. The practice of solitary reading, which had got off to a good start thanks to Thomas à Kempis's *The Imitation of Christ*, finally took wing, although for a long time fictional texts would still be primarily read aloud.

Books that were printed before 1501 are called incunabula, or cradle editions, because they date from the infancy of book printing. There are about half a million surviving copies of such books, which first rolled off the presses in Germany and Venice. The Low Countries also played their part, and the French-speaking Colard Mansion was one of the leading stationers of Bruges. Mansion got along well with William Caxton, a shrewd Englishman who had cut quite a dash in Flanders as a textile merchant. After having been appointed English trade representative, Caxton often came in contact with members of the Burgundian court, especially with his compatriot Duchess Margaret of York.

A few years before, during a visit to the castle of Hesdin that Philip the Good had restored to all its glory, Caxton became enchanted by Melchior Broederlam's wall paintings of Jason's adventures with the Golden Fleece. The instruments at Hesdin that imitated thunder, fog and lightning had already delighted the old duke and now became a pathway to classical Greek legends for the Englishman. One day, Caxton requested an audience with Margaret of York. He wanted to present her with a sample translation of the famous story of Troy. The Burgundian duchess is reported to have spotted a spelling error in Caxton's English version, but was nevertheless enthusiastic enough to commission him to finish his translation of Raoul Lefèvre's *Recueil des histoires de Troyes*. For reasons that have never been made clear, he was then banished to Cologne, where he started work on the translation and became fascinated by Gutenberg's invention. The textile merchant became fully engrossed in language and books.

When he returned to Bruges eighteen months later, he brought with him not only his complete Troy translation but also a printing press. It was under Caxton's supervision that the first English and French books ever printed were produced: *Recuyell of the Historyes of Troy* and *Recueil des histoires de Troyes*, in 1473 and 1474 respectively. In all probability he accomplished this feat in collaboration with Colard Mansion, who, unlike Caxton, operated the printing press himself. Without Philip the Good and Margaret of York, the first book to be printed in French and English would undoubtedly have been another title. It is far from certain whether these two titles were also the first application of Gutenberg's invention in the Low Countries.

Who the very first printer was in the Low Countries is a matter of debate, since Petrus Comestor's *Historia scholastici*, a popular retelling of the Bible, was also published in 1473 by Nicolaus Ketelaer and Gherardus de Leempt in Utrecht. A network of bibliophiles had formed in that city around Bishop David of Burgundy, like the network that had grown up in Bruges around the dukes. It was also in the year of our Lord 1473 that the first book printed by Dirk Maartens appeared in Aalst, *Speculum conversionis peccatorum* (Mirror of the Conversion of Sinners) by Dionysius the Carthusian.[6] Interestingly enough, few books were printed in the Dutch vernacular, and not in Bruges but in Gouda, Oudenaarde and Delft. These included Latin-Dutch textbooks, the works of rhetorician Anthonis de Roovere and the Delft Bible of 1477, possibly the oldest printed book in Middle Dutch, made about twenty-five years after the Gutenberg Bible.

So while we might safely announce, with a bit of fanfare, that the art of printing in the Low Countries was born in 1473 during the time of Charles the Bold, it certainly doesn't mean that everything changed in one fell swoop. Handwritten books did very well for themselves until roughly 1500. Colard Mansion continued to produce manuscripts in Bruges for the Burgundian elite, works that were more expensive because they were unique. But he also used his printing press for writings that were cheaper because their print run brought the costs down. He even made so-called hybrid books in which part was printed and the rest handwritten. Sometimes he left a white space at the beginning of a chapter to allow for the addition of hand-drawn miniatures, depending on the customer's budget. More than once these spaces were actually left empty.

The word 'miniature' originally had nothing to do with 'mini', by the way. *Miniatura* is the future participle of *miniare* (to paint red), a typical Latin part of speech that here means something like 'what is going to be painted red'. This is further based on *minium*, the red pigment that medieval calligraphers used to colour in the beautifully decorated initial letter of a chapter. These letters, the original miniatures, were gradually accompanied by necessarily small illustrations that eventually came to be known as 'miniatures'. Just as an entire story is contained in the most beautiful miniatures, so a whole series of lines converge in this etymological history.

Mansion continued to work closely with William Caxton in Bruges until the latter swapped Flanders for England in 1476, where he built the country's oldest known printing house from scratch. From then on Mansion's hands were free, and in that same year he added these words to the back of the first book he printed on his own, showing that he was well aware of his pioneering role: '*Primum opus impressum per Colardum Mansion*' – 'The first work printed by Colard Mansion'.[7]

Mansion rented a room right next to St Donatian's church, gathered a few copyists, miniaturists and bookbinders about him and over the next ten years would introduce important technical innovations and produce more and more beautiful work. Like other printers, he discovered that mentioning the author's name on the title page was a selling point. Not much later, promotional slogans would appear in addition to the title and the author. Those first printers were clearly salesmen as well as pioneers. A printing press was no small acquisition, a type case even less so, but more than half the budget was spent on paper.

It's striking that Mansion's first typeface was an imitation of the most popular Gothic script that invariably was used in luxury Burgundian manuscripts. You couldn't tell them apart, or at least that was the intention. In his English history of Troy from 1473, Caxton didn't fail to mention that this was indeed a printed work that one could read or have read aloud to you. The Gutenberg Bible also looked as if it had been written by hand with extreme precision, but even so it was a typographical work. Mansion called his first typeface, which in all probability was based on his own elegant handwriting, 'Burgundian bastarda'. Later he came up with a more modern-looking typeface, his 'rotunda', in which, with a measure of goodwill, you can catch a glimpse of typefaces to come, such as Times New Roman and Perpetua, at least in the capital letters.

Gutenberg's invention, alias innovation, seemed to put an end to the mistakes that were caused by the copyist's lack of concentration or surplus of fantasy. That euphoria would later give way to the realization that any residual errors would now be even more widely distributed. In any case, Gutenberg paved the way to intensive textual studies and gave rise to unprecedented intellectual fervour from which the humanists would profit, as well as the Protestants. Not only could they interpret the ancient classics with greater ease and accuracy, or devote themselves to Bible study, but they could also spread their ideas more rapidly. This elicited the following ominous words from Victor Hugo four centuries later: 'Before the invention of printing, reform would have been merely a schism; printing converted it into a revolution.'[8]

*

As duchess, Margaret of York launched a whole range of bibliophilic activities to keep her occupied, but after the death of Charles the Bold she suddenly dropped them all. When Caxton presented her with the first printed book in English, which partly came about thanks to her support, she had only a little more than three years in which to purchase printed works or manuscripts.

In 1474 she ordered a luxury edition of *Les Visions du chevalier Tondal*, a manuscript illuminated with magnificent miniatures that contained the insights of a man named Tondal after a near-death experience. It was a twelfth-century religious story that was still popular in the fifteenth. Sir Tondal was given a glimpse of hell, and after his return to earth he showed much remorse. From then on he would only become involved in peaceful activities, which included the revival of his marriage.

It wasn't surprising that during the long siege of Neuss the duchess would draw courage from the adventures of this repentant knight. Beneath each miniature she had had the initials M and C (for Charles) painted, hopefully entwined. She must have prayed fervently that this enchanting illuminated narrative would inspire her husband to lead a different life. Why couldn't the duke become a new Tondal?

Unfortunately, Charles would no longer have time to concern himself with luxury books, let alone spiritual renewal. His star would continue to shine in all its intensity before being inexorably snuffed out.

DEATH IN THE SNOW

*Or how Charles the Bold failed as a commander, blundered at
Neuss, lost his treasure at Grandson, his army at Murten and
his life at Nancy – in short, how inevitable fate can be.*

EVERY NOW AND then a cannonball shot from the town of Neuss
would fly over the heads of the Burgundians at a remarkable
height. Some of them reached the other side of the Rhine, where
the Cologne allies of the besieged city had set up camp. There were
messages attached to the cannonballs, one of which is still on file in
the Cologne archives: 'Unless we are quickly and decisively rescued
we are headed for a complete catastrophe. Only God can deliver
us. If no other help reaches us in the near future, we will begin to
negotiate in order to avoid the loss of our lives and our possessions.'[1]
If the Burgundians had got their hands on this message they would
have taken heart, for on 18 March 1475 the siege was still firmly
entrenched.

Charles the Bold had been maintaining an impressive siege
of Neuss since 29 July 1474. The Archbishop of Cologne had been
coming under increased pressure, and the duke had decided to
intervene. After capturing a few small cities, he had finally decided
to bring Cologne itself under his yoke and turn this electorate
into a Burgundian protectorate. Neuss would be the first nibble
of this German meal. Olivier de la Marche also described it in
terms of a banquet. 'It was the most beautiful and luxurious siege
in living memory [...] our camp was like a city, there were all
sorts of things there, medicinal herbs [...] craftsmen, wholesalers,
textile merchants, fish mongers, grocers, barbers, carpenters,
knife makers, camp followers, labourers, lamplighters, drivers.
[...] Everyone fulfilled his own calling [...] and lived with dignity
in fine tents. [...] They seemed to have been set up to last forever
[...] some looked like towers, others had moats and drawbridges
around them.'[2] There were also windmills, fives courts, taverns
and bathhouses. The better sort of Flemish polyphony was

performed in Charles's chapel at set times. Prostitutes relieved the needs of the body, priests those of the spirit. There were weddings, baptisms and sex. But no progress was made.

Philip de Croy, the lost sheep who had made his way back to the Burgundian camp, seemed to be having less fun and complained about the infernal noise of the artillery, the knee-deep mud and what he regarded as a deficient number of ladies of easy virtue. The pairing of pleasure and death did not particularly appeal to him. The duke, for his part, was blissfully happy, filling his days and nights with inspections, launching attacks and digging trenches... but he found receiving international delegates, and in full armour, just as pleasing as if he were back at Coudenberg Palace. While his camp was being transformed into the official capital of Burgundy, the months slipped by and Charles's enemies set the trap that would lead to his demise.

'God Has Clouded His Common Sense'

To begin with, the Alsatians had had just about enough of Peter von Hagenbach, their crude Burgundian governor. Sigismund, who had sold his principality out of a need for ready cash, was given the necessary money by Strasbourg, Basel, Sélestat and Colmar in order to buy back Upper Alsace and thus to put an end to Hagenbach's reign of terror. But Charles flatly refused to resell his new property.

Another addition to this so-called Lower League – the *Niedere Vereinigung* – were the Swiss, who were gradually beginning to feel the Burgundians breathing down their necks in Bern and decided they would much rather see the ineffective Sigismund on their borders once again. They supported a rebellion in Alsace, which led to the imprisonment of Peter von Hagenbach. He was executed in Breisach on 9 May 1474. The man was already so mutilated that he had to be carried to the Great Market in a wheelbarrow. The place was packed. Everyone wanted to see the monster get what was coming to him. The most gruesome stories about him were making the rounds: from scalping his opponents and nailing their heads to their houses, to having his wife's pubic hair shaved off and added to the evening meal. Hagenbach was seen as the devil incarnate, and the crowd cheered when his head rolled off the chopping block.

Charles was very keen to restore his authority in Alsace, but he was just about to leave for Neuss. So he decided he'd cross that bridge when he got to it. But the Lower League were very efficient in using the time they had been granted. After Charles's refusal to resell Upper Alsace, the allies formally declared war on Charles the Bold on 29 October 1474. By way of warning, they laid siege to the Burgundian castle of Héricourt in the Franche-Comté. With the help of the Ostrich, an immense cannon along the lines of Dulle Griet, the castle was theirs for the taking. Konrad Pfettisheim of Strasbourg wrote a rhymed chronicle of the last Burgundian wars in which he described the 'buzzing sound' made by the Ostrich and its wild dance. 'When it had a crop full of powder, then it laid hard eggs.'[3] The Swiss crushed the Burgundian troops who tried to relieve the siege and left more than a thousand dead on the battlefield. Mercifully for Charles the Bold winter arrived, and the Swiss went back to their mountains.

In early January 1475 an English delegation arrived at Neuss. Did the Burgundian duke remember what he had agreed to with king and brother-in-law Edward IV? Of course, nodded Charles, and moreover, England had no cause for alarm. Before 1 July he would appear at Calais with a force of 10,000 soldiers to join Edward in defeating the French king in the mother of all battles. Charles would then recognize him as King of France. Four months later, when the Burgundian was still persisting in his relentless siege, the English monarch began to get suspicious.

On 9 May, another herald of René II stood before Charles's velvet tent. The Duke of Lorraine was no longer willing to grant passage to the Burgundian troops. Charles, seated on his throne and smartly decked out as usual, listened impassively. The herald tossed a blood-spattered glove on the ground. It was supposed to be a telling gesture, but Charles's appearance had made such an impression that all the poor man could do was stammer out the rest. 'Blood and fire be upon you, your lands, your allies.[4] A declaration of war, even a faltering one, is still a declaration of war. The weak René, whom the duke thought he could manipulate like a puppet, had torn himself loose from his influence. Charles's reaction was hilarious. 'Your words bring me great joy, and to demonstrate that I will give you my tunic as gift.[5] As incomprehensible as it may seem, the Grand Duke of the West was genuinely happy to have an objective reason to capture Lorraine once and for all. He even sent a knight to guard the herald on his homeward journey so that Charles's words would be properly conveyed. Completely flabbergasted, the envoy from Lorraine rode away, one luxury tunic and 500 gold pieces richer. Remarkably enough, Charles actually felt emboldened now that everyone had taken a stand against him like a single bloc. 'God has clouded his common sense,'[6] wrote his former friend Commynes.

In the meantime, the Swiss were intensifying their efforts. They signed a pact with Louis XI of France, who promised to slip them 20,000 francs a year to add to their war chest. The king himself politely waited until the truce with Burgundy expired on 1 May 1475, only to discover with relief that the duke was still at Neuss, and profiting from the fact by immediately attacking the Somme towns. Charles the Bold shrugged this off as a minor annoyance, but he had lost Montdidier, Roye, Corbie and other strategically important cities.

In the meantime, after countless bombardments and more than sixty stormings, he still found himself at the gates of Neuss with nothing to show for his efforts. Although only a handful of the city's hundreds of cows were still alive, and the population had begun feeding on snails and weeds, the residents of Neuss refused to throw in the towel. While bitter fighting was taking place on the walls, processions were being conducted through the streets to pray for a miraculous rescue. And then, just in the nick of time, Frederick III decided to send in troops to save the city. In May, the imperial soldiers found themselves face to face with Charles's army. The only problem was that except for a few skirmishes no one dared start the great battle, which had been so overblown by the Burgundian propagandists that it seemed as if Charles had single-handedly forced the entire assembled host of the Holy

Roman Empire to accept a humiliating truce. Finally, a treaty was signed on 28 June, and Charles the Bold left the principality of Cologne.

The man who, as almost-king and Grand Duke of the West, had wanted to bend the principality of Cologne to his will in a rapid campaign, was obliged to turn around empty-handed just over ten months later – almost 10 per cent of the total length of his reign. The fact that the Caesar of his age had been defeated by a little German town that had managed to resist him was extremely damaging to his image. Perhaps he took comfort in the thought that centuries before, Charlemagne hadn't been able to cut Neuss down to size either, but it was cold comfort to be sure. The Swiss and the Alsatians, the people of Lorraine and of France, had joined forces and were ready to grab him by the throat.

Then a remarkable incident occurred that proved that his star was still shining, even after the signing of the treaty at Neuss. Hundreds of German soldiers queued up to behold the terrible, almost legendary Charles the Bold. The enemy gaped at the Burgundian duke in wonder. Jean-Pierre Panigarola, ambassador of the Duke of Milan, couldn't believe his eyes. 'They threw themselves on the ground and worshipped him as if he had been a saint on his throne.'[7] To avoid chaos, it even became necessary to organize a '*sens de la visite*' – a carefully structured visit. Charles sat on his princely throne in full regalia, the object of an extraordinary cult. The admirers trickled in from one side in orderly fashion, abandoned themselves to adoration when they reached the throne, and then filed out in total silence. The Bold One continued to capture the imagination. Need it be said that such expressions of veneration inflated his dangerous sense of hubris out of all proportion?

'Die Or Triumph'

Charles sent his army on to Lorraine, and he himself took a small armed escort to Calais to meet Edward IV. On the way he stopped at Bruges to address the States of Flanders; the county was still the core of the Burgundian Netherlands, certainly when it came to finances. On 11 July he tore into them. It was their fault that he hadn't been able to take Neuss, he said. Where were the labourers and pikemen he had asked for? Didn't they realize that 'when they slept, he kept watch; when they were warm, he braved the cold; when they were asleep in their houses, he was riding through the rain; when they filled their bellies, he fasted?'[8] But they would have a chance to make up for their failure. They had fourteen days to mobilize a massive army. Or heads would roll!

The Flemings were thunderstruck, but they refused to take it lying down. Why should they take part in his campaigns of conquest? They were tradesmen. If they didn't keep Flanders afloat economically, he could kiss his taxes goodbye, and then how would he pay for his foreign wars? In the past Charles would have drawn his sword and crushed so much resistance, but he already had so many fires to put out on so many fronts that all he could do was leave and slam the door behind him.

There was no getting around it: his expenses vastly exceeded his income. Yet in a sense he was more frugal than his father, who was constantly handing out inappropriate, expensive gifts and sums of money. He himself greatly minimized the well-known ducal generosity, but he would not hesitate to spend more when it came to princely display. Philip the Good had been able to enhance his authority by means of splendour and pageantry, but by the time Charles came along the balance was tipped and dazzling propaganda worked to the disadvantage of both his image *and* his treasury. In his memoirs, Olivier de la Marche had to admit that few were able to understand such obstinacy. 'What on earth possessed the grand duke, who owned so many domains, lands and riches? Why the insistence on incurring the wrath of his neighbours? Why the desire to conquer the world?'[9] These were the same questions that some would ask during Napoleon's last fatal imperialistic years.

A few days later he finally saw his wife again. It would be the last time they met. Margaret of York had been able to keep her angry brother Edward IV happy, at least for a while (where was that Charles and his army?). Now it was up to Charles to face his brother-in-law on his own. Edward quickly realized that Charles was not going to keep his promises and had only come to butter him up. The duke slapped him good-naturedly on the shoulder and said in his best English that Edward's army was so magnificent that he didn't need Burgundy's help. The English king would have to defeat Louis himself. Charles would do the same with Lorraine, and afterwards they would meet each other at Edward's coronation in Reims. Charles was just saying whatever came into his head.

So it wasn't surprising when Edward signed an agreement with the French king a few weeks later. On 29 August 1475 the two sovereigns, who were on the point of tearing each other apart, met on a bridge over the Somme near Picquigny. Louis promised that he would cover all the costs of Edward's expedition if Edward would quickly return to England. He began by calling for food and drink for the entire army. The French king was very keen to put Edward in a good mood. The whole operation must have cost him a fortune in the end, but his crown was saved.

Remarkably enough, Louis also signed a peace treaty with Charles the Bold two weeks later. The essence of their pact was that they would not fight each other, not even if they clashed with one of their allies. So the duke and the king agreed not to rush to the aid of their supporters if those supporters were attacked by the other. This hypocritical agreement gave Louis the chance to observe from the sidelines and secretly to continue supporting Charles's enemies, who would be doing his dirty work for him.

Now that his hands were free, a relieved Charles rushed to Nancy and occupied it fairly quickly. After Neuss, which had all the speed of a funeral procession, this raid was over in a flash, although it must be said that the defence of the capital of Lorraine was not exactly impressive. Yet it was a triumph in any case, because with it Charles the Bold finally succeeded in connecting 'the lands hither' with 'the lands thither', the Burgundian Netherlands in the north and old Burgundy in the south. The great Burgundy now constituted one continuous whole. The duke could travel from Boulogne to Luxembourg and from Mâcon to Amsterdam without crossing a single border. Although he was under pressure from all sides, no one could deny that the Burgundian Middle Empire was a fact. Charles the Bold could finally call himself the true heir of King Gundobad. Whether he would remain so was very much in doubt, but at least now it gave him wings: surely the title of king would soon be his!

He entered Nancy like a Renaissance prince: self-confident and flashy. But for once he was forgiving. The residents of Nancy trembled when they recalled the fate of the people of Liège and Dinant. But the Burgundian duke seemed to have big plans for them. In one of his last impassioned speeches, he even talked about declaring Nancy the capital of all his lands.

Despite the debacle at Neuss, Charles the Bold found himself at the top of his game at Christmas 1475. If the Fates had told the duke during those glorious days that he had only one year to live, he would have laughed out loud.

*

Resting on his laurels was not his style. Charles was eager to teach those tiresome Swiss a lesson, and the sooner the better. It was at this time that the designation Switzeri or *Switsois* became fashionable as synonyms for *Eidgenossen* or 'oath fellowship', the confederacy of the Waldstätte cantons Uri, Unterwalden and Schwyz, with the latter imparting its name to the whole. After their formation at the end of the thirteenth century, the local communities of Zug and Glarus would eventually be added, as well as cities such as Bern, Lucerne and Zürich – in short, the core of what would later become Switzerland.

They were not led by a sovereign but by a federal council consisting of representatives from each part of the confederacy. They called themselves Upper Germans and saw themselves as part of the German empire. There was still no sense of Swiss identity, yet something like unity did develop based on the form of independence they had achieved from the Habsburgs. The fact that in 1307 a man named William Tell was said to have shot an apple from the head of his young son at the command of the Habsburg governor Gessler, whom Tell later shot and killed, was a legend that gave wings to the sense of anti-Habsburg solidarity.

This was something that Sigismund of Habsburg experienced

in 1469. If he failed to come up with the money he owed, the Swiss would be all over him. Charles the Bold came to his rescue by purchasing Upper Alsace, but during Hagenbach's reign of terror Sigismund's old subjects soon began longing for their previous governor. After their execution of the hated tyrant, their resentment really intensified. While at first they had aimed their arrows at the Habsburg, now the Burgundian was their target. The fact that this is how Charles got into trouble, and that the Habsburgs would profit from it, is one of the ironies of history.

What the Swiss blamed the duke for was what the Burgundians had done in scores of places throughout the past century: expand their sphere of influence. At the same time the *Eidgenossen* were beginning to look westward, which they saw as an interesting market. So they did all they could to fend off foreign intervention between the Alps and the Rhine. It was inevitable that they would find Charles standing in their way, although the opposite could also be argued: it was inevitable that he would come up against the Swiss.

The actual provocation for an armed encounter took place on 30 April 1475, when Swiss militias took the village of Grandson. Located on Lake Neuchâtel, it was among the possessions belonging to Charles's vassal Louis de Chalon. In the months that followed, the *Eidgenossen* stationed a number of garrisons at the lake as well as in Grandson. When this Canton of Vaud was captured, Charles's direct line of connection with Italy was broken. This made things difficult for Charles because for quite some time he had been relying on Italian mercenaries to reinforce his standing army. In early January 1476, Charles went to Lake Neuchâtel in order to deal with his Swiss tormentors. He was hoping for one big battle that would allow him to incorporate the *Eidgenossen*'s entire territory into his Burgundian empire in one fell swoop.

On 21 February he easily captured Grandson castle. The soldiers guarding it were ruthlessly slaughtered. 'He ordered three executioners to hang four hundred men in the nearby trees. The rest were drowned in the lake,'[10] noted the Burgundian chronicler Jean Molinet, successor to Georges Chastellain. Chastellain had died in the autumn of 1475, thereby just missing the demise of the Burgundy that he had written about in such glowing terms. Of course, this unnecessary and typical brutality would only strengthen the anti-Burgundian zeal of the Swiss.

On 2 March 1476, Charles moved further along the shoreline while the enemy made their way over the hills. The Burgundians and the Swiss knew they were in each other's proximity, but they didn't know their respective positions. They were groping in the dark. Suddenly, the *Eidgenossen*'s advance guard, while peering through the foliage, saw the army of Charles the Bold marching right below them, and they pounced on them with savage determination. Despite being taken by surprise, the Burgundians responded with ferocity – except the duke made a fatal mistake. In order to lure the Swiss more deeply into the valley and to better position his own artillery, he ordered his troops to pull back a little. Unfortunately, the rest of his army thought the soldiers were fleeing and looked on in shock. Now what? Should they too turn and run? At that very moment, ominous sounds could be heard from the forests above them. It was the rest of the Swiss troops, announcing their arrival with horns. The Burgundians were confused and demoralized. The fearful blast turned Charles's tactical withdrawal into a chaotic rout.

The duke must have been just as bewildered as the Swiss by how soon the battle was over (and strictly speaking it didn't deserve to be called a battle at all). Ranting and raving, he tried in desperation to turn the tide by holding back the flood of Burgundians with the flat of his sword... but it was useless. Charles was relentlessly pulled along by the unstoppable energy of his fleeing troops.

What really gave the fiasco a bitter aftertaste was the fact that they weren't even being pursued. Most of the Swiss were foot soldiers and barely had enough cavalry to give chase to their enemy. While Charles, riding his black charger El Moro, began the most disorienting horse race of his life, the Swiss turned their full attention to one of the richest spoils of war in military history. Why Charles had filled so many carts with priceless treasures and then transported them to the edge of the battlefield remains a mystery. Apparently he demanded that his entire royal household be at his beck and call at all times, even on military campaigns. During a siege is one thing, but during a battle?

The Swiss farmers' sons were barely able to grasp what it was that lay before them. One of them picked up Charles's famous diamond – one of the largest in Europe – smiled, closed the case in which it was held and unsuspectingly tossed the whole thing on the ground. An ox-cart rolled over it as if it were a lump of clay, after which the soldier dug it up again and sold it to a priest for a handful of florins. The diamond was worth 20,000 florins.

Astonished, the Swiss army got lost among the precious relics, silver and gold monstrances, dinnerware, brocade vestments, velvet garments, dazzling wall tapestries, rare manuscripts, countless gold pieces, precious stones and other valuables... The duke's parade sword, his ducal seal and his chain of the Order of the Golden Fleece went from hand to hand. Even Charles's legendary diamond- and pearl-encrusted hat ended up on the head of some Swiss drover. Soldiers fought each other to sit in his silver bathtub or on his gilded throne. This was as close as they would ever come to the most famous ruler of their age. In addition, dozens of luxurious tents and hundreds of horses, lances, swords, pikes, banners, flags and Burgundian artillery pieces were seized. Naturally, they feasted on the provisions they found, which lasted for weeks. Why in the world would the Burgundians leave them behind? They found themselves in an earthly paradise.

Chroniclers made mention of 4,000 young bawds, as if Charles's army had been one big mobile brothel. That seems like an exaggeration when you think of the duke's strict instructions, which allowed only thirty women per company. Either the Burgundian army was incredibly large – which it wasn't, with around 20,000 soldiers – or the duke's moral stranglehold on his troops had weakened considerably. It's also possible that the *Eidgenossen* were so intoxicated by all the grandeur that they were no longer able to count.

Most of the Burgundian treasure has been lost. The Swiss herdsmen and burghers hadn't the vaguest idea what extraordinary goods had fallen into their hands, and their leaders argued among themselves about what to do with it all. Most of it was hopelessly squandered. The city of Basel, for example, settled its debts by peddling off Charles's hat, and as a result one of the most famous head coverings from the Late Middle Ages disappeared into the mists of time. An engraving of the hat has been preserved in the Bibliothèque Nationale in Paris, on the basis of which a reproduction was made that you can admire in Grandson Castle.

Displayed in the Bern Historical Museum, along with the seized flags and banners, is the extraordinarily beautiful *Tapisserie aux Mille Fleurs* featuring the coat of arms of Philip the Good – garlanded with the Golden Fleece, of course – amid thousands of flowers. The old duke bought this tapestry from the Brussels weaver Jan de Haze in 1466. In Grandson it graced the interior of Charles the Bold's army tent. Standing in front of this masterpiece, you find yourself reeling from all the gold decoration and ornament, which renders any overview impossible: a dazzling summary of the Burgundian empire at the height of its existence. Any more exuberance and the whole tapestry would burst at the seams.

*

Not much later, the Swiss discovered the 400 bodies hanging from the trees in Grandson and were sorry they had let the brute escape so easily. Next time they wouldn't hesitate. But would there be a next time?

Of course there would. Charles was beside himself after having been insulted so badly. His splendid army had been beaten by a bunch of ploughmen, a fact that must have been more than he could stomach. Panigarola commented that Charles was furious at the Swiss bumpkins, but no more than at his own army for having fled in such a cowardly fashion. 'He says that in order to restore his honour he will have to die on the battlefield or triumph.'[11] After this umpteenth example of grandstanding, he went to Lausanne and turned all his attention once more to organizing his army. He mobilized, recruited and reformed. Over the course of April and May his soldiers came flocking in. At 20,000, they easily outnumbered the local population, which caused a certain amount of friction. The question was just how motivated this motley jumble of professional soldiers, mercenaries and vassals would be. The Swiss were much stronger in that regard. Certainly, now that the duke had designs on Bern itself, they were prepared to defend their land to the last gasp.

By this time, Charles no longer resembled the handsome Adonis that Rogier van der Weyden had immortalized almost fifteen years earlier. In the 1474 portrait housed in the Museum of Fine Arts in Dijon, you can see that the anonymous painter did not try to disguise how much weight Charles had gained in his face. Look at the double chin, the heavy eyelids. In Dijon, the painting hangs as fourth in a series of portraits, following those of Philip the Bold, John the Fearless and Philip the Good. For the uninformed visitor, there is nothing in this Charles the Bold that is particularly impressive. It could even be mistaken for the work of a mediocre artist. But there is something else that is equally undeniable: this is the exhausted Charles at the end of his life, a man with a dull gaze, more soldier than duke. Only his armour is still gleaming.

After Grandson, the duke, always so meticulous, let his beard grow for the first time. He began to drink his wine undiluted, although he had always watered it down in the past. As if to confirm that these were signs of real decline, he soon shut himself away and no longer let himself be seen. He collapsed. Today we would say he had had a nervous breakdown. The chroniclers called it 'the duke's melancholy', and let it go at that. Not that it was a complete surprise. The beard. The frustration. The incessant shouting and ranting. The obsessive reorganization of his army. Clearly, he had not been able to process the setback at Grandson. His spirit was willing, but his flesh protested.

In the night of 10 to 11 April 1476, the psychological blow was followed by physical symptoms, and he was plagued by terrible stomach cramps. Was there something wrong with the tea he drank to relieve his 'melancholy'? Or could he have been poisoned? In any case, his health was quickly going downhill. Two weeks later he lay gasping in a semi-conscious state, while his legs became terrifyingly swollen. His life hung by a thread for days. Leeches, prayers, purgatives – nothing seemed to help. Someone shaved off his beard. But just when it looked as if the end had come, he got better. In early May, he could even leave his sickbed. Pale and wan, he returned to the land of the living.

With one last spark of statesmanship, an emaciated Charles succeeded in sealing the contract of marriage between his daughter, Mary, and Maximilian of Austria. After the Treaty of Neuss, all seemed well between the duke and the emperor. Charles even seemed genuinely happy that the wedding was taking place. He never said another word about his desire to become king. After Grandson, the chess board looked quite different.

On 9 May he held a big review of his troops. Like a reborn fragment of sheer brutality, he rode past the lines for hours, dressed in a silk tunic woven with gold thread. He screamed out orders as if he were personally pounding in every detail of his new military organization. Soldiers who weren't lined up neatly were given a firm rap with his stick. His expression was one of merciless rage.

The next day he published his new military decree, although he planned to go on the warpath in less than two weeks. Everyone around him advised him to delay, to rest, to give this some thought and to ask himself whether the Swiss were really worth it. He didn't listen to anyone any more; all he could think of was revenge. His men looked with fear at his clouded gaze. By the beginning of June he regarded himself as sufficiently recovered, and he sent his troops ahead, determined not to make any mistakes this time.

Everyone in Dijon, Bruges, Ghent, Brussels and The Hague held their breath. What did fate have in store for their unrestrained duke? Charles was being sent less and less financial support and fewer and fewer troops from the Low Countries. At a meeting of the States General on 26 April in Ghent, his chancellor, Guillaume Hugonet, had demanded that the Low Countries send 10,000 soldiers without delay. But no matter how much he threatened them, Hugonet came home disappointed.

Charles's daughter, Mary, and his wife, Margaret, were also extremely concerned. Was their father and husband, who was always absent, still capable of properly assessing the situation? What would they do if something happened to him? Were they prepared for every eventuality? Even the people of Lyon looked on nervously. After all, King Louis XI of France was residing there temporarily, close enough to intervene in this Swiss campaign if necessary.

Only in Rome did they play dumb – either that or they really did live on another planet. Pope Sixtus IV managed to send Charles a most improbable summons at this critical hour: it was high time the Burgundian duke began working on a Crusade against the Turks!

'I Took Action'

Although most of the Swiss soldiers had travelled dozens of kilometres on foot to get there and had only just arrived, that didn't stop them from going into battle on the early morning of 22 June 1476. They set off in the direction of Murten, a village in the Swiss lake country about thirty kilometres from Bern and right on the language border between French and German. It was at that symbolic spot that the weapons would clash: *Charles le Téméraire* against *les Switsois, Karl der Kühne* versus *die Schweizerische Eidgenossenschaft*, Charles the Bold face to face with the Swiss Confederacy.

The opponents of the Burgundians consisted largely of ploughmen and herdsmen, but the part played by the city militias from Bern, Basel and Zürich was certainly not to be underestimated. Peasants or burghers, the Swiss army was one of the most formidable of its time. In the spirit of the ancient Greek infantries they formed themselves into compact squares, closed off by large shields with five-metre pikes sticking up behind them. The units moved across the battlefield like giant steel hedgehogs. Nothing more was needed to inspire awe in the enemy. Machiavelli, who was seven years old at the time, would sing the praises of the Swiss phalanxes many years later in his *Dell'arte della guerra* (1520): 'the [Swiss] have assumed so much audacity, that fifteen or twenty thousand of them would assault any great number of horse.'[12] The pike squares were made up of hardened warriors who were prepared to give their lives to defend the fatherland. Because they had scarcely any artillery, the *Eidgenossen* could move with extraordinary speed. The cannons of Charles the Bold were the best in Europe but were rather cumbersome and involved fairly complex logistics that inevitably slowed his army down. In mountainous Switzerland, rapid mobility played an important role in the waging of war. Yet another striking difference: the Burgundian army was a mobile Tower of Babel, while the Swiss all spoke the same language. And naturally they had a much better knowledge of the terrain.

The duke had arrived at Murten nine days earlier, and as usual he hoped for one big decisive battle. That's just what he would get. He knew that the Swiss had entered the area on 20 June and he expected a major attack the following day, since the *Eidgenossen* didn't have enough resources to conduct a long campaign. He spent the whole day carefully preparing his army in order to neutralize the dreaded pike squares, no matter what action they undertook. But nothing happened that day – the duke thought it was because they were terrified – and then that night the heavens opened up. Charles was sure that after such a deluge the Swiss would not attack immediately, and he gave his men the opportunity to rest after the first light of day. Such a nonchalant attitude would prove his undoing. It must be said, however, that the Swiss were very lucky. Because some of their troops had yet to arrive they decided to hold back, and when they did launch their attack the enemy was caught napping.

Charles had left at least part of his vanguard out in the field, and they suddenly became aware of the presence of the Swiss hedgehogs. There was shouting, shrieking, messengers hurrying to their commander. But the horse had already bolted. The bulk of his army were quickly seized. The duke was helped into his armour, and just in the nick of time. He actually had to be told three or four times that the Swiss were coming. The great strategist refused to accept it without question because it didn't accord with what he himself had in mind. He had little choice but to jump on his beloved horse El Moro for the second time in just a few months and try to save his own skin. In contrast to what happened in Grandson, the vengeance-hungry Swiss had equipped themselves with cavalry this time. The Burgundians had to run for their lives.

It was like an implausible scene from a B-movie: dozing soldiers having to scramble to find their horses and swords, barely able to defend themselves against an army that was much more numerous than they thought it would be. Because of their lack of concentration and motivation, the Burgundians were doomed from the start; the sheer determination and numerical superiority of the Swiss did the rest. Just as in Grandson, the battle deteriorated into a rout, with this difference: the only escape route soon became so clogged that the confusion ended in slaughter. The Burgundians dived into Lake Murten and climbed the trees… all of them sitting ducks. They either drowned or were shot like fish in a barrel. Jan van Luxemberg, one of Charles's military commanders, became trapped, fell to his knees and begged to be spared in exchange for 25,000 gold ducats. His appeal was answered with an axe planted in his skull. The duke lost most of his army's staff, while he himself miraculously escaped.

Charles the Bold may have been a visionary administrator, a manager *hors catégorie*, an inspired theoretician, but in practice he turned out to be a less than mediocre commander. By thinking everything out in advance down to the minutest detail, he immediately lost his balance when reality challenged his plans. Improvising was not his forte, while spontaneous readjustment of tactics was often what was called for. He lived so much in his own head that he was too careless when it came to reconnoitring and spent too little time assessing the numerical strength and tactics of the enemy. Not that he realized this. On the contrary, until the bitter end he saw himself as a brilliant military leader.

Nine years later, a monument was erected in Murten, a charnel house containing the bones of thousands of victims. An inscription was added later on that began with these words: 'Helvetians, stop! Here lies the army that laid waste to Liège and shook the throne of France…'

*

In the meantime, René II of Lorraine had not been idle and had retaken almost his entire principality. He had also finally driven the Burgundians out of Nancy, the capital city. While Charles was licking his wounds, the connecting link of his Middle Empire disappeared. He refused to go to the safety of the north to regain his strength, but instead, with the courage born of desperation, cobbled together the last army of his life, provoking Louis XI to utter the very telling words, 'He has gone mad.'[13] Like a spider waiting at the edges of the web he himself had spun, the king looked on, determined to make his move only when his prey was cornered.

Ambassador Panigarola, who was looking forward to having the adventure of a lifetime, would soon abandon Charles because his employer, the Duke of Milan, had defected to the King of France. The adventurous envoy also seemed to have lost his confidence in the duke's sanity. 'He laughs, he makes jokes, he says that God has given him an empire with so many reserves that he would really have to take a beating before ruination struck.'[14] Charles had now completely lost contact with reality. He began speaking gibberish and seemed to live in a parallel universe. But no one could shake him from his idée fixe: reconquer Nancy, rehabilitation, blind fury. All the rest was idle chatter.

Undeterred, he travelled to Dijon to raise funds and recruit soldiers. It wasn't easy. Chancellor Hugonet in the north let it be known that there was no more money to be had in Ghent, Bruges, Brussels or The Hague. Yet he managed to wangle a large loan from the Medici Bank, thanks to the unquestioning support of Tommaso Portinari. As banker, he overplayed his hand by overrating the duke's creditworthiness and issuing unsecured loans. So Charles collected the money he needed to cover the cost of bringing about 10,000 soldiers, haphazardly gathered, to the capital of Lorraine.

If Portinari, who had commissioned Hugo van der Goes to make one of the most impressive triptychs of the century, had strictly followed the directives of his superiors in Florence, Charles would never have gone to Nancy.

★

On 22 October 1476, Charles began the siege of Nancy, even though his troop numbers were incomplete. Small groups of soldiers reported every day, but in the first week of December, René II succeeded in cutting off the only Burgundian connecting route to Luxembourg via the friendly bishopric of Metz. Now Charles was entirely on his own. The Italian mercenary leader Campobasso was behaving very strangely. Could he be trusted? Not at all, as it turned out. Campobasso was already reaching out to René II, from whom more money could be obtained on short notice, but Charles either couldn't see it or didn't want to. The inhabitants of Nancy fought for their lives. They would never give up their city, not for all the money in the world. Nor would the tyrant Charles be generous with them a second time. For now the Burgundians were fighting a losing battle, but they knew the little capital of Lorraine couldn't endure the siege for more than two months. Would a saviour finally step in to liberate the people of Nancy?

René did all he could to assemble a relief force. In early December, the Swiss declared that it was too cold to fight. That was no lie, but it was also a way of raising their price. René's grandmother, who was critically ill, made part of her legacy available to him in order to incentivize the *Eidgenossen*. King Louis XI of France finally came through with some money, again in deepest secret, since essentially he was still allied to Burgundy through the peace treaty. Without a dying grandmother and a devious king, history would have taken quite a different turn.

At the last moment the dreaded Swiss army did show up, this time driven solely by cash and the promise of more booty. As far as the latter was concerned, simply uttering the word 'Grandson' worked like a charm. Initially the force was fairly modest in size, but it grew steadily. As soon as the *Eidgenossen* crossed the border they were joined by Alsatians and Lorrainers, 20,000 soldiers in all. On 5 January 1477, Burgundy's nemesis came marching up in a snowstorm.

*

Charles's remaining commanders begged their leader to raise the siege in order to give the exhausted troops a rest, to let them get through the winter and regain their strength. The Great Bastard, his half-brother Anthony, looked him deep in the eyes. René II doesn't have nearly enough money to pay his troops that long. So we'll take care of him when spring comes, right? Philip de Croÿ, the man responsible for the break with his father twenty years before, made an especially passionate argument. He might just as well have been talking to the tomb of Philip the Bold. Charles barely heard what his devoted associates proposed. 'Even if I have to fight the Swiss alone, I will still go into battle.'[15]

The duke went on to outline his tactics – that is to say, he imposed them. He would occupy the hill between Jarville and Neuville, accompanied by the bulk of his troops. Then he would cleverly position his cannon and count on their striking power. The fact that Charles was not able to count on the artillery lost at Grandson and Muren, which had been equipped with the latest refinements, and had had to rely on cast-offs scrounged from past battles, was of little interest to him. He was equally indifferent to the fact that for weeks his soldiers had been facing the real possibility of freezing to death. And the numerous forests that made it so difficult to see if the enemy was coming didn't faze him in the least. Fearless or reckless? Call it audacious, yes – even suicidal. His headstrong perseverance began to look like a suicide mission. But maybe that's what he had in mind. Tempting fate in a way that would never be forgotten. Securing the place of a blood-drenched martyr in the history books.

In addition, he had to manage with scarcely 5,000 soldiers. A substantial number of his troops had deserted, and many others had succumbed to disease, cold and hardship. The traitor Campobasso had shown his true colours two days earlier. He had defected to the enemy and naturally had told them all about the misery in the Burgundian camp. René now knew he had no time to lose. If the duke were to leave for the north, it would be a missed opportunity.

On the morning of 5 January, Charles prepared himself for battle. He looked as if he knew this would be his last. When he put on his helmet, the crest – which featured the figure of a rampant lion – fell mournfully to the floor. *'Hoc est signum Dei,'*[16] said the duke with an air of foreboding. 'This is a sign from God.'

So there he sat, the almost-king, the Grand Duke of the West, the intriguing Charles the Bold. Hunted like a beast, sequestered in the snow, hidden behind a ridge, shivering with cold, waiting until the enemy, who were warmed from marching, should appear in his field of vision.

Except the clever Swiss had split their army into two parts. The first part went forward, heading straight for the Burgundians' dilapidated artillery. The second group walked all the way round to the left with slow and cautious steps, aided by the snow that fell noiselessly on the army and the forests. Owing to this sound-deadening carpet, Charles and his men did not hear them. A thick mist had settled in, which also worked to the advantage of the alliance of Lorrainers, Alsatians and especially the *Eidgenossen*.

At about one o'clock in the afternoon, three hellish horn blasts resounded. Icy, lingering notes, as long as the trained lungs could keep it up. The signal of the accursed Swiss. The Burgundian cannon immediately responded. The cannonballs flew through the air. No one had any idea if they had hit their target or not. At that very moment, the allies' second force pounced on the unsuspecting right wing of Charles the Bold. Of course, he hadn't thought to send scouts in that direction. What must have gone through his head when he saw his last plan go up in smoke as well? There they stood, his cannon, positioned with the utmost care but aimed in the wrong direction.

Quickly he organized his troops for the final struggle, but when the Swiss moved in for a frontal attack there was no stopping them. For the third time in a year, the once so powerful Burgundian army took to their heels. Charles too put spurs to his horse. El Moro sprinted and leaped, a jet-black steed without equal. The last warriors to catch a glimpse of the duke saw him with raised sword, slashing his way out of this inferno. He had to keep swerving, since the escape route was filled with groaning soldiers. In one such manoeuvre El Moro must have stumbled. The duke fell to the ground.

The raging Swiss behind him did not recognize the man who had fallen in the snow. A battle-axe was raised. Perhaps, like his grandfather John the Fearless, he lay on his back and was able to look death in the eye. The Montereau bridge, the snow of Nancy. Two key Burgundian moments, each with the same outcome. A cry, a last scuffle, a split skull. Charles must have died instantly.

Free of his restless burden, his charger walked on alone. Zigzagging between the bodies, El Moro disappeared into the mist. Beside the lifeless duke lay his banner, the fluttering snow covering his gold-embroidered motto. His legendary slogan, *'Je lay emprins'* – 'I took action', was soon completely obliterated.

PART IV

'Mary of Burgundy lies in Bruges in bronze;
Ilaria del Caretto in Lucca sweetly prone,
her waxen face forever carved in stone,
like Medea Colleoni in Bergamo [...]

How came your body here to lie, O how?
What earthly thing now occupies your name?
What stone, what copper here replace your frame?
Only my words and what I write them on.'

Christine D'haen, from: Onyx, 1983

A DECISIVE YEAR

1482

---

*Or how, after the death of Charles the Bold and despite
all the subsequent misery, the Low Countries under Mary
of Burgundy opted for continuity and acquired the first
'constitution' in history, and how the painter Hugo van der
Goes made it through those complex years, but especially how
the marriage and tragic death of the new duchess hastened the
age of the Habsburgs.*

'I GLORIFY THE true God, summon the people, rally the clergy, mourn the dead, dispel the plague, enliven feasts.' These are the words imprinted on the bell that was cast in 1481 for the church in the Frisian village of Sondel. In that year, the plague did indeed wreak havoc in the Low Countries, from Ypres, Bruges and Turnhout, by way of Durbuy, Liège and Maastricht, all the way to Friesland. The new outbreak came on the heels of an exceedingly severe winter. The Burgundian chronicler Jean Molinet witnessed 'the birds falling dead from the sky, the trees perishing where they stood and riders freezing to death on their horses'.[1] To make matters worse, the following winter would also be very harsh. At the start of 1482, the Low Countries looked back on a year of death and destruction.

While the population in these regions was suffering a serious demographic contraction, Mary of Burgundy and her consort, Maximilian of Austria, withdrew to the Prinsenhof in Bruges. Unlike King Afonso V of Portugal, who succumbed to the plague on 28 August 1481, they managed to escape the clutches of death, which made the Burgundian winter feasts all the more exuberant when the new year arrived. On three occasions, the couple had invited the best knights to take part in tournaments on Bruges's Great Market.

King Louis XI of France, still eager to flush out what was left of Burgundy, had declared a salt blockade. This common preservative became so expensive that even the ever-popular salt herring was no longer available. The fact that the ordinary Bruggian was stupefied with hunger and cold did nothing to spoil the Burgundian fun. Maximilian donned his best suit of armour and outdid himself on the playing field while the populace snarled.

He cast a proud glance at his beloved Mary, who looked on from Craenenburg, the house where, six years later, Maximilian would spend the least pleasant moments of his rule. In the restaurant of the same name, which retains the ancient roof trusses and cellar, today's tourists eat beef stew prepared with the aptly named *Bourgogne des Flandres* beer.

Despite all the misery, Mary succeeded in preventing the complete downfall of Burgundy after her father's terrible debacle. Things looked relatively good in 1482, certainly with Maximilian at her side. The festive gathering of the Order of the Golden Fleece six months earlier in 's-Hertogenbosch had evoked the glory of the olden days. Afterwards, Mary also made her way to the same city, and what followed was the ducal couple's Joyous Entry. During that inauguration, one of the public grandstands suddenly began to totter, and a few seconds later the entire construction collapsed. Thankfully, no one was killed. Although months later some self-proclaimed seers would announce that they had heard the call of destiny back in 's-Hertogenbosch, all signs looked positive at that point for Mary and Maximilian.

Between the New Year's festivities, the couple spent their time skating on the *meersen*, the low-lying, flooded and frozen marshes south of Bruges. Mary was wildly enthusiastic, and as soon as the freezing temperatures allowed she would strap on her skates, never letting a few tumbles get in her way. Maximilian did his best to keep up. The skating fun came to an end with the March thaw, but one amusement made way for another. Adolph of Cleves, Lord of Ravenstein, who had served as governor-general of the Burgundian lands for several years, decided to organize a dignified celebration of the arrival of spring and planned a great hunt on his estate, Wijnendale, to take place on 13 March 1482. He hoped that Mary and Maximilian would brighten up his festive event as guests of honour.

The couple quickly let him know that they would be coming from Bruges, for both the duke and the duchess were mad about hunting. Adolph immediately ordered the cleaning of the huge grills in his monumental fireplaces. He chuckled at the very thought of all the excitement in store, and he could already smell the fragrance of roast game. Not a detail escaped his attention. This hunt was going to be a day to remember.

Ravenstein's intention would amply succeed, so much so that it would make the pages of the history books, to his great sorrow.

'Faithful Unto Death'

When the news of the debacle of her father's army reached her sometime in January 1477, Mary of Burgundy was left in the dark as to his fate. Charles the Bold was said to have fled, but no one knew where. His horse El Moro was soon located, but there was no sign of his master in any nearby fields or roadways. For forty-eight hours the duke's whereabouts were unknown. Then an Italian page, Baptiste Colonna, claimed he knew where Charles could be found.

Lying near the place where he had seen him fall were more than a dozen frozen corpses, expertly stripped by robbers. The naked bodies were turned over one by one until the Italian stopped shaking his head no. 'Alas, this is my good lord and master,'[2] said Colonna. He recognized him from his scars, missing teeth and long fingernails. Charles's head was frozen into the ice of a small lake, his skull was split from his ears to his teeth, someone had clearly thrust a lance up his anus, his arms and limbs had been trampled by horses' hooves, and worst of all: one of his cheeks had been torn from his face by a wolf. In the centuries to come, Charles's name would often be mentioned in the same breath with the words 'eaten by wolves'.

What if he had won at Grandson or Murten? That might have happened despite the failure, even in Nancy. Think of the totally unexpected French defeat at Poitiers in 1356. Of course, you can't explain the past by wondering what would have happened if, say, Napoleon had lost at Austerlitz. But it's true that Charles, who had all the makings of a failed Napoleon, paid the price for his hubris much earlier than the Corsican would three centuries later. History teaches that rulers with too much pepper in their ambition are bound to come to grief some day. The only question is when.

If Nancy was the last Burgundian battle, then with a bit of goodwill you can call Poitiers the first: the courage of Philip the Bold gave him both his epithet *and* the old duchy. At Nancy, great-grandson Charles forfeited not only his life but the original duchy as well. It was there that his epithet took on a lustre of agelessness. He would always be known as '*le Téméraire*', the reckless.

French spies informed Louis XI of the tragic news on 8 January, scarcely a day after the body had been found, two weeks before the news reached the new duchess at the Prinsenhof in Ghent. He sent no condolences but immediately invaded both the old Burgundian duchy and the Franche-Comté. Any memory of holding baby Mary over the baptismal font in Coudenberg Palace in Brussels twenty years before had long been forgotten. He saw his opportunity. Finally he would be able to reclaim Picardy, Artois, Burgundy and Flanders, which had been associated with France since time immemorial.

While Louis was preparing his advance, Margaret and Mary wondered when Charles the Bold would show up to rectify the situation. At first they refused to believe that he had disappeared. And they weren't the only ones. A few usurers floated loans that were to be paid back on the day of Charles's return. Everyone tried to benefit from the situation, although in this last case the borrowers were the ones who profited.

Mary had no time to speculate. When the news was confirmed on 25 January, she found herself with her back to the wall. Despite the great sadness that befell her, she had no choice but to quickly conclude an agreement with her subjects, or Louis XI would gobble up the entire Burgundian state. Fortunately, the States General, which had convened in Ghent, declared that it 'would be faithful to her unto death'.[3] But it was all quid pro quo.

The irritation that had been building over Charles's management came gushing out all at once. Cities and states wanted to formulate their own policy as much as possible, steering clear of anything that smacked too much of centralism. So to start off, the members of the States General abolished the Mechelen Parlement and replaced it with another travelling Great Council. This council had fewer far-reaching powers and had to work with judges from all the sub-regions who had a firm grasp of Dutch and who could not disregard local laws. On the other hand, it remained an overarching judicial authority. Other central bodies also survived the reforms. The regional courts of auditors and council chambers in Lille, Brussels and The Hague continued working as before, although they were made up of officials appointed by the late Charles the Bold.

The most important changes were laid down in the Great Privilege, signed by Mary on 11 February 1477. The result was striking for its attention to detail and for the individual regional provisions. The general text consisted of 20 articles. In Flanders there followed another separate charter with 47 additional provisions, Holland and Zeeland added another 60 and Brabant no fewer than 108. The latter figure is not surprising. Brabant can safely be regarded as the birthplace of joint management in the Low Countries. A distant Brabant precursor of the Great Privilege was the Charter of Kortenberg of 1312. In an attempt to simplify the complex succession of John II at that time, pledges were made to the nobility and the cities. This was now taking place on a grand scale.

Henceforth, Mary could not marry, wage war or levy taxes without the approval of the States General, which also could meet on its own initiative. Her official enactments were to be drafted in Dutch if that was the language of the residents. The language question would remain a sensitive issue.

The Burgundian Netherlands acquired what today you might call a federal structure, with more authority for the regions and with a more balanced division of power between the estates and the sovereign. The Great Privilege, which applied to all 'lands hither', can be regarded as the first constitution for the Low Countries, a legal framework that would often be referred to during the revolt against the Spanish in the sixteenth century. It was basically a way of saying: this is how the relationship between sovereign and subjects ought to be.

The right to resist and to refuse military service in the event that Mary were to violate the Privilege's provisions was a European first. This right applied to all burghers and villagers. For the first time, everyone – and not only the vassals of the prince, as was customary under feudal law – could resist unjust actions by the government, and everyone also had the right to have their privileges restored. This was so groundbreaking that even the drafters of the Belgian constitution in 1831 consulted the Great Privilege one last time.

After this breakthrough, the various regions said that they were prepared to recruit troops to stop the advance of the French king. Despite all the resentment against Charles the Bold, most of the Low Countries were eager to preserve the Burgundian dynasty. Only the recently annexed principalities of Guelders and Liège wanted to continue on their own, with the return of the former duke and prince-bishop. After the crimes of Charles the Bold, you can hardly blame the people of Liège for having their reservations.

Although the centralism of the deceased duke was axed, the attack of the French triggered what seemed like a 'national' reflex. Hadn't the Brabantians in the States General said that 'men should be brothers and remain united' in order 'to preserve' the 'true union and concord' of the Burgundian lands?[4] Hadn't everyone nodded their heads in assent? Put these words to music and romantic souls would actually speak of a first national anthem of the Low Countries, with that 'faithful unto death' mentioned earlier to add punch to the refrain.

To bring us back to earth, it should be said that the members of the States General usually defended their own region or city first of all, just as they do today in that federation known as Belgium. The concept of 'nation' was always more applicable to, say, Brabant or Holland than to the Burgundian Netherlands as a whole. The Great Privilege put an end to the stadholderate of 'foreigners'. As stadtholder of Holland and Zeeland, Bruggian Louis de Gruuthuse had to step aside for the Zeeuw Wolfert van Borselen.

Nevertheless, the cohesion of the States General meant much more than regulated interregional neighbourliness. Certainly in times of great crisis, the people of the Burgundian Netherlands spoke and acted as one. There's also the fact that the old Burgundian duchy had fallen into the hands of Louis XI. After a bit of grumbling, Dijon had completely surrendered. Mary and her descendants continued to dream of retaking the homeland some day, but in the meantime, slowly but surely, the name Burgundy became disconnected from its ancient history and forever entwined with that of the Low Countries. Essentially, Mary of Burgundy had become Queen of the Netherlands.

'A Small Nose, A Small Forehead, Drooping Eyelids'

Mary may have been able to salvage whatever she could, but it would take more than the Great Privilege to siphon off the people's anger. Their frustration sought and found a violent outlet. Exactly ten years after her father had addressed the populace from the window of the Hooghuis in Ghent, Mary stood in the same place and pleaded for mercy for Chancellor Hugonet. As a loyal follower of her father, he had to pay the piper. No matter how moving her intervention may have been, Mary would quickly come to understand that an unleashed mob was almost unstoppable. On Holy Thursday, Hugonet was beheaded, as was councillor Guy de Brimeu, stadtholder of Liège and Luxembourg. Now that the many-headed hydra known as 'the people' had had its revenge, the Great Privilege could do its work.

Mary turned her back on perilous Ghent and travelled to Bruges in the company of Louis de Gruuthuse, her tower of strength. There she saw the necessity of having a strong husband at her side. Countless candidates were vetted, but she remained stubbornly faithful to the will of her father and chose Maximilian of Austria. A strategic marriage with the French dauphin might have defused the complex situation with her godfather Louis XI, but sleeping with the enemy? Delicate as she may have been, the twenty-year-old Mary held her ground.

She chose as her motto *'En vous me fye'*. There was nothing frivolous about this 'In you I trust'. Indeed, it was now up to the Habsburg to rescue the Low Countries from the clutches of France. Maximilian was received with open arms.

★

Maximilian actually should have been called Constantine, after the obsession of his father Frederick III with the liberation of Constantinople. Earlier, the emperor had rechristened Maximilian's mother, Eleonora of Portugal, with the name Helen. He himself was thinking of replacing the Portugal in her name with Troy. Deep down, the melancholy emperor was a dreamer. His Helen died in 1467, making little Maximilian a semi-orphan at the age of eight. This did not help his exceptional shyness. For a while it was feared that after his mother's death he would never speak another word, but all was well once he found his true calling: to become a widely acclaimed knight. It's not surprising that while in Trier he was completely captivated by the pomp and splendour of the sovereign of the Golden Fleece, so that entering into marriage with his daughter, Mary, later on was like a dream come true.

When he first arrived in the Low Countries, it was almost too much to take in. So many big cities so close together was something he had never seen before. But hidden behind all the hustle and bustle was a destitute Burgundian state. Charles the Bold had blown his entire fortune on three disastrous campaigns. At the sight of the empty coffers it dawned on Maximilian that despite all the glistening court ritual, the dukes were no kings. In his own case he had the title of King of the Romans to look forward to. Apart from that, he, like most princes, would live on credit. The Low Countries – Flanders, Brabant and Holland at the top – were quite rich, and with the taxes approved by the States General he ultimately would have more money at his disposal than anything he could ever expect in Austria.

The wedding took place on 18 August 1477 in the chapel of the Prinsenhof in Ghent. Because the mourning period after Charles's death was not yet over, the wedding was held in a minor key (which was good in a way because there wasn't enough money for anything else). The nuptials of Mary's father, Charles, and her stepmother, Margaret, nine years earlier had been a celebration straight out of The Thousand and One Nights, making the un-Burgundian simplicity all the harder to bear. On the other hand, it seemed to make the tie between the newly-weds that much stronger, a sharp contrast with the rather detached relationship between Charles the Bold and his last wife.

Three weeks later, Maximilian wrote a lyrical letter to an Austrian friend in which, like a florid poetaster, he raved about Mary's 'pale skin, as white as snow' and her 'thick, red lips'. He went on to describe her as a woman with 'a small nose and a small forehead and slightly drooping eyelids, as if she had just woken up'. But the drooping eyelids are 'barely noticeable', he hastened to add. He decided that she was 'the most beautiful woman' he had ever seen.[5] The fact that he himself had excessively long legs, an oversized chin and a hooked nose didn't seem to dampen Mary's enthusiasm, although she did have to use sign language at first in order to understand him. She would teach him French, he would teach her German. Margaret of York tried to teach the archduke Dutch. The ladies' linguistic diligence was not very effective, however. Their Austrian pupil made little effort to master Dutch, and even his French remained substandard. The mistrust that his subjects would feel towards him in the coming years was only exacerbated by his language handicap.

*

In addition to the executions mentioned earlier there were still more purges, and countless others were driven from their positions. Everyone tried to save their skin. Anthony of Burgundy, Charles's half-brother and one of his most important army commanders, was taken prisoner at Nancy by René of Lorraine and passed on to the King of France. There, Anthony swapped his allegiance for his life. From then on, he would serve as advisor to Louis XI. He wasn't the only knight of the Golden Fleece to commit treason and defect to the enemy, whether by choice or necessity.

Because of his risky loans to Charles the Bold, banker Tommaso Portinari was compelled to close the branch of the Medici Bank in Bruges. After this failure he went through some hard times, but two years later the survivor resurfaced as ambassador to the Spanish court. In the meantime, Hugo van der Goes had all but finished his *Portinari Altarpiece*, except for one detail: the head of Portinari, who commissioned the work, was missing. Van der

Goes was probably holding it back until the final payment was made. Now that Portinari was strapped for cash, the painter would have to be patient – a real setback for him, since he too was in financial straits.

The fact that Van der Goes had worked for Charles the Bold put him under a cloud of suspicion after Charles's death. And the fact that in all probability his *Adoration of the Magi* (c.1473) had been commissioned by the beheaded Chancellor Hugonet – who didn't want to be outdone by Rolin and his Madonna – did not work to the artist's advantage either. On top of that, there were plenty of others who couldn't wait to show the door to someone with as much talent and success as Van der Goes. No one approached him to work on the decorations for the wedding of Mary and Maximilian. That honour was given to the now forgotten Matthijs van Roden.

It must have been very difficult for the painter, who was melancholic by nature, for at the end of 1477 he decided to answer a late calling, left Ghent and entered a monastery as a lay brother. At the Red Cloister in the Sonian Forest near Auderghem, he was received with open arms. After all, he was one of the greatest artists of his time. His half-brother Nicholas had entered the order years before and gave the disoriented Hugo a warm welcome. Nevertheless, he had four trying years ahead.

'From The Emperor's Seed'

On 13 March 1482 the company of Burgundians set off on their hunting trip in the forests of Wijnendale. Galloping through the woods along with Adolph of Ravenstein, Louis de Gruuthuse, Olivier de la Marche and of course Maximilian was Mary of Burgundy. The group were in high spirits and turned all their attention to the ancient hunting ritual. Everything went smoothly until the duchess saw a heron standing on the other side of a brook.

In a flash she removed the hood from her trained falcon and tossed him into the air. She then spurred her horse towards the water and urged him to jump to the other side. For an experienced horsewoman like Mary it was a routine manoeuvre. This time, however, the animal stumbled on a fallen tree trunk and slid. And there Mary of Burgundy took the most widely discussed fall in the history of the Low Countries, with the exception of the fatal plunge of King Albert I of Belgium in 1934. Unfortunately, she landed on the same tree trunk. But it was the tumbling of the horse that proved fatal. He landed with his full weight on the duchess's right side.

Maximilian, Louis, Olivier and Adolph raced up to attend to her. The duchess did not appear to be injured, yet the pain was unbearable. The journey back to Bruges must have been a dreadful torture for her. No doctor or surgeon could ease her suffering. No one knew exactly what the cause was. Maximilian was frantic and inconsolable.

It wasn't until 1979 that a paleo-pathological examination of Mary's skeleton was carried out, revealing that when she fell she broke not only both wrists but also three ribs, which penetrated her chest cavity and struck her right lung. That must have triggered a lung infection. The examination also showed that she had extremely bad teeth, eleven of which were missing. This was probably a combination of poor dental hygiene and royal inbreeding. Now a person with bad teeth, or few of them, could easily live a long life, but a perforated lung that went undiagnosed, let alone treated, was quite a different matter.

In an act of desperation, a procession was organized in Bruges. Perhaps carrying the relic of the Holy Blood would bring about a miracle. But the terrible pain continued unabated. Her situation worsened, and three days before her death she summoned her most important advisors to her bedside. The first chamberlain, Louis de Gruuthuse, was also present. She begged them to accept Maximilian as regent and guardian of her son, Philip, who was not yet four years old. Everyone nodded in agreement, but the subject would later generate much emotion.

So many things must have gone through the poor woman's mind. Her father, the most powerful man in Europe, had suffered a tragic death and sowed nothing but chaos and misery, and just when the future had begun to look rosy again after the Low

Countries had almost unanimously opted for dynastic continuity, she found herself facing certain death. When she looked at her husband she saw an impetuous knight of the old school, a Habsburgian replica of her father. When her eyes turned to her son she saw a four-year-old toddler, much too young to take the helm.

*

Fortunately, the barely twenty-five-year-old Mary had produced an heir. Within a year of her marriage, on 22 June 1478, Philip came into the world and was named after the old Grand Duke of the West. Both the court and the populace received the news with delight, while the King of France must have stifled a curse. In an effort to spoil the festive mood, Louis XI could think of nothing better than to have spies circulate the rumour that the child was not a son but a daughter, which at that time was seen as significantly less positive.

The unflappable grandmother, Margaret of York, made quick work of the false reports. One anonymous chronicler described her removing little Philip's clothing in the middle of the Bruges market and holding him up *'naect'* (naked) for all to see. *'Si nam sijn cullekens in haer hants ende si sprak: kinderen siet hier uwen nieuwen gheboren here den iongen Philippus van des keysers sade.'*[6] Translated into modern English, this sounds as bombastic as it does comical: 'She took his little balls in her hands and said: my children, behold your newborn lord, the boy Philip, from the emperor's seed.' Then Mary took the baby in her arms, kissed him tenderly and handed the crown prince to a deeply affected Maximilian, who proclaimed in just the right words: 'O noble Burgundian blood!' The joy that followed proved how much the people had come to embrace the once so alien Burgundians as their own.

This Philip would go down in history as 'the Handsome' and would be popular in the Low Countries. Of this there is no doubt. But was he really as attractive as his epithet suggests? He looks rather good in his portraits, at least by our standards of beauty. A Venetian diplomat and contemporary unhesitatingly used the words '*bello di corpo, gagliardo e prospero*' to describe him.[7] In any event, with this 'handsome, strapping and rich' youth the world was one Burgundian womanizer richer. The typical jutting 'Habsburg jaw' was not so prominent in his case. As sometimes happens with hereditary characteristics that tend to skip a generation, the condition would affect his son all the more. From an early age, Philip did have strikingly thick lips, as you can still read about in the Royal Library of Belgium. '*Cest livre appartient à Philippe, dict autrement Lippeque*'[8] is charmingly inscribed in one of the books belonging to him. You can just hear Mary of Burgundy speaking those words. But *Lippeque*!

His grandmother Margaret stood by him during his early years, but she wasn't alone. Olivier de la Marche, who was ransomed after the Battle of Nancy, sided with Mary, helped her negotiate the marriage with Maximilian and would supervise the upbringing of her son, Philip. In the introduction to his memoirs, he expressed the hope that knowledge of the past would show the young archduke the way to a just future.

Only two months after Philip's birth, his father, Maximilian, was back in his armour and pressing his dear son to his chest. Up until then he had been fully occupied with the French, whom he defeated in 1479 at Guinegatte, today's Enguinegatte, a village between Béthune and Boulogne-sur-mer. In doing so, he saved Flanders from the web of 'the big spider' Louis XI. In Holland, the Hooks and the Cods were at each other's throats again, but the archduke managed to bring those disputes under control as well. Although Maximilian complained in his letters of 'hunger and thirst, fear, fatigue and hard labour',[9] he thought he could make his old dream of knighthood come true on the battlefield. His subjects had no interest in such ambitions. Not only did all that sabre-rattling cost barrels of money, but the people were hungry for peace. Between battles, the commander sired a daughter, Margaret of Austria, who was to become so important for the Low Countries. A third child, a son, did not live long. Only a few months later, Death came knocking for Mary herself.

'*Adieu Margrite, edel bloemen reyn / mijn liefste dochter bid voor mi / mijn hert is in grooten weyn,*' ('Adieu Margaret, pure flower that thou art / my dearest daughter, pray for me / how filled with sorrow is my heart') are the words that an anonymous rhetorician put in the mouth of Mary of Burgundy at her leave-taking from her children. '*Adieu Philips, lieve sone mijn / Ick schyde nog veel te vroech van dijn*' ('Adieu Philip, dear son of mine, / I take my leave far too soon from thine').[10] Mary must have had enough time to take Margaret and Philip in her arms once more. On 27 March 1482, two weeks after her fall at Wijnendale, she died from the effects of her injuries. What now? Duke Charles had passed away five years earlier, and now Mary, scarcely twenty-five years old. What was to become of tormented Burgundy?

The members of the States General had sworn to her to be 'faithful unto death', but there was no scenario for what would happen afterwards. They gave Archduke Maximilian powers of regency over the four-year-old Philip, although the commitment was fraught with difficulties. As prince consort he had been readily embraced, but as guardian, let alone as head of state, he was viewed with considerable suspicion. In exchange he would have to dance to the tune of the States General. What Maximilian wanted most of all was to keep on fighting, but the States were aiming for a truce with France. Their vote was decisive.

On 23 December 1482 the Treaty of Arras was signed, which went against everything Maximilian stood for. But the Burgundian Netherlands, especially Flanders, were willing to go to great lengths to finally live in peace and quiet. To speed this up, Maximilian's two-year-old daughter ended up in French hands as a sort of peace collateral. She was engaged to marry the dauphin Charles, but for now the little mite was relocated to the Loire region to be moulded into the next French queen. As a dowry she was given Artois and the Franche-Comté. Clearly, the Burgundian Netherlands wanted to go it alone from now on.

To prevent Philip from becoming an unpredictable Austrian eccentric like his father, it was decided that the little prince would be given a Burgundian upbringing. So the States General, goaded by the Flemings, deprived Maximilian of his son as well. Every four months, Philip would be entrusted to the good care of a different region of his empire. After the intense grief that fell to him following the loss of his beloved wife, he was now given two more major setbacks to deal with.

At the start of the new year, the various domains looked back with satisfaction on the way the transfer of power had been negotiated. The States General, who had more or less taken control, had the archduke right where they wanted him. For the first time in the history of the Low Countries, a representative body, which you could hardly call democratically elected, had managed to curtail the authority of a sitting monarch in a way that was legally binding.

This central organ, which would foster the unification of the Low Countries, consisted of important members of the clergy and nobility who were directly summoned by the ducal chancellery, but it was mainly made up of representatives of the principal cities that chose their own delegation. The only region to send representation from the countryside was Flanders. In short, the voices of the rich city-dwellers carried the most weight. If you count the number of members per region, Flanders comes out as the most heavily represented. At a well-attended meeting in April 1493, thirty-five of the eighty-four members present were from this region. The exact composition of the States General fluctuated, depending primarily on the agenda. But it might just as well have depended on the weather. In the winter of 1477, the Holland delegates were late in reaching Ghent on account of the severe climatic conditions.

The tenacity with which the States General got the upper hand and held on tight was a source of great irritation to Maximilian. As a Habsburg, he had been raised to think that men with no blue blood in their veins were deserving of contempt. And by the way, didn't the Burgundian Netherlands have him to thank for not having been gobbled up by France?

*

Hugo van der Goes spent most of Mary's reign in the Red Cloister. He tried to live according to *The Imitation of Christ* by Thomas à Kempis, and devoted himself to moderate asceticism. Thanks to the sympathetic prior, Thomas van Vessem, he was given a special position that allowed him to paint and receive visitors. He was even permitted to drink wine with them in the guest quarters, an exceptional privilege. Because of his fame, a great many prominent people called at the Red Cloister. Van der Goes proved to be something of a prestigious signboard.

Even governor Maximilian honoured the painter with a few occasional visits. As a seasoned hunter, the archduke frequently passed through the Sonian Forest, and the monastery was on his way. In all probability, Tommaso Portinari, or at least one of his envoys, also came by to settle the outstanding bill for his monumental triptych. It is not even inconceivable that Maximilian, who was in debt to Portinari, made the last payment in his name. *The Portinari Altarpiece* would finally end up in Florence in 1483. It's still quite obvious that the head of the patron was not added until the work was finished, after the payment was made, most probably in the Red Cloister. Van der Goes misjudged the measurements of Portinari's head and left too little space for it. To compensate, he had to make a slight notch in the patron's coiffure to keep from covering over St Thomas's left little finger.

In 1480, the Leuven city council asked him to assess the value of the last unfinished painting by Dirk Bouts, who had died five years before. The council did not know how much to pay his widow, and who better than Van der Goes to make such a determination? The artist received more and more visits and commissions. It was difficult for him to combine his increasingly busy life with his private devotions and celebration of the Mass. He was worried that he'd never be able to finish his last works. The sensitive Van der Goes was consumed by stress.

To help him relax, Prior van Vessem gave the painter permission to travel to Cologne. The journey went very well until the return trip, when Van der Goes underwent a mental collapse and began wailing that he was damned. Had he actually enjoyed the flashy city life in Cologne, and did he dread returning to the monastery? Did he feel guilty about his inability to live according to the teachings of Thomas à Kempis? Was the combination of an exhausted body and a tormented spirit taking its toll? In any event, he felt so existentially burdened that he would have ended his life then and there if his fellow brothers had not stopped him.

Back then, people like Van der Goes were usually locked up in one of the few madhouses, or sent on pilgrimage to Geel, where you could venerate the relics of St Dymphna for relief from madness. Novenas were often said for the insane in an attempt to exorcise the devil. Some of the sick stayed in Geel. These 'lunatics' or 'fools' were taken in by the local people. Over time, the town became widely renowned as a model of home care for psychiatric patients, a reputation it would maintain well into the twentieth century. Even though there were reportedly two hundred boarders staying in Geel at the end of the fifteenth century, and the Kempian town was barely three days' walking distance from Auderghem, the good-hearted prior insisted on caring for Van der Goes himself. Perhaps this approach was an expression of the humaneness widely preached by Devotio Moderna, the spiritual movement to which the order of the Red Cloister belonged. After all, the first madhouses in the Low Countries were founded partly thanks to Thomas à Kempis, the famous follower of Devotio Moderna, who contended that people who were different were also worthy of decent care.

After a period of observation, Prior van Vessem came to the conclusion that Van der Goes was suffering from the same condition that afflicted the despondent King Saul of the Old Testament. Hadn't he asked the young David to ease his melancholy by playing on his lyre? The Bible said the endeavour had been successful, so the prior prescribed music. Although it was probably the oldest example of music therapy in Europe, it didn't do any good. But it did provide the inspiration for a famous painting by Emile Wauters. In *The Madness of Hugo van der Goes* (1872), in which he portrays the wide-eyed painter listening to a few musicians and singers, Wauters captured the image of the deranged Van der Goes for posterity. The legends were numerous: that his brain had given out after he realized he could never match the beauty of the *Ghent Altarpiece*, that a sordid love affair did him in, that he died after a terrible fit of madness.

Van der Goes emerged from his breakdown, and during his recovery he painted *Death of the Virgin* (1482), one of his greatest masterpieces. With the Grim Reaper peeking over his shoulder, he turned his hand to the passing of the Mother of God as described in the apocryphal gospels. A blue robe, a white headdress and a pale countenance. Here, Mary lies on a bed surrounded by the grief-stricken apostles. The works of the Flemish Primitives that hang alongside Van der Goes's final opus in the Groeningemuseum in Bruges radiate a full range of colours, while the painter-monastic opted for subdued tints. No splendour and glory here; only sadness at the death of what once was so great.

In the context of our story, the mind of the viewer turns instinctively to the death of that other Mary. The grief suffered by Archduke Maximilian, Louis de Gruuthuse, Olivier de la Marche and Adolph of Ravenstein was no less intense than that of the apostles. In the year of Duchess Mary's death, and certainly without meaning to do so, the grand master movingly gave expression to the decline of the once so glorious Burgundians. After this last spasm of his genius, the successor to Jan van Eyck and Rogier van der Weyden himself passed away.

In the middle foreground of the painting, Van der Goes painted himself as one of the apostles. He is the only figure looking us straight in the eyes. He seems tired, with deep bags under his eyes, but his sadness seems to have settled into a pious form of resignation, the realization that everything eventually comes to an end, even the most beautiful stories. But you can also read in it the faith of the confident Christian, who knows that after death the best is yet to come.

PART V

'Between Dijon and Beaune in early September
I visited a cemetery, it lay in the heart
Of a vineyard, the harvest had begun.'

Leonard Nolens: *Een dichter in Antwerpen en andere gedichten*
[*A Poet in Antwerp and Other Poems*], 2005

A MEMORABLE DAY
20 OCTOBER 1496

---

*Or how Philip the Handsome was married in the
Brabant city of Lier and the world seemed to be on the
point of turning in a whole new direction.*

As Bishop of Cambrai, Henry of Bergen had hired Desiderius Erasmus as his secretary in 1493. Following in the footsteps of his master, the humanist would become acquainted not only with the southern Low Countries but also with the circles of spiritual and political power. Eventually, the Rotterdammer was given permission to study theology in Paris. Later, Erasmus would write an epitaph for his old employer. The brilliant bishop had an irreproachable record of service. He had recently been appointed chancellor of the Order of the Golden Fleece and, as if that weren't enough, first counsellor of Philip the Handsome. As the ultimate tribute, Henry of Bergen was asked to officiate at the wedding of his sovereign in Lier on 20 October 1496 – without doubt the ceremonial high point of his career.

In 1493 the Emperor Frederick III had died. As King of the Romans, his son Maximilian was now the strong man of the Holy Roman Empire. With all that to worry about, he decided to transfer power in the Low Countries to his fifteen-year-old heir apparent, Philip the Handsome. This was met with applause from Ypres to 's-Hertogenbosch, not only because it meant that a home-grown, 'natural' sovereign was taking over who spoke the right language, but also because Maximilian had done everything he could to ride roughshod over the Great Privilege.

He didn't even attend the solemnities in Lier. The Low Countries had been the bane of his existence for the past few years, and he preferred not to let himself be seen there. Philip didn't mind. He would much rather go his own way and steer his lands into more peaceful waters than the turbulent seas his exhaustingly ambitious father had chosen. The heir had a playful disposition and did very well for himself as a card player, archer and stick fighter. But the boisterousness he displayed during those activities disappeared when it was time for him to take the helm. Inexperienced as he was, he made sure he was surrounded by carefully chosen advisors. Olivier de la Marche christened him *Philippe Croit Conseil* – Philip the Believer in Counsel. As governor, he regularly followed the advice of his counsellors, something at which his grandfather Charles the Bold had failed miserably. Much to Maximilian's irritation, he listened sympathetically to the call for peace. Maximilian couldn't bear knowing that his son was forging peace agreements with the odious French while he himself was waging war with Charles VIII.

Was Philip a pawn in his counsellors' game? Was he a slacker who had little interest in anything that was going on? Or did he follow his own steady course against the advice of his own father? Whatever the answer, his approach did result in peaceful years that earned him the love of his people. This was a leader who really did seem to care about the welfare of the lands entrusted to him. Taxes were reduced, an attempt was made to seek a balance between central power and public participation, and the States General of the Low Countries convened on a regular basis. The fact that its members did this on their own initiative was proof that mutual cohesion had improved, as did the desire to consult each other on a variety of issues. As accommodating as Philip may have been, he certainly was no puppet of regional tendencies. He reinstated the Mechelen Parlement, this time as the Great Council of Mechelen. It was something most minds finally seemed ready for. No one objected to a centrally located, super-regional court of appeals – an important psychological hurdle in the unification story.

It must have come as a breath of fresh air. Philip the Handsome gave the Low Countries the chance to develop independently by conducting a national Burgundian policy. He himself identified much more as the heir to the dynasty Philip the Bold had established than as a Habsburg. He didn't even work on mastering German, even though one day he would have to succeed his father. It was as if he sensed that history would decide otherwise, and that every effort in that regard was pointless. In the meantime, his father kept trying to make his opinion known, but to no avail. His son needed to look at the bigger picture.

On the day of the wedding, 20 October 1496, Philip felt like a fish in water. He had met his future spouse Joanna on the 19th, and immediately the erotic sparks began to fly. Legend has it that before anyone could stop them the two slipped away, accosted a priest in the street and compelled him to join them in matrimony then and there, after which they went to the Hof van Mechelen in Lier and surrendered to the mating call of an all-consuming love. As implausible as it may sound, this popular folk tale charmingly expresses the impression that most sources corroborate. The people of Lier and the invited guests couldn't help but notice the feverish longing in the eyes of Joanna of Aragon and Castile and of Philip of Burgundy and Habsburg. Only an exceptional leader could be born of a union like this one.

That being said, Philip the Handsome would soon delight other women with his virile potency. Ten years later that would lead to another implausible story, but this time a true one.

'It Is Better To Destroy A Land Than Lose It'

In Lier, however, everything clicked between Philip and Joanna. Lier was able to wrap itself in an aura of peace and tranquillity. It was the festive confirmation of the calm that had returned to the Low Countries. On 20 October 1496, Lier really did rhyme with cheer, all the more so because the decade after the death of Philip's mother had been pure hell.

All Maximilian wanted to do was to integrate the Low Countries into the greater Holy Roman Empire. What did he care about the private demands of the burghers and the local nobility? Why should he respect the treaty with France, like some kind of pushover? No, he was still a real commander, a knight of the old school, cut from indestructible feudal cloth, the leader of a great empire – of course that helped. So he dreamed of getting his own back, not only with the unavoidable French but also with the States General of the Low Countries.

After the death of Louis XI in 1483, France found itself saddled with a problem. The dauphin, Charles VIII, was only thirteen years old and barely ready to assume his responsibilities. Maximilian saw this as his chance to crush the French claim to the Burgundian inheritance once and for all. The King of the Romans emerged as a second Charles the Bold, a ruthless bully who would aim his arrows at his own people as well as his foreign enemies, and who almost succeeded in levying more taxes than his late lamented predecessor. This resulted in years of executions, fines and violent raids.

Is it any surprise that the greatest resistance took place in Ghent and Bruges? To begin with, the Ghentenars refused to turn over his son, Philip, still a little boy, to the more accommodating Brabant after the specified deadline had passed because they feared he would fall into his father's hands again. It wasn't until the summer of 1485, with the help of German troops, that Maximilian was finally able to embrace his son. The seven-year-old Philip was a bit apprehensive at the first sight of his father, who was armed to the teeth. Maximilian pressed the boy fondly against his armour and then sent him to Mechelen, where he was entrusted to the loving care of the indestructible Margaret of York. Her palace, part of which has been preserved, is now the beautiful Mechelen Theatre. She received her guests exactly where the theatregoers now sit.

In the meantime, the conflict with France continued to breed bad blood, especially in Flanders, which had traditionally maintained close ties with the kingdom and could be counted on to provide the lion's share of its war costs. To keep the resistance there from spreading unchecked into the rest of the Low Countries, Maximilian called a meeting of the States General in Bruges in late January 1488. It didn't work out as he had hoped. The level of frustration in the city was already high because of so much wasted tax money, but there was even more grumbling about the economic decline, the feeling that Bruges, the queen of the Burgundian cities, was gradually being dethroned by Antwerp.

As incomprehensible as it sounds, the brave Bruggians simply decided to take their governor prisoner. Since his election to the Imperial Diet of 1486, Maximilian had held the rank of king, but clearly that did not deter them. He was staying at Craenenburg, where he was put under house arrest. Guild militias stood guard. The fact that there was a spice shop on the ground floor of the building made it all the more painful. For three months, the royal courts of Europe didn't know what to make of the situation: should they refuse to believe it or suppress their laughter? Dignity was all-important to Maximilian, and there he was, locked up amid the poppy seeds, cinnamon, saffron and summer savoury. The humiliation could not have been more pungent.

The Bruggians, actively backed by the Ghentenars and passively by the rest of the Low Countries, issued clear demands: end the war with France, remove all Germans and Burgundians from public office, grant Ghent and Bruges a monopoly on textiles and allow self-government under Philip. In Flanders, a gold coin was even struck in Philip's name.

When Maximilian stubbornly refused, the Bruggians came up with plan B. At the same spot on the Great Market where Mary had gone into raptures over the chivalrous bravura of her consort six years earlier, he was now forced to look on as his supporters were tortured and beheaded. By 12 May the King of the Romans had had enough, and he conceded on all fronts. The Bruggians responded by rushing in the relics of the Holy Blood, on which the prisoner was made to swear. Only then was Maximilian freed from the fragrance of cloves and cinnamon.

No sooner had he left the city than he reneged on his oath and began a devastating war with Flanders. Breaking his promise did not go down well. With an army of insurgents, Maximilian's old confidant Philip of Cleves was able to rally a large part of the Low Countries behind him. Only when Emperor Frederick III sent troops to his son could Maximilian retake his cities in Hainaut, Holland and Zeeland. The county of Flanders was dealt the most blows.

After years of bloodshed, the civil war came to an end in 1492. Not much later Emperor Frederick died, Maximilian took the throne, and he never showed his face again in the Low Countries except once. Even the marriage of his heir could not entice him to return, although for him that was the pinnacle in a series of negotiations that were as long as they were important.

*

The system of channels that connected Bruges with the outer harbours of Damme and Sluis was silting up badly, and in recent decades it was becoming more and more difficult for big ships to unload their cargo. Invariably, the cargo had to be trans-shipped on smaller boats, and these in turn had to struggle with a steadily decreasing flow. The Zwin – the inlet that had formed after a major storm in 1134 – had clogged up and the silting was an unstoppable phenomenon. The seawater that had difficulty flowing inland during high tide had even more trouble flowing back when the tide was out. The remaining tidal channels, pitiful as they were, could hardly be regarded as reliable shipping lanes.

This process had been going on for quite some time, and Bruges had spent a fortune dredging its canals. It was an approach that had been paying off, not only because the city had sufficient funds available but also because Antwerp continued to be difficult to reach by way of the Western Scheldt, which was blessed with countless sandbanks. The great floods that occurred at the end of the fourteenth and beginning of the fifteenth centuries changed all that. The extension of the Scheldt became navigable for seagoing ships, which were increasing in size.

What had long been set in motion by nature would now reach its definite conclusion because of current political events. After his triumph, Maximilian took revenge through executions, exorbitant fines and withdrawal of privileges, and from then on the cities of Flanders would be kept on a short leash. Three-quarters of the landed estates around Ghent lay fallow, countless villages had become ghost towns. The Bruges harbour had been blockaded for years because of the war, the textile trade had practically come to a standstill and the city coffers were empty on account of the heavy fines. As ultimate retaliation, Maximilian called on international traders to leave the city and settle in Antwerp, in the old duchy of Brabant, which dealt a death blow to Bruges. The Brabantians had remained loyal to the archduke. They had refused to draw the French card, which certainly didn't do them any harm. The merchants, opportunists that they were, opted for the safety of Antwerp, which seemed to have the wind in its sails.

'There is really no part of the world whose finest products

'cannot be found here,'¹ the Cordoban traveller Pero Tafur wrote
back in 1438, but those great riches evaporated into thin air. The
European quarter, within walking distance of the Great Market,
with the consulates of Genoa, Florence, Venice, Catalonia,
Portugal, Scotland and England, to name but a few, packed their
bags and relocated to the city on the Scheldt. That put an end to
the period in which Scandinavian wood was known everywhere
as 'Flemish wood', only because so much of it was traded in
Bruges.

The Bruges *Kontor*, the city's headquarters of the Hanseatic
League, dug in its heels, but in 1500 even this international
merchants' guild opted for the more spacious waters of Antwerp;
the city's total demise seemed just a question of time. The
Hanseatic League, in which almost two hundred north German
trading cities were first represented, had been a privileged partner
of Bruges since 1253, and it too would soon have to face the fact that
its glory days were over. Antwerp, on the other hand, succeeded
in connecting with the rising world power of Spain. Everything
was shifting.

The demise was all the more spectacular when you realize that
until 1480 Bruges was by far the richest city in the Low Countries.
When it came to paying taxes, Bruges far surpassed Ghent, even
in absolute terms, while that city had approximately 20,000
more residents. Even the money business, which will always be
etymologically indebted to the inn in Bruges run by the Van der
Beurze family, moved its headquarters. The people of Bruges could
only look back with nostalgia to the time when magnates held
sway. Dino Rapondi (moneylender to Philip the Bold and John the
Fearless), Giovanni Arnolfini (financier to Philip the Good who
was long seen as the man featured in the famous Arnolfini painting
by Jan van Eyck) and Tommaso Portinari (sponsor of Charles the
Bold, patron of Hugo van der Goes and Hans Memling) had all
faded into spectres from the past.

Not only that, but building a career as an artisan was easier
in Antwerp. The influence of the guilds was not as great and you
didn't have to stem from a line of master craftsmen to advance
to the highest ranks, as you did in Bruges and Ghent. Artisans

were glad they could escape the dynastic master's title by moving to the Brabant city. Businessmen, bankers and workmen poured in. Partly thanks to the Austrian Habsburg Maximilian, loyal Antwerp consigned the Flemish-Burgundian Bruges to political, financial and economic purgatory, although the city managed to prolong its death throes until around 1530.

Hidden behind that conspicuous change was an even greater transformation. The centre of gravity of the Low Countries shifted to Brabant in its entirety. The once so rich and powerful county of Flanders began its trek through the wilderness. 'It is better to destroy a land than lose it,'² as Maximilian so tersely summarized the situation.

The final upheaval at the end of the fifteenth century was abrupt and spectacular, but Brabant had been trying to catch up for quite some time. If you look at the portion of the income of the Burgundian dukes that came from Flanders, you see that in 1445 it still amounted to one-third as opposed to barely 10 per cent for Brabant, and that by 1473 Brabant and Flanders each accounted for a quarter of the benevolences collected that year. Under the Burgundians, the volume of trade in the Low Countries – which was borne mainly by Flanders, Brabant, Holland and Zeeland (the rest being mainly agrarian areas) – almost doubled. The greatest recorded rise was once again in Brabant, owing especially to the yearly markets in Antwerp and Bergen-op-Zoom. This trend was also reflected in the population figures. Bruges would never exceed the 50,000 mark, while Antwerp confidently reached the magic border of 100,000 souls over the course of the sixteenth century.

The city on the Scheldt broadcast its success with a spectacular architectural symbol. It was the only city in the region to complete at least one tower of its monumental Gothic church – the tallest in Europe at 123 metres. Since its completion in 1521, the Antwerp Church of Our Lady (it didn't become a cathedral until 1559) has always been regarded as a climax of Brabant Gothic, as triumphant as it is breathtaking, and a veritable high point in the history of the Low Countries.

It was indisputable. The Low Countries had undergone an

economic heart transplant. Scarcely one century later, the multiple bypass to Amsterdam would follow.

*

The man who witnessed Bruges's swansong first-hand was Hans Memling. Born in Seligenstadt, Memling learned to paint from Van der Weyden in Brussels and had the good fortune to catch the last golden period. Beginning in 1465 he worked mainly on commissions for foreign merchants and bankers, mostly rich Italian expatriates of the Tommaso Portinari sort. He had less contact with Burgundian rulers, although Anthony of Burgundy, whose 1463 portrait by Rogier van der Weyden is one of the most beautiful in the history of portraiture, turned to him after Van der Weyden's death. Perhaps Van der Weyden had alerted this most famous of Philip the Good's illegitimate sons to Memling's qualities.

Like his contemporaries Van der Goes and Bouts, Memling continued the legacy of Van Eyck and Van der Weyden, but in his own way. His work is characterized by fewer paint layers, which were applied in flowing strokes and sweeps. Sometimes you can dimly detect the underlying drawing. Just when having your portrait painted was becoming fashionable, he would be the first to begin experimenting with portraits against a landscape backdrop. In that regard, Da Vinci's *Mona Lisa* (*c*.1503–19) is unmistakably indebted to Memling.

You don't immediately find references in his work to the turbulent Burgundian period that coincided with his career. All we know is that like every other affluent burgher, he had to contribute to Maximilian's unpopular campaign against France. Compared with the work of his predecessors, his oeuvre contains a surprisingly large number of shields, helmets, banners, flags and speech scrolls. And sometimes they afford us a glance behind the scenes. A striking example of this can be found in one of his most famous works, the *Shrine of St Ursula*, which he made in 1489 for the Hospital of St John in Bruges (where miraculously it remains on display). On the sixth panel he painted the martyrdom of Ursula. As legend has it, she was a Catholic martyr who was killed by Attila for refusing to marry the godless Hun. On the banner flapping in the background the attentive viewer can see the wing of a black eagle, an obvious nod to the coat of arms of the Holy Roman Empire. This small detail suggests that in the eyes of Memling, Maximilian was a devious ruler, at least the equivalent of the bloodthirsty Attila. With just a few brushstrokes, he shows the downfall of Bruges and the bankruptcy of Flanders as reflected in the martyrdom of St Ursula.

The fact that so many of Memling's paintings have survived – around a hundred panels – attests to his great popularity. But even he fell on hard times after the collapse of the Bruges economy. At his death in 1494, the famous grand master lacked the means to have himself buried in the Church of St Giles, as every member of the better Bruges circles usually did at that time. Memling ended up in the public cemetery as an ordinary mortal.

In the year of Memling's death, King Charles VIII of France crossed the Alps on the way to Italy and his well-to-do city-states. Another very telling event. Here, too, the devastated Flanders, which had fought itself to death, was forced to stand back and watch. In the coming decades, the French king, the German emperor and the new superpower Spain would compete against each other in Italy. After all, there were fortunes to be made!

And in sixty years' time they would ruin the prosperity of the cities there as well.

'Anno 1496 Philippus Pulcher Lyrae, In Collegiali Sancti Gummari...'

Maximilian's son, Philip the Handsome, who thought he deserved the label 'the Good' far more than his illustrious great-grandfather, was not interested in following suit. The heir to the throne only had eyes for the Low Countries. To rectify the situation, Maximilian sought inspiration from Philip the Bold. Hadn't he united his two oldest children with the House of Bavaria in a double wedding, thereby laying the basis for a successful dynasty? What if he now did the same: offer Philip and Margaret to the royal house that had made so much spectacular progress in recent years?

And so he let his gaze fall upon Spain, where Isabella of Castile and Ferdinand of Aragon had placed the entire Iberian peninsula under their rule, with the exception of Portugal. They even succeeded in recapturing the last small portion of their land from the Moors in 1492. Charles Martel, who had halted the advance of the Moors at Poitiers in 732 and driven the heretics back across the Pyrenees, must have danced in his grave with joy. As if that triumph wasn't enough, the end of this *Reconquista* just so happened to coincide with the beginning of the new *Conquista*, for the eccentric Christopher Columbus sent out by Ferdinand and Isabella would discover America that same year. Finally, the Spanish had access to their own land – and to the whole New World as well.

Maximilian sensed that now was the time to act, at the beginning of the Spanish success story, so he offered his two children, Philip and Margaret, to the Catholic Monarchs. Ferdinand and Isabella had earned this honorary title by virtue of their struggle against the Muslims, but also because they intended to propagate the true faith on the other side of the ocean.

They jumped at the opportunity. Who would be foolish enough to scorn the coveted Burgundian-Habsburg legacy? Maximilian could rub his hands with glee. He had found the perfect partner to defeat the French, for the Spanish were just as much at loggerheads with Charles VIII as he was. Now his son had no choice but to make his international political contribution, or so he thought.

The double wedding occurred in two acts. Margaret would be married to John of Asturias, the heir to the Spanish throne, on 3 April 1497 in Burgos. But first it was Philip's turn. On 20 October 1496 he was wed to Joanna of Castile, the third child and second daughter of Ferdinand and Isabella.

The attentive reader will no doubt remember that as a young girl, Margaret had been destined to become the Queen of France – a marital plan that was intended to serve as a guarantee for peace. 'I, *Marguerite*, the most beautiful of flowers, blossomed in the French court, where I would grow to be as great as the French fleur-de-lis'³ were the words to a song by master composer Pierre de la Rue, already a great name in Flemish polyphony, who, in the best Burgundian tradition, would build his career at court. Even Josquin des Prez wrote compositions for Philip and Margaret. Like their grandfather, they attached great importance to the high standards of the court chapel.

So how did poor Margaret, who was being pushed like a pawn around the chessboard of her father's dreams, end up in a Spanish bed? Again, it all had to do with her progenitor's growing anti-French attitude, which expressed itself in his determination to marry Margaret to the Spanish heir, much to her distress. What followed was like a scene from a whimsical melodrama, albeit with international repercussions.

To play a nasty trick on the infernal Maximilian, Charles VIII decided to marry the Duchess of Brittany, the woman whom the King of the Romans himself had finally chosen as his own new consort. It was a move that rivalled his spicy imprisonment in Craenenburg. Not only did Charles VIII win over Maximilian's future bride, but he also rejected his daughter, Margaret, with whom he had been expected to probe the delights of marriage. More than ever, the Austrian was bent on revenge.

To start off with, he managed to snag the fabulously rich Bianca Sforza, who reportedly was neither big on brains nor especially good-looking. She was the daughter of Galeazzo Sforza, Duke of Milan, who was murdered in 1476, and niece of the later duke Ludovico Sforza, who acted as patron for Leonardo da Vinci in his free time. With Bianca at his side, he went to Maastricht to embrace his fourteen-year-old daughter. It was the first time he had seen her since she had been taken to live in Amboise at the age of two. Unlike her brother, Philip, she got on well with her father. The great rejection had made her cynical, so she was a better interlocutor than Philip.

Now that he had his two children under his care, Maximilian could start planning the spectacular double wedding. Brother and sister were split up again. The distance between Lier and Burgos was no less than 1,300 kilometres as the crow flies.

*

Ever since 1369, Lier had been blessed with one of the most elegant bell towers in the Low Countries. This slender spike of stone is still the highlight of the charming Great Market. Bell towers as such were rather exceptional in Brabant; they were much more common in Flanders. This has to do with a greater measure of participatory decision-making. In Flanders, when the count granted a city its charter, it was almost obligatory to seal it with the erection of a bell tower, while the duke gave the Brabantians more freedom. They could do whatever they liked. Often a monumental church served as a bell tower. The small city of Lier, which lay right between Antwerp and Mechelen, must have seen the building of a bell tower as an expression of resolute self-confidence.

Lier had gained a measure of wealth through the textile industry. It was considered the gateway to the Campine, where thousands of sheep grazed on an almost endless expanse of heather. While Flanders depended on wool from England, the people of Lier kept their looms busy with the wool from animals they heard bleating in the distance. Over time, they would also switch to the better quality product from England and Scotland. When the Lier textile business went through a rough patch in the second half of the fifteenth century, the city succeeded in transitioning to beer brewing by imitating the successful Holland hops beer. In 1436, a delegate was even sent from Leuven 'to learn the method used there of brewing from hops'.[4] For centuries, Lier would be known as the city of beer. By around 1700 more than twenty breweries had set up shop in the city centre. The last closed its doors in 1967.

Today, the city's residents proudly call themselves 'Sheep Heads' (*Schappenkoppen*), which they even use as the city logo. Remarkably, that nickname has nothing to do with the textile industry but with the fact that, according to legend, the people of Lier preferred the pleasures of livestock to those of the intellect. At the beginning of the fourteenth century, Duke John II, who was grateful to them for their support during his struggle with Mechelen, offered them a choice: a livestock market or a university. When they chose the first, the duke allegedly sighed and said, 'O, those sheep heads!' But as it turned out, it wasn't such a bad choice after all. For a long time, Lier was the only city for miles around that had the right to organize a livestock market.

There isn't a scrap of historical evidence to prove the veracity of this story – although the privilege actually was granted in 1309 – but the people of Lier still get a kick out of saying that if they had opted for the university back then, the Leuven Alma Mater would be located in Lier today. You get the impression that any historical importance this lovely Brabant town can lay claim to depends on a mountain of legend. But all you need to do to discover a true Lier story of the first order, now quite forgotten, is to travel back in time to 20 October 1496.

*

'*Anno 1496 Philippus Pulcher Lyrae, in collegiali Sancti Gummari, solemniter ducit Johannam.*'⁵ You can still read these words in the archive of the St Gummarus Church, and that's exactly what happened. Philip the Handsome did indeed receive the sacrament of marriage with Joanna in the collegiate church in question.

The fact that the wedding did not take place in Ghent or Bruges is no more than natural, in view of the events. But in Lier, a modest town with a total population of 5,000 'Sheep Heads'? Why not in Antwerp? Perhaps there was a desire not to arouse jealousy and frustration by granting such a high honour to a successful metropolis in the making. But why not a large city in Holland? There were relatively fewer courtiers and knights from the northern regions in Philip's household, so any argument in favour of a 'Holland' marriage had little going for it. In addition, the nobility there were extremely divided because of the resurgence of animosity between the Hooks and the Cods. How about Mechelen then, the capital city? Mechelen had already had its share of fun. That was where Margaret had been married without her John in attendance, stretched out on a bed with the marital proxy Don Francisco de Rojas, who was said to have left one leg exposed. That was understood to count as the symbolic celebration of the marriage. The nuptials having been settled, the real feast could now take place in Spain.

But first on to Lier, as surprising as it was modest. The people of Lier today still wonder to what they owed this honour. Lier and Antwerp were the only cities in Brabant that had taken Maximilian's side during the civil war, which already put them in the top drawer of the archduke's administration. It was rumoured that the family of the preacher Henry of Bergen had had many connections in Lier. But the key to the actual situation lay with Margaret of York. Her preference was the deciding factor.

The church where the vows would be exchanged was dedicated to St Gummarus, the saint who had drawn the widow of Charles the Bold to the town in 1475. Two years later she even took part in the local Gummarus Procession, touching his relics repeatedly and with great emotion. Why so much zeal? St Gummarus, who once miraculously succeeded in rejoining the two parts of a felled oak, was invoked for all sorts of fractures, small, large, double, even triple… He was also said to heal not only broken legs but also broken marriages. This explains the devotion of Margaret, who was unhappily married to Charles and suffered greatly from it. So she begged various legendary figures for help, from the knight Tondal to St Gummarus, gentlemen who symbolized reunion and reconciliation. As a deeply devout grandmother, she wanted to show her grandson the way to a marriage more successful than her own.

On 20 October, the town of Lier was packed. One of the bridges over the Nete couldn't bear the weight of the teeming throng and collapsed. A few unfortunate locals were drowned in the Nete's torrential waters, a tragic human sacrifice on the altar of the betrothed. The feast went on as planned.

The local dramatic societies performed their burlesques with fervour, the tradesmen made impressive torches and fires. The butchers did their work with extraordinary skill, and each was rewarded with a castrated ram. The double beer and Rhenish flowed in rivers. The well-lubricated voices burst forth in song. It was certainly a festive occasion, at least for the Austrian Habsburgs and the Catholic Spanish. But by Burgundian standards it was a sober affair, especially when compared with the exuberant feasts of Philip the Good and Charles the Bold.

The involvement of the public was so great that a huge number of people stationed themselves at the Hof van Mechelen, where the newly-weds would spend their first night. Could anything be heard? Was the marriage being appropriately celebrated in the bedroom as well? That was one thing that the people of Lier and Margaret of York didn't have to worry about. The marriage would produce six children. '*Potens in terra erit semen eorum.*'[6] During the Solemn Mass, Henry of Bergen read aloud from the Book of Psalms, for which his secretary Erasmus would later provide detailed commentary: 'His descendants will be mighty in the land.'

St Gummarus may have provided a fruitful marital union, but apart from that there was little joy. Although the two beamed like giggly teenagers on 20 October 1496, the hormonal excitement on Philip's side would soon dissipate, while Joanna developed a morbid love for her husband. Add to that adultery and jealousy and you end up with the wrong sparks.

But in Lier everything was glorious. The eighteen-year-old Philip looked to the future with a broad grin on his face. As Duke of Burgundy (for that is how he saw himself), he hoped to serve as lord of the Low Countries for many years to come. If his father was blessed with a great age, he'd be able to run things here for a long time to come. His sister, Margaret, was destined to become the new Queen of Spain, but that would have little impact on the House of the Burgundian-Habsburgs. His union with the third child of Ferdinand and Isabella would not disrupt his life as governor of the Low Countries in any way.

Except that's not how things turned out, not by a long shot. Due to circumstances, the modest Lier wedding was destined to become the most important dynastic coupling of the millennium. It was as if Old Europe had had an appointment in the St Gummarus Church with its modern alter ego.

'*Potens in terra erit semen eorum.*'

EPILOGUE

'Emperor Charles moans like Mary of Burgundy's toothache. His father Philip the Handsome is lying in his coffin, waiting in vain for Joanna the Mad. She no longer kisses him on his foul-smelling mouth. She reads Lorca by the dark cypresses.'

Peter Holvoet-Hanssen, from: 'Inferno IX', *Dwangbuis van Houdini* [*Houdini's Straitjacket*], 1998

THE LAST BURGUNDIAN

Or how the conclusion and resolution of this long story converge in a man who rules over an empire on which the sun never sets.

Twenty years later, Maximilian went to the Low Countries for the last time. He did not travel alone but in the company of his grandson Charles. On 24 January 1516, the two attended a Solemn Mass at the St Gummarus Church in Lier. Charles's thoughts must have turned to his parents, who were married there two decades earlier. For the first time, he found himself standing on the spot that was so closely connected to his birth and his existence. Perhaps he asked himself what was supposed to happen now. Destiny had shuffled the cards so thoroughly over the past years that it must have left the almost sixteen-year-old Charles reeling.

The people in attendance watched as the two bowed before the choir, which had just been completed. Gleaming there, as a finishing touch, were the five imposing stained-glass windows that were consecrated on this occasion and remain the pride of the church five hundred years later. The windows depicted the House of Burgundy-Habsburg in all its glory. In the centre was the fifty-six-year-old Emperor Maximilian of Austria himself; at his side was Mary of Burgundy, who had died more than thirty years earlier and had long been replaced in the marital bed by someone else. The old pair now symbolized the merging of two illustrious dynasties. Their children, Philip and Margaret, were pictured as well, of course, as were their grandchildren Ferdinand and especially Charles, on whom all eyes were focused.

His grandfather Maximilian looked exhausted. After the civil war in the Low Countries he had devoted himself to a reformation of the Holy Roman Empire, to fighting the French over northern Italy, and, thanks to another double wedding, to ensuring that both Hungary and Bohemia would soon become part of the

Empire as well. His best years were clearly behind him. Charles, who knelt beside him and gazed at the stained-glass windows, possessed at least one quality that the emperor lacked: he was young. Otherwise, he certainly was not bursting with vitality and energy. His movements were slow, his face pale, and when he opened his mouth he could barely make himself understood. That had to do with his exceptionally large jaw, which was even more impressive than Maximilian's. And on top of all that, he was blessed with a gaping mouth. Later on, Charles would camouflage those defects by growing a manly, curling beard and dressing like a Roman ruler, but in 1516 he was still a long-haired but beardless Habsburg, of average height and skinny as a rail.

The objective observer noticed two important absentees. Where were Charles's parents? Philip the Handsome had died unexpectedly in 1506 of complications of pneumonia, barely twenty-eight years old. Unlike her faithless husband, Joanna was always as much in love as she was on the day of their nuptials in Lier. Her legendary jealousy led to terrible scenes, but during the ten days he spent at his sickbed she finally had Philip entirely to herself. She was extravagant in her care and affection. The grief that overtook Joanna when he died was so great that she surrendered to the madness that had revealed itself to her in occasional flashes earlier in her life. She wandered through Castile in the company of her husband's coffin, repeatedly ordering the servants to open it so she could speak to him. She also lit a whole shipload of candles, which twice resulted in a fire. Philip's mortal remains came within an inch of incineration. Charles's mother fiercely resisted his father's death. She wanted to have her husband with her forever. Consumed with adoration, obsessed, distraught and heavily pregnant to boot, Joanna gave birth to her daughter Catherine and was finally able to let her husband go. Joanna the Mad would spend the rest of her days under lock and key, and not until half a century later would she depart this life, deeply depressed.

'My God, why hast thou forsaken me?' cried Maximilian when he heard the news of Philip's death. Doubtless Charles must have thought the same thing. His father dead, his mother mentally ill, he the oldest son and uncontested heir to the throne. He was scarcely six years old when all this befell him. His aunt Margaret of Austria would serve as regent for ten years and rule over the Low Countries. This enabled Charles to calmly prepare himself for what was unquestionably the most extensive job description of the century. For it wasn't only the Holy Roman Empire and the Low Countries that awaited him. Other even more important possessions had unexpectedly fallen to him. Charles's Joyous Entry as Duke of Brabant is still celebrated in Lier, but that was a mere trifle beside all the other titles.

His aunt Margaret, as part of the double wedding in Burgos, married the Spanish heir to the throne John of Asturias, who died unexpectedly in 1497. The shock of John's death caused the pregnant Margaret to miscarry. One year later, John's eldest sister Isabella died, and in July 1500 her son, Miguel, the boy who had become the new crown prince following all the previous deaths, also passed away. As improbable as it may seem, the situation at the dawn of the sixteenth century was none other than this: Joanna became the heir to the Spanish throne and Philip the Handsome, great-grandson of Philip the Good, could prepare himself to assume the title of king. When this realization filtered down to them, the two were still calmly ruling the Low Countries and had just become the proud parents of Charles. Margaret of York, the old widow of Charles the Bold, after whom the infant was named, had carried him to the baptismal font. Six months after his birth, it was certain that if this baby grew to healthy adulthood he would one day rule over an immense empire. The fact that his father died young and his mother was muddling along in a state of insanity meant that the moment arrived sooner than anyone could have wished for.

All these accidents of history must have run through Charles's head over and over again on 24 January 1516. The rise of the Habsburgs under Frederick III was only really achieved by his grandfather Maximilian. The Low Countries had finally taken shape under Philip the Good, and now Spain, united by his maternal grandparents Ferdinand of Aragon and Isabella of Castile, as well as its vast overseas possessions, had fallen into his lap. His mentally incapacitated mother may well have been titular queen, but in reality he would have to do all the ruling there as well. He could only hope that his grandfather Maximilian would live a bit longer.

But that hope was soon dashed. Barely three years after his journey to Lier, the bone-weary Maximilian also died. Charles let himself be elected King of the Romans and then was anointed Holy Roman Emperor, and the dynastic lineages and unified possessions of several royal houses converged in a way that was unprecedented. Charles inherited the harvest of countless battles, reforms and political marriages. He was the symbol of what the elite of the European aristocracy had accomplished over the last hundred years.

It was just then that the continent was confronted by two phenomena that would profoundly influence the future: the emergence of a colonial empire and the eruption of the Reformation. Columbus had died in 1506, but the empire on the other side of the ocean was still very much alive. Charles would carry on a pointless struggle with his own colonists, who trampled the rights of the natives underfoot in the most lamentable way. With great sorrow, the Christian monarch was forced to witness endless debates over whether the savages had souls or not. On the other hand, the *Conquista* provided Spain with both prestige and vast stores of silver. This made it possible for Charles to finance the relentless wars that were triggered by the political and religious upheavals in Europe.

In 1517 Luther did not nail his ninety-five theses on the abuses in the church to the Wittenberg church door – a legend of major proportions – but he did send them to the Bishop of Brandenburg and Archbishop Albert of Mainz. Luther's ideas were initially intended to provoke a discussion within the confines of the church hierarchy, but thanks to the invention of the printing press they soon spread like wildfire. As if that were not enough, King Francis I of France would be a thorn in Charles's side for the rest of his life, and the Turks, who had dealt his forefather John the Fearless such a merciless blow in 1396, were making deep and terrifying inroads into Europe.

Charles V would have to have been a demi-god to manage all this successfully. But the future of Europe lay in the hands of a twenty-year-old youth who was blessed with a delicate constitution and a mediocre intelligence.

'My Heart Has Always Been Hither'

Half a century after Charles's death, the Italian Girolamo Fabrizi reported that he spoke several languages effortlessly and always made the appropriate choice: 'in Spanish to God, in Italian to courtiers, in French to women and in Dutch [*Nederduits*] to horses'.[2] It is generally assumed that in this context the reference is to Middle Dutch and not German, although as emperor he certainly must have spoken the language of his grandfather Maximilian. Owing to the conquest of Milan, Lombardy, Naples, Sicily and Sardinia, he felt obliged to utter a few words of Italian every now and then. So it's not surprising that a much-quoted defence of multilingualism is often attributed to him: 'The more languages you speak, the more human you are.' The fact that several languages converged in the figure of Charles V corresponds nicely with the historic reality in the Low Countries, namely that the linguistic situation there at the start of the modern era was varied in shape and form: French was the language of the Walloon regions and a large portion of the elite, Spanish would soon be the language of those in command, and Dutch that of the remaining inhabitants.

Whatever his reflections in Lier on that day in 1516, they would have been in French. Although he had been surrounded by Spanish- and Dutch-speaking teachers from an early age, he continued to correspond with his sister in French until his last breath. It was not his mother's language yet it was his mother tongue, and it was also the language of the elite in the Southern Netherlands, thanks to the Burgundians. The importance of French also meant that the Burgundian influence in the north, where the upper echelon barely spoke that language, would always be less prevalent. Later on in Belgium, French would retain its privileged position until well into the twentieth century.

Not only did the emperor speak the language of his Burgundian ancestors, but he also regarded himself as one of them. His most important titles may have been King Charles I of Spain and Emperor Charles V of the Holy Roman Empire, but he was equally comfortable with Charles II of Burgundy. Although the old duchy had become part of France again in 1477, the emperor-king insisted on being called the Duke of Burgundy as well. He would be the last descendant of Philip the Bold to lay claim to that title, and it was not a matter of gratuitous vanity.

After the death of her third husband, Margaret of Austria had not only become the governor of the Low Countries but she was also given custody of the children of her brother, Philip. At the beginning of the sixteenth century she began building a large collection of Late Medieval masters, painters who had been able to develop exponentially thanks to the Burgundian patronage of her forefathers. Her nephew Charles was witness to her collector's passion. He had been raised with the idea of a rich Burgundian culture and it would never vanish from his thoughts.

Charles grew up in Mechelen and would find it difficult to thrive in the rigidity of Catholic Spain. During his first years, the 'Burgundians', as they were called, were the objects of outright hatred on the Iberian peninsula. When Charles made his Joyous Entry he treated the Spanish aristocracy to an old-fashioned jousting tournament with all the concomitant Burgundian pageantry. It did not go down well. What ostentation! The Spanish had long questioned the point of such spectacles. Their knights, who had no time for frivolous displays, were mainly interested in rolling up their sleeves and getting to work. They owed their success to that attitude: driving the last of the Moors from Granada in 1492, making one colonial conquest after another, which now demanded all their attention. The new king would do well to keep that in mind, and he could start by learning Spanish.

There it was again: a leader should speak the language of his people. This reproach had prompted Philip the Bold to have his son John the Fearless learn Dutch. John's offspring would do the same. When Maximilian came along, the Low Countries were saddled once again with a leader who did not understand their language, which only made the conflicts more corrosive. Now it was Charles's turn to be given a linguistic dressing-down. The experience of his ancestors taught him that he had best acquire Spanish as quickly and as fluently as possible – the lessons from his youth were far from sufficient. But beneath the thin layer of Spanish that gilded his kingship was his old identity, stubbornly holding on.

When he turned forty, Charles ordered a Castilian translation of *Le chevalier délibéré* (*The Confident Knight*), an allegorical tale of chivalry that the former Burgundian court chronicler Olivier de la Marche had written in 1483. This was the dream world that the emperor loved to inhabit. Just as his forefather Philip the Good had done with the brother of the English king, he would challenge King Francis I of France to a duel with all the necessary bombast. He'd even do it twice. The fact was that in his heart of hearts Charles would always remain a Burgundian knight.

Ever since the redistribution of Charlemagne's legacy and the downfall of the Middle Kingdom in the ninth century, the border between the kingdom of France and the Holy Roman Empire, the dividing line between what would later be France and Germany, seemed destined to last forever. Yet the Burgundians succeeded in building a state that incorporated principalities from both sides of that border. Once the unification had taken place, however, and Charles the Bold was killed, the French reclaimed Burgundy and the Habsburg Netherlands made no effort to keep the old duchy on board, as if the catalyst that had caused a chemical reaction and created a new compound was then being rejected. Even Charles V was unable to rectify the situation.

Yet the emperor did dream of retaking the old duchy from the French so he could be interred in the ancestral vault at Champmol, beside Philip the Bold, John the Fearless and Philip the Good, in the shadow of masterpieces by Sluter, Broederlam and Maelwael. In 1526 he had the return of the duchy included as an unconditional demand in the Treaty of Madrid that he signed with France. That wish was sacred to him, but as a statesman he realized that apart from his nostalgia there were no conceivable economic or political reasons to invest anything in such a recapture.

In the end, two women would succeed in bringing about a temporary peace between France and the Holy Roman Empire. In 1529, Louise of Savoy, the mother of Francis I, and Margaret of Austria, the aunt of Charles V, agreed that it was time for all parties to lay down their arms and that the Burgundian duchy would go to France once and for all. It was a fine example of realpolitik, for it must have grieved Charles and Margaret, who both had Burgundian souls, to give up the old tribal ground in exchange for international stability.

Now that the stunningly beautiful tombs of Champmol were in the hands of the enemy, the emperor made every effort to transfer the remains of his late lamented great-grandfather Charles the Bold from Nancy to Bruges. In 1550 he finally pulled it off. Three years later the remains were united with those of Charles's grandmother Mary of Burgundy in Bruges's Church of Our Lady. The fact that we have these two bronze tombs to admire is owing to the perseverance of Charles V. We've forgotten that when the bronze monuments were gilded, poisonous vapours were released that cost the lives of several craftsmen. Here we are only interested in meditating on the collapse of the Burgundian empire. For its origins we have to go back to Dijon, where Sluter's pleurants are standing guard over the patriarch Philip the Bold and his son John the Fearless – the irony of fate being that Philip the Good, the one and only Grand Duke of the West, has to do without such an imposing tomb. In the best of all possible worlds, Charles would have had them all interred together. But the current situation still tells a lovely story: the time traveller makes his way from the south to the north, from the artistic bud to the unification of the Low Countries and finally to the decline of Burgundy.

After the death of Margaret, Charles's sister Mary of Hungary ruled over the Low Countries on his behalf. Although the emperor had entrusted the task of governing to two women, he consulted with them the entire time and would make all the major decisions. Charles stayed in his native region on a regular basis. He saw the Burgundian Netherlands as his true fatherland. 'My heart has always been hither,'[3] he said in an address to the States General in Brussels in 1520. Hither – *herwaarts* – here. What a difference between him and his son Philip II, who scarcely showed his face in the north. As a Spanish prince, he had no emotional or linguistic tie with what for him were merely conquered lands, let alone with the idea of Burgundy, which in his eyes had been pulverized to oblivion and had meant so much to his father. It was partly this lack of empathy and historical awareness that made it possible for Lutheranism to grow into such a fatally divisive element in the Low Countries. After the split between north and south, only the Southern Netherlands bore the unique Roman-German double identity that later on, through the work of historians such as Henri Pirenne, would earn Belgium the designation 'crossroads of Europe'.

'Belgium, Netherlands And Flanders'

Burgundy may have been lost, but Charles did all he could to get the Low Countries into Habsburg hands. He conquered the Sticht Utrecht and the Oversticht, brought Guelders (seized by Charles the Bold at an earlier date) back into the Netherlandish fold, and even subjugated areas like Groningen and Friesland that had never been ruled by the Burgundians. From 1543 on he had all the Low Countries in his possession, with the exception of the prince-bishopric of Liège, which was as good as autonomous. In another effort to relive the past, he renamed the Habsburg Netherlands the Burgundian Circle, which also included the Franche-Comté, the county that had been part of Burgundy since the time of Philip the Bold but was now floating at a distance like an alien satellite.

The 'Seventeen Provinces' were complete. Recent research has shown that this term, which in historical records is usually uttered in one and the same breath along with Charles V, had actually been in use since Charles the Bold – proof that the commonality of the Low Countries had already given rise to one all-embracing title under the Burgundians. The use of the word 'province' was much better at conveying a sense of unity than, say, the 'Seventeen Principalities' would have done. On the other hand, the plural clearly indicates that the provinces always retained a measure of autonomy. The fact that the Franche-Comté was never included suggests once again that in practice this was strictly a northern union.

Originally, the Low Countries – the Netherlands – was purely a geographic concept: literally the lands on the lower reaches of the Meuse, the Rhine and the Scheldt. The term '*daz Niderlant*' appeared in the *Nibelungenlied*, which was inspired by the experiences of the old Burgundians. There is also mention of the '*Niderlanden*' in a fourteenth-century Limburg chronicle. And in a chronicle from the county of Holland, the anonymous author speaks of himself as having been born in '*de lagen landen bi de zee*' – 'the low countries by the sea'.[4] Thanks to the Burgundians, this ancient geographical region also acquired national, political, monetary and juridical unity. They boosted this sense of commonality by organizing banquets and entries that were as consolidating as they were resplendent, by uniting the aristocratic upper crust in the Order of the Golden Fleece, and by commissioning historic chronicles. As mentioned earlier, this unity came about as a result of the continuous interplay between the dukes and the urban elite. It ensured that the existing trade relationships would increase and flourish.

The Burgundians usually spoke of 'the lands hither', which meant something like 'the lands here' – 'here' being the place where Philip the Good spent most of his time, i.e. the north. The dukes themselves expressed this by means of the French variant, of course. So the rather exotic '*les pays de par deçà*' can be regarded as the first official term used by a government to refer to the Low Countries, although it was only common within the Burgundian administration.

Slightly confusing is the fact that at the end of the sixteenth century, Justus Lipsius labelled Duke Philip the Good '*Conditor Belgii*'. This certainly did not mean that he saw him as the founder of Belgium, a country that didn't even exist yet, but of the Low Countries. This was Lipsius's nod to Caesar, who called the *Belgae* the bravest of all the Gauls. And where did those famous old Belgians live? Between the Seine and the Rhine. In imitation of Caesar, people began using the Latin term *Belgium*, and even the plural *Belga*, to refer to the Low Countries as a whole. When chronicler Gilbert Roy translated his *Nederlandtscher Oorlogen, Troublen en Oproeren (The Netherlandish Wars, Troubles and Rebellions)* of 1580 into French, he spoke of both '*le Pais belgique*' and '*pays bas*'. In around 1575, the Mechelen engraver Frans Hogenberg labelled his map of the Low Countries with four different names – in Latin, Italian, Dutch and French – which can therefore be regarded as synonyms: *Belgium, Il paese basso, Niderlandt, le Pays Bas*.

Interestingly enough, '*Flandre(s)*' was still the most commonly used term. Flanders emerged as a kind of all-encompassing entity associated with Bruges, the international hub, and also as an outpost of what lay beyond it... and was consequently applied to all the Low Countries. Thus Charles V's famous Capilla Flamenca consisted of musicians from every corner of the Low Countries. One Spanish author, writing in 1518, spoke of '*los Belgas vulgarmente llamados Flamencas*',[5] by which he meant that by and large the subjects from the Low Countries were called Flemings. Although the Brabantians had taken over the managerial role of the old county, no one used the label 'Brabant' when speaking of the Seventeen Provinces. A letter to governor Mary of Hungary written in 1543 was simply addressed to '*Flandres*', yet it was delivered in good order to the addressee in Brussels, which had taken the place of Mechelen as 'capital of the Netherlands' after the death of Margaret of Austria. The sixteenth-century lexicographer Cornelis Kiliaen summarized this confusing question in this way: 'Belgium, commonly called the Netherlands, is also known as Flanders throughout practically all of Christendom, taking the part for the whole.'[6]

In any case, the creation of 'the Seventeen Provinces' was an attempt to put an end to the terminological confusion, although another soon appeared to take its place. Actually, the whole never consisted of seventeen parts, no matter how many attempts were made over the centuries to put the puzzle together in this way. Seventeen was simply a biblical number that denoted a large empire, and such an impressive whole should always be united, at least according to Charles V. To reinforce that argument, he issued the Pragmatic Sanction of 1549 in which the right of succession was laid down for the Seventeen Provinces, which were forthwith to pass through history as one indivisible whole. Charles believed this would secure the future of the Low Countries within the Holy Roman Empire. Barely three decades later, however, the Low Countries would split into two parts: the Spanish Netherlands (from 1713 on, the Austrian Netherlands) and the Republic of the United Netherlands. In the south, power would be exercised by the central authority, in the north by the urban elites, while under the Burgundians the interaction between the two had worked quite well.

Even after the division, terms such as *Vlaenderen*, *Nederlandt* and *Pais Belgique* would long be used interchangeably to stand for the whole. The *Leo Belgicus* is a cartographical convention widely known in the Low Countries in which the Seventeen Provinces are drawn in the shape of a lion. Between 1583 and 1800, approximately 120 different editions of the map were issued. For the official division in 1648, which in reality had been a fact since the fall of Antwerp in 1585, just two maps were made of the north alone, and only one of the south. The unity persisted in people's minds longer than the official dates suggest. The stubborn survival of the *Leo Belgicus* can even be seen as a symbol of the hope of a possible reunification.

Gradually, the words *Olanda* and *Olandesi* popped up in church documents in reference to the heretical empire in the north and its inhabitants – Holland as the synecdoche for the whole. In the eighteenth century, the Austrian court used the word 'Netherlands' when speaking of the Southern Netherlands as opposed to 'Holland' for the north. When the French invaded the south in 1792, they addressed the inhabitants in their broadsheets as '*Belges*', which the inhabitants translated as 'Netherlanders'.

After the temporary reunion under William I from 1815 to 1830 (when the Belgian Revolution took place), the French-speaking elite of the infant Belgium would narrow their use of the words *Belgique* and *Belges* to refer to the south alone, which not much later were translated back into Dutch as '*België*' (Belgium) and '*Belgen*' (Belgians). But it wasn't until the nineteenth century that the distinction finally emerged between Belgians/Belgium and the Dutch/the Netherlands, as we know it today (Dutch being the English translation of *Nederlanders*, which is how the Dutch refer to themselves). Yet it was then that the term 'Flemish Primitives' entered the lexicon, even though the painters in question were not all Flemings by any means: Dirk Bouts may have come from Haarlem, Gerard David from Oudewater near Gouda, Van Eyck from Maaseik and Van der Weyden from Tournai, but the magic of the pars pro toto 'Flanders' did not vanish overnight.

In the 1840s, the connotations of 'primitive' were not necessarily negative. 'Primitive' also suggested 'purity' and 'Christian tenderness'. Originally, the word was used in relation to the art of Fra Angelico and other early Italian painters. To specify northern painters, the general adjective 'Flemish' was attached to it. The real breakthrough in this designation came in 1902, when almost four hundred works by the Late Medieval painters from the northern regions were brought together in the great retrospective *Les primitifs flamands* in Bruges. The lasting impression that it made on Johan Huizinga can probably be regarded as the creative germ for his world-famous *Autumntide of the Middle Ages* (1919/2020). Originally called *The Century of Burgundy*, its point of departure was 'the need to gain a better understanding of the art of the Van Eycks and their followers'.[7]

*

The split that occurred after 1585 seemed to lend plausibility to the idea that the resulting breach was a logical border, which it wasn't. There had never been a sharp distinction between north and south in the Burgundian and Habsburg Netherlands. The 'national' feeling actually originated in the heart of the Low Countries, in the core regions of Flanders-Brabant-Holland-Zeeland, where the elite built a mainly urban network and, stimulated by the dukes, an early form of global thinking emerged.

That evolution was also fuelled by the struggle with common enemies, first the French and later the Spanish. When the armies of Louis XI advanced after the death of Charles the Bold, expressions like 'the common fatherland' emerged – '*het gemeyne vaderlant*' in Middle Dutch and '*patria*' in Latin. A century later it was 'het verdruckte vaderlant', 'the oppressed fatherland'. These slogans could be heard mainly in the centre. The largely agrarian periphery felt that solidarity less strongly. The outskirts of the empire, from Friesland to Luxembourg via Overijssel, Guelders and Limburg, were more secluded and sent few representatives to the States General. When Joyous Entries were planned, the Burgundians focused mainly on the cities in the centre and far less, if ever, on those in the periphery. It was no different with the Habsburgs. They knew who they were dealing with: in 1473 the core regions were good for three-quarters of the taxes and benevolences; by 1548, that had risen to 80 per cent.

Any logical division that may have existed ran along a west–east line and not a north–south line. The gap between north and south put an end to the socio-economic ties that had always existed. And there are more things that run counter to what is automatically assumed today. Who is aware that Protestantism first caught on in the south, that the uprising against Catholic Spain took root in the southern provinces, and that Flanders and Brabant also signed the Act of Abjuration (the *Acte van Verlatinghe*, or the declaration of independence of the Netherlands drawn up in 1581)? That remarkably enough, the south was long known as '*Nederland*'? That 'Belgium' and even 'Flanders' were names applied to all the Low Countries? That in view of the economic and political shifts taking place at that time, a province with a name like Flemish Brabant would have sounded downright hilarious to a mortal from the Late Middle Ages?

Even the fact that the Low Countries under Emperor Charles V were as good as complete is something we conclude from the perspective of the present day. Actually, he could just as well have added other eastern principalities from the Rhineland. After all, they were part of the Holy Roman Empire too. Hadn't the same dukes, or their relatives, ruled over Jülich, Berg, Cleves and Mark? But after some hesitation, Charles drew the dividing line that later would become the eastern border of the Netherlands. A city like Duisberg might just as well be located in the Netherlands today, and Roermond in Germany. So in the end it was not only the north–south gap but also the eastern border that severed relations people thought would last forever.

The historian Wim Blockmans is correct when he says that 'few prejudices are as strong as those that turn present-day states into unquestioned interpretative frameworks for historical developments'.[8] It is tempting but misleading to look at the past from the distorted perspective of today, to think that the provisional ending we know down to the last detail was meant to be that way, let alone that it always was that way. But there is one thing we can soundly endorse as we reach our story's end: the national dimension of the Low Countries is a Burgundian project that was further developed by the Habsburgs and was torn in two by the conflicts of a divided religion, notably the response of Charles V and Philip II to those conflicts. Yet the chalk lines would long remain visible, and the idea would survive the centuries.

In 1815, Gijsbert Karel van Hogendorp was one of the framers of the constitution of the United Kingdom of the Netherlands. He himself witnessed the reunification of the Low Countries after the Battle of Waterloo as the rebirth of the Burgundian Netherlands. But a pragmatic sobriety also prevailed at that time that had little to do with the romantic evocation of a centuries-old story. The new unity would soon fall apart in 1830, the mayonnaise didn't hold, and no one felt the need to liberate the Burgundians from the dusty archives to justify an unstable union. Even the Orangists, traditionalists who supported the House of Orange in opposition to the more liberal Republicans, had little regard for the Seventeen Provinces; their main concerns were commercial. As mentioned earlier in this book, Belgian historians – with Pirenne leading the way – began searching for a foundation on which to base the new Belgian kingdom, and they held up Philip the Good as the Father of the Nation. In the Netherlands, Philip was regarded as the French-speaking opponent of urban liberty and was branded the man who had pointed the way to division a century before the Eighty Years War (1568–1648), when the Seventeen Provinces revolted against Philip II of Spain, but Spain was allowed by the Peace of Münster to retain the southern Provinces.

In the 1930s 'Burgundy' cropped up again, this time within extreme right and Catholic circles. Admiration for the old dukes took on a nasty edge. In the darkest days of Belgian history, the fascist Rex leader and wartime collaborator Léon Degrelle bent over backwards to attract Hitler's attention and approval. Who knew, maybe the Nazi leader would appoint him as his successor? A fop and fantasist, Degrelle was given the name 'Modest I, duc de Bourgogne' by his legionnaires and fancied himself the descendant of Philip the Good. He was totally committed to resurrecting the empire of the Grand Duke of the West from its ashes and breathing new life into the splendour of the Golden Fleece. He adorned the banners of his Walloon Legion with the Burgundian cross and hung an enlarged version of that emblem on the wall of his home, as you can see in the TV interviews he gave at the end of his life in Franco's Spain. The Generalísimo had granted asylum to the 'Führer of Bouillon'.

The Belgian fascist dreamed of 'a Middle Dutch ideal, inspired by the great Burgundy' and swooned nostalgically over the memory of the powerful Bruges and 'the studios of our Memlings, our Van Eycks'.[9] He was convinced that the reunited Burgundian Netherlands could be an important partner of Nazi Germany. Why would a return of the great ducal empire – including the Somme towns! – be impossible to achieve? In any event, from the end of the 1930s Degrelle was ready to become the great leader of a Germanized Burgundia. Would he have known that the ancestors of his venerated Burgundians let themselves be Romanized voluntarily, that not only did they give up their Germanic language but proceeded to forget it for good? No matter how fanatical Degrelle was, his Burgundian balloon would never get off the ground.

In the early twentieth century, Pirenne and Huizinga breathed new life into Burgundian studies in a most impressive way. Partly thanks to such scholars as Richard Vaughan, Bertrand Schnerb, Walter Prevenier and Wim Blockmans, this research has flourished once again in recent decades, but their important efforts rarely extended beyond the circles of specialists or well-versed enthusiasts. Unexpected change may yet be in the offing, however. While concentrating on completing this book, I learned to my astonishment that two beautiful Burgundian 'lieux de mémoire' would soon be coming to Mechelen and Brussels, places of remembrance where a direct connection would be sought with the part of our cultural memory that I had been trying to unravel in my writing. The hope, of course, was that hundreds of thousands of tourists from all over the world would pour in to marvel at the Late Medieval grandeur, but to my knowledge it was the first time that millions of euros had been invested in drawing attention to the fact that Belgian history took root in the subsoil of the Burgundian Netherlands. Now that 'the' world would be making more inroads into 'our' world, wasn't it possible that, apart from any mercantile motives, a greater need would arise to grant more prominence to our little-known history?

In the summer of 2018, after an extensive restoration, the Hof van Busleydan in Mechelen was repurposed as a museum whose aim is to bring to light Mechelen's Burgundian-Habsburg past as well as that of the region in general, and to explore the significance of that history for today. At least as impressive is the brand-new Museum of the Royal Library of Belgium. In 2020, the entire Burgundian era – starting with the world-famous Library of the Dukes of Burgundy, a manuscript collection of breathtaking beauty – was placed on permanent display there. It is located in Brussels, right near the site of Coudenberg Palace, the place where Philip the Good spent countless hours and right on the very last route taken by Emperor Charles.

'Magnificent And Luxurious'

In 1515 Desiderius Erasmus wrote a 'mirror for princes' for Charles, a vade mecum for the future leader, a moral and political talisman. 'He should then consider how desirable, how honourable, how wholesome a thing is peace; on the other hand, how calamitous as well as wicked a thing is war, and how even the most just of wars brings with it a train of evils – if indeed any war can really be called just.'[10] Charles would carry these words with him all his life as a kind of compass. There was nothing he desired more than a general peace, as if a naive goodness was lodged somewhere within him.

On 25 October 1555, Charles V, groaning with gout, abdicated the throne in the great hall of Coudenberg Palace in Brussels. In the place where Philip the Good had listened to the scabrous *Cent nouvelles nouvelles* a century earlier and had roared with laughter, his great-great-grandson bitterly took stock of his situation. That he had waged so many wars despite Erasmus's advice should not be held against him: it was always done against his will, and the blame lay with his enemies. Yet he asked the States General, with a quivering voice and tears in his eyes, to forgive him his faults. The members had never before seen such humility in so great a prince, and they must have granted their forgiveness with deep emotion.

It was not without resentment that Charles, influenced by dynastic tension within his own family, felt obliged to divide the immense empire into two parts. The Holy Roman Empire went to his brother Ferdinand, the patriarch of the Austrian branch. In Brussels, Charles transferred the rest of his power to his son, Philip, the future leader of the Spanish branch. Philip II managed to mangle four sentences of French in Brussels and then to give the floor to an advisor who was fluent in the language. The assembled guests were unanimous in their opinion: what a disgraceful performance! Immediately a fly in the ointment. In the meantime, the members looked on as their beloved, withered Charles found support on the sturdy shoulders of the mostly French-speaking William of Orange. In Brussels, this William was the man who kept the wavering emperor on his feet, but soon he would lead the Northern Netherlands in revolt.

The members had never seen a leader abandon power of his own free will. What a model of self-knowledge and sacrifice! Perhaps this is where the legend of the good Charles took root, a myth that in the Southern Netherlands would lead to countless folk tales in which the emperor is presented as a great man, someone who effortlessly fraternized with the common people, a bon vivant who never passed up a beautiful woman, a tasty meal or a cool pint. The fact that he was said to have breakfasted not only on eel pie but also on *waterzooi* – chicken and vegetables stewed in milk – was a source of great admiration. This Burgundian was a *bourgondiër* – he really knew how to enjoy himself!

Thanks to their banquets, the dukes earned themselves an entry in the Van Dale *Groot woordenboek van de Nederlandse taal*, the OED of the Dutch language. Gourmands – be they Charles V or one's own father – are known as 'real burgundians' (with a lower-case 'b'). Naturally, Philip and his people must have profited from the riches of Flanders and the abundance of products that washed ashore in Bruges in order to live so extravagantly, but if they hadn't made such propagandistic works of art out of their feasts we would have had to come up with another word today to describe a preference for gastronomic pleasures.

Charles's contemporary Pieter Brueghel the Elder, with his paintings of fairground scenes, zoomed in on the peasant component of the debauched character on which the average Belgian still prides himself centuries later. Charles de Coster depicted that soul of the south in 1867 with Lamme Goedzak and his 'Flemish fat, fed by battles, hard work and exhaustion'.[11] And in 1968 Jacques Brel expanded on both these ideas when he sang 'between London and Berlin it smells like beer'.[12] Although these three artists opted for an overwhelmingly plebeian interpretation, all of them were elaborating on the Burgundian ideal of the dukes, who so elegantly combined the elevated with the common, the pious with the overfed. It's the sensual contradiction with which the Southern Netherlands seems to correspond, at least in the imagination: 'burgundian' as the hot-blooded counterpart to 'Calvinistic', the adjective that would come to symbolize the north so acutely.

On the Market Square in the village of Olen there are three monumental jugs – actually, they're gigantic tankards – symbolizing the enduring love that the Southern Netherlands has for Emperor Charles, an affection that goes by way of the stomach. Charles visited the village three times. On his first visit he was offered a jug with a single handle, which the innkeeper held when serving it to him, so the emperor was forced to grasp the jug awkwardly with both hands. Shocking! On his next visit the emperor was given a jug with two handles, both of which the innkeeper managed to hold when offering it to his guest. Shocking again! But the good emperor deigned to return once more to visit his beloved subjects in Olen. The innkeeper was so terrified of committing another blunder that he succeeded in having a jug made with three handles, and he held only one of them when serving the emperor. The good-natured prince is said to have joked that the next time the poor man would have to come up with a jug with four handles. It is not known whether Charles ever paid another visit to Olen. Indeed, there is considerable doubt as to whether the emperor ever visited Olen at all. But his reputation was set. The legend of the three jugs has become part of the collective memory of Flanders.

In reality, Charles was not at all the affable fellow that legend makes him out to be. In 1540, when the Ghentenars refused to go on sponsoring his French wars, he crushed them in a way that would have put Philip the Good to shame. It sealed the city's fate: the old metropolis dwindled into a lethargic provincial town whose inhabitants would always be known as 'noose bearers' – *stroppendragers* – which is how the five hundred aldermen and guildsmen were forced to appear before him. He fought one war after another with France with an even heavier hand, always over the coveted north of Italy. With unfortunate obstinacy he responded to Luther and his followers in exactly the wrong way, leaving behind a totally divided church. He must have cursed himself more than once as the last emperor to be anointed by a pope, for the papal blessing obliged him to defend Catholicism with fire and sword. It was a burden he did not deal with very well. Charles was deeply religious but lacked theological training, and he lost himself in his own rigidity. But it was that Catholic stubbornness that would furnish him with an aura of Christian goodness after the successful passage of the Counter-Reformation through the south. That honour would be denied him in the Reformed north, although as the hapless warrior against Lutheranism and the father of the accursed Philip II he does belong to that region's canon of historical figures.

When he finally passed away, exhausted by asthma, diabetes, haemorrhoids and the ever-present gout, it was 21 September 1558. Three months later, an impressive funeral procession passed through the streets of Brussels in honour of the emperor. From

Coudenberg Palace to the Church of St Gudula, which was illuminated by 3,000 candles (and did not become a cathedral until the twentieth century), a huge crowd of spectators gathered behind the wooden barricades and stared in fascination. It was as if Olivier de la Marche had risen from the dead and turned the procession into a macabre counterpart to the Feast of the Pheasant.

We can read the 'magnificent and luxurious' details in the masterfully illustrated report *La magnifique et sumptueuse pompe funèbre* (1558), printed by Christoffel Plantijn in Antwerp. There we see dignitaries still proudly wearing the chain of the Order of the Golden Fleece 128 years after its founding in 1430. Philip the Good's order would survive the turbulent commotion of the centuries. Even today it remains an especially prestigious distinction for European aristocrats. The two former Belgian kings, Baudouin and Albert II, had the honour of calling themselves knights of the Golden Fleece, and Queen Beatrix of the Netherlands was also received into the order.

The pièce de résistance and direct counterpart to the whale that made such a splash at the wedding of Charles the Bold in 1468 was a parade float in the shape of an immense galleon. The vessel was apparently being drawn by two seahorses but was actually being dragged by two invisible men, like slaves in the belly of a ship – an unintentional symbol of what was happening to the indigenous peoples and the black slaves in the colonial empire. The colossus was decorated with flags from all of Charles's possessions, which included twenty-seven kings' crowns, thirteen duchies, twenty-two counties, a handful of seigniories and symbolic titles like 'King of Jerusalem'.

At the top of the mast was a crucifix. The identification of Charles with the Son of God was entirely consistent with how Philip the Good, at his Joyous Entry in Ghent in 1458, must have related to the Messiah enthroned in the living imitation of the *Adoration of the Mystic Lamb* (the *Ghent Altarpiece*). Behind the galleon were two elephant seals dragging the pillars of Hercules, antiquity's classical ending of the world, which was now consigned to the archives. Scores of banners bore Charles's French motto '*plus oultre*', which left no room for doubt: ever further!

The splendour of the multicoloured decorations, banners, chasubles, caparisons and other saddle blankets stood in stark contrast with the black mourning attire of the guests. How different from the sombre cortège that had recently passed through the streets of Brussels. The tribute to the deceased Mary Tudor, second wife of Philip II, was shrouded in English restraint and Spanish austerity.

So the exuberant funeral procession of Emperor Charles V on 29 December 1558 seemed to communicate one great message: take a good look – the last Burgundian is being laid to rest.

*

It would have been a beautiful, somewhat romantic ending to this book, but the truth has its rights. After Charles V, countless Burgundians would pass through this life. The duchy still existed, after all; it was just reconnected to France. Ever since Richard the Justiciar defeated the Vikings at Chartres in 911 and was given the title of duke by the French king as a reward, Burgundy had belonged to the French crown. That situation was restored after the death of Charles the Bold.

From now on, the rebel Burgundy would no longer play a significant role in French history. Like one of the many satellites that revolved around Paris, it was silently absorbed into the rigid centralism of the kingdom. Although the French are quite skilled at keeping their history alive, the memory of that unruly duchy has never been cultivated. Burgundy was given an unenviable position in the national narrative. Wasn't it true that the dukes had almost brought Eternal France to the brink of extinction? In 1789, the revolutionaries dealt with the matter by simply abolishing the 'Généralite de Bourgogne', as the principality had been known in the French administrative records since 1542. In its place came the departments Côte d'Or (Dijon), Saône-et-Loire (Mâcon), Yonne (Auxerre) and Nièvre (Nevers).

Even the casks of wine, the absolute pride of Burgundy, seemed to roll across the land with an unimaginative tedium. In the end, only folklorists showed any interest in the once so famous region. Then in the 1930s, the winegrowers decided enough was enough. They founded the *Confrérie des Chevaliers du Tastevin* (Brotherhood of the Knights of the Wine-Tasting Cup) and began taking pride once more in the time-honoured tradition of good food and good wine. They had great success with their *dîners-spectacles*, dousing their coq-au-vin with the most delicious Burgundian crus in the extravagant style of the ducal banquets. They took their example from Philip the Good, and it worked. Busloads of connoisseurs and journalists descended on the old duchy and let themselves be pampered by experts.

Suddenly, everybody remembered that in his later years, the Sun King, Louis XIV, had partaken of wine from Nuits-Saint-Georges as a sort of elixir. That Napoleon lugged bottles of Chambertin all the way to Egypt, Moscow and Waterloo. That the writer-revolutionary Alphonse de Lamartine, one of France's great literary figures and legendary presidential candidate, had written the following words to his Burgundian home base from the barricades in 1848: 'Care for and press my vintage in the three vineyards. [...] Tell my winegrowers that I am with them in my thoughts. I am no poet. I am a great winegrower.'[13] Nor could it have been accidental that the French hero Ardan from Jules Verne's novel *Autour de la Lune* (*Around the Moon*, 1870) uncorked a 'Côte de Nuits' during his space journey. If a Frenchman was making a successful moonshot, it would have to be celebrated with the appropriate wine.

Such anecdotes made everyone happy, especially potential customers. And that was only right, cried the Burgundians. Grapevines had been planted in the region around Dijon ever since the time of the Romans. After a Germanic people from the island of Bornholm, alias Burgundarholmr, settled here, the brew that would grow into the world's most famous wine acquired its name and was free to begin its success story as *vin de bourgogne*. King Gundobad had devoted several lines to it in his famous *Lex Burgundionum* (502). But the importance of Philip the Bold in particular cannot be underestimated. Not only did he promote the Pinot Noir as the Burgundian grape par excellence, but as ambassador of Beaune's better casks he also knew how to gain an international reputation. When the direct connection between the

Low Countries and Burgundy was lost after 1477, that reputation quickly faded. Moreover, wine from Bordeaux was being transported overseas, which was a great deal cheaper than the overland journey that Burgundian casks had to travel. This partly explains why Flemings became Bordeaux lovers for the most part, and why the Walloons continued to swear by Burgundy. In France itself, even though the dukes had faded from memory by the twentieth century, their region once again became synonymous with the liquid that had heralded its fame.

In 1972, the name 'Burgundy', which had been eradicated in the eighteenth century, finally resurfaced as the region comprising the departments created by the Revolution. On 1 January 2016 this entire area fused with the Franche-Comté, the former Free County of Burgundy.

Can you hear King Gundobad chuckling from the great beyond? With this recent territorial revision, the new all-encompassing region of Bourgogne-Franche-Comté is beginning to look suspiciously like the mythical kingdom of the fifth and sixth centuries, the kingdom that Charles the Bold tried to emulate and where this long tale began so many pages ago. Give it some time, you hear Gundobad thinking, give it some time, and everything goes back to the way it once was.

ENDNOTES

With a book like this one it's easy to generate a vast number of endnotes. That struck me as pointless. My main aim was to provide the origin of the quoted material. This is almost exclusively taken from the testimonies of chroniclers from those bygone days and is hardly ever the view of historians, although the opinions of Michelet, Pirenne, Huizinga and Blockmans do constitute the rare exceptions. Quotes from Middle Dutch (*Diets*) and Middle French are all translated into English. Of course, I have read and consulted more works than those listed here. These can be found in the descriptive and the enumerative bibliography.

PROLOGUE

1 Jean Schoonjans and Jean-Léon Huens, *'s Lands Glorie: Vulgarisatie van de geschiedenis van België door het beeld*, vol. III, p. 9.
2 Ibid. p. 23.
3 Ibid. p. 44.
4 Ibid. vol. I, p. 9.
5 Ibid. p. 41.
6 Ibid. vol. III, p. 15.
7 Hugo de Schepper, *Belgium dat is Nederlandt*, p. 17.

PART I. THE FORGOTTEN MILLENNIUM
FROM KINGDOM TO DUCHY

1 Edward Gibbon, *History of the Decline and Fall of the Roman Empire*, Project Gutenberg Edition.
www.gutenberg.org/files/25717/25717-h/25717-h.htm

2   www.eupedia.com/europe/Haplogroup_Q_Y-DNA.shtml
    Recently, a number of historians and archaeologists have called into
    question the story of Bornholm as the island from which the Burgundians
    originated. They suggest that while the island may have had a Burgundian
    settlement, the settlers themselves first came from the Oder region. They
    regard these Burgundians not so much as an ethnic group but as a political
    conglomerate. Clearly, the last word on this subject has yet to be spoken.

3   Katalin Escher, *Les Burgondes, Ier-VIe siècles apr. J.-C.*, p. 89.

4   Jean-Robert Pitte, *Dictionnaire amoureux de Bourgogne*, p. 147. Also see
    Jean-François Bazin, *Histoire du Vin de Bourgogne*, p. 11.

5   Historians are still divided on the exact date, but all agree that it must
    have happened sometime between 496 and 508. In 1996 France celebrated
    the 1500th anniversary of Clovis's baptism. But since then more and more
    voices have spoken out in favour of dating the baptism to 506, since any
    other date would make the chronology of his life problematic. Cf. Justin
    Favrod, *Les Burgondes: Un royaume oublié au coeur de l'Europe*, pp. 83–5
    and Katalin Escher, op. cit., p. 119.

6   Gregory of Tours, *History of the Franks*, book II, chapter 31. E-text of
    the translation made by Earnest Brehaut in 1916. A Fordham University
    Medieval Sourcebook: sourcebooks.fordham.edu/basis/gregory-hist.asp

7   Ibid. book II, chapter 30.

8   Ibid.

9   Ibid. book II, chapter 37.

10 Ibid. book III, chapter 5.

11 Escher, op cit., p. 132.

12 For a very short period there was a kingdom known as Arelat, which
    united the Franche-Comté with the county of Provence, two parts of
    Gundobad's former kingdom of Burgundy. Arelat (named after its capital,
    Arles) ceased to exist in 1032 and was also called the Kingdom of the Two
    Burgundies. Cf. Norman Davies, *Vanished Kingdoms: The History of Half-
    Forgotten Europe*, pp. 130ff.

FROM BURGUNDY TO FLANDERS

1   Georges Duby, *The Age of the Cathedrals: Art and Society, 980–1420*, p. 65.

2   Jacques Le Goff, *Medieval Civilization*, p. 59.

3   The Rule of St Benedict, chapter 40. Also see: Henri D'Arbois De
    Jubainville, 'De la nourriture des Cisterciens, principalement à Clairvaux,
    aux XII et au XIII siècle' in *Bibliothèque de l'École des Chartes*, 1858, 19, p.
    277.

4 Barbara Tuchman, *A Distant Mirror*, p. 144.

5 Ibid. p. 150.

6 Ibid.

7 Jules Michelet, *Histoire de France, vol. 3: Philippe le Bel. Charles V*, p. 192.

8 Vic De Donder, *In de naam van Vlaanderen*, p. 70.

9 Wim Blockmans, *Metropolen aan de Noordzee*, p. 223.

10 Clément-Janin, *Les pestes en Bourgogne 1349–1636*, p. 5.

11 Bertrand Schnerb, *L'État bourguignon*, p. 37.

12 Robert Stein, *De hertog en zijn staten*, p. 32.

PART II. THE BURGUNDIAN CENTURY

RISING FROM THE MUD

1 Bertrand Schnerb, *Jean Sans Peur: Le prince meurtrier*, p. 23.

2 Edward de Maesschalk, *De graven van Vlaanderen (861–1384)*, p. 57.

3 Dante, *The Divine Comedy*, vol. 1: *Inferno*, canto XV, p. 205.

4 William Shakespeare, *King Lear*, Act 1, Scene 1: 'Not all the dukes of waterish Burgundy / Can buy this unprized precious maid of me.'

5 Tuchman, op. cit. p. 76.

6 Ibid. Barbara Tuchman attributes the quote to Matthew of Westminster, an author who is regarded by many as never having existed. It most probably was Matthew of Paris.

7 Michael Pye, *The Edge of the World: How the North Sea Made Us What We Are*, p. 263.

8 August Vermeylen, 'Vlaamse en Europese Beweging,' in *Verzameld Werk*, vol. 2, 162.

9 David Nicholas, *Medieval Flanders*, p. 223.

GHENT THE FEARLESS

1 Pitte, op. cit. p. 25. See also Bazin, op. cit.

2 Schnerb, op. cit. p. 447.

3 *Chronique du religieux de Saint-Denys, le règne de Charles VI, de 1380–1422*, vol. I, p. 91.

4 Geoffrey Chaucer, *The Canterbury Tales*, General Prologue, line 448.

5 Tuchman, op. cit. p. 363, and Patrice Guennifey, *Les derniers jours des rois*, p. 108.

6 Tuchman, op. cit. p. 364.

7 Frans Hugaerts, *Heel dit Vlaamse land: Of hoe de Franse hofdichter*

Eustache Deschamps Vlaanderen zag in de laatste jaren van de veertiende eeuw, p. 27. I have translated Hugaert's anthologized writings from Middle French into Dutch.

8   Jean Froissart, *Chroniques*, books I and II, p. 863.

9   Jean-Philippe Lecat, *Quand flamboyait la Toison d'or*, p. 34.

10 Ibid. p. 33.

11 Prospère Barante, *Histoire des ducs de Bourgogne de la Maison de Valois (1364–1477)*, p. 63.

12 Leah DeVun, *Prophecy, Alchemy and the End of Time: John of Rupescissa in the Late Middle Ages*, p. 35.

13 Hugaerts, op. cit. p. 31.

14 Ibid. p. 35.

15 Froissart, op. cit. p. 914. For the Battle of Westrozebeke, see also *La Chronique du bon duc Loys de Bourbon*.

16 Ibid.

1789 AVANT LA LETTRE

1   Ibid. pp. 925–6.

2   Ibid. p. 926.

3   Ibid. p. 927.

4   Hugaerts, op. cit. p. 47.

5   Dante, *The Divine Comedy*, vol. 3: *Paradise*, canto XV, p. 181.

6   Frans Hugaerts / Deschamps, pp. 43–4.

7   Ibid. p. 46.

8   Pitte, op. cit. pp. 451–2.

9   Froissart, op. cit. p. 928.

10 Hugaerts, op cit. p. 45.

LOW COUNTRIES IN THE MAKING

1   Ben Speet, *De tijd van de steden*, p. 54.

2   Schnerb, op. cit. p. 41.

3   Froissart, op. cit. pp. 986–8.

4   Ibid.

5   Bernard of Clairvaux, 'Apologia', p. 169.

6   Froissart, op. cit. pp. 986–8.

7   Bernard of Clairvaux, 'In Praise of the New Knighthood', p. 132.

8   Schnerb, op. cit. p. 506.

FRANCE AS THE DRAUGHT HORSE OF BURGUNDY

1   Amédée Gouêt, *Histoire des règnes de Charles VI et VII: 1380–1460, d'après les documents originaux*, p. 71.
2   Barante, op. cit. p. 96.
3   Jean Froissart, *Chroniques*, vol. 2, p. 316 (Jean Alexandre Buchon edition, 1840).
4   Hugaerts, op. cit. p. 65.
5   Ibid. p. 74.
6   Ibid. p. 68.
7   Albrecht Rodenbach, from 'Fierheid' (Pride), published in *Eerste gedichten*.
8   Bertrand Schnerb, *L'État bourguignon*, p. 85.
9   Jan Van Dixmude, *Dits de Cronike ende Genealogie van den prinsen ende Graven van den Foreeste van Buc, dat heet Vlaenderlant, van 863 tot 1436*, p. 284.
10 Nicholas, op. cit. p. 323.
11 *La Chronique du bon duc Loys de Bourbon*, p. 181.
12 Hugaerts, op. cit. pp. 86–8 (also see Froissart and Deschamps).
13 Barante, op. cit. p. 110.
14 Hugaerts, op. cit. pp. 103–4.
15 Catharina Ipes, *Petrarca in de Nederlandse letterkunde*, pp. 3–4.
16 Hugaerts, op. cit. p. 122.
17 The third brother, Louis of Anjou, also a member of the regency council, had died during a violent Neapolitan campaign of conquest in 1384.
18 Joseph Calmette, *Les grands ducs de Bourgogne*, p. 80.
19 Bart Van Loo, *O vermiljoenen spleet! Seks, erotiek en literatuur*, p. 21. English translation by Nancy Forest-Flier.
20 Hugaerts, op. cit. pp. 132–3. English translation by Nancy Forest-Flier.

BEAUTY AND MADNESS

1   In the Burgundian records there is no trace of the Middle Dutch name Claes, but we do find the name 'Claux'. 'Claus' is used today in both English and French, which is the practice followed here.
2   Michel Pintoin, *Chronique du Religieux de Saint Denis*, actually written in Latin, *Historia Karoli Sexti Francorum regis* (The History of Charles VI), folio 189, cited by Michelet, op cit. p. 50.
3   Michelet, op. cit. p. 50. He is citing Froissart.
4   Bernard Guenée, *La folie de Charles VI*, p. 17.
5   Lecat, op. cit. p. 111.
6   Tuchman, op cit. p. 513. Also see Guenée and Michelet.

7   Schnerb, op. cit., p. 66. He is citing Froissart.

8   Aloysius Bertrans in the prologue to *Gaspard de la nuit*, 1842.

OSTENTATION AND PROPAGANDA

1   Schnerb, op. cit. p. 74.

2   Jean Froissart, *Chroniques*, books III and IV, p. 535.

3   Lecat, op. cit. p. 112.

4   Schnerb, op. cit. p. 91.

5   Tuchman, op. cit. p. 576.

6   Froissart: op. cit. p. 613. Also see Marie-Gaëtane Martenet, 'Le récit de la bataille de Nicopolis (1396) dans les Chroniques de Jean Froissart: de l'échec à la gloire' in *Questes*, 30, 2015, pp. 125–39.

7   Philip, the third son of Philip the Bold, not to be confused with his grandson Philip, the later Philip the Good.

8   Today the city lies in Flemish Brabant, but during most of the Middle Ages it was part of the county of Hainaut.

9   Anthony married Johanna of Luxembourg, and his brother Philip married Bonne of Artois. Their sisters Catharine and Mary married Leopold IV of Austria and Amadeus VIII of Savoy respectively.

10   These are quite probably the work of the former court sculptor, Jean de Marville.

11   Remarkably, he is misidentified there as 'Jan Sluter'. On the southern wall he is shown between towers VII and VIII. When I asked for clarification from the Rijksmuseum, I was given the following answer: 'In view of the image shown in the window, this must be the same figure. What we see here is a medieval sculptor. It is true that you do not come across the name Jan Sluter in the literature, so probably this is an outdated and incorrect understanding of the first name of Claus/Claes Sluter.' (e-mail dated 17/8/2017)

12   From the elegy that Christine de Pizan wrote in 1404 in response to Philip's death. Schnerb quotes it in its entirety in *L'État bourguignon*, pp. 141–2.

MURDER AND THE LANGUAGE WARS

1   Enguerrand de Monstrelet, *La Chronique en deux livres avec pièces justificatives 1400–1444*, book 1, p. 156.

2   All quotes from the attack are taken from the work cited in note 1. Also see: Schnerb, op. cit. p. 209.

3   Barante, op. cit. p. 221.

4   Pierre Cochon, in Auguste Vallet de Viriville (ed.), *Chronique de la Pucelle ou Chronique de Cousinot, suivie de la Chronique normande de P. Cochon relatives aux règnes de Charles VI et Charles VII*, p. 381.

5   Monstrelet, op. cit. p. 162.

6   Barante, op. cit. p. 222.

7   Lecat, op. cit. p. 124.

8   Blockmans, op. cit., p. 171.

9   Jacob van Maerlant, *Spiegel Historiael*, part 4, book I, chapter XXIX, line 27.

10 Hendrik Conscience, *De Leeuw van Vlaanderen*, p. 273.

11 Quote from the Antwerp writer Jan van Boendale from *c.*1330.

12 Nicholas, op. cit. p. 347.

13 Schnerb, op. cit. p. 30.

14 Corpus Gysseling, compiled by the Ghent linguist Maurits Gysseling (1977–8).

15 Monstrelet, op. cit. pp. 242–3.

ARRANGED MARRIAGES, UNCONTROLLABLE TUMULT

1   Monstrelet, op. cit. p. 352.

2   Culverins were portable cannon. Ribaudequins were multiple gun barrels that could be fired all at once.

3   Monstrelet, op. cit. p. 363.

4   Ibid. p. 364.

5   Ibid. p. 398.

6   His father, Henry IV, had died of leprosy or diabetes in 1413.

7   Monstrelet, op. cit. p. 404.

8   Charles of Orléans, translated by Nancy Forest-Flier from a Dutch translation by Hella S. Haasse in *Het woud der verwachting*, p. 5.

9   Enguerrand de Monstrelet, *La Chronique en deux livres avec pièces justificatives 1400–1444*, book 3, pp. 226–30. Schnerb, op. cit. p. 661.

10 Jim Bradbury, *The Medieval Siege*, p. 170. Also quoted by other authors who all note the chronicler Juvenal des Ursins as a primary source.

SEVERED HAND, CLEFT SKULL

1   Not very long ago, this derailed conversation was reconstructed on the basis of eyewitness Jean Séguinat, secretary to John the Fearless. It can be read in Schnerb, op. cit. pp. 683–4.

2   Lecat, op. cit. p. 157.

3 Ignace Van der Hey, *Histoire des comtes de Flandre depuis l'établissement de ses souverains, jusqu'à présent*, p. 136. Also cited by Jean-Philippe Lecat, op. cit. p. 157 and Renée-Paul Guillot, *Les ducs de Bourgogne*, p. 115. Also see Joseph Calmette, op cit. p. 178.

4 Lecat, op. cit. p. 157.

5 Bertrand Schnerb, *Jean Sans Peur Le prince meurtrier*, p. 716.

THREE COUNTIES, ONE DUKE

1 Richard Vaughan, *Philip the Good: The Apogee of Burgundy*, p. 132.

2 Johan Huizinga, *Autumntide of the Middle Ages,* p. 149.

3 Georges Chastellain, *Oeuvres*, vol. 7, p. 221 (Kervyn de Lettenhove edition).

4 Emmanuel Bourassin, *Philippe le Bon: Le Grand Lion des Flandres*, p. 39.

5 Translated from the text in Antheun Janse, *Een pion voor een dame: Jacoba van Beieren (1401–1436)*, pp. 225–7. Also see Wim Blockmans, *De Bourgondiërs*, p. 90, and Léopold Devillers, *Cartulaire des comtes de Hainaut, de l'avènement de Guillaume II à la mort de Jacqueline de Bavière*, vol. IV, pp. 473, 474 and 475.

6 Georges Bordonove, *Joan of Arc et la Guerre de Cent Ans*, p. 110.

7 Ibid. p. 97.

THE BATTLE FOR HOLLAND AND ZEELAND

1 Janse, op. cit. p. 245.

2 Because of the counting of 'hearths' (the old name for a house, with the hearth as *pars pro toto*), surnames, most of which were still patronymics, slowly came into administrative use between 1200 and 1400.

3 Wim Blockmans, *Metropolen aan de Noordzee*, p. 290.

4 Vaughan, op. cit. p. 43.

5 Janse, op. cit. p. 248.

6 Ibid. p. 256.

7 Ibid. p. 264.

8 Ibid. p. 271.

9 Blockmans, *Metropolen aan de Noordzee*, p. 400.

AS WOMAN OR AS MAN?

1 De Meung, *The Romance of the Rose, The Continuation*, chap. LI, p. 210.

2 Christine de Pizan, *The Book of the City of Ladies*, p. 256.

3   Ibid. p. 35.

4   Bordonove, op. cit. p. 121.

5   Ibid. p. 113.

6   Ibid. p. 121.

7   Olivier Bouzy, *Joan of Arc: Mythes et réalités*, p. 58.

GOLDEN GLITTER

1   Michelet, *Histoire de France, Jeanne d'Arc, Charles VII*. vol. V, p. 69.

2   Paul Jubault, *D'Azincourt à Joan of Arc*, p. 277.

3   Léon de Laborde, *Les ducs de Bourgogne. Études sur les lettres, les arts et l'industrie pendant le XVe siècle, t. I (Preuves)*, p. 206. Also see Till-Holger Borchert, Dorine Duyster, Stephan Kemperdick & Friso Lammertse (eds.), *De weg naar Van Eyck*, p. 85.

4   These can be found in the Turin-Milan Book of Hours (partially destroyed in 1904, but some black-and-white photographs of the destroyed part do exist), containing page-size miniatures of John of Bavaria, among others, who is shown praying with his retinue on the beach at Scheveningen. Although it is not entirely certain, specialists attribute a number of the miniatures to Jan or his brother Hubert van Eyck.

5   The response that Napoleon made on 1 May 1802 in an attempt to silence the critics of his Légion d'honneur. He was proved right by his opponents themselves, who soon stood in line to receive his little trinket.

THE BURIAL PIT AND THE STAKE

1   Georges Chastellain, *Pages choisies*, p. 54.

2   Chastellain, *Chroniques*, part II, chap. 14.

3   Enguerrand de Monstrelet, *La Chonique d'Enguerrand de Monstrelet en deux livres avec pieces justificatives 1400–1444*, part II, chap. 86.

4   *Procès de condamnation de Joan of Arc*, vol. II, p. 126. W.P. Barrett (trans.), *The Trial of Joan of Arc*.

5   Blockmans, *Metropolen aan de Noordzee*, p. 403.

6   Louis Guillemin, *Jeanne dite Joan of Arc*, pp. 306–7.

7   Jules Michelet, *Joan of Arc*, p. 8.

8   Guillemin, op. cit. p. 309.

9   Bordonove, op. cit. p. 296.

10   Guillemin, op. cit. p. 265.

11   Bordonove, op. cit. p. 252.

BEAUTY AND PEACE

1   Bernhard Ridderbos, *Schilderkunst in de Bourgondische Nederlanden*, p. 55.

2   In the most recent art historical articles and books (Dhanens, among others), Philip's presence at the installation of the *Ghent Altarpiece* is either taken for granted or accepted with certain reservations. Ridderbos, for example, notes it with a few caveats. Wim Blockmans openly doubts the possibility and argues that, on the basis of household accounts, the duke would have been in Burgundy at the time. I have opted to follow the interpretation of most art historians, because it seems logical to me that he must have been there for the baptism of his possible successor. But we can't be sure. Another question over which there is some disagreement is whether the *Ghent Altarpiece* was completely finished in 1432. Art historian Hugo van der Velden, in two articles from 2011 (see bibliography), maintains that the quatrain on the frame (dated 1432) only pertains to the lower zone of the interior. Clearly, the mystery of the *Ghent Altarpiece* is far from being resolved.

3   Marcus van Vaernewyck, *Van die beroerlicke tijden in die Nederlanden en voornamelick in Ghendt 1566–1568*, chapter IV, p. 146.

4   Jan Walch, *Karel de Stoute*, p. 9.

5   Stephan Kemperdick and Friso Lammertse, *De weg naar Van Eyck*, p. 87 (chapter by Till-Holger Borchert: 'Jan van Eyck: Mythe en documenten').

6   Elisabeth Dhanens, *Hubert and Jan Van Eyck*, pp. 287, 290.

7   Bernhard Ridderbos, *De Melancholie van de kunstenaar: Hugo van der Goes en de Oudnederlandse schilderkunst*, p. 94.

8   Dhanens, op. cit. p. 58.

9   And not on 9 July, as is constantly insisted. That day was when the annual Mass was said. As Dhanens points out in her groundbreaking book, there are other known examples of annual Masses that are celebrated on a day other than that of the person's death (p. 57).

THE BURGUNDIAN DREAM

1   Barante, op. cit. p. 369.

2   *Sinxenwoensdach*. *Sinxen* means 'Whitsun', as it still does in most Flemish dialects. Cited from Jan Dumolyn, '*Rebelheden ende vergaderinghen*: Twee Brugse documenten uit de grote opstand van 1436–1438', *Bulletin de la Commission Royale d'Histoire*, 1996, 162, pp. 297–323.

3   Generally accepted as a statement made by Justus Lipsius, although specialists claim it was Pontus Heuterus who said it first. Whoever it was, Henri Pirenne was all too glad to quote Lipsius's remark in his famous

Histoire de Belgique (p. 342). Remarkably enough, Pirenne translated the words in another work (*La fin du Moyen Age*, p. 459) as '*fondateur de la Belgique*', an intentional anachronism by this Belgian nationalist. It is not surprising that Schoonjans, who is quoted here in the prologue, was a disciple of Pirenne. For the confusion that arose between Belgium, the Netherlands and the Low Countries over the course of the years, I refer the reader to the epilogue of this book.

4   Stein, *De hertog en zijn Staten*, p. 94.

5   Ibid. p. 123.

6   Ibid. p. 129.

7   J.J. Steyaert, *Beschryving der stad Gend, of Geschiedkundig overzigt van die stad en hare bewooners, de merkweerdige gebouwen, gestichten en maetschappyen, de beroemde Gentenaren, enz*, p. 69.

8   Stein, op. cit. p. 265.

9   Schnerb, *L'État bourguignon*, p. 382.

10 Nicholas, op cit. p. 330.

11 Blockmans, 'La répression de révoltes urbaines comme méthode de centralisation dans les Pays-Bas bourguignons', in *Publications du Centre Européen d'Études Bourguignonnes*, pp. 5–9.

12 Blockmans, *De Bourgondiërs*, p. 193.

13 Ibid. p. 165.

PHEASANT AND FOX

1   Jacques du Clercq, *Memoires de J. Du Clercq, sur le règne de Philippe le Bon, Duc de Bourgogne*, vol. 3, p. 203.

2   Lecat, op. cit. p. 246.

3   Thomas à Kempis, *Soliloquium animae, Opera Omnia*, vol. I, p. 230.

4   Thomas à Kempis, *Sermones et novitios* (no. 28), *Opera Omnia*, M.J. Pohl (ed.), Freiburg 1902–1910, vol. VI, p. 287. Also see Huizinga, *Autumntide of the Middle Ages*, p. 391.

5   All other quotes are taken from Thomas à Kempis, *The Imitation of Christ*, translated by Anthony Hoskins in around 1613.

6   Olivier de la Marche, 'Les Voeux du Faisan' in *Splendeurs de Bourgogne: Récits et chroniques*, p. 1141.

7   Ibid. pp. 1145–8. Her words formed the inspiration for the famous *Lamentatio sanctae matris ecclesiae Constantinopolitanae* ('Lament of the Holy Mother Church of Constantinople') by Guillaume Dufay. Quite possibly this beautiful Latin composition was sung at the banquet, although it is not known for certain.

8   Ibid. pp. 1157–63.

9   Between Sigismund's and Frederick's reign, the imperial crown had graced the head of Albert II of Habsburg for less than a year. Albert was married to Sigismund's only daughter. Frederick III was also a Habsburg. He was a full cousin of the short-lived emperor Albert II, who died in 1439 during a battle against the Turks.

10   Georges Chastellain, 'Le duc vainqueur: l'entrée à Utrecht' in *Splendeurs de la Cour de Bourgogne: Récits et chroniques*, p. 814.

11   Georges Minois, *Charles le Téméraire*, p. 64.

12   Ibid. p. 66.

13   Georges Chastellain, 'Comment le duc se rendit à Bruxelles, et des grands honneurs qu'il fit au Dauphin' in *Splendeurs de la Cour de Bourgogne: Récits et Chroniques*, p. 828.

FATHERS AND SONS

1   All quotes from this episode are taken from Chastellain, 'La colère de Philippe: une aventure qui faillit mal tourner' in *Splendeurs de la Cour de Bourgogne, Récits et Chroniques*, pp. 831–49.

2   Huizinga, op. cit. p. 427.

3   *Les cent nouvelles nouvelles* (critical edition by F.P. Sweetser), p. 410.

4   Huizinga, op. cit. p. 20.

5   *Les cent nouvelles nouvelles*, op cit. p. 83.

6   *Complete Poems of François Villon*, translated by Beram Saklatvala, New York: Dutton, 1968. '*Ballades des menus propos*' ('A Ballade of Little Sayings'), p. 160.

7   Ibid. 'Villon's Epitaph for himself, being *A Ballade of the Hanged*', pp. 179–80.

8   Ibid., 'A Ballade of Ladies of Former Times' ('*Ballade des dames du temps jadis*'), p. 37.

9   Minois, op. cit. p. 125.

10   Arnout van Cruyningen, *De Staten-Generaal: vijfenhalve eeuw geschiedenis van het parlement*, p. 19.

11   The name did not become official until 1477.

12   Picardy had just been sold back to France by the ailing Philip the Good. In the more remote Limburg and Luxembourg there would never be much enthusiasm for the States General. See the Epilogue.

13   Henri Dubois, *Charles le Téméraire*, p. 113.

14   Bourassin, op. cit. p. 352.

15   Dhanens, *Rogier van der Weyden, Revisie van de documenten*, p. 65.

16   Dirk de Vos, *Rogier van der Weyden*, p. 56.

17   'Le temps a laissié son manteau', www.everypoet.com/archive/poetry/ Charles_d_orleans/index.htm

PART III. THE FATAL DECADE

JOYOUS ENTRY, SOMBRE RECEPTION

1   Olivier de la Marche, *Les mémoires de messire Olivier de la Marche*, p. 487.

2   Georges Chastellain, 'La mort de Philippe le Bon' in *Splendeurs de la Cour de Bourgogne: Récits et chroniques*, p. 902.

3   Georges Chastellain, *Chronique des ducs de Bourgogne*, p. 512.

4   Georges Bordonove, *Louis XI, Le diplomate*, p. 129.

5   Chastellain, op. cit. p. 519.

6   With its famous Middle Dutch opening: '*Egidius waer bestu bleven / Mi lanct na di gheselle mijn / Du coors die doot du liets mi tleven.*' (Egidius, where have you gone? / I long for you, my friend. / You've chosen death, left me among the living.)

7   Chastellain, op. cit.

8   Ibid. p. 522.

9   Minois, op. cit. p. 179.

10   Michelet, *Histoire de France: Jeanne d'Arc. Charles VII.* pp. 302–3 (note 2).

11   Dhanens, *Hugo van der Goes*, p. 39. A sign at number 158 recalls the creation of this work.

12   Thanks to several accounts, we know that Rogier van der Weyden had put his name on the frame of one of his justice scenes – *Rogerius pinxit*. The work was lost in a fire. Nowhere else do we find a similar signature.

13   Hugo Claus, *Gedichten (1948–1993)*, p. 423.

14   De la Marche, op cit. p. 520.

15   Minois, op. cit. 184.

THE CROWN FOR THE TAKING

1   *Mémoires de Commynes*, p. 86.

2   Juliaan van Belle, *Les Pays de par deçà: De Bourgondische Nederlanden*, vol. 2, p. 57.

3   *Mémoires de Commynes*, p. 146.

4   Claus, op. cit. p. 425.

5   Henri Pirenne, *Histoire de L'Europe: Des invasions au XVIe siècle*, p. 349.

RENEWAL AND INNOVATION

1   Richard Vaughan, *Valois Burgundy*, p. 195.

2   Stein, op. cit. p. 165.

3   *Memorieboek der stad Ghent van 't jaar 1301 tot 1588*, p. 279.

4   Minois, op. cit. p. 273.

5   Only a small area east of the Scheldt was feudally connected to the Holy Roman Empire.

6   A 'mirror' was often a didactic-moralizing text whose aim was to enlarge human knowledge and self-knowledge by holding a figurative mirror up to the reader.

7   Yet at the end of the nineteenth century, Albrecht De Vriendt, in consultation with the Bruges city council, chose to honour Mansion's fellow printer Jan Brito on the monumental wall painting that graces the Gothic hall in Bruges city hall. Six of Brito's books have survived, as opposed to more than twenty-five by Mansion. It would have been logical to highlight Caxton, Mansion and Brito as the holy trinity of the art of printing in Bruges – and by extension all of Burgundy.

8   Victor Hugo, *Notre-Dame de Paris, also known as the Hunchback of Notre Dame*, Project Gutenberg e-book, www.gutenberg.org/files/2610/2610–h/2610–h.htm. From the famous chapter 'This Will Kill That', in which he also says, 'The invention of printing is the greatest event in history'.

DEATH IN THE SNOW

1   Minois, op. cit. p. 414.

2   *Les mémoires de messire Olivier de la Marche*, pp. 512 and 515. Also see Jean Molinet, *Chroniques*, vol. I, pp. 65–6.

3   Vaughan, op. cit. p. 208.

4   Dubois, op. cit. p. 358.

5   Ibid. p. 426.

6   *Mémoires de Commynes*, p. 168.

7   Minois, op. cit. p. 437.

8   Gachard, *Collection de documents inédits concernant l'histoire de la Belgique*, vol. I, p. 252.

9   *Les mémoires de messire Olivier de la Marche*, p. 85, particularly in his introduction to Philip the Fair, whom La Marche always directly addresses. In this passage he is talking about 'the great reversal at the end of the reign of your grandfather'. With regard to this introduction, see part 5 of this book.

10 Jean Molinet, *Chroniques*, vol. I, p. 191.

11 *Dépêches des ambassadeurs milanais sur les campagnes de Charles-le-Hardi*, vol. I, p. 318 (similar statement on p. 214).

12 Niccolo Machiavelli, *The Art of War*, book II, trans. Henry Neville, https://oll.libertyfund.org/titles/machiavelli-the-art-of-war-neville-trans

13 'Ma per la fede mia el e matto', letter from Franceso Petrasanta to the Duke of Milan dated 2 September 1476. *Archiv für Kunde österreichischer Geschichtsquellen*, vol. 6, Vienna, 1856, p. 197.

14 *Dépêches des ambassadeurs milanais sur les campagnes de Charles-le-Hardi*, vol. II, p. 340.

15 Jean Molinet, 'La journée de Nancy', in *Splendeurs de la Cour de Bourgogne*, p. 964.

16 Van Belle, op. cit. book II, p. 250.

PART IV. A DECISIVE YEAR

1 Ibid. book III, p. 223.

2 Anonymous, 'Chronique de Lorraine' in *Splendeurs de la Cour de Bourgogne*, p. 1015.

3 Paul Morren, *Van Karel de Stoute tot Karel V*, p. 32.

4 Jaap ter Haar, *Geschiedenis van de Lage Landen*, p. 167.

5 Van Belle, op. cit. III, p. 247.

6 Blockmans, *De Bourgondiërs*, p. 231.

7 Eugenio Albèri (ed.), *Relazioni degli ambasciatori veneti al senato*, vol. I, p. 5.

8 'This book belongs to Philip, whom they call Lippeke.' Joseph Casier and Paul Berghmans, *L'art ancien dans les Flandres*, p. 56.

9 Victor von Kraus (ed.), *Maximilians I: Vertraulicher Briefwechsel*, p. 39.

10 G. Degroote, *Vier Vlaams-Bourgondische gedichten (1496–1497)*.

PART V. A MEMORABLE DAY

1 Blockmans, *Metropolen aan de Noordzee*, p. 547.

2 Maesschalk, op. cit. p. 208.

3 Monika Triest, *Macht, vrouwen en politiek (1477–1558)*, p. 97. Text by court poet Octavien de Saint-Gelais, set to music by Pierre de la Rue.

4 Erik Aerts, *Het bier van Lier: De economische ontwikkeling van de bierindustrie in een middelgrote Brabantse stad eind 14de-begin 19de eeuw*, p. 120.

5 Henri D'Hulst, *Het huwelijk van Filips de Schone met Johanna van Castilië*, p. 44.

6 Ibid. p. 17.

EPILOGUE

1 Hermann Wiesflecker, *Kaiser Maximilian I: Das Reich, Österreich und Europa an der Wende zur Neuzeit*, vol. V, p. 425.

2 Luc de Grauwe, 'Welke taal sprak keizer Karel' in *Handelingen der maatschappij voor geschiedenis en oudheidkunde*, p. 17. Also see Blockmans, *Karel V*, p. 245.

3 Wim Blockmans, 'Rijke steden, steile dijken: Bourgondisch en Calvinistisch' in *Het geheugen van de Lage Landen*, p. 358.

4 Hugo de Schepper, *Belgium dat is Nederlandt*, p. 17. Also see Blockmans, *Metropolen aan de Noordzee*, pp. 17–18.

5 Ibid. p. 22.

6 Ibid. pp. 22 and 38. Actually, Kiliaen's translation had to do with an analysis written in Italian that had already appeared in Spanish. In a seventeenth-century reissue, the text was given a title that seems surreal to modern eyes but was quite logical at the time: 'Belgium: that is to say, the Netherlands'.

7 Huizinga, op. cit., p. 3. Art experts today have a preference for Ars Nova, but the use of the term 'Flemish Primitives' seems ineradicable, at least for the time being.

8 Johan Frieswijk (ed.), 'Fryslân: Staat en macht 1450–1650', contributions to the Leeuwarden Historical Congress of 3–5 June 1998, p. 12.

9 From 'Cheminement de l'idée bourguignonne', text by Degrelle written during his exile in Spain. To be found in the chapter 'Le mythe bourguignon, Bourgogne fondatrice, "Grande Bourgogne" dévoyée' in *La Belgique et ses démons* by Luc Beyer de Ryke.

10 *Erasmus, The Education of a Christian Prince*, translated by Neil M. Cheshire and Michael J. Heath, Cambridge, UK: Cambridge University Press, 1997, p. 103.

11 Charles de Coster, *La Légende et les aventures héroïques, joyeuses et glorieuses d'Ulenspiegel et de Lamme Goedzak au pays de Flandres et ailleurs*, p. 379.

12 Jacques Brel, 'La Bière', 1968.

13 Letter to his sister Cécile (21 September 1848).

BIBLIOGRAPHY

THE BIBLIOGRAPHY I am presenting here is a typical alphabetical listing of the sources, articles, books and literary works that were of help to me in the writing of *The Burgundians*. It is useful to know that most of the titles dating from before 1900 can be found online.

Perhaps you'd like to read more about the era of the dukes? Since it's easy to get lost in an enumerative catalogue like this one, I have drawn up a brief vade mecum with a few concrete reading tips. This is followed by the more exhaustive bibliography as well as a list of historical novels, for gluttons with more insatiable appetites.

*

Let's begin with two books for those who'd really like to lose themselves in the Middle Ages in general. In the highly acclaimed *La civilisation de l'occident médieval* (1964, translated as *Medieval Civilisation*), the well-known French medievalist Jacques Le Goff provides both a synthesis and an analysis of the millennium that unfolded between roughly 476 and 1453. In the Dutch language there is the excellent *Eeuwen des onderscheids: Een geschiedenis van middeleeuws Europa* (2002) by Wim Blockmans and Peter Hoppenbrouwers.

Zeroing in on the later Middle Ages (starting in about the year 1000), two books by Georges Duby are definitely worth looking into. In *Le temps des cathédrales* (1976, translated as *The Age of the Cathedral Builders*), the author conjures up an entire worldview based on medieval architecture (monastery, cathedral, palace). In *Art et Société au Moyen Âge* (1995, translated as *Art and Society in the Middle Ages*, 2000), which has a narrower focus, he interweaves the evolution of medieval thought with that of the fine arts. Although he does not write about the Burgundians specifically, his book has helped me to better understand the significance of the ducal patronage system.

Less academic but all the more fascinating, and no less informative, is *Middeleeuwers tussen hoop en vrees* (2015) by Cas van Houtert, highly recommended for those who'd like to be introduced to the Middle Ages by a good storyteller. The author does this by exploring big themes such as the Vikings, the Crusades and the cathedrals. In one of his chapters he treats the problem of the year 1000, a complex subject that Tom Holland deals with extensively in his book *Millennium: The End of the World and the Forging of Christendom* (2008).

Finally, in her engaging little book *Pour en finir avec le Moyen Âge* (1979, translated as *Those Terrible Middle Ages!*, 2000), Régine Pernoud makes short shrift of a number of negative clichés about the Middle Ages.

When it comes to the early history of the Burgundians, and by that I mean the Germanic tribe that made a long trek across Europe and founded a kingdom east of what later became France, the chapter 'Burgundy' in Norman Davies's *Vanished Kingdoms* (2011) is a good place to start. Davies deals with Burgundy in all its guises throughout the course of history, and he also spends a bit of time on the ancient kingdom. More details can be found in the academic studies by the two most important specialists in the field: *Un royaume oublié au coeur de l'Europe* (2002) by Justin Favrod and *Les Burgondes* (2006) by Katalin Escher. Favrod's work contains fewer details and is consequently more accessible, which probably makes it an ideal place to start.

For insight into the chaos of the Hundred Years War, *The Hundred Years War* (1988) by Christopher Allmand and *La Guerre de Cent Ans* by Michel Mollat du Jourdin (1992) are both recommended. The difference between the two is immediately evident in the subtitle of the latter work – *vue par ceux qui l'ont vécue*, seen by those who experienced it, from kings, knights and soldiers to peasants and townspeople. In short, the decision-makers, the warriors and those who endured it all. Indispensable to this discussion is *A Distant Mirror* (1978) by Barbara Tuchman, which masterfully chronicles the first half of the Hundred Years War as well as its entire context, marked by plague, schism and misrule. The first fifty pages of Joseph Calmette's *Les grands ducs de Bourgogne* (1949) is an illuminating study of the Burgundian Capetians and is also required reading for those interested in delving deeper into the history of the famous Valois dukes. And that brings me to the heart of the matter.

I am fully aware that I never could have written this book without the work of several generations of medievalists who sank their teeth into the Burgundian period. From Henri Pirenne (especially the sections 'L'unification des Pays-Bas' and 'L'État Bourguignon' in his multi-volume *Histoire de Belgique*, 1948) through Johan Huizinga (*Autumntide of the Middle Ages*, 1919/2020) to Walter Prevenier and Wim Blockmans, who together wrote *In de ban van Bourgondië* (1988), later thoroughly revised, as well as the illustrated tome *De Bourgondische Nederlanden*, published by Mercatorfonds in 1983. Prevenier and Blockmans have given a new impetus to Burgundian studies in recent decades and inspired a whole string of disciples to engage in a deeper exploration of their beloved subject. Anyone interested in reading more on the early history of the Low Countries in general should turn to Wim Blockmans' masterwork *Metropolen aan de Noordzee (1100–1560)*, 750 pages of facts and insight in one massive volume. The fact that his name is most frequently listed in this bibliography is not surprising. Finally, it would be showing a serious lack of respect if I failed to include the Briton Richard Vaughan and the Frenchman Bertrand Schnerb in the row of important Burgundian specialists.

It is remarkable that for a long time Bertrand Schnerb's *L'État bourguignon* (1999), along with Calmette's work cited above, were the only real surveys of French origin. All that changed in 2016 with *Le royaume inachevé des ducs de Bourgogne* by Élodie Lecuppre-Desjardin, although her book is not a chronological overview but a thematic reflection on propaganda, chivalric loyalty (and disloyalty) and military organization. Because of that approach, and the fact that she openly enters into discussions with the greatest specialists in the field, the readers she addresses will mostly be people familiar with the material. Unlike Schnerb, who actually speaks of a 'Burgundian state', Lecuppre-Desjardins doubts whether you can ascribe any political ambitions to the dukes, let alone political accomplishments. What her fine work neither denies nor demonstrates is one of the central theses of my book: that thanks to the Burgundian displays of power in the northern regions, a new entity emerged between France and the Holy Roman Empire – the Low Countries, the cradle of what later became Belgium and the Netherlands.

For anyone in search of biographical facts and anecdotal details, *Quand flamboyait la Toison d'or* (1982) by Jean-Philippe Lecat is a good choice. Richard Vaughan's *Philip the Bold* (1962) is a dry, more academic work, but it's an especially accurate biography that zooms in on Philip's political dimension. He does the same with the following three dukes: *John the Fearless* (1966), *Philip the Good* (1970) and *Charles the Bold* (1972). Other than Vaughan's book, which is more than fifty years old, there is no recent publication on Philip the Bold, who usually – and very undeservedly – comes off badly in historical works. The same holds true for John the Fearless. But Bertrand Schnerb redresses the situation with his *Jean sans Peur* from 2005, which is as excellent as it is academically sound. For Philip the Good (in addition to Vaughan's work), there is the highly readable but not definitive biography by Emmanuel Bourassin from 1983, the ever informative *Philippe-le-Bon* by Paul Bonenfant from 1943, and the first volume of Juliaan van Belle's *Les pays de par deçà: De Bourgondische Nederlanden* (1984). As the publication years suggest, it's time for a new, in-depth biography of the founding father of the Low Countries. In 1985 and 1986, Van Belle added two more volumes on Charles the Bold and Mary of Burgundy. The beautifully illustrated book by Edward de Maesschalk on *De Bourgondische vorsten* (2008) also makes for fascinating reading. Interestingly, Charles the Bold can rejoice in having received the most attention. In past years, biographies have been published by Jean-Pierre Soisson (1997), Henri Dubois (2004) and Georges Minois (2015). I suggest you start with the last, which is lively and very comprehensive. Is it possible that the French have allowed themselves to revel in the final collapse of the once so threatening Burgundy? That tragic figure has also appealed to the German imagination (*Karl der Kühne* by Werner Paravicini from 1976, among others, followed a year later by K. Schelle's work from 1977) as well as the Belgian and the Dutch. Not only was Schelle's book translated into Dutch in the late seventies, but in 2016 Uitgeverij Aspect actually reissued the biography by Jan Walch from 1940, and with the pre-war spelling intact. For those who can't get enough of biographies, there are also books about other important protagonists mentioned in *The Burgundians*. One such work, and quite an extraordinary one, is *Nobel streven* (2017), in which Frits van Oostrom describes the adventurous life of Jan van Brederode (*c*.1372–1415) in a splendid portrait of an era. Brederode was a contemporary of Philip the Bold and John the Fearless.

Finally, the indispensable classic from 175 years ago that is still worth the effort for anyone interested in this era, if only on account of its writing style: the *Histoire de France* by Jules Michelet, especially volumes IV (published in 1840), V (1841) and VI (1844), which cover the periods of Charles VI, Charles VII and Louis XI. The anti-Burgundian tone of this passionate champion of the French *roman national* should be accepted for what it is. The insanity of Charles VI takes fascinating shape in the fourth volume of Michelet's monumental history of France. Readers who want to delve more deeply into the madness of the king will find *La folie de Charles VI* (2004) much to their liking, a rather dry but accurate work by Bernard Guenée.

In *Een pion voor een dame: Jacoba van Beieren* (2009), Antheun Janse untangles all the novelistic lines that have often reduced the life of Jacqueline of Bavaria to a courtly romance, and he's quite strict in specifying what we can know with certainty about her life. In doing so he correctly notes the importance of her mother, Margaret of Burgundy, the clever and aggressive sister of John the Fearless. For more information on Jacqueline's contemporary, Joan of Arc, it might be useful to start with the general work by Georges Bordonove – her story embedded in that of the Hundred Years War – and go on to the classic nineteenth-century perspective by Michelet (volume V of his *Histoire de France*), and then to finish on YouTube by watching the six-and-a-half-hour masterclass by the controversial but riveting historian Henri Guillemin from 1970, who also published his book *Jeanne, dite Joan of Arc* that same year.

As for the Burgundification of the Low Countries, Blockmans and Prevenier remain the essential guides, but my view of the unification of the Burgundian Netherlands was also shaped by Robert Stein's clear and detailed analysis in *De Hertog en zijn Staten* (2014). For those with the necessary background knowledge, this work has much to recommend it. The source of names such as the Netherlands, Belgium, the Low Countries, Flanders and Holland is explored in *Belgium dat is Nederlandt* (2014) by Hugo de Schepper.

Artists are mentioned in both the classical and the academic works on the Burgundian period, of course, but their role is never really fully developed. That is remarkable. Huizinga has been put on a pedestal, but the main idea behind his *Autumntide of the Middle Ages* has been largely overlooked, as interesting as it was: to try to understand the Late Middle Ages by focusing your attention on art and culture. In this book I have attempted to connect Huizinga's inspiring line of thought with the current state of historical research, and to give artists the place that is rightfully theirs. And although little is known about the lives of Sluter, Van Eyck, Van der Weyden or Van der Goes, I have studied them with the same attention that I paid to the dukes themselves. Indeed, the work of sculptors and painters gave me immediate access to the past. The work of art as time machine.

L'art à la cour de Bourgogne: Le mécénat de Philippe le Hardi et de Jean sans Peur (1363–1419) is a collective work from 2004 in which more than fifty specialists shed light on the role of patron in the Burgundian court. We have little specific information on the life of Sluter, and *Claus Sluter* by Henri David from 1951 remains an indispensable publication, although the substantial English-language work by Kathleen Morand, published in 1991, has made an interesting contribution with regard to Sluter's younger years. As for the early painting at the Burgundian court, the catalogue for the Maelwael exhibition at the Rijksmuseum (2017) in Amsterdam is well worth perusing. A great deal has been written about Van Eyck, but if you have to pick one book out of the whole stack, go for the hefty reference work *Hubert and Jan van Eyck* by Elisabeth Dhanens from 1980, and of course the magnificent catalogue from the Ghent exhibition (2020), which unfortunately was cut short due to the Covid crisis. Amusing, erudite and surprising is the recent *L'affaire Arnolfini* (2016) in which Jean-Philippe Postel attempts to solve the mystery of one of Van Eyck's most famous works. I also took great pleasure in reading Dhanens's *Hugo van der Goes* (1998) and her illustrated *Rogier van der Weyden: Revisie van de documenten* (1995), in which she takes a critical look at the known facts about the artist. And of course the monograph on Van der Weyden by Dirk de Vos from 1999 is also required reading.

While statues and paintings guided me on my journey to the past, so did Late Medieval texts: the works of Burgundian and Middle Dutch chroniclers, one more florid and poetic, the other more journalistic in style. Without Jean Froissart, Enguerrand de Monstrelet, Georges Chastellain, Jacques du Clercq, Olivier de la Marche, Michel Pintoin, Jan and Olivier van Dixmude, Jan van Boendale, Eustache Deschamps, Jean Molinet, Philippe de Commynes and less illustrious chroniclers, every story about the Middle Ages would be drained of its colour and anecdotes. A number of them have the honour of appearing in French pocket editions, others are available as e-books, and several chroniclers are anthologized in the voluminous *Splendeurs de la Cour de Bourgogne: Récits et chroniques* (edited by Régnier-Bohler, 1995). Almost all their works can be found online. Reading a few pages by these chroniclers is highly recommended as a way of gaining a sense of the era's atmosphere. One surprising discovery was *Heel dit valse land* (1984) by Frans Hugaerts, in which the French-Burgundian-Flemish crisis of the 1380s is shown through the eyes of the forgotten poet-chronicler Eustache Deschamps. I eagerly drew on Hugaerts's anthology, and my Dutch translations of Deschamps's late medieval French are based on his inspiration.

For those with a greater interest in literature, there are the two reference works by Frits van Oostrom (*Stemmen op schrift*, to 1300) and Herman Pleij (*Het gevleugelde woord*, 1400–1560) that are monumental in scope and well worth reading, and that cast a light on the Dutch literature of the Middle Ages. In Paul Verhuyck's beautiful *Minuten middeleeuwen* (2018), the author recalls his career as a teacher of medieval French literature, sharing his broad erudition in a way that is both elegant and personal.

Finally, if a historical novel is what you're after, you can't do better than Hella S. Haasse's *In a Dark Wood Wandering: A Novel of the Middle Ages* (1989; *Het woud der verwachting*, 1949). In it she tells the story of the duke and poet Charles of Orléans as if she herself had been there. A number of the historical figures from *The Burgundians* play prominent roles in her majestic novel, which takes place between 1395 and 1465. Reading it is like bumping into old friends.

For those who took pleasure in reading this book but found themselves mixing up the names: I have made a podcast with Rolly Smeets and Annick Lesage van Klara in which I tell the core story of the book in a way that is both exciting and instructive. The narrative is told against a splendid soundtrack that includes the clatter of hoofs and the clashing of swords and is interspersed with lovely examples of polyphonic music. It's a way of experiencing the story anew and familiarizing yourself with its protagonists.

*

Aerts, Erik, *Het bier van Lier: De economische ontwikkeling van de bierindustrie in een middelgrote Brabantse stad einde 14de–begin 19de eeuw* (Brussels: KAWLSK, 1988).

Aerts, Erik and Herman Van der Wee, *Geschiedenis van Lier: Welvaart en samenleving van het ontstaan van de stad tot de Eerste Wereldoorlog* (Lier: Gilde Heren van Lier VZW, 2016).

Albèri, Eugenio, *Relazioni degli ambasciatori veneti al senato* (Florence, 1839).

Allmand, Christopher, *The Hundred Years War* (Cambridge, UK: Cambridge University Press, 1988).

Anagnostopoulos, Pierre and Jean Houssiau, *Het voormalige Coudenbergpaleis* (Brussels: Monumenten en Landschappen, 2010).

Bange, Petty, *De wereld van de Bourgondiërs (1363–1477)* (Amersfoort/Bruges: Bekking & Blitz, 2011).

Barante, Prospère, *Histoire des ducs de Bourgogne de la Maison de Valois (1364–1477)* (Paris: Laffont, 1969; revised edition of the original work from 1826).

Barrett, W.P. (trans.), *The Trial of Joan of Arc* (Gotham House, Inc., 1932). https://sourcebooks.fordham.edu/basis/joanofarc-trial.asp

Bauer, Raoul, *De Lage Landen: Een geschiedenis in de spiegel van Europa* (Tielt: Lannoo, 1994).

— *Tussen rampspoed en vernieuwing: Een Europese cultuurgeschiedenis van de veertiende en de vijftiende eeuw* (Kapellen: Pelckmans, 2004).

Bazin, Jean-François, *Histoire du Vin de Bourgogne* (Paris: Éditions Jean-Paul Gisserot, 2002).

Beck, Corinne, Patrice Beck and François Duceppe-Lamarre, 'Les parcs et jardins des ducs de Bourgogne au XIVe siècle: Réalités et représentations', *Actes des Congrès de la Société d'Archéologie Médiévale*, 7 (2001), pp. 97–111.

Becker, Uwe, *Maatschappij, macht, Nederlandse politiek: Een inleiding in de politieke wetenschap* (Amsterdam: Het Spinhuis, 1996).

Bernard of Clairvaux, 'Apologia' (*c*.1125), in G. G. Coulton (ed. and trans.), *Life in the Middle Ages*, vol. 4, Cambridge, UK: Cambridge University Press, 1929–30, pp. 169–74.

— 'In Praise of the New Knighthood', in Daniel O' Donovan (trans.), *The Works of Bernard of Clairvaux*, vol. 7, Kalamazoo, MI: Cistercian Publications, 1977, pp. 125–68.

Berthier, Marie-Thérèse and John-Thomas Sweeney, *Le chancelier Rolin (1376–1462)* (Précy-sous-Thil: Éditions de l'Armançon, 1998).

Besson, F. *et al.*, *Actuel Moyen Âge: Et si la modernité était ailleurs?* (Paris: Arkhé, 2017).

Beyaert, Marc, *De Dulle Griet of het Groot Kanon te Gent: Casus van de vijftiende-eeuwse krijgskunst en technologie* (Ghent: Skribis, 2020).

Beyer De Ryke, Luc, *La Belgique et ses démons: Mythes fondateurs et destructeurs* (Wavre: Éditions Mols, 2011).

Blockmans, Wim, 'La répression de révoltes urbaines comme méthode de centralisation dans les Pays-Bas bourguignons', *Publications du Centre Européen d'Études Bourguignonnes*, 28.

— 'The Devotion of a Lonely Duchess', in *Margaret of York, Simon Marmion and* The *Visions of Tondal: Papers Delivered at a Symposium Organized by the Department of Manuscripts of the J. Paul Getty Museum in collaboration with the Huntington Library and Art Collections*, Malibu, CA: J. Paul Getty Museum, 1992, pp. 29–64.

— 'Rijke steden, steile dijken: Bourgondisch en Calvinistisch', in *Het geheugen van de Lage Landen*, Rekkem: Ons Erfdeel, 2009.

— *Metropolen aan de Noordzee: De geschiedenis van Nederland (1100–1560)* (Amsterdam: Bert Bakker, 2010).

— Karel V. *Keizer van een wereldrijk (1500–1558)* (Utrecht: Uitgeverij Omniboek, 2012).

— 'The Medieval Roots of the Constitution of the United Provinces', *The Medieval Low Countries*, vol. 4 (2017), pp. 215–28.

— 'Jacques de Lalaing: The Vitality of the Chivalric Ideal in the Burgundian Netherlands', in *A Knight for Ages: Jacques de Lalaing and the Art of Chivalry*, Los Angeles: J. Paul Getty Museum, 2018, pp. 53–64.

Blockmans, Wim and Peter Hoppenbrouwers, *Eeuwen des onderscheids: Een geschiedenis van middeleeuws Europa* (Amsterdam: Bert Bakker, 2002).

Blockmans, Wim and Walter Prevenier, *De Bourgondische Nederlanden* (Antwerp: Mercatorfonds, 1983).

— *In de ban van Bourgondië* (Houten: Fibula, 1988) (revised and expanded as *De Bourgondiërs: De Nederlanden op weg naar eenheid* [Amsterdam: Meulenhoff/Kritak, 1997]).

Blockmans, Wim *et al.*, *Studiën betreffende de sociale structuren te Brugge, en Gent in de 14e en 15e eeuw* (Heule: UGA, 1971).

Blockmans, Wim *et al.*, *Staging the Court of Burgundy, Proceedings of the Conference 'The Splendour of Burgundy'* (Bruges: Groeningemuseum, 2009).

Blockmans, Wim and Herman Pleij (eds.), *Plaatsen van herinnering: Nederland van prehistorie tot Beeldenstorm* (Amsterdam: Bert Bakker, 2007).

Blok, Dirk Peter (ed.), *Algemene geschiedenis der Nederlanden: Middeleeuwen* (vols. 1–4) (Haarlem: Fibula-Van Dishoeck, 1977–83).

Blokker, Jan, Jan Blokker Jr and Bas Blokker (with classroom illustrations by Johan Herman Isings), *Het vooroudergevoel: De vaderlandse geschiedenis* (Amsterdam/Antwerp: Contact, 2005).

Boehme, Olivier, *Europa: Een geschiedenis van grensnaties* (Antwerp: Polis, 2016).

Bonenfant, Paul, *Philippe-le-Bon* (Brussels: La Renaissance du Livre, 1943).

Boone, Marc, *Gent en de Bourgondische hertogen c.1384 – c.1453: Een sociaal-politieke studie van een staatsvormingsproces* (Brussels: Paleis der Academieën, 1990).

— *De Bourgondische Nederlanden: Een hoorcollege over de cultuurgeschiedenis van de Lage Landen (1384–1482)* (The Hague: Home Academy, 2020).

Borchert, Till-Holger, *Van Eyck* (Cologne: Taschen, 2008).

Borchert, Till-Holger *et al.* (eds.), *De weg naar Van Eyck* (Rotterdam: Museum Boijmans Van Beuningen, 2012–13).

Bordonove, Georges, *Louis XI: Le diplomate* (Paris: Pygmalion, 1986).

— *Jeanne d'Arc et la Guerre de Cent ans* (Paris: Pygmalion, 1994).

Bourassin, Emmanuel, *Philippe le Bon: Le Grand Lion des Flandres* (Paris: Tallandier, 1983).

Bouzy, Olivier, *Jeanne d'Arc: Mythes et réalités* (Paris: Atelier de l'Archer, 1999).

Bradbury, Jim, *The Medieval Siege* (Woodbridge, UK: Boydell & Brewer, 1992).

Brel, Jacques, *L'oeuvre intégrale* (Paris: Robert Laffont, 1982).

Brocvielle, Vincent and François Reynaert, *L'art et l'histoire du Nord-Pas-de-Calais* (Paris: Flammarion, 2014).

Brouwer, J., *Johanna de Waanzinnige* (Amsterdam: Meulenhoff, 1940).

Brown, Andrew and Jan Dumolyn, *Medieval Bruges (c.850–1550)* (Palmerston North, New Zealand and Ghent: Massey University and Ghent University, 2018).

Buylaert, F. and E. Verroken, 'Een adellijk altaarstuk: de sociaal-historische studie van de ontstaanscontext van het Lam Godsretabel', in *Het Lam Gods: Kunst, Geschiedenis, Wetenschap en Religie*, Brussels: Hannibal, 2018.

Calmette, Joseph, *Les grands ducs de Bourgogne* (Paris: Albin Michel, 1949).

Caron, Marie-Thérèse, '17 février 1454: le Banquet du Faisan, fête de cour et stratégies du pouvoir', *Revue du Nord*, 315 (1996), pp. 269–88.

Carson, Patricia, *The Fair Face of Flanders* (Tielt: Lannoo, 2001).

Casier, Joseph and Paul Berghmans, *L'art ancien dans les Flandres (région de l'Escaut)* (Brussels: G. Van Oest & Cie, 1921).

Cauchies, Jean-Marie, *Louis XI et Charles le Hardi: De Péronne à Nancy (1468–1477)* (Brussels: De Boeck-Université, 1996).

— *Philippe le Beau: le dernier duc de Bourgogne* (Turnhout: Brepols, 2003).

Cazaux, Yves, *Marie de Bourgogne* (Paris: Albin Michel, 1967).

Chastellain, Georges, *Pages Choisies* (Paris: Éditions Universitaires, 1949).

— *Chroniques* (Brussels: Académie Royale des Sciences, des Letters et des Beaux-Arts de Belgique, 1863–66).

Chaucer, Geoffrey, *The Canterbury Tales*. Translated into Modern English by Nevill Coghill (London: Penguin Classics, 2003).

Claes, Paul (trans.), *De tuin van de Franse poëzie: Een canon in 100 gedichten* (Amsterdam: Athenaeum-Polak & Van Gennep, 2011).

Claus, Hugo, *Gedichten (1948–1993)* (Amsterdam: De Bezige Bij, 1965).

Clairvaux, Bernardus van, *Verweerschrift: Brief in den regen* (translated and with an introduction by Anton van Duinkerken) (Amsterdam: De Spiegel, 1938).

Clément-Janin, Michel-Hilaire, *Les pestes en Bourgogne 1349–1636* (Dijon: Imprimerie et Litographie Carré, 1879).

Cochon, Pierre, 'Chronique normande', in A. Vallet de Viriville (ed.): *Chronique de la Pucelle ou Chronique de Cousinot, suivie de la Chronique normande de P. Cochon relatives aux règnes de Charles VI et Charles VII*, Paris: Adolphe Delahays, 1859, pp. 343–6.

Commeaux, Charles, *La vie quotidienne en Bourgogne au temps des ducs de Valois (1364–1477)* (Paris: Hachette, 1979).

Commynes, Philippe de, *Mémoires de Commynes* (Paris: Belin-Leprieur, 1843).

Comtois, Marc A., *Burgundians in the Mist* (Los Gatos, CA: Smashwords Editions, 2011).

Conscience, Hendrik, *De Leeuw van Vlaanderen* (Leiden: A.W. Sijthoff, 1879).

Damen, Mario, 'Ridders en toernooien (1000–1300)', in *Cultuurgeschiedenis van de middeleeuwen*, pp. 171–88. Zwolle: W Books, 2015.

Damen, Mario and Louis Sicking (eds.), *Bourgondië voorbij: De Nederlanden 1250–1650* (Hilversum: Verloren, 2010).

Dante, *The Divine Comedy*, translated by Mark Musa (New York: Penguin Books, 2003).

D'Arbois De Jubainville, Henri, 'De la nourriture des Cisterciens, principalement à Clairvaux, aux XII et au XIII siècle', *Bibliothèque des Chartes*, 19 (1858).

David, Henri, *Claus Sluter* (Paris: Éditions Pierre Tisné, 1951).

Davies, Norman, *Vanished Kingdoms: The History of Half-Forgotten Europe* (London: Allen Lane, 2011).

De Bruyn, Anna and Hanna De Vos, *Haute lecture by Colard Mansion: Vernieuwing van tekst en beeld in middeleeuws Brugge* (Ghent: Openbaar Kunstbezit Vlaanderen [56], 2018).

De Coster, Charles, *La Légende et les aventures héroïques, joyeuses et glorieuses d'Ulenspiegel et de Lamme Goedzak au pays de Flandres et ailleurs* (Brussels: Editions de la Toison d'Or, 1942).

De Donder, Vic, *In de naam van Vlaanderen: Een historie (8ste–21ste eeuw)* (Leuven: Davidsfonds, 2007).

Degroote, G., *Vier Vlaams-Bourgondische gedichten (1496–1497)* (Antwerp: Nederlandse Boekhandel, 1950).

De La Marche, Olivier, *Les mémoires de messire Olivier de la Marche* (Ghent: Chez Gerard De Salenson, 1567).

De Gingins de la Sarra, Frédéric, *Dépêches des ambassadeurs milanais sur les campagnes de Charles-le-Hardi*, vol. I (Paris-Geneva: Cherbuliez, 1858).

De Grauwe, Luc, 'Welke taal sprak keizer Karel?', *Handelingen der maatschappij voor geschiedenis en oudheidkunde*, 2000, pp. 17–29.

De Gruben, Françoise, *Les chapitres de la Toison d'or à l'époque bourguignonne (1430–1477)* (Leuven: Leuven University Press, Mediaevalia Lovaniensia, 1997).

De Laborde, Léon, *Les ducs de Bourgogne: Études sur les lettres, les arts et l'industrie pendant le XVe siècle*, vol. I (Preuves) (Paris: Plon, 1849).

De Maesschalk, Edward, *De Bourgondische vorsten (1315–1530)* (Leuven: Davidsfonds, 2008).

— *De graven van Vlaanderen (861–1384)* (Leuven: Davidsfonds, 2012).

De Meung, Jean, *The Romance of the Rose (Le Roman de la Rose), The Continuation* (1275), translated by A.S. Kline. *Poetry In Translation* (www.poetryintranslation.com), 2019.

De Pizan, Christine, *La Cité des dames* (1404). Translated as *The Book of the City of Ladies* by Earl Jeffrey Richards (New York: Persea Books, 1982).

De Reiffenberg, Frédéric-Auguste, *Histoire de l'Ordre de la Toison d'Or depuis sa fondation jusqu'à la cessation des chapitres généraux* (Vienna/Brussels, 1831).

Deschamps, Eustache, *Poésies morales et historiques* (Paris: Crapelet, 1833).

De Schepper, Hugo, *Belgium dat is Nederlandt: Identiteiten en identiteitenbesef in de Lage Landen* (Breda: Papieren Tijger, 2014).

Devillers, Léopold, *Cartulaire des comtes de Hainaut, de l'avènement de Guillaume II à la mort de Jacqueline de Bavière*, vol. IV (Brussels: Hayez, 1889).

De Voldere, Luc, *Tegen de kruideniers: Over talen, Europa en geheugen* (Antwerp/Amsterdam: De Bezige Bij, 2014).

De Vos, Dirk, *Rogier van der Weyden: Het volledige oeuvre* (Antwerp: Mercatorfonds, 1999).

— *De Vlaamse primitieven: De meesterwerken* (Antwerp: Mercatorfonds, 2002).

De Vos, Dirk, Willy Le Loup and Dominique Marechal, *Hans Memling*, catalogue (Brussels: Ludion, 1994).

DeVun, Leah, *Prophecy, Alchemy and the End of Time: John of Rupescissa in the Late Middle Ages* (New York: Columbia University Press, 2014).

Dhanens, Elisabeth, *Hubert and Jan van Eyck* (New York: Tabard Press, 1980).

— *Rogier van der Weyden: Revisie van de documenten* (Brussels: AWLSK, 1995).

— *Hugo van der Goes* (Antwerp: Mercatorfonds, 1998).

D'Hulst, Henri, *Het huwelijk van Filips de Schone met Johanna van Castilië te Lier op 20 oktober 1496* (Antwerp/Amsterdam: Standaard Boekhandel, 1956).

D'Orville, Jean-Cabaret, *La Chronique du bon duc Loys de Bourbon*, published by Alphonse-Martial Chazaud (Paris: Renouard, 1876).

Drouot, H., 'L'atelier de Dijon et l'exécution du tombeau de Philippe le Hardi', *Revue belge d'archéologie de l'art*, 9 (1932), pp. 11–39.

Dubois, Henri, *Charles le Téméraire* (Paris: Fayard, 2004).

Duby, Georges, *Le temps des cathédrales: L'art et la société (980–1420)* (Paris: Gallimard, 1976). Translated as *The Age of the Cathedrals: Art and Society, 980–1420* (Chicago: University of Chicago Press, 1981).

— *Art et société au Moyen Âge* (Paris: Seuil, 1995). Translated as *Art and Society in the Middle Ages* (Cambridge, UK: Polity Press, 2000).

Du Clercq, Jacques, *Mémoires de J. Du Clercq, sur le règne de Philippe le Bon, Duc de Bourgogne*, first published by Baron de Reiffenberg, second edition (Brussels: J.M. Lacrosse Libraire-Éditeur, 1836).

Dumolyn, Jan, *De Brugse opstand van 1436–1438* (Heule: UGA, 1997).

— 'Adel en nobiliteringsprocessen in het laatmiddeleeuwse Vlaanderen: Een status quaestionis' (with F. van Tricht), *Bijdragen en Mededelingen voor de Geschiedenis van de Nederlanden*, 115 (2000), pp. 197–222.

Érasme (Erasmus), Didier (Desiderius), *Eloge de la Folie, Adages, Colloques, Réflexions sur l'art, l'éducation, la religion, la guerre, la philosophie, Correspondance* (Claude Blum, André Godin, Jean-Claude Margolin and Daniel Ménager, eds.) (Paris: Robert Laffont, 1992).

Erasmus, *The Education of a Christian Prince*, translated by Neil M. Cheshire and Michael J. Heath (Cambridge, UK: Cambridge University Press, 1997).

Escher, Katalin, *Les Burgondes, Ier-VIe siècles apr. J.-C.* (Paris: Errance, 2006).

Escher, Katalin and Iaroslav Lebedynsky, *Le dossier Attila* (Arles: Actes Sud, 2007).

Falter, Rolf, *België: Een geschiedenis zonder land* (Antwerp/Amsterdam: De Bezige Bij, 2012).

Favrod, Justin, *Les Burgondes: Un royaume oublié au coeur de l'Europe* (Lausanne: Presses polytechniques et universitaires romandes, 2002).

Frédéric, Pierre, *5 janvier 1477: La Mort de Charles le Téméraire* (Paris: Gallimard, 1966).

Frieswijk, Johan (ed.), *Fryslân: Staat en macht 1450–1650, bijdragen aan het historisch congres te Leeuwarden van 3 tot 5 juni 1998* (Leeuwarden: Fryske Akademy, 1999).

Froissart, Jean, *Chroniques*, books I, II, III and IV (Paris: Livre de Poche, 2004).

Gachard, Louis Prosper, *Collection de documents inédits concernant l'histoire de la Belgique*, vol. 1 (Brussels: Louis Hauman, 1833).

Garnot, Benoît and Alain Rauwel, *Histoire de la Bourgogne* (Paris: Éditions Jean-Paul Gisserot, 2011).

Genet, Jean-Philippe, *Le monde au Moyen Âge: Espaces, pouvoirs, civilisations* (Paris: Hachette, 1991).

Gibbon, Edward, *The History of the Decline and Fall of the Roman Empire*, Project Gutenberg Edition, 1782/1845. www.gutenberg.org/files/25717/25717-h/25717-h.htm

Goetinck, Marc, 'De ontluikende boekdrukkunst in Brugge (*c.*1474–1484): William Caxton, Colard Mansion en Jan Brito', *Vlaanderen*, 43 (1994), pp. 25–132.

Gombrich, Ernst, *The Story of Art* (London: Phaidon, 1950).

Gouêt, Amédée, *Histoire des règnes de Charles VI et VII, 1380–1460, d'après les documents originaux* (Brussels: Lebègue et cie, 1870).

Gregory of Tours, *History of the Franks*, translated by Earnest Brehaut, 1916. A Fordham University Medieval Sourcebook: sourcebooks.fordham.edu/basis/gregory-hist.asp

Guemriche, Salah, *Abd er-Rahman contre Charles Martel: La véritable histoire de la bataille de Poitiers* (Paris: Perrin, 2010).

Guenée, Bernard, *La folie de Charles VI* (Paris: Perrin, 2004).

Guennifey, Patrice (ed.), *Les derniers jours des rois: De Charlemagne à Napoléon III* (Paris: Perrin, 2014).

Guillemin, Henri, *Jeanne dite Jeanne d'Arc* (Paris: Gallimard, 1970).

Guillot, Renée-Paul, *Les ducs de Bourgogne* (Paris: Fernand Lanore, 1998).

Guyotjeannin, Olivier, *Population et démographie au Moyen Âge* (Paris: Editions du CTHS, 1995).

Haemers, Jelle, *For the Common Good: State Power and Urban Revolts in the Reign of Mary of Burgundy (1477–1482)* (Turnhout: Brepols, 2009).

— *De strijd om het regentschap over Filips de Schone: Opstand, facties en geweld in Brugge, Gent en Ieper (1482–1488)* (Ghent: Academia Press, 2014).

Haemers, Jelle, Andrea Bardyn and Chanelle Delameillieure (eds.), *Wijvenwereld: Vrouwen in de middeleeuwse stad* (Antwerp: Vrijdag, 2019).

Hagopian van Buren, Anne, 'Reality and Literary Romance in the Park of Hesdin', in *Medieval Gardens: Colloquium on the History of Landscape Architecture*, Washington: Dumbarton Oaks Research Library and Collection, 1986, pp. 115–34.

Heers, Jacques, 'Les limites des méthodes statistiques pour les recherches de démographie médiévale', *Annales de Démographie Historique*, 1968, pp. 43–72.

Higounet-Naval, Arlette, 'La démographie des villes françaises au Moyen Âge', *Annales de Démographie Historique*, 1980, pp. 187–211.

Holland, Tom, *Millennium: The End of the World and the Forging of Christendom* (New York: Random House, 2008).

Huens, Jean-Léon and Jean Schoonjans, *'s Lands Glorie: Vulgarisatie van de geschiedenis van België door het beeld*. Artis Historia, 1949–61.

Hugaerts, Frans, *Heel dit valse land: Of hoe de Franse hofdichter Eustache Deschamps Vlaanderen zag in de laatste jaren van de veertiende eeuw* (Zele: Reinaert Uitgaven, 1984).

Hugo, Victor, *Notre-Dame de Paris, also known as The Hunchback of Notre Dame*, translated by Isabel F. Hapgood, The Gutenberg Project e-book, www.gutenberg.org/files/2610/2610–h/2610–h.htm

Huizinga, Johan. *Herfsttij der middeleeuwen: Studie over levensen gedichtenvormen der veertiende en vijftiende eeuw in Frankrijk en de Nederlanden* (Amsterdam: Wolders-Noordhoff, 1919/1984). Translated as *Autumntide of the Middle Ages: A Study of Forms of Life and Thought of the Fourteenth and Fifteenth Centuries in France and the Low Countries* by Diane Webb, edited by Graeme Small and Anton van der Lem (Leiden: Leiden University Press, 2020).

Ipes, Catharina, *Petrarca in de Nederlandse letterkunde* (Amsterdam: De Spiegel, 1934).

Israel, Jonathan, *The Dutch Republic: Its Rise, Greatness and Fall 1477–1806* (Oxford: Oxford University Press, 1995).

Janse, Antheun, *Een pion voor een dame: Jacoba van Beieren (1401–1436)* (Amsterdam: Balans, 2009).

Joubert, Fabienne, 'Le tombeau de Philippe le Hardi: Une méditation monumentale', *Dossier de l'Art* 203 (2001), pp. 48–63.

Jubault, Paul, *D'Azincourt à Jeanne d'Arc* (Paris: Moulet, 1968).

Kempis, Thomas à, *The Imitation of Christ*, translated by Anthony Hoskins (Oxford: Oxford University Press, 1613/1903). Revised edition published by The Folio Society, London, 2009.

— *Soliloqium animae, Opera Omnia*, edited by M.J. Pohl (Freiburg, 1902–10).

Kogen, Helena, 'De l'Imitatio Christi aux Opera Thomae de Jean de Roigny (1549): Lectures de Thomas a Kempis en France à l'époque prémoderne', in *Ouvrages phares de la Réforme et de la Contre-Réforme dans les collections montréalaises*, Québec: Presses Universitaires, pp. 229–46.

Koldeweij, Jos, Alexandra Hermesdorf and Paul Huvenne, *De Schilderkunst der Lage Landen*, vol. 1., *De Middeleeuwen en de zestiende eeuw* (Amsterdam: Amsterdam University Press, 2006).

Kuipers, Jan J.B. and Robbert Jan Swiers, *Het verhaal van Zeeland* (Hilversum: Verloren, 2005).

Lacerda, Daniel, *Isabelle de Portugal, duchesse de Bourgogne (1397–1471): Une femme de pouvoir au cour de l'Europe du Moyen Âge* (Paris: Éditions Lanore, 2008).

Lafortune-Martel, Agatha, *Fête noble en Bourgogne au XVe siècle: Le banquet du Faisan* (Montréal/Paris: Bellarmin-Vrin, 1984).

Laurioux, Bruno, *Le Moyen Âge à table* (Paris: Adam Biro, 1989).

Lecat, Jean-Philippe, *Quand flamboyait la Toison d'or* (Paris: Fayard, 1982).

Lecuppre-Desjardin, Élodie, *Le royaume inachevé des ducs de Bourgogne (XIVe et XVe siècle)* (Paris: Belin, 2017).

Le Goff, Jacques, *La Civilisation de l'Occident médiéval* (Paris: Arthaud, 1964). Translated as *Medieval Civilisation* (London: The Folio Society, 2011) by Julia Barrow.

— *Le Moyen Âge expliqué aux enfants* (Paris: Seuil, 2006).

Leguay, Jean-Pierre, *Vivre en ville au Moyen Âge* (Paris: Éditions Jean-Paul Gisserot, 2012).

Lemaire, L., 'La mort de Philippe le Bon, duc de bourgogne (15 juin 1467)', *Revue du Nord*, 1–4 (1910), pp. 321–6.

Lernout, Geert, *Een beknopte geschiedenis van het boek* (Antwerp/Amsterdam: De Bezige Bij, 2009).

Loeb Brice, Deborah and Susie Nash, 'Le puits de Moïse. Sluter à son apogée', *Dossier de l'Art*, 203 (2001), pp. 20–43.

Machiavelli, Niccolo, *The Art of War*, translated by Henry Neville, https://oll.libertyfund.org/titles/machiavelli-the-art-of-war-neville-trans

Maddens, Nicolaas (ed.), *De geschiedenis van Kortrijk* (Kortrijk: West-Vlaamse Gidsenkring, 1983).

Mak, Geert, *Een kleine geschiedenis van Amsterdam* (Amsterdam: Olympus, 1995).

Martenet, Marie-Gaëtane, 'Le récit de la bataille de Nicopolis (1396) dans les Chroniques de Jean Froissart: de l'échec à la gloire', *Questes*, 30 (2015).

Martens, Birgitte, *Digitaal of oud papier* (Antwerp/Amsterdam: De Bezige Bij/Manteau/Ludion, 2012).

Mesqui, Jean, *Les châteaux forts: De la guerre à la paix* (Paris: Gallimard, 1995).

Michelet, Jules, *Histoire de France IV: Charles VI* (Paris: Éditions des Équateurs, 2014).

— *Histoire de France V: Jeanne d'Arc, Charles VII* (Paris: Éditions des Équateurs, 2014).

— *Histoire de France VI: Louis XI* (Paris: Éditions des Équateurs, 2014).

Milis, Ludo, 'Vlaanderen in het jaar duizend', *De Franse Nederlanden / Les Pays-Bas Français*, annual published by the Ons Erfdeel Foundation, 2002, pp. 91–141.

Minois, Georges, *Charles le Téméraire* (Paris: Perrin, 2015).

Molinet, Jean, *Chroniques* (Paris: Verdière, 1827).

Mollat du Jourdin, Michel, *La guerre de Cent Ans vue par ceux qui l'ont vécue* (Paris: Seuil, 1992).

Monstrelet, Enguerrand de, *La Chronique d'Enguerrand de Monstrelet en deux livres avec pieces justificatives 1400–1444,* 6 vols (Paris: Société de l'Histoire de France, 1857–62).

Morand, Kathleen, *Claus Sluter: Artist at the Court of Burgundy* (Austin, TX: University of Texas Press, 1991).

Morren, Paul, *Van Karel de Stoute tot Karel V (1477–1519)* (Antwerp/Apeldoorn: Garant, 2004).

Mus, Octaaf, *De geschiedenis van de middeleeuwse grootstad Ieper: Van Karolingische villa tot de destructie in 1914* (Ypres: Stad Ieper, 2010).

Nadot, Sébastien, *Rompez les lances! Chevaliers et tournois au Moyen Âge* (Paris: Autrement, 2010).

Nash, Susie, 'Claus Sluter's "Well of Moses" for the Chartreuse de Champmol Reconsidered' (part I), *The Burlington Magazine,* 147 (2005), pp. 798–809.

— (part II), *The Burlington Magazine,* 148 (2006), pp. 456–69.

— (part III), *The Burlington Magazine,* 150 (2008), pp. 724–41.

Neefs, Hugo, *Lier 1496: Een huwelijk in Europees perspectief* (Lier: Comité Lier Kermis, 1981).

Nicholas, David, *Medieval Flanders* (London: Longman Group UK Limited, 1992).

The Nibelungenlied, Translated into Rhymed English Verse in the Metre of the Original, translated by George Henry Needler, Project Gutenberg e-book, first posted 2003. www.gutenberg.org/files/7321/7321-h/7321-h.htm

Offenstadt, Nicolas, *Faire la paix au Moyen Âge: discours et gestes de paix pendant la Guerre de Cent Ans* (Paris: Odile Jacob, 2017).

Paravicini, Werner, *Karl der Kühne: Das Ende des Hauses Burgund* (Northeim, Germany: Muster-Schmidt Verlag, 1976).

Pernoud, Régine, *Jeanne d'Arc par elle-même et par ses témoins* (Paris: Seuil, 1962).

— *Pour en finir avec le Moyen Âge* (Paris: Seuil, 1979). Translated as *Those Terrible Middle Ages! Debunking the Myths* (San Francisco: Ignatius Press, 2000).

Pinette, Matthieu, *Le château de Germolles* (Germolles, 2015).

Pintoin, Michel, *Chronique du religieux de Saint-Denys, le règne de Charles VI, de 1380–1422* (Paris: Imprimerie de Crapelet, 1839). Research has shown that Pintoin is the principal author of this chronicle.

Pirenne, Henri, *La fin du moyen âge: la désagrégation du monde médiéval (1285–1453)* (Paris: PUF, 1931).

— *Histoire de Belgique: Des origines à l'État bourguignon* (Brussels: La Renaissance du Livre, 1948).

— *Histoire de l'Europe des invasions au XVIe siècle* (Paris: Alcan, 1936).

Pitte, Jean-Robert, *Dictionnaire amoureux de la Bourgogne* (Paris: Plon, 2015).

Pleij, Herman, *Dromen van Cocagne: Middeleeuwse fantasieën over het volmaakte leven* (Amsterdam: Prometheus, 1997).

— *Het gevleugelde woord: Geschiedenis van de Nederlandse literatuur (1400–1560)* (Amsterdam: Bert Bakker, 2007).

Postel, Jean-Philippe, *L'affaire Arnolfini* (Arles: Actes Sud, 2016).

Power, Eileen, *Medieval People* (London: Penguin Books, 1924).

Prevenier, Walter (ed.), *Prinsen en poorters* (Antwerp: Mercatorfonds, 1998).

Prevenier, Walter and Peter Arnade, *Onze gratie en genade: Misdaad en vergiffenis in de Bourgondische Nederlanden* (Antwerp/Utrecht: Houtekiet-Omniboek, 2015).

Procès de condamnation de Jeanne d'Arc, translation and notes by Pierre Tisset (Paris: Klincksieck, 1970).

Pye, Michael, *The Edge of the World: How the North Sea Made Us Who We Are* (London: Penguin Books, 2014).

Quéruel, Danielle, 'Des entremets aux intermèdes dans les banquets bourguignons', in *Banquets et manières de table au Moyen-Âge*, Aix-en-Provence: Presses Universitaires, 2014, pp. 141–57.

Raedts, Peter, *De ontdekking van de middeleeuwen: Geschiedenis van een illusie* (Amsterdam: Wereldbibliotheek, 2011).

Rambourg, Patrick, *De la cuisine à la gastronomie* (Paris: Audibert, 2005).

Recht, Roland, 'La révolution artistique de Claus Sluter', *Dossier de l'Art*, 203 (2001), pp. 2–11.

Régnier-Bohler (ed.), *Splendeurs de la Cour de Bourgogne Récits et chroniques* (Paris: Robert Laffont (Bouquins), 1995).

Reynebeau, Marc, *De Droom van Vlaanderen: Of het toeval van de geschiedenis* (Antwerp: Manteau, 2002).

Ridderbos, Bernhard, *De melancholie van de kunstenaar: Hugo van der Goes en de Oudnederlandse schilderkunst* (The Hague: Sdu Uitgevers, 1991).

— *Schilderkunst in de Bourgondische Nederlanden* (Leuven: Davidsfonds, 2014).

Rodenbach, Albrecht, *Eerste gedichten* (Roeselare: Den Wijngaert, 1980). Originally published in 1878.

Rottier, Honoré, *Rondreis door middeleeuws Vlaanderen* (Leuven: Davidsfonds, 1996).

Schelle, Klaus, *Karel de Stoute: Leven en dood van een Boergondische hertog* (Nijmegen: Gottmer, 1978).

Schmelzer, Björn, 'Agricola's aesthetics of the blind'. Liner notes for the CD *Cecus* by Graindelavoix (with music by Pierre de la Rue, Alexander Agricola and others), 2010.

— 'Binchois, Father of Joy'. Liner notes for the CD *Joye* by Graindelavoix (with music by Gilles Binchois), 2006.

Schnerb, Bertrand, *Armagnacs et Bourguignons: La maudite guerre (1407–1435)* (Paris: Perrin, 1988).

— *L'État bourguignon* (Paris: Perrin, 1999).

— *Jean sans Peur: Le prince meurtrier* (Paris: Payot, 2005).

— 'La piété et les dévotions de Philippe le Bon, duc de Bourgogne (1419–1467)', *Comptes rendus des séances de l'Académie des Inscriptions et Belles-Lettres*, 2005 (149–4), pp. 1319–44.

Serdon, Valérie, *La guerre au Moyen Âge* (Paris: Éditions Jean-Paul Gisserot, 2017).

Shakespeare, William, *King Lear* (London: Wordsworth Editions, 1994).

Sleiderink, Remco, 'Dichters aan het Brabantse hof (1356–1406)', *De nieuwe taalgids*, 86 (1993), pp. 1–16.

Smith, Robert Douglas and Kelly DeVries, *The Artillery of the Dukes of Burgundy, 1363–1477* (Woodbridge, UK, 2005).

Soisson, Jean-Pierre, *Charles le Téméraire* (Paris: Grasset, 1997).

— *Marguerite: Princesse de Bourgogne* (Paris: Grasset, 2002).

Speet, Ben, *Kleine geschiedenis van Nederland: De tijd van steden en staten (1000–1500)* (Zwolle: Waanders, 2008).

Stein, Robert, *De hertog en zijn staten: Eenwording van de Bourgondische Nederlanden (c.1380–c.1480)* (Hilversum: Verloren, 2014).

Steyaert, J.J., *Volledige beschryving van Gent, of geschiedkundige beschouwing van deze stad en hare bewooners, de merkwaerdige gebouwen, gestichten en maetschappyen, de beroemde gentenaren, enz.* (Ghent: Boeken Steendrukkery Van Doosselaere, 1857).

Suckale, Robert *et al.*, *Gotiek* (Cologne: Taschen, 2007).

Sweetser, Franklin P. (ed.), *Les cent nouvelles nouvelles* (Geneva: Librairie Droz, 1996).

Tang, Frank, *De Middeleeuwen: Een kleine geschiedenis* (Amsterdam: Prometheus, 2014).

Ter Haar, Jaap, *Geschiedenis van de Lage Landen* (Weesp: Fibula-Van Dishoeck, 1985).

Tollebeek, Jo and Henk te Velde, *Het geheugen van de Lage Landen* (Rekkem: Ons Erfdeel, 2009).

Triest, Monika, *Macht, vrouwen en politiek, 1477–1558: Maria van Bourgondië, Margaretha van Oostenrijk, Maria van Hongarije* (Antwerp: Van Halewyck, 2000).

Tuchman, Barbara, *A Distant Mirror: The Calamitous 14th Century* (New York: Knopf, 1978).

Vallet, Françoise, *De Clovis à Dagobert: Les Mérovingiens* (Paris: Gallimard, 1995).

Van Belle, Juliaan, *Les Pays de par deçà: De Bourgondische Nederlanden*, 3 vols: *Filips de Goede, Karel de Stoute* and *Maria van Bourgondië* (Torhout: Flandria Nostra, 1984–86).

Van Boendale, Jan, *De Brabantse yeesten* (Brussels: Mayez, 1939–69).

Van Cruyningen, Arnout, *De Staten-Generaal: Vijfenhalve eeuw geschiedenis van het parlement* (Utrecht: Omniboek, 2013).

Van Den Heuvel, M.E., 'De verdediging van bastaarden door Olivier de la Marche, een vijftiende-eeuwse Bourgondische hoveling', *Handelingen der Maatschappij voor Geschiedenis en Oudheidkunde te Gent* (January 1991), pp. 33–68.

Van der Hey, Ignace, *Histoire des comtes de Flandre depuis l'établissement de ses souverains, jusqu'à présent* (Antwerp, 1733).

Van der Velden, Hugo, 'The Quatrain of the Ghent Altarpiece', *Simiolus* 35 (2011), pp. 5–39.

— 'A Reply to Volker Herzner and a Note on the Putative Author of the Ghent Quatrain', *Simiolus* 35 (2011), pp. 131–41.

Van Dyck, Maarten, *In de ban van de tijd* (Ghent: De Boekentoren, 2017).

Van Hautert, Cas, *Middeleeuwers tussen hoop en vrees* (Utrecht: IJzer, 2015).

Van Loo, Bart, *Als kok in Frankrijk: Literaire recepten en culinaire verhalen* (Amsterdam/Antwerp: De Bezige Bij, 2008).

— *O vermiljoenen spleet! Seks, erotiek en literatuur* (Amsterdam/ Antwerp: De Bezige Bij, 2010).

Van den Bergen-Pantens, Christiane (ed.), *L'ordre de la Toison d'or, de Philippe le Bon à Philippe le Beau (1430–1505): Idéal ou reflet d'une société?* (Brussels: Bibliothèque royale, 1996).

Van Dixmude, Jan, *Dits de Cronike ende Genealogie van den prinsen ende Graven van den Foreeste van Buc, dat heet Vlaenderlant, van 863 tot 1436* (Ypres: Drukkerij Van Lambin en zoon, 1839).

Van Dixmude, Olivier, *Merkwaerdige gebeurtenissen, vooral in Vlaenderen en Brabant, en ook in de aengrenzende landstreken van 1377 tot 1443* (Ypres: Drukkerij Van Lambin en zoon, 1835).

Van Heule, Andreas, *Memorieboek der stad Ghent van 't jaar 1301 tot 1588*, vol. 1 (Ghent: C. Annoot-Braeckman, 1852).

Van Maerlant, Jacob, *Spiegel Historiael.* https://www.dbnl.org/tekst/ maer002spie04_01/maer002spie04_01_0002.php?q=scone%20 walsche%20valsche%20poeten#hl1

Van Oostrom, Frits, *Maerlants wereld* (Amsterdam: Prometheus, 1996).

— *Stemmen op schrift: De geschiedenis van de Nederlandse literatuur vanaf het begin tot 1300* (Amsterdam: Prometheus, 2013).

— *Nobel Streven: Het onwaarschijnlijke maar waargebeurde verhaal van ridder Jan van Brederode* (Amsterdam: Prometheus, 2017).

Van Vaernewyck, Marcus, *Van die beroerlicke tijden in die Nederlanden en voornamelick in Ghendt 1566–1568*, edited by Ferdinand Vanderhaeghe (Ghent: Maetschappy der Vlaemsche Bibliophilen, 1872–81).

Vaughan, Richard, *Philip the Bold: The Formation of the Burgundian State* (London: Boydell Press, 2002 (reissue of the original work from 1962).

— *John the Fearless: The Growth of Burgundian Power* (London: Boydell Press, 2002) (reissue of the original work from 1966).

— *Philip the Good: The Apogee of the Burgundian State* (London: Boydell Press, 2002) (reissue of the original work from 1970).

— *Charles the Bold: The Last Valois Duke of Burgundy* (London: Boydell Press, 2002) (reissue of the original work from 1972).

— *Valois Burgundy* (London: Allen Lane, 1975).

Vélissariou, Alexandra, 'L'espace et le jeu des Cent Nouvelle nouvelles', *Le Moyen Âge: Revue d'Histoire et de Philologie*, 2 (2008), pp. 239–54.

Verdon, Jean, *La femme au Moyen Âge* (Paris: Éditions Jean-Paul Gisserot, 1999).

Verhulst, A., *Landbouw en landschap in middeleeuws Vlaanderen* (Brussels: Gemeentekrediet, 1995).

Verhuyck, Paul, *Minuten middeleeuwen* (Antwerp: Vrijdag, 2018).

Viard, Jules, 'Philippe XI de Valois: Début de règne (février-juillet 1328)', *Bibliothèque de l'École des Chartes*, 95 (1934), pp. 259–83.

Villon, François, *Complete Poems of François Villon*, translated by Beram Saklatvala (New York: Dutton, 1968).

Walch, Jan, *Karel de Stoute* (Soesterberg: Aspect, 2016) (reissue of the work from 1940).

Weidmann, Franz Carl, *Panorama der Österreichischen Monarchie* (Vienna: Archiv-Verlag, 2001 (reissue of the work from 1846).

Wheaton, Barbara Ketcham, *Savoring the Past: The French Kitchen and Table from 1300 to 1789* (New York: Touchstone Books, 1983).

Von Kraus, Victor (ed.), *Maximilians I: Vertraulicher Briefwechsel mit Sigmund Prüschenk Freiherrn zu Stettenberg* (Innsbruck: Wagnersche Verlag, 1875) (reissued 2012).

Wiesflecker, Hermann, *Kaiser Maximilian I: Das Reich, Österreich und Europa an der Wende zur Neuzeit*, 5 vols. (Munich: Oldenburg, 1971–86).

Witte, Els, *De constructie van België (1828–1847)* (Tielt: Lannoo, 2006).

CATALOGUES

L'art à la cour de Bourgogne: Le mécénat de Philippe le Hardi et de Jean sans Peur (1364–1419) (Dijon and Cleveland: Musée des Beaux-Arts and The Cleveland Museum of Art, 2004–5).

Claus Sluter en Bourgogne (Dijon: Musée des Beaux-Arts, 2004).

Colard Mansion: Incunabula, prints and manuscripts in Medieval Bruges. Exhibition *Haute lecture by Colard Mansion* (Bruges: Groeningemuseum, 2018).

Dames met Klasse: Margaretha van York, Margaretha van Oostenrijk (Mechelen: Congresen erfgoedcentrum Lamot, 2005).

De eeuw van Van Eyck (1430–1530): De Vlaamse Primitieven en het Zuiden (Bruges: Groeningemuseum, 2002).

De Librije van Filips de Goede (Brussels: Albert I-Bibliotheek, 1967).

De Vlaamse miniatuur: Het mecenaat van Filips de Goede (1445–1475) (Brussels: Paleis voor Schone Kunsten, 1959).

De weg naar Van Eyck (Rotterdam: Museum Boijmans Van Beuningen, 2012–2013).

Eenheid op papier: De Nederlanden in kaart van keizer Karel tot Willem I (Leuven: Lieve-Vrouw-ter-Predikheren, 1994).

Handschriften met miniaturen van de 9de eeuw tot het begin van de 15de eeuw (Brussels: Koninklijke Bibliotheek, 1985).

Johan Maelwael: Nijmegen-Paris-Dijon, Kunst rond 1400 (Amsterdam: Rijksmuseum, 2017).

Karel de Stoute (1433–1477): Pracht en praal in Bourgondië (Bruges: Groeningemuseum, 2009).

La Toison d'Or: Cinq siècles d'Art et d'Histoire (Bruges: Groeningemuseum, 1962).

Pleurants des tombeaux des ducs de Bourgogne (Dijon: Musée des Beaux-Arts, 1971).

Rogier van der Weyden, Rogier de le Pasture: Official painter to the city of Brussels, Portrait painter of the Burgundian Court (Brussels: City Museum, 1979).

Van Eyck: Een optische revolutie (Ghent: Hannibal, 2020).

Vlaamse miniaturen (1404–1482) (Brussels: Koninklijke Bibliotheek van België/Paris: Bibliothèque nationale de France, 2011–12).

HISTORICAL NOVELS

D'Aillon, Jean, *Une étude en écarlate* (Paris: 10/18, 2015). The age of John the Fearless and the civil war between the Burgundians and the Armagnacs.

— *Le chien des Basqueville* (Paris: 10/18, 2016). Same time frame as above.

— *La ville de la peur* (Paris: 10/18, 2017). Same time frame as above.

Anker, Robert, *In de wereld* (Amsterdam: Querido, 2017). The age of Charles the Bold, Mary of Burgundy and Philip the Handsome.

Beckman, Thea, *Geef me de ruimte!* (Rotterdam: Lemniscaat, 1976). See Prologue.

— *Triomf van de verschroeide aarde* (Rotterdam: Lemniscaat, 1977). See Prologue.

— *Rad van fortuin* (Rotterdam: Lemniscaat, 1978). See Prologue.

Bélorgey, Élisabeth, *Autoportrait de Van Eyck* (Paris: Fayard, 2000). Fictional autobiography of Jan van Eyck.

Benzoni, Juliette, *Il suffit d'un amour* (Paris: Pocket, 2015). First part of a five-part series of novels from 1963 set in the age of Philip the Good.

Bourin, Jeanne, *La dame de beauté* (Paris: La Table Ronde, 1970). The age of Charles VII and Agnès Sorel.

Chevalier, Tracy, *The Lady and the Unicorn* (London: Harper Collins, 2003). The age of Charles VIII.

Compère, Gaston, *Je soussigné, Charles le Téméraire* (Brussels: Labort, 1989). Fictional autobiography of Charles the Bold.

Druon, Maurice, *Quand un roi perd la France* (Paris: Livre de Poche, 1977). The age of John the Good and the Battle of Poitiers. Seventh and last part of the series of compelling novels *Les rois maudits*.

Dupuy-Mazuel, Henry, *Le miracle des loups* (Paris: Albin Michel, 1924). The age of Louis XI and Charles the Bold.

Grafteaux, Serge, *Philippe le Hardi* (Paris: Editions Universitaire, 1979). The life of Philip the Bold in novel form.

— *Jean sans Peur* (Paris: Editions Universitaire, 1980). The life of John the Fearless in novel form.

— *Philippe le Bon* (Paris: Editions Universitaire, 1981). The life of Philip the Good in novel form.

— *Charles le Téméraire* (Paris: Editions Universitaire, 1981). The life of Charles the Bold in novel form.

Haasse, Hella, *In a Dark Wood Wandering: A Novel of the Middle Ages* (Chicago: Academy Chicago Publishers, 1989). Originally published as *Het woud der verwachting: Het leven van Charles d'Orleans* (Amsterdam: Querido, 1949).

Hill, Tobias, *The Love of Stones* (London: Faber and Faber, 2002). Fictional quest for a jewel belonging to John the Fearless.

Povel, Wim, *Het felle leven van Jacoba van Beieren* (Schoorl: Uitgeverij Conserve, 1991). Novel about the life of the countess of Hainaut, Holland and Zeeland. Also see Joyce Tulkens and Simone van der Vlugt.

— *De laatsten der Bourgondiërs* (Schoorl: Uitgeverij Conserve, 1993). The age of Philip the Good and Charles the Bold.

Rufin, Jean-Christophe, *Le grand Coeur* (Paris: Gallimard, 2012). The age of Charles VII, Agnès Sorel and Jacques Coeur.

Sinoué, Gilbert, *L'enfant de Bruges* (Paris: Gallimard, 1999). The age of Jan van Eyck and Philip the Good.

Tulkens, Joyce, *Jacoba van Beieren: De nicht van de bisschop* (Schoorl: Conserve, 2001).

Van Aken, Jan, *De ommegang* (Amsterdam: Querido, 2018). Set between 1373 and 1415.

Van der Vlugt, Simone, *Jacoba, dochter van Holland* (Amsterdam: Ambo/Anthos, 2016).

CHRONOLOGY

1050	Marriage of Matilda of Flanders and William the Conqueror
1066	Battle of Hastings; William the Conqueror King of England
1098	Creation of the Abbey of Cîteaux
c.1100	Otto II named first count of *Habsburg*
1152	Henry Plantagenet marries Eleanor of Aquitaine, sowing the seeds of the Hundred Years War
1153	Death of Bernard of Clairvaux
1214	Battle of Bouvines
1215	Magna Carta
1230–40	Ypres Cloth Hall and Belfry of Bruges (stone tower, 1280)
from 1253 on	All official documents in Ghent written in Middle Dutch, the rest of the Low Countries will follow suit
c.1285	Van der Beurze inn in Bruges
c.1300	Death of Jacob van Maerlant
1302	Battle of the Golden Spurs (Kortrijk)
1309	Pope Clement V moves the papacy to Avignon
1328	Branch of the Valois family occupies the French throne, Philip VI
1334	Flood, the islands of Walcheren and Wulpen in Zeeland inundated
1337	Official beginning of the Hundred Years War
1338–45	Jacob van Artevelde, strong man of Flanders
1346	Battle of Crécy / Louis of Male, Count of Flanders
1348	Beginning of the plague epidemic in Europe
1356	Battle of Poitiers (Hundred Years War)
1357	Étienne Marcel (Paris Uprising)
1360	Treaty of Brétigny (truce)
1363	John the Good gives Burgundy to Philip the Bold, founding father of the Valois-Burgundians
1369	Marriage of Philip the Bold and Margaret of Male
1371	Birth of John the Fearless
1375	Flood, Koudekerke and Elmare wiped off the map
1377	Philip the Bold purchases land in Champmol / death of Edward III
1378	Western Schism (Rome versus Avignon, two popes)
1379–85	French-Flemish crisis
1379	Ghent puts an end to the construction of Bruges canal
1380	Death of Charles V
1382	Battle of Westrozebeke / death of Philip van Artevelde
1383	Siege of Ypres / first stone laid of monastery of Champmol
1384	Death of Louis of Male → Philip the Bold Count of Flanders
1385	Double wedding in Cambrai / siege of Damme / Peace of Tournai
1386	Failed invasion of England from Sluis

1388	Expedition against the Duke of Guelders
1389	Battle of Kosovo / Joyous Entry of Isabeau of Bavaria in Paris / Claus Sluter becomes court sculptor of Philip the Bold
1390	Christine de Pizan is widowed / beginning of the career of the 'first' female writer
1390–9	Retable of the Crucifixion and Altar of Saints and Martyrs by painter Melchior Broederlam and woodcarver Jacob de Baerze
1392	Charles VI suffers his first attack of madness
1394	Death of Clement VII → Benedict XIII / flood / Oostende forced to move inland
1395	Great wine law of Philip the Bold / Claus Sluter starts work on the *Well of Moses*
1396	Crusade of John the Fearless / Battle of Nicopolis / marriage of Richard II and Isabella of Valois / truce (Hundred Years War) signed
1397	Johan Maelwael becomes court painter for Philip the Bold
1400	Death of Richard II / Philip the Bold creates his *Cour amoureuse* / Johan Maelwael's *Large Round Pietà*
1404	Death of Philip the Bold → John the Fearless comes to power / death of Jean Froissart and Eustache Deschamps
1405	Alliance between Burgundy, Brabant-Limburg and Holland-Zeeland-Hainaut / Joyous Entry of John the Fearless / language facilities for the Flemings
1406	Death of Claus Sluter / Claus van de Werve completes the tomb of Philip the Bold / Anthony of Burgundy (brother of John the Fearless) becomes Duke of Brabant
1407	Murder of Louis of Orléans
1407–35	Civil war between the Burgundians and the Armagnacs (high point: 1407–20)
1408	Battle of Othée
1410	Erection of the Tower of John the Fearless in Paris
1411	Philip the Good (then simply Count of Charolais) becomes permanent representative of his father in Ghent
1413	Revolt of the Cabochiens / John the Fearless flees Paris / death of Henry IV
1414–18	Council of Constance: end of the Western Schism / Jan Hus burned at the stake / John the Fearless acquitted of all theological blame
1415	Battle of Agincourt / death of Jan Maelwael, Hendrik Bellechose becomes court painter for John the Fearless, starts work on his *Saint Denis Altarpiece*
1416	John IV becomes Duke of Brabant and Limburg (nephew of John the Fearless)

1417	Death of William of Hainaut, Holland and Zeeland → Jacqueline of Bavaria (niece of John the Fearless) becomes Countess of Holland, Zeeland and Hainaut
1418	Marriage of John and Jacqueline / Holland, Zeeland, Hainaut, Brabant and Limburg enter more deeply into Burgundian waters / Burgundians back in Paris / death of Bernard of Armagnac
1419	Murder of John the Fearless → Philip the Good in power
1420	Treaty of Troyes, France in English hands
1421	St Elizabeth's flood / dozens of villages disappear under water
1422	Death of Henry V → his son, Henry VI, new King of England and France / death of Charles VI, dauphin Charles VII's failed attempt to claim the throne / founding of the University of Dole
1425	Founding of the University of Leuven / John of Bavaria dies, Jan van Eyck becomes Burgundian court painter / Philip the Good challenges Humphrey of Gloucester / Jacqueline of Bavaria loses Hainaut (siege of Mons) / imprisoned in Ghent / she escapes to Holland / beginning of Philip the Good's war with Holland / Joan of Arc hears her 'voices' for the first time / Jacqueline of Bavaria wins the first battle at Alphen aan den Rijn
1426	Battle of Brouwershaven (Philip the Good victorious) / Haarlem besieged by Jacqueline of Bavaria (failed) / second Battle of Alphen (Jacqueline of Bavaria victorious) / Battle of Hoorn (Philip the Good victorious)
1427	Siege of Zevenbergen (Philip the Good victorious) / naval battle of Wieringen (Philip the Good victorious) / death of John IV of Brabant
1428	Pope declares marriage of Jacqueline of Bavaria and Humphrey of Gloucester invalid / siege of Gouda / Kiss of Delft / Joan of Arc to Vaucouleurs, driven by her 'voices'
1429	'Battle of the Herrings', defeat of the French against the English / Joan of Arc to Chinon, convinces Charles VII of her cause / Joan of Arc relieves Orléans and crowns Charles VII at Reims / Jan van Eyck in Portugal, portrait of Isabella of Portugal / county of Namur in Burgundian hands
1430	Marriage of Philip the Good with Isabella of Portugal / founding of the Order of the Golden Fleece / Joan of Arc in Burgundian and then in English hands / *Portrait of a Man with a Blue Chaperon* (Jan van Eyck) / death of Philip of Saint-Pol, Duke of Brabant / Philip the Good becomes Duke of Brabant and Limburg
1431	Joan of Arc burned at the stake (Rouen)
1432	Installation of the *Ghent Altarpiece* (Van Eyck brothers)
1433	Birth of Charles the Bold / *Portrait of a Man in a Red Turban* (probably a self-portrait by Jan van Eyck)

1434   The *Arnolfini Portrait* (Jan van Eyck) / first Burgundian common currency, the *vierlander* (four lands), in general circulation from 1443 on

1435   Treaty of Arras (France and Burgundy)

1435–6 *The Madonna of Chancellor Rolin* (Jan van Eyck)

1436   Death of Jacqueline of Bavaria / *Virgin and Child with Canon van der Paele* (Jan van Eyck)

1436–8 Bruges Rebellion

1438   *Portrait of Cardinal Niccolò Albergati* (Jan van Eyck, based on a drawing from 1435)

1439   Flemish-English and Holland-English trade pact

*c.*1440 Bladelin House (Pieter de Leestmaker) on Naaldenstraat in Bruges

1441   Death of Jan van Eyck / Luxembourg in Burgundian hands (from 1451 also under the law of succession)

1443   Truce between Burgundy and England / first stone laid for the Hôtel-Dieu in Beaune

1445–8 *Bladelin Triptych* by Rogier van der Weyden

1447   The Ghent salt dispute, beginning of the great Revolt of Ghent

1452   Opening of the Hôtel-Dieu in Beaune (Nicolas Rolin and Guigone de Salins) / *The Last Judgement* (Rogier van der Weyden)

1453   Battle of Castillon, end of the Hundred Years War (29 May) / fall of Constantinople, end of the Eastern Roman Empire (17 July) / battle of Gavere, end of the Revolt of Ghent (23 July)

1454   Feast of the Pheasant in Lille (17 February) / Imperial Diet in Regensburg / marriage of Charles the Bold with Isabella of Bourbon

1456   Siege of Utrecht, siege of Deventer / French Dauphin Louis requests and is granted political asylum in Burgundy

1457   Legendary quarrel between Philip the Good and Charles the Bold / birth of Mary of Burgundy

1457–61 *Les cent nouvelles nouvelles*

1461   Death of Charles VII / Louis XI new King of France / Henry VI deposed / Edward IV new King of England

1462   Death of Nicolas Rolin

1461–2 *Portrait of Charles the Bold* (Rogier van der Weyden)

1463   François Villon, 'A Ballade of the Hanged'

1464   First States General of the Low Countries / death of Charles of Orléans and Rogier van der Weyden

1465   Battle of Montlhéry

1466   Destruction of Dinant

1467   Death of Philip the Good / Joyous Entry of Charles the Bold in Ghent (revolt)

1468	Marriage of Charles the Bold with Margaret of York / Treaty of Péronne / destruction of Liège
1469	Charles the Bold purchases Upper Alsace
1470–71	Henry VI, King of England for only a few months, dies in 1471, Edward IV back on the throne
1472	Charles the Bold conquers the duchy of Guelders (and county of Zutphen) / meeting of Charles the Bold with Emperor Frederick III in Trier / Ordinance of Thionville, financial, military and judicial reforms, the Parlement of Mechelen (becomes the capital of the northern domains)
1473–7	*Adoration of the Shepherds* (*Portinari Triptych*, Hugo van der Goes)
1474	Speech of Charles the Bold in Dijon
1474–5	Siege of Neuss, Frederick III sends in a relief force / execution of Peter von Hagenbach / René of Lorraine declares war / Swiss and Alsatian cities declare war
1475	Successful siege of Nancy / Lorraine in Burgundian hands / States General of the Low Countries refuses to continue financial support for Charles's wars
1476	Battle of Grandson (March) / battle of Murten (June) / beginning of the siege of Nancy (October)
1477	Battle of Nancy (5 January) / death of Charles the Bold / Great Privilege / marriage of Mary of Burgundy and Maximilian of Austria / Hugo van der Goes enters the monastery (Red Cloister, Auderghem)
1482	Death of Mary of Burgundy / Treaty of Arras / *Death of the Virgin* (Hugo van der Goes) / death of Hugo van der Goes
1483	Death of Louis XI → Charles VIII King of France / death of Edward IV → Richard III King of England (after a very brief intermezzo with Edward V as king, who was imprisoned in the Tower of London and probably murdered)
1486	Maximilian elected King of the Romans
1488	Maximilian imprisoned in Bruges
1489	Shrine of St Ursula (Hans Memling)
1492	Columbus discovers America
1493	Death of Frederick III → Maximilian head of the Holy Roman Empire
1494	Death of Hans Memling / opening phase of the Italian wars between the Habsburgs and the kings of France (which drag on until 1559)
1496	Marriage of Philip the Handsome and Joanna of Castile
1498	Death of Charles VIII of France → Louis XII
1506	Death of Philip the Handsome
1507–15	Margaret of Austria (sister of Philip the Handsome) governor of the Habsburg Netherlands

1515	Philip's son Charles becomes ruler of the Low Countries / death of Louis XII → Francis I King of France
1516	Death of Ferdinand of Aragon → Charles King of Spain
1517	Luther's ninety-five theses / beginning of the Reformation
1517–30	Margaret reappointed governor of the Low Countries
1519	Charles V elected King of the Romans
1520	Charles V crowned emperor in Aachen
1521	Completion of the Church of Our Lady in Antwerp (became a cathedral in 1559)
1529	Ladies' Peace of Cambrai (between France and the Holy Roman Empire)
1530	Death of Margaret of Austria
1530–55	Mary of Hungary (sister of Charles V) governor of the Habsburg Netherlands
1547	Death of Francis I
1549	Pragmatic Sanction (the Low Countries shall henceforth be inherited intact, one and indivisible)
1555	Abdication of Charles V in the Low Countries
1556	Abdication of Charles in Spain and renunciation of the emperorship
1558	Death of Charles V
1566	Iconoclastic Fury
1581	Act of Abjuration
1585	Fall of Antwerp, beginning of the division between north and south

HISTORIC FIGURES

Aetius (c.390–454), supreme commander of the Roman army who, along with the Burgundians, defeated the Huns in 451

Albert of Bavaria (1336–1404), Count of Hainaut, Holland and Zeeland, grandfather of both Jacqueline of Bavaria and Philip the Good

Anthony of Burgundy (1384–1415), Duke of Brabant and Limburg, brother of John the Fearless

Anthony of Burgundy (1421–1504), the Great Bastard, bastard son of Philip the Good, important commander under Charles the Bold

Attila (c.406–53), King of the Huns, enemy of the Burgundians

Baldwin Iron Arm (c.840–79), first Count of Flanders

Baldwin van der Nieppe (c.1345–1410), tutor of John the Fearless, provost of St Donatian's church in Bruges

Bernard van Armagnac (1360–1418), father-in-law of Charles of Orléans, count of Armagnac, leader of the anti-Burgundian party, rival of John the Fearless

Bertrand du Guesclin (1320–80), famous French commander in the Hundred Years War

Capetians (Burgundian), descendants of Hugo Capet's grandson Robert, who would govern the Burgundian duchy from 1032 for more than three centuries (the last is Philip of Rouvres, who dies in 1361)

Capetians (French), French royal family who will occupy the throne for eight centuries, first directly (from Hugo Capet, 987), then via the Valois branch (from Philip VI, 1328), and finally via the Bourbon division (from Henry IV, 1589)

Charlemagne (c.747–814), king and emperor of the Franks

Charles the Bold (1433–77), Duke of Burgundy, son of Philip the Good, father of Mary of Burgundy

Charles Martel (c.689–741), major-domo of the Frankish empire, founding father of the Carolingians, stopped the advance of the Moors at Poitiers (732), grandfather of Charlemagne

Charles of Orléans (1394–1465), son of Louis of Orléans, whose death he set out to avenge, also a well-known medieval poet

Charles V (1338–80), King of France, brother of Philip the Bold

Charles VI (1368–1422), mad King of France, nephew of his regent Philip the Bold, cousin of John the Fearless

Charles VII (1403–61), King of France; as dauphin he gave the order to murder John the Fearless; ended the Hundred Years War, partly thanks to Joan of Arc, whom he then deserted; opponent of Philip the Good

Charles VIII (1470–98), King of France, started the Italian Wars (1494–1559)

Claus Sluter (1350–1406), sculptor at the court of Philip the Bold, born in Haarlem

Claus van de Werve (c.1380–1439), cousin and, as sculptor, assistant of and successor to Claus Sluter

Clothilde (480–545), Catholic wife of Clovis, Burgundian princess, niece of Gundobad

Clovis (c.466–511), King of the Franks, converted to Christianity, married the Burgundian princess Clothilde

Croy, family of, influential clan at the Burgundian court of Philip the Good

David of Burgundy (1427–96), Bishop of Utrecht, bastard son of Philip the Good

Edward III (1312–77), King of England who set off the Hundred Years War in 1337

Eustache Deschamps (c.1340–c.1404), poet, but also author of historical writings in verse

Francis I (1494–1547), King of France, rival of Emperor Charles V

François Villon (1431–after 1463), most important French poet of the Middle Ages

Frederick III (1415–93), Holy Roman Emperor, Habsburg, father of Maximilian of Austria

Georges Chastellain (†1475), chronicler at the court of Philip the Good and Charles the Bold

Gundobad (†516), King of the Burgundians, driving force behind the *Lex Burgondionum*

Henry V (1386–1422), King of England, victor at the Battle of Agincourt, father of Henry VI and son of Henry IV

Hugo Capet (941–96), considered the first King of the Franks (see Capetians)

Hugo van der Goes (†1482), one of the most important painters of the so-called Flemish Primitives, part of the generation that succeeded Van Eyck and Van der Weyden

Humphrey of Gloucester (1390–1447), third husband of Jacqueline of Bavaria, brother of King Henry V of England

Isabeau of Bavaria (c.1371–1435), Queen of France, spouse of Charles VI, mistress of Louis of Orléans

Isabella of Portugal (1397–1471), Duchess of Burgundy, third wife of Philip the Good

Jacqueline of Bavaria (1401–36), Countess of Hainaut, Holland and Zeeland, in conflict with Philip the Good

Jan van Eyck (c.1390–1441), court painter for Philip the Good; he and his brother Hubert painted the *Ghent Altarpiece* (1432)

Jean Froissart (c.1337–c.1405), one of the most important chroniclers of the Late Middle Ages

Jean Molinet (1432–1507), Burgundian chronicler, successor to Georges Chastellain

Joan of Arc (c.1412–31), also known as the Maid of Orléans, played a key role in the Hundred Years War, paved the way to the coronation of Charles VII in Reims, burned at the stake (Rouen)

Joanna of Brabant (1322–1406), Duchess of Brabant and Limburg, key mediator for the double wedding at Cambrai of 1385

Johan Maelwael (c.1370–1415), court painter for Philip the Bold and John the Fearless, also considered the first famous Dutch painter

Johannes Canard (c.1350–1407), chancellor of Burgundy under Philip the Bold

John of Bavaria (1374–1425), prince-bishop-elect of Liège, later briefly the Count of Hainaut, Holland and Zeeland, which was disputed by Jacqueline of Bavaria; also called John the Pitiless

John of Berry (1340–1416), Duke of Berry, brother of Philip the Bold, commissioned the famous book of hours *Les très riches heures du duc de Berry* (Limbourg brothers)

John IV of Brabant (1403–27), Duke of Brabant and Limburg, cousin of Philip the Good, second husband of Jacqueline of Bavaria

John the Fearless (1371–1419), Duke of Burgundy, son of Philip the Bold, father of Philip the Good

John the Good (1319–64), King of France, father of Philip the Bold, defeated at the Battle of Poitiers (1356)

Joos Vijd and his wife, Elisabeth Borluut, patrons of the *Ghent Altarpiece*

Louis de Gruuthuse (1422–92), councillor and confidant of Charles the Bold and Mary of Burgundy, great bibliophile

Louis of Male (1330–84), Count of Flanders, father-in-law of Philip the Bold

Louis of Orléans (1372–1407), brother of King Charles VI of France, cousin and rival of John the Fearless

Louis XI (1423–83), King of France, enemy of Charles the Bold, also in conflict with his own father, Charles VII

Margaret of Austria (1480–1530), governor of the Habsburg Netherlands, sister of Philip the Handsome, daughter of Mary of Burgundy, aunt of Emperor Charles V

Margaret of Bavaria (1363–1423), Duchess of Burgundy, spouse of John the Fearless

Margaret of Male (1350–1405), consort of Philip the Bold, Countess of Flanders

Margaret of York (1446–1503), Duchess of Burgundy, consort of Charles the Bold, sister of the English kings Edward IV and Richard III

Mary of Burgundy (1457–82), Duchess of Burgundy, daughter of Charles the Bold; in a certain sense she was 'Queen of the Netherlands'

Maximilian of Austria (1459–1519), first Archduke of Austria, later Holy Roman Emperor

Melchior Broederlam (†c.1410), most important Flemish painter of the generation before Jan van Eyck, worked at the court of Louis of Male and of Philip the Bold

Nicolas Rolin (c.1376–1462), most important chancellor of Burgundy under Philip the Good, builder of *Les Hospices de Beaune* (Hôtel-Dieu)

Olivier de la Marche (1426–1502), diplomat-poet-chronicler at the Burgundian court

Philip van Artevelde (1340–82), leader of Ghent, governor of Flanders, son of Jacob van Artevelde

Philip the Bold (1342–1404), Duke of Burgundy, son of King John the Good of France, father of John the Fearless

Philip the Fair (*Philippe le Bel*, 1268–1314), King of France at the time of the Battle of the Golden Spurs, responsible for the Schism and the annihilation of the order of the Knights Templar

Philip the Good (1396–1467), Duke of Burgundy, son of John the Fearless, father of Charles the Bold

Philip the Handsome (*Philippe le Beau*, 1478–1506), son of Maximilian of Austria and Mary of Burgundy, archduke, governor of the Low Countries, father of Emperor Charles V

Philip of Saint-Pol (1404–30), Duke of Brabant and Limburg, younger brother of John IV of Brabant, cousin of Philip the Good

Philippe de Commynes (1447–1511), Burgundian diplomat and chronicler-writer who defected to King Louis XI of France

Richard the Justiciar (858–921), first Duke of Burgundy, stopped the advance of the Vikings at Chartres (911)

Rogier van der Weyden (c.1400–64), along with Jan van Eyck, the most important painters of the so-called Flemish Primitives; worked for the Burgundian court

Rollo (c.846–933), Viking warlord, defeated by the Burgundians at Chartres, 'founder' of Normandy

Sigismund (†524), King of Burgundy, son of Gundobad, first German to convert to Christianity

Sigismund of Luxembourg (1368–1437), as King of Hungary, one of the driving forces behind the Crusade to Nicopolis, later Holy Roman Emperor

Thomas à Kempis (c.1380–1471), author of *The Imitation of Christ*, prominent member of the Devotio Moderna spiritual movement

Timur (also Amir Timur, Tamerlane and Timur the Lame, 1336–1405), Turkish-Mongol warlord

Tommaso Portinari (c.1430–1501), Florentine banker, patron of the arts (Van der Goes, Memling) and financier of Charles the Bold

Valois (Burgundian), after the Burgundian Capetian line became extinct, the throne went to Philip the Bold in 1364; Philip was the son of the French Valois king John the Good; this branch ruled Burgundy until 1477, and afterwards only the Low Countries; the dynasty was subsumed into the House of Habsburg

Valois (French), after the direct Capetian line became extinct, the throne went to the cadet branch of the Valois; they would occupy the French throne from 1328 to 1589 (see Capetians)

William of Bavaria (1365–1417), Count of Hainaut, Holland and Zeeland, married Margaret of Burgundy, sister of John the Fearless, father of Jacqueline of Bavaria

William the Conqueror (c.1028–87), Duke of Normandy, King of England

ILLUSTRATION CREDITS

SECTION 1

p. 1 above: Barbarians cross the Rhine. Print by Alphonse de Neuville from *History of France* by François Guizot.

p. 1 below: The baptism of Clovis. Saint Remigius binding. Musée de Picardie Médieval, Amiens.

p. 2 above: The execution of Sigismund. Bibliothèque municipale de Valenciennes.

p. 2 below: Battle of the Golden Spurs. Royal Library of Belgium, Brussels. From the *Grandes Chroniques de France*, ms. 5, vol. 329v.

p. 3: The murder of Jacob van Artevelde. Librairie de Blois, Bibliothèque nationale de France, Paris.

p. 4: Portrait of John the Good. Bibliothèque nationale de France, Paris, dép. des Estampes, in the collection of the Musée du Louvre.

p. 5: Battle of Poitiers. IRHT-CNRS, Bibliothèque municipale de Besançon, Ms 864.

p. 6 above: Edward III. British Library, London.

p. 6 below: The plague; flagellants in Tournai. Jean-Louis Torsin, IRPA. fol.16 v.

p. 7 upper left: Philip the Bold. Musée des Beaux-Arts de Dijon.

p. 7 upper right: Margaret of Male. Musée Hospice Comtesse, Lille.

p. 7 below: Marriage of Philip the Bold and Margaret of Flanders. From the *Grandes Chroniques de France,* Bibliothèque nationale de France, Paris, Ms 2615 f399.

p. 8 above: Louis of Male and Humphrey of Gloucester. From *Recueil d'Arras*, Bibliothèque nationale de France/Médiathèque Arras-Pas de Calais, Ms fr 266.

p. 8 below: John IV and Philip of Saint-Pol. Royal Library of Belgium, Brussels, hs II 1862/1.

p. 9: Battle of Westrozebeke. Niday Picture Library – Alamy Stock Photo.

p. 10 above: *Well of Moses* (Sluter). Musée des Beaux-Arts de Dijon.

p. 10 below: *Pleurants* (Sluter). Musée des Beaux-Arts de Dijon/François Jay.

p. 11: *Large Round Pietà* (Maelwael). Musée du Louvre, Paris – Alamy Stock Photo.

p. 12: *Altar of Saints and Martyrs* (Baerze and Broederlam). Musée des Beaux-Arts de Dijon.

p. 13 left: John the Fearless. Musée du Louvre, Paris.

p. 13 right: Margaret of Bavaria. Museum of Fine Arts, Ghent (Lukas – Art in Flanders VZW).

p. 14: Jousting Tournament (Master of Margaret of York). Bibliothèque nationale de France, Paris, Mss, fr. 87, f. 58v.

p. 15: The Fury of Charles VI. Librairie de Blois, Bibliothèque nationale de France, Paris, Ms 2615 f399.

p. 16 above: Nicopolis. Bibliothèque nationale de France, Paris, Ms 2646 f255v.

p. 16 below: Murder of Louis of Orléans. Bibliothèque nationale de France, Paris.

SECTION 2

p. 1: Murder of John the Fearless. Librairie de Blois, Bibliothèque nationale de France, Paris, Ms 2680, f293.

p. 2: Jacqueline of Bavaria (copy of portrait by Lambert van Eyck). Kunsthistorisches Museum Wien, Vienna.

p. 3 above: *The Madonna of Chancellor Rolin* (Jan Van Eyck). Musée du Louvre, Paris.

p. 3 below: *Portrait of a Man in a Red Turban* (Jan van Eyck, self-portrait). The National Gallery, London – Alamy Stock Photo.

p. 4 above: *Les Très Riches Heures du Duc de Berry*. Musée de Condé, Chantilly.

p. 4 below: Joan of Arc taken prisoner. Bibliothèque nationale de France, Paris, MS 5054, f70r.

p. 5: Philip the Good humiliating the Ghentenars. Master of the Privileges of Ghent and Flanders, Österreichische Nationalbibliothek, Vienna, Cod 2583, folio 349.

p. 6 left: Isabella of Portugal (copy of original by Van der Weyden). J. Paul Getty Museum, Los Angeles.

pp. 6–7: Philip the Good, his son, and Chancellor Rolin (Van der Weyden). Royal Library of Belgium, Brussels, hs.9242, fol. 1.

p. 8: The dream of Philip the Good, the Crusade. Bibliothèque nationale de France, Paris, Arsenal, Ms5702 Rés. f. 349v.

pp. 8–9: The Great Council of Mechelen. Bibliothèque nationale de France, Paris, Réserve OB-10-Fol, ff.38v–39.

p. 10: Charles the Bold (Van der Weyden). Staatliche Museen zu Berlin, Berlin, Preussischer Kulturbesitz cat.nr. 545.

p. 11: *The Last Judgement* (Van der Weyden). Hospices de Beaune.

p. 12: *Portinari Altarpiece* (Van der Goes). Uffizi, Florence.

p. 13 above: Coudenberg Palace (Brueghel the Younger). Prado, Madrid.

p. 13 below: Margaret of York. Musée du Louvre, Paris.

p. 14: The famous hat of Charles the Bold. Historisches Museum Basel, Basel. Photo: P. Portner.

p. 15 above: Charles VII (Fouquet). Musée du Louvre, Paris.

p. 15 below: Louis XI. Brooklyn Museum, New York.

p. 16 upper left: Maximilian family portrait. Kunsthistorisches Museum Wien, Vienna.

p. 16 upper right: Philip the Handsome (anonymous). Rijksmuseum, Amsterdam.

p. 16 below: The young Charles V (Van Orly). Szépművészeti Múzeum, Budapest.

ACKNOWLEDGEMENTS

My grateful thanks to everyone who helped me in the writing of this book, especially Wim Blockmans. In conducting my research, I frequently ran into questions to which I could not find an answer. My search for clarity brought me in contact with Professor Blockmans, one of our most important medievalists and *the* European authority on the Burgundians. He said he was willing to act as a sounding board. This meant bothering him with all kinds of questions, big and small, during the writing process, to which he always responded in his great wisdom with speed and efficiency. Afterwards, he generously offered to give the book a thorough reading. Naturally, I take responsibility for any remaining inaccuracies. I would also like to thank Haye Koningsveld of the De Bezige Bij publishing house, who knew how an idea could develop into a book and was always there to help me with calm consistency, good tips and relevant editorial advice. I received a working grant from Flanders Literature, and thanks to the Passa Porta international house of literature in Brussels I was able to spend two weeks as a resident in the Lijsternest of Stijn Streuvels in Anzegem. Gert Dooreman designed a splendid cover for the book, Stephan Vanfleteren was actually able to shake a colour portrait out of his black-and-white lens, Koen D'haene guided me through the files of the interlibrary loan system, and my indispensable companion Kris Lauwerys read the provisional, unfinished versions of my book over and over again. Of course there was Coraline, who had rarely seen me work so hard. There seemed to be no end in sight and the mountain of information kept on growing, but she patiently encouraged me, fully confident that I could pull it off. The enthusiasm of our clever Clémence was

ACKNOWLEDGEMENTS

contagious. On one particular day, when I had lost sight of the light in the darkness of my Middle Ages, I decided to sort out our collection of light bulbs in an act of pure desperation. I had to do something! Almost all of them were of the Philips brand. As I was putting them in order, our three-and-a-half-year-old daughter took an interest in what I was doing. Without realizing it, I began talking out loud. 'Philips, Philips, Philips... Philips...,' she heard me say. Suddenly she interrupted me and shouted, 'Philip the Bold!' I burst out laughing and went straight back to work.

INDEX

ABOUT THE AUTHOR

Bart Van Loo has developed a rare twin talent over the years. While drawing big crowds in the theatre, he is also the author of the universally praised *France Trilogy*, and the bestseller *Chanson: A sung history of France*. Friend and foe alike have to admit that Van Loo is a born storyteller, with a unique ability to combine enthusiasm, humour and expertise. *The Burgundians* is the first of his books to be translated into English.

ABOUT THE TRANSLATOR

Nancy Forest-Flier grew up in a Dutch-American milieu in the United States and studied English literature and creative writing at Hope College, Michigan before settling in the Netherlands in 1982. She works as a freelance English-language editor and Dutch-English translator.